Handbook of
MARKETING
AND
SOCIETY

Handbook of
MARKETING
AND
SOCIETY

PAUL N. BLOOM
GREGORY T. GUNDLACH
Editors

Sage Publications, Inc.
International Educational and Professional Publisher
Thousand Oaks ▪ London ▪ New Delhi

For information:

 Sage Publications, Inc.
2455 Teller Road
Thousand Oaks, California 91320
E-mail: order@sagepub.com

Sage Publications Ltd.
6 Bonhill Street
London EC2A 4PU
United Kingdom

Sage Publications India Pvt. Ltd.
M-32 Market
Greater Kailash I
New Delhi 110 048 India

Printed in the United States of America

Library of Congress Cataloging-in-Publication Data

Bloom, Paul N.
   Handbook of marketing and society / by Paul N. Bloom and Gregory T.
Gundlach.
       p. cm.
Includes bibliographical references and index.
  ISBN 0-7619-1626-1 (acid-free paper)
 1. Social marketing.   I. Gundlach, Gregory T. (Gregory Thomas) II.
Title.
  HF5414 .B55 2000
  658.8′02—dc21

                                  00-009055

This book is printed on acid-free paper.

01 02 03 04 05 06 07 7 6 5 4 3 2 1

Acquisition Editors:	Marquita Flemming
Editorial Assistant:	Mary Ann Veil
Production Editor:	Diane S. Foster
Editorial Assistant:	Candice Crosetti
Typesetter:	Rebecca Evans
Indexer:	Juniee Oneida
Cover Designer:	Michele Lee

Contents

Foreword

It is both sobering and inspiring to realize that, as citizens of the developed world, we have been given the opportunity to participate in one of the most exciting periods in the entire history of civilization. As marketing academics, moreover, one might think that we would be especially alert to monitoring the contributions our field has been making to the world during this time. This has not been the prime emphasis of marketing studies, however, and many of us probably are not as aware of some matters as we might desire. This fine undertaking by Paul Bloom, Greg Gundlach, and this handbook's chapter contributors will go a long way toward informing us on these issues. In this regard, for the past few years, I have been fortunate to be engaged in a large-scale academic project aimed at comprehending more about the role and performance of marketing in our modern world. This has led to several new insights for me—insights that relate directly to the chapters here. In their Introduction, the editors do a fine job of laying out the contents of this handbook, arranged around a new and interesting framework by which to conceptualize this area. In this Foreword, therefore, I focus on a few of my background perspectives on the topic of marketing and society in general.

Background: A Century in Perspective

It may be merely trite to point out that the world is changing and that marketing is an active participant in this process. It is *not* trite, however, to inquire into the nature of such change—to delve more deeply into the history, substance, and controversies concerning marketing's roles in society. It is *stimulating,* moreover, to pursue the implications of all of this for our present and our future. For example, let us briefly consider that the formal academic field of marketing began just about 100 years ago, at the turn of the last century, with the first offerings of courses on "market distribution" (Bartels 1998). Substantively, these courses reflected the realities of their time and place (e.g., courses in the Midwest tended to stress the distribution system for agricultural and other products, those on the urban East Coast covered distribution and merchandising). Theoretically, interest was on pursuing benefits flowing from distributive activities that had been missed by those economic thinkers concentrating on land, labor, and capital. In reading the literature of that time, it is clear that issues of marketing's performance on behalf of its society were quite a central concern for this fledgling field.

Of course, the "society" at hand was much less developed, and consumer life-styles were very different, at that time. For example, the typical U.S. housewife carried 9,000 gallons of water into the house each year, and she then had to boil the water before using it because only 25% of homes had running water (and only 3% had electricity). Cooking, baking, and food preservation required some 42 hours per week. Central heating would not arrive until the 1920s, so many households heated only the kitchen for the winter, using fuel hauled in daily by family members. On the health front, infant mortality was common—about 1 in every 10 births—and life expectancy was only 47 years (Wilkie and Moore 1999). By contrast, in today's U.S. society, life expectancy is nearing 80 years, gross domestic product is some 400 times greater, and time spent gathering and preparing food has dropped to less than 10 hours per week. Typical homes are filled with comforts and conveniences based on electricity and water. And autos, airplanes, television, and the Internet have stretched our personal borders far beyond the distance we could reach with a day's walk or ride on horseback.

This recognition of historical change serves to make the academic challenge in the study of marketing and society a bit more daunting than we might at first imagine. We know beyond doubt that the world (society) has changed greatly and that the aggregate marketing system (marketing) also has changed greatly. But what about the *relationship* between the two? What about *marketing's relationship to society?* Has it changed as well, or is it in some larger sense immutable? Either answer will, of course, be interesting. If *immutable* is correct, then merely clarifying this answer will itself be a heroic achievement. If *has changed* is our answer, then what exactly are our present and future goals for the relationship of marketing to society, and who (what) is taking us toward meeting them? Altogether, this is a worthy challenge, and one that this handbook will help us to address.

The Central Role of the Aggregate Marketing System: What Type of World Do We Desire?

Another of the hidden challenges to this area is the decision as to which level of aggregation will best serve the purposes of a given research undertaking. The recent strengths of academic marketing have been at the individual firm and decision-maker (manager) level, whether this be in a business, government agency, or consumer household. This holds true in much of the present handbook as well. However, I would like to suggest that the reader also explicitly consider other levels of aggregation for future research undertakings.

For example, in a recent article on marketing's contributions to society, Elizabeth Moore and I centered our analysis on the "aggregate marketing system" (AGMS) of the United States. The AGMS itself is huge and includes all relevant aspects of business operations (including both profit and not-for-profit), relevant centers of government operations, and all consuming units. Not only did this concept seem necessary to capture the many facets of marketing and society, but we also found it to be quite useful in placing familiar topics in new perspective and in reorienting our thoughts about fruitful avenues for further exploration (Wilkie and Moore 1999). In initially assessing our AGMS concept, moreover, three key lessons appear especially relevant to this handbook:

1. A society's AGMS holds extraordinary potential for developing and transitional economies. It can literally change the world in which people live.

2. Every AGMS is likely to be quite imperfect, with problems ranging from inferior performances, to frauds and deceits, to unacceptable dangers and risks to others, to environments.

3. Appropriate analyses of AGMSs should properly go beyond a mere emphasis on technology, economics, and the material side of a society's existence. Many of the vibrant issues also are concerned with softer "quality of life" dimensions.

These three lessons are significant to me in that they nicely bridge the AGMS concept with much of the work that historically has been pursued in the marketing and society arena and that is reported in this handbook.

Such work implicitly rests on the question, "What type of society do we wish to create and inhabit?" Here, we find the many issues involved in assessing permissible and/or desirable marketer actions including discussions of marketing ethics, probes of marketing mix activities such as limitations for persuasion or pricing practices, and explorations of the roles for business self-regulation. We also see numerous topics involving the interplay of the three primary parties in a society's AGMS—marketers, government, and consumers—revolving around issues of societal incentives for marketers as well as societal constraints on marketing activities. Increasing attention also has been given to the benefits of marketing expertise and technology for overtly pro-social purposes (social marketing). One further topic that I have not seen pursued, but that does seem to me to be of potentially great interest, would investigate the question "What does it mean to *be* a marketing person?" by examining the psychological satisfactions and stressors experienced by the millions of marketers at work in our system on a daily basis. My sense is that asking this question will force us to look closely at actual marketing actions and trade-offs as well as at their real contexts and the forces at work in the marketplace. My expectation is that we will admire much of what we find but that we also will uncover areas that cause some discomfort and could lead to needed improvements.

Fragmentation, Marginalization, and Learning Lost

As a final background perspective, I feel the need to raise the paradoxical current status of this academic area within the field of marketing for our brief but direct attention. There is no question that the subfield of *marketing and society* has flourished during recent years, with a genuine infrastructure (e.g., journals, conferences, organizations) available to welcome and assist further academic contributions. For those persons working *within* this area, there is legitimate excitement, appeal, and opportunity.

At the same time, however, the mainstream of marketing academia has for some time been fragmenting into increasingly narrow areas of specialization. This process, while having some positive aspects, is leaving a generation of young scholars at risk of learning little or nothing about some other areas within marketing including this one. As I have commented elsewhere, the danger is that knowledge outside a person's specialization may first be viewed as noninstrumental, then as nonessential, then as nonimportant, then finally as nonexistent. In a very real sense, knowledge is being lost from the field because the younger scholars at the tail of such a process never will even be exposed to key questions and insights about their own discipline. To examine this possibility, Moore and I recently conducted a survey of American Marketing Association doctoral consortium participants (Wilkie and Moore 1997). We found that fewer than 1 in 10 current Ph.D. students in marketing has taken even a single course in this area at any level of training and that virtually all self-rate their proficiency as *low* or, at best, *moderate*. By contrast, we were surprised to see the interest expressed in learning about this area; two-thirds of the consortium candidates reported that they held a personal interest in learning about marketing and society. If this can happen, then we will be effective in stemming the loss of knowledge that currently is occurring.

Roles for This Handbook

I feel as though my comments to this point have already implicitly communicated my views about the important role that this handbook can play for development of this area of study, so I will be brief here. As the reader will see, given its broad scope, it is not surprising that a huge number of viable topics exist to be pursued and that an interesting and elaborate academic infrastructure has arisen to pursue them, with marketing as only one of the players. For those persons already at work in this field, this handbook will serve as a useful source through which to broaden and deepen our understanding of the various key topics in the area. Furthermore, as just noted, there is a serious need within marketing for a basis through which to educate future scholars, and the handbook will perform a wonderful service in this regard as well. In general, I perceive a real need to "center" the field of marketing—to provide a basis for rigorous scholarship while preserving a keen eye on relevance for important issues in the world. I believe that this handbook will serve this need well, and for this I salute Paul Bloom, Greg Gundlach, and the contributors of the work herein.

William L. Wilkie
University of Notre Dame

References

Bartels, Robert (1998), *The History of Marketing Thought,* 3rd ed. Columbus, OH: Publishing Horizons.

Wilkie, William L. and Elizabeth S. Moore (1997), "Consortium Survey on Marketing and Society Issues: Summary and Results," *Journal of Macromarketing,* 17 (2), 89-95.

———— and ———— (1999), "Marketing's Contributions to Society," *Journal of Marketing,* 63, 198-218. (Special millennium issue)

Acknowledgments

Our biggest debt of gratitude is to the chapter authors of this handbook, who contributed so much of their valuable time and intellectual resources. We also thank William Wilkie for writing the Foreword. Thanks also is due to Harry Briggs at Sage Publications, who had the original idea to assemble this handbook and encouraged us in the early going. In addition, we thank Marquita Flemming at Sage for seeing the handbook through the production and distribution process. Finally, we are indebted to all those individuals who provided reviews of chapters for us, helping us to guide the chapter authors in fine-tuning their manuscripts. Many of the authors helped out by reviewing the chapters of others. Moreover, the following individuals also completed reviews for us:

Dana Alden, University of Hawaii

Joseph Cannon, Colorado State University

Gary Ford, American University

Stuart Hart, University of North Carolina

Easwar Iyer, University of Massachusetts

Donald Lichtenstein, University of Colorado

Kent Monroe, University of Illinois

Michael Rothschild, University of Wisconsin

Al Segars, University of North Carolina

Charles Weinberg, University of British Columbia

George Zinkhan, University of Georgia

Introduction

Paul N. Bloom
Gregory T. Gundlach

The marketing discipline has had a long history of conducting research on how marketing affects the welfare of society. Early marketing scholars frequently addressed questions such as the following. Does distribution cost too much? (Barger 1955; Cox 1965; Hollander 1963; Stewart and Dewhurst 1939). Does advertising increase consumer prices? (Backman 1967; Borden 1942). Should product differentiation be restricted? (Root 1972; Stern and Dunfee 1973). More recently, numerous marketing scholars have gravitated toward subfields such as marketing and public policy, macromarketing, social marketing, nonprofit marketing, and marketing ethics. These subfields have developed their own specialized journals and conferences, each of which serves as a catalyst for additional knowledge creation and dissemination. For example, the *Journal of Public Policy & Marketing,* started in 1982, has become a well-respected outlet, scoring very highly in citation frequency counts compared to most other marketing journals. In addition, the annual Marketing and Public Policy Conference, first held in 1989, is now regularly drawing more than 150 scholars for a two-day event that takes place every spring.

Indeed, a significant body of work has developed, looking beyond marketing's impact on the corporate bottom line toward how marketing can affect competition in markets, economic growth and development, and consumer welfare. However, the large and growing amount of research concerned with the relationship between marketing and society has expanded in many different directions. A wide variety of topics are being pursued, and a diverse assortment of journals and proceedings are becoming avenues for dissemination of this research. Although there have been a few texts that addressed aspects of this body of knowledge (e.g., Laczniak and Murphy 1993 on ethics; Cohen 1995 and Stern and Eovaldi 1984 on law), little has been published that takes both a comprehensive and an in-depth look at this body of scholarly research. There is a need for a volume to pull this research together to facilitate the assessment of what we have learned and what we need to study further. This handbook represents an attempt to fill this need. It contains chapters that offer reviews, summaries, and perspectives of the state of knowledge in 22 different topic areas. The various topic areas are organized to be consistent with the model introduced in the next section.

Presented in this fashion, the chapters attempt to offer an organized basis for understanding the contributions of marketing knowledge and research to society.

How Marketing Affects Societal Welfare

Our model of how marketing can affect societal welfare is shown in Figure I-1. The model proposes that marketing may affect societal welfare through two initial mechanisms. First, marketing *knowledge,* as published in journals and as presented through conference presentations, teaching, or consulting, can affect the way in which decisions are made by public policy makers, corporate marketers, and nonprofit marketers. These decision makers may then make decisions that contribute to or detract from societal welfare based on what they have learned from being exposed to marketing knowledge. Second, the marketing *decisions* of corporate, nonprofit, and social marketers, whether they have been influenced by marketing knowledge or not, can affect how well society functions in terms of competition in certain markets, economic growth and development, and consumer welfare.

As the model shows, there are many linkages (numbered 1 to 13) among marketing knowledge, decisions by policy makers and managers, and social outcomes. In the paragraphs that follow, the central research questions raised by each linkage are identified along with examples of past research and some thoughts on how well previous research has done in addressing these questions. Against this backdrop, each handbook chapter is introduced and its contributions are highlighted.

An effort was made to have at least one handbook chapter address topics related to each linkage. However, as might be expected, not all of the linkages and questions have been addressed in the field, and therefore, not all of the linkages have handbook chapters associated with them (e.g., Linkage 2). For those linkages that *are* addressed, the objective of each chapter is to provide a review, summary, or perspective on what is known about a specifically defined subarea without attempting to cover all of the research that could be related to a particular linkage. Authors were granted leeway in covering chapters in their own creative way using their own unique expertise, producing chapters that vary somewhat in the approaches taken.

Each linkage from Figure I-1 is presented in the following paragraphs in the order in which it appears in the model rather than in the order of its relevance or importance for understanding how marketing affects societal welfare.

Linkage 1: The Effect of Knowledge about Marketing on Public Policy Decisions

What is known about the ways in which public policy makers use the findings and approaches offered by the marketing discipline? Marketing thought has gone from getting little attention from public policy makers in Washington,

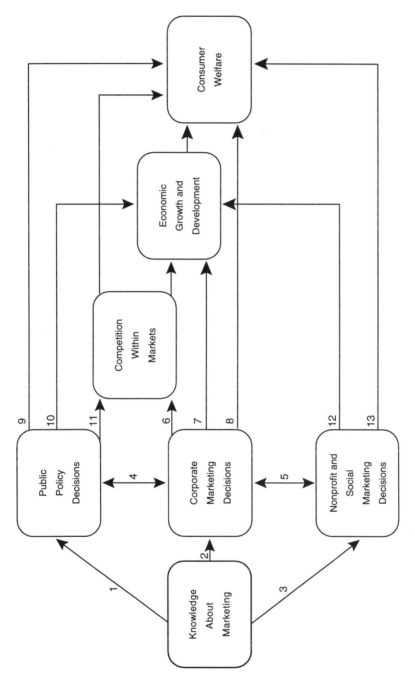

Figure Intro-1. Paths through Which Marketing Affects Societal Welfare

D. C. (Greyser 1973; Wilkie and Gardner 1974) to being an integral part of decision making at U.S. agencies such as the Federal Trade Commission (FTC) and the Food and Drug Administration. Several articles have documented how marketing thought has come into play in rule making, court decisions, and legislation (Bernhardt and Stiff 1980; Murphy 1990). Both marketing theories and marketing research methods are being increasingly relied on in deliberations involving deceptive advertising, trademark infringement, and other issues. These applications of marketing knowledge often have helped public policy makers to reach decisions that have improved competition, economic growth and development, and consumer welfare (i.e., they have helped to make Linkages 9, 10, and 11 more positive).

Three of the chapters in this handbook are especially relevant for understanding Linkage 1 and are *indirectly* relevant for understanding Linkages 9, 10, and 11. Andrews (Chapter 1) provides an examination of what is known about how public policy makers in the consumer protection area have been influenced and helped by thinking and research from the marketing discipline. Based on his own experiences and on interviews with staff members at the FTC, Andrews offers various frameworks for understanding the use of marketing knowledge in the formulation of consumer protection policy and in the enforcement of such policy. Gundlach (Chapter 2) provides a perspective on the nature of antitrust law as an area of public policy and its relationship to marketing. In his chapter, the complementary nature of marketing thought to emerging perspectives in antitrust is advanced to suggest the increasing importance and role of marketing in antitrust policy development and practice. Finally, Bloom, Edell, and Staelin (Chapter 3) start their chapter with an exploration of the ways in which public policy makers in various arenas use empirical research studies on the effects of marketing communications. They then provide a review and enumeration of the most appropriate research methods to use for providing public policy makers with evidence about the effects of marketing communications.

Linkage 2: The Effect of Knowledge about Marketing on Corporate Marketing Decisions

What is known about the ways in which corporate marketers use the findings and approaches offered by the marketing discipline? Several researchers have examined how corporate marketing practitioners use knowledge developed in the marketing discipline, with some evidence of such use having been identified (see, e.g., Bloom 1986). The use of marketing knowledge by corporate managers may indeed be subsequently leading to improvements in competition, economic growth and development, and consumer welfare. However, little research has examined the way in which corporate marketing decisions have become more socially beneficial (i.e., Linkages 6, 7, and 8 have become more positive) as a result of the application of marketing knowledge. Hence, there is not a chapter in this handbook associated with Linkage 2.

Linkage 3: The Effect of Knowledge about Marketing on Nonprofit and Social Marketing Decisions

What is known about the ways in which nonprofit and social marketers use the findings and approaches offered by the marketing discipline? Several researchers have examined how nonprofit and social marketing practitioners use knowledge developed in the marketing discipline to affect competition, economic growth and development, and consumer welfare (Andreasen 1995; Fox and Kotler 1980). The use of marketing knowledge has grown during recent years in the nonprofit and social sectors, as Andreasen (Chapter 4) observes in his chapter. He also includes the suggestion that decisions by nonprofit and social managers have become *more* socially beneficial (i.e., Linkages 12 and 13 have become more positive) due to the application of marketing knowledge. However, Andreasen recognizes that there is potential for much more "intersector transfer" of marketing knowledge in the future.

Linkage 4: The Reciprocal Effects of Public Policy Decisions and Corporate Marketing Decisions on Each Other

What is known about how laws, regulations, and public programs affect the decisions of corporate marketers? What is known about how the actions of corporate marketers affect public policy? There have been several studies that examined how corporate marketers responded to new laws and regulations such as Moorman's (1998) work on how food manufacturers changed their product and promotion strategies in response to the new nutritional labeling law. Other work includes Bloom, Heinzelmann, and Alt's (1986) study of how petroleum marketers responded to franchisee protection laws. In general, these studies have looked at how the responses of marketers to the laws have affected competition (Linkage 6), economic growth (Linkage 7), and consumer welfare (Linkage 8). As might be expected, these studies have not shown a clear pattern suggesting that public policy initiatives always lead marketers to make more socially beneficial decisions. In fact, some studies have suggested that laws and regulations might have backfired and led marketers to make less socially beneficial decisions (Ringold and Calfee 1989).

Two of the chapters in this handbook are especially relevant to the first question addressed under this linkage. Moorman (Chapter 5) reviews, among other things, what is known about how corporations have modified their marketing programs in response to public policy initiatives that seek to supply consumers with more information to assist in their buying decisions (e.g., nutritional labeling). Sheffet (Chapter 6) overviews what has been learned about how corporations have modified their marketing programs in response to changes in antitrust enforcement and judicial opinions.

Little is known about how the marketing practices of corporations affect public policy decisions. There has been some descriptive work that has tried to explain how certain agencies set priorities and choose cases (Murphy 1984), and there has been some work on how self-regulation of advertising affected the deceptive advertising policies of the FTC (Armstrong and Ozanne 1983). Additional work in this last vein, exploring how corporate marketing practices (e.g., pursuing self-regulation) could lead to better public policy decisions (i.e., making Linkages 9, 10, and 11 more positive), would be valuable. There is not a handbook chapter that addresses this topic.

Linkage 5: The Reciprocal Effects of Nonprofit/Social Marketing Decisions and Corporate Marketing Decisions

What is known about how the marketing actions of nonprofit and social organizations affect corporate marketers? What is known about how the actions of corporate marketers affect nonprofit and social organizations? There are a number of studies that have been done on how corporate marketers have responded to the marketing and advocacy actions of consumer and public interest groups (Smith 1990), exploring whether more socially beneficial marketing decisions (i.e., making Linkages 6, 7, and 8 more positive) came out of these challenges. In addition, there have been several studies of how collaboration between corporate marketers and nonprofit/social marketers can lead to positive social outcomes (i.e., making Linkages 6, 7, 8, 12, and 13 more positive) (Bloom, Hussein, and Szykman 1995).

Two chapters are relevant to this linkage. Smith (Chapter 7) provides a review of what is known about how corporations have modified their marketing practices in response to pressures from public interest groups and advocacy organizations. He focuses on the role of consumer boycotts in promoting corporate social responsibility. Drumwright and Murphy (Chapter 8) further the extant understanding of corporate societal marketing through offering their perspective on its meaning and identifying the various ways in which it can yield benefits for companies, nonprofits, organizations, consumers, and society at large (through Linkages 6, 7, and 8). Among other things, they discuss what is known about alliances between corporations and nonprofit or social organizations (this is relevant to understanding Linkage 5). They also examine what is known about solo corporate social initiatives (this is relevant to understanding the next set of linkages).

Linkages 6, 7, and 8: The Effects of Corporate Marketing Decisions on Competition, Economic Growth and Development, and Consumer Welfare

What is known about the ways in which corporate marketing actions affect competition, economic growth and development, and consumer welfare? There have been several streams of research that have addressed this question. There has been considerable research on the effects of advertising on competition and prices showing that, with some notable exceptions, advertising tends to enhance competition and lower prices (Albion and Farris 1981). There also has been much research on what deceives or misleads consumers in the marketplace

(Bernhardt, Kinnear, and Mazis 1986; Kinnear and Root 1988). Another frequently examined topic (by researchers from the macromarketing subfield) is how marketing can enhance economic growth and development. More recently, there have been several studies exploring the competitive effects associated with relationship marketing (Kalwani and Narayandas 1995), marketing channel practices (see, e.g., Bloom, Gundlach, and Cannon 2000 on slotting fees; Dutta, Heide, and Bergen 1999 on vertical territorial restrictions), and pricing (Guiltinan and Gundlach 1996).

In addition to Drumwright and Murphy's chapter, which contains an examination of corporate societal marketing, there are five other chapters that are relevant to these linkages. Abela and Farris (Chapter 9) provide a critical review of recent literature and an assessment of what is known about the impact of advertising on competition and (in particular) prices. Kaufmann (Chapter 10) provides a retrospective on 25 years of knowledge development directed at the impact of franchise distribution on competition and consumer welfare. Guiltinan and Sawyer (Chapter 11) provide an examination of perspectives from the marketing field that are relevant for understanding the impact of pricing strategies and tactics on competition and consumer welfare. Klein and Nason (Chapter 12) provide a review of the wide-ranging research completed on the relationship between marketing and economic growth and development. Hagerty (Chapter 13) provides a perspective on the long-term impact of corporate marketing on various measures of consumer welfare.

Linkages 9, 10, and 11: The Effects of Public Policy Decisions on Competition, Economic Growth and Development, and Consumer Welfare

What is known about the ways in which public policy actions contribute to competition, economic growth and development, and consumer welfare? The types of studies discussed earlier for Linkage 4 all are relevant, as are any studies that have shown that marketing thinking helped produce laws, regulations, or enforcement practices that worked better than what was tried previously (as discussed earlier for Linkage 1).

Seven additional chapters are relevant to these linkages. Simonson (Chapter 14) provides a perspective on corporate branding as protected under trademark and copyright public policy. He also discusses the legal system's method for handling scientific evidence in determining the course of brand and trade dress protection cases. Stewart, Folkes, and Martin (Chapter 15) provide a summary and discussion of current knowledge about the consumer impact of government-regulated and voluntary product warnings and other types of product hazard information. Derby and Levy (Chapter 16) provide a review of what is known about the effects on consumers of government-mandated food labeling. Mayer, Lewis, and Scammon (Chapter 17) provide a review of what is known about the nature and effectiveness of government-regulated and voluntary environmental marketing claims. Calfee (Chapter 18) provides an appraisal of the impact of consumer research on the effectiveness of deceptive advertising regulation in the United States. Morgan (Chapter 19) provides a review of the regulatory and judicial processes through which product safety regulation goals evolve including an examination of the costs and benefits of both systems. Milne (Chapter 20) provides a review and assessment of what is known about privacy protection, most of which emerges from self-regulation and does not involve government initiatives.

Linkages 12 and 13: The Effects of Nonprofit/Social Marketing Decisions on Economic Growth and Development and Consumer Welfare

What is known about the ways in which nonprofit and social marketing actions have contributed to economic growth and development and consumer welfare? Studies that would be relevant to this question include a wide range of evaluation research efforts that have been done on social marketing programs all over the world (Andreasen 1995). Although many of the studies have detected favorable results, an attempt needs to be made to extract generalizable principles about social marketing's most effective tools and approaches.

We are hopeful that two chapters in this handbook provide a start for achieving this objective. Dholakia and Dholakia (Chapter 21) provide a review of what has been learned about the impact of social marketing programs on economic growth and development. In addition, Lefebvre (Chapter 22) provides a summary and assessment of the various theories that have been used to inform preventive health social marketing programs.

Conclusion

Our model of how marketing affects societal welfare provides a way of organizing and thinking about the contributions that scholars have made to marketing and society. The chapters in this handbook contain carefully developed reviews, summaries, and perspectives of these contributions. Together, the chapters provide a basis for enhancing our understanding of the interplay between marketing and society. Overall, the chapters reveal the impressive development and scholarly contributions that define this growing field of inquiry. We are hopeful that the handbook is found to be a useful guide for understanding this development and providing clear direction for future knowledge generation efforts.

References

Albion, Mark S. and Paul W. Farris (1981), *The Advertising Controversy.* Boston: Auburn House.

Andreasen, Alan R. (1995), *Marketing Social Change.* San Francisco: Jossey-Bass.

Armstrong, Gary M. and Julie L. Ozanne (1983), "An Evaluation of the NAD/NARB Purpose and Performance," *Journal of Advertising,* 12 (3), 15-26.

Backman, Jules (1967), *Advertising and Competition.* New York: New York University Press.

Barger, H. (1955), *Distribution's Place in the American Economy.* New York: National Bureau of Economic Research.

Bernhardt, Kenneth L., Thomas C. Kinnear, and Michael B. Mazis (1986), "A Field Study of Corrective Advertising Effectiveness," *Journal of Public Policy & Marketing,* 15 (1), 146-62.

———— and Ronald Stiff (1980), "Public Policy Update: Perspectives on the Federal Trade Commission," in *Advances in Consumer Research,* Vol. 8, Kent B. Monroe, ed. Ann Arbor, MI: Association for Consumer Research, 452-54.

Bloom, Paul N. (1986), *Knowledge Development in Marketing: The MSI Experience.* Lexington, MA: Lexington Books.

————, Gregory T. Gundlach, and Joseph P. Cannon (2000), "Slotting Allowances and Fees: Schools of Thought and the Views of Practicing Managers," *Journal of Marketing,* 64 (April), 92-108.

————, Richard Heinzelmann, and Frank B. Alt (1986), "An Evaluation of Franchisee-Protection Legislation in the Petroleum Industry," *Journal of Public Policy & Marketing,* 5 (1), 105-122.

————, Pattie Yu Hussein, and Lisa R. Szykman (1995), "Benefiting Society and the Bottom Line," *Marketing Management,* 4 (Winter), 8-18.

Borden, Neil H. (1942), *The Economic Effects of Advertising.* Chicago: Irwin.

Cohen, Dorothy (1995), *Legal Issues in Marketing Decision Making.* Cincinnati, OH: South-Western.

Cox, Reavis (1965), *Distribution in a High-Level Economy.* Englewood Cliffs, NJ: Prentice Hall.

Dutta, Shantanu, Jan B. Heide, and Mark Bergen (1999), "Vertical Restrictions and Public Policy: Theories and Industry Evidence," 63 (4), 121-34.

Fox, Karen and Philip Kotler (1980), "The Marketing of Social Causes: The First Ten Years," *Journal of Marketing,* 44 (October), 24-33.

Greyser, Stephen A. (1973), "Public Policy and the Marketing Practitioner: Toward Bridging the Gap," in *Public Policy and Marketing Practices,* Fred C. Allvine, ed. Chicago: American Marketing Association, 219-32.

Guiltinan, Joseph P. and Gregory T. Gundlach (1996), "Aggressive and Predatory Pricing: A Framework for Analysis," *Journal of Marketing,* 60 (July), 87-102.

Hollander, Stanley C. (1963), "Measuring the Cost and Value of Marketing," in *Marketing and the Behavioral Sciences,* Perry Bliss, ed. Boston: Allyn & Bacon, 529-43.

Kalwani, Manohar U. and Narakesari Narayandas (1995), "Long-Term Manufacturer-Supplier Relationships: Do They Pay Off for Supplier Firms?" *Journal of Marketing,* 59 (January), 1-16.

Kinnear, Thomas C. and Ann R. Root (1988), "The FTC and Deceptive Advertising in the 1980's: Are Consumers Being Adequately Protected?" *Journal of Public Policy & Marketing,* 7 (1), 40-48.

Laczniak, Gene R. and Patrick E. Murphy (1993), *Ethical Marketing Decisions: The Higher Road.* Boston: Allyn & Bacon.

Moorman, Christine (1998), "Market-Level Impacts of Information: Competitive Responses and Consumer Dynamics," *Journal of Marketing Research,* 35 (February), 82-98.

Murphy, Patrick E. (1984), "Strategic Planning at the FTC," *Journal of Public Policy & Marketing,* 3 (1), 56-66.

———— (1990), "Past FTC Participation by Marketing Academics," in *Marketing and Advertising Regulation: The Federal Trade Commission in the 1990s,* Patrick E.

Murphy and William L. Wilkie, eds. Notre Dame, IN: University of Notre Dame Press, 205-15.

Ringold, Debra Jones and John E. Calfee (1989), "The Informational Content of Cigarette Advertising: 1926-1986," *Journal of Public Policy & Marketing,* 8 (1), 1-23.

Root, H. Paul (1972), "Should Product Differentiation Be Restricted?" *Journal of Marketing,* 36 (July), 3-9.

Smith, N. Craig (1990), *Morality and the Market: Consumer Pressure for Corporate Accountability.* London: Routledge.

Stern, Louis W. and Thomas W. Dunfee (1973), "Public Policy Implications of Non-Price Marketing and De-Oligopolization of the Cereal Industry," in *Public Policy and Marketing Practices,* Fred C. Allvine, ed. Chicago: American Marketing Association, 271-87.

———— and Thomas L. Eovaldi (1984), *Legal Aspects of Marketing Strategy.* Englewood Cliffs, NJ: Prentice Hall.

Stewart, Paul W. and J. Frederick Dewhurst (1939), *Does Distribution Cost Too Much?* New York: Twentieth Century Fund.

Wilkie, William L. and David M. Gardner (1974), "The Role of Marketing Research in Public Policy Decision Making," *Journal of Marketing,* 38 (January), 38-47.

Chapter 1

The Use of Marketing Knowledge in Formulating and Enforcing Consumer Protection Policy

J. Craig Andrews

The purpose of this first chapter of the handbook is to discuss how the findings and approaches offered by the marketing discipline are used in consumer protection policy. Thus, the link between marketing knowledge and public policy decisions is examined as it pertains to consumer protection, and as depicted in this handbook's model of the paths through which marketing affects societal wefare (see pag xv). The focus of this discussion is on the Federal Trade Commission (FTC), the primary federal regulatory agency of business in the United States. However, other agencies involved in consumer protection at the federal level are mentioned as well (e.g., Food and Drug Administration [FDA]).

As it has been so aptly described in the past, "marketers should recognize that public policy will continue to be created, with or without their research" (Wilkie and Gardner 1974, p. 38). No doubt, our work is appreciated and integrated into many public policy decisions. However, it is in our best interest to examine more completely how our discipline's research is used (and can be used) in the formulation, enforcement, and evaluation of public policy. In this regard, this chapter offers two separate frameworks detailing the use of marketing knowledge in the formulation and enforcement of public policy decisions. Then, examples of spe-

AUTHOR'S NOTE: The author gratefully acknowledges the assistance of Lee Peeler, associate director; Anne Maher, assistant director; and the staff in the Division of Advertising Practices at the Federal Trade Commission. He also appreciates the helpful comments of Ross Petty, Terry Shimp, Judy Wilkenfeld, two anonymous reviewers, and the two editors on a previous version of this chapter.

cific research applications (e.g., nutrition labeling and claims, deceptive advertising and remedies) and theoretical frameworks are cited in which our discipline has contributed to consumer protection missions of agencies. Finally, cautions and suggestions in conducting research in marketing and public policy are examined, and future research opportunities are explored.

History of Marketing Knowledge Use in Consumer Protection Policy

The Early Years: 1970s

The history of contributions from the marketing discipline to public policy spans the entire 20th century (cf. Hollander, Keep, and Dickinson 1999; Wilkie and Moore 1999). However, many of the contributions from the marketing field to public policy have taken place within the past three decades and focus on work with the FTC (for a history of the FTC, see Zuckerman 1990). Three focal areas for FTC decisions on consumer protection matters are policy planning, enforcement, and evaluation (Bernhardt and Stiff 1981; Jones and Silverman 1973; Wilkie and Gardner 1974). In 1969, the Nader and American Bar Association reports on the effectiveness of the FTC's consumer protection mission cited weaknesses in these basic decision areas. Specifically, case selection on trivial problems, time delays in investigation and enforcement, and ineffective remedies were mentioned (cf. Wilkie and Gardner 1974). The establishment of the Office of Policy Planning and Evaluation and a more streamlined information system were used to help with these concerns. Commissioner Mary Gardiner Jones, among others, believed that input from marketing academics could help in the areas of planning, enforcement, and evaluation (Jones 1990; Jones and Silverman 1973). So in 1971, Commissioner Jones initiated the process by which many marketing academics served at the FTC in roles such as advising commissioners and bureau directors, assisting attorneys with cases, conducting planning and evaluation studies, providing economic analyses of cases, and serving as experts in rule making (cf. Murphy 1990). During the early years, contributions of marketing academics to *planning* and *formulation* of policy were evident in aiding the efficient allocation of limited resources (e.g., rule making, guides, information disclosure programs). For example, marketing academics were instrumental in formulating the FTC's (1979) policy on consumer information remedies. However, formal input into the planning function declined during the 1980s when the separately formed Office of Policy Planning was disbanded (Maronick 1990).

Although contributions from marketing academics to the *enforcement* mission of the FTC have continued since the early days of participation, it has not always been an easy task to communicate such contributions. As indicated by Jones and Silverman (1973), barriers exist limiting the contributions of research to ongoing judicial and legal proceedings. Such barriers include research that is viewed as offering tentative and inconclusive results, exactly the opposite of what is preferable in a legal setting. Moreover, during this time, copy test research used in ad deception and unfairness cases sometimes was described as the "battle of the tests" pitting researchers against one another in court (Jones and Silverman 1973; more recently, see Jacoby and Szybillo 1995; Stewart 1995; and Sudman 1995 regarding the Kraft Inc. 1991 case). Others described the inability of researchers to adequately explain to presiding officers, administrative law judges (ALJs), and attorneys in proceedings exactly what was conducted in the research and why it should be given weight in court (Bernhardt and Stiff 1981). Improvements in research methodology were needed to avoid criticisms such as small samples, inappropriate selection, and weak controls. Reviews of FTC and Lanham Act deceptive ad cases showed that many of these methodological problems persisted through the 1980s (cf. Preston 1987, 1992). This was especially important in Lanham Act cases between competitors involving implied claims in which extrinsic evidence of deception is required (Cohen 1995).

However, in reviews of early contributions to the FTC's mission, both Bernhardt and Stiff (1981) and Wilkie and Gardner (1974) indicated that public policy officials shared a sincere interest in contributions from marketing and consumer research. Consumer protection activities such as case and area selection, rule making, case investigations, fact finding, remedy alternatives, and evaluation of remedies all were enhanced as a result of input from marketing academics. As suggested by Bernhardt and Stiff (1981), discussions among FTC staff now included methodological issues such as statistical significance, sample size requirements and procedures, and multivariate analysis techniques. However, formidable gaps existed in knowledge, communication, and interpretation of the marketing evidence between those in the marketing discipline and public policy decision makers. Wilkie and Gardner (1974) cited misconceptions of consumers operating under the "economic man" assumption, a lack of concern for consumer psychological needs, the assumption that "more information is better," little attention to the quality of message content, and the assumption that all information is processed the same by all consumers, among others. Other constraints, such as the limited time necessary to conduct investigations, little training in the legal and economics professions in behavioral sciences, and the struggle between internal and external validity of research, contributed to the gap between the marketing profession and public policy decisions during the early years.

Perhaps the most important lesson from such misinterpretations on the part of all parties is the need for a better understanding of the different disciplines involved in public policy decisions. For example, in the examination of labeling research, Mazis (1980) proposed four different perspectives on the issue, with each perspective frequently studying the topic from its own myopic viewpoint. The psychological perspective stressed maximizing labeling benefits by improving the consumer impact (e.g., comprehension) of the information presented. The economic perspective focused on minimizing costs to sellers in the marketplace, whereas the legal perspective was concerned with cost minimization in litigation and violation of law. Finally, the consumerist perspective focused on the benefits of providing as much information to consumers as possible (e.g., enhancing consumers' "right to know"). Obviously, a better understanding and integration of these different perspectives would serve to improve public policy decisions.

A Decade of Change: 1980s

Although the number of enforcement actions declined during the 1980s, it was apparent that the role of marketing and consumer research had been elevated in such actions (Ford and Calfee 1986; Petty 1992, p. 58). For example, although not required per se in the evaluation of deceptive ad cases, the use of extrinsic evidence (e.g., copy tests) became increasingly important in FTC cases. In *Thompson Medical Company Inc.* (1984), the FTC indicated, "The evidence we prefer to use and to which we give great weight is direct evidence of what consumers actually thought upon reading the advertisement in question" (p. 789). Moreover, former FTC commissioner Jones (1990), suggested many additional opportunities for marketing academics in this new environment, including the need for input on information disclosures, consumer vulnerability to ad deception, and effective methods of relief. However, she recommended that the Commission take a further step by formally recognizing our discipline through the establishment of a Bureau of Consumer Behavior Research. Other ideas offered for increasing involvement of our field in public policy decisions included inviting staff and commissioners to conferences, sending in copies of research articles, and participating in FTC hearings.

A review by Maronick (1990) provided direct insight into the role of consumer research at the FTC during the 1980s. Major changes cited by Maronick included the disbanding of the Office of Policy Planning and a reduced emphasis on trade regulation rules (TRRs). The political environment, the need for explicit cost-benefit analysis, scarce funding, and evaluation problems in long-term tracking all contributed to a decline in TRRs and, therefore, resulted in less activity for the Office of Impact Evaluation in baseline and follow-up studies of TRRs. An increased reliance on an evaluation committee in the Bureau of Consumer Protection occurred in which the committee enforced its "100-hour rule" requiring approval for cases before they moved to a full-phase status (Maronick 1990). The Commission also relied more on "mini-studies" during this period in deceptive ad investigations. Such copy tests included, on average, only 20 to 40 consumers in a single location and were substantially less expensive than normal copy test projects. The advantage was that such a test gave a quick and inexpensive read for the staff on potential cases. However, this approach was open to criticism regarding the generalizability of the findings and offered potential problems if introduced into case proceedings.

Renewed Activity: 1990s and Beyond

The 1990s showed an increase in enforcement actions, policy statements, and guides (although not rules) at the Commission. In terms of the marketing academic roles at the FTC described by Murphy (1990), contributions during the

1990s were primarily in assisting attorneys with cases and in administering contract research. Other roles included advising commissioners and bureau directors (sometimes through staff and advisers) as well as providing assistance with rules, guides, policy statements, reports, and hearings. Other activities popular during the 1970s at the bureau and commission level, such as conducting planning studies and participating in policy review sessions, were not part of the everyday routine of academics at the Commission during the 1990s. However, due to the specialized and decentralized structure of the FTC at this time, opinions of marketing academics regarding planning and policy were sought at the *division level* (e.g., Division of Ad Practices), where initial investigations are launched. The reliance on economic analysis and input continued as applied to rules, guides, and policy statements (e.g., environmental marketing guides [FTC 1992]). However, the following rules, guides, policy statements, reports, and associated hearings all received input and review by specialists in the marketing discipline: environmental marketing guides (FTC 1992 [and 1996 revision]), "900 number" disclosure rule (FTC 1993), enforcement policy statement on food advertising (FTC 1994), telemarketing sales rule (FTC 1995b), dietary supplement advertising guides (FTC 1998a), and privacy on-line report to Congress (FTC 1998d). In addition, the marketing discipline played an important part in providing consumer research for the FDA's (1996) regulations restricting the sale and distribution of cigarettes to children and adolescents, for everyday activities at the FDA's Center for Food Science and Nutrition, and for the FDA's over-the-counter (OTC) drug advertising and labeling. At the FTC, the marketing field played a valuable role in providing copy test evidence and in expert witness testimony in the *Stouffer Foods Corporation* (1994) (see review by Andrews and Maronick 1995) and *Novartis Corporation* ("Doan's Pills") (1999) trials. In turn, key public policy officials actively solicited the help of the marketing profession with calls for research on a wide variety of consumer protection topics (cf. Bernstein 1996; Schultz 1996; Starek 1993; Steiger 1994). Thus, the 1990s saw a resurgence of activity at the FTC as well as in the solicitation and use of marketing knowledge in consumer protection policy and decisions.

On the academic side, the marketing and public policy discipline flourished during the 1990s, with important contributions from the *Journal of Public Policy & Marketing* (*JPP&M*), the continued success of the annual Marketing and Public Policy Conference, and the start of the Marketing and Society special interest group of the American Marketing Association (Mazis 1997). A mentor program currently matches scholars in the marketing and public policy field with doctoral students and new Ph.D.s expressing an interest in the discipline. Recent texts on legal decision making in marketing (Cohen 1995) and edited volumes addressing research on consumer issues in public policy (Bloom and Gundlach 2000; Hill 1996; Macklin and Carlson 1999) are valued resources for our profession. Finally, a series of retrospective articles in *JPP&M* described historical viewpoints of six leading marketing and public policy scholars (Andreasen 1997; Bloom 1997; Greyser 1997; Kinnear 1997, Mazis 1997; Wilkie 1997) and represent important reading for anyone considering a contribution to public policy.

Marketing Knowledge and the Formulation of Consumer Protection Policy

Knowledge Development in Policy Formulation

As indicated by Hunt (1978, 1991), the primary directive for scholarly research in marketing and other disciplines is to seek knowledge. Knowledge must be "intersubjectively certifiable and capable of describing, explaining, and predicting phenomena" (Hunt 1978, p. 109). Possible audiences for such marketing knowledge may be marketing managers, educators and scholars, public policy officials, special interest groups, and consumers (Monroe et al. 1986; Shimp 1994). Contributions to knowledge can be classified as theoretical, empirical, methodological, or critical and can be diffused in a multitude of ways (e.g., academic journals, fellow academics, texts, students, seminars, consulting, expert witnessing [Shimp 1994]). Thus, there are many routes of relevance for marketing knowledge and for its application to public policy. The ultimate contribution of such knowledge will depend on the degree to which the research is representative of the issue that is being studied (Shimp 1994).

A Framework for the Formulation of Consumer Protection Policy

The following framework displays a variety of relevant routes for marketing knowledge in the formulation of consumer protection policy. It is based on direct experience of the author in serving at the FTC and on interviews with FTC personnel. It also uses the author's experiences with the FDA in its use of marketing knowledge in rule-making procedures. In comparison to in-house initiatives at the FTC during the late 1970s (e.g., the children's advertising rule), the starting point during recent years often has been a "change agent" (e.g., Congress, Center for Science in the Public Interest [CSPI], Center for Media Education, National Association of Attorneys General) that has precipitated action. For example, both the "900 number rule" (FTC 1993) and the telemarketing sales rule (FTC 1995b) were motivated by legislative acts of Congress directing FTC involvement. Similarly, although FTC hearings and workshops on privacy occurred since 1995, the FTC's (1998d) privacy on-line report to Congress responded to inquiries by Senator McCain and Representative Bliley for their respective congressional commerce committees. However, other consumer and industry groups (e.g., Children's Advertising Review Unit, Direct Marketing Association, Center for Media Education) played instrumental roles with respect to the formulation of proposed rules for notice, choice, access, and security of information collected from children over the Internet (cf. the FTC's [1999b] children's on-line privacy protection rule). In a similar fashion, the FTC's (1994) operating policy statement on food advertising was influenced by the passage of the Nutritional Labeling and Education Act (1990), maintaining consistency with the FDA's (1993) nutritional labeling regulations and addressing enforcement criticisms suggested by the CSPI's (1994) *Food Advertising*

Chaos: The Case for Reform. In the case of the environmental marketing guides, the FTC (1992) received petitions from industry members and trade associations to issue guides. Also, a task force of state attorneys general strongly recommended that uniform environmental marketing standards be issued at the federal level. As a final example, the Clinton administration and public health community represented important change agents in supporting the issuance of the FDA's (1996) proposed tobacco regulations. Although the Supreme Court ruled recently that the FDA lacked the authority to regulate tobacco at this time (*FDA v. Brown & Williamson Tobacco Corporation* 2000), this does not necessarily preclude Congress from taking action in the future.

Trade regulation rules, guides, and operating policy statements at the FTC usually are the result of industry-wide problems that would make the traditional case-by-case enforcement approach inefficient. As indicated in Figure 1.1, prior legal precedent, case law, and jurisdiction in the formulation of such rules, guides, and policy statements provide the framework for FTC staff and commission action. For example, in the enforcement policy statement on food advertising (FTC 1994), the FTC, FDA, and U.S. Department of Agriculture all share jurisdiction in the regulation of food product claims. However, a 1954 memorandum of understanding between the FDA and FTC assigns the FTC the responsibility for regulating food advertising, whereas the FDA has taken primary responsibility (except for meat and poultry products) in regulating food labeling. In addition, the FTC's legal authority in regulating the practice in question usually is outlined in the rule, guide, or policy statement. In the case of food ad claims, the FTC has statutory authority to prohibit deceptive acts or practices under Section 5 of the FTC Act. The FTC's deception policy statement (reprinted in *Cliffdale Associates Inc.* 1984, pp. 110, 176) and advertising substantiation policy (reprinted in *Thompson Medical* 1984, pp. 648, 839) normally are cited to set the stage for regulation or policy with respect to deceptive ad claims in a given industry. Although not as common, the FTC's unfairness policy (FTC Act Amendments 1994) can be applied as support for rules, guides, or operating policy if unfairness exists (Preston 1995; Simonson 1995).

Direct Contributions to Policy Formation

It is within this context that marketing knowledge and information provided by marketing consultants is valued and used in the formation of rules, guides, and policy statements (Figure 1.1). At times, this information is *directly* incorporated into the formal release statements. For example, in the case of the FTC's (1993) "900 number rule," the Commission wished to allow more flexibility in the size and presence of sweepstakes disclosures. Direct evidence was cited (FTC 1993, 132 ff.), based on research by Bhalla and Lastovicka (1984) and Petty and Cacioppo (1986), to indicate that disclosure size variability might be desirable in some cases to reduce "wear-out" and enhance ad noticeability. Similarly, marketing and advertising research (Barlow and Wogalter 1993; Hoy and Stankey 1993; Murray, Manrai, and Manrai 1993) is cited directly in the recent policy statement proposal regarding the applicability of rules and guides to elec-

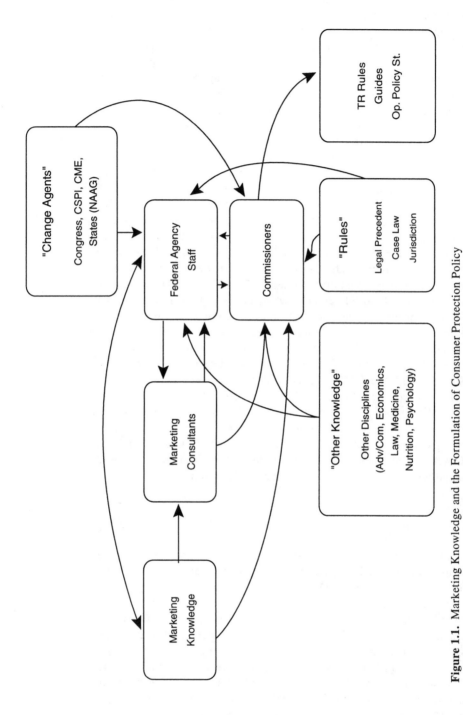

Figure 1.1. Marketing Knowledge and the Formulation of Consumer Protection Policy

NOTE: CME = Center for Media Education; NAAG = National Association of Attorneys General; Adv/Com = advertising and communications; TR Rules = trade regulation rules; Op. Policy St. = operating policy statements.

tronic media (FTC 1998c, p. 28003) to indicate a preference for the simultaneous use of visual and audio modes in disclosures. An examination of the FTC's (1998d) privacy on-line report to Congress reveals substantial reliance on marketing and demographic studies in explaining the extent of Internet use. Finally, the FDA's (1996) tobacco rules to protect children and adolescents contained numerous cites to marketing, advertising, and social psychology research. For example, research by Lutz and Lutz (1977) was offered on the role of ad imagery (FDA 1996, p. 44467); Petty and Cacioppo's (1986) elaboration likelihood model was examined in the context of peripheral route imagery (FDA 1996, p. 44468); and Lavidge and Steiner (1961), McGuire (1962), and Pechmann and Ratneshwar (1994) were cited with respect to ad persuasion and belief processes. Different positions on the effectiveness of cigarette ad bans were offered directly in the tobacco rule (Boddewyn 1994; Cohen 1990).

Indirect Contributions to Policy Formation

Because research studies often are not available at the time of the issuance of rules or guides on emerging public policy issues, marketing knowledge and information from marketing consultants frequently plays an *indirect* role in the formulation of consumer protection policy. For example, the FTC usually posts a 60-day request for comments on proposed rules or guides. In-house (and sometimes external) marketing consultants will review the proposal. Next, hearings and workshops often are planned, with a 60-day period offered to indicate a willingness to participate. Quite often, the consultants will be helpful in suggesting and evaluating proposed questions for the workshops or hearings. In the case of a recent proposed workshop on the interpretation of FTC rules and guides for electronic media (FTC 1999a), a series of questions for researchers were offered in the interpretation of the "clear and conspicuous standard" for disclosures as applied in electronic media. Alternatively, marketing knowledge may have an impact in hearings and workshops conducted *prior to* the issuance of the rules or guides. For example, extensive hearings were held in 1995 in conjunction with the planned revision of the FTC (1992) environmental marketing guides. At the hearings, consumer researchers provided helpful evidence in the form of tracking studies on environmental claim use across product categories and geographical areas (Mayer et al. 1995).

Calls for consumer research by public policy officials often occur in conjunction with the issuance of rules and guides. As an example of this, the question of whether consumers will generalize from nutrient and health claims in advertising given the omission of an important negative nutrient was raised on several occasions (e.g., Bernstein 1996; Starek 1993). If such generalizations occurred, the FTC then raised the question, "What kind of disclosure best conveys the presence and significance of the risk-increasing nutrient—a numerical disclosure of the percent[age] of daily value of fat contained in each serving, a concise verbalization, or some other disclosure format?" (Bernstein 1996, p. 313). To answer this question, a series of studies were conducted by researchers in marketing and economics (cf. Andrews, Netemeyer, and Burton 1998; FTC 1998b).

Evidence from one study shows that consumers do indeed generalize from such ad claims, although this generalization is dependent on the product category, ad claim specificity, consumer nutrition knowledge, and disclosure type used (Andrews, Netemeyer, and Burton 1998). In other instances, marketing consultants (and their knowledge) have had an impact in discussions during joint meetings with staff attorneys and industry and trade representatives with respect to details of trade rules and guides. Similarly, marketing consultants serve an important function in the coordination and implementation of certain rules and guides (e.g., environmental marketing) with other federal agencies and in discussions with consumer protection personnel from other countries (e.g., Canada, Russia).

Marketing Knowledge and the Enforcement of Consumer Protection Policy

A Framework for the Use of Marketing Knowledge in the Ad Enforcement Process

Introductory Stages

Based on direct experiences and observations by the author, as well as input from staff attorneys, Figure 1.2 offers insight as to how marketing knowledge is used in the advertising enforcement process at the FTC. The figure focuses primarily on contributions at the division level (i.e., Division of Ad Practices) and on external influences in the process, as other frameworks have been offered tracing the internal steps of FTC staff, commissioners, and ALJs in the case process (cf. Wilkie, McNeil, and Mazis 1984, p. 18). The starting point in Figure 1.2 is similar to the notion of change agents in Figure 1.1; however, in this case, the petitions to the FTC from complaint sources reflect the narrower focus on a specific, potential violator. For example, in "Campbell Soup Company" (1992), complaints to the FTC about the company's "heart healthy" campaign surfaced from the American Heart Association and the CSPI due to the omission of relatively high sodium levels in the advertised soup products. Alternatively, a refusal to abide by self-regulatory bodies, such as the National Advertising Review Board, might indicate the need for action at the federal level (e.g., *Eggland's Best Inc.* 1994). On occasion, actions are initiated due to order violations found by the FTC's Division of Enforcement (e.g., *Hasbro Inc.* 1993, 1996). The state attorneys general and citizen complaints also represent important sources for beginning possible enforcement actions. In 1997, the FTC joined with many state attorneys general offices in conducting sweeps and bringing actions against fraudulent providers of promotional and telemarketing services. Contrary to popular belief, however, the FTC does not have the resources to monitor all ads appearing across print, broadcast, and electronic media. Thus, a reliance on, and a close relationship with, external complaint sources is important in tracking practices that are potentially deceptive or unfair.

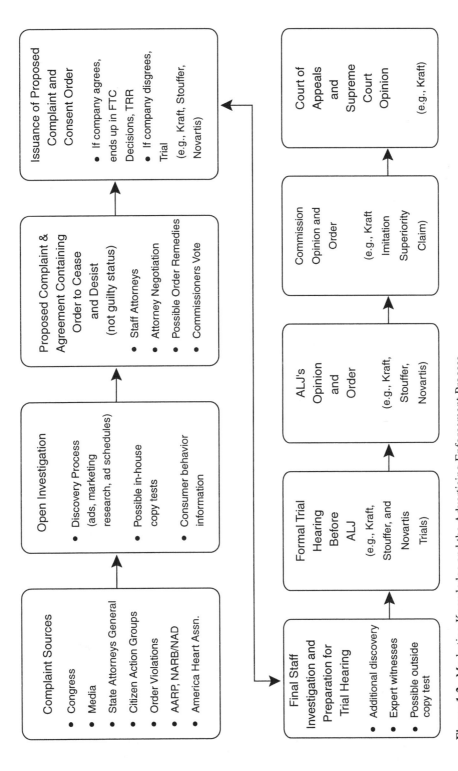

Figure 1.2. Marketing Knowledge and the Advertising Enforcement Process

NOTE: AARP = American Association of Retired Persons; NARB/NAD = National Advertising Review Board, National Advertising Division.

The next step in Figure 1.2 is that an investigation is opened if the case is within the FTC's jurisdiction under the FTC Act, involves interstate commerce and the public interest, and deserves allocation of the Commission's limited resources. The first stage in the discovery process of the investigation is for the staff attorneys assigned to the case to send an access letter to the company requesting all materials pertaining to the campaign in question (e.g., ads disseminated, marketing research, ad schedules). An investigation of these materials is important in establishing whether the claims were made and in bringing forth any intent to make the claims by the company (see introductions to *Kraft* 1991; *Novartis* 1999; *Stouffer Foods* 1994). (Note that intent is not required but represents a presumption of materiality if found [see deception policy appended to *Cliffdale Associates* 1984, pp. 182-183].) Next, an in-house copy test or other preliminary marketing or consumer behavior evidence may be brought to bear on the case. Normally, in-house marketing consultants conduct such tests, although many outside marketing consultants have been valuable in this capacity. Such an analysis is important to screen out potentially weak cases that might absorb Commission resources. If a copy test is proposed, then the research challenge is to construct the most appropriate test possible given limited resources at this juncture (see "mini-studies" in Maronick 1990).

Following initial evidence from the discovery process, in-house copy tests, and consumer research in general, a decision may be made by the staff attorneys to recommend to the bureau director that a proposed complaint be developed (Figure 1.2). The staff economists are likely to provide important evidence and analysis at this stage as well. The eventual complaint that is developed is accompanied by an order, often to cease and desist from the practice in question. The breadth of product coverage in the order usually is determined by the nature of the violation and is open to negotiation between the staff attorneys and the company at this stage. Depending on the nature of the offense, the order may contain possible remedies such as triggered disclosures, corrective advertising, and consumer redress (for remedy effectiveness issues, see Wilkie, McNeil, and Mazis 1984). At this point, input from marketing consultants, armed with knowledge on the planning, development, and implementation of remedies, can be valuable in determining the success of the enforcement action. At times, staff attorneys may seek an injunction in federal court at this stage (e.g., to freeze assets of a firm involved in fraud or revoke an Internet domain name for a fraudulent Internet advertiser). The commissioners then will vote on the complaint and order provisions (also known as a *consent agreement*). If the company agrees to the consent agreement, they retain a "not guilty status" yet must abide by the order provisions. The result then is published in *FTC Decisions* and the *Trade Regulation Reporter*. However, if the company disagrees, then the case goes to trial before an FTC Administrative Law Judge (ALJ) (see, e.g., *Kraft* 1991; *Novartis* 1999; *Stouffer Foods* 1994).

Preparation for Trial

As indicated in Figure 1.2, if the company elects to go to trial, then the FTC engages in final staff investigation and preparation for the trial hearing. This entails additional discovery and the collection of extrinsic evidence for the trial.

Although such evidence is not required per se, it is nonetheless considered and given substantial weight in cases involving potentially deceptive implied claims (*Thompson Medical* 1984, p. 789). Extrinsic evidence can include expert witness testimony, common use of terms, generally accepted principles in marketing research, and methodologically sound consumer research studies (e.g., ad copy tests) (*Kraft* 1991, pp. 121-122). For example, in the *Stouffer Foods* (1994) trial before the ALJ, the complaint counsel (i.e., FTC staff attorneys) relied on an outside copy test, expert testimony on consumer behavior principles (e.g., priming, relational processing of ads), and expert review of disclosure research. The defendant used an outside copy test and expert testimony. Thus, because most cases moving to trial involve implied claims in question, the role of extrinsic evidence and the use of marketing knowledge have become increasingly important in FTC cases over the years.

Following the trial before the ALJ and the ALJ's opinion and order, the Commission will issue its separate opinion and order based on its expertise and evidence presented at the trial (Figure 1.2). At times, the commissioners might disagree with part or all of the ALJ's ruling, as happened in the *Kraft* (1991) case. In Kraft, although the commissioners agreed with most of the ALJ's decision (e.g., involving the challenged "milk equivalency" claim), they made two major changes in their ruling. First, the commissioners did not see evidence implicating Kraft's "class picture/5-ounce" ads as making the challenged "imitation superiority" claim. However, they broadened their order to include a wider range of cheese products. Kraft appealed the decision, but the FTC decision was upheld in the 7th Circuit (*Kraft v. FTC* 1992). On further appeal, the Supreme Court refused to hear the case, leaving the 7th Circuit decision to stand.

Contributions to Consumer Protection Policy

Application Areas

Although a wide variety of specific contributions to consumer protection policy are mentioned in previous reviews (cf. Andreasen 1997; Andrews 1996; Bloom 1997; Mazis 1997), the purpose of this section is to highlight six important application areas where the collective research from our profession has made a difference. The review of these areas and contributors is not meant to be exhaustive (see, e.g., the past 19 volumes of *JPP&M* for more complete coverage); rather, it is intended to provide several examples of research programs that have contributed to consumer protection policy.

Deceptive Advertising, Remedies, and Unfairness

As indicated in the preceding section, although not required per se, extrinsic evidence is nonetheless considered in the case of potentially deceptive ad claims at the FTC, especially when they are of an implied nature. During recent years, ad copy tests have represented the primary form of extrinsic evidence offered in deceptive ad cases at the Commission and in Lanham Act cases (cf. Cohen 1995; *Kraft* 1991; *Novartis* 1999; *Stouffer Foods* 1994; *Thompson Medical* 1984). As such, an important contribution from the work of Preston (1987, 1992) is a historical review and analysis of prior extrinsic evidence including what elements the Commission and courts have given greater weight in the proceedings. (For a thorough review of ad regulation in the European Union [EU] vs. the United States, see Petty 1997. A detailed comparison of Lanham Act vs. FTC cases can be found in Petty 1992.) In the Commission's consideration of extrinsic evidence, adherence to generally accepted principles is perhaps the most important criterion for researchers to remember. These principles evolve from FTC case precedent (see above) and reviews and analysis in marketing and legal research (cf. Andrews and Maronick 1995; Jacoby and Szybillo 1995; Maronick 1991; Morgan 1990; Owen and Plyler 1991; Plevan and Siroky 1991; Preston 1987, 1992; Stewart 1995). Issues such as the universe, sample drawn, method of questioning, experience in design and execution, controls, data collection, and analysis represent fertile ground for challenges in FTC legal proceedings. Although such general standards or principles exist, their operationalization to the case situation often is very different from researcher to researcher.

There are several examples of contributions from the marketing discipline in the direct study of the FTC's deception policy statement (appended to *Cliffdale Associates* 1984). For example, Ford and Calfee (1986) offered a thorough analysis of the 1983 change in deception policy at the Commission including the likely outcomes of such a change. Others examine the three important elements of deception policy: (1) misleadingness, (2) the reasonable consumer, and (3) materiality. Specifically, the first element in the FTC deception policy concerns whether a representation, omission, or practice is likely to mislead consumers. Examples of such misleadingness include misrepresentations that are contrary to fact and misleading omissions. Effects of misleading advertising and remedies have been analyzed in several consumer research studies, often in an experimental setting (cf. Andrews, Netemeyer, and Burton 1998; Burke et al. 1988; Johar 1995; Olson and Dover 1978; Pechmann 1996; Russo, Metcalf, and Stephens 1981). The second element examines the potentially deceptive practice from the perspective of a consumer acting reasonably under the circumstances (e.g., a member of the target market). Researchers have studied the role of product expertise and involvement levels associated with the reasonable consumer element in deceptive advertising (Laczniak and Grossbart 1990). Finally, the third element in the FTC deception policy requires that the representation, omission, or practice be a "material" one. That is, the issue is whether the act or practice is likely to affect the consumer's conduct or decision regarding the product or service in question. Although materiality often falls under presumptive elements (e.g., health and safety concerns, intent, seller knowledge), considerable debate has ensued regarding this element in deception, especially in conjunction with the challenged "milk equivalency" claim in *Kraft* (1991; see also Jacoby and Szybillo 1995; Stewart 1995; Sudman 1995).

In addition, the Commission has relied on economic evaluations of deception (Pappalardo 1997). For example, economics of information theory posits that consumers tend to be less skeptical of search claims than of experience claims (i.e., when the product cannot be inspected prior to purchase) and most skeptical of credence claims (i.e., when consumers lack the expertise or time to verify the claims) (Ford, Smith, and Swasy 1990; Nelson 1974; Smith 1990). *Kraft* (1991) and *Novartis* (1999) are examples of FTC cases for which credence claims are at issue because reasonable consumers lack the ability to evaluate material claims on health and back pain.

As suggested by former Commissoner Jones (1990; Jones and Silverman 1973), perhaps one of the more important contributions from the marketing field is the expertise that is provided on *remedies* to deceptive practices. A wide variety of remedies are possible as part of deceptive ad orders including affirmative and triggered disclosures (cf. Wilkie 1985), warnings (cf. Stewart and Martin 1994), consumer redress, and corrective advertising (cf. Wilkie, McNeil, and Mazis 1984). The latter remedy, corrective advertising, remains an extremely important tool for the Commission today and recently was applied in the *Novartis* (1999) case. Researchers working in this area are encouraged to read Wilkie, McNeil, and Mazis (1984) for a thorough review of corrective advertising history and its overall effectiveness.

Legal marketing scholars have examined recent changes in the FTC's unfairness policy that amended the FTC Act in 1994 (Preston 1995; Simonson 1995; for unfairness history, see Cohen 1982). Unfairness elements of (1) substantial injury to consumers that are (2) not reasonably avoidable by consumers themselves and (3) not outweighed by countervailing benefits to consumers or competition have been evaluated by these scholars, as have unfairness application areas (e.g., children, TRRs, substantiation theory) and the likely impact of the 1994 changes. Finally, discussion of the FTC's policy planning protocol for substantiation actions can be found in Cohen (1980).

Tobacco Advertising, Promotion, and Regulation

A variety of studies in consumer behavior and economics thoroughly examine the effectiveness of past tobacco regulatory initiatives and the difficulty of measuring cause-and-effect relationships (cf. Calfee 1986; Cohen 1990). Numerous research studies from the medical and advertising professions have studied effects of the "Old Joe the Camel" campaign on children's logo recognition rates, brand recall, preferences, and market share estimates (for a listing of seven of these, see Andrews 1996). Recent testimony before the FTC on the Old Joe campaign has applied important consumer behavior principles in evaluating the impact of the campaign (Cohen 1998). In light of increased litigation and proposed FDA regulations, many states initiated a settlement with the tobacco industry to recoup medical and other costs. Goldberg and Kozlowski (1997) and Petty (1999) provided critical analyses of this 1997 tobacco agreement with the state attorneys general. No doubt, future work will examine other tobacco regulations such as those proposed by the FDA (1996). Recently, consumer research on adolescents has suggested that exposure to anti-smoking ads makes salient prior beliefs about smoking risks and leads to less favorable thoughts about smokers (Pechmann and Ratneshwar 1994). This experimental research also has suggested that exposure to cigarette ads results in more favorable thoughts about smokers. Other recent consumer research has shown the effectiveness of processing interventions in anti-smoking appeals (Keller and Block 1996) and that young adult perceptions of addiction and financial risks are directly related to smoking status (Rindfleisch and Crockett 1999). Future research is likely to systematically examine the many existing state anti-smoking campaigns (cf. Pechmann and Goldberg 1998). Finally, several studies have used meta-analyses and market share estimation to examine the overall impact of tobacco advertising (Andrews and Franke 1991; Pollay et al. 1996).

Understanding Children's Advertising and Promotion

This topic attracted a considerable amount of interest by researchers (and resources at the FTC) during the late 1970s to early 1980s (cf. FTC 1978, 1981). Extensive hearings were held during this time to examine young children's difficulties in understanding and processing televised advertising messages and reactions to promotions. An example of one important contribution at this time is the identification of different processing levels of children (e.g., strategic, cued, limited) varying by age and based on storage and retrieval differences (Roedder 1981). Such research offered clear and specific public policy alternatives (p. 150), although political changes led to the termination of the FTC initiatives (FTC 1981). However, research programs continued, studying questions such as the formulation and use of cognitive defenses to promotion (Brucks, Armstrong, and Goldberg 1988) and adaptive decision making on behalf of children (Gregan-Paxton and Roedder John 1997). Early experimental research included examinations of snack commercials and public service announcements (Goldberg, Gorn, and Gibson 1978) and whether young children understood the selling intent of commercials (Macklin 1985). Recently, Martin (1997) performed a meta-analysis of findings with respect to this latter inquiry. Also, researchers are encouraged to examine new findings and perspectives on children's advertising in Macklin and Carlson (1999). Extensions of past research to new issues such as privacy regulations for children's personally identifiable information on the Internet are likely.

Environmental Marketing Claims

A major initiative by the FTC in 1992 was the issuance of the environmental marketing guides. Extensive hearings took place in December 1995 with respect to the revision of the guides. As part of the request for comments for the hearings (FTC 1995a), the Commission released several studies conducted by consumer researchers on perceptions of ozone and environmentally friendly claims (cf. Maronick and Andrews 1999) and interpretations of recyclable claims. Several consumer researchers participated in the hearings by discussing tracking studies on environmental claim use across product categories and geographical areas (Mayer et al. 1995). In addition, an entire issue of the *Journal of Advertising* (Summer 1995) was devoted to research on environmental marketing claims (see also Morris, Hastak, and Mazis 1995). One of the studies provided a thorough analysis of federal, state, and local agency policies with respect to environmental marketing claim regulation (Scammon and Mayer 1995). Recent discussion of fuel cell vehicles, life-cycle analysis, environmental seal systems, and new environmental marketing activities no doubt will provide researchers with opportunities for further study.

Nutrition Labeling and Health Claims

The implementation of the Nutrition Labeling and Education Act (1990) by the FDA's (1993) food labeling regulations and the FTC's (1994) operating policy statement on food advertising created many opportunities for researchers to examine unanswered questions. For example, a major section of the Spring 1996 issue of *JPP&M* was devoted to addressing nutrition issues such as the effectiveness of alternative labeling formats (Levy, Fein, and Schucker 1996), consumer processing of nutrient and health claims on packages (Ford et al. 1996), acquisition and comprehension of nutrition information (Moorman 1996), demographic profiles and food shopping preferences (Mathios 1996), and alternative reference points for the provision of daily reference value information (Barone et al. 1996). Additional studies varied nutrition labeling format information (Burton, Biswas, and Netemeyer 1994; Viswanathan 1994), studied age effects (Burton and Andrews 1996), conducted experimental and field studies of nutrient and health claim information (Andrews, Netemeyer, and Burton 1998; FTC 1998b; Ippolito and Mathios 1991; Roe, Levy, and Derby 1999), and examined interactions between claims and labeling (Keller et al. 1997; Mitra et al. 1999; Szykman, Bloom, and Levy 1997). In sum, it is apparent from prior research that nutrition information modality (e.g., labeling vs. claims), labeling and disclosure format (e.g., adjectival, percentage value, absolute value), message content (e.g., reference value strength, nutrients included), and consumer characteristics (e.g., motivation, nutrition and health knowledge, age, opportunity) all play important roles in the effectiveness of nutrition labeling and claims. New venues for the application of these factors and associated theory are likely in the areas of dietary supplements and functional foods.

Warnings and Disclosures

A rich history of contributions exists on warnings and disclosures from our field and predates many of the nutrition studies just discussed. For example, special conferences on issues relating to warnings and disclosures (e.g., labeling and health risks [Mazis 1980]) were held several years ago, with numerous contributors and disciplines involved. However, similar to the recent special *JPP&M* section on nutrition, a special issue of *JPP&M* recently was devoted to the topic of warnings and disclosures (for contributors, see Spring 1998 issue of *JPP&M*). This issue examined retail price disclosures, odds disclosures, superimposed video information, trademark disclaimers, alcohol warnings, OTC drug labeling, and the legal duty to warn. In general, a starting point for researchers in this area is to read Stewart and Martin's (1994) thorough examination of the intended and unintended consequences of warnings (see also the update by Stewart, Folkes, and Martin in this volume [Chapter 15]). In addition, Andrews and Netemeyer (1996) provided a review of the numerous alcohol warning research studies and examined related addiction issues and policy alternatives. For those interested in enhancing the effectiveness of product warning labels, the Bettman, Payne, and Staelin (1986) article offers many suggestions based on theories of information processing. No doubt, perceptual differences play an important role in the assessment and handling of risk from warnings, as indicated in Slovic, Fischhoff, and Lichtenstein (1980). Finally, Cox and colleagues (1997) offered a meta-analysis of the influence of warnings on behavior revealing the many difficulties of this relationship.

Disclosure research can be split into (1) the study of regulatory issues and (2) experimental work, especially in the area of advertising. For a thorough examination of the role of affirmative disclosures at the FTC, researchers are encouraged to read the series of studies offered by Wilkie in *JPP&M* (e.g., in 1985). Other influential research includes Hoy and Stankey's (1993) extensive content analysis of advertising disclosures in the study of applications of the FTC's "clear and conspicuous standard." At present, the clear and conspicuous standard is being examined in light of the application of Commission rules and guides in new electronic media formats (FTC 1998c). Experimental work on advertising print disclosures can be found in Foxman, Muehling, and Moore (1988) and shows that disclosures can play an important role in highlighting the importance of associated ad copy. Finally, if clearly and prominently displayed, experimental manipulation of various ad disclosure statements has revealed that "evaluative" disclosures can have a stronger effect on nutrition beliefs than "absolute" or "relative" disclosure statements (Andrews, Netemeyer, and Burton 1998; see also FTC 1998b). In sum, and as found with studies of nutrition labeling and claims, research on warning and disclosure effectiveness ultimately depends on the strength of the message content, modality, format, source, and consumer factors.

Theoretical Contributions to Consumer Protection Policy

Numerous theoretical contributions to consumer protection policy have been made from the fields of psychology, marketing and consumer behavior, economics, and law. This section highlights examples of some of these contributions as extended and applied by scholars working in the marketing and consumer behavior disciplines.

Perhaps one of the most enduring contributions over the years has been the *stages of information processing,* as introduced by McGuire (1976, 1980). These eight stages (exposure, attention, comprehension, agreement, retention, retrieval, decision making, and action), coupled with communication factors (source, receiver, message, and modality), have been quite helpful in assessing the impact of deceptive and unfair ad campaigns, copy tests of such campaigns, and new public policy initiatives (e.g., trade rules, warning labels). Aspects of information processing apply to the study of information overload (Scammon 1977); comprehension, perception; and memory (Bettman 1979); miscomprehension (Jacoby and Hoyer 1982); learning processes (Mitchell 1983); and imagery (Lutz and Lutz 1977; Paivio 1969; Rossiter 1982). For example, studies of imagery and the dual coding of visual and verbal information have played an important role in the FDA's (1996) proposed tobacco regulations and the FTC's clear and conspicuous standard. Also, information-processing principles have been extended to children's advertising (Roedder 1981), package labeling (Bettman, Payne, and Staelin 1986), and warnings (Andrews and Netemeyer 1996; Hilton 1993; Stewart and Martin 1994).

A second area of impact has been the application of several *theories of persuasion*. Specifically, the *hierarchy of effects model* (Lavidge and Steiner 1961) outlines the process of awareness, knowledge, liking, preference, conviction, and purchase as well as later variations of cognitive, affective, and conative components (Barry 1987). This model is useful in measuring effects in deceptive and unfair ad cases (e.g., Cohen 1998). Other studies have extended knowledge of attribution, conformity, and susceptibility theories in the study of persuasive factors important in substance abuse intervention programs (Rose, Bearden, and Manning 1996). Comprehensive theoretical models in persuasion, such as the *elaboration likelihood model* (ELM) (Petty and Cacioppo 1986) and its extensions (Batra and Ray 1986; MacInnis and Jaworski 1989; Meyers-Levy and Malaviya 1999) and the *theory of reasoned action* (Ajzen and Fishbein 1980; Fishbein and Ajzen 1975), have integrated a multitude of persuasive theories and helped to explain consumer motivation, opportunity, ability, and experiences in processing marketing communications. Such information has been helpful in evaluating the success of consumer protection campaigns and regulations (e.g., nutrition information, energy labels, tobacco marketing restrictions). Theoretical frameworks of coping behavior and fear persuasion, such as the *protection motivation model* (Rogers 1975; Tanner, Hunt, and Eppright 1991), the *parallel response model* (Leventhal 1970), and risk perception research (Slovic, Fischhoff, and Lichtenstein 1980), have aided our understanding of the processing of warning labels and prevention programs. Likewise, *prospect theory* (Tversky and Kahneman 1981) can assist our knowledge of the weighing of negative and positive information in disclosures. Finally, *psychological reactance theory* (Brehm 1966) offers much insight into situations where consumers' personal freedom is believed to be restricted due to regulations (cf. Mazis 1975).

A third contributing area is theoretical research on *ad claim processing*. Specifically, ad claims in question may interact with other consumer "evidence" such as prior experience, involvement levels, and package labeling. The *integrated information response model* (Smith and Swinyard 1982) helps to explain consumer processing in such an interactive environment. Similarly, research by Deighton (1984) and Hoch and Ha (1986) examined the integration between advertising and trial experience, especially under varying levels of evidence ambiguity. Darley and Smith's (1993) "*claim objectivity classification*" has helped researchers in experimental studies on deceptive advertising. Similarly, *economics of information theory* (Ford, Smith, and Swasy 1990; Nelson 1974; Smith 1990) provides an important classification of ad claims according to search, experience, and credence attributes. For example, researchers comparing Lanham Act and FTC cases have applied this classification (Petty 1992), and economics of information theory has been used extensively in its application to FTC nutrition and environmental cases. Finally, contributions from the *ad inferencing* literature have provided critical linguistic and legal analyses of deceptive advertising content (Harris, Dubitsky, and Bruno 1983; Richards 1990; Shimp 1978, 1983).

A fourth area of theoretical contributions to consumer protection policy is the study of *source effects*. For example, Alba and Hutchinson's (1987) hypothesized effects on consumer expertise and knowledge and Kelman's (1961) *model of source attributes* (credibility, attractiveness, and power) and *receiver processing modes* (internalization, identification, and compliance) are helpful resources for the study of endorsements and testimonial advertising (FTC 1980; see also Kertz and Ohanian 1992).

Cautions and Suggestions for Marketing and Public Policy Researchers

To enhance contributions to consumer protection policy, several cautions and suggestions for marketing and consumer researchers are offered in this section. One general recommendation is that marketing and consumer researchers might try to become greater advocates of the many theoretical contributions studied in our field and applied in consumer protection policy. As shown in Figure 1.1, such marketing knowledge is likely to compete with long-standing theories from economics and law for the attention of consumer protection agency personnel. Thus, it is up to marketing scholars to demonstrate the value of theory from the marketing discipline in policy formation. The following specific suggestions apply both for those conducting academic research on public policy issues and for those involved in contract research (e.g., copy tests, rule evaluation) for consumer protection agencies.

Issue Immersion

The first suggestion to enhance contributions for consumer protection policy is that, before any research is conducted, it might be helpful to take the time to fully understand the nuances of the issue and why past research is deemed to be useful or irrelevant. Thus, it is very important to become *immersed* with the substantive public policy issue at hand and its many complexities. One method to accomplish this is to thoroughly examine the multiple sides and viewpoints on the issue (e.g., by speaking to staff attorneys, economists, and industry representatives). Information gained from agency sites on the Internet, conferences, hearings, special issues, retrospective sections (e.g., Spring 1997 *JPP&M*), and calls for research can be an invaluable planning tool. However, researchers might be cautious when secondary data sets become available in that the data might dictate the study objectives rather than the theory or public policy issue being examined. In such a scenario, a forcing of theory or public policy questions into the existing data set might be very transparent to consumer protection personnel and eventual reviewers.

Differing Perspectives

When researchers enter the consumer protection arena, there exist two play-ers—attorneys and economists—that already have established rules of proce-dure and conduct. The greatest chance of having an impact is to test public pol-icy issues with an appreciation of their language and frameworks (e.g., legal process, legal cites, economic principles and analysis). Thus, enhancing one's familiarity with the economic and legal theories involved in a given public pol-icy issue or case is a good idea. At the same time, with such an understanding of differing perspectives (cf. Mazis 1980), marketing and consumer researchers should be comfortable in effectively communicating the contributions from our field to other disciplines.

Theoretical Grounding

Another suggestion is that researchers might consider carefully the role of theory in the *formation* of studies on consumer protection topics. The consider-ation of theory firmly grounds our application tests about public policy in offer-ing a systematic structure (e.g., nomological network of relationships) capable of explaining and predicting future issues and events (cf. Hunt 1991, p. 4). With-out theory, our tests might be applicable only in isolation and will not offer the richer program of research afforded by links to a network of predicted relation-ships useful in research extensions. This reliance also bolsters the discussion of contract studies under cross-examination by integrating the study findings within the larger network of research associated with the theory (or theories). Moreover, many avenues exist for the role of theory in marketing and public pol-icy research. For example, theoretical frameworks may be subjected to specific application tests in the context of a marketing and public policy issue. Alterna-tively, a series of public policy application tests may help to form or alter present theories through the process of induction. Or, one might wish to pit theory against theory in an application test in the spirit of "strong inference" (Platt 1964). For example, a multitude of theories exist helping to explain and predict effects in conducting warnings, disclosures, and ad claim studies (e.g., activa-tion theory, adaptation-level theory, economics of information, the ELM, inte-grated information response theory, legal theories, parallel response theory, prospect theory, protection motivation model, theory of reasoned action [or behavior]).

Striking a Balance

One caution in theory development work, however, is that it is possible to oversimplify the public policy issue in question (Wilkie 1997). As indicated by Petty and Cacioppo (1996), researchers might attempt to develop not only the theoretical aspects of their work but also try to link these with having a substan-tive impact on society. Moreover, the very nature of a theory is that it is *empiri-cally testable* (Hunt 1991), and in our field this means a closer representation and linkage with the specific public policy issues in question (Shimp 1994). In so doing, however, researchers face a difficult balancing act in trying to address concerns of both internal validity (e.g., with causal inferences) and external validity (e.g., generalizability of the findings to other settings) in studies (Cook and Campbell 1979). As suggested previously, issue immersion, the use of a realistic methodology, and consideration of the appropriate theoretical domain are likely to help in achieving such a balance.

Research Design and Rigor

Some have suggested that if the data are likely to be used by consumer protection agencies involved in litigation (e.g., a FTC trial), then a researcher should think of the most thorough journal review that he or she has ever received. Under the discovery process, one's data, questionnaires, and pretest results will be made available to the other side, which will hire an expert to find flaws in one's research. If the case proceeds to trial, then the researcher might be subjected to a cross-examination of the materials and prior deposition comments. In general, and in the context of providing extrinsic evidence for enforcement actions, the researcher's adherence to "generally accepted principles" and maintaining of independence (as opposed to advocacy) are important practices in ensuring a successful outcome (Maronick 1991). Also, in the design of studies for consumer protection agencies, the objectives for the study might be at odds with the researcher's own objectives, training, and methods in performing such studies. If the goal is eventual journal publication of the study (assuming that it is made public), then this might alter the beginning strategy for the design. For example, there might be pressure to test a multitude of warning and disclosure cells based on pending case scenarios rather than to use a systematic variation of content, control groups, and ties to theory. On the other hand, the use of realistic stimuli, procedures, and a representative sample of the policy issue being studied helps to enhance the usefulness of the results for consumer protection policy and to increase its chances for journal publication.

Multiple Approaches and Programmatic Research

With respect to methodology, the consideration of multiple approaches (e.g., surveys, qualitative studies, experimentation in the field and laboratories, meta-analyses, legal and policy analyses, and case studies) is encouraged in addressing a given public policy issue. For example, the combination of ethnographic fieldwork and a follow-up study using experimental variables discovered from the first study might provide additional insight into the issue. Also, as advocated elsewhere (cf. Andreasen 1997; Bloom 1997), the study of actual behavior with respect to the policy issue can enhance the contribution of the research. Such multiple approaches add value to the contributions from the marketing discipline to both policy formation and policy enforcement.

Another observation is that some of the more influential articles contributing to consumer protection policy and thought are the products of long-term programmatic research in an area. This is evident in the review of contributors mentioned in this chapter on multiple occasions in a given policy area. Finally, researchers are encouraged to "stay the course" over the years in addressing public policy research, even though funding might fluctuate according to the political interest levels in public policy activity. The reason is that if a proposed study is well done, then support usually will follow.

Future Research Directions

There are several needs for research on consumer protection issues that are likely to continue for some time and are addressed in this final section. However, one way in which to keep abreast of consumer protection issues is to be a frequent visitor to congressional, federal agency, consumer group, and trade association Web sites that are likely to share current topics of importance.

The issue of privacy of personal information offered, required, or captured in e-commerce, computer sensors and microchip technology, children's Web sites, Internet banking, electronic transfer of medical records, on-line profiling (FTC 1999c), and information transfer between countries with varying privacy policies is likely to be debated for some time (see Spring 2000 issue of *JPP&M*). For example, the FTC's (1999b) recent children's advertising privacy protection rule is a result of congressional action in this area. Parental verification is needed before companies can collect personally identifiable information on the Internet from children under 13 years of age. However, there exists little consumer research as to how children might respond to disclosures and requests for parental approval on Web sites. A rich body of theory on children's processing of information exists (cf. Macklin and Carlson 1999) and might be applied in this setting or in other policy issues with children (e.g., reactions to disclosures of violence found in video games). Also, the study of "opt-in" versus "opt-out" strategies for protecting the privacy of information might be examined, especially if there are differences in other parts of the world (e.g., EU).

A related topic that has received some attention recently is the applicability of FTC rules and guides in electronic media (FTC 1999a). However, little is known about how consumers process Web sites, ad banners, and corporate public relations pages over the Internet. Exactly where should disclosures be placed in Web-based advertising? Is it important that consumers understand the corporate sources of the sites? How will deception and unfairness policies apply in this new environment? An understanding of underlying economic principles (e.g., economics of information) also might be important in the FTC's application of e-commerce issues. For example, economics of information principles would argue that more resources should be applied to cases of fraud over the Internet than to shopper- or search-related Internet issues. Whereas such a trade-off certainly is open to debate, marketers might consider the underlying principles that could be applied in such a policy analysis.

Corrective advertising represents a potentially important remedy tool at the FTC. Recently, the final order in the *Novartis* (1999) case required ads and packaging for Doan's Pills to include, in a clear and conspicuous manner, the following message: "Although Doan's is an effective pain reliever, there is no evidence that Doan's is more effective than other pain relievers for back pain." The corrective statement was to be carried on all packaging and ads for one year (except radio and television ads of 15 seconds or less) and until Novartis expended a total of $8 million on Doan's advertising. In general, research questions remain regarding the necessary length of time and impact of lingering beliefs needed for corrective ad remedies. Also, opportunities exist to examine systematically the effectiveness of different corrective ad language, measures, formats, and media placements.

In addition to the need for study of consumer perceptions of dietary supplement claims (FTC 1998a), little is known regarding how consumers will respond to claims, evidence, and disclosures for functional foods appearing in the marketplace. Such promotion might be viewed in the same category as a material credence claim due to its focus on health issues; therefore, it might receive greater scrutiny. Functional foods have added herbs, additives, cultures, and vitamins with medicinal claims of aiding depression, lessening symptoms of colds, improving one's ability to concentrate, and so on (Brophy and Schardt 1999). However, little research exists as to how consumers will react to such claims, evidence, and disclosures. Do consumers have the necessary knowledge to interpret the safety and efficacy of evidence advertised about such foods? Do they understand the difference between "structure function claims" (e.g., "promotes a healthy heart"—yet with high levels of fat) versus health claims (e.g., "may reduce the risk of heart disease"—meeting disqualifying levels for negative nutrients such as total fat)?

Other topics for possible research include debates regarding the trade-offs between domestic consumer protection laws and international trade agreements (e.g., North American Free Trade Agreement, World Trade Organization [WTO]). Similarly, marked differences exist between the United States and other countries on the determination and regulation of deceptive, unfair, and comparative advertising (Petty 1997). As partnerships, agreements, and markets evolve (e.g., EU, WTO), is a harmonization and consistency of ad regulations best for consumers and competition? Finally, much can be done in the study of the effectiveness of different anti-tobacco (as well as anti-alcohol abuse and anti-gambling) ads that differ in their types of appeals used across jurisdictions (cf. Pechmann and Goldberg 1998). Thus, many opportunities exist for public policy scholars on consumer protection matters. It is in our best interest as a field, which is valued by consumer protection officials, to play a proactive role in contributing knowledge in this area.

References

Ajzen, Icek and Martin Fishbein (1980), *Understanding Attitudes and Predicting Social Behavior.* Englewood Cliffs, NJ: Prentice Hall.

Alba, Joseph W. and J. Wesley Hutchinson (1987), "Dimensions of Consumer Expertise," *Journal of Consumer Research,* 13 (March), 411-54.

Andreasen, Alan R. (1997), "From Ghetto Marketing to Social Marketing: Bringing Social Relevance to Mainstream Marketing," *Journal of Public Policy & Marketing,* 16 (Spring), 129-31.

Andrews, J. Craig (1996), "Overview: The Role of Consumer Research in National Advertising Regulation," *Advertising Law Anthology,* 19 (Part 1, January-June), xix-xxvii.

——— and Thomas J. Maronick (1995), "Advertising Research Issues from *FTC versus Stouffer Foods Corporation,*" *Journal of Public Policy & Marketing,* 14 (Fall), 301-9.

——— and Richard G. Netemeyer (1996), "Alcohol Warning Label Effects: Socialization, Addiction, and Public Policy Issues," in *Marketing and Consumer Research in the Public Interest,* Ronald Paul Hill, ed. Thousand Oaks, CA: Sage, 153-75.

———, ———, and Scot Burton (1998), "Consumer Generalization of Nutrient Content Claims in Advertising," *Journal of Marketing,* 62 (October), 62-75.

Andrews, Rick and George R. Franke (1991), "The Determinants of Cigarette Consumption: A Meta-Analysis," *Journal of Public Policy & Marketing,* 10 (Spring), 81-100.

Barlow, Todd and Michael S. Wogalter (1993), "Alcoholic Beverage Warnings in Magazine and Television Advertisements," *Journal of Consumer Research,* 20, 147-56.

Barone, Michael J., Randall L. Rose, Kenneth C. Manning, and Paul W. Miniard (1996), "Another Look at the Impact of Reference Information on Consumer Impressions of Nutrition Information," *Journal of Public Policy & Marketing,* 15 (Spring), 55-62.

Barry, Thomas E. (1987), "The Development of the Hierarchy of Effects," in *Current Issues and Research in Advertising,* James H. Leigh and Claude R. Martin, Jr., eds. Ann Arbor: University of Michigan Press, 251-96.

Batra, Rajeev and Michael L. Ray (1986), "Situational Effects of Advertising Repetition: The Moderating Influence of Motivation, Ability, and Opportunity to Respond," *Journal of Consumer Research,* 12 (March), 432-45.

Bernhardt, Kenneth L. and Ronald Stiff (1981), "Public Policy Update: Perspective in the Federal Trade Commission," in *Advances in Consumer Research,* Vol. 8, Kent B. Monroe, ed. Ann Arbor, MI: Association for Consumer Research, 452-54.

Bernstein, Joan Z. (1996), "Federal Trade Commission Solicits Consumer Research," in *Advances in Consumer Research,* Vol. 23, Kim P. Corfman and John G. Lynch, Jr., eds. Provo, UT: Association for Consumer Research, 313-15.

Bettman, James R. (1979), *An Information Processing Theory of Consumer Choice.* Reading, MA: Addison-Wesley.

———, John W. Payne, and Richard Staelin (1986), "Cognitive Considerations in Designing Effective Labels for Presenting Risk Information," *Journal of Public Policy & Marketing,* 5, 1-28.

Bhalla, Gaurav and John L. Lastovicka (1984), "The Impact of Changing Cigarette Warning Message Content and Format," in *Advances in Consumer Research,* Vol. 11, Thomas C. Kinnear, ed. Provo, UT: Association for Consumer Research, 305-10.

Bloom, Paul N. (1997), "Field of Marketing and Public Policy: Introduction and Overview," *Journal of Public Policy & Marketing,* 16 (Spring), 126-28.

——— and Gregory T. Gundlach, eds. (2000), *Handbook of Marketing and Society.* Thousand Oaks, CA: Sage.

Boddewyn, J. J. (1994), "Cigarette Advertising Bans and Smoking: The Flawed Policy Connections," *International Journal of Advertising,* 13 (4), 311-32.

Brehm, Jack W. (1966), *A Theory of Psychological Reactance.* New York: Academic Press.

Brophy, Beth and David Schardt (1999), "Functional Foods," *Nutrition Action Healthletter,* April, 3-7.

Brucks, Merrie, Gary M. Armstrong, and Marvin E. Goldberg (1988), "Children's Use of Cognitive Defenses against Television Advertising: A Cognitive Response Approach," *Journal of Consumer Research,* 14 (4), 471-82.

Burke, Raymond R., Wayne S. DeSarbo, Richard L. Oliver, and Thomas S. Robertson (1988), "Deception by Implication: An Experimental Investigation," *Journal of Consumer Research,* 14 (March), 483-94.

Burton, Scot and J. Craig Andrews (1996), "An Examination of Age, Product Nutrition, and Nutrition Label Effects on Consumer Perceptions and Product Evaluations," *Journal of Consumer Affairs,* 30 (Summer), 68-89.

———, Abe Biswas, and Richard G. Netemeyer (1994), "Effects of Alternative Nutrition Label Formats and Nutrition Reference Information on Consumer Perceptions, Comprehension, and Product Evaluations," *Journal of Public Policy & Marketing,* 13 (Spring), 36-47.

Calfee, John E. (1986), "The Ghost of Cigarette Advertising Past," *Regulation,* November-December, 35-45.

"Campbell Soup Company and the Federal Trade Commission" (1992), in *Ethics in Marketing,* N. Craig Smith and John A. Quelch, eds. Homewood, IL: Irwin, 636-40.

Center for Science in the Public Interest (1994), *Food Advertising Chaos: The Case for Reform.* Washington, DC: CSPI.

Cliffdale Associates Inc. (1984), 103 FTC 110-202.

Cohen, Dorothy (1980), "The FTC's Advertising Substantiation Program," *Journal of Marketing,* 44 (Winter), 26-35.

——— (1982), "Unfairness in Advertising Revisited," *Journal of Marketing,* 46 (Winter), 73-80.

——— (1995), *Legal Issues in Marketing Decision Making.* Cincinnati, OH: South-Western.

Cohen, Joel B. (1990), "Charting a Public Policy Agenda for Cigarettes," in *Marketing and Advertising Regulation: The Federal Trade Commission in the 1990s,* Patrick E. Murphy and William L. Wilkie, eds. Notre Dame, IN: University of Notre Dame Press, 234-54.

——— (1998), Expert Testimony in the Matter of R. J. Reynolds Tobacco Company, FTC Docket No. 9285, November 16, 1-66.

Cook, Thomas D. and Donald T. Campbell (1979), *Quasi-Experimentation: Design and Analysis Issues for Field Settings.* Boston: Houghton Mifflin.

Cox, Eli P., III, Michael S. Wogalter, Sara L. Stokes, and Elizabeth J. Tipton Murff (1997), "Do Product Warnings Increase Safe Behavior? A Meta-Analysis," *Journal of Public Policy & Marketing,* 16 (Fall), 195-204.

Darley, William K. and Robert E. Smith (1993), "Advertising Claim Objectivity: Antecedents and Effects," *Journal of Marketing,* 57 (October), 100-13.

Deighton, John (1984), "The Interaction of Advertising and Evidence," *Journal of Consumer Research,* 11 (December), 763-70.

Eggland's Best Inc. (1994), FTC Docket No. C-3520 (consent agreement), August 15.

Federal Trade Commission (1978), *FTC Staff Report on Television Advertising to Children.* Washington, DC: FTC.

——— (1979), *Policy on Consumer Information Remedies.* Washington, DC: FTC.

——— (1980), *Guides Concerning Use of Endorsement and Testimonials in Advertising,* 16 *CFR* 255.

——— (1981), "Children's Advertising: Termination of Federal Trade Commission Rulemaking Proceeding," *Federal Register,* October 2, 48710-14.

——— (1992), *Guides for the Use of Environmental Claims.* Washington, DC: FTC. (Revised 1996, 1998)

———(1993), *Trade Rule Pursuant to the Telephone Disclosure and Dispute Resolution Act* (900 number rule), 16 *CFR* 308, August 9, 42364-406.

——— (1994), *Enforcement Policy Statement on Food Advertising.* Washington, DC: FTC.

———(1995a), *FTC Survey" (n. 6), in "Request for Comment Concerning Environmental Marketing Guides,* 16 *CFR,* Part 260, 1-4.

——— (1995b), *Telemarketing Sales Rule,* 16 *CFR* 310.

——— (1998a), *Dietary Supplements: An Advertising Guide for Industry.* Washington, DC: FTC.

——— (1998b), *Generic Copy Test of Food Health Claims in Advertising.* Washington, DC: FTC.

——— (1998c), *Interpretation of Rules and Guides for Electronic Media: Request for Comment,* 16 *CFR,* Chapter 1, May 6, 24996-5005.

——— (1998d), *Privacy Online Report to Congress.* Washington, DC: FTC.

——— (1999a), *Announcement of Date of Public Workshop on the Interpretation of Rules and Guides for Electronic Media, Procedure for Requesting to Participate, and Request for Submission of Advertisements.* Washington, DC: FTC.

———(1999b), *Children's Online Privacy Protection Rule,* 16 *CFR* 312, November 3.

——— (1999c), *Notice on Department of Commerce and Federal Trade Commission Public Workshop on Online Profiling,* Docket No. 990811219-9219-01, September 15.

Federal Trade Commission Act Amendments of 1994, *Statutes at Large,* 108, 1691. (Public Law 103-312).

Fishbein, Martin and Icek Ajzen (1975), *Belief, Attitude, Intention, and Behavior: An Introduction to Theory and Research.* Reading, MA: Addison-Wesley.

Food and Drug Administration (1993), *Food Labeling; General Provisions . . . Final Rules,* 21 *CFR,* Part 1, January 6, 2302-964.

——— (1996), *Regulations Restricting the Sale and Distribution of Cigarettes and Smokeless Tobacco to Protect Children and Adolescents: Final Rule,* 21 *CFR* 801, Part 2, August 28, 44396-5318.

Food and Drug Administration v. Brown & Williamson Tobacco Corporation (2000), 120 S.Ct., 1291-333.

Ford, Gary T. and John E. Calfee (1986), "Recent Developments in FTC Policy on Deception," *Journal of Marketing,* 50 (July), 82-103.

———, Manoj Hastak, Anusree Mitra, and Debra J. Ringold (1996), "Can Consumers Interpret Nutrition Information in the Presence of a Health Claim? A Laboratory Investigation," *Journal of Public Policy & Marketing,* 15 (Spring), 16-27.

———, Darlene B. Smith, and John L. Swasy (1990), "Consumer Skepticism of Advertising Claims: Testing Hypotheses from Economics of Information," *Journal of Consumer Research,* 16 (March), 433-41.

Foxman, Ellen, Darrel D. Muehling, and Patrick A. Moore (1988), "Disclaimer Footnotes in Ads: Discrepancies between Purpose and Performance," *Journal of Public Policy & Marketing,* 7, 127-37.

Goldberg, Marvin E., Gerald J. Gorn, and Wendy Gibson (1978), "TV Messages for Snack and Breakfast Foods: Do They Influence Children's Preferences?" *Journal of Consumer Research,* 5 (September), 73-81.

——— and Lynn T. Kozlowski (1997), "Loopholes and Lapses in the '1997 Tobacco Agreement': Some Devils in the Marketing Details," *Journal of Public Policy & Marketing,* 16 (Fall), 345-51.

Gregan-Paxton, Jennifer and Deborah Roedder John (1997), "The Emergence of Adaptive Decision Making in Children," *Journal of Consumer Research,* 24 (June), 43-56.

Greyser, Stephen A. (1997), "Consumer Research and the Public Policy Process: Then and Now," *Journal of Public Policy & Marketing,* 16 (Spring), 137-38.

Harris, Richard Jackson, Tony M. Dubitsky, and Kristin Jo Bruno (1983), "Psycholinguistic Studies of Misleading Advertising," in *Information Processing Research in Advertising,* Richard J. Harris, ed. Hillsdale, NJ: Lawrence Erlbaum, 241-62.

Hasbro Inc. (1993), FTC File No. 912-3369 (consent agreement), April 15.

———(1996), FTC Docket No. C-3447, Civil Action No. 96-451P (order violation and civil penalty), August 7.

Hill, Ronald Paul, ed. (1996), *Marketing and Consumer Research in the Public Interest.* Thousand Oaks, CA: Sage.

Hilton, Michael E. (1993), "An Overview of Recent Findings on Alcoholic Beverage Warning Labels," *Journal of Public Policy & Marketing,* 12 (Spring), 1-9.

Hoch, Stephen J. and Young-Won Ha (1986), "Consumer Learning: Advertising and the Ambiguity of Product Experience," *Journal of Consumer Research,* 13 (September), 221-32.

Hollander, Stanley C., William W. Keep, and Roger Dickinson (1999), "Marketing Public Policy and the Evolving Role of Marketing Academics: An Historical Perspective," *Journal of Public Policy & Marketing,* 18 (Fall), 265-69.

Hoy, Maria Grubbs and Michael J. Stankey (1993), "Structural Characteristics of Televised Advertising Disclosures: A Comparison with the FTC Clear and Conspicuous Standard," *Journal of Advertising,* 22 (June), 47-59.

Hunt, Shelby D. (1978), "A General Paradigm of Marketing: In Support of the Three Dichotomies Model," *Journal of Marketing,* 40 (July), 107-10.

———(1991), *Modern Marketing Theory: Critical Issues in the Philosophy of Marketing Science.* Cincinnati, OH: South-Western.

Ippolito, Pauline M. and Alan D. Mathios (1991), "Health Claims in Food Marketing: Evidence on Knowledge and Behavior in the Cereal Market," *Journal of Public Policy & Marketing,* 10 (1), 15-32.

Jacoby, Jacob and Wayne D. Hoyer (1982), "Viewer Miscomprehension of Televised Communication: Selected Findings," *Journal of Marketing,* 46 (Fall), 12-26.

———and George J. Szybillo (1995), "Consumer Research in *FTC v. Kraft:* A Case of Heads We Win, Tails You Lose?" *Journal of Public Policy & Marketing,* 14 (Spring), 1-14.

Johar, Gita Venkataramani (1995), "Consumer Involvement and Deception from Implied Advertising Claims," *Journal of Marketing Research,* 32 (August), 267-79.

Jones, Mary Gardiner (1990), "Marketing Academics at the FTC: Reflections and Recommendations," in *Marketing and Advertising Regulation: The Federal Trade Commission in the 1990s,* Patrick E. Murphy and William L. Wilkie, eds. Notre Dame, IN: University of Notre Dame Press, 216-20.

———and Murray Silverman (1973), "Is There a Role for Research in the Federal Trade Commission?" in *Proceedings of Workshop on Public Policy and Marketing Practices,* Fred C. Allvine, ed. Chicago: American Marketing Association, 69-81.

Keller, Punam Anand and Lauren Goldberg Block (1996), "Increasing the Persuasiveness of Fear Appeals: The Effect of Arousal and Elaboration," *Journal of Consumer Research,* 22 (March), 448-59.

Keller, Scott B., Mike Landry, Jeanne Olson, Anne M. Velliquette, Scot Burton, and J. Craig Andrews (1997), "The Effects of Nutrition Package Claims, Nutrition Facts Panels, and Motivation to Process Nutrition Information on Consumer Product Evaluations," *Journal of Public Policy & Marketing,* 16 (Fall), 256-69.

Kelman, Herbert C. (1961), "Processes of Opinion Change," *Public Opinion Quarterly,* 25 (Spring), 57-58.

Kertz, Consuelo Lauda and Roobina Ohanian (1992), "Source Credibility, Legal Liability, and the Law of Endorsements," *Journal of Public Policy & Marketing,* 11 (Spring), 12-23.

Kinnear, Thomas C. (1997), "An Historic Perspective on the Quantity and Quality of Marketing and Public Policy Research," *Journal of Marketing & Public Policy,* 16 (Spring), 144-46.

Kraft Inc. (1991), Commision Decision, 114 FTC 40-46, 116-51; *aff'd, Kraft Inc. v. FTC* (1992), 970 F.2d 311 (7th Cir.), 311-28; *cert. denied* (1993), 113 S.Ct., 1254.

Laczniak, Russell N. and Sanford Grossbart (1990), "An Assessment of Assumptions Underlying the Reasonable Consumer Element in Deceptive Advertising Policy," *Journal of Public Policy & Marketing,* 9, 85-99.

Lavidge, Robert J. and Gary A. Steiner (1961), "A Model for Predictive Measurements of Advertising Effectiveness," *Journal of Marketing,* 25 (October), 59-62.

Leventhal, Howard (1970), "Findings and Theory in the Study of Fear Communications," in *Advances in Experimental Social Psychology,* Vol. 5, Leonard Berkowitz, ed. New York: Academic Press, 119-86.

Levy, Alan S., Sara B. Fein, and Raymond E. Schucker (1996), "Performance Characteristics of Seven Nutrition Label Formats," *Journal of Public Policy & Marketing,* 15 (1), 1-15.

Lutz, Kathy A. and Richard J. Lutz (1977), "The Effects of Interactive Imagery on Learning: Application to Advertising," *Journal of Applied Psychology,* 62 (August), 493-98.

MacInnis, Deborah J. and Bernard J. Jaworski (1989), "Information Processing from Advertisements: Toward an Integrative Framework," *Journal of Marketing,* 53 (October), 1-23.

Macklin, M. Carole (1985), "Do Young Children Understand the Selling Intent of Commercials?" *Journal of Consumer Affairs,* 19 (2), 293-304.

——— and Les Carlson, eds. (1999), *Advertising to Children: Concepts and Controversies.* Thousand Oaks, CA: Sage.

Maronick, Thomas J. (1990), "Current Role of Research at the Federal Trade Commission," in *Marketing and Advertising Regulation: The Federal Trade Commission in the 1990s,* Patrick E. Murphy and William L. Wilkie, eds. Notre Dame, IN: University of Notre Dame Press, 345-55.

——— (1991), "Copy Tests in FTC Deception Cases: Guidelines for Researchers," *Journal of Advertising Research,* 31 (December), 9-17.

——— and J. Craig Andrews (1999), "The Role of Qualifying Language on Consumer Perceptions of Environmental Claims," *Journal of Consumer Affairs,* 33 (Winter), 297-320.

Martin, Mary C. (1997), "Children's Understanding of the Intent of Advertising: A Meta-Analysis," *Journal of Public Policy & Marketing,* 16 (Fall), 205-16.

Mathios, Alan D. (1996), "Socioeconomic Factors, Nutrition, and Food Choices: An Analysis of the Food Dressing Market," *Journal of Public Policy & Marketing,* 15 (Spring), 45-54.

Mayer, Robert N., Jason Gray-Lee, Debra L. Scammon, and Brenda J. Cude (1995), *Trends in Environmental Marketing Claims since the FTC Guides.* Salt Lake City: University of Utah, Department of Family and Consumer Studies.

Mazis, Michael B. (1975), "Antipollution Measures and Psychological Reactance Theory: A Field Experiment," *Journal of Personality and Social Psychology,* 31, 654-60.

——— (1980), "An Overview of Product Labeling and Health Risks," in *Banbury Report 6: Product Labeling and Health Risks,* Louis A. Morris, Michael B. Mazis, and Ivan Barofsky, eds. Cold Spring Harbor, NY: Cold Spring Harbor Laboratory, 3-11.

———— (1997), "Marketing and Public Policy: Prospects for the Future," *Journal of Public Policy & Marketing,* 16 (Spring), 139-43.

McGuire, William J. (1962), "Persistence of the Resistance to Persuasion Induced by Various Types of Prior Belief Defenses," *Journal of Abnormal and Social Psychology,* 64, 241-48.

———— (1976), "Some Internal Psychological Factors Influencing Consumer Choice," *Journal of Consumer Research,* 4 (March), 302-19.

———— (1980), "The Communication-Persuasion Model and Health-Risk Labeling," in *Banbury Report 6: Product Labeling and Health Risks,* Louis A. Morris, Michael B. Mazis, and Ivan Barofsky, eds. Cold Spring Harbor, NY: Cold Spring Harbor Laboratory, 99-122.

Meyers-Levy, Joan and Prashant Malaviya (1999), "Consumers' Processing of Persuasive Advertisements: An Integrative Framework of Persuasion Theories," *Journal of Marketing,* 63 (Special Issue), 45-60.

Mitchell, Andrew A. (1983), "Cognitive Processes Initiated by Exposure to Advertising," in *Information Processing Research in Advertising,* Richard Jackson Harris, ed. Hillsdale, NJ: Lawrence Erlbaum, 13-42.

Mitra, Anusree, Manoj Hastak, Gary T. Ford, and Debra Jones Ringold (1999), "Can the Educationally Disadvantaged Interpret the FDA-Mandated Nutrition Facts Panel in the Presence of an Implied Health Claim?" *Journal of Public Policy & Marketing,* 18 (Spring), 106-17.

Monroe, Kent B., William L. Wilkie, Linda J. McAleer, and Albert R. Wildt (1986), "Report of the AMA Task on the Development of Marketing Thought," in *Marketing Education: Knowledge Development, Dissemination, and Utilization,* Joseph Guiltinan and Dale Archabal, eds. Chicago: American Marketing Association, 8-9.

Moorman, Christine (1996), "A Quasi-Experiment to Assess the Consumer and Informational Determinants of Nutrition Information Processing Activities: The Case of the Nutrition Labeling and Education Act," *Journal of Public Policy & Marketing,* 15 (Spring), 28-44.

Morgan, Fred W. (1990), "Judicial Standards for Survey Research: An Update and Guidelines," *Journal of Marketing,* 54 (January), 59-70.

Morris, Louis, Manoj Hastak, and Michael Mazis (1995), "Consumer Comprehension of Environmental Advertising and Labeling Claims," *Journal of Consumer Affairs,* 29 (2), 328-50.

Murphy, Patrick E. (1990), "Past FTC Participation by Marketing Academics," in *Marketing and Advertising Regulation: The Federal Trade Commission in the 1990s,* Patrick E. Murphy and William L. Wilkie, eds. Notre Dame, IN: University of Notre Dame Press, 205-15.

Murray, Noel M., Lalita A. Manrai, and Ajay K. Manrai (1993), "Public Policy Relating to Consumer Comprehension of Television Commercials: A Review and Some Empirical Results," *Journal of Consumer Policy,* 16 (2), 145-70.

Nelson, Phillip (1974), "Advertising as Information," *Journal of Political Economy,* 78 (March-April), 729-54.

Novartis Corporation (1999), Commission Decision, FTC Docket No. 9279, May 27, 1-38.

Nutrition Labeling and Education Act (1990), Public Law 101-535, 21 U.S.C. 301, November 8.

Olson, Jerry C. and Philip A. Dover (1978), "Cognitive Effects of Deceptive Advertising," *Journal of Marketing Research,* 15 (February), 29-38.

Owen, Debra K. and Joyce E. Plyler (1991), "The Role of Empirical Evidence in the Federal Regulation of Advertising," *Journal of Public Policy & Marketing,* 10 (1), 1-14.

Paivio, Allan (1969), "Mental Imagery in Associative Learning and Memory," *Psychological Review,* 76 (May), 241-63.

Pappalardo, Janis K. (1997), "The Role of Consumer Research in Evaluating Deception: An Economist's Perspective," *Antitrust Law Journal,* 65, 793-812.

Pechmann, Cornelia (1996), "Do Consumers Overgeneralize One-Sided Comparative Price Claims, and Are More Stringent Regulations Needed?" *Journal of Marketing Research,* 33 (May), 150-62.

———— and Marvin E. Goldberg (1998), "Should Anti-Smoking Ads Attempt to Denormalize Tobacco Use? Alternative Perspectives and Theoretical Frameworks," paper presented at the meeting of the Association for Consumer Research, October, Montreal.

———— and S. Ratneshwar (1994), "The Effects of Antismoking and Cigarette Advertising on Adolescents' Perceptions of Peers Who Smoke," *Journal of Consumer Research,* 21 (September), 236-51.

Petty, Richard E. and John T. Cacioppo (1986), *Communication and Persuasion: Central and Peripheral Routes to Attitude Change.* New York: Springer-Verlag.

———— and ———— (1996), "Addressing Disturbing and Disturbed Consumer Behavior: Is It Necessary to Change the Way We Conduct Behavior Science?" *Journal of Marketing Research,* 33 (February), 1-8.

Petty, Ross D. (1992), *The Impact of Advertising Law on Business and Public Policy.* Westport, CT: Quorum Books.

———— (1997), "Advertising Law in the United States and the European Union," *Journal of Public Policy & Marketing,* 16 (Spring), 2-13.

———— (1999), "Tobacco Marketing Restrictions in the Multistate Attorneys General Settlement: Is This Good Public Policy?" *Journal of Public Policy & Marketing,* 18 (Fall), 249-57.

Platt, John (1964), "Strong Inference," *Science,* October, 347-53.

Plevan, Kenneth A. and Miriam L. Siroky (1991), *Advertising Compliance Handbook,* 2nd ed. New York: Practicing Law Institute.

Pollay, Richard W., S. Siddarth, Michael Siegel, Anne Haddix, Robert Merritt, Gary A. Giovino, and Michael Ericksen (1996), "The Last Straw? Cigarette Advertising and Realized Market Shares among Youths and Adults, 1979-1993," *Journal of Marketing,* 60 (April), 1-16.

Preston, Ivan L. (1987), "Extrinsic Evidence in Federal Trade Commission Deceptiveness Cases," *Columbia Business Law Review,* 3, 633-94.

———— (1992), "The Scandalous Record of Avoidable Errors in Expert Evidence Offered in FTC and Lanham Act Deceptiveness Cases," in *Proceedings of the 1992 Marketing and Public Policy Conference,* Paul N. Bloom and Richard G. Starr, Jr., eds. Chapel Hill: University of North Carolina Press, 2-19.

———— (1995), "Unfairness Developments in FTC Advertising Cases," *Journal of Public Policy & Marketing,* 14 (Fall), 318-20.

Richards, Jef I. (1990), *Deceptive Advertising: Behavioral Study of a Legal Concept.* Hillsdale, NJ: Lawrence Erlbaum.

Rindfleisch, Aric and David Crockett (1999), "Cigarette Smoking and Perceived Risk: A Multidimensional Investigation," *Journal of Public Policy & Marketing,* 18 (Fall), 159-71.

Roe, Brian, Alan S. Levy, and Brenda M. Derby (1999), "The Impact of Health Claims on Consumer Search and Product Evaluation Outcomes: Results from FDA Experimental Data," *Journal of Public Policy & Marketing,* 18 (Spring), 89-105.

Roedder, Deborah L. (1981), "Age Differences in Children's Responses to Television Advertising: An Information-Processing Approach," *Journal of Consumer Research,* 8 (September), 144-53.

Rogers, Ronald W. (1975), "A Protection Motivation Theory of Fear Appeals and Attitude Change," *Journal of Psychology,* 91, 93-114.

Rose, Randall L., William O. Bearden, and Kenneth C. Manning (1996), "Using Individual Differences to Segment the 'Market' for an Attribution-Based Substance Abuse Intervention Program," *Journal of Public Policy & Marketing,* 15 (Fall), 252-62.

Rossiter, John R. (1982), "Visual Imagery: Applications to Advertising," in *Advances in Consumer Research,* Vol. 9, Andrew A. Mitchell, ed. Ann Arbor, MI: Association for Consumer Research, 101-6.

Russo, J. Edward, Barbara L. Metcalf, and Debra Stephens (1981), "Identifying Misleading Advertising," *Journal of Consumer Research,* 8 (September), 119-31.

Scammon, Debra L. (1977), " 'Information Load' and Consumers," *Journal of Consumer Research,* 4 (December), 148-55.

——— and Robert N. Mayer (1995), "Agency Review of Environmental Claims: Case-by-Case Decomposition of the Issues," *Journal of Advertising,* 24 (Summer), 33-43.

Schultz, William B. (1996), "Food and Drug Administration's Suggested Consumer Research Ideas," in *Advances in Consumer Research,* Vol. 23, Kim P. Corfman and John G. Lynch, Jr., eds. Provo, UT: Association for Consumer Research, 316.

Shimp, Terence A. (1978), "Do Incomplete Comparisons Mislead?" *Journal of Advertising Research,* 18, 21-27.

——— (1983), "Evaluative Verbal Content and Deception in Advertising: A Review and Critical Analysis," in *Information Processing Research in Advertising,* Richard J. Harris, ed. Hillsdale, NJ: Lawrence Erlbaum, 195-216.

——— (1994), "Academic Appalachia and the Discipline of Consumer Research," in *Advances in Consumer Research,* Vol. 21, Chris T. Allen and Deborah Roedder John, eds. Provo, UT: Association for Consumer Research, 1-7.

Simonson, Alexander (1995), " 'Unfair' Advertising and the FTC: Structural Evolution of the Law and Implications for Marketing and Public Policy," *Journal of Marketing & Public Policy,* 14 (Fall), 321-27.

Slovic, Paul, Baruch Fischhoff, and Sarah Lichtenstein (1980), "Informing People about Risk," in *Banbury Report 6: Product Labeling and Health Risks,* Louis Morris, Michael Mazis, and Ivan Barofsky, eds. Cold Spring Harbor, NY: Cold Spring Harbor Laboratory, 165-81.

Smith, Darlene Brannigan (1990), "The Economics of Information: An Empirical Approach to Nelson's Search-Experience Framework," *Journal of Public Policy & Marketing,* 9, 111-28.

Smith, Robert E. and William R. Swinyard (1982), "Information Response Models: An Integrated Approach," *Journal of Marketing,* 46 (Winter), 81-93.

Starek, Roscoe B., III (1993), "Ross Starek's Wish List: Or, a Call for Extrinsic Evidence," prepared remarks made at the Marketing and Public Policy Conference, June, East Lansing, MI.

Steiger, Janet D. (1994), "Keynote Address," presented at Marketing and Public Policy Conference, May, Washington, DC.

Stewart, David W. (1995), "Deception, Materiality, and Survey Research: Some Lessons from Kraft," *Journal of Public Policy & Marketing,* 14 (Spring), 15-28.

——— and Ingrid M. Martin (1994), "Intended and Unintended Consequences of Warning Messages: A Review and Synthesis of Empirical Research," *Journal of Public Policy & Marketing,* 13 (Spring), 1-19.

Stouffer Foods Corporation (1994), Commission Decision, FTC Docket No. 9250, slip opinion, October 4, 1-21.

Sudman, Seymour (1995), "When Experts Disagree: Comments on the Articles by Jacoby and Szybillo and Stewart," *Journal of Public Policy & Marketing,* 14 (Spring), 29-34.

Szykman, Lisa R., Paul N. Bloom, and Alan S. Levy (1997), "A Proposed Model of the Use of Package Claims and Nutrition Labels," *Journal of Public Policy & Marketing,* 16 (Fall), 228-41.

Tanner, John F., Jr., James B. Hunt, and David E. Eppright (1991), "The Protection Motivation Model: A Normative Model of Fear Appeals," *Journal of Marketing,* 55 (July), 36-45.

Thompson Medical Company Inc. (1984), 104 FTC, 648-844.

Tversky, Amos and Daniel Kahneman (1981), "The Framing of Decisions and the Psychology of Choice," *Science,* January, 453-58.

Viswanathan, Madhubalan (1994), "The Influence of Summary Information on Usage of Nutrition Information," *Journal of Public Policy & Marketing,* 13 (Spring), 48-60.

Wilkie, William L. (1985), "Affirmative Disclosure at the FTC: Objectives for the Remedy and Outcome of Past Orders," *Journal of Public Policy & Marketing,* 4, 91-111.

—— (1997), "Developing Research on Public Policy and Marketing," *Journal of Public Policy & Marketing,* 16 (Spring), 132-36.

—— and David M. Gardner (1974), "The Role of Marketing Research in Public Policy Decision Making," *Journal of Marketing,* 38 (January), 38-47.

——, Dennis L. McNeil, and Michael B. Mazis (1984), "Marketing's 'Scarlet Letter': The Theory and Practice of Corrective Advertising," *Journal of Marketing,* 48 (Spring), 11-31.

—— and Elizabeth S. Moore (1999), "Marketing's Contributions to Society," *Journal of Marketing,* 63 (Special Issue), 198-218.

Zuckerman, Mary Ellen (1990), "The Federal Trade Commission in Historical Perspective: The First Fifty Years," in *Marketing and Advertising Regulation: The Federal Trade Commission in the 1990s,* Patrick E. Murphy and William L. Wilkie, eds. Notre Dame, IN: University of Notre Dame Press, 169-202.

Marketing and Modern Antitrust Thought

Gregory T. Gundlach

Two vital areas of public policy that relate to marketing are consumer protection and antitrust. Consumer protection involves public policy and law directed at protecting consumers from deceptive acts and other marketing practices, whereas antitrust attempts to encourage competitive conduct and protect competition among marketplace rivals (Cohen 1995; Stern and Eovaldi 1985). Although marketing scholarship has played a role in each of these areas, its contributions have tended to be emphasized primarily in the development of consumer protection. Indeed, considerable scholarship in marketing now underlies and informs much of the policy and law of consumer protection.

Curiously, the field of antitrust has failed to attract a similar level of scholarly emphasis by marketers, nor have its academic contributions been applied as extensively to the development of antitrust policy and law. Given the relevance of competition to marketing and the interplay of both in the marketplace, two key questions regard (1) why marketing scholarship has not played a larger role in the development of antitrust policy and law and (2) how this important area of public policy might benefit from insights obtained from marketing.

To address these questions, this chapter examines the nature of antitrust law as an area of public policy and contemplates its relationship to marketing. Highlighting antitrust's long-standing association with economics and the ongoing debate regarding the nature of economic theory best suited to inform modern

AUTHOR'S NOTE: The author expresses his appreciation to colleagues in the Department of Marketing at the University of Notre Dame for their helpful suggestions and support.

antitrust thought, the chapter considers the relevance of marketing and marketing scholarship to antitrust. Inspecting key lines of development distinguishing the two most recent schools of antitrust economics (i.e., Chicago and Post-Chicago schools), the chapter advances the complementary nature of marketing thought to emerging perspectives in antitrust, suggesting its role for informing modern antitrust.

Antitrust's Economic Foundations

As a general public policy goal, the law of antitrust endeavors is to promote consumer welfare through encouraging competitive conduct and protecting the process of competition (Sullivan 1983). Philosophical interpretation of the specific approach for advancing this goal, however, has been the focus of considerable historical debate. On one level, this debate centers on the extent to which an exclusively economic approach should govern the analysis of anticompetitive behavior versus the inclusion of other, more interpretive approaches as well.

Advocates of a purely economic approach to antitrust contend that consumer welfare should be narrowly conceived of in explicitly economic terms as economic efficiency (Bork 1993). According to these advocates, the careful definitions and parsimonious logical structure of economic theory yield the required intellectual rigor necessary for understanding competitive behavior. Those advocating a more interpretive approach argue for a broadened definition of consumer welfare to include concerns beyond economic efficiency (e.g., protection of small business, fairness). In the view of these advocates, the antitrust laws originally were enacted to address various social and political problems (Jacobs 1995).

Although most scholars and policy makers now endorse an economic view of consumer welfare, the nature of economic theory informing this interpretation now is under critical debate. The nature and evolution of discourse for this debate provides the basis for understanding the evolving association of antitrust law and economic thought and is suggestive of the potential role of marketing scholarship for informing antitrust policy and law.

Antitrust Economics

Although the Supreme Court has not fully endorsed an economic interpretation of consumer welfare, at present a largely economic approach to antitrust has been adopted by the federal administrative agencies and most courts. Under this approach, consumer welfare is conceived in terms of economic efficiency, with the antitrust laws informed and interpreted for the most part through economic thought (Brodley 1987). Wealth maximization is considered the dominant goal of antitrust, with antitrust enforcement striving to achieve the highest practical level of consumer welfare. Antitrust analysis involves the application of economic theory to an understanding of market and firm behavior and the evaluation of potentially anticompetitive practices.

The current debate in antitrust centers on the nature of economic theory best suited to inform antitrust analysis (Jacobs 1995). Two schools of thought dominate this debate. Key differences in substantive thought and methodology distinguish these two schools. These differences largely center on the workings and efficiency of the "market" mechanism and the proper approach for antitrust enforcement.

Chicago School

On one hand is the "Chicago" school, which holds to the core belief that markets, by nature, tend toward efficiency and that market imperfections generally are transitory in nature and, for the most part, self-correcting (Posner 1979). Adopting such assumptions and working from a model of perfect competition originating in neoclassical price theory, much of competitively ambiguous conduct under the Chicago school is viewed as the manifestation of efficient market behavior.

For example, as price theory adopts profit maximization as the underlying driver of firm behavior, conspiracies generally are considered inherently unstable, monopoly markets self-correcting, and entry barriers inadequate to undermine the efficiency of the market. Under such theoretical prescriptions, antitrust enforcement is viewed as simply distinguishing between activities that increase wealth through efficiency and those that decrease wealth through restriction of output. The resultant enforcement posture is a strictly cautious approach to antitrust to avoid mistakenly condemning behavior that is believed, in theory, to promote consumer welfare.

The implication of the Chicago school for antitrust is at once its rationalization and its clarity. Through defining behavior purely in terms of output (and price), enforcement authorities and the courts are viewed to be equipped with simple and objective tests for determining the effect of marketplace conduct on consumer welfare. Whereas expanded output and lower prices enhance consumer welfare, restraints on output and higher prices do not. An important offshoot of this simplification is the ability of firms to predict more accurately what might be considered suspect conduct and to avoid such conduct in favor of activities leading to the enhancement of consumer welfare.

Adoption of the Chicago school thinking and its implied enforcement approach is observable in the federal administrative agency and judicial activities of the 1980s and early 1990s. During this time, what might be labeled a "minimalist" approach to antitrust underlied enforcement activities (Jacobs 1995).

Post-Chicago School

In contrast to "Chicagoans," proponents of the "Post-Chicago" school believe that markets are largely imperfect and that market failures are not necessarily self-correcting (Baker 1989; Hovenkamp 1985). According to this view, firms can and do take advantage of these imperfections resulting in inefficient results. The resultant posture is the belief that antitrust enforcement must take a more active role through heightened scrutiny of a wider range of marketplace conduct to promote and ensure consumer welfare (Ross 1992).

Much of the Post-Chicago thinking and challenge to the Chicago school reflects progressive changes in the field of economics itself and, more particularly, the field of industrial organization (Jacobs 1995). During the 1980s, focus within industrial organization shifted from studies of industry structure, conduct, and performance to focus on the strategic behavior of firms within imperfectly competitive markets.

Informing this new generation of industrial organization thinking is a host of new approaches for analyzing the questions central to antitrust that go beyond simple price theory (Ordover and Saloner 1989). These game theoretic approaches and other perspectives for explaining and understanding firm behavior reflect a very different view of human nature, firm behavior, and the efficiency of the market (Porter 1991).

In contrast to the Chicago school's price theory-based perspective, the Post-Chicago approach views market imperfections (particularly information asymmetry) as a pervasive and durable phenomenon that, rather than dissolving under the pressures of the market, tends to corrode its efficiencies over time (Kaplow 1985). Moreover, in contrast to a static view of firm behavior as held by the Chicago school, under the Post-Chicago view strategizing firms accentuate, perpetuate, and exploit market imperfections hampering competitive balance (Baker 1989).

To some, the Post-Chicago approach to antitrust is simply a refinement and advancement of prior Chicago school thinking to include a more accurate picture of marketplace behavior and the inclusion of more sensitive tools for detecting inefficient behavior. Others view the approach as representing a very different perspective and posture for antitrust policy development and practice (Jacobs 1995).

Consequences for Antitrust

The implication of the Post-Chicago school's adoption of new thinking in industrial organization is to challenge prior antitrust doctrine and practice (Hovenkamp 1985). This includes important doctrinal areas such as the relevant measures for assessing market power, the competitive effects of vertical restraints, the plausibility and occurrence of predatory pricing, and the lasting durability of cartels and oligopolies. Differences between the Chicago and Post-Chicago schools also pose more general implications for the methodology and cost of antitrust practice (Arthur 1994).

Antitrust Doctrine

Market power, a central doctrine of antitrust, is defined as the ability of a firm to profitably raise prices through reducing output. Under the Chicago school, market power is largely inferred from market concentration and is measured through simple market share calculations while making allowance for entry conditions and other aspects of industry structure. Post-Chicago school economists adopt a more complicated view of market power beyond concentration and market share and, although requiring more empirical investigation, claim to provide a more accurate picture of the substance and dynamics of this important concept (Arthur 1994).

The competitive effects of vertical restraints also are viewed differently under the two schools. Vertical restraints characterize various forms of conduct on the part of one firm that attempts to restrict the independent business activities of another vertically related firm. Tying arrangements involving the sale or lease of one product or service on the condition that the buyer take a second product or service as well are an example of a vertical restraint. Exclusive contracts, another example, involve arrangements in which one party agrees to purchase all of its market requirements from another party.

Under the Chicago school, widespread skepticism exists as to the competitive harm generated through vertical restraints, viewing them instead as generally yielding productive competitive efficiencies (Bork 1993). The invocation of an anticompetitively restrictive practice is theorized to be largely unprofitable given that a party whose actions would be restricted would insist on compensation for such limitations on its behavior. As a result, a general explanation for the occurrence of such restrictive practices under the Chicago school is that they are more efficient than alternative arrangements. Post-Chicago explanations for the occurrence of vertical restraints view them as more often privately profitable to the imposing firm and potentially socially inefficient (Brodley and Ma 1993).

Similar differences between the two schools also underlie thinking toward predatory pricing. Predatory pricing occurs when one firm prices below cost in an effort to drive a rival from the market or otherwise discipline its competitive conduct (Sullivan 1983). Chicago scholars doubt the occurrence of predatory pricing based on the logic that a predatory firm would be unable to recoup losses from its actions in a competitive market (Easterbrook 1981). The occurrence of price reductions results from rivalrous conduct yielding immediate benefits to consumers. Alternately, Post-Chicago thinking adopts a more plausible belief of the possibility of recoupment and the long-range anticompetitive effect of predatory pricing (Ordover and Saloner 1989).

Finally, in attempting to understand oligopolistic behavior, the Chicago school adopts a largely static model of either perfect competition or monopoly. To the contrary, the Post-Chicago school envisions a variety of dynamic models of strategic firm conduct to explain oligopolistic behavior (Jacobs 1995). These models are argued to yield a richer and more complex understanding of firm behavior and to suggest a greater scope for antitrust intervention.

Antitrust Practice

Overall, differences in economic thinking between the Chicago and Post-Chicago schools pose contrary implications for both the methodology and cost of antitrust practice. The streamlined methodology and lower costs of the Chicago school contrast markedly with the more complicated methodology and costly approach of the Post-Chicago school.

Under the Chicago school, the generally simple principles of neoclassical price theory are argued to offer a coherent set of explanations for many forms of business conduct central to antitrust that may be easily applied by the courts employing neutral-based decisional criteria. The explanatory power of these simple principles, however, is challenged on the grounds that they do not always reflect market reality. Alternately, the more complicated models of the Post-Chicago school are argued to yield a more comprehensive explanation of marketplace behavior but demand a more complex methodology and costly approach for antitrust. Jacobs (1995) described this state of affairs during the mid-1990s as follows:

> Each school claims a more accurate vision of the marketplace and a more effective enforcement policy, and each promotes its vision as the linchpin of competition law. Chicago's streamlined methodology rests on an optimistic vision of the market and a pessimistic view of the judiciary's ability to cope with complex economic data. Post-Chicago sees competition as more fragile, market imperfections as more descriptive, and the judicial process as more capable—all of which, in its opinion, warrant a more probing enforcement policy. (p. 250)

A key question regards which school of thought will inform antitrust economics in the 21st century.

The Future of Antitrust Economics

Recent trends suggest that antitrust's association with economic thought is progressively tilting in favor of the Post-Chicago school. As reflected in a series of influential decisions of the Supreme Court, the Court appears to favor the newer thinking of the Post-Chicago school. Increasing reliance by the administrative agencies on Post-Chicago theories also is suggestive of the widening acceptance of this newer thinking. Finally, the continuing focus of antitrust scholars on Post-Chicago-based developments in theory and application suggests this trend.

Beginning in *Eastman Kodak Company v. Image Technical Services Inc.* (1992), the Supreme Court announced rules that suggest greater reliance on the more complicated, fact-intensive approach to antitrust advocated by the Post-Chicago school and less resort to the simplified methodology and streamlined approach of the Chicago school. Reflecting indirectly on the distinction of the two schools in terms of abstract theory and their association with market realities, the court announced in *Kodak* that "legal presumptions that rest on formalistic distinctions rather than actual market realities are generally disfavored in antitrust law." The court went on to reiterate its preference for analyzing antitrust claims on a case-by-case basis, focusing on the "particular facts disclosed by the record."

Similarly, in another decision, *Brooke Group Ltd. v. Brown & Williamson Tobacco Corporation* (1993), the Supreme Court announced its requirement, as part of a test for predatory pricing, that plaintiffs demonstrate "the extent and duration of the alleged predation, the relative financial strength of the predator and its intended victim, and their respective incentives and will." The court's requirement of proof as to the "respective incentives and will" is regarded as

requiring a more subjective and factually intensive standard of proof associated
with the Post-Chicago school.

Together, the various pronouncements of the Supreme Court generally are interpreted by commentators to suggest the beginning of the Court's shift away
from the abstract deductive generalities of the Chicago school approach to the
more open, fact-intensive analysis favored by the Post-Chicago school (Sullivan
1995). Decisions of the lower courts, although not fully consistent, also are suggestive of this trend.

In addition to the Supreme Court's posture, the trend toward acceptance of
the Post-Chicago school of thought also appears to be reflected in the activities
of the administrative agencies. An increasing number of high-profile cases by
both the Department of Justice (DOJ) and the Federal Trade Commission (FTC)
incorporate Post-Chicago thinking. These include *FTC v. Toys 'R' Us* (1998) and
the commission's investigation of the proposed merger of Staples and Office Depot (*FTC v. Staples Inc.* 1997). The DOJ's case against Microsoft (*United States
v. Microsoft Corporation* 1998) also incorporates many aspects of Post-Chicago
thought.

Finally, the trend toward Post-Chicago thinking also is detectable in the literature on antitrust economics and law. Although an imperfect measure, this literature focuses increasingly on Post-Chicago-based developments in theory and
their application to antitrust policy and law.

Antitrust as an Interdisciplinary Field

The ascendancy of the Post-Chicago school of antitrust economics highlights
the increasing breadth of theory applicable to antitrust policy and the rising importance of factual inquiry in antitrust adjudication. These advancements set the
stage for future improvements to the rationality and consistency of antitrust policy and enforcement. This progression also portends antitrust's expansion beyond its purely economic foundations to include wider application of theories
from other disciplines to antitrust policy development and the employment of
additional empirical methodologies in antitrust adjudication.

Various scholars have long suggested that antitrust might be best served
through acknowledgment of its interdisciplinary foundations and a deeper
understanding of the issues. As Williamson (1979) observed more than 20 years
ago, "Antitrust is an interdisciplinary field that is best served by acknowledging
that a deeper understanding of the issues will result by addressing the subject
from several points of view" (p. 991).

To adequately address the complexities of antitrust, some scholars contend
that additional modes of understanding outside of economics are required (cf.
Gerla 1985). In this respect, many sources of wisdom have been suggested to
have relevance to antitrust including the other social sciences, the humanities,
and traditional legal analysis (Sullivan 1977). In the next section, marketing is
examined for its relevance to antitrust. Reflecting on the current evolution in antitrust economics and the emerging perspective of the Post-Chicago school,

marketing is advanced as a complementary base of knowledge for understanding and analyzing competitive exchange.

Marketing and Modern Antitrust

Evolving developments in the economics informing antitrust are reflected in changes from the Chicago to the Post-Chicago school of antitrust. Inspection of the main lines of development between these two schools reveals an increasing degree of correspondence between the Post-Chicago view of competitive exchange and that found in marketing. Table 2.1 summarizes the perspectives and incremental contributions of each school and marketing across four antitrust dimensions: interpreting consumer welfare, assumptions about marketplace behavior, understanding competition and competitive behavior, and analyzing competitively ambiguous conduct. The complementary nature and incremental contributions of marketing suggest its role for informing antitrust analysis and practice.

Interpreting Consumer Welfare

Extending from price theoretic interpretations of competitive behavior, the Chicago school stands in favor of the narrow proposition that antitrust's goal of enhancing consumer welfare should be defined exclusively by economic efficiency and, in particular, by productive and allocative efficiency. Firms achieve higher levels of productive efficiency by building efficient plants, developing cost-saving procedures, using employees more effectively, and other measures. Allocative efficiency refers to the welfare of society as a whole and is defined as the ratio of a firm's outputs to its inputs. Often assessed in "potential" terms, allocative efficiency addresses the following question: Given a set amount of inputs or resources, what use and assignment of these resources will make society best off? (Bork 1993). Under the Chicago school, price and output provide the basic formulation for assessing the implications of competitive conduct for efficiency.

Those in the Post-Chicago school, informed by more dynamic conceptions of competition, favor expansion of the operationalization of consumer welfare to include, beyond productive and allocative efficiency, dynamic efficiency or gains to consumer welfare extending from improvements to existing market conditions as precipitated through innovation. To a lesser degree, proponents of the Post-Chicago school also see some virtue in acknowledgment of the non-efficiency-based goals of antitrust that appear to have been originally contemplated by Congress in development of the Sherman Act (and over time) through the passage of other antitrust-related legislation. These include, among other goals, maximization of consumer wealth, protection of small businesses from larger competitors, protection of easy entry into business, concern about large accumulations of economic or political power, prevention of the impersonality or "facelessness" of giant corporations, and encouragement of morality or "fairness" in business practices.

TABLE 2.1 Perspectives and Incremental Contributions of Chicago School, Post-Chicago School, and Marketing

Antitrust Dimension	Chicago School	Post-Chicago School	Marketing Perspective
Interpreting consumer welfare	Economic efficiency • Allocative efficiency • Productive efficiency	Economic efficiency • Allocative efficiency • Productive efficiency • Dynamic efficiency	Economic efficiency • Allocative efficiency • Productive efficiency • Dynamic efficiency Noneconomic considerations • Variety • Quality • Other interests
Assumptions about market-place behavior	"Market" • "Atomistic" market • Price competition • Assets are fluid • Perfect information • Actors are rational • Profit maximization goals	Imperfect "market" • "Nonatomistic" market • Price and nonprice competition • Assets are not fluid • Imperfect information • Actors are rational • Profit maximization goals	Imperfect "market" • "Nonatomistic" market • Price and nonprice competition • Assets are not fluid • Imperfect information • Actors are not always rational • Profit maximization and other goals
Understanding competition and competitive behavior	Neoclassical price theory • Perfect competition	Game theory • Strategic business behavior	Cross-discipline theory • Economics • Sociology • Psychology • Anthropology • Biology • Other disciplines
Analyzing competitively ambiguous conduct	Norm-based approach • Deductive • Abstract Static analysis Firm-level analysis	Fact-based approach • Inductive • Empirical Dynamic analysis Firm-level analysis	Fact-based approach • Inductive • Empirical Dynamic analysis Actor-level analysis

Marketing

A marketing-oriented view of consumer welfare both complements and extends views held by the Chicago and Post-Chicago schools of antitrust economics. Marketing shares the perspective that consumer welfare is enhanced by healthy competition and not through arbitrarily preserving weak competitors for their own sake. In contrast to the Chicago school, however, marketing views the benefits of competition to extend beyond those captured through the simple metrics of price and output. As with the Post-Chicago school, marketing views the additional competitive benefits extending from innovation as critically important. Future improvements in existing market conditions precipitated through innovation add markedly to competition.

Marketing, however, extends the Post-Chicago perspective through consideration of additional nonprice benefits. Finding that nonprice competition often is the most vibrant aspect of many markets, marketers argue that markets containing both price and nonprice competitors best serve the welfare of consumers (Guiltinan and Gundlach 1996). Indeed, much of marketing thought is directed at understanding the nature of benefits to be derived by consumers through such nonprice competition and how marketers might provide such benefits. For antitrust, more fully understanding the nature and consequences of nonprice competition could enhance its grasp of the nature and welfare implications of competitive exchange.

Finally, marketing also concerns itself with the broader consequences of competitive exchange including societal implications and moral issues. The "societal marketing" concept holds that a firm's task is to engage in marketing exchanges in a way that preserves or enhances consumers' and society's well-being (Kotler 2000). A significant number of scholars in marketing also address ethical issues that attend to exchange (Laczniak and Murphy 1993). This broadened view of competitive exchange parallels emergent views within the Post-Chicago movement that acknowledge the non-efficiency-based goals of antitrust.

Assumptions about Marketplace Behavior

For understanding exchange behavior and its implications for the various forms of economic efficiency, both the Chicago and Post-Chicago schools adopt various market assumptions including, among others, assumptions regarding the number of sellers; the nature of marketplace goods exchanged; the form of assets held by exchange actors; and the motives, knowledge, and degree of rationality held by each actor. Basic differences across these assumptions, in part, account for the different views of the two schools.

The Chicago school works from the assumptions underlying a model of perfect competition in an attempt to understand and explain the antitrust consequences of marketplace exchange. This model adopts the view that exchange takes place in a market composed of a sufficient number of sellers roughly equal in size and acting independently such that no one seller can affect market output or price through its own production or pricing decisions. Products in this marketplace are assumed to be homogeneous, each with the same mix of physical characteristics, quality, and service. Price is the main determinant of sales in this market. Sellers are assumed to possess homogeneous assets that are nonspecific to any one use and that are infinitely divisible and capable of flowing from one defined market to another depending on demand. Both sellers and buyers involved in exchange are believed to be motivated through rational attempts at profit (or individual utility in the case of consumers) maximization. These actors also are thought to possess perfect and instantaneous information regarding all relevant market conditions including not only price but also the costs of manufacturing and marketing. Together, these assumptions identify the prerequisites for efficient market performance under perfect competition (Scherer and Ross 1990). Working from these assumptions, the Chicago school attempts to explain how deviations from perfect competition affect market efficiency.

Under the Post-Chicago school, some of the assumptions underlying perfectly competitive markets are relaxed to take into account various market imperfections and other forces that alter market outcomes. Many of these adopted assumptions reflect those employed in the application of game theory to an understanding of competitive interaction (Ordover and Saloner 1989). These include, for example, the assumption that individual firms acting independently can affect market outcomes such as output and price; that, beyond price, sellers' nonprice strategies can affect sales in the market; that sellers in the market often possess assets that are nondivisible and nontransferable (e.g., sunk costs); and that, because the marginal cost of information is positive, both sellers and buyers rarely acquire complete information but rather often are asymmetrically or imperfectly disadvantaged in their knowledge of relevant market conditions (e.g., price, costs). Other market imperfections also are considered such as those extending from consideration of assumptions toward consumers, for example, the presence of network externalities[1] and the presence of an installed customer base (Ross 1992). Working from these assumptions and applying dynamic models of competitive behavior, the Post-Chicago school attempts to interpret the efficiency consequences of competitive conduct (Baker 1989).

Marketing

Compared to both the Chicago and Post-Chicago schools, marketing tends to be even less circumscribed in its marketplace assumptions. Like the Post-Chicago school, marketing adopts the view that markets are largely imperfect in terms of the ability of independent firms to affect market outcomes. It also views that firms do this through both price and nonprice competition and that firms operate in the market under the constraints of sunk costs and less than full information. The degree of imperfection assumed to be present in the market, however, generally is considered by marketers to be even more extensive than thought by either the Chicago or Post-Chicago school of antitrust.

Marketing, for example, views the actors involved in exchange to often be more "imperfect" in their behavior than believed by either the Chicago or Post-Chicago school. Consumers, in particular, are viewed to vary greatly in what motivates their behavior and often are thought to act less than rational in their consumption behaviors. Marketers commonly view the market as composed of different segments of consumers, each possessing different needs and wants, acting on different motivations, and varying in degrees of rationality. Indeed, a significant subfield of marketing focuses on specifically understanding the nature and varying aspects of consumers and their behavior (e.g., consumer behavior). Understanding more fully the nature of consumers should help antitrust to understand better the nature of consumer welfare and the reactions of con-sumers to the conduct of competitors.

Viewed from the perspective of managers, firms themselves also are thought to be motivated by a variety of factors beyond profit maximization including pri-vate goals and noneconomic motives. Managers within these firms are assumed to be more imperfectly rational in how they go about following their motives and fulfilling their goals. Through studying individual managers, marketers attempt to identify and understand these motives, goals, and (ir)rationality processes (Urbany and Dickson 1994). Such an understanding could be helpful to antitrust in better understanding the nature and purpose of competitive conduct and its implications.

Understanding Competition
and Competitive Behavior

Through the Chicago school, the substance of antitrust is largely circum-scribed to an understanding of competition and competitive behavior drawn from the static framework of neoclassical price theory (Scherer and Ross 1990). Applying this framework, market forces are thought to generally discipline anticompetitive or inefficient behavior and to correct for periodic imbalances to competition. Unless facilitated by market power, competitively ambiguous con-duct is believed to be accounted for largely as the drive for greater efficiency (Posner 1979).

Following the Chicago school, markets generally are viewed as competitive even if they contain relatively few sellers. Monopoly, when it does exist, is con-sidered self-correcting given that a firm obtaining higher profits in one market automatically will attract new entrants. "Natural" barriers to entry are more imagined than real, as resource investments are thought to easily flow from one market to another. "Unnatural" or governmentally sanctioned barriers to entry exist but are deemed inefficient. Conspiracies are inherently unstable given that the profit maximization goals of competing managers tend to undermine them. Even where so inclined, firms are thought to have little incentive to attempt monopolization of vertically related markets given that their own profits will be maximized when their downstream and upstream markets are competitive. Sim-ilarly, monopolists are thought to be incapable of leveraging their position in one market to foreclose access to a vertically related market (Bork 1993).

Employing more complicated and dynamic models for understanding com-petition and competitive behavior, the Post-Chicago school sees far more poten-tial for the inhibition of competitive processes by rival firms (Baker 1989). Broadly influenced by game theory (e.g., the study of profit-maximizing strate-gic behavior of firms in imperfectly competitive markets), these models take into account various market imperfections, external forces, and the potential for strategic behavior in a more elaborate fashion than that found for the Chicago school. Rather than competitively ambiguous behavior being attributed unskep-tically to efficiency, anticompetitive effects are considered in more depth (Ross 1992).

Under the Post-Chicago school, for example, market power is considered more ubiquitous, with firms thought to be able to unilaterally restrict competition in ways considered unattainable by those subscribing to the Chicago school. Emphasizing dynamic behavior and the cost of information, barriers to entry also are considered more prevalent. In addition, collusive behavior is thought to be potentially more durable, and vertical practices are thought to be more suspect for their efficiency consequences. Although managers still are believed to be motivated through profit maximization, they are thought to think strategically about how to maximize profit, leading to alternative explanations for competitive conduct.

Marketing

The Chicago school differs from the Post-Chicago school in that, through the adoption of a more sophisticated interpretation of the marketplace, it finds the marketplace more complex and finds competitive behavior more ambiguous. A similar view of the marketplace is found in marketing. As with the Post-Chicago school, competitive behavior is considered a dynamic process of rivalry among firms attempting to best fulfill the needs and wants of consumers. Marketing, however, is even more eclectic in its attempt to understand the conduct of actors engaged in this process, including competitively ambiguous conduct.

As a cross-disciplinary science, marketing casts its net broadly in an attempt to explain how consumers and marketers behave in exchange (Deshpandé 1983). Borrowing from a multitude of disciplines, beyond economic interpretations of exchange, marketing also incorporates the added understanding of the other sciences. These include sociology, psychology, anthropology, and biology, among others. Viewing marketers and consumers through the lens of theories from their fields, marketing attempts to interpret marketplace behavior and to understand exchange conduct. As a result, the view that much of competitive conduct is based solely on the drive for economic efficiency is held even less sanguine than by the Post-Chicago school.

Although acknowledging the drive for economic efficiency as an important procompetitive explanation for competitive conduct, marketing, like the Post-Chicago school, accepts a variety of explanations for such conduct, including those that might be anticompetitive. Given the breadth of theory used to inform marketing understanding, these explanations often take into account even more interpretations than those offered by the Post-Chicago school through its game theoretic view of competitive exchange. As a result, from a marketing perspective, concepts such as market power and entry barriers are viewed as potentially even more omnipresent, with competitive behavior such as collusion and exclusion thought to be attributable to other explanations beyond efficiency. In general, applying such understanding to antitrust is likely to increase its explanatory power.

Analyzing Competitively Ambiguous Conduct

For the analysis of exchange behavior, differences in the Chicago and Post-Chicago schools of antitrust reflect underlying distinctions between neoclassical and industrial organization microeconomics. Although both interpret consumer welfare through the lens of efficiency, for assessing competitively ambiguous conduct, the Chicago school method relies generally on "deductive analysis based on a sequence of truisms expressed through highly abstracted modes of reality"(Sullivan 1995, p. 670). Applying a static, norm-based approach, the purpose and effect of competitively ambiguous conduct, no matter what factual circumstances are present, is assumed to be determinable through deduction from the analytical generalizations of neoclassical price theory.

Relying almost exclusively on the deductive logic of abstract models derived from neoclassical price theory, the Chicago school sees limited utility in deep empirical inquiry. Fearing the administrative complexities of extensive fact finding and favoring judicial efficiency, in practice, economic "filters" (based on market share) and generalized defenses often are relied on to screen out "theoretically" implausible claims (Sullivan 1995). Many claims are dismissed early in adjudication through motions for summary judgments and are based on normative resolution, thereby closing the door on extensive fact-based inquiry.

In contrast to the Chicago school, the Post-Chicago school method employs a dynamic and more inductive, exploratory approach, "dig[ging] into empirical material in an effort to fathom the significance of observed distinctions between classic models and the configuration of the particular market under examination" (Sullivan 1995, p. 670). The purpose and effect of competitively ambiguous conduct are viewed as best determined through reliance on the facts and empirical inquiry and analysis. Theory, although important, provides merely a framework and pathway through which to analyze competitive conduct and its welfare implications.

Although admittedly raising the complexity of antitrust adjudication, the Post-Chicago school believes that the Chicago school approach exalts economic theory over facts and often results in the premature disposition of meritorious claims (Sullivan 1995). Through emphasizing detailed factual analysis, the role of theory is considered to highlight the potential of market imperfections and to justify empirical investigation rather than provide for the disposition of a particular case. Adjudicated cases under the Post-Chicago school more often involve contextually specific forensic evidence offered by certified experts in an attempt to explain the purpose and effect of competitively ambiguous conduct.

Marketing

The Chicago school approach offers simplicity, elegance, and generally simple answers to difficult antitrust questions. By contrast, the Post-Chicago school yields more complex, coarse, and often ambiguous answers to the hard questions of antitrust. A marketing perspective on antitrust follows more closely the dynamic, inductive, empirical model advanced by the Post-Chicago school. Although some areas of marketing adopt a static normative approach, knowledge and understanding in marketing are steeped in a tradition of inductive reasoning and empirical methodology. Marketing uses an extensive array of methodologies for understanding exchange behavior including reliance on primary and secondary data; use of laboratory, simulation, and field settings; experimental, quasi-experimental, and survey methodologies; and a variety of analytic techniques ranging from econometric, to multivariate, to interpretive forms of analysis. Realizing the limitations and complexities of each approach, each of these methodologies might be usefully applied for analyzing and understanding the effects of competitive conduct in the context of antitrust.

Another distinction regards the basic difference between economics and marketing relative to the primary unit of analysis emphasized in analyzing competitive exchange. Although not distinctive to either the Chicago or Post-Chicago school, this difference further illuminates marketing's complementary role for informing antitrust. As a science, antitrust economics, informed by industrial organization economics, tends to focus on the behavior of the firm within a market. By contrast, marketing as a "science of exchange" emphasizes the individual actor (e.g., manager within a firm or consumer in the context of an exchange within a market). Although considerable overlap is present across marketing and economics, for antitrust, the complementary nature of each perspective's emphasis provides the basis for more fully understanding the nature and implications of competitively ambiguous exchange conduct.

Conclusion

Recent developments in antitrust economics, as reflected in the two schools of economic thought currently informing antitrust, foretell considerable opportunity for marketing scholarship in antitrust. Compared to the Chicago school, the emergent view of the Post-Chicago school corresponds in many ways with a marketing perspective of competitive exchange. Both view exchange as involving the complex interaction of actors in an imperfect marketplace. Both attempt to understand these interactions calling on a broader base of theory. Both focus on the interplay of theory and facts to understand the implications of such exchanges. Finally, both define consumer welfare as including economic efficiency as well as other goals. Although this correspondence is necessarily incomplete given the fundamental differences of economics and marketing, the complementary nature of marketing to the Post-Chicago school perspective is suggestive of the role of marketing in modern antitrust. Both public policy makers and marketing scholars are encouraged to embrace this role.

Note

1. This concept refers to the benefits that one individual gets by being part of a network of many individuals who purchase the same product. For example, the advantages flowing to a consumer from choosing a VHS format for a VCR rather than a beta or laser disk format include access to a larger set of prerecorded tapes.

References

Arthur, Thomas C. (1994), "The Costly Quest for Perfect Competition: Kodak and Nonstructural Market Power," *New York University Law Review,* 69, 1-61.

Baker, Jonathan B. (1989), "Recent Developments in Economics that Challenge Chicago School Views," *Antitrust Law Journal,* 58, 645-55.

Bork, Robert H. (1993), *The Antitrust Paradox: A Policy at War with Itself,* 2nd ed. New York: Basic Books.

Brodley, Joseph F. (1987), "The Economic Goals of Antitrust: Efficiency, Consumer Welfare, and Technological Progress," *New York University Law Review,* 62 (November), 1020-53.

———— and Ching-to Albert Ma (1993), "Contract Penalties, Monopolizing Strategies, and Antitrust Policy," *Stanford Law Review,* 45, 1161-213.

Brooke Group Ltd. v. Brown & Williamson Tobacco Corporation (1993), 113 S.Ct. 2578.

Cohen, Dorothy (1995), *Legal Issues in Marketing Decision Making.* Cincinnati OH: South-Western.

Deshpandé, Rohit (1983), " 'Paradigms Lost': On Theory and Method in Research in Marketing," *Journal of Marketing,* 47 (Fall), 101-10.

Easterbrook, Frank A. (1981), "Predatory Strategies and Counterstrategies," *University of Chicago Law Review,* 48, 263-320.

Eastman Kodak Company v. Image Technical Services Inc. (1992), 112 S.Ct. 2072.

FTC v. Staples Inc. (1997), 970 F. Supp. 1066.

FTC v. Toys 'R' Us (1998), FTC Docket No. 9278, opinion and final order (October 13, 1998); appeal filed, Docket No. 98-4107, 7th Cir. (December 7, 1998).

Gerla, Harry S. (1985), "The Psychology of Predatory Pricing: Why Predatory Pricing Pays," *Southwestern Law Journal,* 39, 755-80.

Guiltinan, Joseph P. and Gregory T. Gundlach (1996), "Aggressive and Predatory Pricing: A Framework for Analysis," *Journal of Marketing,* 60 (July), 87-102.

Hovenkamp, Herbert (1985), "Antitrust Policy after Chicago," *Michigan Law Review,* 84, 213-84.

Jacobs, Michael S. (1995), "An Essay on the Normative Foundations of Antitrust Economics," *North Carolina Law Review,* 74, 219-66.

Kaplow, Louis (1985), "Extension of Monopoly Power through Leverage," *Columbia Law Review,* 85, 515-56.

Kotler, Philip (2000), *Marketing Management.* Upper Saddle River, NJ: Prentice Hall.

Laczniak, Gene R. and Patrick E. Murphy (1993), *Ethical Marketing Decisions.* Boston: Allyn & Bacon.

Ordover, Janusz A. and Garth Saloner (1989), "Predation, Monopolization, and Antitrust," in *Handbook of Industrial Organization,* Richard Schmalensee and Robert D. Willig, eds. Amsterdam: Elsevier Science, 537-96.

Porter, Robert H. (1991), "A Review Essay on Handbook of Industrial Organization," *Journal of Economic Literature,* 29, 553-72.

Posner, Richard A. (1979), "The Chicago School of Antitrust Analysis," *University of Pennsylvania Law Review,* 127, 925-52.

Ross, Stephen (1992), "Post-Chicago Analysis after Kodak: Interview with Professor Steven C. Salop," *Antitrust,* Fall-Winter, 20-22.

Scherer, F. M. and David Ross (1990), *Industrial Market Structure and Economic Performance,* 3rd ed. Chicago: Rand McNally.

Stern, Louis W. and Thomas L. Eovaldi (1985), *Legal Aspects of Marketing Strategy.* Englewood Cliffs, NJ: Prentice Hall.

Sullivan, Lawrence A. (1977), "Economics and More Humanistic Disciplines: What Are the Sources of Wisdom for Antitrust?" *University of Pennsylvania Law Review,* 125, 1214-43.

———— (1983), *Antitrust.* St. Paul, MN: West.

———— (1995), "Post-Chicago Economics: Economists, Lawyers, Judges, and Enforcement Officials in a Less Determinate Theoretical World," *Antitrust Law Journal,* 63, 669-81.

United States v. Microsoft Corporation (1998), 147 F.3d 935 (D.C. Cir.).

Urbany, Joel and Peter Dickson (1994), "Evidence on the Risk Taking of Price Setters," *Journal of Economic Psychology,* 15 (1), 127-48.

Williamson, Oliver E. (1979), "Assessing Vertical Market Restrictions: Antitrust Ramifications of the Transaction Cost Approach," *University of Pennsylvania Law Review,* 127, 953-93.

Chapter 3

Criteria for Assessing the Public Policy Relevance of Research on the Effects of Marketing Communications

Paul N. Bloom
Julie Edell
Richard Staelin

Legislators, as well as public policy regulators and influencers, have had a long-standing interest in better understanding the effects of marketing communications. Their primary concerns have been (1) to encourage marketers (e.g., manufacturers, service providers, retailers) to provide full and valid information and (2) to scrutinize and regulate messages sent by these marketers to the public. Empirical research often plays an important role in advancing this understanding. For example, the results of an empirical study on a particular communications practice can provide the stimulus for an investigation or even a congressional hearing. In addition, policy makers can use empirical results to better understand the links between the relevant marketing communications and the behavior of interest, thereby facilitating the design of regulations and the identification of appropriate remedies. Furthermore, judges, juries, and regulatory agency officials can use empirical results as evidence when deciding the fates of certain cases.

AUTHORS' NOTE: The authors thank the Marketing Science Institute, Advertising Research Foundation, Association of National Advertisers, and American Association of Advertising Agencies for their support of this research.

Empirical research on marketing communications often is highly complex. Because many parties interested in the effects of marketing communications are personally untrained in social science research methods, it can be difficult for them to assess and interpret such research. Not surprisingly, then, the "instrumental" use of empirical research, where study results provide the main justification for a public policy action, is rare (Deshpandé and Zaltman 1982; Florio and Demartini 1993; Rich 1977; Weiss 1980). Instead, "affective" or "conceptual" use of empirical research, where study results influence the frames of reference and the ways in which policy makers think about issues, is more likely to occur.

Because public policy decision makers often do not have the technical training to evaluate the validity of research and the generalizability of results, they frequently call on research-trained colleagues, support staff, or consultants to make policy recommendations for them. Or, they rely on interpretations of research results reported in the media. Or, they form their own interpretations of the value of studies based only on who paid for the research or on whether the results confirm their prior opinions. Well-conducted research might be dismissed because a policy maker views a study's sponsor as representing the untrustworthy "other side."

To encourage more evaluation and use of empirical research on marketing communications among public policy makers, this chapter presents criteria for assessing research on marketing communications and, thereby, evaluating the potential contributions of an empirical research study. Employing these criteria should allow policy makers to more easily determine whether the descriptions, associations, or causal inferences reported in a research study should provide a basis for a regulatory or policy decision. These criteria also should be useful to the media in their efforts to determine how much coverage and publicity to give to a particular study.

We recognize that most empirical studies will not meet all of our criteria for valid research. Even so, such studies can provide useful information. That being said, it is our belief that a study meeting more criteria should be given more weight or coverage than a study having significant research flaws, especially flaws that can produce biased or nongeneralizable results. Moreover, we believe that our criteria will help public policy makers to better understand when study results can be used for the following purposes:

1. describing a current situation (e.g., 75% of children under five years of age eat sugar-coated cereals);

2. determining the strength of an association (e.g., youths exposed to more beer advertisements consume more beer); and

3. determining causality (e.g., the new food labels result in consumers having a better knowledge of the nutritional content of packaged foods).

More broadly, our hope is that the criteria given here reduce the confusion about research studies often exhibited by policy makers, their staffs, and the media. We believe that they can improve the ability of decision makers to assess the

TABLE 3.1 Individuals Interviewed in Preparation of the Criteria

- Staff from both the Democratic and Republican sides of the U.S. House of Representatives' Subcommittee on Transportation and Hazardous Materials

- A staff member from the Democratic side of the U.S. House of Representatives' Subcommittee on Health and the Environment

- Staff from both the Democratic and Republican sides of the U.S. Senate's Consumer Committee

- Staff in the consumer protection area from the Federal Trade Commission

- Staff in the drug advertising area from the Food and Drug Administration

- Staff from the Center for Science and the Public Interest

- A staff member from the Consumers Union

- Staff from the Association of National Advertisers, American Association of Advertising Agencies, and Advertising Research Foundation

- Academics who have conducted empirical research on marketing communications and public policy issues

- Business executives working for firms that often are affected by communication legislation

quality of studies and their generalizability before they are widely publicized and/or used in public policy decisions. Although exposure to all relevant research results is valuable, users might be unduly influenced by the viewpoint supported by the largest number of studies regardless of their validity or by those studies conducted by researchers who are perceived as being the most "independent." To the extent possible, policy decisions should be guided by the stronger, more valid, reliable, and generalizable empirical studies. Moreover, users need to understand what a particular study has actually shown and whether it can be used appropriately to support a viewpoint, establish a relationship, or suggest other conclusions.

The criteria presented here are the result of a collaborative effort. We began by interviewing potential users of the criteria as well as producers of empirical research on the effects of marketing communications. Table 3.1 shows the individuals interviewed. They included regulatory agency officials, congressional staffers, consumer advocates, business executives, marketing professors, and business trade association representatives (who indirectly provided the financial support for this project). These individuals were questioned about research use in public policy making, the need for criteria, and the features desired in the criteria.

Following the interviews, we conducted a review to identify situations in which public policy makers actively considered empirical studies on advertising and marketing communications. This review gave us insight into the types of controversies that have emerged over research approaches and methods. Next, we wrote a draft of this report and sent it to those we originally had interviewed as well as other interested people. We also presented this draft for public comment at the 1994 Marketing and Public Policy Conference and at a workshop organized by the Marketing Science Institute. The comments we received were used to formulate the final wording of the report and these criteria.

The balance of this chapter is organized as follows. First, we discuss the public policy making process, describing the different ways in which empirical research is used to guide decision making. Next, we present a model of the marketing communications process. This model provides the needed background and concepts for the subsequent presentation of the actual criteria. Finally, we present the criteria. We organize them according to the purpose of the study. We start with those that are applicable to all studies. Next, we present criteria for assessing studies seeking to determine either the strength or the causality of an association. Finally, we detail the criteria needed to establish a cause-and-effect relationship. We conclude with criteria for assessing appropriate researcher behavior.

The Public Policy-Making Process

Our interviews and discussions suggest that there is no consistent pattern to the process by which public policy concerning marketing communications is formulated. Moreover, we found great variation in how empirical research is used in formulating policy. Nevertheless, three uses of empirical research appear common:

1. as a stimulus for an investigation or hearing,

2. as information to be considered in writing new laws or regulations, and

3. as evidence to be weighed in reaching a court decision.

In what follows, we elaborate on each of these uses, briefly discussing how the criteria presented in this chapter can apply to each of them.

Research as a Stimulus to Scrutiny

Research studies are receiving more and more attention in the media (Crossen 1994). From the front-page diagrams in *USA Today* to stories on television programs such as *60 Minutes,* the American public is regularly presented with reports about the latest scientific research findings and public opinion polls. Recognizing the media's appetite for research studies, policy advocates and lobbyists do what they can to "feed" the media research results that they believe support their positions. These groups might conduct studies themselves, provide funding to academics and others to do original studies, or search the literature for completed studies that support their causes. Industry groups, for example, sometimes publicize studies that support eliminating certain laws or regulations. Consumer advocacy groups often publicize studies showing the harm of specific products or marketing approaches. More generally, such practices, if successful at attracting press coverage, can create enough public clamor over an issue to stimulate a regulatory agency or congressperson to initiate an investigation or to hold hearings about the issue.

Although such studies often trigger detailed investigations and hearings to determine the veracity and generalizability of the initial findings, such investigations and hearings can be expensive, not only for the government bodies conducting them but also for the companies and organizations that must prepare testimony and responses to defend their interests. If the media use the criteria presented here to evaluate studies, then they might be less inclined to publicize a poorly conducted study that could overstate or understate a problem. Likewise, if public policy makers use these criteria, then they might be more inclined to give their attention to well-executed studies before taking action. Of course, what constitutes a well-designed and well-executed study varies. As these criteria suggest, if a study is concerned with describing a current condition (e.g., the number of consumers who exhibit a certain behavior), then the research design and methods required to produce valid and reliable findings are less extensive than those required of a study designed to show that a specific communication caused that behavior.

Research to Help Write New Laws and Regulations

Once Congress or a regulatory agency has decided to scrutinize a marketing communications practice, empirical research may be used to help determine the appropriate legal response, if any, that should be taken. Normally, any study that prompted an investigation or a hearing will be examined further. In addition, the regulatory agency and congressional staffers work hard to expose policy makers to a wide range of research results so that all points of view can be considered. The assumption is that, by presenting all of the research evidence and considering all of the arguments, better laws or regulations will emerge.

The record of the hearings for H.R. 4493, a bill submitted by Representative Joseph Kennedy in 1990, suggests how staffers attempt to introduce a wide range of research findings into the policy debate. Had this bill passed, it would have required health warnings to be included in alcoholic beverage advertisements (U.S. House of Representatives 1990). Results from a variety of studies found their way into this record in the form of summaries, commentaries, tables, and graphs including the following:

- The language of the bill itself refers to several studies. These include a 1981 federally funded study that "found a significant relationship between youth exposure to alcoholic beverage advertising and drinking behaviors," a 1988 Opinion Research Corporation survey that found that 80% of 2,000 adults surveyed "believe that alcohol advertising influences underage youth[s] to drink alcoholic beverages," and a 1989 *Wall Street Journal* poll that found that two-thirds of those surveyed "favor requiring warnings about the dangers of drinking on both alcoholic beverage containers and in alcohol advertisements" (U.S. House of Representatives 1990).

- Janet Steiger, chairman of the Federal Trade Commission (FTC), testified about what the commission staff had learned from a review of the literature on the effects of alcoholic beverage advertising. She disagreed with the statement in the bill about the 1981 study, stating that "the commission believes that the evidence is inconclusive on the issue of the linkage between alcohol advertising and consumption." She also testified about what the FTC had learned about warning labels based on the experience with cigarette labels. Drawing on Bettman, Payne, and Staelin's (1986) review of labeling research, which originally was conducted under a grant from the Environmental Protection Agency, Steiger provided several suggestions including keeping messages short and direct (U.S. House of Representatives 1990).

- James Sanders, president of the Beer Institute (a trade association and lobbying group), cited numerous studies in his testimony including one by Strickland (1982) that found no effect of exposure to televised alcoholic beverage advertising on the level of consumption among teenagers.

- Lawrence Wallack of the University of California, Berkeley, testified about a study he had completed based on a sample of 10- to 13-year-olds. He reported significant associations between how much exposure to beer commercials the children reported (through watching sports programming and other television programs) and how well they could name brands of beer and match slogans with correct brands. Those with greater exposure had higher expectations that they would drink as adults (Wallack, Cassady, and Grube 1990).

Reading the record of the hearings for H.R. 4493, it becomes clear that members of Congress and their staffs frequently encounter a bewildering and conflicting array of research results. Understandably, they are unsure whether the correct questions are being addressed in research and which researchers or research methods they should trust. The following exchange between Kennedy (the bill's sponsor) and Representative Dan Schaefer, which took place at the beginning of the hearings, demonstrates the type of confusion that exists:

Mr. Schaefer: Mr. Chairman, I would just like to add that the Roper organization did a poll, and in this poll, 67 percent of those polled said warnings in advertisements would be one of the least effective measures in countering alcohol abuse, 61 percent of the American public believes that warnings for alcoholic beverage advertising will not reduce alcohol abuse, and 57 percent feel that very little will change if such labels were mandated.

Mr. Kennedy: Mr. Schaefer, could I address that briefly?

Mr. Schaefer: Oh, please.

Mr. Kennedy: Sixty-eight percent of all high school students in America say they are influenced by alcohol advertising on television and radio. I have seen those studies, and every time I see them, they are twisted even more in terms of what the actual questions are and what the actual results are. Certainly I believe, and I'm sure every member of the panel believes, that if we could have direct intervention, if we could have alcohol treatment centers set up around the country, that's going to be more effective than placing alcohol warning label on advertisements. I believe that, and I'm sure any logical person believes that.

> Does that mean we shouldn't have alcohol warnings on alcohol advertise-
> ments? That's what that study suggested. So, I think we should be accurate. I'm
> sure you're being accurate, but I think the industry has really been pumping that
> study, which I think is seriously flawed in terms of the overall specific results that it
> was trying to achieve. (U.S. House of Representatives 1990, p. 18)

This example illustrates the many different types of studies used (e.g., descriptive, associational, causal) and the confusion that occurs when research is
being evaluated. Although there is value in making sure that each study is evaluated and considered, we believe that it is useful to have criteria for assessing the
validity and generalizability of each study. Perhaps more important, these criteria can be used to delineate what types of conclusions can validly be drawn from
a study given its design and execution. For example, can the study be used only
to describe a situation? To show the strength of an association? To show how
changing the marketing communication will change some consumer response?

Research to Guide Court Decisions

Once laws or regulations have been passed and are being enforced, research is
used differently. For example, enforcement often leads to trials or hearings before judges or regulatory agency commissioners. The research submitted in
these proceedings often is used to try to prove that a legal violation did or did not
occur. As a result, the research findings become a basis for a decision, and the
methods employed in these studies have to be able to withstand challenges by
opposing counsel and their expert witnesses.

Such occurrences have led to a body of case precedents and regulatory
agency procedures. In essence, guidelines already exist on how to assess the empirical research used in many court proceedings. For example, the FTC has laid
out recommendations for conducting research on the deceptiveness of an implied advertising claim in several cases (*American Home Products* 1981; *Bristol-
Myers Company* 1975; *Kraft Inc.* 1991; *Thompson Medical* 1984; see also
Maronick 1991; Richards and Preston 1992). Similarly, the Food and Drug Administration has developed procedures for evaluating the deceptiveness of prescription drug advertising. Still, controversies erupt over what constitutes appropriate methodology. In the *Kraft* (1991) case, for example, opposing experts
disagreed over how to measure the materiality of Kraft's claims about the calcium content of its American cheese food "singles" slices (Jacoby and Szybillo
1994; Stewart 1994).

The judges and commissioners who rule on cases usually already have considerable guidance to help them assess the quality of research studies. Nevertheless, we believe that the criteria presented in this chapter can provide additional
assistance. Our goal is to present criteria that are easier to understand and then to
apply some of the existing guidelines and recommendations (see Appendix).
Moreover, our criteria pay special attention to the problem of establishing causality. Although we recognize that there are many cases in which establishing
that a communication *caused* a change in beliefs, attitudes, or behavior is not an
issue (e.g., many deceptive advertising cases), there still are an ample number of

cases in which demonstrating whether a cause-and-effect relationship exists can resolve a controversy. We believe that using these criteria to assess the inferences and generalizability of the research evidence presented can help judges, legislators, commissioners, and others to make decisions.

Summary

So far, we have tried to show when our criteria might be useful in assessing marketing communications research that attempts to influence public policy. However, because many public policy actions are predicated on the existence of a causal link, we next provide a framework that can be used to understand how marketing communications affect consumers' beliefs and behavior. Our objective is to show that there are many influences, in addition to the communication itself, that may affect the outcome of interest. The influences should be taken into account in the research design or in limiting the scope of the findings.

Conceptual Framework

We start with the premise that the study being evaluated or considered is concerned with determining the effects of advertising, labels, telemarketing, and/or some other marketing communication. Normally these effects are studied in two areas: consumer beliefs and consumer behavior.

The focus on consumer beliefs is based on the idea of consumer sovereignty. That is, each individual consumer is at liberty to select those goods and services that best satisfy his or her needs and wants. Consumer sovereignty implies that consumers should have unlimited access to any and all information necessary for them to form correct beliefs about their options, the logic being that if consumers do not receive information on which to form correct beliefs about the costs and benefits to them of choosing a particular product or service, then their ability to "rule" the marketplace begins to break down.

The focus on consumer behavior is based on the behaviorist perspective that only overt observable behavior is the proper subject of investigation. Included in this perspective is the idea that information has value only when it affects behavior. Thus, if consumers engage in a behavior that is detrimental to their health, then it is not enough to inform them that their behavior is detrimental (change their beliefs); intervention is required to change the behavior itself.

Figure 3.1 details our conceptualization of how marketing communications affect beliefs and behavior. The model starts with the marketing communication, which can take a variety of forms including direct selling and promotion as well as advertisements and labels. This conceptualization recognizes that marketing communications do not operate in a vacuum. Instead, marketing communications both affect and are affected by (1) the environment in which the communication is delivered and (2) the characteristics and experiences of the recipient. We discuss these environmental and recipient characteristics in more depth after we present the other elements of our conceptual framework.

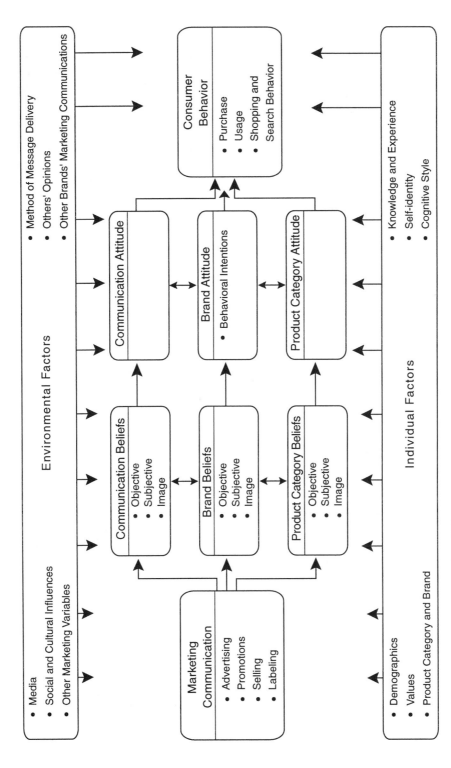

Figure 3.1. Marketing Communications Effects

59

The first effect in our conceptualization is the recipients' beliefs. These beliefs can be about the marketing communication itself, about the brand sponsoring the communication, or about the product category to which the brand belongs. Moreover, these beliefs can be influenced by objective factors such as the advertisement's spokesperson and the brand's color, more subjective factors such as the brand's taste and the product category's efficacy, or image factors such as the type of person who purchases from that product category and the feelings individuals are supposed to have when they consume the brand.

One implication of this representation concerns the common approach of assessing the efficacy of an ad by measuring consumers' brand beliefs after being exposed to the communication. Clearly, such a procedure could lead to erroneous conclusions if one does not consider that category beliefs also can influence brand beliefs. Furthermore, there are at least two mechanisms by which messages influence beliefs. One occurs in situations where consumers process the marketing communications without critically evaluating the information. For example, when consumers see a television commercial, they might only briefly compare its claims with what they already believe. If the content is counter to their existing beliefs, then consumers often discount the message entirely because it does not "ring true" for them. If it rings true, then they might accept it on faith.

In cases where the motivation to resolve the discrepancy between a new message and existing beliefs is stronger, consumers may use their existing beliefs to argue against the message claim. These counterarguments are likely to negatively affect the brand's evaluation. If a communication contains new information about the offering that is believable, then consumers might update their beliefs about the brand and the category. Because category beliefs also can affect beliefs about *any* brand in the category, one brand's communications can influence beliefs about another brand in the same category. This pattern reinforces the point that measuring consumers' beliefs about a brand does not necessarily establish that these beliefs were formed based on that brand's communications.

It is important to note that beliefs are not always based entirely on the information conveyed in the communication. Rather, beliefs may be formed based on inferences that consumers draw from the message and their own experiences. One type of inference of particular interest to policy makers is that based on the implied claims in a brand's marketing communications. For example, an advertisement might show the brand being used by attractive, well-dressed people having fun. Some viewers of the ad might infer that they will be considered "cool" and will have more fun if they use this brand. Although the ad does not explicitly make these claims, it might encourage these inferences to be formed on the part of viewers by the use of particular images or phrases.

The next element in our model is attitudes. Attitudes are summary evaluations of consumers' beliefs and inferences. These summary evaluations are important because consumers do not usually act directly on their beliefs or even consciously recall most of these beliefs when they decide to take actions. Instead, they find it easier simply to recall their overall attitudes. Attitudes may take the form of behavioral intentions (e.g., "The next time I need X, I will use the Brand Y"), or they may simply summarize their evaluation of the object (e.g., "Product Category Z is terrible"). It is these summary measures or attitudes, not actual beliefs, that typically guide behavior.

Normally, consumers form interrelated attitudes. They often form attitudes toward the communication itself, toward the brand sponsoring the communication, and even toward the product category to which the sponsoring brand belongs. These attitudes can influence each other. In many studies, the attitude toward the communication or its likability has been shown to be the primary determinant of brand attitudes and the best predictor of whether an ad affects sales volume (Haley and Baldinger 1991). Similarly, attitudes about the product category can have a strong influence on the attitude formed about a brand from that category. Thus, in examining brand attitudes, it is important to include measures of attitude toward the communication and product category as well.

Once attitudes are formed, they are fairly stable (Fishbein and Ajzen 1975). Changes in attitudes happen only gradually, and these changes might not be detectable by typically crude attitude measurement scales used after individuals have been exposed to a new message only a few times or over short intervals of time. Therefore, researchers interested in showing a causal link between the communication and attitudes need to use a longitudinal research design and/or more sensitive measures to accurately assess the impact of the communication on attitudes.

The final component of our model is consumers' actual behavior. This behavior can take many forms such as purchasing and regularly using the brand, searching for more information about a product category, and suggesting that others use the brand. As Figure 3.1 shows, the process through which a marketing communication affects behavior is more complex than the process through which it affects beliefs. Behavior is affected not only by consumers' attitudes but also by a multitude of environmental and individual factors. Moreover, the impact of any message might not be immediate. For example, exposure to an advertising campaign might affect a 5-year-old child's belief structure and attitude about a brand yet not influence the child's behavior until he or she is 15 years old. This pattern might hold particularly for products used primarily by older consumers such as cigarettes, alcohol, some types of foods, and durables (e.g., automobiles, appliances). In fact, one of the main reasons why researchers measure factors other than behavior is that the link between exposure to the marketing communication and actual behavior can be affected by so many factors and over such long time periods that it often is difficult to establish the true influences of the messages, if any, on behavior.

This discussion brings us to the two aspects of the model introduced earlier: the environmental influences and consumer characteristics that play critical roles in determining the effects of marketing communications. Environmental factors and consumer characteristics have a tremendous impact throughout the communication process. Moreover, this impact relative to the impact of the communication increases the closer one comes to actual behavior. Second, many of the environmental influences and consumer characteristics are not under the control of either the communicator or the public policy decision maker. For example, more knowledgeable consumers (i.e., those with an extensive background of information about a particular category) often will form beliefs and attitudes and will make choices different from those of less knowledgeable consumers. Likewise, cultural and familial influences play significant roles in determining what communications are received; how they are processed to form beliefs, inferences, and attitudes; and how behavior is affected. Thus, any research aimed at measuring the influence of a communication on behavior or beliefs must take these outside influences into account.

In summary, our conceptual model lays out the different linkages between the marketing communication and the ultimate behavior. As this conceptualization shows, the path is not straightforward. Moreover, in addition to the communication, other factors can influence beliefs, attitudes, and behavior. Therefore, in evaluating research that addresses the question of whether marketing communications affect some belief, attitude, or behavior, users must be aware of the complex relationships shown in the model and the fact that other factors can influence the measures of interest. Even when the research is concerned only with description or association, consideration of the environmental and individual factors can be useful in determining the adequacy of the research sample and in interpreting the findings.

Research Criteria

Because the intent of an empirical study can vary from establishing a particular level of an occurrence (e.g., a particular level of beliefs or behavior) to determining the strength of the causal link between a communication and some behavior, we organize our criteria to reflect differences in research objectives. We start with those that apply to all empirical studies involving primary data collection. Such studies include the use of focus groups, observational studies, in-depth interviews, survey research, laboratory experiments, and field experiments. Next, we list criteria that are appropriate when the intent is to show association and/or causation. We conclude with criteria associated with researchers' behaviors and interpretations. A listing of all the criteria is found in Table 3.2.

These criteria are not novel. Indeed, most market research books (see, e.g., Aaker and Day 1990; Churchill 1991; Lehmann 1989) address the same issues, although their emphasis is on how to conduct the research. Our approach, by contrast, is to provide those interested in the public policy implications of a marketing communications study with a checklist that they can use to determine the validity, generalizability, and reliability of the research results. Broadly speaking, this first set of criteria can be grouped into two categories: (1) those associated with ensuring that the researcher "talked" to the correct group of people so as to reflect the views and behaviors of the relevant target group and (2) those associated with ensuring that the information obtained from these people accurately reflects their views and behaviors.

TABLE 3.2 Research Criteria

Criteria generally applicable to all studies

Sample selection criteria

1. The sampling frame should reflect the population of interest, and the conclusions drawn and generalizations made should be limited to this sampling frame.
2. The sample should be representative of the population from which it is drawn.
3. The sample size should be large enough to provide reasonably precise estimates for all subgroups being studied.
4. Nonresponse rates should be reported, and the effects of nonresponse should be estimated.

Measurement criteria

5. Individuals gathering and coding the data should not know the purpose, hypotheses, or sponsor of the research study.
6. The data collection instrument or questionnaire should be pretested.
7. The measures, procedures, and questions should not suggest a response.
8. Wording and topics in the data collection instrument or questionnaire should be unambiguous and easily understood by the target population.
9. Whenever possible, several methods and measures should be used to assess beliefs, attitudes, or behavior.

Additional criteria for associative and causal research

10. Whenever possible, associative and causal studies should use different methods and scales to measure the constructs under investigation.
11. Associative and causal studies should report the test statistics used and their level of significance.

Additional criteria for causal research

12. Research designed to establish causality should rule out spurious associations caused by unobserved variables.
13. Research designed to establish causality should rule out reverse causality.
14. Research designed to establish causality should rule out simultaneous causality.
15. Research designed to examine constructs (e.g., behavior) that are distant in time from the communication should give strong emphasis to controlling additional factors.
16. Designs using a control group should ensure that the control and treatment groups are not different prior to the treatment.
17. When different groups cannot be controlled for a priori, the study should control for differences statistically.

Criteria for conduct of researcher

18. The researcher should publicly acknowledge all research sponsors and affiliations that might have had input into the research.
19. The researcher should make available at no charge (or at a nominal charge) the research instruments, the sampling plan, and the analysis plan to any interested party.
20. When generalizing the findings to broader contexts, the researcher should temper the conclusions to reflect the study's limitations.

Sample Selection Criteria

- *The sampling frame should reflect the population of interest, and the conclusions drawn and generalizations made should be limited to this sampling frame.*

One of the most critical decisions for those conducting communications research with public policy implications is from whom to gather the data. This decision is important because it determines the limit to which the results can be generalized. The sample of people contacted by the researcher to participate in the study usually is only a subset of the people in whom the researcher is interested. For example, a study was conducted by contacting a random sample of subscribers to the *New England Journal of Medicine.* The purpose of the study was to determine the extent to which pharmaceutical advertising in medical journals is causing doctors in the United States to prescribe inappropriately. However, the sample was drawn not from all doctors in the United States (the population) who write prescriptions but rather from a much smaller subset— those who subscribe to the *New England Journal of Medicine* (the sampling frame). The subscriber base might include individuals who are not prescribing doctors and might exclude those prescribing doctors who do not happen to subscribe to the journal.

The estimate of the extent of misprescribing obtained from this study cannot be used to unambiguously describe the misprescribing rate of doctors in general. Rather, the conclusions drawn from this study should be limited to the subscriber base from which the sample was drawn.

- *The sample should be representative of the population from which it is drawn.*

In addition to the problems just discussed, error can be introduced into the results if the sample is selected in a way that does not ensure representativeness. One standard approach is to use probability sampling. This procedure (1) requires that every individual in the sampling frame have a known nonzero probability of being selected to be in the sample; and (2) guarantees that as the size of the sample increases, the sampling error will decrease. Thus more precise estimates of the relationships being investigated will be obtained. For example, if there are 200,000 members of the American Medical Association (AMA) and the researcher draws a simple random sample of 200, then the probability of each member being selected to be in the study is 1 chance in 1,000. Using such a probability sample allows a researcher to statistically project the confidence of the findings from the sample of 200 members to the total sampling frame of 200,000 AMA members. Thus, in this example, if it is found that 12% of the doctors in the sample preferred Drug A to Drug B, then the researcher could use probability theory to establish that there is a 95% probability that the true percentage of doctors preferring Drug A will be between 10% and 14%.

If a nonprobability sampling method is used, then an explanation and justification should be presented to explain how the researcher ensured representativeness of the sample. For example, because researchers sometimes obtain their samples by stopping people in malls, they cannot assign an a priori probability to each person in the sampling frame of mall shoppers being selected. However, these mall intercept procedures can be modified to improve their representativeness (of mall shoppers) by using procedures that approximate random sampling such as selecting every *n*th person who walks into the mall. Additional criteria (e.g., age groups, gender, income categories) may be added to ensure that the sample is diverse, at least on the additional criteria. If the researcher knows the proportion of men and women of different ages in the population of interest, then he or she can prescribe that the sample also have these proportions of men and women in the various age groups. To the extent that age and gender are related to the topic being researched, adding these criteria will make nonprobability samples more representative. However, unlike a probability sample, such quota procedures will not allow the researcher to attach a degree of precision associated to any given estimate using standard statistical techniques.

■ *The sample size should be large enough to provide reasonably precise estimates for all subgroups being studied.*

The size of the sample that is appropriate for a public policy research project depends on many factors. The absolute size of the sample is less important than whether the sample is representative of the population. If a probability sampling procedure is used, then increasing the number of respondents will yield more precise information about the topic of interest. Sample size and representativeness are related. Yet, having a large sample will not make up for drawing the sample from a frame that does not adequately match the population of interest. Furthermore, increasing the size of a nonprobability sample will not necessarily increase the confidence that the information obtained from the sample validly captures the views and behaviors of the desired population.

In deciding on the adequacy of the sample size drawn, it is important for the researcher to examine the degree of variability in the population on the topic of interest. If the researcher believes that population members have widely differing opinions, attitudes, or behavior concerning the topic of interest, or if the factors that might influence these constructs vary widely, then larger samples are required. For example, if the purpose of the study is to examine the mechanisms by which ad-induced feelings influence brand evaluations, then it might be acceptable to use smaller samples because general memory mechanisms do not differ significantly across people. However, if the study's goal is to understand whether regular exposure to alcohol advertising in sports arenas and stadiums influences young people to start drinking at an earlier age, then a much larger sample probably is needed. Two factors cause this variability. First, it is necessary to capture the variability in exposure to the alcohol advertising by young people. Second, large differences exist in the social and environmental factors in these youths' environments that influence the strength of the relationship between exposure and initiation of drinking activities, but normally these are not measured. Therefore, it often is necessary to treat these unmeasured factors as "random noise." More generally, the more the random noise, the larger the sample size needs to be to ensure precision.

It is important to consider not only the size of the total sample drawn to investigate a topic but also the size of subsamples within the total sample for which the researcher wants to make specific statements. For example, if the study compares the prescribing behavior of older rural doctors to that of younger urban doctors, then the study must use a large enough overall sample to ensure that the smallest subsample to be considered has enough members. One rule of thumb is that the smallest subsample must contain at least 20 members (Sudman 1976, p. 30). It should be remembered, however, that such small sample sizes usually are associated with large sampling error (i.e., less precision). It should be standard procedure for the researcher to report not only the estimated value but also the magnitude of the sampling error. (Remember, the researcher can only do this when a probability sample has been used.)

- *Nonresponse rates should be reported, and the effects of nonresponse should be estimated.*

Not every person selected to be a member of a sample or every shopper stopped in a mall will be willing or able to participate in research. People with more extreme opinions, greater interest in the topic, and more time are more likely to participate. Thus, nonrespondents can be much different from those who agree to participate, resulting in what is called nonresponse bias. The larger the percentage of nonrespondents, the greater the likelihood of nonresponse bias in the measures of interest. Several strategies are available to estimate the size of the nonresponse bias. These include callbacks to a subsample of nonrespondents, analyzing the trend between those responding on the first contact and those responding on a later contact, use of subjective estimates, and weighing of responses by demographic characteristics to project to nonrespondents (Chapman 1976). In any case, the researcher should report the number or percentage of nonrespondents and should address the issue of the extent to which nonresponse might alter the obtained results.

Measurement Criteria

- *Individuals gathering and coding the data should not know the purpose, hypotheses, or sponsor of the research study.*

The individuals collecting information (either in person or over the telephone), the individuals classifying or coding the interviewees' responses, and those analyzing the content of marketing communications should not know the purpose of the research, its hypotheses, or the identity of the sponsoring organization. This knowledge might influence the interviewers to interact differently with some respondents, thereby introducing interviewer bias into respondents' replies. Coders of the information received from respondents or coders of a communication's content might interpret or classify responses differently if they know the purpose or sponsor of the study. These biases can occur even when the interviewers and coders are highly trained professionals. These biases can be unintentional and can occur unconsciously. When coding of information is believed to be subjective or open to interpretation, it is good practice for the researcher to use multiple independent coders and to report the degree to which these coders were in agreement.

- *The data collection instrument or questionnaire should be pretested.*

The data collection instrument should be pretested to ensure that it can be administered properly, that it is easily understood by the target population, and that it will adequately provide the necessary information. All components of the questionnaire should be tested including instructions, layout, sequencing, content, and wording. At least some of the pretests should be conducted via interviews with members of the target population. Interviewees should be encouraged to provide their reactions to the data collection instrument as they are completing it, and the interviewer should probe nonverbal reactions that might indicate confusion or uncertainty.

- *The measures, procedures, and questions should not suggest a response.*

The data collection instrument and procedures are in themselves a form of communication. Because the questions asked can change respondents' beliefs and attitudes, the research instrument and procedures should be constructed in such a way that they accurately reflect the true beliefs, attitudes, or behavior of each respondent without suggesting a response or divulging the purpose of the research. Many times, this can be accomplished by asking less directed questions, at least initially. For example, if a study is exploring the effects of beer commercials, then it might be better to start by asking respondents "For what product categories do you remember seeing ads?" rather than "Do you remember seeing any advertisements for alcoholic beverages?" The latter question primes the respondent to recall an alcoholic beverage ad. This general, open-ended question could be followed by a question that provides a list of five or six product categories in addition to alcoholic beverages and asks respondents to mark all categories for which they remember seeing ads. Here, the researcher is providing a memory cue, but one that is less focused than a cue asking solely about alcoholic beverage ads.

Another way in which researchers reduce question bias is to give respondents "don't know," "no opinion," and/or "no preference" options on questions asking for knowledge, opinions, or preferences. This practice reduces the amount of guessing as well as the tendency of respondents to respond affirmatively (i.e., "yea-saying"). Researchers also can reduce guessing by explicitly instructing respondents not to guess. Another approach is to use balanced phrasing of a question (e.g., "Do you or do you not . . . .?"), which can reduce the extent of false agreement (Jacoby and Szybillo 1994).

- *Wording and topics in the data collection instrument or questionnaire should be unambiguous and easily understood by the target population.*

Respondents, especially those personally interviewed, do not want to appear stupid or uninformed. They will respond to nearly any question asked, whether or not they are clear about the question to which they are responding. The questions should clearly indicate what is to be included and what is not to be included. For example, asking respondents "How frequently do you consider the nutritional information before making a food purchase?" could be interpreted by respondents in many different ways. "Consider" might be interpreted by some to mean that they compare the nutritional content labels of all brands before making purchases, whereas to others it might mean that they think about the calorie or fat content of items before ordering them in restaurants. By "nutritional information," the researcher might mean only the data on the side panel of packaged food products, whereas the respondents might include advertised claims and menu information in their definitions of the same term. Frequency response categories also can be fraught with differences of interpretation. For some "occasionally" might mean one time out of five, whereas to others it might mean once a year. Careful pretesting allows the researcher to adapt the language to the target population and the topic under investigation.

- ■ *Whenever possible, several methods and measures should be used to assess beliefs, attitudes, or behavior.*

Because most responses are a fallible measure of the individual's true underlying belief or behavior, having different measures of the variables of interest provides a means for assessing the validity and reliability of the measures. For example, if a number of different measures, obtained with very different methods, all yield similar results, then the user can be more confident that the results in fact reflect the underlying variable of interest. Conversely, if each measure yields a very different answer, then there is less reason to believe the veracity of any one response.

More generally, there is great value in having results from a number of different studies, done by different researchers, using different methods. Using different methods and different researchers reduces the possibility that each study is biased by the same flaw. If all of the studies yield approximately the same answers, then the decision maker can be more confident in the results. However, having a number of studies yielding similar results does not, by itself, indicate that the results are valid. If all of these studies with similar results do not meet the standards set by our criteria (e.g., if researchers talk to the wrong reference group or use faulty procedures), then the cumulative weight afforded these studies should be small. Finding compatible results is not a substitute for determining whether the studies meet the research criteria.

Thus far, the criteria have centered on assessing the accuracy and generalizability of the obtained responses. In this way, they address cases in which the researcher is interested in describing a given situation such as the current level of a belief or the percentage of consumers who exhibit a particular type of behavior. However, some studies also are interested in determining relationships between constructs. For example, a study might report a link or an association between a marketing communication and some belief, attitude, or behavior. The validity of such a statement can be assessed by applying the next set of criteria.

Additional Criteria for Associative and Causal Research

Two variables are said to be associated when the obtained responses to one variable move in a predictable way with the obtained responses from the other variable. For example, a telephone survey of respondents might show that consumers' responses to viewing a particular advertisement are positively related to their responses concerning a specific type of shopping or use behavior. The question then becomes "Why do these two variables move together, that is, why do they covary?"

There are many potential reasons for this observed association. One is that one variable causes the other (i.e., there is a causal link). In the next section, we discuss in more detail what is needed to show causal links. Another reason is that, although there is no causal link, the two variables move together because both are related to a third variable, which in turn dictates the movement of the two variables being studied. For example, suppose that both the number of auto advertisements aired and the number of cars bought were positively influenced by the state of the economy. Then, as the economy becomes stronger, we would see the number of auto advertisements and the number of cars bought increase. Thus, changes in the economy would lead to a positive association between the two variables.

Finally, some associations are not caused by external factors such as the economy but instead are artifacts of the research. More specifically, these associations will "go away" if the measures or methods of obtaining the answers are varied. This leads to our first criterion for assessing associations.

- *Whenever possible, associative and causal studies should use different methods and scales to measure the constructs under investigation.*

Measuring constructs using the same general approach can lead to a positive association for no other reason than that they were measured with a similar instrument or method (i.e., common methods bias). Said differently, the method influenced both responses, causing them to covary. For example, if attitude and purchase intentions both are measured using similar 5-point Likert scales, then the positive association between them might result in part from the similarity of the measurement scales and the proximity of the questions on the survey. When possible, items to be related to each other should be separated from each other and measured using different formats.

- *Associative and causal studies should report the test statistics used and their level of significance.*

In assessing whether a relationship between a marketing communication and a belief, attitude, or behavior is important and in need of additional investigation, it is important to know the direction, size, and statistical significance of the association. Tests such as chi-square, *t* test, and correlation are appropriate for assessing the relationship between two constructs. Multivariate tests such as analysis of variance, regression, and discriminant analysis are used to examine the relationship when there are more than two constructs involved.

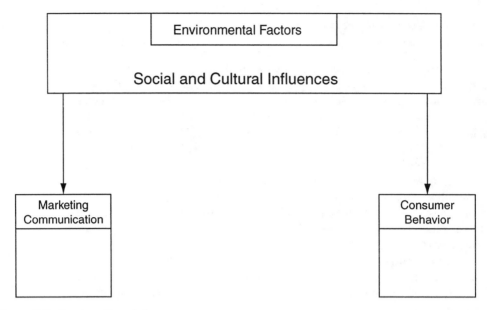

Figure 3.2. Spurious Association

Additional Criteria for Causal Research

Even when researchers eliminate the problem of common methods bias, it is possible that two constructs are related and yet there is no causal linkage between them. In Figure 3.2, which is both a simplification and a variant of our conceptual model of marketing communication effects, we show social values influencing both marketing communication and behavior. For example, changes in social values might alter children's behavior as well as the nature of what a firm communicates to this target group. As social values change, so will the nature of the communication message and the children's behavior. However, there is no causal link between the change in the communication and behavior. Instead, the relationship is spurious, being caused by the third variable, social values. Thus, if public policy makers were to intervene in this example and require changes in the communication, then this new policy would *not* result in a change in behavior because there is no causal link between this communication and the behavior. (This example is conceptually the same as the prior discussion concerning the spurious association caused by using a common measure.)

This discussion leads to our first criterion for research designed to establish causal links.

- *Research designed to establish causality should rule out spurious associations caused by unobserved variables.*

A second variant of this problem is shown in Figure 3.3. In this case, the arrows representing causality are reversed, indicating that changes in behavior

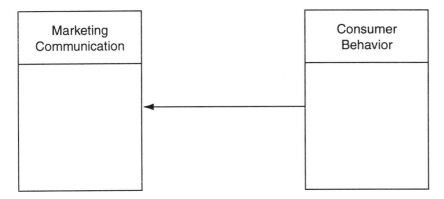

Figure 3.3. Reverse Causality

cause changes in the communication. For example, a firm, after determining that consumers are using its product in a particular way, might alter its communication message to reflect this new use. Just as in our previous example, one would find that changes in the communication message are associated with changes in behavior. However, altering the firm's communications policy in this second case would not affect consumer behavior because the communication did not *cause* the behavior. In fact, the relationship is just the opposite.

- *Research designed to establish causality should rule out reverse causality.*

A third variant of this problem is shown in Figure 3.4. In this case, there is a link between communications and behavior: Increases in the frequency of encountering the communication will cause a change in behavior. However, in this example, we see that social values also influence behavior. Let us assume that shifting social values alter women's use behavior toward a specific product class (i.e., such behavior becomes more acceptable relative to what it was before). This pattern means that a larger portion of women begin to use the product class. Sensing these shifts in social values and women's behavior, firms find it in their best interests to increase the funds allocated to communicate to this particular market segment. In such a situation, one would see both an increase in use behavior of the product class (and the communicating brand) and an increase in product class and brand advertising. In this case, however, the increase in advertising did not initially cause the change in use behavior. Instead, changing social values altered women's behavior, causing firms to modify their advertising.

The point of this example is that although one might observe changes in communication expenditures and in behavior (or in other measures of interest), it is not necessarily true that the changes in communication caused the initial changes in overall use behavior. Instead, these changes might be caused by some other factor (e.g., social values) affecting consumer and firm behavior. Without proper controls, however, a researcher might misattribute all of the influence to the changes in communication policy.

■ *Research designed to establish causality should rule out simultaneous causality.*

A final variant of this discussion is concerned with the time frame between the communication and the measure of interest. Some policy makers focus their attention on constructs such as beliefs and attitudes, which are more immediately related to a communication. Such an emphasis reduces the number of outside factors that could confound the results. However, many studies focus on the link between the communication and some behavior that is potentially distant in time from the communication. As Figure 3.1 shows, environmental and individual factors become more influential as the temporal distance from the communication increases. In addition, differences in beliefs and attitudes will have a greater influence on these behaviors. The greater the time interval between the communication and the measure of interest, the greater the need to institute the proper controls.

■ *Research designed to examine constructs (e.g., behavior) that are distant in time from the communication should give strong emphasis to controlling additional factors.*

Because the issues of causality are so complex and the approaches used to obtain the proper controls are so diverse, we next briefly discuss some approaches that often are used by researchers interested in establishing causality. In each case, we specify criteria useful in assessing the veracity of the particular type of approach.

Controlled Experiments

One way in which to address the problems just discussed is to conduct a controlled experiment using one of the standard experimental designs (for a detailed discussion of these designs, see Campbell and Stanley 1963). Assume, for example, that one group, the treatment group, is exposed to the communication and that the other, the control group, is not. The effects of the communication are determined by examining the difference between the two groups on the variables of interest after the treatment group has seen the communication.

This design has several essential features. First, by having two groups, the researcher can rule out the influence of additional variables causing spurious relationships. Even if additional variables affect the treatment group, they also affect the control group; by looking at the difference in responses between the two groups, the effects of all additional variables are removed. Second, because the communication was given prior to the measurement, the researcher can rule out the hypothesis of reverse causality. Finally, because the decision to give the communication and the appropriate level of communication were determined prior to observing the behavior, simultaneous causality is not a concern.

It also should be noted that for the control group to be a true control group, it is critical that the individuals assigned to the treatment and control groups be "identical" before the treatment. Otherwise, the differences between the two groups might be caused by factors other than the treatment.

- *Designs using a control group should ensure that the control and treatment groups are not different prior to the treatment.*

There are several ways in which researchers can establish equality of groups. One is to randomly assign participants to each group. This approach can provide equality of groups if a large number of participants are available. When the number of participants is limited, matching of groups is required. Matching is done by taking measures prior to the treatment, thereby allowing the researcher to adjust for any prior differences that are not completely controlled for via randomization. (The pros and cons of taking premeasures are discussed more fully in Campbell and Stanley 1963.)

Sometimes, it is impossible to randomly assign people to control and treatment groups, especially in controlled experiments conducted "in the field." For example, in a field study looking at the effects of new labels, consumers need to be spatially distant because it would be impossible to have a store carry both types of labels. In such a situation, the treatment and control groups should be matched a priori on all variables that are believed to influence their shopping habits and their use of nutritional information. Such a procedure increases confidence that any observed differences were caused by the difference in the labels and not by some other variable associated with the fact that the groups are spatially distant.

Naturally Occurring Field Studies

The experiments just discussed obtained control by assigning people to groups a priori and then providing a treatment to one of the groups. This often is not possible, however, particularly when researchers are interested in assessing causality after the fact or when both Action A and Behavior B already have taken place. One approach that researchers often take is to look for different groups of individuals who have naturally been exposed to different levels of the communication. This approach often is referred to as a cross-sectional design. For example, if a researcher were interested in the effects of beer or cigarette advertisements at sporting events on young adults, then he or she could look at the smoking and drinking behavior of young adults who do and do not go to sporting events and, therefore, are and are not exposed to such messages, respectively. The difficulty here is that the two groups of people cannot be randomly assigned, nor can they be matched a priori on other characteristics. Thus, differences in the two groups also could be caused by additional variables such as personality or cultural differences that affect both going to sporting events and smoking and drinking behavior.

A second type of natural experiment occurs when events change over time. For example, it is possible to look at changes in the number of advertisements for a designated driver and the changes in the number of auto deaths due to drinking while under the influence. Here again, the researcher has less control over the situation than if he or she ran an experiment. The researcher cannot explicitly control for the fact that some third variable, such as a change in the way in which police report the causes of automobile deaths, might account for a change in one or both of the variables of interest.

Given the possibility that the association between two variables is caused by some third variable and not a causal link, researchers using a naturally occurring design often will measure factors believed to affect both the communication level and the behavior or belief of interest, thereby allowing them to control for these other factors. For example, many researchers look at variations in exposure to cigarette advertising over time and the associated variations in smoking behavior. In addition, they measure other variables thought to influence the behavior of interest such as social values, parental smoking habits, education, and changes in the cigarette tax. They then adjust statistically for possible group differences.

There are numerous ways in which to accomplish this statistical adjustment. As before, the need for careful adjustment increases as the number of possible other influences increases. The particular type of statistical adjustment also depends on whether or not the researcher can obtain accurate measures for these other variables. For example, in our sporting event example, we mentioned that variables such as personality traits and cultural norms may affect both the probability of being exposed to the message and smoking and drinking behavior. However, such measures are normally not available. In such cases, it still is possible to obtain control if the researcher obtains measures of the communication levels and behavior for the same individual over time. (This approach often is referred to as a longitudinal cross-sectional study.) The researcher then rules out all factors that remain fixed over the time of the study (e.g., personality traits) by relating changes in behavior and changes in the communication for each individual. In this way, the individual acts as his or her own control. Note, however, that before making any causality claims, the researcher needs to determine that other relevant factors have not changed over time because changes in these factors and not the change in message level also could cause a shift in behavior. (For a more complete discussion of these issues, see Boulding and Staelin 1994.)

One standard approach for circumventing this last problem is to alter the order of when the treatment is received across individuals. For example, some individuals might see an increase in the number of messages from Period 1 to Period 2, whereas others might see a decrease. This approach allows the researcher to control for the observed change being due to additional variables that vary over time. The preceding discussion leads us to our next criterion.

- *When different groups cannot be controlled for a priori, the study should control for differences statistically.*

Meeting this criterion requires obtaining measures on all additional factors believed to influence the communication and the measure of interest or using the longitudinal aspects of the data to remove or control for fixed or varying unmeasured factors.

Criteria for Conduct of Research

Thus far, we have provided criteria for assessing the procedures used during research. In addition, there are several other criteria that users of public policy research might find helpful when assessing an empirical study. These criteria have less to do with the research process than with the conduct of the researcher.

- *The researcher should publicly acknowledge all research sponsors and any affiliations that might have had input into the research.*

As mentioned earlier, it is common for special interest groups to sponsor studies in the hope that the findings can be used to support their positions. It is our belief that the sponsorship of a study should not be used to judge the veracity of its results. Nevertheless, it can alert the user of the study to critically evaluate the study methodology (using the previously mentioned criteria).

- *The researcher should make available at no charge (or at a nominal charge) the research instruments, the sampling plan, and the analysis plan to any interested party.*

For policy makers to use our criteria for evaluating research, the details of the research design, measures, and procedures must be described in detail and/or provided on request. It is standard research policy to provide information to others so that they can replicate the study. Often, this is done by publishing the needed information with the study results. In addition, it is accepted practice to make the raw data available. This practice allows others to critically review the analyses and to perform additional analyses. The only exception to this practice occurs when the data involve company secrets or other private data. Even in these instances, there often are ways in which to ensure that others can gain access to the data without compromising their confidentiality. Finally, it should be noted that in many instances the researchers need to promise respondents personal confidentiality. Thus, others should not expect to be able to link specific respondents to specific responses.

- *When generalizing the findings to broader contexts, the researcher should temper the conclusions to reflect the study's limitations.*

Public policy research often is associated with emotionally laden issues. Some people might draw implications from the results that overstep the actual findings. Many of our prior criteria are aimed at helping the user to delineate the limitations of a study. That being said, it is important to remember that no single study is likely to be perfect and that every study provides some insights. The bottom line in evaluating any study is "What useful information should be obtained from the study, and how should it be weighed relative to other existing evidence?" We hope that the criteria presented in this chapter will help in answering this question.

Appendix

The criteria presented in this chapter cover some of the same issues and topics that have been treated in other publications. Organizations such as the Advertising Research Foundation (ARF, which helped to fund this study), the Council of American Survey Research Organizations (CASRO), and the Federal Trade Commission (FTC) have issued research guidelines for various reasons including trying to steer public policy makers away from reliance on poorly conducted research. Table 3.3 presents a comparison between the topics covered in our criteria and those covered in several similar efforts. Topics that we believe fall under one of our four headings are shown in the same row in the table as that heading. Additional comments on how our criteria differ from each of the other sets of guidelines are offered in what follows. Further details about the other guidelines can be obtained by examining the original documents.

We believe that our criteria differ from others in three respects. First, we have tried to make ours particularly relevant to research related to marketing communications. Second, we have emphasized the importance of being careful in making causal inferences. Third, we have tried to make our wording and discussion as accessible as possible to those not trained in research methodology. We do not mean to suggest that the other efforts lack elements of these features, only that our criteria stress them more explicitly.

Many of the other guidelines contain more specific details about negative features of research studies. For example, the 1981 ARF guidelines, titled *Guidelines for the Public Use of Market and Opinion Research,* contain a long list of detailed questions to consider in assessing the quality of a study (ARF, 1981). The questions treat issues that range from research design (e.g., "If the research calls for continuing panels or repeated studies, are there unbiased ways to update or rotate the original sample?"), to execution (e.g., "Were objective tests made to determine how completing the balance of the sample would have changed the results?"), to interpretation (e.g., "Does the report specifically qualify any data that depend on the respondents' memories over time or their ability to predict future behavior?"). The 1984 ARF guidelines, titled *ARF Criteria for Marketing and Advertising Research,* cover much the same ground as the 1981 guidelines but in a different format (ARF, 1984). The questions that this latter report recommends using to assess a study are not as lengthy or detailed as in the previous ARF work, and they are accompanied by more explanatory text.

The 1985 CASRO guidelines, titled *Guidelines for Conducting Forensic Research,* contain a list of detailed recommendations, although the treatment is not as lengthy and technical as the ARF material (CASRO, 1985). Recommendations deal with topics such as interviewing (e.g., "Careful, thorough records of the field experience should be maintained"), coding (e.g., "The study director should code some of the questionnaires—especially at the start of coding—to make sure the codes are appropriate"), and data processing (e.g., "Complex, hard-to-explain analytical techniques should be avoided, if possible"). Another CASRO document, its *Code of Standards for Survey Research,* is essentially a set of ethical guidelines, although several of its statements provide guidance on

TABLE 3.3 Comparison of Topics of Research Criteria

MSI	ARF 1981	ARF 1984	CASRO 1985	CASRO 1992	FTC/Maronick 1991	Morgan 1990
Sample Selection	• Design • Execution • Stability	• The Sample	• Research Design		• Sampling	• Sample Selection
Measurement	• Design • Execution	• The Research Plan • The Questionnaire • The Fieldwork • Data Processing	• Research Design • Questionnaire Design • Interviewing • Coding		• Interviewers • Leading Questions	• Instrument Administration • Interviewers
Determining Association and Causality	• Design • Applicability • Meaning	• Data Processing • Treatment of Data • Presentation	• Data Processing		• Control Groups • Experimental Settings	• Data Analysis
Conduct of the Researcher	• Origin • Candor	• Origin and Purpose • Presentation • Summary of Limitations	• Reporting • Materials Retention	• Responsibilities	• Researcher-Attorney Relations • Researcher Credentials	• Project Administration

how to assess research (e.g., "The basis for any specific 'completion rate' percentages should be fully documented and described") (CASRO, 1992).

The final two efforts covered in Table 3.3 were published as journal articles written by marketing academics. The work by Maronick (1991) presents a summary of FTC guidelines that have been articulated in several cases that the agency has pursued against deceptive advertising claims. Maronick's emphasis is on providing advice to researchers who might be investigating how deceptive an advertising claim might be. He offers nine simple statements about how to design studies that will stand up to legal challenges. The other journal article, by Morgan (1990), also is concerned about research that will withstand legal challenges. This work deals with survey research, offering 27 statements about survey methodology that cover sampling (e.g., "Convenience and nonprobability sampling must be justifiable"), instrument design (e.g., "Objective questions must include properly stated, complete sets of response scales"), and data analysis (e.g., "The frequencies and order of mention of multiple responses to a question should be avoided").

References

Aaker, David A. and George S. Day (1990), *Marketing Research,* 4th ed. New York: John Wiley.

Advertising Research Foundation (1981), *Guidelines for the Public Use of Market and Opinion Research.* New York: ARF.

——— (1984), *ARF Criteria for Marketing and Advertising Research.* New York: ARF.

American Home Products (1981), 98 FTC 136.

Bettman, James R., John W. Payne, and Richard Staelin (1986), "Cognitive Considerations in Designing Effective Labels for Presenting Risk Information," *Journal of Public Policy & Marketing,* 5, 1-28.

Boulding, William and Richard Staelin (1994), "How to Identify Strategic Empirical Generalizations: The Case of Returns to R&D Spending," working paper, Duke University.

Bristol-Myers Company (1975), 85 FTC 688.

Campbell, Donald T. and Julian C. Stanley (1963), *Experimental and Quasi-Experimental Designs for Research.* Chicago: Rand McNally.

Chapman, D. W. (1976), "Survey of Nonresponse Imputation Procedures," in *Proceedings of the Social Statistics Section, American Statistical Association, Part 1.* Washington, DC: American Statistical Association, 245-51.

Churchill, Gilbert A., Jr. (1991), *Marketing Research: Methodological Foundations,* 5th ed. Chicago: Dryden.

Council of American Survey Research Organizations (1985), *Guidelines for Conducting Forensic Research.* Port Jefferson, NY: CASRO.

——— (1992), *Code of Standards for Survey Research.* Port Jefferson, NY: CASRO.

Crossen, Cynthia (1994), "How 'Tactical Research' Muddied Diaper Debate," *The Wall Street Journal,* May 17, B1.

Deshpandé, Rohit and Gerald Zaltman (1982), "Factors Affecting the Use of Market Research Information: A Path Analysis," *Journal of Marketing Research,* 19 (February), 14-31.

Fishbein, Martin and Icek Ajzen (1975), *Belief, Attitude, Intention, and Behavior.* Reading, MA: Addison-Wesley.

Florio, Evelyn and Joseph R. Demartini (1993), "The Use of Information by Policymakers at the Local Community Level." *Knowledge: Creation, Diffusion, Utilization,* 15 (September), 106-23.

Haley, Russell I. and Allan L. Baldinger (1991), "The ARF Copy Research Validity Project," *Journal of Advertising Research,* 31 (April-May), 11-32.

Jacoby, Jacob and George J. Szybillo (1994), "The Implications of Relying on Deceptive Research to Determine Deceptive Advertising," working paper, New York University.

Kraft Inc. (1991), Docket No. 9208, FTC Lexis 38, January 30.

Lehmann, Donald R. (1989), *Marketing Research and Analysis,* 3rd ed. Homewood, IL: Irwin.

Maronick, Thomas J. (1991), "Copy Tests in FTC Deception Cases: Guidelines for Researchers," *Journal of Advertising Research,* 31 (December), 9-17.

Morgan, Fred W. (1990), "Judicial Standards for Survey Research: An Update and Guidelines," *Journal of Marketing,* 54 (January), 59-70.

Rich, Robert F. (1977), "Uses of Social Science Information by Federal Bureaucrats: Knowledge for Action vs. Knowledge for Understanding," in *Using Social Science Research in Public Policy Making,* Carol H. Weiss, ed. Lexington, MA: D. C. Heath, 199-211.

Richards, Jef I. and Ivan L. Preston (1992), "Proving and Disproving Materiality of Deceptive Advertising Claims," *Journal of Public Policy & Marketing,* 11 (2), 45-56.

Stewart, David W. (1994), "Deception, Materiality, and the Role of Survey Research: On the Difference between Evidence and Desire," working paper, University of Southern California.

Strickland, Donald E. (1982), "Alcohol Advertising: Orientations and Influence," *International Journal of Advertising,* 1 (October-December), 307-19.

Sudman, Seymour (1976), *Applied Sampling.* New York: Academic Press.

Thompson Medical Company Inc. (1984), 104 FTC 648.

U.S. House of Representatives (1990), *Health Warnings on Alcoholic Beverage Advertisements.* Hearing on H.R. 4493 before the Subcommittee on Transportation and Hazardous Materials, Committee on Energy and Commerce, U.S. House of Representatives, Serial No. 101-173. Washington, DC: Government Printing Office.

Wallack, Lawrence, Diana Cassady, and Joel Grube (1990), *TV Beer Commercials and Children: Exposure, Attention, Beliefs, and Expectations about Drinking as an Adult.* Washington, DC: AAA Foundation for Traffic Safety.

Weiss, Carol H. (1980), "Knowledge Creep and Decision Accretion," *Knowledge: Creation, Diffusion, Utilization,* 1 (March), 381-404.

Intersector Transfer of Marketing Knowledge

Alan R. Andreasen

Marketing is, at base, simply an activity carried out by individuals and organizations to achieve certain personal and social ends, just as preaching, plumbing, automobile repair, and surgery also are activities to achieve personal and social ends. Societies grow and develop as their members get better at such activities, especially if such activities are central to their welfare. Wilkie and Moore (1999) made the persuasive argument that marketing clearly meets the test of contributing significantly to a great many dimensions of social welfare.

Activities clearly improve with practice, as any athlete will attest. But great leaps forward in practice areas typically follow major intellectual breakthroughs that stimulate new ways of thinking about and carrying out those activities. Although there are many sources of intellectual breakthroughs, a common pattern is for concepts and tools from one discipline to migrate into a new domain where they can afford major benefits. One could argue that this describes athletics where athletes have benefited enormously from improved understanding of nutrition, muscle mechanics, and body chemistry. Similarly, international political analysis has profited greatly from the introduction of game theory from mathematics, agriculture has profited greatly from gene research and the sociology of innovation, and management and economic theory have profited greatly from Darwinian theories of evolution.

Introduction

It is the central thesis of this chapter that the migration of basic concepts and tools from private sector marketing to the nonprofit sector *has the potential to profoundly affect the ways in which the latter operates.* In my view, there already have been important cross-sector contributions, but the potential for major breakthroughs still is just that—a potential. In the sections to follow, I briefly describe the beginnings of attention to the nonprofit and government sectors within mainstream marketing thinking. I then sketch the ways in which marketing thinking penetrated the nonprofit sector, hypothesizing that the rate of adoption is affected by the nature of organizations and exchanges involved from this initial breakout to the present. This leads to a discussion of where the major impacts have been on the field of public and nonprofit management as well as some of the reciprocal influences on commercial thinking and practice. The chapter concludes with suggestions for where and how we should proceed to reinvigorate the cross-sector transfer of these valuable tools.

It must be noted that this chapter does not purport to be comprehensive in its treatment of the vast literature on nonprofit and government marketing. Furthermore, the tracing of the development of the field reflects my own experience and perceptions. The chapter seeks to give the reader a sense of the origins of the field, its general progress, and where it stands at present. Although testing of the suppositions, hypotheses, and speculations presented here might be a useful future enterprise for scholars, there are many more conceptual and methodological issues that deserve more immediate attention.

The Origins

The year 1969 marked a watershed in the way in which marketing scholars and practitioners thought about the field of marketing and its relationship to noncommercial organizations. Prior to 1969, scholars conceived of marketing as an economic activity in which business enterprises competed to provide goods and services to consumers so as to maximize the enterprises' returns on investment. This economic activity necessarily involved the public sector, but only as facilitator (e.g., trade missions to foreign markets) or regulator (e.g., rules and actions of Food and Drug Administration, Federal Trade Commission, and U.S. Department of Agriculture).

During the pre-1969 era, commentators took one of three perspectives. In its earliest years, marketing was viewed from either an *institutional* or a *functional* perspective. Both of these approaches were descriptive, treating marketing as a basic activity that was carried out by entities in societies and about which authors and researchers needed models and theories to explain, predict, and (often) criticize it. To the extent that analysis of marketing resulted in prescriptive recommendations, these were for societal actors such as the public or governmental agencies that needed to curb market excesses.

After World War II, and particularly after 1950, the dominant marketing perspective became *managerial*. Marketing was seen as a set of activities that managers in enterprises did to achieve corporate goals. It was acknowledged that there were better and worse ways of carrying out these responsibilities and that one needed models and theories to tell managers how to optimize impact and profits through customer choices. Although there still were scholars who adopted a societal perspective during this period, this perspective more often was directed at evaluating managerial actions and making normative recommendations about how to regulate or otherwise influence such actions for the social good.

In 1969, Kotler and Levy lobbed a conceptual grenade into this comfortable domain of marketing scholarship. In a classic article (Kotler and Levy 1969a), they argued,

> Marketing is a pervasive societal activity that goes considerably beyond the selling of toothpaste, soap, and steel. . . . [An] increasing amount of society's work is being performed by organizations other than business firms . . ., [and] every organization performs marketing-like activities whether or not they are recognized as such. (p. 10)

This expanded perspective did not sit well with the scholarly establishment at the time, whose members argued that the "broadening" of marketing was taking the field well beyond where it properly belonged. For example, Luck (1969) argued that marketing obviously involved markets, and this meant buying and selling. "Prominent scholars" who were trying to expand beyond this frame might find that their "self-image is pleasurably inflated," but they will be ignoring important issues still to be resolved within the traditional domain. Broadening the field would divert attention from critical issues and encroach on other disciplines (Luck 1969). Kotler and Levy (1969b) responded that marketing was about transactions, not just *market* transactions.

Luck's (1969) position, as well as that of Bartels (1974) and others who supported him, did not prevail. The broadened conception rapidly gained widespread acceptance within marketing academic circles. During the early 1970s, Nickels (1974) surveyed 74 marketing professors and found that 95% thought that the scope of the field should be broadened in the ways in which Kotler and Levy proposed. But the "broadening movement" threw the field into some confusion and sparked debate as to just what the essence of marketing really was. Kotler coined the term "Consciousness 3" to advance his argument that the modern view of marketing is a natural progression and that it follows from (1) a definition that restricted the field to market transactions as a business subject (Consciousness 1) and (2) a somewhat broader definition that permitted organization-client transactions not involving money (Consciousness 2). Consciousness 3, by contrast, incorporates "an organization's attempts to relate to all of its publics, not just its consuming publics" (Kotler 1972, p. 48). Bartels (1974), a marketing historian, stated that this debate suggested that the field was in an "identity crisis" and needed to decide whether marketing was defined by its technology (the Kotler-Levy position) or by the class(es) of behaviors toward which it was directed (the Luck position). In the year 2000, it is clear that the "technology school" has prevailed.

Early Developments

Because Kotler saw marketing as a technology, he and his colleagues set out to ask what it would mean if one applied it to noneconomic settings (cf. Elliott 1991). In a frequently quoted argument, Kotler and Zaltman (1971) explored what it would mean to apply the technology to social issues where, they suggested, it could be called "social marketing." At the same time, the original provocateurs, Levy and Kotler (1969), speculated on whether it was possible to do away with the troublesome noun "market" altogether. Their proposed solution was to say that what marketers really did was "furthering" and that this might be a better way in which to think about (and perhaps define) the field. It turned out that marketing academics were happy to broaden themselves but not to relabel themselves as "furtherers," and the term never caught on (Nickels 1974). However, the term social marketing did have a much longer life.

Over the subsequent 30 years, the issue became noncontroversial. Nonprofit and social marketing subjects came to be widely accepted, discussed, researched, and taught. Indeed, courses now are routinely taught on the application of marketing to nonprofit organizations. Textbooks on marketing management are available for business school courses in the United States (Kotler and Andreasen 1996; Rados 1996) and abroad (Sargeant 1999) and for the general practitioner (Herron 1997; Radtke 1998). There now are journals devoted to nonprofit marketing in general[1] as well as specialized journals.[2] There are texts in specific institutional or topical areas including education (Kotler and Fox 1995), economic development (Kotler, Jatusripitak, and Maesincee 1997), the arts (Kotler and Scheff 1997), places (Kotler, Haider, and Rein 1993), health care (Kotler and Clarke 1986), and social marketing (Andreasen 1995b; Fine 1990; Kotler and Roberto 1989; Manoff 1985).

On the other hand, it remains the case that the broadening movement still has some distance to go, both in the nonprofit sector (where the concepts can be applied) and in academic institutions (where the concepts can be researched and taught). Marketing still is limited in its applications in the noncommercial sector and suffers from a negative connotation in many quarters. Nonprofit marketing as an academic subject is found in only a limited number of business schools and is rare in M.B.A. programs. Today, it can be considered only a minor specialty for scholars and researchers. For example, there is no special interest group within the American Marketing Association devoted to nonprofit marketing, no regular conference on nonprofit topics, no first- or second-tier journal, and no academic job description that seeks a specialist on the topic. On the other hand, commercial marketing concepts and tools have had an important impact on the study and practice of nonprofit management.

To understand these contributions and the gaps in the institutional and intellectual structure of this special topic area today, one first needs to understand something of the historical progression of the nonprofit market and the factors that appear to be driving it forward—and holding it back.

Some Definitions

In the discussion that follows, the terms *nonprofit marketing* and *social marketing* are used to distinguish organizational perspectives from program perspectives. As I have defined elsewhere, social marketing is the application of commercial marketing concepts and tools to *programs* designed to influence the voluntary behavior of target audiences, where the primary objective is to improve the welfare of the target audiences and/or the society of which they are a part (Andreasen 1994). Social marketing can be carried out by nonprofit and public sector *organizations*. The management of the latter (lumped together here as *nonprofit organizations*) involves many more issues than those that typically are the focus in social marketing such as recruiting volunteers, creating and managing boards, fund-raising, and organization-level strategic planning.

Factors Affecting the Broadening of Marketing

In their classic "broadening" article, Kotler and Levy (1969a) asserted that that "the business heritage of marketing provides a useful set of concepts for guiding all organizations," that is, organizations not in the commercial sector (p. 15). However, applying commercial concepts and tools to the nonprofit world is not frictionless. One problem is that, as a number of authors have made clear (e.g., Andreasen 1995b; Bloom and Novelli 1981; Fox and Kotler 1980), the nonprofit organizational world is different in important ways from the commercial world, and if one wants to apply for-profit concepts and tools, then one must adapt to these differences. The problem, I argue here, is compounded by the fact that cross-sector transfers encompass not only new types of organizations *but also new types of transactions.* Much of the discussion around the Kotler-Levy challenge confounds these two important contingencies.

What has transpired as a result of the broadening movement is that marketing now is assumed to be useful to (1) new types of organizations and (2) new types of transactions. The former comprise both public and nonprofit organizations that are formally distinguished from commercial organizations in the way in which they are funded and to whom they are responsible. The new types of transactions have major noneconomic components in that they do not involve exchanges in which consumers pay for the economic offerings of the organization.[3] In both commercial and nonprofit worlds, we can distinguish four classes of transactions at the consumer level:

A. transactions involving the exchange of money for goods and services (e.g., sales of United Airlines tickets, Big Macs, and Girl Scout cookies);

B. transactions involving the exchange of money for intangible benefits (e.g., donations of money to the American Red Cross);

A + B. transactions involving the exchange of money for goods and services and an intangible social benefit (e.g., sales of Big Macs where 5% of sales goes to the American Red Cross), often called "cause-related marketing"; and

C. transactions involving the exchange of intangible costs for intangible benefits (e.g., going on a diet, giving up smoking).

In addition to these consumer transactions, there are organization-to-organization transactions involving the commercial and nonprofit sectors. Elsewhere, I have suggested that there are two variations: *joint promotions* and *licensing* (Andreasen 1996). The former is the case in which a commercial organization and a nonprofit organization form a partnership to achieve some social objective (e.g., *Glamour* magazine and various health agencies promoting "breast health" among young women). Licensing is the case in which a commercial organization pays a fee to a nonprofit in return for permission to use the nonprofit's name and/or logo on commercial products or services. An example would be the American Cancer Society's agreement with SmithKlineBeecham allowing the latter to use the American Cancer Society logo in advertisements for NicoDerm patches. In return, SmithKlineBeecham paid the American Cancer Society a fixed licensing fee.

In my view, the transfer of commercial marketing concepts and tools to nonprofit contexts can be explained in terms of these distinctions. Thus, I would propose the following hypotheses:

Hypothesis 1: The greater the similarity of the nonprofit *organizational environment* to a commercial environment, the earlier and more extensive the adoption of commercial marketing concepts and tools.

Hypothesis 2: The greater the similarity of the nonprofit's focal *transaction* to an economic transaction, the earlier and more extensive the adoption of commercial marketing concepts and tools.

To understand the impact of the factors, we must consider, in turn, the ways in which organizations and transactions differ between the sectors.[4]

Differences in Organizational Environment

Structural Differences

A number of authors have sought to explore the differences between the for-profit and nonprofit sectors (Bloom and Novelli 1981; Kotler and Andreasen 1996; Rothschild 1979). Among the unique characteristics frequently found in nonprofits are the following (Andreasen 1995b, pp. 59-63):

1. *Funding by nonowners.* Nonprofit organizations are funded directly by individual and corporate donors, foundations, and government grants as well as by revenues

from sales (Weisbrod 1998). They also are indirectly funded by tax concessions, donations of goods and services, and voluntary labor. Those who provide these resources often have limited—or zero—direct influence on organizational decision making. They also receive no distribution of organizational surpluses, so their commitment to organizational success must come about in other ways.

2. *No simple bottom-line metric.* Commercial marketers have very clear and relatively simple metrics by which to guide and evaluate their efforts such as sales, market share, and profits. Nonprofit marketers often are challenged to achieve difficult to measure goals such as reducing spousal abuse, increasing physical activity, and making the end-of-life years less stressful. Such challenges are hard to measure, very long term, and subject to all sorts of influences outside marketers' control.

3. *Public scrutiny that constrains risk taking.* Nonprofits receive donations and tax concessions because they are believed to be acting to improve the general welfare. As a consequence, it is typical that some form of formal or informal public scrutiny will be accorded their performance. This scrutiny may be by the government, a funding source, and/or the general public as represented by the press or academic researchers and critics. This scrutiny, among other effects, makes risk taking more difficult for nonprofit marketers and increases the importance of "politics" and "public relations" in the marketing mix.

4. *Multiple publics.* The constant need for outside assistance and/or the constant oversight by other individuals and agencies increase the need for nonprofits to market simultaneously to target customers and to those who are giving assistance or regulating activities.

5. *Limited budgets yet daunting goals.* Commercial marketers often have generous budgets to meet given challenges. On the other hand, nonprofit marketers typically have severely restricted promotional budgets and big challenges (e.g., eliminating hunger). In addition, their ability to invest in building greater long-term capacity is limited by watchdog groups who are suspicious of expenditures on "overhead." They think that an organization that pays too high salaries or "wastes" too much money on overhead, advertising, and/or sales commissions is somehow not being frugal with taxpayers' money or donations (Cordes et al. 1999; Letts, Ryan, and Grossman, 1999).

6. *Fewer opportunities to modify offerings.* Many nonprofits market in environments where desired behaviors involve offerings that are relatively fixed and less than desirable from the customers' perspective. Quitting smoking or drugs is neither pleasant nor easy. Condoms are the major (current) method of preventing sexually transmitted diseases. Wagner's Ring Cycle is very long. In each case, marketers must devise strategies where they are "stuck" with a product or behavior that cannot easily be modified. In the private sector, resources and science more often are available to make such changes.

The inference from the preceding characteristics is that one might be expected to find more adoption of commercial sector marketing concepts and tools where the following exist:

- Less public scrutiny

- Fewer publics to accommodate (e.g., fewer donors, no political jurisdictional problems)

- More generous budgets

- More opportunities to modify products or services

- Clear, short-term, and traceable objectives

Cultural Differences

A second set of factors influencing the rate of adoption of marketing knowledge across organizations is the attitude toward marketing within the organization or industry. As Manning and I pointed out elsewhere (Andreasen and Manning 1987), many social marketing organizations are affected by a basic conflict between two or more "cultures." Many nonprofit and public sector marketing organizations were founded to achieve basic social service missions. They want to eliminate homelessness, reduce child abuse, or improve the physical and mental well-being of the very elderly. Their managers care deeply about this mission and often are willing to overlook waste, misdirection, and inefficiency if they are "in a good cause." Those with this "social service" orientation frequently conflict with marketers who come from a "corporate culture." The latter often enter organizations many years after their founding and attempt to increase the efficiency and effectiveness of the organizations and sometimes dramatically increase the number and range of programs offered. The concerns of those inhabiting the corporate culture mind-set often are seen by the social service people as heartless, uncaring, or even immoral. For their part, the corporate people often see their counterparts as ill focused, wasteful, and somewhere on "Cloud 9." Conflicts between the two cultures can have highly debilitating effects on social marketing programs if not resolved.

These cultural differences would predict that, other things being equal, one would find more rapid adoption of commercial marketing concepts and tools in organizational categories where the following exists.

- Less hostility toward marketing

Similarities and Differences between Economic and Noneconomic Transactions

Many nonprofits sell goods and services as a major revenue source, one that is becoming more and more important during the 21st century (Weisbrod 1998). However, as Kotler and Levy (1969a) noted originally, what is unique about recent broadening is the transfer of marketing concepts and tools to transactions that are not economic exchanges of goods and services for money. This occurs at two critical junctures. First, the majority of nonprofits raise funds through charitable donations or foundation grants. These might be called quasi-economic transactions in that there is money exchanged but the "other side" of the transaction does not involve goods and services.[5] This is not to say that there are not important returns to donors or funders in psychic and social satisfaction. Indeed, one of the important challenges for nonprofit marketers is to craft effective "psychic benefit packages" that produce desired exchange levels.

The second juncture at which purely market exchanges are absent is in the core mission or specific programs of many, if not most, nonprofits. This is clearest for nonprofits promoting transactions in which the "payment" by the target audience is the undertaking of some behavior that incurs nonmonetary costs such as psychic pain, social embarrassment, and significant time commitments. These types of transactions are the principal focus of many social marketing programs (Andreasen 1994; Goldberg, Fishbein, and Middlestadt 1997).

In addition to the fact that quasi-economic and noneconomic transactions minimize the role of money, they often display a number of other unique characteristics:

1. *Negative demand.* It is rare for a private sector marketer to be asked to market a product or service for which the target audience has a clear distaste. Yet, as Kotler and Andreasen (1996) noted, nonprofit marketers "must try to entice 'macho men' into wearing seat belts, timid souls into giving blood or taking medication around which swirl rumors about devastating effects on sexual potency, or aging citizens to finally admit they are infirm or otherwise need assistance" (p. 27).

2. *High-involvement issues.* Most of the behaviors that nonprofit marketers are asked to influence are much more highly *involving* than those found in the private sector. Asking parents to begin to regulate family size or asking rural mothers to regularly weigh their children and expose the fact that their families have little food is much more serious than asking them to buy bicycles or new furniture. One consequence of this very high level of involvement is that it often makes it very hard for nonprofit marketers to carry out the customer research that they need to be effective. As Bloom and Novelli (1981) noted, "While people are generally willing to be interviewed about these [nonprofit marketing] topics, they are more likely to give inaccurate, self-serving, or socially desirable answers to such questions than to questions about cake mixes, soft drinks, or cereals" (p. 80).

3. *Invisible benefits.* Whereas in the private sector, it usually is relatively clear what benefits one is likely to get with a Hilton Hotel room or a new Xerox machine, nonprofit marketers often are encouraging behaviors for which there is no obvious immediate benefit—*nothing happens.* Immunization is supposed to prevent disease, and birth control is supposed to prevent pregnancies. In each of these cases, the *absence* of outcomes is a sign of success. This does not mean that one cannot find ways in which to talk about the benefits of those absences (e.g., the freedom of not having "too many" children). It also is the case that some commercial organizations must market products for which nothing happens (e.g., using a deodorant means that no one will criticize you).

4. *Benefits in the future.* Many behaviors require immediate costs but promise only long-term benefits. Stopping smoking or increasing physical activity will result in a longer life and happier "senior years." Not "smacking" a child will mean that he or she will grow up with more self-confidence and less psychic damage.

5. *Benefits to third parties.* Some behaviors advocated by nonprofit marketers have payoffs for third parties such as poor people or society in general and not to the person undertaking the behavior. This is the case, for example, for energy conservation and obedience to speed laws.

Again, other things being equal, one might expect to find more adoption of commercial sector marketing concepts and tools where the following exist:

- There is no negative avoidance of the proposed transaction.
- The behavioral domain is not particularly involving.
- The benefits of the behavior are visible.
- The changes in behavior result in relatively immediate benefits.
- The benefits of the behavior are primarily—or totally—to the target audience.

The History of Intellectual Transfer

There are two dimensions along which one can observe the transfer of commercial marketing concepts and tools. First, one can observe the types of organizations that adopted marketing concepts early and late as well as the types of transactions to which marketing was applied. Second, one can observe the concepts and tools that were widely adopted early and late.

Organizations Adopting Marketing

One way in which to trace the organizational acceptance of marketing concepts and tools is to look at the published literature, particularly published texts, cases, and articles during the period following the Kotler and Levy (1969a) broadening article. This reveals that the earliest response to the broadening challenge was the development of texts, readings books, and cases on nonprofit marketing *in general.* The first text was Kotler's (1975) *Marketing for Nonprofit Organizations.*[6] The topical organization of this text followed the general structure of Kotler's very popular general marketing management texts but with public and nonprofit sector examples. Not surprisingly, a great many of the examples in Kotler's original edition were in higher education. Although this orientation reflects Kotler's own interests and experience, it also fits the predictions of this chapter in that the central transaction in higher education is very much like a traditional services-for-money business. Indeed, many commercial consultants today prosper by offering high-priced workshops and seminars, and executive education is a highly lucrative cash cow for nonprofit business schools.

The first major case involving nonprofit marketing that received widespread use in M.B.A. programs was Rangun's case of contraceptive marketing in Bangladesh. This also was a predictable early extension of commercial marketing ideas because the case very much involved the selling of condoms and other contraceptive products, albeit at a highly subsidized price.

The first book to take marketing concepts and apply them to a particular organizational specialty was by MacStravic (1977), a health care specialist who produced *Marketing Health Care.* This was followed by a readings book by Cooper

(1979). These volumes were consistent with our hypotheses in that they focused on the selling of hospital services, an industry that features a significant mix of for-profit and nonprofit competitors (Marmor, Schlesinger, and Smithey 1987).

A third area into which marketing concepts filtered during the early years was arts marketing (Andreasen 1995a; Kotler and Kotler 1998; Kotler and Scheff 1997; McLean 1998; Mokwa, Dawson, and Priere 1980). Here, a number of researchers looked into how and where individuals might be persuaded to attend symphonies, theaters, and museums. These settings also involved semieconomic transactions with consumers paying for services. The one area in which this involved ventures beyond this realm was at museums, where entry often was free.

Nonprofit Exchanges Where Marketing Is Applied

In the organizational settings and transactions just described, applications of marketing were to products (contraceptives) and services (hospital care) that did not differ in important conceptual ways from commercial transactions. However, there were early developments in which the transactions were different in important ways. First, there was very rapid growth in applications to fundraising. In these cases, target audiences were asked to give money where the benefits of such actions were ephemeral, hard to portray, in the distant future, and/or benefits to other third parties. In my estimation, the early adoption of marketing ideas here was in the rather narrow domain of direct marketing, where nonprofit practitioners could see the real value of an array of marketing concepts. But the applications were more tactical than strategic.

Different strategic thinking, however, was required in two other areas of interest during the late 1970s and 1980s: blood donations and recycling. However, unlike the examples just mentioned, both of these domains presented new challenges for marketing thinking because they were fully noneconomic and reflected many of the characteristics of such transactions cited earlier. This growing focus on noneconomic transactions led to journal articles that began to explore the differences between the two sectors. In 1979, Rothschild wrote about "Why It's so Hard to Sell Brotherhood Like Soap" (Rothschild 1979), and two years later, Bloom and Novelli (1981) sought to define the special problems inherent in social marketing.

The most recent applications in nonprofit marketing have been in an area where the transactions typically are not economic, as in the case of many social marketing programs and campaigns. Although social marketing of "pure behaviors" (as opposed to social marketing of contraceptives) has been around since the earlier 1970s with the participation of marketers in the National High Blood Pressure Education Program, its growth has been phenomenal during the past 15 years (Andreasen 1995b; Novelli 1990). At this point, social marketing has been adopted by a wide range of private, public, and private nonprofit organizations and institutions worldwide including the Centers for Disease Control and Prevention, the U.S. Agency for International Development, the U.S. Department of Agriculture, the National Cancer Institute, and the American Association of Retired Persons. There now are social marketing textbooks (Andreasen 1995b; Fine 1981; Kotler and Roberto 1989; Manoff 1985), readings books (Fine 1990;

Goldberg, Fishbein, and Middlestadt 1997), chapters within mainstream texts (Kotler and Andreasen 1996), and a Harvard teaching note (Rangun and Karim 1991). There have been reviews of the accomplishments of social marketing (Fox and Kotler 1980; Malafarina and Loken 1993) and presidential addresses for two different consumer behavior organizations calling for researchers and academics to become more deeply involved in studies of social marketing (Andreasen 1993; Goldberg 1996). Centers for social marketing now are present or proposed in Tampa, Forida; Ottawa, Ontario; and Glasgow, Scotland. A social marketing "listserver" now has more than 600 participants, and there are several social marketing Web sites.

The Role of Academic Institutions

There was relatively slow growth in the number and range of nonprofit texts and materials that were developed during the 1980s and early 1990s. This reflected a greater focus on private sector growth and on personal self-centeredness during the Reagan years. It also reflected a shift in the interests of the scholars and researchers who produced the early work in this area in the face of the realities of academic life in schools of business during the 1980s. First, in most schools of business, it was relatively rare for students to consider careers in nonprofit marketing. Most undergraduates were interested in private sector careers and saw few role models in the nonprofit sector. Furthermore, they were unlikely to think far enough ahead to the time when they might be on nonprofit boards and could benefit from exposure to the nonprofit world as undergraduates. For their part, M.B.A. students could appreciate the possibility of a future board role, but they too were oriented toward private sector careers. Thus, business schools did not seek—or reward—faculty who wanted to teach about nonprofit marketing or do research on the topic.[7]

During the 1990s, several forces resulted in something of a rebirth of interest in work in this area. First, some business schools have learned the value of research that stretches their faculty and have rewarded seminal contributions in this domain. Second, business schools have taken a greater interest in issues involving social responsibility and have observed that more corporations are becoming involved in social initiatives. Thus, the late 1980s and 1990s witnessed the reappearance of nonprofit marketing texts that were first written during the early 1980s (Lovelock and Weinberg 1989; Rados 1996) as well as the continued revision and publication of the original Kotler text, now coauthored by me (Kotler and Andreasen 1996). There also has been some growth in the number of papers and presentations at marketing academic conferences on nonprofit and social marketing topics.

In the absence of interest by business schools in teaching nonprofit management (with the major exception of Yale University), the 1990s saw the emergence of a number of nonprofit degree programs outside of business schools at places such as Case Western Reserve, Indiana University, and the University of San Francisco. On the other hand, a review of the curricula in such nonprofit programs indicates that courses with marketing titles still are relatively rare.

Finally, scholarship on nonprofit marketing topics has been aided by the growth in the number of nonprofit managers who have experience in the private sector and who can appreciate marketing as a management tool. The latter two forces have spawned a significant market for nonprofit marketing texts that are written in a much more popular and accessible style. Publishers have been quick to fill this gap, particularly Jossey-Bass, the leading publisher in this area. A June 1999 search of the Amazon.com Web site turned up 21 books under "non-profit marketing." Of these, only 4 were by scholars identified by me to be in marketing departments or business schools.

Conceptual Contributions to Nonprofit Marketing Management

I have argued that marketing can best be thought of as a mind-set, a process, and a set of concepts and tools (Andreasen 1995b). In my view. the conceptual contributions from the commercial to the nonprofit worlds have been in all three areas.

The Customer Mind-Set

It is possible to enumerate only some of the more important conceptual contributions that commercial marketing has made to nonprofit and social marketing management. Probably the single most important contribution of marketing to the nonprofit world is in teaching what has been called the "customer mind-set." For many years, often under quasi-monopoly conditions, nonprofits thought that all they really needed to do to get patients, donors, or volunteers to do what the organizations wanted was simply to announce the opportunities and tell the intended target audiences about the benefits of the proposed actions (e.g., giving money to the United Way, volunteering at the YMCA, quitting smoking). The so-called marketers knew what the problems or needs were and thought that relatively simple communication vehicles, such as clever direct mail, would achieve their ends. This organization-centered mind-set often led the managers in the case of program failure to think of the customers as the enemy, and this got in the way of organizations developing a research orientation and being willing to make significant changes in their offerings. Their solution to a lack of success was simply to say to themselves that somehow they "have to tell our story better."

The adaptation of a customer mind-set by the more sophisticated nonprofits has led to increased use of a wide range of research techniques at three stages of the typical marketing campaign. First, nonprofit and social marketing organizations more often are conducting formative research to guide them in the development of their initial plans and tactics. Second, organizations more often are likely to pretest their major tactical elements before committing them to the field. Finally, a few organizations have seen the importance of continuing customer research to track performance and to adjust strategies and tactics.

A customer mind-set has led to the exploration of many consumer behavior models from mainstream marketing (or that are used by mainstream marketing thinkers) in an attempt to understand how people make decisions to act in socially important situations. Works by Ajzen and Fishbein (1980) and Bagozzi and Warshaw (1990) have been particularly useful.

One of the areas that has made extensive use of "customer research" is political marketing (Newman 1994). Here, major and minor campaigns of politicians and issues commonly use "focus groups" to understand target audiences and to test out possible positions and potential advertisements. Regular polling (often overnight) has become a mainstay of politics, particularly at the national level.

The Marketing Planning Process

A number of authors have focused on how to introduce marketing more deeply into nonprofit organizations (Kotler 1979), and a number of nonprofit organizations have learned to make extensive use of marketing planning processes (Andreasen 1990, 1992). These processes are of two types. First, there is organization-level planning in which the institution plots its course of action over an extended period of time. Many of the components of this process, such as the development of mission statements, SWOT (strengths, weaknesses, opportunities, threats) analyses, and portfolio models, are drawn from standard management and strategy texts and articles. Marketing thinking also has pervaded the planning process in the following respects:

- Marketers make clear that communications is only one element of the marketing mix. Too many nonprofit managers think that (1) marketing is just communications and (2) this is all that one needs to influence behavior. Yet, many nonprofit communications are failures because of inadequate attention to the design of products or "benefit packages," the pricing of offerings, or the distribution of behavioral opportunities.

- The concept of the marketing audit (Kotler, Gregor, and Rodgers 1977) has been found to be helpful in a number of nonprofit and social marketing programs (Andreasen 1978; Berkowitz and Flexner 1978; Herron 1978).

- Marketers have emphasized the importance of tracking systems to assess organization and program performance. For example, during the 1980s, family planning programs in developing countries sought to develop retail audit methodologies for contraceptive sales to give themselves better information and to help answer questions about the overall market effects of their programs[8] (Andreasen 1988b).

- Marketers have introduced the concept of brand management as an alternative form of organization for nonprofits.

Marketing Concepts and Tools

There also have been important developments in transferring concepts and tools in specific areas from the commercial sector to the nonprofit sector. Among these are segmentation, branding, and alliance building.

Segmentation

For many years, the nonprofit world segmented markets relatively crudely on the basis of standard demographics. However, during recent years, contact with private sector organizations and consultants has led to more sophisticated approaches. A good case in point is the imaginative use of geodemographic clustering and related segmentation techniques by Currence and her colleagues at the American Cancer Society. The American Cancer Society now routinely uses the PRIZM system to improve the efficiency and effectiveness of its fundraising efforts by tailoring messages and effort levels to the 62 neighborhood clusters established by Claritas, the consumer marketing information firm. The researchers also have begun to use this approach for their health intervention programs. For example, a recent project discovered through this technology that programs to increase the frequency with which women obtained mammograms in specific urban areas could be focused on only four PRIZM clusters in which mammogram rates were particularly low and clusters had other characteristics identifying them as underserved (Currence 1997).

Branding

Two forces have led nonprofits to become much more interested in the branding possibilities inherent in their names and reputations. The first is the growing importance of alliances in the nonprofit sector, where negotiations inevitably involve considerations of the value of the nonprofit brand, particularly the value to specific partners. Second, branding has become more important as nonprofits face more competition. Competition always has existed in traditional areas such as fund-raising and volunteer recruitment. However, many more nonprofits have entered heretofore exclusively commercial markets with products and services. Between 1977 and 1996, the number of nonprofits increased 36%, while the revenues of those in the so-called independent sector[9] increased more than fivefold (Independent Sector 1998). This means that nonprofits must fight each other harder for traditional financial and human resources. But as many supplement their revenues with for-profit ventures, they also are faced with competition from the private sector itself. Finally, many nonprofits are finding that domains they once considered their own preserve now face competition from the private sector, for example, in areas such as hospital and long-term care and worker training as well as in public services such as prisons, waste removal, and transportation (Weisbrod 1998).

As a consequence of these competitive pressures, nonprofits have come to realize that they could be more successful if they had a clearer idea of (1) how they were perceived, (2) the dimensions on which those perceptions are formed, (3) how they differ from competitors on these dimensions, and (4) what gains might be obtained from various repositioning strategies. One of the top 10 U.S. nonprofits recently hired a major consulting organization to carry out branding and positioning research for the organization and each of its major resource attraction and service delivery areas. This exercise made significant use of laddering concepts from the private sector to understand fundamental values that undergirded impressions of the organization. As in the private sector, these fundamental values, then, are becoming the basis of many of the organization's present and planned marketing initiatives (Ritchie, Swami, and Weinberg 1999).

Alliance Building

Nonprofits have become increasingly involved in alliances with commercial organizations. There have, of course, been such alliances for many years in the areas of advertising and volunteer service. Campaigns by the Advertising Council have produced some of our most memorable ad copy and most enduring icons. For example, consider the following tag lines:

- This is your brain on drugs.
- A mind is a terrible thing to waste.
- Only you can prevent forest fires.
- Take a bite out of crime.
- Friends don't let friends drive drunk.

Advertising Council campaigns have given us Smokey Bear, McGruff the crime-fighting dog, and the crash test dummies.

What has changed in the relationship between nonprofit and private sector organizations recently is the shift in corporate philanthropy from giving programs to strategic investments (Burlingame and Young 1996; Smith 1994). This has changed nonprofit approaches to corporations from begging to partnering (Austin 2000; Weeden 1998). Corporations have realized that alliances with nonprofits can have important effects on sales, company image, and employee morale. Alliances also can help in the political battles that many corporations face. Beginning with creative insights from American Express, these new alliances first took the form of cause-related marketing activities (Varadarajan and Menon 1988), where transactions were tied to charitable contributions. As companies began to see the strategic advantages of these partnerships, they began to create alliances that I have labeled joint issue promotion (Andreasen 1995b), where both parties (e.g., Avon and various breast cancer organizations) pursue the same social goals. Finally, there has been a recent spate of licensing arrangements, for example, where the American Cancer Society has allowed its name to be used by the marketers of NicoDerm and Florida orange juice in the belief that such use of the American Cancer Society brand will increase the number of people undertaking important cancer prevention behaviors.

Marketing alliances have proven to be a mixed blessing for some partners, and many observers have raised questions about the ethics of such relationships, particularly licensing. Leaders of the American Medical Association found themselves in significant trouble with members over the agreement that the association signed with Sunbeam Corporation. Recently, attorneys general from 16 states and the District of Columbia issued an advisory opinion to regulate some of the activities in this new area of collaborative promotion between nonprofit and for-profit organizations.

Reciprocal Intellectual Benefits

As I have argued elsewhere (Andreasen 1993), the transfer of knowledge is not unidirectional. Mainstream marketing has benefited in important ways from the broadening experience. In the developing world, this is because nonprofit marketers and their consultants have diffused management and research concepts to commercial organizations that were unfamiliar with them.[10] More generally, Drucker (1989) argued that mainstream management, even in the developing world, has much to learn from nonprofits that "are practicing what most American businesses only preach" (p. 88).

In the area of scholarship and research, the nonprofit domain has yielded—and can yield—important intellectual contributions to mainstream marketers and can offer even more in the future. I offer a limited number of examples.

Foot-in-the-Door Theory

Marketers always have faced the challenge of motivating people to take actions where the payoffs to the actors are vague and long term, for example, convincing a promising brand assistant to take a position in Myanmar because of the "growth opportunities." As noted previously, the nonprofit world is replete with challenges wherein marketers must induce target audiences to take actions for which there are no obvious personal concrete payoffs. It is not surprising, therefore, to find that fundamental research on securing compliance with requests was done in a nonprofit context. Pioneering work on the foot-in-the-door technique was carried out during the 1970s and early 1980s (Scott 1977) on what it would take to get householders to help out with a social cause and later by Reingen (1978) and others on soliciting charitable donations. This early research then was extended to the creation of strategies to get people to respond to marketing research survey requests (Allen, Schewe, and Wijk 1980) in the private sector.

Exchange Theory

I believe that it can be argued convincingly that one of the most fundamental changes in the way in which we understand and study marketing came about because of the broadening trend in the field during the 1970s. Bagozzi's (1974, 1978) pioneering work on exchange theory was, in fact, an essential for marketing to venture beyond the traditional confines of economic transactions. To make it possible to apply marketing to charitable giving or getting people to stop smoking, we needed to develop a way of thinking about the "exchanges" that marketers were trying to solicit as something other than offers of economic goods or services for financial payments. The field also had to allow for transactions that went beyond simple two-way exchanges to account for the fact that, in some cases, the prime beneficiaries of exchanges (especially in the nonprofit world) were third parties, for example, when recycling benefits not the recycler (who mostly has costs) but rather the society as a whole. Bagozzi was able to develop a fundamental framework that would account for these differing exchange models. Exchange theory now is fundamental to most basic marketing and consumer behavior texts and to much research in both mainstream and nonprofit marketing.

Other Past and Potential Reciprocal Contributions

The fact that many nonprofits have limited budgets yet are urged by their mentors to engage in customer research during early years creates considerable frustration. As a result, I wrote a series of articles and a textbook, *Cheap but Good Marketing Research* (Andreasen 1988a), to help such managers. One of the articles introduced the concept of "backward" marketing research (Andreasen 1985) as a process for ensuring that research would have maximum usefulness—and thus minimize the waste of limited resources. Both publications have seen wide use in the private sector (and the classroom), and the backward approach was adopted at one point as standard procedure at DDB Needham's research department.

Social marketers often are charged with influencing highly sensitive behaviors in foreign environments. As a consequence, they have had to develop approaches that would allow them to obtain deep understanding of culture-bound behaviors with limited budgets. To achieve this, several social marketing programs have developed a technique called "rapid ethnography," which involves applying many of the in-depth interviewing and observational techniques of cultural anthropologists over a very short time span to topics such as the treatment of diarrheal disorders in developing countries (Kendall 1985). Such approaches would seem to have considerable potential for mainstream marketers with limited budgets—or immediate deadlines—serving unique but poorly understood cultures.

Because the language and culture of many target audiences represent unfamiliar terrain for nonprofit marketers, social marketers have become adept at perfecting community-based approaches to the development of research instruments, communications messages, and other intervention components. A common technique is to involve the target audience itself in the design process. For example, a campaign by the Porter Novelli agency in Tijuana effectively solicited the help of female sex workers in the development of a series of comic books intended to teach skills for dealing with various types of clients who did not want to use condoms (Ramah and Cassidy 1992). Such customer-created instruments capture well the basic marketing concept and deserve wider adoption in the commercial sector.

Summary and Future Directions

This review of selected aspects of knowledge development in the nonprofit sector permits the following tentative conclusions:

1. No one in the marketing or academic communities today seriously questions whether the marketing concept should be broadened to include the nonprofit and public sectors.

2. Managers in the nonprofit sector have learned much from the commercial sector in terms of the following:

   - The customer mind-set
   - The marketing planning process
   - A wide array of concepts and tools

3. Adoption of these commercial sector concepts and tools was—and is—most likely to come about where the organizational environment and the exchanges involved are most like the private sector. For example, adoption of marketing technology in the nonprofit sector appears to have taken place first in settings where the transactions involved are largely economic in character and only more recently in settings where transactions do not involve the exchange of money in either direction.

4. Transfer of this knowledge to the nonprofit sector has been carried out both by business school scholars and professors and by scholars in other disciplines.

5. Although they are shrinking in number, some practitioners in the nonprofit and public sectors resist the adoption of marketing technology in areas where it might be appropriate. This can be attributable to an unclear conception of what *good* marketing is all about.

6. Despite the growth in importance of the nonprofit sector, nonprofit courses rarely are found in business schools. (It also is true that the major professional association in marketing, the American Marketing Association, offers little institutional support for the topic.)

7. Although the "slack" in management education for nonprofits has been taken up by schools other than business schools, nonprofit marketing courses still are relatively rare.

8. Knowledge transfer between the sectors is not one-way; it is better conceived as an *interpenetration* of marketing ideas. Research and conceptualization about the unique problems of marketing in the nonprofit sector have yielded important conceptual breakthroughs of value to the commercial sector as well as to the nonprofit sector.

Although there has been a substantial amount of interpenetration between the sectors, the potential for further knowledge growth in both directions is significant. A number of steps need to be taken:

1. Business schools should recognize the growing importance of the nonprofit sector and the potential value of marketing technology to individuals who will work, consult, or serve on boards in that sector. Therefore, business schools should do the following:

   - More frequently offer courses in nonprofit marketing in undergraduate, graduate, and executive programs
   - More frequently offer short courses and workshops on nonprofit marketing as part of their executive education offerings

2. The American Marketing Association also should recognize the growth of the non-profit sector and the potential value of developments in that area for the commercial sector. As such, it should do the following:

   ■ Actively solicit members from the nonprofit world

   ■ Establish a Special Interest Group on nonprofit marketing

   ■ Fund, or at least facilitate, periodic (or annual) conferences on nonprofit marketing

3. Faculty who are mentoring doctoral students should seriously consider nonprofit contexts in which to study phenomena of general relevance to marketing. Among the topics for which this context might provide breakthrough mainstream insights are the following:

   ■ Long-term acquisition of new behavior patterns or lifestyles (e.g., hobbies, sports)

   ■ Research methodologies for nonliterate or low-education targets

   ■ Modeling alliance formation, evolution, and management

   ■ Ethical issues across diverse stakeholder groups

   ■ Private-public-nonprofit competition

4. Marketing teachers, textbook writers, and consultants should investigate the transfer potential of many additional research and planning tools being widely adopted in the private sector but rare in the nonprofit world. Nonprofit managers are, in fact, eager to learn more about topics such as the following:

   ■ Electronic commerce

   ■ Horizontal alliances among marketers

   ■ Co-branding by nonprofits

   ■ Relationship marketing

   ■ Mathematical modeling of decisions about distribution, pricing (especially across segments), and promotional spending[11]

   ■ Advertising schedule optimizers (as more nonprofits pay for advertising instead of relying on public service spots)

5. Commercial marketing professionals should be encouraged to lend their talents to nonprofits so as to facilitate one-to-one transfer of marketing thinking.

Concluding Comment

A future marked by increased transfer of marketing knowledge from the commercial sector to the nonprofit and public sectors seems to be a certainty. Typical of what is happening today was an August 1999 news story in *The Nonprofit Times* describing a two-year reorganization effort of the American Heart Association. This initiative forced the organization into making a "redefinition of [its] driving forces." The organization concluded that the four major forces on which it needs to concentrate for future success are the following:

- Generating resources

- Communicating its key message to medical and lay audiences

- Advocating for the general public

- Determining where the organization's biggest impact would be from the stand-point of focusing resources

Because three of these factors clearly imply major marketing efforts, it is not surprising that the article concluded, "In addition to taking advantage of techno-logical advancement, the [American Heart Association] also decided to bring in more marketing expertise" (McNamara 1999).

This is an organizational trend that can be expected to be repeated frequently throughout this sector in the coming decades. It is a trend that can support accel-erated transfer of marketing concepts and tools—in *both* directions.

Notes

1. Examples include *Journal of Non-Profit and Public Sector Marketing* and *International Journal of Nonprofit and Voluntary Sector Marketing.*

2. Examples include *Health Marketing Quarterly, Journal of Hospital Marketing, Social Marketing Quarterly,* and *Journal of Marketing for Higher Education.*

3. Of course, the promotion of noneconomic behaviors has *indirect* economic conse-quences for nonprofits. Many institutions that do not charge directly for their services (e.g., public libraries, museums) obtain indirect economic benefits in that their budgets bear direct relationships to the levels of service provided.

4. Material in the next few sections is adapted from Andreasen (1995b).

5. Of course, many donations yield some tangible returns in goods and services such as access to special events, subscriptions to newsletters, commemorative T-shirts, and coffee mugs.

6. It was a measure of limited significance of the nonprofit marketing field that the publisher, Prentice Hall, did not bother to create a teaching manual for the book until its fourth edition.

7. An informal Public Interest Affinity Group has emerged during recent years to ex-plore more systematically the possible role of nonprofit issues, training, and research in M.B.A. programs. Early meetings of this group were funded by the Aspen and Kellogg foundations.

8. A persistent question of such programs was whether subsidized contraceptive sales were merely taking sales from the commercial sector.

9. These are organizations classified by the Internal Revenue Service as 501.c.3 or 501.c.4 and religious organizations.

10. I once interviewed a commercial marketer in south Asia about his role in carrying out a contraceptive social marketing program. When I asked about the benefits he re-ceived from this involvement, he was most enthusiastic about learning about focus group research, which he assured me he was going to employ regularly in his commercial ven-ture.

11. For example, could airline yield management models be helpful to those in the theater or arts?

References

Ajzen, Icek and Martin Fishbein (1980), *Understanding Attitudes and Predicting Social Behavior.* Englewood Cliffs, NJ: Prentice Hall.

Allen, Chris T., Charles D. Schewe, and Gosta Wijk (1980), "More on Self-Perception Theory's Foot-in-the-Door Technique in the Pre-Call/Mail Survey Setting," *Journal of Marketing Research,* 17 (November), 498-502.

Andreasen, Alan R. (1978), *A Marketing Audit of the Smoking and Breast Cancer Program of the Office of Cancer Communications, National Cancer Institute.* Washington, DC: National Cancer Institute.

———(1985), " 'Backward' Marketing Research," *Harvard Business Review,* 85 (May-June), 176-82.

——— (1988a), *Cheap but Good Marketing Research.* Homewood, IL: Dow Jones/Irwin.

———(1988b), *Conducting an Effective Retail Audit.* Washington, DC: SOMARC/The Futures Group.

———(1990), *Strategic Marketing Planning Workbook.* Alexandria, VA: United Way of America.

——— (1992), *The Strategic Marketing Planning Guidebook.* Atlanta, GA: American Cancer Society.

——— (1993), "Presidential Address: A Social Marketing Research Agenda for Consumer Behavior Researchers," in *Advances in Consumer Research,* Vol. 20, Michael Rothschild and Leigh McAlister, eds. Provo, UT: Association for Consumer Research, 1-5.

——— (1994), "Social Marketing: Definition and Domain," *Journal of Marketing and Public Policy,* 13 (Spring), 108-14.

——— (1995a), *Expanding the Audience for the Performing Arts.* Washington, DC: Seven Locks Press.

——— (1995b), *Marketing Social Change.* San Francisco: Jossey-Bass.

———(1996), "Profits for Nonprofits: Find a Corporate Partner," *Harvard Business Review,* 74 (November-December), 47-59.

——— and Jean Manning (1987), "Culture Conflict in Health Care Marketing," *Journal of Health Care Marketing,* 7 (March), 2-8.

Austin, James E. (2000), *The Collaboration Challenge.* San Francisco: Jossey-Bass.

Bagozzi, Richard P. (1974), "Marketing as an Organized Behavioral System of Exchange," *Journal of Marketing,* 38 (October), 77-81.

——— (1978), "Marketing as Exchange," *American Behavioral Scientist,* 21 (March-April), 535-56.

——— and Paul Warshaw (1990), "Trying to Consume," *Journal of Consumer Research,* 17, 127-40.

Bartels, Robert (1974), "The Identity Crisis in Marketing," *Journal of Marketing,* 38 (October), 73-76.

Berkowitz, Eric N. and William A. Flexner (1978), "The Marketing Audit: A Tool for Health Service Organizations," *HCM Review,* Fall, 55-56.

Bloom, Paul N. and William D. Novelli (1981), "Problems and Challenges of Social Marketing," *Journal of Marketing,* 45 (Spring), 79-88.

Burlingame, Dwight F. and Dennis R. Young, eds. (1996), *Corporate Philanthropy at the Crossroads.* Bloomington: Indiana University Press.

Cooper, Philip D. (1979), *Health Care Marketing: Issues and Trends.* Germantown, MD: Aspen Systems.

Cordes, Joseph J., Jeffrey R. Henig, Eric C. Twombly, and Jennifer L. Saunders (1999), "The Effects of Expanded Donor Choice in United Way Campaigns on Nonprofit Human Service Providers in the Washington, D.C., Metropolitan Area," *Nonprofit and Voluntary Sector Quarterly,* 28 (June), 127-51.

Currence, Cynthia (1997), "Demographic and Lifestyle Data: A Practical Application to Stimulating Compliance with Mammography Guidelines among Poor Women," in *Social Marketing: Theoretical and Practical Perspectives,* Marvin Goldberg, Martin Fishbein, and Susan Middlestadt, eds. Mahwah, NJ: Lawrence Erlbaum, 111-20.

Drucker, Peter F. (1989), "What Business Can Learn from Nonprofits," *Harvard Business Review,* 89 (July-August), 88-93.

Elliott, Barrie J. (1991), *A Re-examination of the Social Marketing Concept.* Sydney, Australia: Elliott & Shanahan Research.

Fine, Seymour (1981), *The Marketing of Ideas and Social Issues.* New York: Praeger.

———, ed. (1990), *Social Marketing: Promoting the Causes of Public and Nonprofit Agencies.* Boston: Allyn & Bacon.

Fox, Karen F. A. and Philip Kotler (1980), "The Marketing of Social Causes: The First Ten Years," *Journal of Marketing,* 44 (Fall), 24-33.

Goldberg, Marvin (1996), "Social Marketing: Are We Fiddling While Rome Burns?" *Journal of Consumer Psychology,* 4 (4), 347-70.

———, Martin Fishbein, and Susan Middlestadt, eds. (1997), *Social Marketing: Theoretical and Practical Perspectives.* Mahwah, NJ: Lawrence Erlbaum.

Herron, Douglas B. (1978), "Developing a Marketing Audit for Social Service Organizations," in *Readings in Public and Nonprofit Marketing,* Charles B. Weinberg and Christopher H. Lovelock, eds. Palo Alto, CA: Scientific Press, 269-71.

——— (1997), *Marketing Nonprofit Programs and Services: Proven and Practical Strategies to Get More Customers, Members, and Donors.* San Francisco: Jossey-Bass.

Independent Sector (1998), *America's Nonprofit Sector in Brief.* Washington, DC: Independent Sector.

Kendall, Carl (1985), "Ethnomedicine and Oral Rehydration Therapy: A Case of Ethnomedical Investigation and Program Planning," *Social Science and Medicine,* 39, 253-60.

Kotler, Neil and Philip Kotler (1998), *Museum Strategy and Marketing.* San Francisco: Jossey-Bass.

Kotler, Philip (1972), "A Generic Concept of Marketing," *Journal of Marketing,* 36 (April), 46-54.

——— (1975), *Marketing for Nonprofit Organizations.* Englewood Cliffs, NJ: Prentice Hall.

——— (1979), "Strategies for Introducing Marketing into Nonprofit Organizations," *Journal of Marketing,* 43 (January), 37-44.

——— and A. R. Andreasen (1996), *Strategic Marketing for Nonprofit Marketing,* 5th ed. Englewood Cliffs, NJ: Prentice Hall.

——— and Roberta N. Clarke (1986), *Marketing for Health Care Organizations.* Englewood Cliffs, NJ: Prentice Hall.

——— and Karen F. A. Fox (1995), *Strategic Marketing for Educational Organizations,* 2nd ed. Englewood Cliffs, NJ: Prentice Hall.

———, William Gregor, and William Rodgers (1977), "The Marketing Audit Comes of Age," *Sloan Management Review,* 18 (Winter), 25-43.

———, Donald H. Haider, and Irving Rein (1993), *Marketing Places: Attracting Investment, Industry, and Tourism to Cities, States, and Nations.* New York: Free Press.

————, Somkid Jatusripitak, and Suvit Maesincee (1997), *The Marketing of Nations: A Strategic Approach to Building National Wealth.* New York: Free Press.

———— and Sidney J. Levy (1969a), "Broadening the Concept of Marketing," *Journal of Marketing,* 33 (January), 10-15.

———— and ———— (1969b), "A New Form of Marketing Myopia: Rejoinder to Professor Luck," *Journal of Marketing,* 33 (July), 55-57.

———— and Eduardo Roberto (1989), *Social Marketing: Strategies for Changing Public Behavior.* New York: Free Press.

———— and Joanne Scheff (1997), *Standing Room Only: Strategies for Marketing the Performing Arts.* Boston: Harvard Business School Press.

———— and Gerald Zaltman (1971), "Social Marketing: An Approach to Planned Social Change," *Journal of Marketing,* 35 (July), 3-12.

Letts, Christine W., William P. Ryan, and Allen S. Grossman (1999), *High Performance Nonprofit Organizations: Managing Upstream for Greater Impact.* New York: John Wiley.

Levy, Sidney J. and Philip Kotler (1969), "Beyond Marketing: The Furthering Concept," *California Management Review,* 12 (Winter), 67-73.

Lovelock, Christopher H. and Charles B. Weinberg (1989), *Marketing for Public and Nonprofit Managers,* 2nd ed. Palo Alto, CA: Scientific Press.

Luck, David J. (1969), "Broadening the Concept of Marketing—Too Far," *Journal of Marketing,* 33 (July), 53-55.

MacStravic, Robin E. (1977), *Marketing Health Care.* Germantown, MD: Aspen Systems.

Malafarina, K. and B. Loken (1993), "Progress and Limitations of Social Marketing: A Review of Empirical Literature on the Consumption of Social Ideas," in *Advances in Consumer Research,* Vol. 20, M. Rothschild and L. McAlister, eds. Provo, UT: Association for Consumer Research, 397-404.

Manoff, Robert K. (1985), *Social Marketing.* New York: Praeger.

Marmor, T. R., M. Schlesinger, and R. W. Smithey (1987), "Nonprofit Organizations and Health Care," in *The Nonprofit Sector: A Research Handbook,* Walter W. Powell, ed. New Haven, CT: Yale University Press, 221-39.

McLean, F. (1998), "Corporate Identity: What Does It Mean for Museums?" *International Journal of Nonprofit and Voluntary Sector Marketing,* 3 (1), 11-21.

McNamara, Don (1999), "AHA's Restructuring Centralizes Management," *Nonprofit Times,* August, 4.

Mokwa, Michael P., William D. Dawson, and E. Arthur Priere, eds. (1980), *Marketing the Arts.* New York: Praeger.

Newman, Bruce I. (1994), *The Marketing of the President: Political Marketing as Campaign Strategy.* Thousand Oaks, CA: Sage.

Nickels, William G. (1974), "Conceptual Conflicts in Marketing," *Journal of Economics and Business,* 27 (Winter), 140-43.

Novelli, William D. (1990), "Applying Social Marketing to Health Promotion and Disease Prevention," in *Health Behavior and Health Education,* K. Glanz, F. M. Lewis, and B. K. Rimer, eds. San Francisco: Jossey-Bass, 342-69.

Rados, David (1996), *Marketing for Non-Profit Organizations,* 2nd ed. Boston: Auburn House.

Radtke, Janel M. (1998), *Strategic Communications for Nonprofit Organizations: Seven Steps to Creating a Successful Plan.* San Francisco: Jossey-Bass.

Ramah, Michael and C. M. Cassidy (1992), *Social Marketing and the Prevention of AIDS.* Washington, DC: AIDSCOM/Academy for Educational Development.

Rangun, V. K. and S. Karim (1991), *Teaching Note: Focusing the Concept of Social Marketing.* Boston: Harvard Business School Press.

Reingen, Peter H. (1978), "On Inducing Compliance with Request," *Journal of Consumer Research,* 5 (September), 96-102.

Ritchie, Robin J. B., Sanjeev Swami, and Charles B. Weinberg (1999), "A Brand New World for Nonprofits," *International Journal of Nonprofit and Voluntary Sector Marketing,* 4 (1), 26-42.

Rothschild, M. D. (1979), "Marketing Communications in Nonbusiness Situations, or Why It's so Hard to Sell Brotherhood Like Soap," *Journal of Marketing,* 43 (Spring), 11-20.

Sargeant, Adrian (1999). *Marketing Management for Nonprofit Organizations.* Oxford, UK: Oxford University Press.

Scott, Carol A. (1977), "Modifying Socially Conscious Behavior: The Foot-in-the-Door Technique," *Journal of Consumer Research,* 4 (December), 156-64.

Smith, Craig (1994), "The New Corporate Philanthropy," *Harvard Business Review,* 94 (May-June), 105-16.

Varadarajan, P. Rajan and Anil Menon (1988), "Cause-Related Marketing: A Coalignment of Marketing Strategy and Corporate Philanthropy," *Journal of Marketing,* 52 (July), 58-74.

Weeden, Curt (1998), *Corporate Social Investing.* San Francisco: Berrett-Koehler.

Weisbrod, Burton A., ed. (1998), *To Profit or Not to Profit: The Commercialization of the Nonprofit Sector.* Cambridge, MA: Harvard University Press.

Wilkie, William L. and Elizabeth Moore (1999), "Marketing's Contributions to Society," *Journal of Marketing,* 63 (October), 198-218.

Chapter 5

Firm Responses to Consumer Information Policy

Christine Moorman

There is a class of informational problems that arise in markets that cause price to be a poor signal of quality. These problems may emanate with the customer, the product, the seller, the nature of the transaction, or some combination of these factors. As a result, markets become inefficient (i.e., price and quality do not correlate), consumers make suboptimal choices, and market equilibrium is not achieved. The solution to these problems is not firm specific. Instead, an industry-wide solution, typically in the form of self-regulation or government regulation, is required to solve the problem.

This chapter is concerned with the use of a class of governmental remedies referred to as *consumer information remedies*. Consumer information remedies are defined as regulation that seeks to increase the number of speakers providing information (speaker remedies) and those affecting the content of the information provided by sellers (message remedies) (Federal Trade Commission [FTC] 1979, pp. 184-89). The function of these remedies is to improve the free flow of accurate information to consumers who may, in turn, increase their knowledge base or change their search and/or purchase behaviors.

Consumer information remedies are distinct from market restraint remedies that constrain the level of quality that firms offer to the market (Stern and

AUTHOR'S NOTE: Special thanks go to Pauline Ippolito and Paul N. Bloom for their comments on a previous version of this chapter.

Eovaldi 1984). Market restraint remedies, therefore, often involve banning or restricting the manufacture and sale of products and services in the market.

In this chapter, I examine firm responses to consumer information remedies. I have several goals. First, I provide a summary of the literature describing firm responses to consumer information remedies and develop a typology that identifies general types of firm responses. Second, I describe a set of mechanisms underlying firm responses to consumer information remedies. These include mechanisms reflecting compatible incentives, the strategic use of regulation, sensemaking and enacting, interorganizational learning, market orientation, and consumer signaling. Third, drawing on these mechanisms influencing firm responses, I offer a set of recommendations for the design of consumer information remedies. Finally, I close the chapter by offering a set of recommendations for improving research on the topic of firm responses to consumer information remedies.

The Impact of Consumer Information Remedies on the Market

Firm responses to consumer information remedies are critical to market-level changes. The market-level changes of concern in this chapter are improved product quality, increased market efficiency (i.e., the correlation of price and quality), and greater competition (as revealed in lower prices and more rivalry). Linking information remedies, firm responses, and market-level outcomes such as these is a complex research problem and policy design question. As a result, it should not be surprising that most consumer information policies involve a series of typically untested assumptions about these linkages (FTC 1979). Figure 5.1, borrowed in part from Bloom (1997) and drawing on economic, organizational, and marketing literature, highlights several of the key linkages assumed to occur when information required from a consumer information remedy enters markets.

Speaker and message remedies are assumed to reduce the costs of information search by consumers (Russo, Staelin, Nolan, Russell, and Metcalf 1986). In the case of speaker remedies, this cost reduction occurs because information is easier to collect; in the case of message remedies, it occurs because information is easier to process. Both of these effects, in turn, make it easier for consumers to compare choice alternatives. With information search costs reduced, consumers are in a better position to make informed choices and perhaps to make utility-maximizing choices. Better choices are the bonanza of information remedies and are not seen as a necessary condition in the evaluation of most information programs. Therefore, following Bettman (1975), consumer cognitive responses to information (e.g., better awareness, enhanced comprehension) are distinguished from behavioral responses to information (e.g., better choices, brand switching) (Step 1 in Figure 5.1). In an ideal word, cognitive responses and behavioral responses would be reinforcing. In other words, informed consumers would search for more information and make better choices, and more search and better choices might increase consumers' information levels (from experi-

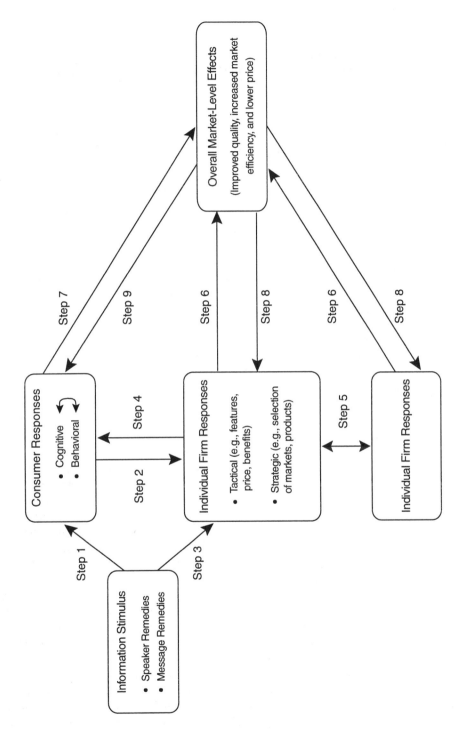

Figure 5.1. Linkages among Consumer Responses, Firm Responses, and Overall Market-Level Effects in Response to Consumer Information Remedies

107

ence in both using products and searching for products). I use a reciprocal arrow within the consumer response box to depict this relationship.

The model shows that firms, like consumers, have reactions to information remedies. Sometimes, these responses are due to new consumer behaviors resulting from the information remedy (e.g., shifting choice patterns) (Step 2). Other times, they are due to firms' direct reactions to the information regulation (Step 3). In this latter condition, firms anticipate consumer or competitive reactions to the information and respond with a variety of marketing responses (discussed in detail later).[1]

Firm responses, in turn, can influence the nature and degree of consumer responses (Step 4). For example, firms may decide to make the subject of the information remedy a prominent part of their marketing strategies. If this occurs, then they may stimulate consumers to search more. For example, following the removal of advertising restrictions on professional price advertising, the number of low-cost/high-volume optometry service providers increased dramatically (Parker 1995).

This model suggests that firms also can learn how to respond to information remedies from other firms, not by making direct connections with consumer behavior or the original information policy (Step 5). These types of effects are due to diffusion and imitation and are discussed in detail later. To cite an example, the impact of the *Business Week* ratings on the design and delivery of M.B.A. programs (Bloom and Szykman 1998) is likely to be driven by lower-performing schools attempting to imitate higher-performing schools.

Step 6 depicts firm responses to consumer information responses as a critical mediating factor in determining whether an information remedy will have an impact on the market. This means that firm responses, either directly or indirectly (via consumer responses), to information regulation are central to the market-level effects.

Step 7 in Figure 5.1 suggests, on the other hand, that even if firms do not change, market performance can be directly influenced by consumer behavior. In this view, sales of products that perform well on featured attributes are purchased at higher rates and perhaps at higher margins by consumers interested in these qualities. The increase in sales for low-tar and low-nicotine cigarettes described by Mazis and colleagues (1981) is a good example of the direct impact of consumer behavior on market performance without firm response mediating this effect. It is true, however, that the market performance of low-tar and low-nicotine cigarettes prompted the development of more brands with this feature. This feedback effect is shown in Step 8.

Finally, changes in the overall market also can influence consumer responses (Step 9) (Moorman and Price 1989). For example, if consumers observe changes to the market (e.g., improved product quality or information), then they might display less skepticism and increased confidence in the quality of products and the effective functioning of markets. Moreover, consumers might learn that price is a good signal of quality or learn about various product quality features when a large number of firms respond in the market. These experiences, in turn, are likely to change consumer responses (Moorman 1996).

A Typology of Firm Responses to Consumer Information Remedies

Overview Points

Table 5.1 summarizes the extant literature describing how firms respond to information remedies. The nature of the information stimulus is identified, and firm responses are documented where available. One of the surprising conclusions of this table is the relatively small number of studies of firm responses to consumer information remedies that have been conducted.

Wilkie (1985, 1986) provided an excellent description and categorization of the types of firm responses to FTC-ordered information remedies that occurred between 1970 and 1977. He observed that 36% of the affirmative disclosure orders issued by the FTC resulted in firms deciding to stop marketing the products or services. Wilkie (1985) noted that, in most cases, these were "smaller firms which had relied heavily on the allegedly deceptive practice to obtain customers" (p. 107). In 38% of the cases studied, firms made some alterations to the products or services in response to the information disclosure.

Firm responses can be categorized into a typology such as Table 5.2. There are two dimensions associated with this typology. The first dimension involves the distinction between firm responses that are linked specifically to the information remedy (e.g., energy efficiency ratings linked to energy labels on home appliances) and those responses that are not linked to the information remedy (e.g., aesthetic features on home appliances linked to energy labels) but that are spurred by responses to the information remedy.

The second dimension is the distinction between tactical and strategic firm responses. Tactical-level changes are focused on changes to existing products and focus on marketing mix features (e.g., promotion, advertising, price). Strategic-level changes involve consideration of markets, product development, product management, and broader activities that a firm might undertake in response to an information remedy (e.g., forming an alliance with other manufacturers).

Firm Responses Directly Linked to Information Remedy Content

Regarding tactical responses within the marketing mix, firms can display a variety of responses. In the case where the information remedy content is focused on product features, firms can respond in one of three ways. First, firm responses can involve adding new product attributes (e.g., calcium to orange juice) or removing attributes (e.g., cigarettes with no tar). Second, firms can increase levels of current attributes (e.g., fiber content in ready-to-eat cereals) or decrease attributes (e.g., fat or sodium levels in food products). Third, firms can respond to information disclosure by changing the emphasis on benefits linked to product attributes. This could involve reducing risks (e.g., describing a

TABLE 5.1 Sample of Firm Responses to Consumer Information Remedies

Focal Area	Consumer Information Remedy	Citation	Research Findings on Firm Responses
Nutrition information	1973 nutritional labelling laws requiring the provision of re-commended daily allowance information	Mazis et al. (1981)	An increase in vitamin fortification in ready-to-eat cereals was noted.
	Allowance of fiber health claims for ready-to-eat cereals	Ippolito and Mathios (1990, 1991)	Statistically significant increases in fiber content were noted between the pre-advertising period (1.64 grams per ounce) and the post-advertising period (1.75 grams per ounce) and in fiber content of new cereal introductions between the pre-advertising period (1.70 grams per ounce) and the post-advertising period (2.59 grams per ounce). Cereals also reflected a significant reduction in sodium content (14.7 milligrams/ounce vs. 178.6 milligrams/ounce).
	1990 Nutrition Labeling and Education Act	Moorman (1998)	Results from a longitudinal quasi-experiment showed a statistically significant increase in positive nutrients among firms' current brands and a reduction in nutrients among firms' brand extensions. A significant interaction between price promotion activity and healthiness of the product category also was discovered, revealing a significant increase in price promotion for unhealthy brands pre- and post-NLEA but no change in price promotion activity for healthy brands during the two time periods.
		Moorman and Slotegraaf (1999)	Results from a longitudinal quasi-experiment showed that firm characteristics influenced the amount and speed of firm responses to the information produced by the NLEA. Specifically, firms with a complementarity of product marketing and product technology skills were likely to make more changes to product quality and to make those changes faster than were firms without such capabilities. Moreover, this interaction effect was discovered only during the post-NLEA period and not during the pre-NLEA period.
		Ghani and Childs (1999)	Using a standard event study methodology, results showed a reduction in shareholder wealth following the passage of the NLEA for a sample of large U.S. multinational food corporations.

Product	Label/Policy	Citation	Findings
Saccharin	Saccharin warning label	Schucker et al. (1984)	Media and retailer advertising expenditures for diet soft drinks and regular soft drinks increased significantly over the pre-warning label period, excluding 1978 (when a great deal of the negative news coverage occurred). Price also increased during the same time period.
Beef	U.S. Department of Agriculture beef grading information	Miller, Topel, and Rust (1976)	No firm responses were examined.
Baby food	Ingredient labels on baby food	Mazis et al. (1981)	A reduction in salt and artificial ingredients was devised.
Alcoholic beverages	Alcohol warning labels describing risks involved in consumption	Mazis, Morris, and Swasy (1991); Scammon, Mayer, and Smith (1991)	No firm responses were examined.
Professional advertising including price advertising	*Bates v. State Bar of Arizona* resulted in allowance of professional price advertising, beginning with lawyers and extending to veterinarians, optometrists/ophthalmologists, accountants, funeral homes, and physicians	Benham (1972); Benham and Benham (1975)	The removal of advertising restrictions increased expansion of low-cost/high-volume advertisers (e.g., retail firm operations), had no effect on medical quality, and decreased service prices.
		Schroeter, Smith, and Cox (1987)	It was found that advertising for routine legal services increased the demand elasticity, holding other possible influencing factors constant.
		Haas-Wilson (1986)	A statistically significant reduction in optometrist prices for states allowing media advertising (26.3% to 33.1% reduction) was noted.
		Parker (1995)	Longitudinal evidence indicated that price advertising had the effect of reducing the quality of optometry services, although consumers felt more satisfied with quality.
		Kwon, Safranski, and Kim (1993)	Evidence indicated that professional advertising raised prices in markets for dental services.

TABLE 5.1 Continued

Focal Area	Consumer Information Remedy	Citation	Research Findings on Firm Responses
		Rizzo and Zeckhauser (1992)	A significant increase in price and quality of physician services was noted. There was no control of market effects, only coded advertising.
		FTC (1979); Feldman and Begun (1978)	Price was found to be 5% higher in states that banned optometry advertising, holding quality constant. A ban on optician price advertising raised price 10%. An interaction effect between price and optometry advertising was found, and prices were significantly higher in states that banned both types of advertising.
Separation of diagnosis and treatment	1978 FTC separation of diagnosis (prescription) and treatment (getting eyeglasses made and fitted) rule (the eyeglass rule)	FTC (1979); Mazis et al. (1981)	No firm responses were examined.
Prescription drugs	Removal of price advertising ban for prescription drugs (*Virginia Citizens Council Inc. v. State Board of Pharmacy*)	Cady (1976)	Following removal of the restriction, retail prescription drug prices were more than 5% higher in states that restricted retail prescription drug price advertising than in states that did not.
	FDA's requirement for a patient packet insert for oral contraceptives	FTC (1979); Morris, Mazis, and Gordon (1977)	No firm responses were examined.
	1985 FDA lifting of its moratorium on direct-to-consumer advertising	Kopp and Sheffet (1997); Sheffet and Kopp (1990)	Retail gross margins for pharmaceuticals advertised directly to consumers were significantly lower.
M.B.A. programs	*Business Week* ratings of M.B.A. programs	Bloom and Szykman (1998)	Ratings increased the price charged for quality schools.

Category	Topic	Citation	Findings
Unit pricing of products	Unit pricing information in stores	Russo (1977)	A 1% to 3% reduction in consumer expenditures, some of which might include price reductions, was noted. A 5% increase in the market share for store brands also was noted.
Energy efficiency	Energy Policy and Conservation Act, which required the use of energy efficiency ratings on all home appliances	McNeill and Wilkie (1979)	No firm responses were examined.
	FTC's lumens disclosure, which contains information about light bulb brightness and average life disclosure in number of hours	FTC (1979); Katz and Rose (1976)	A positive effect on the development of long-lasting light bulbs was reported.
Credit and insurance	Consumer Credit Protection Act's truth in lending provision requiring all sources of consumer credit to disclose the annual percentage rate and the dollar finance charges for any consumer credit transaction	Day and Brandt (1974)	No firm responses were examined.
	National Association of Insurance Commissioners' life insurance cost disclosure package	FTC (1979); Mazis and Staelin (1981)	No firm responses were examined.
Hospitals and HMOs	1986 Health Care Financing Administration hospital mortality information dissemination	Rudd and Glanz (1991)	No firm responses were examined.
	HMO quality ratings	Bloom and Syzkman (1999)	Convergence of HMOs in terms of price and quality indicators was noted. High-quality/high-price firms and low-quality/low-price firms converged.
Automobile tires	National Highway Traffic Safety Administration's uniform grading system for tires	Bucklin (1974)	It was speculated to reduce entry barriers due to product differentiation, large-scale dollar investments in advertising, and brand loyalties created through association with automobile manufacturers.
Gasoline	Petroleum Marketing Practices Act requiring the posting of octane ratings (the octane rule)	FTC (1979)	No firm responses were examined.

TABLE 5.1 Continued

Focal Area	Consumer Information Remedy	Citation	Research Findings on Firm Responses
Garment labeling	Care labeling for garments	FTC (1979)	No firm responses were examined.
Funeral prices	Funeral rule requiring funeral directors to disseminate price information on the telephone, thereby reducing search costs	FTC (1979)	No firm responses were examined.
Tobacco	1954 cigarette advertising guides that prohibited reference to the physical effects of tobacco and all unsubstantiated tar and nicotine claims in advertising	Calfee (1997); Scheraga and Calfee (1996)	Event analyses of stock returns for tobacco firms showed negative returns (−2.3%) for all firms and no difference between large and small firms.
	1957 ratings of tar and nicotine content of tobacco products in third-party sources such as *Reader's Digest* and *Consumer Reports*	Ringold and Calfee (1989) Calfee (1997)	Content analyses of cigarette advertising indicated a significant reduction in the use of health claims and a significant increase in claims about taste and cigarette design. Tar and nicotine levels (sales weighted) dropped nearly 40% between mid-1957 and the end of 1959.
	1960 FTC "voluntary" ban on tar and nicotine claims in advertising	Calfee (1997); Scheraga and Calfee (1996)	Event analyses of stock returns for tobacco firms showed a significant positive effect for the entire industry. There also was a statistical difference between the average large firm (+1.8%) and the average small firm (+0.5%). Calfee (1997) noted that the "steep decline in tar and nicotine content was virtually halted" (p. 44).
	1964 cigarette labeling law requiring standardized measurement and communication of tar and nicotine content of tobacco products	FTC (1979); Mazis et al. (1981)	It was found that the average cigarette contained 37 milligrams of tar and more than 2 milligrams of nicotine in 1957. By 1977, the average tar per cigarette had dropped to about 17 milligrams, and the average nicotine had dropped to 1.1 milligrams.

	Scheraga and Calfee (1996)	Event analyses of stock returns for tobacco firms showed no change in the returns for firms.
1970 congressional ban on cigarette advertising on television and radio	Eckard (1991)	Longitudinal examination of industry indicators pre- and post-ban indicated that firm and brand shares were more stable after the ban, that measures of industry concentration that were decreasing before the ban began to increase after the ban, and that new brand entry virtually ceased during the first four years after the ban.
	Holak and Reddy (1986)	In examining a sample of 10 major cigarette brands from 1950 to 1979, it was found that brand loyalty was higher and price elasticities were higher after the ban.
	Mitchell and Mulherin (1988)	Monthly stock market returns for 30 months (ending in December 1970) for four of the six large firms were examined. Findings indicated abnormally high, statistically significant returns following the ban.
General advertising	Lifting of strict advertising regulation by the FTC (1971 to 1981) Abernethy and Franke (1998)	An increase in the level of objective information claims in advertising during the subsequent time period (1982 to 1992) was noted.

NOTE: NLEA = Nutrition Labeling and Education Act; FTC = Federal Trade Commission; FDA = Food and Drug Administration; HMO = health maintenance organization.

TABLE 5.2 Typology of Firm Responses to Information Remedies

	Strategic Response	*Tactical Response*
Firm responses directly linked to information remedy content	• Harvesting current brands (e.g., discontinuing high-fat and high-sodium baby foods) • Develop new products (e.g., lower fat, higher vitamin content) • Target new markets (e.g., remedy-sensitive consumers such as healthy consumers) • Use of a differentiated strategy (e.g., different products in a line for unique markets: regular, low-fat, and low-sodium versions)	• Add product attribute (e.g., calcium to juice) • Delete product attribute (e.g., no-tar cigarettes) • Increase product attribute (e.g., fiber to cereals) • Decrease product attribute (e.g., low-fat foods) • Link attribute to benefit (e.g., diet-disease link) • Lower price (e.g., as a result of unit price regulation) • Raise price (e.g., higher price for no-sugar products) • Higher promotion (e.g., greater advertising for low-price, high-volume optometrists)
Firm responses indirectly linked to information remedy content	• Develop entirely new business models (e.g., high-volume/low-cost optometry store concept)	• Focus on related attributes (e.g., change in fat and sodium levels after the allowance of fiber claims) • Focus on competitive attributes (e.g., compete on the basis of low fees for optometry services in line with the high-volume/low-cost store concept)

reduction in cancer threat from the use of high-fiber products) or increasing positive consequences (e.g., linking more efficient appliances to long-term cost savings).

In addition to product features, firms can respond to information remedies related to price, such as unit price requirements, by lowering their prices. On the other hand, a consumer information program related to advertising or promotion could trigger changes in the level of advertising or promotion used. For example, speaker remedies involving the allowance of advertising by professionals resulted in an enormous increase in the level of advertising by lawyers, physicians, and optometrists.

In addition to revising product attribute levels, firms can have more strategic responses to consumer information remedies. For example, firms may respond by introducing entirely new products or line extensions that perform better on the disclosed attributes. Moorman (1998) found, for example, that firms responded to the Nutrition Labeling and Education Act of 1990 (NLEA) by introducing a statistically significant higher level of brand extensions with lower levels of negative nutrients such as sodium, fat, and cholesterol. Likewise, Levy and Stokes (1987) and Ippolito and Mathios (1990, 1991) reported an increase in the fiber content in ready-to-eat cereals in conjunction with the allowance of fiber health claims. Finally, firms respond to informational remedies by changing their targeting strategies. Firms can shift their foci to new target markets (e.g., healthier consumers) so as to gain a competitive advantage. They also can adopt a differentiated strategy that involves targeting multiple segments of consumers with unique products that perform differently on the disclosed attributes. This strategy is likely to involve new products or line extensions, as already noted.

Firm Responses Indirectly Linked to Information Remedy Content

There is evidence that information remedies also can stimulate firm responses that are indirectly linked to the remedies. In terms of tactical-level responses, the best example of this involves Ippolito and Mathios's (1991) finding that the allowance of fiber health claims resulted in a statistically significant decease in ready-to-eat cereal brands' fat and sodium levels. They suggested, "Economic theory predicts that this ability to make health claims on individual health dimensions should increase the competitive pressure on producers to improve all the major health dimensions of their products" (p. 25). In addition, as described in an enormous literature on economics, information remedies involving advertising also can result in changes to price and quality. The level and efficacy of these changes are a contentious issue. However, many intended and unintended changes have been documented in the literature (see, e.g., Table 5.1).

Drivers of Firm Responses to Consumer Information Remedies

This section steps back from the types of firm responses and reviews the mechanisms underlying or driving firms to respond to consumer information remedies. The sections that follow describe each mechanism and link it to the various steps depicted in Figure 5.1.

The Incentive Compatibility Mechanism

One of the underlying drivers of firm response to regulation that has been documented quite a bit in the literature is the degree to which the regulation is compatible with firms' incentive structure, viewed as economic outcomes such as increased shareholder value, revenues, and profits (Ippolito and Scheffman 1986). If the regulation is compatible with firms' incentives, then it should minimize compliance and enforcement costs. As the FTC (1979) noted, this mechanism allows regulation to harness market forces to transform markets. The Commission cited the example of how disclosure of miles per gallon information for automobiles could promote competition in the industry. This mechanism appears in the link between the information regulation and the firm response (Step 3 in Figure 5.1).

Despite the importance of this mechanism, Wilkie (1986) reported that only 4% of all affirmative disclosures mandated by the FTC between 1970 and 1977 were definitely compatible with firms' economic incentives, whereas another 21% were possibly compatible and 75% were definitely incompatible. Wilkie concluded, "The typical affirmative disclosure case had not lent itself to incentive compatible forms of remedy" (p. 134).

The Strategic Use of Regulation Mechanism

Posner (1974) and Stigler (1971, 1974) described an "economic theory of regulation" as opposed to a "public interest theory of regulation." In the former, regulation is viewed as serving an industry agenda without concern for improving public interest. This agenda can include industry benefits from direct subsidies, control over entry, and price fixing. There is scholarly evidence to support this view of regulation. Wood's (1986) historical analysis of the Pure Food and Drug Act of 1906 found, in part, that it served the industry's interests, and there is some evidence that the regulators producing the act were "captured" by the industry. A series of other studies provide similar evidence that the tobacco industry might have supported the ban on broadcast advertising because it eliminated negative advertising (associated with the fair use laws), erected barriers to entry, and reduced costs (Eckard 1991; Holak and Reddy 1986).

Within this economic theory of regulation, Leone (1977) articulated the view that firms do not incur equal costs and benefits associated with regulation. Therefore, even within industries, there are likely to be some firms that experience higher marginal gains or lower marginal costs from information remedies relative to other firms. The idea here is that the remedy provides selective benefits to firms that are advantageously situated relative to other industry members. Mitnick (1980, 1981) provided an excellent summary of the types of firm features that create advantages in responding to regulation. For example, larger firms might be better able to respond to regulation because they have administrative or technical expertise that allows them to act more efficiently or effectively. Other advantages could accrue due to the ownership of particular technologies, locations (e.g., operating in smaller urban centers when pollution regulation occurs), or product market strategies (e.g., a healthy product portfolio in the wake of the NLEA).

Moorman and Slotegraaf (1999) found that firms did make strategic use of the NLEA. They provided empirical evidence that firms with a complementarity of technical and marketing expertise responded with more changes to the nutritional quality of their food products and did so in a significantly faster way.

Scheraga and Calfee (1996) also found evidence that larger tobacco firms benefited more than smaller firms from several regulatory activities over the years. Specifically, the 1955 FTC advertising guides prohibiting the use of fear appeals related to the "presence or absence of any physical effect of smoking" influenced the stock prices of large tobacco companies (e.g., R. J. Reynolds, American Tobacco) in a significantly more positive manner over the three smaller firms in the market at the time. Likewise, the 1960 FTC voluntary ban on tar and nicotine advertising benefited the industry overall but did so mainly by benefiting larger firms. Other events, such as the U.S. Surgeon General's report and the subsequent labeling law, show no differences regarding the impacts on large and small firms.

The strategic use of regulation is likely to occur in Step 6 in Figure 5.1 (firm responses are tied to a differential marketplace benefit).

Sensemaking and Enactment Mechanisms

Another view of firm response is based on the view that regulation, like other environmental occurrences, must be processed and represented in organizations' belief structures or cognitions (Daft and Weick 1984). It is important, therefore, to understand how information regulation is interpreted by organizations. This interpretation process is referred to by Weick (1995) as a "sensemaking" process (see also Huber 1991; Moorman 1995; Sinkula 1994). Jackson and Dutton (1988) and Dutton and Jackson (1987) suggested that top management teams vary in their categorizations of environmental events as opportunities or threats. They found that organizational response is more likely when the event is coded as a threat rather than as an opportunity. Threats appeared to motivate responses, whereas opportunities seemed discretionary. Consistent with this approach, the corporate social responsibility literature also suggests that firms vary in the extent to which they view a threat as something they should resolve proactively or defensively (Post 1978). A defensive interpretation is unlikely to promote firm responses to information and resolution of issues. The sensemaking mechanism occurs in the links among firm responses to information stimulus (Step 3 in Figure 5.1), firm responses to consumer responses (Step 2), and firm responses to changes in the market (Step 8).

The concept of *enactment* follows from an emphasis on how organizations interpret environmental information. Enactment refers to the view that organizations facilitate the creation of environmental occurrences through their own beliefs and behaviors (Rosa et al. 1999). As Weick (1995, p. 30) noted, "In organizational life, people often produce part of the environment they face (Pondy and Mitroff 1979, p. 17)." Therefore, if a firm interprets a type of information regulation as an opportunity, creates new products or targets new markets as a result, and reaps higher revenues or profits, then its actions might have, in fact, contributed to the market response and the ultimate fulfillment of its own interpretation. However, if that same firm had reacted defensively to the remedy and labeled its products without any change to its strategies, then it would not likely have seen these financial gains.

The enactment mechanism appears to be at play in the link going from firm responses to consumer responses (Step 4 in Figure 5.1) and in the link going from firm responses to market-level outcomes (Step 6). In this case, firm beliefs and behaviors lead to changes in consumer beliefs and behaviors. An excellent example of this occurred in the case of Kellogg's decision to focus on the link between fiber and cancer in promoting its ready-to-eat cereal products. Although the linkage was known, the firm experimented with the explicit promotion of this linkage, thereby creating a positive consumer reaction, a great deal of competitive activity, and ultimately the regulation of health claims including diet-disease linkages.

The Consumer Response Mechanism

Information remedies increase the flow of information into markets, making it easier and less costly for consumers to use information (Mitra and Lynch 1995; Russo and Leclerc 1991; Stigler 1961). Some proportion of these consumers will, in turn, make different choices, exit relationships with firms, or express concern over quality levels (Hirschman 1970; Moorman 1998). Theory suggests that these changed search patterns and choice patterns, in turn, stimulate sellers to compete on the basis of the disclosed attribute or quality, resulting in positive market externalities such as improved products and lower prices. For example, the provision of fiber health claim information resulted in changes in consumer purchases, in turn stimulating firms to increase the fiber content in their ready-to-eat cereals (Ippolito and Mathios 1991).

What remains interesting about the impact of consumer behavior on competitive activity is the view that not all consumers in relevant markets need to change their search and choice behaviors. Instead, only a subset of "activist" consumers need to respond to the information. These consumers, because of higher motivation and knowledge levels, have lower information search costs than do typical consumers. Therefore, when information hits markets, these consumers are likely to respond. A number of researchers have discussed the important role that these activist consumers play in keeping markets competitive and in generating externalities that are enjoyed by all consumers (Capon and Lutz 1979, 1983; Dunn and Ray 1980; Padberg 1977; Salop 1976). Moorman (1998) recently provided empirical evidence from a quasi-experiment that information-sensitive consumers are more likely to engage in direct activism behaviors aimed at the channel (e.g., return a product to a retail outlet) and the government (e.g., complain to a government agency) compared to average consumers following the NLEA. This mechanism is captured in the link going from consumer responses to firm responses (Step 2 in Figure 5.1).

The Interorganizational Learning Mechanism

Another perspective of the mechanisms underlying firm responses to information remedies lies in the view that organizations learn from the experiences of other organizations. Therefore, learning is as much an interorganizational phenomenon as it is an intraorganizational phenomenon (Huber 1991). In this view, firm responses are triggered by imitation effects and diffusion of the response within an industry (Baum and Ingram 1998; Miner and Haunschild 1995).

Interorganizational learning can occur by examining or tearing down products through corporate intelligence, leakage from consultants, or information in the popular press. The explosive increase in the number of high-fiber cereals occurring after Kellogg's tested the fiber-cancer health claim attests to the power of these learning effects (Ippolito and Mathios 1991). Another approach involves what Miner and Haunschild (1995) referred to as contact learning. This can occur in a variety of ways such as interfirm alliances or partnerships, grafting or recruitment of personnel, acquisition of the imitatee, and benchmarking.

The transformation of markets due to information remedy effects would be conceptualized by theorists in this area as a "population-level learning" effect, defined by Miner and Haunschild (1995) as a "systematic impact on the nature and mix of organizational action routines in a population of organizations, arising from experience" (p. 118). This mechanism occurs between firms as they learn to respond from one another, not from the original information stimulus (Step 5 in Figure 5.1).

The Market Orientation Mechanism

This final mechanism involves the force of firm values, beliefs, and behaviors to understand and respond to market needs. Referred to as market orientation (Jaworski and Kohli 1993; Kohli and Jaworski 1990; Narver and Slater 1990), customer orientation (Deshpandé, Farley, and Webster 1993), superior customer value (Narver and Slater 1990), or a market-driven focus (Day 1994), the underlying premise is that a market focus will lead to long-term profitability for the firm. In this sense, a market orientation is quite strategic. However, the sensitivity to customers—or, in the case of this chapter's focus, customers' information needs—is distinct from the strategic use of regulation mechanism, which views information as an economic tool without concern for the customer needs that are met or satisfied in the process of achieving economic ends.

There is evidence that some firms are proactive in trying to understand and meet the market's needs (Deshpandé, Farley, and Webster 1993; Jaworski and Kohli 1993; Moorman 1995; Narver and Slater 1990). However, applying this concept to the provision of consumer information programs is more novel. The idea here is that as consumers respond with different search and purchase patterns as a result of the information remedy, firms will respond to these activities both strategically and tactically.

The market orientation mechanism is, by definition, reactive. This mechanism is captured in the linkage going from customer responses to firm responses (Step 2 in Figure 5.1). Therefore, like consumer response, firms are responding to what consumers are doing. However, a market-oriented firm reflects a deeper commitment and value to serving customers' needs. Therefore, consumer information will be systematically acquired, distributed to various firm functions, and acted on. This is contrasted with the consumer response mechanism in which the relationship might be adversarial, the monitoring of the market might be less systematic, and the response might be more tactical and less strategic.

Designing Information Remedies to Trigger Effective Firm Responses and Effective Markets

General

Following from a description of the firm mechanisms and their depiction in Figure 5.1, one important implication is that there are a number of different paths through which firm responses and positive market-level effects may be achieved. They are as follows:

1. information remedy → consumer response → firm response → market response;

2. information remedy → firm response → market response;

3. information remedy → consumer response → market response → firm response;

4. information remedy → firm response → consumer response → market response; and

5. information remedy → firm response → firm response → market response.

Consumer information policies should consider these different paths and their underlying mechanisms in the design and diffusion of the policies. The FTC's (1979) consideration of the "incentive compatibility" motivation driving firms to react positively to information remedies is an important step in this process. However, a deeper consideration of the impact of various mechanisms and how they may play out in the case of a specific remedy is an important next step.

If, for example, an industry is highly competitive and used to the strategic leadership of certain firms, then the information remedy need only convert a few firms toward positive market responses and the remedy is likely to transform competition and consumer welfare in positive ways. On the other hand, in a very heterogeneous industry with diverse sources of power, a focus on stimulating a small group of activist consumers to exit, voice, and loyalty changes might be more effective in transforming the market. Another alternative would be to target firms with less to lose and more to gain from making effective implementation of the information program. For example, as described in Scheraga and Calfee (1997), small tobacco firms had an incentive to develop and promote low-tar and low-nicotine cigarettes relative to the industry leaders who generally would be shifting their own customers to new brands. In this situation, the small firms should be the focus in generating market-level effects.

The sensemaking and enactment mechanisms are useful in engaging firms that can perceive opportunities for new business opportunities and then help facilitate consumer and market responses through their enactment of these ideas. For example, the proliferation of low-cost/high-volume optometry service providers in response to the removal of advertising restrictions is an example of how the speaker remedy prompted the development of a strategy that, in turn, created consumer demand for these types of services. A firm with a strong market orientation may likewise respond early and creatively to consumer information remedies. Finally, industries with proportionally higher market orientation levels (e.g., consumer packaged good firms vs. industrial marketing firms) may respond sooner to consumer information remedies and with greater focus. Understanding and managing these mechanisms more explicitly, therefore, is likely to be important in generating positive market externalities.

One view is that policy should be designed and diffused so that it maximizes the number of these mechanisms it activates. If this occurs, then policy will increase the prospects of positive market-level outcomes such as improved quality, better correlation of price and quality, and more competition. There are important instances of this compatibility between mechanisms. For example, the consumer response and market orientation mechanisms both focus on consumer responses to guide firm reaction. Likewise, the enactment mechanism and the strategic use mechanism both focus on firm capabilities to behave opportunistically in the environment.

However, there also are examples of incompatibility between these different mechanisms. For example, research has suggested that it is hard for firms to be focused on competition and on consumers at the same time (Day and Nedungadi 1994). Likewise, the enactment mechanism is a more proactive view of strategy, whereas the market orientation and consumer response mechanisms tend to be reactive (to consumer responses). Finally, the incentive compatibility mechanism is focused on the ease of industry adoption. However, the strategic use mechanism allows some firms in the industry to benefit from information regulation.

Discussion Issues

This section discusses several issues that arise in designing remedies to trigger firm response.

Market leader defines remedy response. Market leaders, by virtue of their role and strategic benefits, are likely to define the way in which the industry responds to information regulation. If that response is strong and positive, then industry members are likely to respond in a similar way to remain competitive. On the other hand, if an industry leader responds by lowering quality or focusing on less important qualities of the regulation, the industry will likewise respond. Therefore, it is important to examine the leader's incentives and strategic benefit of market-perfecting responses. If they are not aligned, then the effectiveness of a remedy might be questionable.

Market maverick motivates remedy response. A counterpoint to the idea that market leaders must be motivated to lead response to a consumer information remedy is the fact that often the firms that have the greatest incentive to respond to a regulation are the small firms with less power and following in current markets (see, e.g., Moorman 1996; Scheraga and Calfee 1996). Therefore, if information remedies can be designed to induce these firms to innovate products and marketing practices that are frontal assaults on large firms, then markets might be transformed when the remedies increase the chances of their success by giving consumers the opportunity to search more effectively and efficiently.

A lack of activist consumer representativeness exists. The assumption of the consumer response mechanism is that the activist consumers' choices and voices will create positive market externalities that benefit average consumers. However, if markets are transformed in a direction that benefits only highly motivated and knowledgeable consumers, then this might be suboptimal for the market overall.

Firms learn as well from one another as from the market. The value of the interorganizational learning mechanism is premised on the assumption that firms learn equally well from markets as they do from other firms. This might not be correct. Research suggests that firms focused on competitors tend to pay attention to a small set of firms and that they tend to imitate easy-to-copy features, often to the exclusion of true innovation (Kim and Mauborgne 1997). Therefore, if firms use other firms as their primary source of insight about how to respond to an information remedy, then we are likely to see more imitation and less innovation.

The strategic use of regulation may lead to unfair strategic advantages. Recall that the strategic use of regulation mechanism is premised on the idea that firms are differentially capable of responding to regulation. Certain skills, knowledge, or other sources of strategic advantage, therefore, may allow some firms to dominate in the level and speed of their responses (Moorman and Slotegraaf 1999). If this mechanism dominates market-level effects, then concurrent changes to market structure (e.g., increases in market power and consolidation) also are likely to occur. In the end, this change in market structure might have deleterious effects on the functioning of markets.

Manage what consumers are learning from the information remedy. Consumers' beliefs about information regulation might be as important as the information produced by the regulation. Specifically, if consumers believe that the information regulation will result in a more effective market, less deception, and better products, then they might be less vigilant in their searches and complaints (Moorman 1997). Therefore, although this chapter is about firm responses and associated mechanisms, one important consumer mechanism that occurs prior to signaling is the failure of the information remedy to disarm consumers' skepticism beliefs. If these beliefs are weakened, then we might see limited responses from consumers.

Incentive compatibility should be tempered with consumer welfare. Consistent with the incentive structure, Moorman (1998) showed that firms responded to the NLEA in a strategically conservative manner. Specifically, firms increased the levels of vitamins and minerals (positive nutrients) in their current brands and introduced brand extensions with lower levels of fat and sodium (negative nutrients). The approach protected firms' current brands from potentially negative attributions (less fat/sodium and lower taste) while enabling firms to offer brand extensions so as to compete for health-conscious consumers who were willing to make health-taste trade-offs.

Although this approach is strategically effective, the concern is that if the majority of consumers continue to buy the older brands, then health benefits to consumers will not have been maximized. If this were a well-considered choice on the part of consumers, then this outcome could be accepted as reflective of what consumers want in their diets. However, if consumers are using the NLEA as a cue that food quality has improved and, therefore, have reduced their skepticism levels, then this strategic approach that firms are taking is of deep concern.

Recommendations for Future Research

Theoretical Issues

Table 5.1 provides a striking commentary on the lack of research examining firm responses to consumer information remedies. In marketing in particular, we generally have been more concerned with the consumer mechanism underlying firm responses than with the other types of mechanisms. Future research should strive for a greater balance in understanding the nature of firm and consumer responses to regulation. Perhaps even more crucial is research on the overall transformation of markets in which consumer information remedies have been used.

Once a better balance among consumer responses, firm responses, and market transformation occurs, research needs to consider more carefully the interrelationships among them. An empirical test of the mechanisms driving firm responses to consumer information remedies would be very useful. Moorman (1998) provided a test of the direct effect of consumer responses on market transformation. However, it is not clear whether other competitive or economic incentives explained these market changes better.

The possibility that positive market transformation (e.g., higher quality products, greater market efficiency) may be generated by negative changes in market structure and conduct is another reason why examining the underlying mechanisms is important. The operation of the strategic use of regulation mechanism, in particular, is likely to create market dynamics that are not productive over the long run. Likewise, if interorganizational learning drives market-level effects along a dimension that benefits market leaders, then this might not create a healthy outlook for strategic diversity among industry members. The prior section highlights additional issues that might be examined in future research.

Methodological Issues

A critical element of work in this area is the adoption of longitudinal designs. A cross-sectional view of the impact of consumer information regulation is not helpful in identifying the linkages among the remedy, consumers, firms, and the overall market. Furthermore, using a quasi-experimental approach that captures the impact of the information remedy intervention is very important in teasing out the complex set of causal relationships. Without a controlled approach, it is impossible to untangle cause and effect among these elements in the market.

Two additional approaches, in particular, might prove to be very helpful. First, a case study approach involving interviews with managers within firms, activist consumers, and regulators designing and implementing the remedy may provide insight into mechanisms at play in achieving market-level effects. Second, given the proliferation of secondary data now available to researchers, it is increasingly easy to examine actual market-level responses to information, such as changes to product quality and price, as well as promotion expenditures. Combining these data with secondary data regarding firm characteristics and market structure also can lend insight into the interconnections among elements in the model.

Note

1. Although not depicted, organizations, like consumers, have been viewed as having both cognitive and behavioral responses to information. They process information, make sense of it, and sometimes respond (Moorman 1995; Sinkula 1994).

References

Abernethy, Avery M. and George R. Franke (1998), "FTC Regulatory Activity and the Information Content of Advertising," *Journal of Public Policy & Marketing,* 17 (2), 239-56.

Baum, Joel A. C. and Paul Ingram (1998), "Chain Affiliation and the Failure of Manhattan Hotels, 1898-1980," *Administrative Science Quarterly,* 42 (March), 68-102.

Benham, Lee (1972), "The Effect of Advertising on the Price of Eyeglasses," *Journal of Law and Economics,* 15 (October), 337-52.

Benham, Lee and Alexandra Benham (1975), "Regulating through the Professions: A Perspective on Information Control," *Journal of Law and Economics,* 18 (October), 421-47.

Bettman, James R. (1975), "Issues in Designing Consumer Information Environments," *Journal of Consumer Research,* 2 (December), 169-77.

Bloom, Paul (1997), "Studying Consumer Responses to the Changing Information Environment in Health Care: A Research Agenda," in *Advances in Consumer Research,* Vol. 24, Merrie Brucks and Debbie MacInnis, eds. Ann Arbor, MI: Association for Consumer Research, 360-65.

———— and Lisa R. Szykman (1998), "How Comparative Product Information Affects Consumers and Competition: The Effects of the *Business Week* and *U.S. News and World Report* Ratings," in *Advances in Consumer Research,* Vol. 25, Joseph W. Alba and J. Wesley Hutchinson, eds. Provo, UT: Association for Consumer Research, 433-39.

———— and ———— (1999), "How Comparative Product Information Influences the Marketplace: A Study of the Effects of Ratings on the Market for Health Care Insurance and MBA Programs," paper presented at the Marketing and Public Policy Conference, Notre Dame, IN.

Bucklin, Louis P. (1974), "The Uniform Grading System for Tires: Its Effect upon Consumers and Industry Competition," *Antitrust Bulletin,* 19, 783-801.

Cady, John F. (1976), "An Estimate of the Price Effects of Restrictions on Drug Price Advertising," *Economic Inquiry,* 14 (December), 493-510.

Calfee, John E. (1997), "The Ghost of Cigarette Advertising Past," *Regulation* (Summer), 38-45.

Capon, Noel and Richard J. Lutz (1979), "A Model and Methodology for the Development of Consumer Information Programs," *Journal of Marketing,* 43 (January), 58-67.

————— and ————— (1983), "The Marketing of Consumer Information," *Journal of Marketing,* 47 (Summer), 108-12.

Daft, Richard M. and Karl E. Weick (1984), "Toward a Model of Organizations as Interpretation Systems," *Academy of Management Review,* 9 (April), 284-95.

Day, George S. (1994), "The Capabilities of Market-Driven Organizations," *Journal of Marketing,* 58 (October), 37-52.

————— and William K. Brandt (1974), "Consumer Research and the Evaluation of Information Disclosure Requirements: The Case of Truth in Lending," *Journal of Consumer Research,* 1, 21-32.

————— and P. Nedungadi (1994), "Managerial Representations of Competitive Advantage," *Journal of Marketing,* 58 (April), 31-44.

Deshpandé, Rohit, John U. Farley, and Frederick E. Webster, Jr. (1993), "Corporate Culture, Customer Orientation, and Innovativeness in Japanese Firms: A Quadrad Analysis," *Journal of Marketing,* 52 (January), 23-36.

Dunn, Donald A. and Michael L. Ray (1980), "A Plan for Consumer Information System Development, Implementation, and Evaluation," in *Advances in Consumer Research,* Vol. 7, Jerry C. Olson, ed. Ann Arbor, MI: Association for Consumer Research, 250-54.

Dutton, Jane E. and Susan E. Jackson (1987), "The Categorization of Strategic Issues by Decision Makers and Its Links to Organizational Action," *Academy of Management Review,* 12 (January), 76-90.

Eckard, E. Woodrow, Jr. (1991), "Competition and the Cigarette TV Advertising Ban," *Economic Inquiry,* 29 (January), 119-33.

Federal Trade Commission (1979), *Consumer Information Remedies.* Washington, DC: Government Printing Office.

Feldman, Roger and James W. Begun (1978), "The Effects of Advertising Lessons from Optometry," *Journal of Human Resources,* 13 (Suppl.), 247-62.

Ghani, WaQar I. and Nancy M. Childs (1999), "Wealth Effects of the Passage of the Nutrition Labeling and Education Act of 1990 for Large U.S. Multinational Food Companies," *Journal of Public Policy & Marketing,* 18 (Fall), 147-58.

Haas-Wilson, D. (1986), "The Effects of Commercial Practice Restrictions: The Case of Optometry," *Journal of Law and Economics,* 19 (April), 165-86.

Hirschman, Albert O. (1970), *Exit, Voice, and Loyalty: Responses to Decline in Firms, Organizations, and States.* Cambridge, MA: Harvard University Press.

Holak, Susan L. and Srinivas K. Reddy (1986), "Effects of a Television and Radio Advertising Ban: A Study of the Cigarette Industry," *Journal of Marketing,* 50 (October), 219-27.

Huber, George P. (1991), "Organizational Learning: The Contributing Processes and the Literatures," *Organizational Science,* 2 (February), 88-115.

Ippolito, Pauline and Alan Mathios (1990), "Information, Advertising, and Health Choices: A Study of the Cereal Market," *RAND Journal of Economics,* 21 (Autumn), 459-80.

———— and ———— (1991), "Health Claims in Food Marketing: Evidence on Knowledge and Behavior in the Cereal Market," *Journal of Public Policy & Marketing,* 10 (Spring), 15-32.

———— and David T. Scheffman (1986), *Empirical Approaches to Consumer Protection Economics* (proceedings of a conference sponsored by the Bureau of Economics, Federal Trade Commission). Washington, DC: Bureau of Economics.

Jackson, Susan E. and Jane E. Dutton (1988), "Discerning Threats and Opportunities," *Administrative Science Quarterly,* 33 (September), 370-87.

Jaworski, Bernard J. and Ajay K. Kohli (1993), "Market Orientation: Antecedents and Consequences," *Journal of Marketing,* 57 (July), 53-71.

Katz, Benjamin J. and Jane A. Rose (1976), "Information Utilization and the Awareness Criterion in Labeling Regulation," in *Marketing: 1776-1976 and Beyond,* Kenneth L. Bernhardt, ed. Chicago: American Marketing Association, 202-4.

Kim, W. Chan and Renee Mauborgne (1997), "Value Innovation: The Strategic Logic of High Growth," *Harvard Business Review,* 75 (January-February), 103-12.

Kohli, Ajay K. and Bernard J. Jaworski (1990), "Market Orientation: The Construct, Research Propositions, and Managerial Implications," *Journal of Marketing,* 54 (April), 1-18.

Kopp, Steven W. and Mary Jane Sheffet (1997), "The Effect of Direct-to-Consumer Advertising of Prescription Drugs on Retail Gross Margins: Empirical Evidence and Public Policy Implications," *Journal of Public Policy & Marketing,* 16 (2), 270-76.

Kwon, I. W., S. R. Safranski, and J. H. Kim (1993), "The Impact of Advertising on Price and Practice Volume: A Case Study of Dental Markets," *Health Services Management Research,* 6 (1), 52-60.

Leone, Robert A. (1977), "The Real Cost of Regulation," *Harvard Business Review,* 55 (November-December), 57-66.

Levy, Alan S. and Raymond C. Stokes (1987), "The Effects of Health Promotion Advertising Campaigns on Sales of Ready-to-Eat Cereals," *Public Health Reports,* 102 (4), 398-403.

Mazis, Michael B., Louis A. Morris, and John L. Swasy (1991), "An Evaluation of the Alcohol Warning Label: Initial Survey Results," *Journal of Public Policy & Marketing,* 10 (Spring), 229-41.

———— and Richard Staelin (1981), "Using Information-Processing Principles in Public Policymaking," *Journal of Public Policy & Marketing,* 1, 3-13.

————, ————, Howard Beales, and Steven Salop (1981), "A Framework for Evaluating Consumer Information Regulation," *Journal of Marketing,* 45 (Winter), 11-21.

McNeill, Dennis L. and William L. Wilkie (1979), "Public Policy and Consumer Information: Impact of the New Energy Labels," *Journal of Consumer Research,* 6 (1), 1-11.

Miller, John A., David G. Topel, and Robert E. Rust (1976). "USDA Beef Grading: A Failure in Consumer Information?" *Journal of Marketing,* 40 (January), 25-31.

Miner, Anne S. and Pamela R. Haunschild (1995), "Population Level Learning," in *Research in Organizational Behavior,* Vol. 17, L. L. Cummings and B. M. Staw, eds. Greenwich, CT: JAI, 115-66.

Mitchell, M. and H. H. Mulherin (1988), "Finessing the Policy System: The Cigarette Advertising Ban," *Southern Economic Journal,* 54, 855-62.

Mitnick, Barry M. (1980), *The Political Economy of Regulations: Creating, Designing, and Removing Regulatory Forms.* New York: Columbia University Press.

———— (1981), "The Strategic Uses of Regulation and Deregulation," *Business Horizons,* 24, (2), 71-83.

Mitra, Anusree and John G. Lynch, Jr. (1995), "Toward a Reconciliation of Market Power and Information Theories of Advertising Effects on Price Elasticity," *Journal of Consumer Research,* 21 (March), 644-59.

Moorman, Christine (1995), "Organizational Market Information Processes: Cultural Antecedents and New Product Outcomes," *Journal of Marketing Research,* 32 (August), 318-35.

——— (1996), "A Quasi-Experiment to Assess the Consumer and Informational Determinants of Nutrition Information Processing Activities: The Case of the Nutrition Labeling and Education Act," *Journal of Public Policy & Marketing,* 15 (Spring), 28-44.

——— (1997), "Cynical Consumers: Skepticism and Faith in the Marketplace," in *Advances in Consumer Research,* Vol. 25, Joseph W. Alba and J. Wesley Hutchinson, eds. Provo, UT: Association for Consumer Research, 215.

——— (1998), "The Market-Level Impacts of Information: Competitive Responses and Consumer Dynamics," *Journal of Marketing Research,* 34 (February), 82-98.

——— and Linda L. Price (1989), "Consumer Policy Remedies and Consumer Segment Interactions," *Journal of Public Policy & Marketing,* 8, 181-203.

——— and Rebecca J. Slotegraaf (1999), "The Contingency Value of Complementary Capabilities in Product Development," *Journal of Marketing Research,* 36 (May), 239-57.

Morris, Louis, Michael B. Mazis, and Evelyn Gordon (1977), "A Survey of the Effects of Oral Contraceptive Patient Information," *Journal of the American Medical Association,* 238 (December), 2504-8.

Narver, John C. and Stanley F. Slater (1990), "The Effect of a Market Orientation on Business Profitability," *Journal of Marketing,* 54 (October), 20-35.

Padberg, Daniel I. (1977). "Non-Use Benefits of Mandatory Consumer Information Programs," *Journal of Consumer Policy,* 1 (January), 5-14.

Parker, Philip M. (1995). " 'Sweet Lemons': Illusory Quality, Self-Deceivers, Advertising, and Price," *Journal of Marketing Research,* 32 (August), 291-307.

Pondy, L. R. and I. I. Mitroff (1979), "Beyond Open Systems Models of Organization," in *Research in Organizational Behavior,* Vol. 1, Barry M. Staw, ed. Greenwich, CT: JAI, 3-39.

Posner, Richard A. (1974), "Theories of Economic Regulation," *RAND Journal of Economics,* 5 (Autumn), 335-58.

Post, James E. (1978), *Corporate Behavior and Social Change.* Reston, VA: Reston Publishing.

Ringold, Debra Jones and John E. Calfee (1989), "The Informational Content of Cigarette Advertising," *Journal of Public Policy & Marketing,* 8, 1-23.

Rizzo, John A. and Zeckhauser, Richard J. (1992), "Advertising and the Price, Quantity, and Quality of Primary Care Physician Services," *Journal of Human Resources,* 27 (3), 381-421.

Rosa, Jose, Joseph F. Porac, Jelena Runser-Spanjol, and Michael S. Saxon (1999), "Sociocognitive Dynamics in a Product Market," *Journal of Marketing,* 63 (special issue), 64-77.

Rudd, Joel and Karen Glanz (1991), "Providing Consumers with Quality of Health-Care Information: A Critical Review and Media Content Analysis," in *Enhancing Consumer Choice,* R. Mayer, ed. Columbia, MO: American Council on Consumer Interests, 229-38.

Russo, J. E. (1977), "The Value of Unit Price Information," *Journal of Marketing Research,* 14, 193-201.

———— and France Leclerc (1991), "Characteristics of Successful Product Information Programs," *Journal of Social Issues,* 47 (1), 73-92.

————, Richard Staelin, Catherine Nolan, Gary J. Russell, and Barbara L. Metcalf (1986), "Nutrition Information in the Supermarket," *Journal of Consumer Research,* 13 (June), 48-70.

Salop, Steven (1976), "Information and Monopolistic Competition," *American Economic Review,* 66 (May), 240-55.

Scammon, Debra L., Robert N. Mayer, and Ken R. Smith (1991), "Alcohol Warnings: How Do You Know When You Have Had One too Many? *Journal of Public Policy & Marketing,* 10 (1), 214-28.

Scheraga, Carl and John E. Calfee (1996), "The Industry Effects of Information and Regulation in the Cigarette Market: 1950-1965, *Journal of Public Policy & Marketing,* 15, 216-26.

Schroeter, John R., Scott L. Smith, and Steven R. Cox (1987), "Advertising and Competition in Routine Legal Service Markets: An Empirical Investigation," *Journal of Industrial Economics,* 36, 49-60.

Schucker, Raymond E., Raymond C. Stokes, Michael L. Stewart, and Douglas P. Henderson (1984), "The Impact of the Saccharin Warning Label on Sales of Diet Soft Drinks in Supermarkets," *Journal of Public Policy & Marketing,* 2, 46-56.

Sheffet, Mary Jane and Steven W. Kopp (1990), "Advertising Prescription Drugs to the Public: Headache or Relief?" *Journal of Public Policy & Marketing,* 9, 42-61.

Sinkula, James M. (1994), "Market Information Processing and Organizational Learning," *Journal of Marketing,* 58 (January), 35-45.

Stern, Louis and Thomas Eovaldi (1984), *Legal Aspects of Marketing Strategy.* Englewood Cliffs, NJ: Prentice Hall.

Stigler, George (1961), "The Economics of Information," *Journal of Political Economy,* 65 (June), 213-25.

———— (1971), "The Theory of Economic Regulation," *Journal of Economics and Management Science,* 2 (Spring), 3-19.

———— (1974), "Free Riders and Collective Action: An Appendix to Theories of Economic Regulation," *RAND Journal of Economics,* 5 (2), 359-65.

Weick, Karl E. (1995), *Sensemaking in Organizations.* Newbury Park, CA: Sage.

Wilkie, William L. (1985), "Affirmative Disclosure at the FTC: Objectives for the Remedy and Outcomes of Past Orders," *Journal of Public Policy & Marketing,* 4, 91-111.

Wilkie, William L. (1986), "Affirmative Disclosure at the FTC: Strategic Dimensions," *Journal of Public Policy & Marketing,* 5, 123-45.

Wood, Donna J. (1986), *Strategic Uses of Public Policy.* White Plains, NY: Pitman.

Chapter 6

How Corporate Marketing Practices Have Changed in Response to Antitrust Enforcement

Mary Jane Sheffet

Corporations have seen major changes in the regulatory climate over the past 20 years. With the election of Ronald Reagan as president in 1980 came a different focus for federal government enforcement of antitrust. Whereas the 1960s and 1970s saw government charges of "bigness is bad" applied to some proposed mergers, the 1980s saw a different legal climate. During the 1980s, the courts began changing the basis of antitrust judgments by using economic rules of efficiency to judge some business arrangements (e.g., distribution restrictions [*Continental T.V. Inc. v. GTE Sylvania Inc.* 1977]) rather than more legalistic, precedent-driven case law. Under William Baxter, who headed the Department of Justice's (DOJ) Antitrust Division under President Reagan, two major cases were dropped: the *IBM* and *Exxon* cases. These two cases had consumed many years and dollars. The computer market had changed dramatically since the case against IBM had been filed on January 17, 1969 (Streeter 1995), making the government's claims of alleged monopoly by IBM untenable. Exxon's market position also had changed since the case originated. Baxter believed that further pursuit of those cases was not warranted (Streeter 1995).

Although the 1980s saw fewer Antitrust division suits filed against large corporations, corporations were by no means allowed to do as they pleased. The U.S. Supreme Court's decision in *Monsanto Company v. Spray-Rite Service Corporation* (1984) reaffirmed prior anti-resale price maintenance rulings. In addition, merger and acquisition guidelines were developed and promulgated,

TABLE 6.1 Key Antitrust and Product Liability Decisions

Case	Decision	Business Practice Involved
Continental T.V. Inc. v. GTE Sylvania Inc. (1977)	Nonprice distribution restrictions legal	Manufacturer can establish distribution restrictions over its own dealers as long as no resale price maintenance is used and restrictions are enforced unilaterally
Sindell v. Abbott Laboratories et al. (1980)	Market share liability created	A firm must keep records to be able to establish whether it could have been responsible for a plaintiff's injuries even 20 years after a product is distributed
Monsanto Company v. Spray-Rite Corporation (1984)	Minimum resale price maintenance illegal	Manufacturer cannot establish and enforce a minimum retail price for its dealers to charge

and private antitrust actions continued to be filed (U.S. DOJ 1988a, 1988b, 1992). It is interesting to note, however, that there are no studies detailing how business practices have changed in response to the changes in antitrust climate. Although some academics have made suggestions as to how businesses *should* respond to specific changes in the laws or court rulings (see, e.g., Scammon and Sheffet 1986; Sheffet and Scammon 1985; Sheffet 1983), a search of the legal and business literatures reveals no publications reporting on actual business behavior. It is apparent, however, that things have changed. This can be seen by looking at the types of lawsuits and actions filed by both private companies and federal government agencies such as the DOJ and the Federal Trade Commission. Table 6.1 illustrates some key antitrust and product liability decisions from the past 20 years and the business practices they influenced. This chapter reviews those decisions and the business practices that were affected during this time period so that marketing managers can try to prevent future antitrust actions.

Distribution Issues

The landmark decision in the *GTE Sylvania* case allowed *nonprice* vertical restrictions to be placed by manufacturers on their dealers. Thus, manufacturers could limit the distribution of their products and enforce restrictions as to how their products could be sold (i.e., intrabrand nonprice distribution restrictions). If a manufacturer wanted its retailers to provide "full-service" sales and service to its customers, then dealers that failed to provide mandated levels of customer service could be terminated. Manufacturers could not, however, use minimum resale price maintenance without inviting legal problems.

Manufacturers can achieve their desired customer service levels through nonprice vertical restrictions. Thus, manufacturers can require that retailers carry a full line of their brands, maintain a well-trained sales force to assist customers, provide in-store warranty service, and so on. Such requirements can be included in the contract between a manufacturer and its dealers. However, it is up to the manufacturer to establish regular monitoring of the dealers to check on their performance.

Legal actions involving dealer terminations all too often involve discounting of prices as well as service failures. For a manufacturer to substantiate its claims of service failure not related to possible price discounting, detailed monitoring should be done. This means that a manufacturer that wishes to terminate a dealer should make sure that it has records indicating repeated failure of the dealer to perform service-related functions. Dealers should be monitored regularly to ensure that they are performing the contract-demanded levels of customer service. Regular reports should be sent to each dealer rating its performance. Such reports also should contain any necessary warnings if a dealer fails to perform as expected. These reports are essential evidence if a terminated dealer sues for reinstatement. A dealer can be terminated for failure to perform contracted service but not because it was discounting the manufacturer's brand. The manufacturer must have detailed records proving lack of dealer performance of specific agreed-on actions such as warranty service and having in place a well-trained sales force. The courts must be convinced that any dealer termination occurred not because that dealer was engaged in discounting but rather because it failed to live up to contractual obligations to perform nonprice services. Furthermore, it must be demonstrated that the manufacturer acted alone and not in concert with other dealers, as this might be seen as an illegal conspiracy or boycott (Scammon and Sheffet 1986). Thus, a manufacturer can restrict dealer territories and customers and can use exclusive dealing contracts. The one caveat that always applies, however, is that interbrand competition cannot be reduced.

Record Keeping

One of the areas that saw a major change in corporate marketing practices was that of record keeping. Record keeping always has been important to corporations. Traditionally, records were kept on paper, and such files were legion. It was said that the paper files for the *IBM* and *Exxon* cases were so voluminous that the DOJ had to rent additional storage space to house the documents generated by those two cases. During the 1960s, the existence of internal company memorandums on paper outlining certain IBM strategies and practices caused considerable trouble for IBM during the department's discovery prior to trial. This same problem exists at the start of the 21st century. Although firms still use paper, e-mail has become widespread, and much to Bill Gates' chagrin, it can prove to be just as dangerous. In its antitrust case against Microsoft, the DOJ cited internal e-mail messages as evidence of Microsoft's obsession with what it saw as a threat from Netscape's browser (Clark and Gruley 1998). Thus, although the form of internal company communication might have changed from paper to e-mail, the substance of the memos seems to have remained the same, and the danger posed by thoughtless internal communications is just as real. Corporations need to be careful about what they say and write, regardless of where or on what medium it is written.

Regardless of the format, record keeping must be done. Firms must be able to document their practices and maintain records of where their products are distributed. The importance of keeping detailed records of where and to whom products have been sold is amply illustrated by the so-called "delayed manifestation" cases such as those involving a drug known as DES and insulation containing asbestos. In a product liability case, the plaintiff must prove who is responsible for the injury or harm done. The DES and asbestos cases were unique because they involved damage done to consumers long after exposure to the substances (20 years or more) or, in the case of DES, damage done to the children of the mothers who had taken the drug. The problem faced by both plaintiffs and defendants in these cases was the difficulty in proving causation, that is, which company made the substance responsible for the damage. Given the passage of time, some firms had gone out of business and other firms lacked the records needed to substantiate their involvement or innocence. The California Supreme Court decision in *Sindell v. Abbott Laboratories et al.* (1980), which established market share liability, forced surviving defendant manufacturers to either prove that they could not have supplied the plaintiffs or pay a percentage of awarded damages equal to their market share of DES sold as a miscarriage preventative (Sheffet 1983). These delayed manifestation cases showed businesses the importance of keeping detailed records of which products have been distributed to which customers. Such records need to be kept for very long time periods (e.g., more than 20 years) because some injuries and/or damages might not be apparent for many years after the product has been used. Although most firms had kept records of their products, many records did not contain the necessary level of detail and were not kept for long enough time periods. Thus, those firms lacking records to prove that they could not have been responsible for the plaintiff's injuries were included in the defendant pool required to pay the assessed damages.

Fortunately, computer technology has made keeping detailed records easier, however, no one can say for certain how many years a firm should keep such records. To protect itself, a firm should establish a system that allows it to trace each product through its channels of distribution to the final consumer, and such records should be kept for at least 50 years. Such records would be useful not only in the event of a lawsuit but also for aid in completing a product recall if one were necessary. Numerous firms have faced the necessity of recalling their products, usually for safety-related "fixes," and up-to-date records of ownership increase the likelihood of firms' being able to contact their customers. Although it might be difficult for firms to track their products once they have been purchased by consumers, efforts should be made to convince consumers to establish and help maintain accurate product registration records. Technological changes have made record keeping less cumbersome, but it still is time-consuming. For corporations, however, it is essential that time be allocated to continuous record keeping because such records might be an essential part of an antitrust or product liability defense.

Pricing

The area of pricing has seen a recent change in case law. Although the courts still frown on a manufacturer setting a minimum resale price and requiring all dealers to adhere to that price (*Monsanto v. Spray-Rite Service* 1984), the Supreme Court recently eased previous restrictions against maximum price setting. In its unanimous ruling issued on November 4, 1997 (*State Oil Company v. Barkat U. Khan and Khan & Associates Inc.* 1997), the Supreme Court said that each price cap should be evaluated to determine its effect on competition. Only those price ceilings that can be shown to stifle competition should be prohibited. This means that a corporation can tell its dealers that they may not charge more than a stated price. The decision has been called a victory for consumers who are expected to see lower prices across all dealers of a particular brand given that no one dealer is allowed to charge a higher price than that established by the manufacturer (Felsenthal 1997).

Bundling

During recent years, bundling has become a popular method of combining certain products and services. Manufacturers offer bundled packages of goods or services to consumers at a lower price than would be paid if each part of the bundle were purchased separately. This has become widespread in the computer industry in hardware and software packages as well as in other industries where manufacturers or dealers bundle service contracts with product purchases. Manufacturers put together certain products or services and price them to attract consumers, thereby increasing their sales and profits. For example, a local telephone company might offer three services—call waiting, call forwarding, and voice mail messaging—at an attractive package price that is less than the total of the three services priced individually (e.g., $10.95 a month for the bundle of all three, but $3.95 for each service if ordered separately). Computer hardware manufacturers frequently offer packages that include a CPU, monitor, keyboard, printer, and several software programs at a price that is lower than the total price if the consumer were to purchase each piece of the package singly (Eppen, Hanson, and Martin 1991).

In the DOJ's 1997 complaint against Microsoft, bundling has been a major issue. The government charged that Microsoft had bundled Windows 95 with its Internet browser not because it was more efficient or because consumers preferred it that way but rather as a means of eliminating competition. It was the government's position that Microsoft had included Internet Explorer in its Windows 95 program and made it an integral part of the program not to satisfy customer needs but rather to limit its customers' browser options and that such an inclusion was an illegal tying arrangement (Gruley and Wilke 1997). The DOJ's suit also charged that Microsoft had coerced PC manufacturers into making sure that the first screen customers see when their machines are booted is the Microsoft Windows screen. Several state attorneys general also prepared antitrust lawsuits against Microsoft to be filed if they believed that the outcome of the DOJ's suit was unsatisfactory (Donovan 1998). Prior to this suit, Microsoft's settlement of a prior action filed by the department had been upheld by the U.S. Court of Appeals in Washington, DC (Clark and Novak 1995). That action had focused on some practices used by Microsoft that allegedly harmed competing operating systems' sales.

Judge Thomas Penfield Jackson issued his findings of fact in the latest *Microsoft* case on November 5, 1999. Judge Jackson determined that Microsoft has monopoly power in the PC operating systems market and that it used its power to harm competitors and stifle innovation. The judge went on to say that Microsoft had bundled its Internet Explorer program into Windows primarily to protect Windows rather than to benefit consumers (Wilkie and Bank 1999). Microsoft already had signed an agreement on January 22, 1998, that allowed PC manufacturers to install Windows 95 without an Internet Explorer icon (Hamilton 1999). There is widespread speculation on what remedies will be ordered or negotiated.

Microsoft maintained that adding new features and/or programs to its basic Windows operating system is not anticompetitive but rather is done in response to competitive products and to consumer demand. The DOJ countered that Microsoft was using illegal tying arrangements to foreclose competitors from the consumer marketplace. Microsoft said that continuous improvement of its products by adding new programs to Windows is a basic part of its business that benefits both consumers and competition. How Microsoft and its bundling of new programs into its Windows operating system will be affected by the negotiated settlement between it and the DOJ remains to be seen.

For marketers, however, bundling can remain a viable practice. Consumers continue to purchase both products and services that have been bundled together, and so long as the products and services are available separately, there should be no legal problem if the offering firms are not determined to be monopolies. Any large successful firm with more than 50% of the market, however, should beware. Its actions will be carefully scrutinized by competitors and government officials. Both IBM and Microsoft are firms that gained prominence and dominance through new product development. Although IBM no longer is seen as a competitive threat, Microsoft still is. Its pricing, distribution, and product development strategies have been, and will continue to be, watched closely. Any firm with a dominant position in its industry and markets should be particularly careful in designing its marketing strategy. Although competition may have been enlarged to include e-commerce and global competitors, the rules of U.S. antitrust still must be followed. Marketers must take care when establishing dealer relationships, pricing policies, and new product distribution and/or integration strategies. The larger and more successful a firm is, the more care it must take if antitrust problems are to be avoided.

Conclusion

This chapter has discussed some of the areas in which the law has changed and how those changes might affect how businesses proceed. Manufacturers now can establish and maintain distribution networks that allow them better control over their brands. Although nonprice distribution can be used by manufacturers, enforcement of those restrictions must be done unilaterally. If a manufacturer is seen as conspiring with its dealers to terminate another dealer, particularly if the terminated dealer was a discounter, then such actions will be found to be illegal. Manufacturers also must avoid using resale price maintenance to enforce minimum retail prices among its dealers, although setting maximum retail prices for its products is permitted. Bundling products together also may be allowed, but only if consumers also can purchase those products separately.

Although there are no studies currently available that delineate how businesses have responded to the changing antitrust climate, future research examining how specific business practices (e.g., distribution networks, dealer contracts) have changed over time would be useful. For example, a study examining the restrictions contained in dealer contracts before and after the *GTE Sylvania* decision would be interesting. A future study also could look at how product and/or service bundling practices are affected by the Microsoft decision. In addition, future research could focus on changes in record keeping over the past 20 years.

In trying to advise marketing managers on how antitrust and other legal problems can be avoided, the most difficult part is trying to foresee the future. If an antitrust expert were advising a corporation on distribution practices during the early 1970s, the advice would have focused on the form of the restrictions rather than on their effect on intrabrand and interbrand competition. That advice would have changed dramatically after the Supreme Court issued its ruling in *Continental T.V. v. GTE Sylvania* (1977). That decision focused on the competitive effect of intrabrand distribution restrictions rather than on the specific form of the restrictions themselves. Will the Supreme Court continue to use economic efficiency rules when ruling on the legality of business practices such as distribution and pricing restrictions? Although some commentators (e.g., Hovenkamp 1985; Sullivan 1995) believe that economic efficiency has been supplanted as the primary rule and theoretical basis applied by the Supreme Court in deciding antitrust cases, that might not be the case. Some decisions (e.g., *Eastman Kodak Company v. Image Technical Services Inc.* 1992) seem to have been decided using a non-Chicago economic efficiency basis, but it is not clear whether economic efficiency has been abandoned as the primary standard. In *State Oil v. Khan* (1997), the Supreme Court reversed the "per se" standard applied to maximum resale price maintenance in *Albrecht v. Herald Company* (1968). The court held that because the primary purpose of antitrust law is to protect interbrand competition and that, therefore, practices promoting lower consumer prices should be encouraged, such a ban was contrary to consumer interest. Thus, maximum resale price maintenance cases no longer should be decided according to the per se standard of *Albrecht v. Herald* (1968). The court once again relies on economic efficiency and consumer welfare considerations. Predictions about what will happen in future antitrust decisions are dangerous. Personnel changes on the Supreme Court will be made during the coming years. Who is appointed and to what antitrust philosophy they will adhere will depend on which presidential candidate is elected in November 2000. What is certain, however, is that antitrust law will remain an important influence on business practices. Corporations must continue to monitor the legal environment and strive to keep their business practices within the current legal limits.

References

Albrecht v. Herald Company (1968), 390 U.S. 145.

Clark, Don and Bryan Gruley (1998), "Microsoft Launches New Attack against Suits," *The Wall Street Journal,* August 11, A4.

———— and Vivica Novak (1995), "Microsoft Savors Major Victory as Pact on Antitrust Is Reinstated by Judges," *The Wall Street Journal,* June 19, A3.

Continental T.V. Inc. v. GTE Sylvania Inc. (1977), 433 U.S. 36.

Donovan, Karen (1998), "Can U.S., AGs Beat Microsoft?" *National Law Journal,* June 1, 1.

Eastman Kodak Company v. Image Technical Services Inc. (1992), 112 S.Ct. 2072.

Eppen, Gary D., Ward A. Hanson, and R. Kipp Martin (1991), *Sloan Management Review,* Summer, 7-14.

Felsenthal, Edward (1997), "Manufacturers Allowed to Cap Retail Prices," *The Wall Street Journal,* November 5, A3-A4.

Gruley, Bryan and John R. Wilke (1997), "U.S. Sues Microsoft over Browser," *The Wall Street Journal,* October 21, A3.

Hamilton, David P. (1999), "Evolution of the Web Still Tied to Explorer," *The Wall Street Journal,* November 8, A30.

Hovenkamp, Herbert (1985), "Antitrust Policy after Chicago," *Michigan Law Review,* 84, 213-84.

Monsanto Company v. Spray-Rite Service Corporation (1984), 104 S.Ct. 1464, 684 F.2d 1226.

Scammon, Debra L. and Mary Jane Sheffet (1986), "Legal Issues in Channels Modification Decisions: The Question of Refusals to Deal," *Journal of Public Policy & Marketing,* 5, 82-96.

Sheffet, Mary Jane (1983), "Market Share Liability: A New Doctrine of Causation in Product Liability," *Journal of Marketing,* 47 (Winter), 35-43.

———— and Debra L. Scammon (1985), "Resale Price Maintenance: Is It Safe to Suggest Retail Prices?" *Journal of Marketing,* 49 (Fall), 82-91.

Sindell v. Abbott Laboratories et al. (1980), 26 Cal. 3d 588.

State Oil Company v. Barkat U. Khan and Khan & Associates Inc. (1997), 522 U.S. 3.

Streeter, Jon B. (1995), "Antitrust Redux: Microsoft Litigation," *National Law Journal,* April 17, C19-22.

Sullivan, Lawrence A. (1995), "Post-Chicago Economics: Economists, Lawyers, Judges, and Enforcement Officials in a Less Determinate Theoretical World," *Antitrust Law Journal,* 63, 669-81.

U.S. Department of Justice (1988a), "Merger Guidelines—1982," in *Antitrust & Trade Regulation Reporter,* para. 13, 102.

———(1988b), "Merger Guidelines—1984," in *Antitrust & Trade Regulation Reporter,* para. 13, 103.

——— (1992), "Merger Guidelines—1992," in *Antitrust & Trade Regulation Report,* para. 13, 104.

Wilkie, John R. and David Bank (1999), "Microsoft Is Found to Be Predatory Monopolist," *The Wall Street Journal,* November 8, A3, A28.

7 Chapter

Changes in Corporate Practices in Response to Public Interest Advocacy and Actions

The Role of Consumer Boycotts and Socially Responsible Consumption in Promoting Corporate Social Responsibility

N. Craig Smith

The central proposition advanced in this chapter is that corporate practices have changed in response to public interest group use or threat of consumer boycotts and these changes have often benefited societal welfare. The chapter reviews evidence in support of these claims, acknowledging its limitations and, in particular, the paucity of empirical research of consumer boycotts. It highlights the need for further research on this important topic.

The chapter briefly introduces public interest groups and the various pressures they can exert on the corporation and then discusses the concept of corporate social responsibility. Next, it turns to a review of the research and related literatures on consumer boycotts. This discussion focuses on boycotts that protest perceived failings of corporate social responsibility and business ethics (consumer boycotts have been organized to protest other issues, such as price increases). The chapter concludes by identifying opportunities and needs for future research.

Public Interest Groups

Public interest groups are non-profit organizations that have been founded to promote a cause perceived (at least by their organizers) to be in the public

interest. There are many different types of these "promotional" or "ideological"
pressure groups and they stand for a wide spectrum of issues (see Smith 1990,
pp. 100-12). They are differentiated from "sectional" groups that promote the
economic and other interests of a particular group of people by the issues on
which they campaign. As one veteran campaigner (Wilson, 1984, p. 2) puts it:

Public interest groups are nonprofit organizations that have been founded to
promote causes perceived (at least by their organizers) to be in the public interest. There are many different types of these "promotional" or "ideological" pressure groups, and they stand for a wide spectrum of issues (Smith 1990, pp. 100-
12). They are differentiated from "sectional" groups that promote the economic
and other interests of particular groups of people by the issues on which they
campaign. As one veteran campaigner put it,

> Thus . . ., there are two kinds of pressure groups—those whose motivation is a con-
> cern for the health and well-being of the community, and who usually campaign to
> change or improve priorities or policies, and those with vested interests, whose
> cause is usually maintenance of the *status-quo,* or furtherance of policies benefi-
> cial to them, irrespective of the implications for the community. (Wilson 1984,
> p. 2, italics in original)

The executive, the legislature, and public opinion generally are identified as
the primary avenues of pressure for both types of groups. Public interest groups
can be influential when, as Berry (1977) observed, "they have become part of the
political environment and thus part of the equation that explains public policy
outcomes" (pp. 288-89). Some public interest groups have "insider" status and,
thus, influence with government and elected officials (e.g., Sierra Club). Many,
however, are "outsiders" and, thus, rely more on affecting public policy through
their influence on public opinion (e.g., Greenpeace). Public interest groups may
target corporations in their campaigns because this can lead to publicity and in
directly influence public policy. However, Smith (1990, p. 114), noting the prominence and power of business in society, suggested that corporations should be
seen as a fourth avenue of pressure because they also may be the ultimate target
of pressure group activity—with the goal of changing corporate behavior.

Berry (1977, p. 214) identified three categories of tactics used by public interest groups. The first category is direct lobbying or tactics characterized by direct communication between lobbyists and government officials (e.g., personal
presentations, testifying at congressional hearings). The second is trying to
change government policy by influencing elections or altering public opinion
using indirect lobbying (e.g., releasing research results, public relations). The
third is methods by which groups lobby their constituents such as political pro-
tests (e.g., demonstrations, picketing, sit-ins) and letter writing. Tactics used by
public interest groups to lobby corporations include many of the tactics used in
lobbying government (Smith 1990; Vogel 1978). In addition, however, groups
may attempt to influence perceptions of firms and sales of their products and services. Public interest group criticism of corporate practices and calls for consumer boycotts generally reflect concerns about corporate social responsibility.

Corporate Social Responsibility

Corporate social responsibility (CSR) refers to the obligations of the firm to its stakeholders—people affected by corporate policies and practices. These obligations go beyond legal requirements and the firm's duties to its shareholders. Fulfillment of these obligations is intended to minimize any harm and maximize the long-run beneficial impact of the firm on society. As Frederick (1994) put it, "The fundamental idea embedded in 'corporate social responsibility' is that business corporations have an obligation to work for social betterment" (p. 151).

A renewal of interest in CSR occurred during the late 1990s. Whereas there are a number of explanations for this resurgence, two are especially noteworthy. First, the United States and Europe have seen growing recognition of the failure of governments to solve many social problems. Second, for this and other reasons, the scope of government is diminishing. As a result, the private sector is increasingly called on to address social problems and, accordingly, to shoulder greater social responsibilities.

Buchholz (1991) provided a summary of the central ideas of the CSR concept:

> While various definitions of social responsibility have been advocated, there seem to be five key elements in most, if not all, of these definitions: 1) corporations have responsibilities that go beyond the production of goods and services at a profit; 2) these responsibilities involve helping to solve important social problems, especially those they have helped create; 3) corporations have a broader constituency than stockholders alone; 4) corporations have impacts that go beyond simple marketplace transactions; and 5) corporations serve a wider range of human values than can be captured by a sole focus on economic values. (p. 19)

Although there is substantial agreement that CSR entails societal obligations on the part of business, there is much less certainty about what these obligations might be or their scope. Buchholz (1991) was not able to offer much guidance on how business may identify specific responsibilities. Citing Sethi (1975), Frederick (1994) observed, "The content or substance—the operational meaning—of corporate social responsibility is supremely vague" (p. 152). Indeed, it has been suggested that because of this ambiguity, business was able to hijack the CSR concept. As Silk and Vogel (1976) put it, "The doctrine of 'corporate social responsibility' emerged in the United States precisely because it is seen by many businessmen as a way of reducing the role of government in their affairs" (p. 53). Nonetheless, many public interest groups have chosen to offer alternative visions of CSR, at least for specific firms or industries (e.g., Ralph Nader's "public citizen"). Because of these and other problems with the CSR concept, research attention shifted to the concept of corporate social responsiveness, "the capacity of a corporation to respond to social pressures" (Frederick 1994, p. 154).

Frederick (1987) referred to the concepts of CSR and corporate social responsiveness as theories of "corporate social performance" that "try to explain, rationalize, and, in some cases, advocate societal values that are essential to the human condition but are sometimes ignored or overridden by business" (p. 142). Developing this further, Wood (1991) claimed that the concept of corporate social performance provides the integrating framework for the business and society field and defined it as "a business organization's configuration of principles of social responsibility; processes of social responsiveness; and policies, programs, and observable outcomes as they relate to the firm's societal relationships" (p. 693). At a minimum, the corporate social performance perspective acknowledges pressures on the firm to practice CSR.

Pressures on the Firm to Practice CSR

Conflicts between the legitimate goal of shareholder wealth maximization and the interests of other stakeholders of the firm may lead to business decisions that are not socially responsible. In addition, some managers might be tempted to act opportunistically, in disregard of one or more stakeholder groups. Regulatory, civil, and criminal law governing business increases the likelihood of socially responsible business practices and serves as a constraint on opportunism. However, although laws and regulations require conformity with many important societal expectations of business, they are insufficient as mechanisms for ensuring ethical conduct and social responsibility. As Mintzberg (1983) observed, "Legalistic approaches only set crude and minimum standards of behavior, ones easily circumvented by the unscrupulous" (p. 13).

Many managers aspire to high standards of ethical conduct and to make business decisions that are socially responsible. However, in the absence of possible legal or regulatory sanctions, or if moral impulse is insufficient as a motivation, there are other pressures for CSR. These countervailing pressures can come from many different directions. Business leaders such as David Rockefeller, for example, have urged their peers to do more to address pressing social problems (Rockefeller 1996). Often, such calls are based on the recognition that it is in the enlightened self-interest of business to ensure, for example, that it has access to a well-trained and stable workforce. Pressure also may come from investors, either individually or through organizations including the now well-established social investment funds. Even political leaders such as President Clinton have urged "corporate citizenship" and greater business involvement in social problems (Smith 1996).

Pressure for CSR also may come from public interest groups. It can take different forms, ranging from meetings with management, to adverse publicity in the media, to shareholder activism, to consumer boycotts. It may even include organized direct action such as Greenpeace's efforts to hamper the dumping at sea of Shell's Brent Spar oil platform because of the pressure group's environmental concerns (Cowe 1999). Often, these pressures can translate into adverse economic consequences for the firm, and CSR (at least as defined by those promoting the change in corporate behavior) becomes in the firm's economic interest.

These pressures may amount to marketplace sanctions when the firm stands the risk of being penalized in financial or consumer markets for perceived ethical or social responsibility shortcomings. Hence, a positive stock market reaction to a change in packaging policy by McDonald's is attributed to "an anticipation of increased sales to customers supporting a 'socially responsible' company" (McMillan 1996, p. 313). Using standard event methodology, Davidson, El-Jelly, and Worrell (1995) presented a model of reactions to unpopular or irresponsible corporate behavior and then tested the effectiveness of both consumer boycotts and stock divestitures as forms of pressure on the firm. Their empirical research found that product boycott announcements were associated with significant negative market reactions; divestiture announcements resulted in no significant market responses. They also found some evidence of changes in corporate behavior as a result of boycotts.

In sum, the consumer marketplace may be an important source of pressure for CSR. Simply put, firms may be penalized by consumer boycotts—often inspired by public interest groups—for actions that are not considered socially responsible. More positively, firms may be rewarded by increased patronage if they have reputations for being socially responsible. Consumer boycotts are examined in more detail in the next section, together with further evidence for these claims.

Consumer Boycotts

The term *boycott* was coined by James Redpath in late 19th-century Ireland and was used to describe the ostracism of an English land agent, Captain C. C. Boycott. Redpath wrote, "Just say to him that under British law he has the undoubted right to sell his goods to anyone, but that there is no British law to compel you to buy another penny's worth from him, and that you will never do it as long as you live" (quoted in Laidler [1913] 1968, p. 26). Although the term might be relatively recent, boycotts have been used for centuries. Early examples included boycotts of British goods by American colonists during the Revolutionary War, boycotts of slave-made goods by abolitionists, and (going back to 1327) a boycott of the monks of Christ's church by the citizens of Canterbury, England, in an agreement not to "buy, sell, or exchange drinks or victuals with the monastery" (Laidler [1913] 1968, pp. 27-30).

Laidler ([1913] 1968) defined boycotting as "an organized effort to withdraw and induce others to withdraw from social or business relations with another" (p. 27). As this definition suggests, boycotts can take many forms (Smith 1990, pp. 134-66). Sharp's (1973) comprehensive study of nonviolent direct action identified withdrawal of cooperation as one of three broad classes of method. It includes social noncooperation, economic noncooperation, and political noncooperation. Economic noncooperation includes economic boycotts by consumers, workers and producers, middlemen, owners and management, holders of financial resources (e.g., refusal to pay debts or interest), governments (e.g., trade embargo), and strikes. Sharp defined economic boycotts as "the refusal to continue or undertake certain economic relationships, especially the buying, selling, or handling of goods and services" (p. 219).

This chapter is about public interest advocacy and actions; thus, it is focused on economic boycotts by consumers rather than on trade sanctions by governments or labor boycotts by trade unions (which are "sectional" pressure groups). However, it is evident that the use of economic boycotts by workers was a powerful tactic during the early days of trade unions, providing a method whereby unions could pressure businesses to agree to labor organization (Laidler [1913] 1968; Wolman 1916). Once organized, labor was able to make more effective use of the strike tactic, although economic boycotts often continued to be employed. One of the most effective economic boycotts, in terms of achieving a reduction in sales, was the 1965-1970 California grape boycott (Smith 1990, pp. 250-53). It resulted in the unionization of farm workers after all previous efforts had failed. Its success was due, in part, to widespread support for farm workers from consumers, who were concerned about minority rights, poverty, pesticide misuse, and civil rights as well as farm workers' rights to organize.

Consumer boycotts were defined by Friedman (1985) as "an attempt by one or more parties to achieve certain objectives by urging individual consumers to refrain from making selected purchases in the marketplace" (p. 97; see also Friedman 1999, p. 4). This definition captures the "instrumental" function of boycotts but does not refer (at least not directly) to their "expressive" function (Smith 1990, p. 257). Garrett (1987) defined boycotts as "the concerted but nonmandatory refusal by a group of actors (the agents) to conduct marketing transactions with one or more other actors (the targets) for the purpose of communicating displeasure with certain target policies and attempting to coerce the target to modify these policies" (p. 47). This definition recognizes that boycotts generally are intended to "say something" about the targeted firms as well as to influence their practices. Friedman (1999, p. 249), however, suggested that Garrett's (1987) definition is too narrow because it does not include "surrogate" boycotts that target neutral parties to put pressure on other parties (e.g., a hotel chain boycotted to put pressure on its home state legislators).

One reason why it is important to recognize the expressive function of boycotts is that they sometimes are just symbolic and simply involve groups publicizing issues and calling boycotts but making little, if any, effort to organize consumers. These "symbolic" boycotts might not reduce sales (i.e., be "effective"), but they might be successful in helping these groups to achieve their aims nonetheless (Smith 1990, p. 258). More recently, Friedman (1999, p. 11) noted a distinction between boycotts that are "marketplace oriented," including the use of tactics such as picketing or demonstrations at retail stores, and those that are "media oriented," primarily using the news media to attack the images of the targeted firms.

Smith's (1990, pp. 278-82) thesis, in keeping with the central proposition of this chapter, is that consumer boycotts may be viewed as a tool used by public interest groups in their efforts to achieve social control of business. He suggested that such efforts are consistent with and enhance the idea of consumer sovereignty. Accordingly, Smith defined the consumer boycott as "the organized exercising of consumer sovereignty by abstaining from purchase of an offering in order to exert influence on a matter of concern to the consumer and over the institution making the offering" (p. 140).

Smith (1990) suggested that group-organized consumer boycotts are only the most clearly identifiable and deliberate form of a broader phenomenon, which occurs "where people are influenced in purchase by ethical concerns" (pp. 8-9); while Holbrook's (1999) typology of consumer value posits that ethics (including justice, virtue, and morality) is one of eight types of value that consumers may attain in the consumption experience (see also Smith 1999). Consumer boy-cotts organized or inspired by public interest groups are examined more closely in the next section. This is followed by a review of research on ethical concerns in consumer behavior, focusing in particular on the stream of literature that explores "socially responsible consumption."

Public Interest Group-Inspired Consumer Boycotts

During the early 1990s, the business press appeared to agree that consumer boycotts work and were increasing in number. Many of the boycotts reported were over CSR issues (e.g., boycotts of Star-Kist and others over their use of "dolphin-unsafe" tuna, of Exxon over its pollution of the Valdez Sound, and of Nike over its alleged shortfalls in the employment of minorities). *The Economist,* for example, concluded, "Pressure groups are besieging American compa-nies, politicizing business, and often presenting executives with impossible choices. Consumer boycotts are becoming an epidemic for one simple reason: they work" ("Boycotting Corporate America" 1990, p. 69). That judgment still appears to be current (Friedman 1999).

Consumer boycotts continue to be in the news and appear to have had some dramatic effects. Recent and prominent consumer boycotts include the Euro-pean boycott of Shell over its plan to dump the Brent Spar oil platform at sea, the U.S. boycott of Texaco over alleged racial remarks by senior management, and the U.S. boycott of Mitsubishi over alleged sexual harassment in the workplace. All three boycotts achieved most, if not all, of their organizers' goals. Com-menting on the Shell boycott, *The Economist* suggested, "It may be no bad thing . . . for consumers to ask for a higher standard of behavior from the firms they buy from. The best companies . . . make a point of explaining their policies. . . . Shell thought it had done enough explaining, but had not. Regardless of the merits of its case, it made a costly blunder" ("Saints and Sinners" 1995, p. 15). Shell's problems were compounded by public reactions to its involvement in Nigeria and the company's apparent failure to use its influence to prevent the tragic exe-cution of Ken Saro-Wiwa and eight Ogonis by the Nigerian authorities. Criti-cism of Shell by environmentalists and human rights activists and the associated boycotts were said to be key contributors to a fundamental transformation in how the company strives to live up to its social and ethical responsibilities (Cowe 1999; Shell International 1998).

However, if boycotts are to be a force for good, then much depends on percep-tions of corporate conduct and the judgments of its appropriateness made by boycott organizers and consumers. So, for example, it is not clear whether Shell's decision to dismantle the Brent Spar oil platform on land, as a result of the boycott, was a more socially responsible outcome or even more environmen-tally benign than the planned disposal at sea. Moreover, boycotts may be orga-nized by groups with many different values and political persuasions; for exam-ple, contrast the Shell boycott, organized by Greenpeace, with the Disney boycott called by the Southern Baptist Convention over Disney's position on homosexuality including its policy of extending health benefits to partners of homosexual employees. Friedman (1999) showed that boycotts have involved a wide variety of pressure groups, target organizations, and social concerns.

Hence, *The Economist* cautioned that as "boycotts become more widespread . . ., their biggest victim may not be corporate misbehavior, but reason" ("Boycotting Corporate America" 1990, p. 70). In a similar vein, a *Newsweek* article commented, "You can please some of the boycotters, but only some of the time" (Miller et al. 1992, p. 61). Although the success of some boycotts constitutes evidence of public interest groups influencing CSR practices and contributing to improvements in societal welfare, it should not be assumed that all boycotts have such beneficial results, even when successful. As discussed earlier, the operational definition of CSR is uncertain. The definition of boycotters might not be any better than that of the target firm.

Nonetheless, Hayes and Pereira (1990), in a *Wall Street Journal* article, reported a Reebok spokesman as commenting, "More and more in the marketplace, it is our feeling that who you are and what you stand for is as important as the quality of the product you sell" (p. B1). The article also noted that a substantial reduction in sales might not be necessary for a boycott to be successful; even a 5% decline might be considered a cause for concern by a company. Accordingly, a spokesman for Star-Kist (a unit of H. J. Heinz Company) suggested, "Consumer interests . . . have to be recognized. That's just good business" (p. B1).

It was noted earlier that Davidson, El-Jelly, and Worrell (1995) found that product boycott announcements were associated with significant negative stock market reactions, suggesting that investors (at least) believe that the sales of boycott targets can be affected. Some academic researchers have studied boycott effectiveness more directly.

Friedman (1985) reported academic research of 90 U.S. boycotts between 1970 and 1980. He found that boycotts have involved an unusually wide variety of protest groups, target organizations, and social concerns and that boycotts appear to be increasing in number. Friedman was unable to state definitively how many of the boycotts examined were successful, in part because of the difficulty of disentangling the effects of other tactics, such as strikes, that accompanied many of the boycotts studied.

Garrett (1987) suggested that boycotts are important because (1) they are increasing, (2) agents are becoming more sophisticated, (3) targets have only limited refuge from them in the legal system, (4) they are neglected (by marketers) as environmental forces, and (5) they are a double-barreled challenge to marketers—seeking both to change marketing policies and to disrupt exchange relationships. His review of the boycott literature suggested six factors in boycott participation: awareness of consumers, the values of potential consumer participants, boycott goals consistent with participant attitudes, the cost to participate, social pressure, and whether the boycott is promoted by a highly credible leader. He proposed a theory of boycott success, suggesting that the determinants are economic pressure (due to lost sales), (corporate) image pressure (due to adverse publicity), and policy commitment (target's determination not to change the policy in question). Garrett's theory was supported by research of 30 "boycotts" between 1981 and 1984.

Smith (1990) reported case study research including the boycotts of Barclays Bank over its involvement in apartheid South Africa, Nestle over its marketing of infant formula in less developed countries, and the California grape boycott over labor unionization. On the basis of this case research and his review of the boycott literature, Smith identified factors in consumer boycott effectiveness and success including the choice of target (e.g., involvement of the firm in the grievance, its visibility, the connection of the product with the grievance, and its substitutability by competitive offerings), the organization and strategy of the pressure group (e.g., dedication to the cause, use of strategic approach), and responses to the boycott call (e.g., consumers' moral outrage over the grievance, endorsement of the boycott by public figures) (p. 260). More broadly, he suggested that "consumers must be concerned, willing, and able to act" (p. 294) in support of the boycott. He noted, however, that boycotts need not reduce sales substantially to be successful. Firms might comply with boycott demands in response to the moral pressure and concern for their reputations absent any impact on sales.

Friedman (1999, pp. 21-22) drew on "instrumentality theory" (Vroom 1964) to develop an explanation for boycott success. He suggested that before initiating a boycott, a group should ask itself whether (1) consumers care about the boycott issues and objectives, (2) the boycott task is likely to be executed successfully, and (3) the execution of the boycott is likely to lead to the desired consequences specified by the boycott objectives. In keeping with this approach, and based on his extensive knowledge of boycotts, Friedman (1999, pp. 23-32) identified execution and consequence considerations for media-oriented boycotts (e.g., announcements should be made by well-known organizations), marketplace-oriented boycotts (e.g., boycotted products should be easy for consumers to identify), and surrogate boycotts (the more political influence the target companies have, the more likely the government will yield to boycott demands).

In sum, there appears to be evidence of boycott effectiveness leading to changes in corporate CSR practices and hypotheses (at least) as to factors in boycott effectiveness and success. Although there is little empirical research of consumer boycotts, more attention has been given to socially responsible consumption. This literature, discussed in the next section, provides indirect evidence in support of claims about the influence of group-organized consumer boycotts on corporate practices. Furthermore, socially responsible consumption also may be treated as boycotting by individual consumers, even when public interest groups do not organize it. This is consistent with Sharp's (1973) definition of economic boycotts (noted earlier) and use of the term *boycott* elsewhere. For example, Klein, Ettenson, and Morris (1998) referred to boycotts of foreign products because of animosity toward the country of origin. Smith and Cooper-Martin (1997) referred to boycotts of firms because they are perceived to be targeting vulnerable consumers with harmful products. In both cases, these boycotts can take place without pressure group organization.

Research on Socially Responsible Consumption

Interest in CSR prompted a number of marketing scholars to examine whether it might influence consumer purchase behavior. Many of these studies were conducted during the 1970s, although research on the topic was published at least as recently as 1997. In one of the earliest contributions, Kassarjian

(1971) examined consumer reactions to the introduction of a gasoline that was claimed to reduce automotive emissions. Would consumers support CSR in this instance? Kassarjian explained the circumstances and his findings as follows:

> In the early part of 1970, an ideal combination of conditions existed for the intro-duction of . . . a pollution-reducing gasoline. A population existed that was seri-ously concerned about air pollution and willing to try to solve the problem; a prod-uct was available that purportedly aided in the reduction of air pollution; a massive advertising campaign was undertaken; and government officials were prepared to make testimonials. Within six weeks after the introduction of the gasoline, more than half of the population had paid an additional two to 12 cents per gallon to try the new brand. Two-thirds of the people could identify the company marketing the product, and 55% could identify the brand name. (p. 65)

Kassarjian (1971) reasoned that consumer acceptance is very likely for a product that promises some alleviation of pollution problems. Moreover, con-sumers in general are willing to try the product at premium prices and claim to be willing to pay more for it; Kassarjian suggested that there was circumstantial ev-idence indicating that this was true at the time of his study. Advertising of the new product was most effective in reaching members of the high-concern (about air pollution) group in his sample. They could identify the name of the gasoline company and the pollution-reducing additive. Kassarjian concluded, "With a *good* product based on ecological concerns, the potential for a marketer seems to be impressive" (p. 65, italics in original). However, he was unable to identify any market segmentation criteria that would identify the market segment more likely to buy the product beyond the level of concern about the issue (of air pollu-tion) itself.

A subsequent stream of research on socially responsible consumption[1] was directed primarily at identifying the demographic and socioeconomic character-istics of the socially conscious consumer. Clearly, understanding of these char-acteristics might be useful for market segmentation purposes. Anderson and Cunningham (1972) started by citing Friedman's arguments against CSR and then observed that others claim that "with further amplification in the demands for social and environmental responsibility, the cost to the firm of ignoring the social and environmental context in which it operates may not be profit; the cost may well be survival" (p. 23). Accordingly, they assumed that firms must re-spond to demands for greater attention to CSR including those demands from consumers. They continued, "Thus, the issue has shifted from one of corporate social responsibility to a more conventional market segmentation problem: Which consumers constitute the market for products, services, or other corpo-rate actions that promote social and/or environmental well-being?" (p. 23).

To answer this question, Anderson and Cunningham (1972) tested the rela-tive sensitivity of demographic and sociopsychological variables in discriminat-ing degrees of social consciousness. They did not use measures of actual behav-ior to determine social consciousness. Their dependent variable consisted of responses to the Berkowitz and Lutterman (1968) Social Responsibility Scale. Anderson and Cunningham (1972) found that sociopsychological variables are more sensitive discriminators of social consciousness than are demographic variables. More specifically,

> the image of the socially conscious consumer emerging from the research is that of a pre-middle-age adult of relatively high occupational attainment and socio-economic status. He is typically more cosmopolitan but less dogmatic, less conservative, less status conscious, less alienated, and less personally competent than his less socially conscious counterpart. (p. 30)

In an extension of the Anderson and Cunningham (1972) study, Kinnear, Taylor, and Ahmed (1974) explored the relationship between the socioeconomic and personality characteristics of consumers and their level of ecological concern. They suggested that ecologically concerned consumers can be identified, with personality variables (e.g., harm avoidance, openness to new ideas) being better predictors than socioeconomic variables.

Kinnear and Taylor (1973) examined the relationship between the amount of concern for the ecology that buyers indicate and their perceptions of detergent brands. Consumer survey data were analyzed using a multidimensional scaling technique appropriate to the study of brand perceptions. They found that buyers with different levels of ecological concern have different cognitive maps for laundry products. More specifically, "the higher a buyer's ecological concern, the more salient is the ecological dimension in perception, and the greater is the perceived similarity of brands that are ecologically non-destructive" (p. 196). However, although the researchers were able to segment the market on the basis of an ecological dimension (and they noted that this had been done by a number of firms in the laundry products market), the ecologically concerned segment was not very large. Somewhat pessimistically, they concluded, "A large proportion of the sample is not motivated to perceive products on the basis of concern for the ecology. . . . It is unlikely that the purchasing patterns of consumers will shift enough to nonpolluting products to force those products that do pollute off the market" (p. 196). They suggested that other methods, such as legislation and moral pressure on producers, would be necessary to eliminate the polluting products.

Webster (1975) reported an attempt to identify the characteristics of the "socially conscious consumer," somebody who "takes into account the public consequences of his [or] her private consumption or who attempts to use his or her purchasing power to bring about social change" (p. 188). His study found that the socially conscious consumer can be distinguished by a variety of personality, attitude, and socioeconomic variables, although the relationships are somewhat weak. In contrast to Anderson and Cunningham (1972), Webster (1975) developed behavioral measures of socially conscious consumption (e.g., use of recycling, boycott of products involved in labor disputes). He found that Berkowitz and Lutterman's (1968) Social Responsibility Scale is a poor surrogate for these behavioral measures. More specifically, Webster (1975) concluded,

> The socially conscious consumer is not the "pillar of the community" who scores high on measures of social responsibility. . . . He, or more likely *she,* . . . is less ready to judge the values and actions of others. She tends to think business has too

much power, and she tends to have higher household income than her less socially conscious counterpart. (pp. 195-96, italics in original)[2]

More recently, Roberts (1996) reported a large-scale survey of socially responsible consumption and concluded that "large segments of socially responsible consumers do exist" (p. 82), although they are not readily identifiable using demographic characteristics. He suggested that this might indicate that the market for socially responsible products and services is widening. He advised marketers to carefully identify segmentation criteria that distinguish between those who are likely to respond to social and environmental appeals and those who are not.

Pursuing a different line of research, Miller and Sturdivant (1977) reported an empirical test of whether consumers would be likely to penalize questionable corporate conduct. They explained their purpose as follows:

> An assumption that underlies much of the literature treating the social responsibilities of business is that over time "good behavior" will be rewarded in the marketplace. . . . Implicit in this notion that socially responsible firms will be rewarded in the marketplace is the reverse, namely, [that] bad behavior will lead to marketplace sanctions. (p. 1)

Having noted the paucity of research regarding this assumption, Miller and Sturdivant went on to discuss a study that investigated consumer reactions to a boycott of a firm over charges of unsafe working conditions. They concluded that the study provides "limited support for the argument that questionable corporate behavior will influence consumer practices" (p. 7).

Much more recently, Brown and Dacin (1997) reported three studies that explore the relationship between what a person knows about a company ("corporate associations") and perceptions of the company's products. They observed (correctly) that there is a "lack of evidence on how, when, and what types of corporate associations affect product responses" (p. 68). Two types of corporate associations were investigated: corporate ability (CA), or "those associations related to the company's expertise in producing and delivering its outputs" (p. 68), and CSR associations that "reflect the organization's status and activities with respect to its perceived societal obligations" (p. 68).[3] Two laboratory studies and one mall intercept study were described that do the following:

1. "provide empirical validation of the relationship between corporate associations and consumer product evaluations; in short, we demonstrate that what consumers know about a company can influence their evaluations of products introduced by the company" (p. 68);

2. show that "different types of corporate associations . . . can have important influences on company and product evaluations, but . . . the manner in which each type of corporate association affects product responses may be different" (pp. 68-69); and

3. demonstrate that "corporate associations can serve as an important context for the evaluation of a company's products . . .; products introduced by a company with

negative CA associations are not always destined to receive negative product responses" (p. 69).

Brown and Dacin (1997) grounded their studies in the literature on corporate image. They noted that the "handful" of prior empirical studies of the effects of company image on product judgments have equivocal results: "The inconsistent results in the literature leave marketing managers with the intuitive implication that a good image is probably better than a bad image but with little else to guide them as to how particular corporate positioning strategies might influence consumer product responses" (p. 70). Importantly, with respect to this chapter's purpose, they suggested that the inconsistency might be due to the need to distinguish between CA and CSR associations.

Brown and Dacin's (1997) proposed model identifies multiple paths of influence for corporate associations on consumer product responses. CA may influence product evaluation through product sophistication ("degree to which a product exhibits the latest technological advances" [p. 71]) or through corporate evaluation ("when the evaluation of the new product occurs in the presence of corporate information, the corporate associations can create a context for the evaluation of the product" [p. 71]). CSR may influence product evaluation through corporate evaluation or, conceivably ("if a particular product or category were consistently marketed on the basis of social responsibility attributes" [p. 71]), through product social responsibility. The model is largely supported by their studies.

Brown and Dacin (1997) concluded that "what consumers know about a company can influence their reactions to the company's products" (p. 79). More specifically, "all three studies demonstrate that negative CSR associations ultimately can have a detrimental effect on overall product evaluations, whereas positive CSR associations can enhance the product evaluations" (p. 80). This is strong support (subject to the study limitations) for the argument that consumers respond to CSR practices. Brown and Dacin did note, however, that effective communication of positive CSR associations by the firm is necessary if they are to have an effect. The authors referred to the advertising of the Saturn automobile in the United States as an illustrative example.

In keeping with Brown and Dacin's (1997) acknowledgment of the role of corporate image and the studies of socially responsible consumption, a simple model of consumer influence on CSR may be developed. This is shown as Figure 7.1.

Although not directly part of the literature on socially responsible consumption, reference should be made to the widely cited studies of fairness in the marketplace by Kahneman, Knetsch, and Thaler (1986). Brown and Dacin (1997), and most of the studies discussed earlier, examined consumer interest in CSR directly. However, also relevant are the Kahneman, Knetsch, and Thaler (1986) studies that show how considerations of fairness restrict the actions of profit-seeking firms, contrary to conventional economic theory. The studies reported by Kahneman and his colleagues support the notion that there is a "willingness to pay to resist and to punish unfairness" (p. 736). For example, three-quarters of their respondents elected to share $10 evenly with a stranger who had been fair to somebody else in a prior transaction rather than share $12 with somebody who had been unfair previously. Similarly, 69% indicated that they would switch

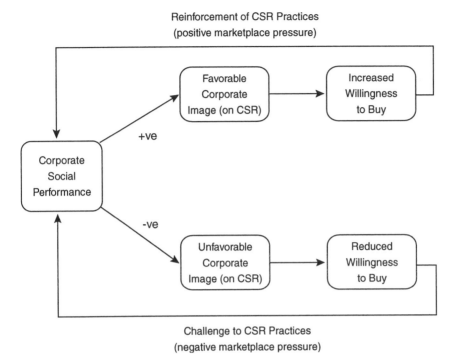

Figure 7.1. A Simple Model of Consumer Influence on Corporate Social Responsibility

NOTE: CSR = corporate social responsibility; + ve = positively perceived corporate social performance; – ve = negatively perceived corporate social performance.

to a convenience store five minutes farther away rather than continue to patronize a store that discriminated against its older workers.

Finally, cause-related marketing also should be considered as evidence of both consumer interest in CSR and a corporate belief that CSR is a source of competitive advantage. Varadarajan and Menon (1988) defined cause-related marketing as "the process of formulating and implementing marketing activities that are characterized by an offer from the firm to contribute a specified amount to a designated cause when customers engage in revenue-providing exchanges that satisfy organizational and individual objectives" (p. 60). More simply, it is a way for a company to do well by doing good, typically by making charitable donations to specified causes in proportion to its sales (Dunfee 1995; Varadarajan and Menon 1988). An early example was a 1983 campaign by American Express, whereby it donated a penny to a renovation fund for the Statue of Liberty for each use of its charge card and a dollar for each new card issued in the United States (Varadarajan and Menon 1988). Cause-related marketing and, more broadly, a new approach to corporate philanthropy that links corporate giving and the larger good of society more clearly to the firm's self-interest are increasing. Smith (1994) observed, "Consumers all over the world are welcoming private-sector activism as never before" (p. 112). The rationale is that "competing on price *and* corporate citizenship is smarter than competing on price alone" (p. 110, italics in original).

Shopping for a Better World

There is also more anecdotal evidence to suggest that the consumer market-place may reward firms for CSR practices as well as penalize firms for perceived CSR shortcomings. Support for favored businesses is well established in the boycott literature. Laidler ([1913] 1968) observed that boycotts can be negative and positive. Negative boycotts involve purchasing from recommended sources: "The primary purpose of negative boycotts is to secure for 'fair' firms the patron-age of labor and its friends. Indirectly, they divert trade from 'unfair' employers" (p. 60). The union label and "white" or "fair" lists assist in this practice, in con-trast to the "unfair" or "we don't patronize" lists. Similarly, Wolman (1916) dif-ferentiated between the indirect and direct boycotts, and Friedman (1999, p. 201) referred to "buycotts" as well as boycotts.

Consumer interest in CSR practices has resulted in a number of consumer guides to assist in shopping. In the United Kingdom, for example, Elkington and Hailes (1988) published *The Green Consumer Guide: High Street Shopping for a Better Environment,* which sold more than 300,000 copies. This was followed by a guide specifically devoted to supermarket shopping (Elkington and Hailes 1989) and another guide for the U.S. market (Elkington, Hailes, and Makower 1990). While in Germany, consumers have had the benefit of the government-supported eco-labeling initiative, the "Blue Angel" program, and similar initia-tives can be found in other countries. The success of these efforts is testament to consumers' interest in at least considering environmental issues in their pur-chase behavior. To the extent that consumers do consider these issues, firms in competitive markets might be expected to respond with more environmentally benign products. However, consumers certainly might get it wrong, as the McDonald's switch away from styrene packaging in response to consumer con-cerns indicates (McMillan 1996).

In the United States, the Council on Economic Priorities (CEP, 1991) pub-lishes *Shopping for a Better World,* a guide covering a wide range of social re-sponsibility issues that has sold more than 1 million copies.[4] The guide rates companies or products on 10 dimensions of social responsibility: giving to char-ity, women's advancement, advancement of minorities, animal testing, disclo-sure of information, community outreach, involvement in South Africa, envi-ronmental impacts, family benefits (for employees), and workplace issues (e.g., outplacement or retraining of employees, unionization). It also notes whether firms have involvement in military contracts or nuclear power. The CEP was founded in 1969. The goal of this nonprofit research organization is "to inform and educate the American public and provide incentives for corporations to be good citizens responsive to the social concerns of all their stakeholders: employ-ees, neighbors, investors, and consumers" (p. 9).

The CEP's work during the 1980s was primarily in support of the ethical in-vesting movement. Providing information to consumers on CSR practices was a logical extension of these efforts. CEP founder Alice Tepper Marlin, in an inter-view with Davids (1990), explained that *Shopping for a Better World* "empow-ers people to support companies and bring products into their homes that coin-cide with their personal values" (p. 40). The CEP's study of buyers of the guide found that 78% said they had switched brands as a result, 64% refer to it regularly, and 97% consider environmental ratings the most important (Davids 1990). The sales of the guide speak to its impact. In addition, it has received praise from many quarters. Semon (1989), for example, wrote that "individual perceptions of good citizenship do influence buying decisions, and this influence will grow." He explained how the guide contributes to consumer pressure for CSR as follows:

> In many product areas, consumers are offered a wide array of virtually indistinguishable me-too brands. . . . Given essentially similar products at similar prices, the buyer will seek other differentiating criteria, and the barrage of corporate-image messages has focused attention on the corporation: Which one would I rather support by buying its product?

Further testament to the scope for positive marketplace pressures for CSR is the success of organizations that have adopted a social responsibility positioning in the consumer marketplace. In the United States, they include the Body Shop, Ben & Jerry's, and Tom's of Maine. However, these companies, more than most, are vulnerable to charges of hypocrisy. As the Body Shop has found, companies that adopt a social responsibility positioning might find that they are subject to attack if they fail to live up to their commitments to CSR practices, even when their social performance overall still is superior to that of most other firms (Smith 1996).

Surveys also regularly appear suggesting that consumer pressure is a force for CSR. A compelling example is a U.S. study by Walker Research and Analysis (1994) that found that 88% of consumers indicated they were much or somewhat *more* likely to buy from a company that is socially responsible and a good corporate citizen if the quality, service, and price are equal to those of competitors; fully 92% said that they would be much or somewhat *less* likely to buy from a company that is not socially responsible. Gildea (1994-95) summarized the Walker Research study by claiming that it is "empirical proof that attention to corporate social responsibility pays off" (p. 20).

The survey confirmed five areas that those surveyed regard as characterizing good corporate citizenship and social responsibility: business practices, community involvement, treatment of employees, environment concerns, and financial stability. In further confirmation of consumer interest in CSR practices, Walker Research and Analysis (1994) found that three-fourths of the sample already were refusing to buy from one or more companies. Gildea (1994-95) quoted Frank Walker, the company's chairman and chief executive officer, as saying,

> As more and more organizations meet the quality requirements of the marketplace, reputation and particularly factors pertaining to being good corporate citizens and socially responsible will differentiate the marketplace. . . . Good quality will be a given. Superior service is a must. Competitive price must be in the formula without question. Successful companies will plainly need to do more. The consumer will want to know what the company behind the product or service stands for in today's society and to make certain that [he or she is] not contributing to any corporation that is harming society, its resources or its people. (p. 21)

The findings of the Walker Research and Analysis (1994) survey and its implications are intuitively appealing and consistent with the argument of consumer pressure as a force for social responsibility. Moreover, they are in keeping with earlier studies by the Roper organization and many studies showing that consumers will say they are influenced by environmental concerns in their purchase decision making. However, these surveys must be viewed with some caution. Academic researchers are careful to minimize demand artifacts in their studies including the potential for respondents to give socially desirable responses when answering survey questions. Accordingly, expressions of environmental concern have not always translated into demand for environmentally benign products.

Conclusions and Directions for Future Research

This chapter has attempted to evaluate evidence for the proposition that corporate practices have changed in response to public interest group use or threat of consumer boycotts, and these changes often have benefited societal welfare. Despite the relative paucity of empirical research of consumer boycotts, it seems reasonable to conclude that consumer pressure is important in leading companies to adopt CSR practices.

From a theoretical standpoint, this consumer behavior may be explained as the exercise of consumer sovereignty (Smith 1990). In competitive markets, firms are driven by the imperative of customer satisfaction. If consumers have concerns about a firm's CSR practices, then they may well choose to support its more responsible competitors. There is ample anecdotal evidence that appears to confirm this claim. Companies have been subject to negative marketplace pressures, where they are penalized for poor CSR practices, in consumer boycotts. Evidence of positive marketplace pressure may be illustrated by the demand for guides such as *Shopping for a Better World* and the success of cause-related marketing. Empirical research provides some measure of support as well (Brown and Dacin 1997; Kahneman, Knetsch, and Thaler 1986; Kassarjian 1971; Kinnear and Taylor 1973; Miller and Sturdivant 1977; Roberts 1996; Webster 1975).

There are limits to the potential for the consumer marketplace to influence CSR practices. First, consumers must be aware of individual firm CSR practices. Friedman (1999) and Smith (1990) highlighted the role of the media and of pressure groups to identify CSR shortcomings, whereas Brown and Dacin (1997) noted that firms should communicate good CSR practices. Second, consumers must be concerned about these practices and willing to consider them within their purchase decision making. The studies of socially responsible consumption (e.g., Webster 1975) are indicative of how consumers may differ in their concern about CSR practices and their willingness to consider CSR in their purchase decision making. Although not all consumers will consider CSR, segments of concerned consumers clearly exist, and in any event, the effect may occur indirectly, with CSR practices forming part of a company's reputation

(Brown and Dacin 1997). Third, consumers must be able to act on their concerns by being in the market for the company's products and having the option of buying from more responsible competitors.

Most consumer markets are competitive, and firms in these markets are looking to find ways of improving their appeal to consumers and of avoiding the possibility of reasons for consumers to shop elsewhere. It is interesting to note that Davidson (1995) suggested that firms might view boycotts as a useful opportunity to build stronger relationships with customers:

> A threatened boycott, though never welcome, may provide an opportunity for a manufacturer to establish a unique relationship with its individual customers. . . . A group of customers will feel they have played a role in shaping the decisions of the company. And the manufacturer will have captured the dominant "mind share" of this group that no traditional marketing strategy . . . could have accomplished. (p. 79)

More fundamentally, a good reputation for CSR could well be a source of competitive advantage, and a poor reputation might place the firm at a disadvantage. Accordingly, Frank Walker, commenting on the Walker Research and Analysis (1994) "corporate character" study, concluded, "There are serious bottom line implications for business in our findings. . . . A strong reputation, built through good citizenship and corporate responsibility, is and will continue to be the trump card for organizations that plan to enter the 21st century in a leadership position" ("National Survey" 1994). This may increasingly be the case as marketers find it more difficult to achieve effective differentiation in today's highly competitive marketplaces. Corporate social performance may make a big difference at the margin.

Nonetheless, not all firms serve consumer markets, other firms have managers who might be less sensitive to consumer preferences, and some firms might serve consumer segments that are not concerned about CSR practices. In other cases, some CSR practices might be seen as too expensive despite the potential loss of competitive advantage if the practice is not adopted. However, there are other pressures on firms to be socially responsible. They might have an important role to play in addition to consumer marketplace sanctions.

Future Research

The topic of consumer boycotts clearly is important and in need of further research. Opportunities for future research include the following.

Consumer responses to boycott announcements. How effective are boycott announcements, and what are the characteristics of more effective boycotts? Friedman (1999, pp. 21-31) proposed many hypotheses as a research agenda. A reliable research study would be fraught with many methodological problems, not least of which are possible demand effects, as discussed earlier. One possibility might be to adapt the event study methodology that has been applied to studies of the effects of CSR on stock market prices. Perhaps using retail scanner data in conjunction with consumer databases, researchers might examine impacts on the consumer marketplace of boycott announcements. Experimental designs represent another approach (Burke, Milberg, and Smith 1993).

Management responses to consumer boycotts. Under what conditions do managers concede to public interest group demands when faced with the threat or call for a boycott of their firms' products? Smith (1990, pp. 266-75) identified responses on the basis of case study research. Survey research might be warranted. Furthermore, in light of management capitulation to group demands that are not ultimately considered socially responsible (e.g., Shell, McDonald's), under what conditions do managers resist such demands, and more preemptively, how can managers avoid such demands being made in the first place?

Consumer motivations for participation in boycotts. Theories of consumer motivation for boycott participation, perhaps along the lines proposed by Friedman (1999, pp. 21-22), could be developed and tested. This might include examination of the differences between boycotts that are group organized and boycotts that are simply individuals "shopping for a better world."

Public interest group strategies and tactics. Research in this area might need to be updated, particularly with public interest groups increasingly targeting firms directly and with the growing use of new information technologies such as Web sites (Friedman 1999, p. 226).

In addition to opportunities for further research on consumer boycotts organized by public interest groups, there remains a need to better understand the broader behavior of socially responsible consumption. Although new studies continue to look at the characteristics of the socially responsible consumer (e.g., Auger, Devinney, and Louviere 1999), perhaps another approach would be to assume that this behavior is not isolated to a given segment of consumers but rather is situation or issue specific. The premise that all consumers potentially may be influenced in their purchase and consumption behaviors by ethical or social responsibility considerations suggests that a useful direction for further research would be the antecedents of such behaviors. What prompts a consumer to exercise his or her "purchase vote" for or against a firm because of ethical or social responsibility considerations associated with the firm or its products? Brown and Dacin (1997), in particular, went some way toward answering this question. Further efforts would appear to be of importance not only to firms that might be affected but also, more generally, because of the potential impact that socially responsible consumption might have on the type of society in which we live.

Notes

1. This also is described as socially conscious consumption, environmentally concerned/responsible consumption, and ecologically concerned/responsible consumption.

2. In a further contribution to the socially conscious consumption literature, Murphy, Kangun, and Locander (1978) found racial variations, with blacks being less likely to respond to ecological issues than whites.

3. Brown and Dacin (1997) suggested that CSR associations often are unrelated to firms' abilities in producing goods and services. This is an important assumption for their studies. However, it is widely believed that firms that are more socially responsible have better managers, which might affect CA. For example, McGuire, Sundgren, and Schneeweis (1988) wrote, "Investors may consider less socially responsible firms to be riskier investments because they see management skills at the firm[s] as low" (p. 856).

4. The latest edition listed by *Books in Print* is 1994.

References

Anderson, W. Thomas, Jr. and William H. Cunningham (1972), "The Socially Conscious Consumer," *Journal of Marketing* 36 (July), 23-31.

Auger, Patrice, Timothy M. Devinney, and Jordan Louviere (1999), "Wither Ethical Consumerism: Do Consumers Value Ethical Attributes?" working paper, Australian Graduate School of Management, University of New South Wales.

Berkowitz, Leonard and Kenneth G. Lutterman (1968), "The Traditional Socially Responsible Personality," *Public Opinion Quarterly,* 32 (Summer), 169-85.

Berry, Jeffrey M. (1977), *Lobbying for the People: The Political Behavior of Public Interest Groups.* Princeton, NJ: Princeton University Press.

"Boycotting Corporate America" (1990), *The Economist,* May 26, 69-70.

Brown, Tom J. and Peter A. Dacin (1997), "The Company and the Product: Corporate Associations and Consumer Product Responses," *Journal of Marketing* 61 (January), 68-84.

Buchholz, Rogene A. (1991), "Corporate Responsibility and the Good Society: From Economics to Ecology—Factors which Influence Corporate Policy Decisions," *Business Horizons,* 34 (4), 19-31.

Burke, Sandra J., Sandra J. Milberg, and N. Craig Smith (1993), "The Role of Ethical Concerns in Consumer Purchase Behavior: Understanding Alternative Processes," in *Advances in Consumer Research,* Vol. 20, L. McAlister and M. L. Rothschild, eds. Provo, UT: Association for Consumer Research, 119-22.

Council on Economic Priorities (1991), *Shopping for a Better World.* New York: Ballantine Books.

Cowe, Roger (1999), "Boardrooms Discover Corporate Ethics," *Guardian Weekly,* March 28, 27.

Davids, Meryl (1990), "The Champion of Corporate Social Responsibility," *Business and Society Review,* 74 (Summer), 40-43.

Davidson, Kirk D. (1995), "Ten Tips for Boycott Targets," *Business Horizons,* March, 77-80.

Davidson, Wallace N., III, Abuzar El-Jelly, and Dan L. Worrell (1995), "Influencing Managers to Change Unpopular Corporate Behavior through Boycotts and Divestitures: A Stock Market Test," *Business & Society,* 34 (2), 171-96.

Dunfee, Thomas W. (1995), "Marketing an Ethical Stance," *Financial Times,* November 17, 13. (Mastering management supplement, Part 4)

Elkington, John and Julia Hailes (1988), *The Green Consumer Guide: High Street Shopping for a Better Environment.* London: Victor Gollancz.

———— and ———— (1989), *The Green Consumer's Supermarket Shopping Guide: Shelf by Shelf Recommendations for Products which Don't Cost the Earth.* London: Victor Gollancz.

————, ————, and Joel Makower (1990), *The Green Consumer.* New York: Penguin.

Frederick, William C. (1987), "Theories of Corporate Social Performance," in *Business and Society: Dimensions of Conflict and Cooperation,* S. Prakash Sethi and Cecilia M. Falbe, eds. Lexington, MA: Lexington Books, 142-61.

———— (1994), "From CSR$_1$ to CSR$_2$: The Maturing of Business-and-Society Thought," *Business & Society,* 33 (2), 150-64.

Friedman, Monroe (1985), "Consumer Boycotts in the United States, 1970-1980: Contemporary Events in Historical Perspective," *Journal of Consumer Affairs,* 19 (1), 96-117.

———— (1999), *Consumer Boycotts.* New York: Routledge.

Garrett, Dennis E. (1987), "The Effectiveness of Marketing Policy Boycotts: Environmental Opposition to Marketing," *Journal of Marketing,* 51 (April), 46-57.

Gildea, Robert L. (1994-95), "Consumer Survey Confirms Corporate Social Action Affects Buying Decisions," *Public Relations Quarterly,* 39 (Winter), 20-21.

Hayes, Arthur S. and Joseph Pereira (1990), "Facing a Boycott, Many Companies Bend," *The Wall Street Journal,* November 8, B1, B8.

Holbrook, Morris B. (1999), *Consumer Value: A Framework for Analysis and Research.* New York: Routledge.

Kahneman, Daniel, Jack L. Knetsch, and Richard Thaler (1986), "Fairness as a Constraint on Profit-Seeking: Entitlements in the Market," *American Economic Review,* 76 (September), 728-41.

Kassarjian, Harold H. (1971), "Incorporating Ecology into Marketing Strategy: The Case of Air Pollution," *Journal of Marketing,* 35 (July), 61-65.

Kinnear, Thomas C. and James R. Taylor (1973), "The Effect of Ecological Concern on Brand Perceptions," *Journal of Marketing Research,* 10 (May), 191-97.

————, ————, and Sadrudin A. Ahmed (1974), "Ecologically Concerned Consumers: Who Are They?" *Journal of Marketing,* 38 (April), 20-24.

Klein, Jill G., Richard Ettenson, and Marlene D. Morris (1998), "The Animosity Model of Foreign Product Purchase: An Empirical Test in the People's Republic of China," *Journal of Marketing,* 62 (January), 89-100.

Laidler, Harry W. (1968), *Boycotts and the Labor Struggle: Economic and Legal Aspects.* New York: Russell & Russell. (Original work published 1913)

McGuire, Jean B., Alison Sundgren, and Thomas Schneeweis (1988), "Corporate Social Responsibility and Firm Financial Performance," *Academy of Management Journal,* 31 (December), 854-72.

McMillan, G. Steven (1996), "Corporate Social Investments: Do They Pay?" *Journal of Business Ethics,* 15, 309-14.

Miller, Annetta, Carolyn Friday, Peter Annin, and Todd Barrett (1992), "Do Boycotts Work?" *Newsweek,* July 6, 58-61.

Miller, Kenneth E. and Frederick D. Sturdivant (1977), "Consumer Responses to Socially Questionable Corporate Behavior: An Empirical Test," *Journal of Consumer Research,* 4 (June), 1-7.

Mintzberg, Henry (1983), "The Case for Corporate Social Responsibility," *Journal of Business Strategy,* 4 (2), 3-15.

Murphy, Patrick E., Norman Kangun, and William B. Locander (1978), "Environmentally Concerned Consumers: Racial Variations," *Journal of Marketing,* 42 (October), 61-66.

"National Survey Finds Public's Concern for Corporate Social Responsibility Is Great Enough to Have Major Impact on Bottom Line" (1994), *Business Wire,* September 22.

Roberts, James A. (1996), "Will the Real Socially Responsible Consumer Please Step Forward?" *Business Horizons,* 39 (January-February), 79-83.

Rockefeller, David (1996), "America after Downsizing: Maximizing Society's Profits," remarks by David Rockefeller at the Economic Club of New York, September 12.

"Saints and Sinners" (1995), *The Economist,* June 24, 15-16.

Semon, Thomas T. (1989), "Consumers Have a Right to Judge Marketers by Their Social Policies," *Marketing News,* July 3.

Sethi, S. Prakash (1975), "Dimensions of Corporate Social Responsibility," *California Management Review,* 17 (3), 58-64.

Sharp, Gene (1973), *The Politics of Nonviolent Action.* Boston: Porter Sargent.

Shell International (1998), *Profits and Principles: Does There Have to Be a Choice?* London: Shell International.

Silk, Leonard and David Vogel (1976), *Ethics and Profits: The Crisis of Confidence in American Business.* New York: Simon & Schuster.

Smith, Craig (1994), "The New Corporate Philanthropy," *Harvard Business Review,* 72 (May-June), 105-16.

Smith, N. Craig (1990), *Morality and the Market: Consumer Pressure for Corporate Accountability.* London: Routledge.

——— (1996), "Corporate Citizens and Their Critics," *The New York Times,* September 8, F11.

——— (1999), "Ethics and the Typology of Consumer Value," in *Consumer Value: A Framework for Analysis and Research,* Morris B. Holbrook, ed. New York: Routledge, 147-58.

——— and Elizabeth Cooper-Martin (1997), "Ethics and Target Marketing: The Role of Product Harm and Consumer Vulnerability," *Journal of Marketing,* 61 (July), 1-20.

Varadarajan, P. Rajan and Anil Menon (1988), "Cause-Related Marketing: A Coalignment of Marketing Strategy and Corporate Philanthropy," *Journal of Marketing,* 52 (July), 58-74.

Vogel, David (1978), *Lobbying the Corporation: Citizen Challenges to Business Authority.* New York: Basic Books.

Vroom, Victor H. (1964), *Work and Motivation.* New York: John Wiley.

Walker Research and Analysis (1994), *Corporate Character: Highlights of a National Survey Measuring the Impact of Corporate Social Responsibility.* Indianapolis, IN: Walker Research and Analysis.

Webster, Frederick E., Jr. (1975), "Determining the Characteristics of the Socially Conscious Consumer," *Journal of Consumer Research,* 2 (December), 188-96.

Wilson, Des (1984), *Pressure: The A-Z of Campaigning in Britain.* London: Heinemann.

Wolman, Leo (1916), *The Boycott in American Trade Unions.* Baltimore, MD: Johns Hopkins University Press.

Wood, Donna J. (1991), "Corporate Social Performance Revisited," *Academy of Management Review,* 16 (4), 691-718.

Corporate Societal Marketing

Minette E. Drumwright
Patrick E. Murphy

- Avon and its 450,000 U.S. sales representatives have raised $22 million during the past five years for breast cancer education and screening efforts through a cause-related marketing initiative known as the Avon Breast Cancer Awareness Crusade.

- Anheuser-Busch spends millions of dollars annually on national advertising that encourages the responsible use of its beer, which translates into less consumption. Sixteen company employees work full-time on moderation campaigns, the best known of which is "Know When to Say When."

- In a Texaco ad, an African American businesswoman, a minority vendor, testifies that Texaco stood by her company through tough times, even when it had nothing to lose in severing the relationship. She insists that this was not tokenism; it was "the right thing to do."

- Ford Motor Company advertises its recycling activities through which items typically considered trash—"soda bottles, beer cans, telephones, tires"—are used to create new auto parts. "We don't just do it to save money. We do it to save the planet."

Each of these initiatives is very different, but the rubric of corporate societal marketing, as understood today, could incorporate all of them. Increasingly, companies are supporting myriad causes through diverse marketing activities. These activities have been described using a variety of terms including cause-related marketing, corporate social marketing, cause branding, cause marketing, cause advertising, issue advocacy, joint issue promotion, mission marketing, passion branding, social alliances, and enviropreneurial marketing. Although the labels are familiar and often used, little attention has been given to specifying the domain of this type of marketing, differentiating among its various forms, or examining how it works. We attempt to undertake these challenges in this chapter. Moreover, although it is ubiquitous, corporate societal marketing (the term we prefer and use in this chapter) has been one of the most controversial aspects of marketing from an ethical perspective. It has been heralded, on the one hand, as one of marketing's greatest contributions to society and has been lambasted, on the other, as marketing's most unabashed exploitation. No discussion of this topic would be complete absent a discussion of ethics. We conclude with a discussion of research needs and priorities.

Specifying the Domain

Corporate societal marketing has it roots in the general societal marketing concept. This concept was developed during the early 1970s by Kotler (1972) and is defined in the latest edition of his textbook as follows:

> The *societal marketing concept* holds that the organization's task is to determine the needs, wants, and interests of target markets and to deliver the desired satisfactions more effectively and efficiently than competitors in a way that preserves or enhances the consumer's and the society's well-being. (Kotler 2000, p. 25, italics in original)

Corporate societal marketing is a part of the broader domain of corporate social responsibility, which Brown and Dacin (1997) defined as the company's "status and activities with respect to its perceived societal obligations" (p. 68).

To specify the domain of corporate societal marketing, we begin with the definition of a corporate social marketing program by Bloom, Hussein, and Szykman (1995a):

> A *corporate social marketing program* is a corporate initiative where significant amounts of time and know-how of the marketing personnel who work for the corporation or one of its agents are applied toward achieving a major goal of persuading people to engage in a socially beneficial behavior. (p. 1, italics in original)

We think that the time has come to expand the definition, and we do so in several ways. First, the initiative could involve many types of company resources in addition to professional time and know-how including money, in-kind contributions, and grassroots volunteer support.

Second, the source of these resources need not be limited to the company's marketing personnel or the marketing budget. Increasingly, marketing tasks are performed by workers who are not officially designated as "marketing" personnel. In fact, this might be most characteristic of companies with higher degrees of market orientation. In addition, it is important to note that corporate societal marketing need not be limited to communications or even to marketing. For example, some aspects of "enviropreneurial" marketing can involve research and development, new product design, and packaging (Menon and Menon 1997; Varadarajan 1992). Certainly, resources from one of the company's agents or partners (e.g., advertising agencies, public relations firms) that are sponsored by the company may be involved as well. It also is important to acknowledge that the resources of the firm and its partners may be combined with those of a non-profit organization or governmental agency. Thus, the sponsorship need not be limited to the for-profit sector.

Third, although an objective related to social welfare must be present, it sometimes is not the sole or even a major objective. In studying company advertising with a social dimension, Drumwright (1996) found that an initiative could contain both economic and noneconomic or social objectives and that the weight given to noneconomic objectives can vary dramatically.[1] In a few cases, the noneconomic objective was all pretense. We do not require that noneconomic objectives dominate economic objectives, but we do require that an initiative have a legitimate noneconomic objective to be considered corporate societal marketing. The effort cannot be entirely cynical. That being said, we do not assert that objectives do not matter, a topic that we discuss as it pertains to measures of effectiveness.

Fourth, the noneconomic objective need not encompass actually persuading people to engage in a socially beneficial behavior, which is one of the final steps in the hierarchy of effects. It may involve an earlier stage in the hierarchy such as merely raising awareness of the cause, creating a favorable attitude toward the cause, or attempting to put the cause on the agendas of individuals, employees, customers, or the organization. For example, Benetton claimed that the purpose of its advertising campaigns with news photos on issues such as immigration, terrorism, violence, and political refugees was to prompt debate of serious social issues (Amos 1994; Coolidge 1994). Likewise, the stated objective of Liz Claiborne's "Women's Work" campaign is to raise awareness of domestic violence among target groups, which vary from year to year and have included college men and parents of preteens (Liz Claiborne Inc. 1996, 1998).

Finally, we use the term *initiative* rather than *program*. The latter connotes a sustained effort with a certain degree of import. An initiative can be more or less important or extensive than a program.

In sum, we offer the following definition: *Corporate societal marketing* encompasses marketing initiatives that have at least one noneconomic objective related to social welfare and use the resources of the company and/or one of its partners.

We believe that it is helpful to distinguish corporate societal marketing from *social marketing* and related terms such as *corporate social marketing* for three additional reasons. First, social marketing has come to connote efforts by non-profit organizations or public agencies in which noneconomic objectives are the primary purpose of the effort (Rangun and Karim 1991), if not the sole purpose (Andreasen 1994). Many of the initiatives falling under the rubric of corporate societal marketing have economic objectives that are weighted as heavily as, if not heavier than, noneconomic objectives. Second, social marketing generally is applied to programs, which are sustained efforts that often encompass multiple campaigns, rather than to less substantial efforts such as individual campaigns

(Andreasen 1994).[2] As noted earlier, our definition of corporate societal marketing encompasses initiatives that are both more and less substantial than programs. Finally, social marketing is designed to influence behavior (Andreasen 1994), as are corporate social marketing programs as defined by Bloom, Hussein, and Szykman (1995a, 1995b). Corporate societal marketing may or may not be so designed. It may involve earlier steps in the hierarchy of effects such as raising awareness or creating positive attitudes toward the cause. However, corporate societal marketing can encompass corporate social marketing programs, which have a dominant noneconomic objective of persuading people to engage in socially beneficial behavior. We now turn to the forms that corporate societal marketing takes.

Forms of Corporate Societal Marketing

The forms that corporate societal marketing takes are many and varied. We focus on 10 forms: traditional philanthropy, strategic philanthropy, sponsorships, advertising with a social dimension, cause-related marketing, licensing agreements, social alliances, traditional volunteerism, strategic volunteerism, and enterprises. We describe the ways in which these forms vary on four key dimensions, which are summarized in Table 8.1: emphasis given to economic objectives, employee involvement, types of resources deployed, and budget source. It is important to note that we describe general tendencies only; there are, of course, exceptions. Also, when various corporate societal marketing initiatives are combined in an integrated communications program, the forms, which are actually hybrids, often take on different characteristics.

Traditional Philanthropy

In a sense, all forms of corporate societal marketing are the progeny of traditional philanthropy, with its social goals, and traditional marketing, with its economic goals. Traditional philanthropy is perhaps the paradigmatic case of a company initiative with low emphasis on economic goals. In many instances, it has consisted largely of ad hoc responses to fund-raising appeals by writing checks, often to causes with which senior managers or their spouses have been personally involved. As such, cash contributions have been made from a philanthropy budget, and there has been little employee involvement. Few would argue that companies have not received any economic benefits from traditional philanthropy, but precisely because these benefits typically are indirect and ambiguous, strategic philanthropy emerged.

Strategic Philanthropy

Strategic philanthropy represents the tying of the philanthropy function and budget to the company's strategic objectives and markets. Although one could argue that traditional philanthropy never has been completely altruistic, during

TABLE 8.1 Corporate Societal Marketing: Forms and Dimensions

Form	Emphasis Given Economic Objectives	Employee Involvement	Types of Resources Deployed	Budget Source
Traditional philanthropy	Low	Low	Money	Philanthropy
Strategic philanthropy	Moderate	Low	Money, in-kind gifts	Philanthropy
Sponsorships	Moderate to high	Low to moderate	Money, in-kind gifts, volunteer support	Marketing
Advertising with a social dimension	Moderate to high	Low	Advertising expertise and expenditures	Marketing
Cause-related marketing	Moderate to high	Low	Advertising expertise and expenditures, money	Marketing
Licensing agreements	High	None	Contractual fees, co-branding support	Corporate, marketing
Social alliances	Low to moderate	Low to high	Advertising expertise and expenditures, personal selling, special events, in-kind gifts, money, professional expertise, volunteer support	Marketing, sales, philanthropy, community relations, corporate
Traditional volunteerism	Low	High	Volunteer support	Community relations
Strategic volunteerism	Moderate	High	Volunteer support, professional expertise, advertising	Community relations, marketing, human resources
Enterprises	Low to high	Low to high	Professional expertise from varied company functions	Corporate, marketing

recent years a pronounced effort has been made to link companies' philanthropic gifts to achieving their business goals. The gifts may even be viewed as a type of "investment" from which the companies hope to attain value (Deutsch 1997). As such, we have characterized strategic philanthropy's emphasis on economic goals as moderate and significantly stronger than that of traditional philanthropy.

Increasingly, contributions are in the form of "in-kind" gifts—products or services. For example, Johnson & Johnson gave away $52 million in cash and $70 million in products in 1997, most of which was directed to hospital-related causes (Deutsch 1997). This option is attractive to companies because they can value the in-kind gifts at their retail prices but manufacture them for significantly less. In addition, in-kind gifts can serve to showcase companies' products. For example, when a company donates cosmetics to a homeless shelter, the products are displayed to social workers, volunteers, and others who might be more likely to be paying customers than are the actual recipients. Like traditional philanthropy, the resources come from the philanthropy budget, and the level of employee involvement typically is low.

We consider strategic philanthropy as falling under the rubric of corporate societal marketing for three reasons. First, the strategic objectives to which it is tied most often include a marketing objective. Second, philanthropy generally becomes "strategic" only when key constituencies are informed of it through marketing communications. Third, many of the corporate social initiatives that we describe later in the chapter are accompanied by a philanthropic component.

Sponsorships

Sponsorships began as an extension of philanthropy to enable companies to tie their names to their contributions more directly. That is, companies make contributions—typically money and in-kind gifts but sometimes volunteer services—to support events with which their names are associated. During recent years, sponsorships have grown in popularity because they enable companies to avoid some of the inefficiencies of traditional advertising such as clutter. Although the majority of dollars spent on corporate sponsorships in North America are directed toward sports (Meenaghan 1998), the arts, education, and social causes also receive support. For example, the Walt Disney Company is a sponsor of the Special Olympics, providing financial and volunteer support. It then features its employees as they volunteer in advertisements that run on network television during family movies. Cigarette manufacturer Philip Morris has sponsored as many as 20 arts and sporting events annually to the tune of $50 million (Kluger 1996).

Crimmins and Horn (1996) explained the value of a sponsorship, which is related to the manner in which it enables a company to segment a market based on interests or psychographics, as follows: "Sponsorship improves the perception of a brand by flanking our beliefs about the brand and linking the brand to an event or organization that the target audience already values highly" (p. 12). We characterize the emphasis on economic goals in sponsorships as moderate to high because of the degree to which companies can receive credit for their support of the cause through the event itself along with its advertising and promotion. Typically, sponsorships are considered marketing initiatives, and their funding comes from the marketing budget rather than from the philanthropy budget. Employee participation ranges from low to moderate. Some employees might be rewarded with tickets and trips to the event, and at times, employees might provide volunteer support.

Advertising with a Social Dimension

Advertising with a social dimension is as diverse as the firms themselves and their interests. It is variously referred to as corporate social advertising, issue advocacy, issue promotion, cause advertising, corporate public service advertising, responsible use advertising, and moderation campaigns. The social dimension often is a part of corporate advertising, which is designed to enhance the company's reputation and to communicate its values and interests rather than to sell products.[3] However, it may appear in product advertising. The social dimension may be overt (e.g., Benetton's ads promoting AIDS awareness), or it may be subtle (e.g., Dow Brands' use of a child with Downs Syndrome as an actor in a Spray 'N Wash commercial). It may be defensive and reactive (e.g., the ad in which a minority businesswoman lauds Texaco for its buying from minority vendors that appeared shortly after Texaco was accused of racial discrimination).

The ads may advocate causes where the companies have an economic interest (e.g., Nike's support of young women and minorities participating in sports), or they may petition support for causes that do not appear to be tied to the companies' economic well-being (e.g., Timberland's campaign to end racism and bring about social justice). Efforts may even resemble public service ads, which once were the sole purview of nonprofit organizations and governmental agencies. For example, the campaign may warn consumers of the hazards of dangerous or addictive products produced by the company, advocating and modeling responsible use. Anheuser-Busch now sponsors commercials encouraging parents to educate their children about alcohol abuse, whereas Philip Morris runs a commercial in which teenagers are told not to smoke and highlights the dangers of smoking on its Web site.

When used by itself rather than in combination with other forms of corporate societal marketing, advertising with a social dimension has come to connote short-term, tactical, often superficial efforts. Because these initiatives often are perceived to be driven largely by commercial purposes, we have categorized the emphasis on economic objectives as moderate to high. The resources deployed on behalf of the cause typically are limited to the advertising expertise and expenditure involved in creating and placing the campaign, which is funded from the marketing budget. There typically is little employee involvement with the cause.

Cause-Related Marketing

Cause-related marketing[4] is perhaps the form most closely identified with corporate societal marketing. Although it typically involves a blending of sales promotion, advertising, and philanthropy, the distinctive characteristic of cause-related marketing is a promise by a company to make a donation to a designated social cause based on revenue-producing transactions by customers (Varadarajan and Menon 1988). It most commonly ties the sale of a specific product or service to a cause, with a portion of the proceeds donated to the cause. At times, a company's sales or profits in the aggregate are tied to a donation to a cause.

The first nationwide example of a cause-related marketing campaign was American Express's "Statue of Liberty" campaign in 1983 (Andreasen 1996). American Express pledged to donate to the restoration of the Statue of Liberty 1 cent every time its card was used in the United States and $1 every time a new card was issued during the fourth quarter. The promise of a donation served as a type of sales promotion, and the offer was widely advertised. As a result, card use increased 28% over the same period in the previous year, and a contribution of $1.7 million was made to the Statue of Liberty renovation.

Today, examples of cause-related marketing abound (see, e.g., the Business for Social Responsibility Web site, http://www.bsr.org). Avon sells pink ribbon pins depicting the international symbol of breast cancer for $2 and donates $1 to the National Alliance of Breast Cancer Organizations. Twice a year, Calphalon, a manufacturer of gourmet cookware, designates a cookware item, and Share Our Strength, an anti-hunger organization, receives $5 for each item sold in the United States. Patagonia donates 1% of its sales to groups focused on environmental protection and restoration. Wild Oats Community Markets donates 5% of sales on the first Wednesday of every month to various charities, some of which are designated by individual stores and others of which are designated by corporate headquarters.

Like advertising with a social dimension, cause-related marketing has gained a reputation for being short term and tactical rather than strategic in nature. The emphasis on economic objectives typically is moderate to high. The resources deployed are advertising expertise and expenditure along with the monetary donation, and these are funded by the marketing budget. Typically, there is little employee involvement.

Licensing Agreements

Licensing agreements enable companies to use nonprofits' names and logos in return for fees or percentages of revenues. Companies pay nonprofit organizations more than $500 million a year for lending their names to their products (Abelson 1999). For example, the American Cancer Society licensed its name and logo to SmithKlineBeecham to use on its NicoDerm CQ nicotine patch. Television ads describe the company and the society as "partners in helping you quit," featuring the society's name and logo. The Arthritis Foundation entered into a licensing agreement with McNeil Consumer Products, a division of Johnson & Johnson, and the result was a line of four pain relievers with the name "Arthritis Foundation Pain Relievers." Licensing agreements involve a strong emphasis on economic objectives and need not encompass much employee involvement beyond negotiating contracts. The resources deployed on behalf of the cause are the contractual fees and the co-branding support, both on packaging and through various other communications efforts. Funding may come from corporate sources as well as marketing budgets.

Social Alliances

Social alliances are collaborative efforts between companies and nonprofits that encompass close, mutually beneficial, long-term partnerships designed to accomplish strategic goals for both entities (Drumwright, Cunningham, and Berger 2000). They involve the sharing of resources, knowledge, and capabilities. Social alliances have been variously referred to as mission marketing, passion branding, cause branding, joint issue promotions, and cause partnerships.

The economic objectives that often figure prominently in social alliances tend to be "company oriented," involving communicating the essence of the companies' missions and values to key constituencies and/or achieving human resource management goals. This aspect is reflected in terms such as *mission marketing*.[5] Because of the close association between the companies and the causes, these initiatives also tend to involve co-branding of the companies and the causes, hence the terms *cause branding* and *passion branding*. This "branding" may be formal or informal.

The ongoing Avon Breast Cancer Awareness Crusade, which began in 1993, has been cited as representing "best practice" in social alliances (Andreasen and Drumwright forthcoming; Fellman 1999). It is based on a partnership between Avon Products Inc. and the National Alliance of Breast Cancer Organizations (NABCO). Through the crusade, Avon sales representatives have raised $22 million for breast cancer education and access to early detection by selling special merchandise such as pins with the insignia of the pink breast cancer ribbon. All profits from the pins are donated to NABCO to be distributed to community programs throughout the United States that promote education and access to screening services for underserved women. In addition, Avon's 450,000 U.S. salespeople have been trained to discuss breast cancer and the importance of early detection with their customers. They have distributed 80 million flyers on breast cancer detection. Some of them volunteer through local breast cancer-related organizations or through special events such as one of the Avon Breast Cancer Walks. The crusade has generated more than one billion media impressions.

Noneconomic objectives typically are given significant weight, but economic objectives may vary from low to high, depending on the alliance. As the Avon Breast Cancer Awareness Crusade illustrates, employee involvement often is moderate to high, particularly when the cause affects many employees. The types of resources deployed may include advertising expertise and expenditures, personal selling, special events, in-kind gifts, money, profession expertise, and volunteer support. Because social alliances often are expansive company-wide efforts, support often comes from multiple sources including the marketing, sales, philanthropy, community relations, and corporate budgets.

Traditional Volunteerism

Increasingly, volunteers are called on to solve some of society's biggest problems. Moreover, corporations are being asked to provide both incentives and venues to prompt their workers to volunteer. The effort led by General Colin Powell resulting from the President's Volunteer Summit is evidence of a trend that has been going on for some time. As a result of the summit, a number of companies announced new volunteer programs, most of which were expansions of existing programs (Barnes 1997). For example, Kimberly-Clark pledged that its workers will help to rebuild 37 playgrounds nationwide, and LensCrafters Inc. promised that its workers will provide free vision care to one million people by the year 2003. General Electric pledged one million employee volunteer hours (Deutsch 1997).

The emphasis on economic objectives is low to moderate, and employee involvement with the cause is high. The company resources deployed range from information and encouragement to paid time off for volunteer work. The budget source typically is community relations.

Strategic Volunteerism

As with philanthropy, volunteerism has evolved as well. Companies have found that volunteer programs can contribute to their competitive advantage and use them strategically, resulting in what Drumwright, Lichtenstein, and Braig (in progress) labelled "strategic volunteerism." They distinguish strategic volunteerism from traditional volunteerism in that it ties the company's volunteer initiatives more directly to its economic objectives. Strategic volunteerism typically involves focusing the company's volunteer efforts on a cause that is related in some way to the company's business and is important to its key constituents. We consider strategic volunteerism to be a form of corporate societal marketing because it becomes strategic when key constituents learn about a company's volunteer contributions. Thus, it must encompass communications efforts. For example, Kraft ran television ads in which its employees were shown volunteering at food banks. Timberland sponsored a print advertising campaign that showcased its philosophy of community action along with its new product lines (Fellman 1999). The ads provided a toll-free line for consumers to call for information about volunteer opportunities and about causes and organizations that Timberland and its employees support.

The emphasis on economic objectives tends to be heavier than traditional volunteerism because of the more overt tie to business goals and the credit that the company receives through the related communications programs. We characterize it as moderate. Like traditional volunteerism, employee involvement is high. Volunteer service events may be organized specifically for company employees, who may receive paid time off for volunteer work. However, because business priorities dominate, support for strategic volunteerism tends to be at a higher level of management than that for traditional volunteerism. Thus, in addition to volunteer support and advertising, the resources deployed on behalf of the nonprofit may include professional expertise such as assistance with management information systems, distribution, and retailing. The source of the support is likely to be not only the community relations budget but also marketing and perhaps human resource budgets.

Enterprises

At times, a company's commitment to a cause can be extended to encompass an enterprise designed to generate revenue. When practiced at the strategic level, enviropreneurial marketing is perhaps the prototypical case of a corporate social enterprise (Menon and Menon 1997; Varadarajan 1992). That is, best practice enviropreneurial marketing combines commitment to the natural environment with entrepreneurship and can spawn revenue-producing enterprises. One of the best-known proponents and exemplars of social enterprise is Tom's of Maine (Chappell 1993). All of the company's products use natural and environmentally safe ingredients. Tom Chappell, the company's founder, bases his business on a concept of goodness that has both practical and spiritual components. As another example, Dupont used the technical expertise that was developed through its in-house pollution prevention program to set up a consulting service for other companies (Kirkpatrick 1990). However, as Menon and Menon (1997) asserted, enviropreneurial marketing can range from tactical to strategic. Likewise, entrepreneurial marketing efforts could be evidenced through virtually any of the forms of corporate societal marketing.

Enterprises also can include nonprofit partners. For example, in 1995, Timberland, the boot and outdoor apparel company, and City Year, a Boston-based youth service corps, collaborated to create a new venture known as "City Gear," a line of apparel featuring the City Year name and logo (Austin and Elias 1996). The effort involved a high degree of joint decision making in the design and marketing of the line.

Because enterprises vary greatly, the emphasis on economic objectives may fluctuate, ranging from low to high. Likewise, the degree of employee involvement may differ substantially. Enterprises enable the deployment of professional resources from various company functions. Typically, support is broader than any single function and is appropriated from corporate coffers as well as from the marketing budget.

Corporate Societal Marketing: A Success?

For companies to sustain corporate societal marketing over time, the initiatives obviously must contribute to achieving, or at least not diminishing, the bottom line. Some firms hope to do this directly through creating breakthrough advertising and/or achieving a differential competitive advantage. Such efforts generally are based on the premise that companies can appeal to a segment of consumers who care about social causes, and there is some evidence that such a segment exists. For example, nationwide surveys have found that a majority of consumers say that they would be more likely to buy a product that supports a cause they care about and that cause marketing creates a positive corporate image (Cone Communications 1993, 1997). Webb and Mohr (1998) identified a segment of socially concerned consumers who react favorably to cause-related marketing even when they perceive the company's motivation as self-centered. However, other competing factors, such as price and convenience, often come into play, and corporate societal marketing is no magic bullet. Breakthrough advertising and sustainable competitive advantage are difficult to achieve in any context, and corporate social initiatives are no exception. In fact, consumers' reactions to corporate social initiatives appear to be particularly complex. They appear to be moderated by a host of factors including consumers' attitudes toward the cause itself, their prior beliefs about the company, their attributions regarding the company's motivations, their attitudes toward corporate social initiatives in general, and the relationship between the cause and the company's business (Brown and Dacin 1997; Blazing and Bloom 1999; Creyer and Ross 1997; Ellen, Mohr, and Webb 1997; Morton 1999; Sen and Bhattacharya 1999). Because of these complexities, sponsorship of socially oriented messages can actually result in a lowering of both attitudes toward a company and purchase intentions among some segments (Blazing and Bloom 1999; Morton 1999; Sen and Bhattacharya 1999). For example, Sen and Bhattacharya (1999) found that corporate social marketing initiatives adversely affected the purchase intentions of consumers who believe that these initiatives are achieved at the expense of a company's ability to produce high-quality products. In short, many companies have been disappointed in the power of corporate societal marketing initiatives to create a differential advantage that enhances the bottom line directly, especially in the short term.

The success of corporate societal marketing when used in a defensive manner—in an attempt to mitigate the damage from other company activities, respond to criticism, or counteract the harm that the company's products can do—is unclear. Although little empirical work has been done assessing the effectiveness of defensive uses of corporate societal marketing, that which has been done suggests that skepticism and negative attitudes toward companies among consumers limit effectiveness. For example, Webb and Mohr (1998) found evidence of a group of consumers who were predisposed to distrust cause-related marketing, whom they labeled "consumer skeptics." Morton (1999) found that when consumers had negative attitudes toward a company, company advertising with a social dimension did not counteract them. Blazing and Bloom (1999) discovered that companies were less effective than nonprofit organizations in influencing the attitudes of some consumers toward a social behavior.

By contrast, corporate societal marketing appears to be much more robust in achieving company-oriented goals such as motivating the workforce and communicating the essence of the company—its mission, values, and reason for being—to key constituents (Drumwright 1996). This effect probably is best explained by an increase in organizational identification or the degree to which workers define themselves by the same characteristics that define the organization. A high degree of organizational identification can result in job satisfaction, organizational commitment, and desirable work-related behaviors (Chatman 1991; Dutton, Dukerich, and Harquail 1994; O'Reilly and Chatman 1986; O'Reilly, Chatman, and Caldwell 1991). Two images or perceptions of a person's work organization shape the strength of organizational identification (Dutton, Dukerich, and Harquail 1994): (1) organizational identity, or what employees believe is distinctive, central, and enduring about the organization; and (2) construed external image, or what employees believe others think about the organization. Corporate societal marketing can affect both images that shape organizational identification.

The concept of organizational identification has been extended to encompass other key organizational constituents including consumers (Bhattacharya and Sen 1999; Lichtenstein, Drumwright, and Braig 2000) and workers in a company's advertising agency (Drumwright 1996). Thus, increases in organizational identification among consumers can enhance a company's reputation, which can translate into an increase in brand image and equity and can result in long-term sales increases.

In summary, there are four possible routes through which corporate societal marketing can enhance the bottom line. One is by creating what consumers perceive to be a differential advantage. A second is by mitigating the effects of criticism and/or problematic behavior by the company or its industry. A third is through increasing organizational identification among employees, which translates into loyalty and job commitment. The fourth is through increasing organizational identification among key consumers and other key external stakeholders. All of this is predicated on the requirement that the corporate societal marketing initiative has a genuinely positive impact on society.

Support for the potential value of corporate societal marketing comes from recent work profiling "visionary companies" (Collins and Porras 1994) and companies that have discovered the "soul of service" (Berry 1999). Chapter titles in these books reveal an underlying social motive, for example, "More than Profit" (Collins and Porras 1994) and "Generosity" (Berry 1999). These companies possess a number of similar characteristics, but one of the most central is the strong commitment to core values and a sense of purpose that leads to a dominant ideology. This consistency drives both the business and noneconomic objectives of the firm.

Companies that practice a "pragmatic idealism" tend to be companies that are more ideologically driven than purely profit driven (Collins and Porras 1994, p. 55). For example, this rationale led Merck to introduce and distribute the drug Mectizan in Africa to cure river blindness, even though the company had to give the drug away. The Johnson & Johnson Credo, the Hewlett-Packard "HP Way," and Motorola's more recent official statement ("For Which We Stand: A Statement of Purpose, Principle, and Ethics" represent well-known U.S. illustrations of firms with such core ideologies.[6]

A similar sentiment was expressed by Berry (1999) in his examination of leading service firms: "What is uncommon is the *centrality* and *depth* of this commitment" (p. 217, emphasis in original). Firms that see their mission and values as grounded in a larger social context behave in ways that reinforce their principles. A number of illustrations, from tuition reimbursement and scholarship plans for employees, to community service activities, to equipment donations and free services such as eyeglass examinations, were discussed. The outcome of these efforts is a creation of "social profit." The conclusion of Berry's study was expressed as follows:

> The central lesson of this book is that humane values power great service companies; generosity continuously reinforces and enriches these humane values. When the product is a performance, winning the hearts of the performers helps companies win the hearts of their customers. (Berry 1999, p. 218)

However, there is no insurance that corporate social responsibility in general or corporate societal marketing in particular will produce the desired results. In fact, the effects of corporate social responsibility on a company's financial performance are equivocal. Across a series of studies, there appears to be, at best, a weak positive relationship (for a review, see Stanwick and Stanwick 1998).

Corporate societal marketing may fail for all the reasons that traditional marketing fails and then some. For example, companies sometimes have blind spots regarding their own behavior, leaving them particularly vulnerable and open to criticism when they position themselves as socially responsible. Managers tend to recognize and give attention to social issues closely related to their organizations' core businesses, often seeming to ignore—or at least be untroubled by—similar issues further removed. For example, whereas managers at an energy company might be on the leading edge of initiatives related to energy conservation, they might be embarrassingly behind on issues of solid waste management. Constituents, expecting consistency across areas of potential social harm, perhaps will judge the energy company more harshly regarding its negligence about solid waste because it is claiming to be responsible on the basis of its energy conservation.

Sometimes, consumers' expectations might even become unrealistically high for companies using corporate societal marketing, expecting companies to be beyond reproach on all issues at all times—a state of perfection that is unachievable. Companies such as the Body Shop and Ben & Jerry's most likely have found consumer and societal expectations to be unreasonably high at times. Finally, a boomerang effect, which creates the opposite of the desired effect, can occur when messages prompt cynical reactions from key constituents, who are dubious of the companies' intent for corporate societal marketing, perceiving the companies as exploiting the causes.

Concerns about exploitation raise the issue of intent. That is, do the company's intentions for engaging in marketing with a social dimension matter? If the outcomes for society are positive, then does it matter that the company's objectives are predominantly or even completely economic? From a managerial perspective, several findings have a bearing on this question (Drumwright 1994, 1996). First, when initiatives have both noneconomic and economic objectives, there is a tendency over time to gravitate toward greater emphasis on the noneconomic objectives. Second, individuals who initially oppose the social initiative but become engaged in it for economic reasons tend to convert. That is, the socially responsible behavior "takes," and commitment to the cause increases. Third, corporate societal marketing, whatever the motivation, can have positive social benefits.

Given these findings, one might argue that intentions might be irrelevant. However, intentions and objectives matter greatly in terms of how success is measured (Drumwright 1996). For example, initiatives with heavily weighted economic objectives often are evaluated using conventional methods such as copy testing, number of media impressions, tracking studies, and sales. The more conventional the measures, the higher the hurdles for corporate societal marketing and the more likely the initiatives are to be "scapegoats" when the company's economic performance is disappointing.

As the emphasis on noneconomic objectives increases, evaluation methods tend to become both more qualitative and more informal as companies assess the initiative's impact on employees and key constituents. Because corporate societal marketing tends to be more robust in meeting objectives related to communicating with and motivating key constituents, it is more likely to be perceived as successful when measured in these terms. When noneconomic objectives are dominant, companies tend to create and use measures related to the cause such as the number of people requesting information, volunteering for the cause, or actually engaging in the socially responsible behavior. Incorporating noneconomic measures ensures that society will benefit as well.

Evidence does exist that a company's intentions or motives regarding its corporate societal marketing matter to consumers. For example, Webb and Mohr (1998) found that the more consumers perceived a company's motives as "other oriented" as opposed to self-oriented, the more receptive they were to cause-related marketing. Blazing and Bloom (1999) found that perceptions that a company's motives were not "pure" can have at least a short-term negative impact on individuals' attitudes toward the social message and even toward the social behavior.

Ethical Challenges

For all its potential for good, corporate societal marketing has been harshly criticized. Moderation campaigns, such as the Anheuser-Busch ads encouraging the use of designated drivers, have been much debated. Critics claim that they are nothing more than brand advertising in disguise (DeJong, Atkin, and Wallack 1992), whereas advocates assert that company-sponsored moderation ads are more effective than public service announcements, especially with young, heavy-drinking males (Ringold 1999). Implied endorsements of company products by nonprofits also have been the target of regulators. Nonprofit organizations involved in licensing with companies typically claim that they endorse no products, a claim that hardly seems plausible. State attorneys general also disagree with the claim. For example, in late 1998, a dozen state attorneys general were concerned that the NicoDerm ads involving a licensing agreement with the American Cancer Society were misleading and misrepresented the organization's involvement with the product (Abelson 1999). SmithKline settled with the states for $2.5 million and now spells out in the ads that "SmithKline makes an annual grant to the American Cancer Society for cancer research and education for the use of its seal." Advertising with a social dimension and cause-related marketing have long been criticized for exploiting causes for commercial purposes. The television ad for Stain Stick from Spray 'N Wash that featured a child with Downs Syndrome was referred to as the "most crassly contrived slice-of-life advertising in history" and was accused of "putting a stain on advertising that no laundry product can remove" (Garfield 1993, p. 50). But others, including activists from the cause community, were ardent defenders of the ad.

In a chapter on ethical issues facing social alliances, Andreasen and Drumwright (forthcoming) discussed a number of ethical issues that are common to corporate societal marketing more generally. They grouped the ethical questions into two general categories: macro ethical issues and micro ethical issues for participants in corporate societal marketing.

Macro ethical issues might not be evident at the level of an individual initiative, but when the aggregate impact of corporate societal marketing on society is considered, they may be quite problematic. For example, what if companies choose to affiliate only with popular, uncontroversial causes and big, well-known nonprofit organizations? This phenomenon is referred to as "cherry picking" and is particularly problematic when one considers that, in many cases, the importance of a cause is not correlated with popularity or attractiveness. Disincentives to support unpopular causes can increase. In addition, corporate support might not mean a bigger pie for social causes. Government might feel "off the hook," and its sense of responsibility and accountability to social issues in general and in particular can be lessened. In this scenario, unpopular causes would be even more disadvantaged.

Variations of the "God and Mammon" question are raised at the macro level. Can social and economic interests be combined without tainting the nonprofit organization and rendering the corporate initiative less than optimally effective? Friedman (1970) anchors one end of the spectrum with his position that the social responsibility of business is to generate profits for stockholders and jobs for workers—period. By contrast, others assert that corporations have multiple stakeholders to whom they are responsible, with society being a prominent one (Donaldson and Dunfee 1995). Bloom, Hussein, and Szykman (1995b) proposed that social marketing initiatives be put to the following two-question test regarding their societal impact: (1) "Is society better off because of this program?" and (2) "Has corporate involvement allowed this program to perform better than it would if it were managed by only a nonprofit or government agency?" (p. 11). Still others hold the position that corporate societal marketing is good for business and can increase a corporation's bottom line (Weeden 1998).

Micro ethical issues for corporate societal marketing participants involve both outcomes and procedures (Andreasen and Drumwright forthcoming). Fund-raising raises a number of potential ethical problems, many of which involve cause-related marketing. Specifically, the manner in which the donation is structured and the proportion of the proceeds that the company keeps for itself can be problematic. This is the case especially if either the nonprofit partner or consumers more generally are misled to think that the donation is much larger than it actually is. For example, problems might arise when the terms of the donation are left unspecified or when the contribution is stated in terms of profits, giving the company leeway in terms of how to allocate costs. These tactics do not represent ethical problems per se, but they can become ethical problems, especially if there is deception. In addition, the donation can be structured as fixed or variable. Timberland committed to provide City Year with a fixed sum of $5 million over five years, not anticipating that it would experience financial difficulties and layoffs. It then was faced with competing demands and interests of shareholders, employees, and City Year and with the difficult task of deciding how to be fair to each group (Austin and Elias 1996). Are companies accountable for their stewardship vis-à-vis causes? It is not clear in such situations what is the most ethical response.

How donations are raised can pose ethical questions. For example, American Express has been heavily criticized for two of its cause-related marketing campaigns, "Charge Against Hunger" and "Statue of Liberty," because far more was spent on advertising the initiatives than was given to the causes. Companies, which often wield more power in the relationship, also have been criticized for imposing unfair requirements and restrictions on nonprofit organizations. These may include "noncompete" or "exclusivity" agreements, which can hinder nonprofits' ability to raise money. Companies also may attempt to place restrictions on grant making or to put pressure, even if subtle, on nonprofit leaders to "hold their tongues" and refrain from speaking out on controversial topics. These requirements and restrictions could substantially alter nonprofits' impact. In short, there always is the possibility of a Faustian bargain. Although nonprofits are unlikely to place overt restrictions on companies because of their characteristically weaker negotiating position, this possibility should not be overlooked given that it could interfere with companies' fiduciary responsibilities.

The company and its business practices can create difficulties for the nonprofit. For example, does a nonprofit organization that participates in a social marketing initiative with a tobacco or alcohol company taint its image or dilute its effectiveness? Moreover, is the association itself unethical if, say, the nonprofit is about the well-being of children? What happens to the credibility of such a nonprofit organization whose corporate partner is exposed for using child labor in Third World countries?

In judging the ethical impact of corporate societal marketing, the well-known ethical theories—consequences-based, duty-based, and principle-based approaches—can provide some guidance. Of course, depending on the ethical paradigm chosen, one sometimes can get different answers. The consequences-based approach, often called utilitarianism, would evaluate a corporate societal marketing initiative according to the outcomes or consequences that it produces. That is, does the initiative produce overall positive outcomes for the company, the nonprofit organization, consumers, and society at large? A duty-based approach would assert that an initiative should be judged not by its consequences but rather by the intentions of the parties involved. It asks what the objectives of the various parties are and whether they are worthy, and it often sets a high and particularly stringent ethical standard. For example, if in cherry-picking causes, companies' intentions were to take the easy way out, then the initiatives would be likely to be judged as unethical. A principle-based approach would examine the basic principles (e.g., justice, truth, compassion) on which the initiative is based. It would attempt to assess whether the initiative upholds or mitigates such principles.

Future Research

Corporate societal marketing appears to be ensconced in the repertoire of marketing strategies and tactics, and there is every reason to expect it to continue to evolve in practice. Although one must be wary of its potential ethical challenges, corporate societal marketing is capable of providing "win-win-win-win" opportunities that create compelling benefits for companies, nonprofits, consumers, and society. However, as the preceding discussion has illustrated, achieving positive results for any one of the parties involved—not to speak of all of them—can be quite complicated. Thus, much more research is needed.

Achieving a win for the organizations involved in corporate societal marketing, whether companies or nonprofits, is largely dependent on the manner in which their various key constituents react. In this context, anticipating consumer reactions is particularly challenging. The reactions are anything but straightforward and can be affected by any number of factors that often vary across segments including attitudes toward the cause itself, prior beliefs about the company, attributions regarding the company's motivation, and attitudes toward corporate societal initiatives in general. Numerous research questions remain. For example, what other factors affect reactions to corporate societal marketing, and how do the various factors interact? How can initiatives be designed and managed to leverage positive reactions and mitigate negative ones? What are the mechanisms through which these initiatives have their desired effects? Organizational identification might be one, but are there others? If so, then how can they be operationalized and measured? How would one do a cost-benefit analysis, encompassing both financial and ethical dimensions, for the organizations involved? When initiatives span across sectors—combining the resources of companies, nonprofits, and government, as they often do—how can the different sectors collaborate to work effectively on these initiatives?

For consumers to win, corporate societal marketing must provide them with compelling benefits that increase their overall welfare. What benefits do corporate societal marketing initiatives *actually* provide consumers? Are they direct benefits such as increased satisfaction with their interactions with commercial or nonprofit organizations? Are they higher levels of intrinsic reward? Are the real benefits to consumers indirect through the betterment of society?

Determining whether there really is a win for society through corporate societal marketing is perhaps the most complicated question of all, but the question must be asked and answers must be attempted. We turn again to the two-question test proposed Bloom, Hussein, and Szykman (1995b): (1) "Is society better off because of this program?" and (2) "Has corporate involvement allowed this program to perform better than it would if it were managed by only a nonprofit or government agency?" (p. 11). The questions are the right ones, but how does one make such determinations? What criteria should one use, and what would be the appropriate measures?

During the past few years, corporate societal marketing has proliferated and expanded in both its scope and the forms that it takes (reconsider Table 8.1). Therefore, we need, at once, to broaden our scope of analysis while being more precise about what form of corporate societal marketing we are examining. Much existing research has focused on the forms with substantial advertising components such as cause-related marketing and advertising with a social dimension. Other forms—especially social enterprises, social alliances, and strategic volunteerism—deserve more attention and research. What is the potential of these less familiar forms, and how should their effect be measured? How can they be designed most effectively? Hybrid initiatives, in which multiple forms are encompassed under the auspices of a single program or initiative, also warrant more investigation. How can the various forms be designed and combined most effectively?

In short, opportunities for research abound. They present both the conventional marketing challenges of assessing and measuring marketing outcomes (e.g., increases in organizational reputation, brand equity, and sales, albeit in a more complicated context) and new challenges related to assessing marketing's impact on broader constituencies including society at large.

To achieve a win-win-win-win for all parties, corporate societal marketing must be better understood and practiced more effectively. In this chapter, we have made a start. We attempted to expand and reconceptualize the domain of corporate societal marketing, which encompasses the many and varied corporate initiatives with a social dimension. We identified the various forms, differentiated among them, and examined how they bring about their desired effects. We raised ethical concerns and questions for future research. Much remains to be done.

Notes

1. A noneconomic objective is related to providing individual benefits or societal benefits or both.

2. For a thorough explication of social marketing, its definition, and its domain, see Andreasen (1994).

3. See Waltzer (1988) for a discussion of corporate advertising and the forms that it takes.

4. Cause-related marketing often is referred to as cause-related advertising or cause marketing.

5. See Duncan and Moriarty (1997, pp. 126-47) for an explication of the "mission marketing" aspect of social alliances.

6. It is interesting and significant that Johnson & Johnson and Hewlett-Packard were ranked Nos. 1 and 3, respectively, in the recent Reputation Quotient survey (Alsop 1999).

References

Abelson, Reed (1999), "Sales Pitches Tied to Charities Attract Scrutiny," *The New York Times,* May 3, A1.

Alsop, Ronald (1999), "The Best Corporate Reputations," *The Wall Street Journal,* September 23, B1, B20.

Amos, Denise Smith (1994), "Bosnia Ad Dips Benetton into Debate Again," *St. Petersburg Times,* March 7, 13. (Business section)

Andreasen, Alan R. (1994), " Social Marketing: Its Definition and Domain," *Journal of Public Policy & Marketing,* 13 (Spring), 108-14.

———— (1996), "Profits for Nonprofits: Find a Corporate Partner," *Harvard Business Review,* 74 (November-December), 47-59.

———— and Minette E. Drumwright (forthcoming), "Alliances and Ethics in Social Marketing," in *Ethical Issues in Social Marketing,* Alan K. Andreasen, ed. Washington, DC: Georgetown University Press.

Austin, James E. and Jaan Elias (1996), *Timberland and Community Involvement* (Harvard Business School Case No. 9-796-156). Boston: Harvard Business School Press.

Barnes, Julian B. (1997), " 'New' Volunteering, or Just Newly Packaged? Hyping Corporate Do-Gooding at the Summit," *U.S. News & World Report,* May 12, 46.

Berry, Leonard (1999), *Discovering the Soul of Service: The Nine Drivers of Sustainable Business Success.* New York: Free Press.

Bhattacharya, C. B. and Sankar Sen (1999), "The Company of a Consumer: The Scope and Relevance of Organizational Identification in Consumer Behavior," working paper, Boston University.

Blazing, Jennifer and Paul N. Bloom (1999), "How Perceptions about the Purity of Sponsor Motives Affect the Persuasiveness of Socially Oriented Communications," working paper, University of North Carolina at Chapel Hill.

Bloom, Paul N., Pattie Yu Hussein, and Lisa Szykman (1995a), "An Assessment of Corporate Social Marketing Programs," in *Proceedings of the Society for Consumer Research: Role of Advertising in Social Marketing.* Washington, DC: Society for Consumer Research, 1-5.

———, ———, and ——— (1995b), "Benefiting Society and the Bottom Line: Businesses Emerge from the Shadows to Promote Social Causes," *Marketing Management,* 4 (Winter), 8-18.

Brown, Tom J. and Peter A. Dacin (1997), "The Company and the Product: Corporate Associations and Consumer Product Responses," *Journal of Marketing,* 61 (January), 68-84.

Chappell, Tom (1993), *The Soul of a Business: Managing for Profit and the Common Good.* New York: Bantam Books.

Chatman, Jennifer A. (1991), "Matching People and Organizations: Selection and Socialization in Public Accounting Firms," *Administrative Science Quarterly,* 36 (September), 459-84.

Collins, James C. and Jerry I. Porras (1994), *Built to Last: Successful Habits of Visionary Companies.* New York: HarperBusiness.

Cone Communications (1993), *Cone/Roper Study: A Benchmark Survey of Consumer Awareness and Attitudes toward Cause-Related Marketing.* Boston: Cone Communications.

——— (1997), *Cone/Roper Cause-Related Trends Report.* Boston: Cone Communications.

Coolidge, Shelley Donald (1994), "Thriving on Controversy, Benetton Stays Out Ahead," *Christian Science Monitor,* May 26, 9.

Creyer, Elizabeth H. and William T. Ross (1997), "The Influence of Firm Behavior on Purchase Intention: Do Consumers Really Care about Business Ethics?" *Journal of Consumer Marketing,* 14 (6), 421-32.

Crimmins, James and Martin Horn (1996), "From Management Ego Trip to Marketing Success," *Journal of Advertising Research,* July-August, 11-21.

DeJong, W., C. K. Atkin, and L. Wallack (1992), "A Critical Analysis of 'Moderation' Advertising Sponsored by the Beer Industry: Are 'Responsible Drinking' Commercials Done Responsibly?" *Milbank Quarterly,* 70 (4), 429-42.

Deutsch, Claudia H. (1997), "Corporations Adopt a Different Attitude: Show Us the Value," *The New York Times on the Web,* December 9.

Donaldson, Thomas and Thomas W. Dunfee (1995), "Integrative Social Contracts Theory: A Communitarian Conception of Economic Ethics," *Economics and Philosophy,* 11 (April), 252-84.

Drumwright, Minette E. (1994), "Socially Responsible Organizational Buying: Environmental Concern as a Noneconomic Buying Criterion," *Journal of Marketing,* 58
(July), 1-19.

——— (1996), "Company Advertising with a Social Dimension: The Role of Noneconomic Criteria," *Journal of Marketing,* 60 (October), 71-87.

———, Peggy H. Cunningham, and Ida E. Berger (2000), "Social Alliances: Company/
Nonprofit Collaboration," Working Paper No. 00-101, Marketing Science Institute.

———, Donald R. Lichtenstein, and Bridgette M. Braig (in progress), "Strategic Corporate Volunteerism," working paper, University of Texas at Austin.

Duncan, Tom and Sandra Moriarty (1997), *Driving Brand Value: Using Integrated Marketing to Manage Profitable Stakeholder Relationships.* New York: McGraw-Hill.

Dutton, Jane E., Janet M. Dukerich, and Celia V. Harquail (1994), "Organizational
Images and Member Identification," *Administrative Science Quarterly,* 39 (June),
239-63.

Ellen, Pam Scholder, Lois A. Mohr, and Deborah J. Webb (1997), "Can Retailers Benefit
from Cause Marketing?" working paper, Georgia State University.

Fellman, Michelle Wirth (1999), "Cause Marketing Takes a Strategic Turn," *Marketing
News,* April 26, 4.

Friedman, Milton (1970), "The Social Responsibility of Business Is to Increase Its
Profits," *The New York Times Magazine,* September 13.

Garfield, Bob (1993), "This Heavy-Handed Ad Exploits Someone New," *Advertising
Age,* May 10, 50.

Kirkpatrick, David (1990), "Environmentalism: The New Crusade," *Fortune,* February
12, 44-54.

Kluger, Richard (1996), *Ashes to Ashes.* New York: Knopf.

Kotler, Philip (1972), "What Consumerism Means for Marketers," *Harvard Business
Review,* 50 (May-June), 48-57.

——— (2000), *Marketing Management,* 10th ed. Upper Saddle River, NJ: Prentice Hall.

Lichtenstein, Donald R., Minette E. Drumwright, and Bridgette M. Braig (2000),
"Increasing Customer-Corporation Identification by Partnering with Nonprofits: A
'Win-Win-Win' for Customer, Corporation, and Nonprofit," working paper, Univer-
sity of Colorado, Boulder.

Liz Claiborne Inc. (1996), "New Liz Claiborne PSA Campaign Uses High Profile College Football Student Athletes to Reposition Relationship Violence as a Men's Issue,"
press release, September 23.

——— (1998). "Starting Early: New Handbook Helps Parents Talk to Pre-Teens about
Healthy Relationships; 60% of Teenagers Have Experienced Some Form of Abuse in
Dating Relationships," press release, November 17.

Meenaghan, Tony (1998), "Current Developments and Future Directions in Sponsorship," *International Journal of Advertising,* 17 (1), 3-28.

Menon, Ajay and Anil Menon (1997), "Enviropreneurial Marketing Strategy: The Emergence of Corporate Environmentalism as Market Strategy," *Journal of Marketing,* 61
(January), 51-67.

Morton, Cynthia R. (1999), "Corporate Social Advertising's Effect On Audience Attitudes toward Company and Cause," unpublished doctoral dissertation, University of
Texas at Austin.

O'Reilly, Charles and Jennifer Chatman (1986), "Organizational Commitment and Psychological Attachment: The Effects of Compliance, Identification, and Internalization on Prosocial Behavior," *Journal of Applied Psychology,* 71 (August), 492-99.

————, ————, and David F. Caldwell (1991), "People and Organizational Culture: A Profile Comparison Approach to Assessing Person-Organization Fit," *Academy of Management Journal,* 34 (September), 487-516.

Rangun, V. Katuri and Sohel Karim (1991), *Teaching Note: Focusing the Concept of Social Marketing.* Boston: Harvard Business School Press.

Ringold, Debra (1999), "Alcohol Advertising and Moderation Campaigns: The Modeling of Normative Drinking Behavior," working paper, Willamette University.

Sen, Sankar and C. B. Bhattacharya (1999), "Does Doing Good Always Lead to Doing Better? Consumer Reactions to Corporate Social Responsibility," working paper, Boston University.

Stanwick, Peter A. and Sarah D. Stanwick (1998), "The Relationship between Corporate Social Performance and Organizational Size, Financial Performance, and Environmental Performance: An Empirical Examination," *Journal of Business Ethics,* 17 (2), 195-204.

Varadarajan, P. Rajan (1992), "Marketing's Contribution to Strategy," *Journal of the Academy of Marketing Science,* 20 (Fall), 335-43.

———— and Anil Menon (1988), "Cause-Related Marketing: A Coalignment of Marketing Strategy and Corporate Philanthropy," *Journal of Marketing,* 52 (July), 58-74.

Waltzer, Herbert (1988), "Corporate Advocacy Advertising and Political Influence," *Public Relations Review,* 14 (Spring), 41-55.

Webb, Deborah J. and Lois A. Mohr (1998), "A Typology of Consumer Responses to Cause-Related Marketing: From Skeptics to Socially Concerned," *Journal of Public Policy & Marketing,* 17 (Fall), 226-38.

Weeden, Curt (1998), *Corporate Social Investing: New Strategies for Giving and Getting Corporate Contributions.* San Francisco: Berrett-Koehler.

Advertising and Competition

Andrew V. Abela
Paul W. Farris

Does advertising increase or decrease competition? Our purpose in this chapter is to advance the understanding of this question, and particularly the impact of advertising on price, by critically reviewing recent research, adding some new insight, and identifying areas for future research. The main conclusions that we draw are that research should focus more on absolute price levels than on relative price differences (price dispersion) and that the significant impact of distribution policy on price needs to be examined more closely.

Accordingly, the chapter is divided into four sections. In the first section, we lay out the question, provide some initial assumptions and definitions, and set the scope for the discussion. In the second section, we summarize the opposing views that typically define debate around the question. In the third section, we provide a critical review of recent work on this question as well as some research that we think brings additional important perspective. In the final section, we present our own conclusions about the question and identify areas for future research.

The Question

Interest in the question of the impact of advertising on prices often starts with the observation that companies with relatively higher advertising budgets also usually charge higher prices. Consumers are willing to pay higher prices for a number of reasons that include advertising as well as superior product quality, better packaging, more favorable user experience, market position, and warranty and/ or service. When these latter nonadvertising factors are assumed equal, we can ask why consumers can be expected to generally pay more for the advertised products. This is a question that invites all sorts of speculation—the implied confidence of manufacturers that are willing to advertise, mere familiarity or reminder effects, and even the psychic value of lifestyles associated with advertised brands. We claim no particular insight into these reasons, but we do find it difficult to believe that consumers would be willing to pay more for a product whose sole distinction is that it is *un*advertised. Therefore, the fact that advertised products tend to have higher prices is not very significant given that the opposite is highly unlikely (Farris and Reibstein 1979, 1997). On the other hand, what conclusions about levels of competition and of absolute retail prices in a market or category can we draw from the observation that prices of advertised brands usually are higher than those of nonadvertised, functionally equivalent products? And why might such differences exist?

In particular, we seek to expand the scope of the discussion to recognize that there are three important groups of actors: consumers, manufacturers, and retailers. We believe that understanding the effect of advertising on consumers' price sensitivity (although a significant challenge) would not be enough to definitely answer the question of whether advertising ultimately makes products more expensive. We need to integrate our knowledge of these effects with assumptions and models of manufacturer (seller) and retailer (middleman) behavior. As retailers, manufacturers, and consumers react to each other, there is no problem in running out of fresh material in this investigation. These interactions create new pricing and promotional strategies, such as yield management, that are more sophisticated methods for delivering targeted discounts. Technology is an enabler of these new strategies, as is the predicted rapid growth of the "friction-less" Internet economy (e.g., "bots" that search the Web for low prices), which adds further complication to the question.

We begin by providing three important assumptions and some definitions of price that will help to establish the scope of this discussion.

Assumptions

The impact of advertising on price competition and, hence, on price is part of the much larger network of effects that determine the degree to which commercial advertising is socially beneficial. We make three assumptions to simplify these effects for the purpose of our analysis.

Assumption 1: Products Are Only Imperfect Substitutes

When we speak of competition in this chapter, we do not have in mind the economic concept of "perfect" competition (an equilibrium condition under which marginal profits equal marginal costs and no manufacturer or supplier has the freedom to raise prices). Instead, we start from the assumption that products are only imperfect substitutes and that most manufacturers and retailers enjoy some limited product differentiation, market power, or other advantage that gives them realistic pricing options. In other words, there is some variation in prices that may result in higher or lower sales volume, but these variations are within the operating range of the company. The whole notion of price comparisons would be rendered invalid if we were to assume, however, that every product was so "different" as to justify whatever price differences were observed. We also need to recognize that each purchase is made at a unique point in time and space and that some different utility is associated with that timing and location. A cold soft drink is worth more on a hot day at a ballpark than on a cold day in a warehouse club store. Unlike classical markets, we accept that imperfect competition results in a certain amount of price dispersion for functionally equivalent products. We need to find ways in which to make sense of this level of dispersion.

Assumption 2: Resellers Play an Important Role in Stocking and Promoting the Product

Given this assumption, our focus is on analyzing advertising's influence on the marketer's ability to raise prices without losing appreciable percentages of sales volume (price inelastic) *or* to gain large increases in sales by only lowering price by a small amount (price elastic). Under different circumstances, either of these options would look good to marketers. Interestingly, the same product can provide both opportunities at different levels in the value chain at a particular point in time. As an example, take a leading product, such as Tylenol, that most retailers would agree absolutely had to be in stock. An increase in the price of this product *to all* retailers is not likely to cause much change in volume sold by all retailers in the short term. A temporary change in the *retail* price of the product by a single highly visible retailer, however, could lead to significant volume change for that particular retailer in the near term if brand switchers were drawn to it and loyal consumers stocked up (or vice versa). Tylenol then would be said to be price inelastic at the manufacturer level and price elastic at the retail level. If the price decrease were perceived by consumers to be permanent, however, then it is less likely that stocking up would occur. Thus, temporary price variations are part of the landscape as well. Indeed, retailers often resort to devices such as "clearance sales" and "going out of business sales" to communicate to consumers that the low prices are a temporary phenomenon and that consumers should "buy now."

Assumption 3: Quality Levels Already Are Established

The third assumption in our analysis of advertising-price relationships is that quality levels and product differences already have been established and, thus, are stable. We recognize that, in reality, these always are changing and that advertising has an essential role in communicating such changes. Over the long term, the incentive to invest in R&D activities that improve product quality and to invest in advertising and promotion programs that bring these innovations to market cannot be completely separated from the ability to use advertising to command higher prices and profit margins. The long-term role of advertising must include the ability of advertising to stimulate new product investments. It may do this by improving the new product introduction process and the diffusion of innovation as well as by providing margins and incentives to invest in marketing and R&D. If innovators could not capture the fruits of their new ideas and risk-taking activities, then the innovation process would suffer. Advertising, especially mass advertising, is helpful for introducing new products quickly and in a way that enables the innovator to capture value. Even if profit margins at any given time are "too high," we also must consider whether the market system that produced these margins is at the same time encouraging the development and introduction of innovative new products. Certain inefficiencies in finding the lowest price for a given quality level are arguably compensated for if the overall result is a productive process of replacing obsolete products.

Premium price strategies create margins that are available to invest in the risky activities of funding R&D projects and launching new products. These prices and margins compensate for the failed innovations as well. To ignore the uncertainties in this process would be to fundamentally misapprehend the management decision process concerning budgets for both. Although this is an essential part of the dynamic process that results in increased advertising and higher prices for certain products, the scope and focus of this chapter compels us to make the strong assumption that quality levels already have been established. Price comparisons are meaningful only when they are made among items of similar quality or among the same items sold at different times or in different markets.

Definitions

Measuring prices sounds simple enough but is complicated quickly by the need to distinguish among different types of prices. Therefore, we provide definitions of some of the different types of prices that we believe are important and yet often overlooked.

For the purpose of this discussion, *manufacturer price* is the manufacturer's selling price. Except in situations where there are intervening parties such as distributors, this price usually is the retailer's purchase price. *Retail price* is the retailer's selling price. As used here, it is synonymous with the consumer's purchase price. *Relative price* is the ratio between the price of the cheapest brand versus the price of the most expensive brand (measured in either retail or manufacturer prices) among functionally equivalent products. To distinguish from relative price, we use the term *absolute price,* which we use to denote the mean of the prices of all such brands (weighted by share of sales). Such an absolute price assumes that we are able to calculate the average price per statistical unit across different sizes, forms, and other product variations in a meaningful way. *Price range* is the difference between the highest and lowest prices available for the functionally equivalent products. There are other more developed measures of price dispersion (Brynjolfsson and Smith 1999), but for a nonempirical discussion, simple differences will suffice. Any empirical examination of these prices also has to deal with the problem of coupons, rebates, manufacturer allowances, and shipping/transportation costs. These complications can confuse measurement. In the extreme, retailers might not be sure of their own selling prices (e.g., when retailers offer to triple the value of manufacturer coupons) or even purchase prices (e.g., when manufacturer rebates are grouped across product lines or are not available until the end of period and contingent on sales goals).

By *functionally equivalent* products, we mean products that are identical in their functional capabilities with regard to normal use and, hence, are substitutable in the eyes of the consumer who cares only about functional benefits (however difficult this type of equivalence might be to determine in practice). At the same time, however, we maintain that such a consumer is not necessarily the typical consumer and that benefits beyond purely functional product benefits can have a significant effect on consumer choice and, therefore, serve as a basis for differentiation. A recent survey of consumer purchasing habits for automobiles and cosmetics conducted for McKinsey & Company, for example, indicated that, in each case, a sizable segment of consumers valued benefits arising from the process of acquiring the product and from their relationship with the company *more than* the product's functional benefits. These segments represented 19% of the automotive buyers and 43% of the cosmetics buyers in the survey (Court et al. 1999).

Scope of Inquiry

We recognize that there are potential effects of advertising at the macro level, both positive and negative, such as driving the growth of new industries and creating a culture of consumption. We also note that the desirability of any given product always will be dependent on the existing technological, political, and cultural environment and that advertising seems to be firmly entrenched as part of our culture. Advertising practices always are evolving, and today there might be more concerns with the idea of how strong brands are priced than with advertising per se. There are other methods of building brands with nontraditional media such as sponsorships and point-of-purchase promotions. For example, limiting tobacco advertising does not seem to have hurt Marlboro. Indeed, some firms fear that the absence of advertising will increase the brand's dominance. The use of the Web to promote brands undoubtedly will become more important and probably more difficult to regulate.

Nevertheless, we limit our exploration to the micro level, and particularly to those situations in which there are no radical technological shifts or new competitors entering. We assume away all of these complications so as to sharpen our focus.

Within the scope of our inquiry, we are primarily interested in whether advertising results in consumers paying higher prices than they otherwise would pay (Figure 9.1). This is related to, but not exactly the same as, the notion of an efficient market as defined by Ratchford and colleagues (1996): a market in which

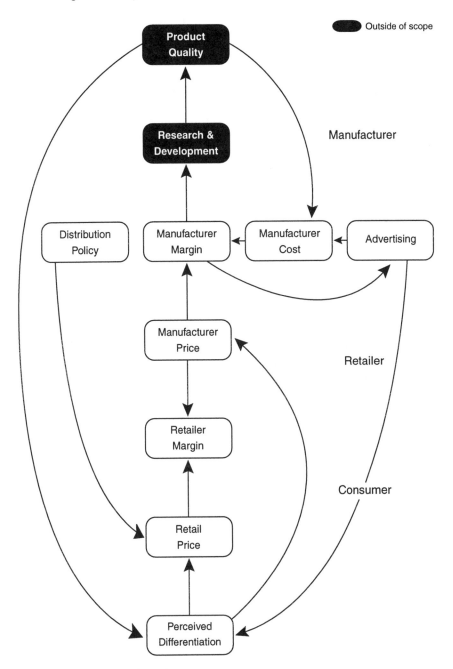

Figure 9.1. Scope of Discussion

"actual or potential losses to individual consumers, which result from imperfect information about alternatives . . ., are or can be large" (p. 168). The imperfect information is about prices and qualities of alternatives.

Opposing Views

Economists have long used two principal models to describe the effects of advertising on price paid, the results of which appear to contradict one another. In the *advertising = market power* model, advertising is thought to influence consumer tastes, establish brand loyalty, and ultimately raise profits and consumer prices by decreasing price sensitivity and competition. In the *advertising = information* model, advertising is seen as providing information to consumers, resulting in increased price sensitivity, lower prices, and reduced monopoly power (Farris and Reibstein 1997). Both models have provided important contributions to the discussion, and both still have their followers.

Market Power Model

Proponents of the market power model argue that advertising too often creates the impression of higher quality where marginal or no product differences exist. There is little doubt that in many cases marketers attempt to justify price premiums and escape the intensity of price competition by using advertising to communicate marginal product benefits to consumers. Some brands, such as Absolut vodka, would not likely be able to charge their current prices without the support of advertising. Vodka is tasteless, colorless, and odorless, making it difficult to find characteristics on which to differentiate. (Thus, vodka manufacturers typically compete on "purity," e.g., asserting that their products are *more* tasteless, colorless, and odorless than the competition.) Perhaps a classic case is Extra Strength Tylenol, which was built on the claim, "You can't buy a more potent pain reliever without a prescription." Strictly speaking, the claim is only one of parity performance, asserting that no stronger product exists, and makes no comment as to whether there are any other products that are equally strong (and, in fact, there are several). Yet, the brand grew steadily with the help of this advertising claim (Strenio 1996).

Information Model

Proponents of the information model argue that our ability to determine whether there really are no differences among products is suspect and that we are better off allowing consumers to make their own decisions. This model argues that advertising makes consumers aware of alternatives and tries to highlight product quality differences that might not otherwise be apparent to the extent that this is possible. For example, to overcome the difficulties of advertising vodka just noted, Gray Goose vodka advertised the results of an "expert panel" that gave its product the highest marks in taste tests including Absolut and several other brands. By becoming more aware of viable alternatives—increasing their "evoked set"—consumers can become more price sensitive (Mitra and Lynch 1995). At the same time, by making real product differences more clear, manufacturers can lead consumers to pay more for certain products when they recognize their unique benefits.

Complications

In addition to the fact that the implications of the two models presented oppose each other, there are several other complications with the current understanding of the advertising and price debate. First, there are several somewhat contradictory ways of understanding the causal relationship between advertising and price. Second, there is significant difficulty in estimating the relationship between advertising and price premium. Third, brand loyalty has ambiguous implications. Fourth, the impact of the Internet promises to add significant complexity.

Causal Relationships

Two popular views see the direction of causality flowing from advertising to higher prices. The first view is that advertising is a "cost." As such, firms that advertise must charge higher prices to cover this cost. Furthermore, it is argued that if advertising were eliminated, then consumer prices could be reduced by the percentage of sales that advertising constitutes—about 2% to 3% for a wide variety of products, but as much as 30% to 40% for some others. Marketers themselves implicitly buy into this argument when they look at advertising and price promotion as competing for a share of marketing budgets instead of as complements. In the extreme, there is some truth in this view.

The second causal view also runs from advertising to prices. We assert that most marketers believe that increased advertising will enable them to charge higher prices (to some degree). Although some marketers might argue that it is higher quality that gives advertisers "something to say" in the advertising to justify higher prices, it need not always be the case that highly advertised products have superior quality. This is particularly true if the superior quality is not easily perceived or is easily believed (Borden 1942). Advertising, in this view, shifts the demand curve out (more volume sold at all possible prices) and may change the slope of the demand curve, making demand less responsive to price at higher prices. Firms with high advertising expenditures might have more options, but even these firms expect lower sales volumes for higher prices. Such firms also must find the combination of price and volume that maximizes (or "satisfices") total profits.

An alternative causal view presents the opposite direction of causality—that higher prices cause increased advertising by increasing the amount that marketers are willing to "pay" for incremental sales. The key intervening variable is gross profit margin. Empirically, it has been found that gross profit margins (before marketing and other fixed costs) are the single most important predictor of higher advertising-to-sales ratios among cross sections of firms and businesses (Buzzell and Farris 1977; Farris and Albion 1981; Farris and Buzzell 1979). Of course, higher gross profit margins also can result from lower costs of distribution or production. Therefore, we believe that, all else being equal, the firm with lower costs usually will advertise more as a percentage of sales. Clearly, the pricing and advertising decisions cannot be easily separated, even for functionally equivalent products. As joint decisions that affect each other, the causality is difficult to conceptualize and does not lend itself to simple empirical tests (Dorfman and Steiner 1954; Farris and Reibstein 1979, 1997).

Advertising and Price Premium Relationship

Even for specific brands, it often can be difficult to tell how advertising works on price premiums and sensitivity to price differences. For example, Quelch (1986) reported the results of a General Electric (GE) experiment on advertising for light bulbs. After GE aired advertising emphasizing the benefits of its soft white bulbs, the percentage of consumers who rated these bulbs as "very good value" increased by at least double the increase for competitive brands when the GE bulbs were priced at parity to competitors. When the GE bulbs were premium priced, their value rating still increased after this advertising, although only marginally. When the competitor bulbs were premium priced, their value ratings declined (p. 408). The implications of such a relationship between advertising and price premium are not clear-cut. Although the marketer could sell more at the higher price, the parity price is relatively more attractive after the advertising than before.

Brand Loyalty

Brand loyalty for the manufacturer also can result in higher or lower price sensitivity, depending on the time frame, on the types of prices, and on whether demand shifts are measured across or between retailers. A brand-loyal consumer is not necessarily less price sensitive. A distinction needs to be made between price differences among different brands and price differences in the same brand over time. Imagine the reaction of two consumers faced with a sale on a product. One is very brand loyal to the product, whereas the other is not. Which consumer is likely to buy more of this product when it is on sale (and, thereby, appear to be more price sensitive)? We assert that the brand-loyal consumer likely will buy more because the nonloyal one is happy to buy whatever goes on sale next week, whereas the loyal one will stock up while the brand is on sale. In this way, brand-loyal consumers can appear to be more price sensitive, at least to price differences for the same brands from week to week and from retailer to retailer. However, the same loyal consumer might continue to buy the brand if prices were increased relative to those for other brands. The reader should consider which price sensitivity is being measured with weekly or daily scanner data on sales and prices.

Impact of the Internet

The question of the impact of advertising on price developed and evolved through an era when the basic issues were defined in terms of the physical shipment of products and their promotion through periodic price reduction events. This question would appear to become more complicated and interesting with the growth of Internet commerce. The promise of frictionless transactions adds a new dimension to the problem while also providing the opportunity for new insights. No simple model explains all of the evidence.

Critical Review of Recent Research

Several recent empirical generalization studies, or meta-analyses, have summarized the findings from the substantial number of studies relevant to our question: Lodish and colleagues (1995) and Vakratsas and Ambler (1999) on advertising effectiveness; Ratchford and colleagues (1996) on market efficiency; Kaul and Wittink (1995) and Mitra and Lynch (1995) on advertising and price. We discuss each of these in turn along with selected individual studies.

Understanding the effect of advertising on price is complicated by the fact that, after 100 years of research, we still are not sure exactly how the effects of advertising occur. Beginning with the first formal advertising model in 1898, advertising has been primarily explained using "hierarchy of effects" models. However, these have been seriously questioned recently. Hierarchy of effects models propose that advertising works through a determined series of effects such as first gaining attention, then peaking interest, then creating desire, and finally motivating action. Yet, Vakratsas and Ambler's (1999) review of 250 journal articles on how advertising affects consumers concluded that there is little support for such hierarchy of effects models. Lodish and colleagues' (1995) meta-analysis of 389 split-cable television advertising experiments between 1982 and 1988 also emphasized how little we know about what makes advertising work. Although conventional wisdom holds that more advertising leads to more sales, Lodish and colleagues found "no obvious relationship between the magnitude of a weight increase [in advertising] and the significance of the impact on sales" (p. 128). They found that "the data explain less than half of the variance in sales changes associated with [television] advertising weight changes" (p. 138).

These two studies would seem to call for a major rethinking of our approaches to understanding the effects of advertising. This rethinking would include our approaches to understanding the impact of advertising on price competition.

Market Efficiency

Part of the difficulty with the debate on the effect of advertising on price has been that, until recently, there was no comprehensive theoretical framework to address consumer welfare aspects of pricing. Ratchford and colleagues (1996) made a significant contribution conceptualizing this problem by proposing a theoretical model to integrate existing findings. The focus is on determining measures of market efficiency, defined in terms of "actual or potential losses to individual consumers" (p. 168) resulting from imperfect information about alternatives. They reviewed the several different measures of market efficiency that have been used in previous studies: price-quality correlations, measures based on a frontier relation between prices and characteristics, and price dispersion. They related each of these to a model of economic welfare and determined that, whereas the first two measures have serious limitations,[1] price dispersion does measure the variance in consumer surplus in this model when there is no variance in quality. Recognizing further limitations, they still concluded that

> the large order of magnitude of efficiency estimates observed in many markets across many studies makes it hard to avoid the conclusion that consumers are often presented with the opportunity to pay higher prices than they need to for a given quality and that many probably do so. (p. 177)

We would argue, however, that the use of price dispersion—relative price—rather than absolute price to measure the impact of prices on consumer welfare is problematic. Ratchford and colleagues (1996) allowed that measurements of market efficiency (including price dispersion) do not take into account the different types of value added offered by different retail outlets: "Retailer services can enhance utility and should be counted . . ., though they rarely are in published data such as the *Consumer Reports* data employed in many studies of market efficiency" (p. 172). We believe that extending the model proposed by Ratchford and colleagues to include space/time utility is a critical next step. Consumers typically are willing to pay a higher price for the identical item from a different retailer because of greater convenience in place or time, for example, or even because the shopping experience is more pleasant. Many varieties of products are available at different times and places where they might not otherwise be without the higher margins required to support them. Aspirin comes in various dosage sizes, coatings, forms (e.g., capsules, tablets, caplets, liquid), and package counts. These variations and their potential importance to different segments mean that we need to develop a theory of price dispersions that takes into account the opportunity that consumers have to purchase products at various prices. Assume, for example, that a small shop in an airport decides to add aspirin to its assortment of other products sold. Such a shop is likely to charge higher prices and margins than do most other retailers. Airport shops are able to do this, not because headaches are more severe in airports but rather because they have local monopolies. Higher income customers for whom time is a premium also are part of the equation. We do not believe that consumers, in the aggregate, are worse off because they now have this additional opportunity to purchase aspirin. Yet, both the average purchase price and the dispersion of prices likely will increase.

The Ratchford and colleagues (1996) studies measured price dispersion of "physically identical items across different outlets in a given retail market" (p. 168). "Physically identical" clearly means items that are physically *functionally* identical; this includes differentially branded and advertised products that nevertheless have the same functional performance. The problem is that highly advertised brands typically will have higher price dispersions because they are more widely distributed across a large number of retail formats with a great variety of margins. Private label products, on the other hand, typically are sold in only one chain and, therefore, have far less price dispersion.

Store Check Illustration

We illustrate our concern with a recent store check (which should not be interpreted as anything except an illustration of the point) and two hypothetical examples. We looked at extra-strength acetaminophen caplets across different distribution channel types, selected for the different levels of convenience they offer (i.e., drug store, warehouse, convenience store, gas station, airport shop). We noted the prices of a major national brand's caplets[2] (Tylenol) and those of store brand caplets in each channel type (where available). Across this sample, the price dispersion of the national brand only was 1.4× (highest to lowest price) for the 24-pack and 1.3× for the 250-pack of caplets (Exhibit 9.1). There was no dispersion across channel type for the store brand because each channel type carried a differentially labeled store brand. Dispersion of all the store brands together was 1.3× for the 50-pack and 2.5× for the 500-pack. Dispersion across the national and store brands combined was 1.7× for the 24-pack and 2.1× for the 250-pack. We also looked at price dispersion across *sizes* (in terms of cost per caplet). The national brand had dispersions of 1.3× (highest to lowest price per caplet) in the convenience store channel and 2.4× in the drug store channel. The store brand dispersion was as high as 4.6× in the warehouse channel. Comparing across brand, channel, *and* size, it is possible to buy extra-strength acetaminophen for as little as 0.8 cents a caplet (warehouse store brand, 500-pack) or as much as 37.5 cents a caplet (airport shop, 2-pack), representing a price dispersion of nearly 50×.

Exhibit 9.1

Variable	Price Dispersion (range)
Channel	1.3× to 2.5×
Brand	1.6× to 2.1×
Size	1.3× to 4.6×

The central problem with price dispersion (relative price) rather than absolute price as a measure of market efficiency is that much of price dispersion could be explained by the legitimate increases in convenience offered by different distribution channels.

Hypothetical Illustration 1

Consider also the case in Exhibit 9.2. This illustrates a hypothetical but not unrealistic situation in which a higher relative price coincides with a lower absolute price. Recall that relative price is the ratio or difference between the price of the most and least expensive of a functionally equivalent product, measured in this case at retail; this is the same as price dispersion. Absolute price is the average price of the same set of products. Scenario A represents a situation in which the advertised brand (typically the national brand) goes on deal (i.e., is discounted by the retailer) frequently. In this case, it is off deal during Week 1 and on deal during Week 2 at a significant retail price discount. In Scenario B, the advertised brand does not go on sale; it is *every day low priced.* The unadvertised brand (typically the private label product) is assumed not to go on deal in either scenario. In addition, we make a simple and realistic assumption that when the advertised brand is on deal, its sales increase at the expense of the unadvertised brand sales as well as at the expense of its own nondeal sales. The resulting situation has Scenario A with a higher relative price but a lower absolute price, whereas the opposite occurs in Scenario B. Which scenario increases consumer welfare? We would argue that consumers are, in aggregate, clearly better off in Scenario A. Although the relative price (or price dispersion) is higher, the average amount paid is lower. Furthermore, the opportunity for consumers to find the product at lower prices is enhanced in Scenario A.

Exhibit 9.2	*Scenario A: Advertised Brand Frequently On Deal*		*Scenario B: Advertised Brand Is Every Day Low Priced*	
	Week 1	*Week 2*	*Week 1*	*Week 2*
Retail price				
Advertised brand	$5.00	$3.00	$4.00	$4.00
Unadvertised brand	$2.90	$2.90	$3.00	$3.00
Units sold				
Advertised brand	5	25	10	10
Unadvertised brand	10	5	10	10
Absolute price		$3.19		$3.50
Relative price		1.67×		1.33×

NOTE: In both scenarios, the unadvertised brand is every day low priced.

Hypothetical Illustration 2

For a twist on the preceding example, imagine a situation in which Scenario A offered a higher relative price (price dispersion) and a higher absolute price, whereas Scenario B offered a lower relative and absolute price. Would Scenario B be the more attractive one in every case? Not necessarily. The lowest price in Scenario A is lower than the lowest price in Scenario B; a very low price is available in Scenario A, for those who desire it, that is not available in Scenario B. We believe that whether the choice to buy at that lowest price is "informed" or "uninformed" cannot be determined merely from the existence of a wide dispersion of prices. Ratchford and colleagues (1996) argued—correctly, we believe—that consumer choice probabilities must be taken into account when evaluating the potential losses from an inefficient market, and this weighting of price by choice probabilities is very similar to our concept of an absolute price.

Increases in Welfare

We also should recall that a wide price dispersion on a particular product can even lead to *increases* in consumer welfare when it helps to serve market segments that could not afford the product if prices were closer to the mean (Schmalensee 1981). Although questions of the effect of price on distributive justice are outside the scope of this chapter, it would be interesting to explore to what extent greater price dispersion can actually benefit society. Such benefits might result from a transfer of wealth from segments that are willing to pay a premium for the same item for services (e.g., convenience) to segments that are willing to go through extra effort (e.g., clipping coupons) to get the cheapest possible price on that item. It seems to us that there is implicit recognition of this in discounts that typically are offered, for example, to seniors and students. Any serious inquiry along these lines must take into account the influences of mobility and education. For example, poorer consumers often have *less* ability to search for the best price (e.g., do not own cars, cannot afford to buy in bulk, cannot afford warehouse club membership fees). As stated earlier, these issues are interesting but outside the scope of this chapter.

The Internet and the Role of Price Dispersion

Recent work on Internet commerce also highlights the inadequacies of price dispersion as a measure of consumer welfare. A study of prices of books and music CDs sold through a number of Internet and traditional retailers found that the price dispersion of CDs sold on-line was approximately equal to that of CDs sold in traditional outlets, whereas the price dispersion of books actually was *higher* over the Internet. This is a surprising finding given the low search costs of the Internet. It led the authors to conjecture that something other than market inefficiency was at work (Brynjolfsson and Smith 1999). Because there probably is far less variation in the mobility, wealth, and education among those buying on-line than among the rest of the population, these findings are particularly interesting.

Overall, although we believe that Ratchford and colleagues (1996) made a significant contribution to the question of market efficiency measurement, we find that price dispersion is an inadequate and potentially misleading measure of impact on consumer welfare.

Reconciling the Market Power and Information Schools

There have been three attempts to reconcile the apparent contradictions between the market power and information schools. These attempts discussed the retailer-manufacturer dynamic, the importance of preference strength and consideration set size, and the difference between price and nonprice advertising. We briefly review each.

Retailer-Manufacturer Dynamic

Albion and Farris (1987) argued the importance of recognizing the retailer-manufacturer dynamic. They noted that manufacturers do not set consumer prices by giving a certain margin to retailers. In fact, the opposite usually is the case, with retail margins being a *result* of the retailers own pricing decisions. The authors argued that retail price decisions can be significantly affected by a manufacturer's advertising if such advertising increases the demand for a product and the amount of retailer competition on that product. Retailers might choose to accept a lower margin on a strongly advertised brand so as to drive traffic, build store image, and/or increase inventory turnover. When retailers take different profit margins on similar products, products with similar manufacturer prices can have significantly different retail prices. In some extreme cases, the manufacturer's price of one product can be higher than that for another, but because of the difference in retail margins, the retail price is *higher* for the product with the *lower* manufacturer's price. In all cases, the effects of promotion, such as coupons and rebates, must be included in the price paid (Ailawadi, Farris, and Shames 1999).

In the just-mentioned work, Albion and Farris (1987) showed that, by and large, the evidence on advertising and price elasticity is consistent with the notion that advertising decreases price elasticity for manufacturers and increases price elasticity for retailers. This earlier work was later buttressed by research showing lower retail gross margins for highly advertised national brands (Albion and Farris 1987). Together with analyses showing higher gross margins and higher relative prices for high-advertising manufacturers, there is support for the argument that advertising helps manufacturers differentiate their products (advertising = market power) but induces greater retail price sensitivity, more intense retail price competition, and lower retail margins (advertising = information).

The mitigating role of the existence of private label products in price also is significant. The best competition involves comparison between brands and between retailers, both interstore and intrastore competition. Private label products are not subject to interstore comparison, but they do provide price control through intrastore competition, offsetting the power of advertising to enable marketers to charge a higher price.

Preference Strength and Consideration Set Size

A second synthesis was provided by Mitra and Lynch (1995), who argued that whether advertising increases or decreases price sensitivity will depend on two mediating variables: relative strength of preference and consideration set size. Advertising provides information about product differences among products, and this can increase consumers' relative strength of preference and, therefore, decrease price elasticity. Advertising also provides information about the availability of substitutes, and this can increase consumers' consideration set and, therefore, increase price sensitivity. In addition, beyond providing information on the existence of substitutes, advertising provides recall cues and, thereby, increases the number of effective substitutes considered at the time of choice. . . . For product markets in which consumers have to rely on memory to generate alternatives, the effects of increased advertising by brands may be to increase price elasticity. (p. 657)

If there are other stimuli increasing the consideration set (e.g., point-of-purchase material), then advertising will not have the same effect on the consideration set.

One concern with this attempted solution is that it is difficult to separate the two types of information (product difference and availability of substitutes). Although different ads were used in the study for reminding and differentiating, Mitra and Lynch (1995) recognized that "some amount of confounding is inevitable" (p. 657). The same advertising message can communicate product difference to one consumer segment and availability as a substitute to another segment. Consumers who already are aware of it as a credible substitute might perceive the ad as a differentiation message, whereas consumers who are not might receive it as an availability message.

A separate limitation in understanding the impact of advertising on price sensitivity is that research typically assumes that buyers know the prices of the products they consider for purchase. When research participants cannot recall the prices of the products being studied, the conclusion often is made that price information was not so relevant in their decisions (Dickson and Sawyer 1990). However, Monroe and Lee (1999) recently argued that what consumers remember explicitly is not necessarily a good indicator of what they know implicitly and that price information that is not remembered consciously still can exert an influence on buying decisions.

Price and Nonprice Advertising

The third attempt at reconciliation is Kaul and Wittink's (1995) empirical generalization of 18 studies. This research highlighted the difference between price and nonprice advertising. The authors found that empirical studies performed across many categories showed that an increase in price advertising leads to increased price sensitivity among consumers. They also found studies of the effect of local advertising on price. These studies concluded that the use of price advertising leads to actual lower prices. (These studies included categories where local advertising was prohibited in some regions and not in others [e.g., legal services, prescription medicines, eyeglasses, eye examinations], allowing for comparisons between regions with and without local advertising for the same products.)

In looking at nonprice advertising, Kaul and Wittink (1995) found several studies showing that an increase in nonprice advertising leads to lower price sensitivity among consumers. Their main argument explaining these results was that "non-price advertising is used for positioning purposes, thus making the brand more differentiated, which, if successful, may result in lower price sensitivity for the brand" (p. G156). However, their thesis was not universally supported by the data; several studies also showed nonprice advertising leading to increased price sensitivity.

Kaul and Wittink (1995) focused on the distinction between price and nonprice advertising. Early on in their article, they recognized that price advertising generally is run by retailers and nonprice advertising is run by manufacturers (p. G153). We interpret their article as relying on the *content* of advertising to determine the difference between retail and manufacturer advertising. In drawing conclusions about the two types of advertising, they consistently assumed that it is the type of advertising (price or nonprice) and not the locus of it (retailer or manufacturer) that is causing the difference in price. Although we have a minor dispute with the notion that price advertising always increases price sensitivity, our major concern is with the question of what causes retailers to advertise price more than do manufacturers.

In the Kaul and Wittink (1995) work, we do not find a recognition of the key role of manufacturer distribution policies as the key intervening variable in the market mechanisms reversing the effects of advertising on price sensitivity for manufacturers and retailers (p. G154). Instead, Kaul and Wittink raised "three considerations that are relevant to the examination of the relationship between advertising and consumer price sensitivity" (p. G158). These considerations refer to the composition of the consumer sample set, the measure of price sensitivity, and the type of consumers. By ignoring the impact of vertical competition on the relationship between advertising and price, Kaul and Wittink—typical of the research in this area—ignored what probably is a key factor in the question of advertising's affect on price, that is, whether manufacturer market power (roughly, the ability to raise prices and margins) translates into more or less reseller (retailer) market power.

Importance of Distribution

We conclude our critical review of the literature by noting an important gap. The impact of advertising on retail prices is significantly moderated by the manufacturer's distribution policy, yet the importance of this vertical competition does not appear to be recognized in the literature. Intensive distribution of strongly advertised brands may lead to intensive price competition among retailers, causing lower retail prices either directly or indirectly as a result of retailers' price-focused advertising. With selective or exclusive distribution, however, such competition is mitigated and retailers are free to take higher margins.

The luxury automobile category provides an example of how exclusive distribution can even override the effects of price advertising on price sensitivity. Although we noted earlier that every case of price advertising identified by Kaul and Wittink (1995) led to increased price sensitivity, the case of Land Rover in North America provides a counterexample. Land Rover used print advertisements with the price of the vehicle clearly stated, yet no one could seriously argue that this increased price sensitivity. In fact, the purpose of price advertising in this case was to allow potential customers to self-select for willingness to pay the significant price premium for this car as well as to build the luxury appeal of the car by showing everyone how much it cost. In the words of the vice president at the agency in charge of the account, "The price drew the right audience. It was self-selecting. . . . It also saved the buyer the step of having to tell his friends how much he paid for this radically new vehicle" (quoted in Fournier 1995, p. 5).

Levi's is an example of the impact of selective distribution on price. Levi's refused to allow Wal-Mart to distribute its jeans for fear of the downward price pressure on the brand's retail price. Another example of selective distribution affecting price is the perfume industry in which premium brands maintain a price premium of 200% to 300% over midrange brands, despite similar product quality and similar product and marketing costs, primarily by limiting their distribution to department stores and staying away from mass merchandisers. Intel is another example of a strong brand that forces computer manufacturers to compete more intensely on price because no computer has an exclusive on the Pentium processor. If one manufacturer had such an exclusive, then prices of that computer certainly would increase (and Intel's prices might be forced down by the manufacturer power).

Conclusions

We draw two conclusions from the forgoing discussion. The first is that research efforts on the question of the impact of advertising on price should focus on absolute, not relative, prices. Price dispersion is not per se evidence of high absolute prices. The second conclusion is that the role of vertical competition needs to be recognized explicitly. Focusing on one stage in the value chain may yield misleading conclusions regarding the role of advertising, branding, and price levels.

Absolute, Not Relative, Prices

First, we believe that the preponderance of evidence and theory supports the notion that advertised products typically sell for higher prices and unadvertised products sell for lower prices, even (or especially) when differences in quality are taken into account. However, although it often is observed that strongly advertised brands tend to *charge more* (Kanetkar, Weinberg, and Weiss 1992), an equally compelling view is that *un*advertised brands *charge less*. In other words, advertised brands set the price ceiling for unadvertised brands. Is this ceiling a "lid" on prices that forces the unadvertised brands to offer consumers even lower prices than otherwise would be available? Or, is the ceiling a "pricing umbrella" under which the advertisers earn comfortable margins and are protected from the rigors of true price competition? (Brown, Lee, and Spreen 1996). We believe that advertised products that are widely available set the price ceiling under which competitors are forced to price their own products and services. In the short term, advertisers may raise or lower this ceiling with quite different effects on "competition."

At the ceiling, in the highest pricing location, sit highly advertised, high-quality, innovative products. Significantly below, in the lowest pricing positions, sit the private labels and "me too" brands. Between the two is a gap or band. Price dispersion measures the width of this band. We believe that such dispersion of prices is a given. We reject the notion that price dispersion is per se evidence of uninformed inefficient markets. Relative prices of brands in a particular set of functionally equivalent products might not tell us much about what the *absolute* (average) price level of the entire set would be without advertising. A variety of prices that offers consumers the opportunity to buy at many different places and at different times is something that few consumers would gladly sacrifice. Variation in price, even among similar products, is not prima facie evidence of reduced consumer welfare. It might even be a healthy indicator of dynamism and innovation in the category, signifying a breadth of retail availability and active price competition.

The more important question to us is the absolute height of this band itself, that is, the absolute price level. This is significantly more difficult to measure in a meaningful way. Measures of profits that capture risk and the cost of investments might provide better insight into the height of the band if they reflect the entire supply chain. It is dangerous to focus on a single link in the supply chain because profits often are inversely related among stages in the supply chain. We believe that a focus of further investigation should be on finding reliable methods for measuring and testing the effect of advertising on absolute prices given the expected variation in prices for different brands with equivalent functional quality and even different prices for the same brands at different retailers.

Role of Vertical Competition

The second conclusion that we draw in this chapter is that the role of middlemen (especially retailers) serves as a pivot point to reverse many conclusions about price sensitivity and monopoly power. We argue that the advertising and price research, with a notable exception of the substantial contributions of Steiner (1973, 1993), generally pays insufficient attention to vertical competition and the dynamics of the relationship between manufacturers and retailers. We believe that the field must move beyond the notion of merely recognizing that retailers and manufacturers are different. It is true that retailers advertise price more often than do manufacturers and that price generally is mentioned in advertising when it is low, not high. However, we believe that it is not just the fact that advertising mentions price or expands the consideration set that determines whether advertising is promoting (increasing) price sensitivity. The discussion needs to be put into the context of a causal explanation for why and how price and nonprice advertising come to dominate different markets.

In particular, it seems to us that the breadth of retailer availability is the primary determinant of the degree to which retailers focus on price or other marketing efforts. Having the same product available in many different retail outlets encourages price competition, especially when consumers regard the different outlets as similar. If a retailer were to enjoy a local monopoly on strong brands such as Heinz ketchup, Tide detergent, and Tylenol, then advertising that increased demand for these products likely would be reflected in higher prices (whether or not price were mentioned or competing brands were included in the consideration set). Of course, manufacturers do not have exclusive or selective distribution policies for these products, and as a result, these brands often are sold by retailers at very low or even negative margins. Many scholars fail to recognize the essential role of broad distribution in creating the conditions for price competition at the retail level. The key point is that the moderating effect of manufacturers' distribution policies determines whether retailers will be able to use increases in demand created by advertising to raise their own selling prices and margins. These distribution policies include promotional policies and allocation of production capacity. Even products with broad distribution but insufficient supply will result in retailers charging higher prices to exploit the shortage.

Directions for Further Research

Based on the forgoing discussion, we believe that several directions can be pursued to shed further light on the impact of advertising on price:

1. A key question that remains unresolved is whether the price of unadvertised brands is being forced down or, on the contrary, pulled up by the price ceiling of advertised brands.

2. Further development of approaches for measurement and comparison of absolute prices—the height of the price band—and lowest prices is required. As already noted, one possibility could be measures of profits that allow for the risk and cost of investments in new product development. Another possibility might be the change in absolute price over time, particularly before and after major changes in the marketing environment for the category such as deregulation and availability of a radical new technology. Comparisons of absolute or lowest prices across countries or large regions also might be useful (in effect, a meta-dispersion measure).

3. The forgoing arguments require the support of empirical study of both the effects of store format on relative prices and the effects of manufacturer distribution policy on relative and absolute prices.

4. Early on, we noted that we needed to limit the scope of this analysis. Extending the analysis to include the long-term impact of advertising in enabling new product development and diffusion also would be valuable.

5. As noted earlier, instead of studying the impact of advertising on price for consumer welfare in the aggregate, it would be interesting to study this and similar questions through the lens of distributive justice, with savings to the less well-off segments of the population valued more than the identical savings to the more well-off segments.

6. Finally, it would be valuable to revisit why this question is important in today's context of building strong global brands with means other than traditional advertising. Is it really advertising or strong brands that concern public policy and consume welfare issues?

We believe that if research efforts are focused on the impact of advertising on absolute price, and if due attention is paid to the impact of intermediaries, then a significant improvement can be made in our understanding of the relationship between advertising and competition.

Notes

1. Price-quality correlation data need to be "augmented by data on the variance in price and quality," and "frontier measures of efficiency will measure the variance in consumer surplus only in the unlikely case of there being a perfect correspondence between the efficiency frontier and the consumer's valuation of each alternative" (Ratchford et al. 1996, p. 177).

2. In all cases, we compared only extra-strength acetaminophen caplets so as to maintain consistency. We did not include variations in strength (e.g., regular strength) or in delivery vehicle (e.g., "gelcaps," tablets).

References

Ailawadi, K., P. W. Farris, and E. Shames (1999), "Trade Promotion: Essential to Selling through Resellers," *Sloan Management Review*, 41 (1), 83-92.

Albion, Mark S. and Paul W. Farris (1987), "Manufacturer Advertising and Retailer Gross Margins," in *Advances in Marketing and Public Policy*, P. Bloom, ed. Greenwich, CT: JAI.

Borden, Neil H. (1942), *The Economic Effects of Advertising*. Chicago: Irwin.

Brown, Mark G., Jonq-Ying Lee, and Thomas H. Spreen (1996). "The Impact of Generic Advertising and the Free Rider Problem: A Look at the U.S. Orange Juice Market and Imports," *Agribusiness*, 12 (4), 309-17.

Brynjolfsson, Erik and Michael D. Smith (1999), "Frictionless Commerce? A Comparison of Internet and Conventional Retailers," working paper, Sloan School of Management, Massachusetts Institute of Technology.

Buzzell, Robert D. and Paul W. Farris (1977), "Marketing Costs in Consumer Goods Industries," in *Strategy + Structure = Performance*, H. B. Thorelli, ed. Bloomington: Indiana University Press.

Court, David, Thomas D. French, Tim I. McGuire, and Michael Partington (1999), "Marketing in 3-D," *McKinsey Quarterly*, No. 4, 6-17.

Dickson, Peter R. and Alan G. Sawyer (1990), "The Price Knowledge and Search of Supermarket Shoppers," *Journal of Marketing*, 54 (3), 42-53.

Dorfman, Robert and Peter O. Steiner (1954), "Optimal Advertising and Optimal Quality," *American Economic Review*, 44, 826-36.

Farris, Paul W. and Mark Albion (1981), "Determinants of the Advertising-to-Sales Ratio," *Journal of Advertising Research*, 21 (1), 19-27.

———— and Robert D. Buzzell (1979), "Variations in Advertising Intensity: Some Cross-Sectional Analyses," *Journal of Marketing*, 43 (Fall), 112-22.

———— and David J. Reibstein (1979), "How Price, Expenditures, and Profits Are Linked," *Harvard Business Review*, 57 (November-December), 173-84.

————and———— (1997), "Consumer Prices and Advertising," in *Encyclopedic Dictionary of Business Ethics*, P. H. Werhane and R. E. Freeman, eds. Cambridge, MA: Blackwell, 139-41.

Fournier, Susan (1995), "Land Rover North America, Inc.," Case 9-596-036, Harvard Business School.

Kanetkar, V., C. Weinberg, and D. Weiss (1992), "Price Sensitivity and Television Advertising Exposures: Some Empirical Findings," *Marketing Science,* 11 (4), 359-72.

Kaul, A. and D. Wittink (1995), "Empirical Generalizations about the Impact of Advertising on Price Sensitivity and Price," *Marketing Science,* 14 (3), G151-61.

Lodish, Leonard M., Magid Abraham, Stuart Kalmenson, Jeanne Livelsberger, Beth Lubkin, Bruce Richardson, and Mary Ellen Stevens (1995), "How TV Advertising Works: A Meta-Analysis of 389 Real World Split Cable TV Advertising Experiments," *Journal of Marketing Research,* 32 (2), 125-40.

Mitra, A. and J. Lynch (1995), "Toward a Reconciliation of Market Power and Information Theories of Advertising Effects on Price Elasticity," *Journal of Consumer Research,* 21 (4), 644-60.

Monroe, K. and A. Lee (1999), "Remembering versus Knowing: Issues in Buyers' Processing of Price Information," *Academy of Marketing Science,* 27 (2), 207-25.

Quelch, John A. (1986), "General Electric Company: Consumer Incandescent Lighting," Case 2-587-014, Harvard Business School.

Ratchford, Brian, Jagdish Agrawal, Pamela E. Grimm, and Narasimhan Srinivasan (1996), "Toward Understanding the Measurement of Market Efficiency," *Journal of Public Policy and Marketing,* 15 (2), 167-84.

Schmalensee, R. (1981), "Output and Welfare Implications of Monopolistic Third-Degree Price Discrimination," *American Economic Review,* 71 (1), 242-47.

Steiner, R. (1973), "Does Advertising Lower Consumer Prices?" *Journal of Marketing,* 37 (October), 19-26.

———— (1993), "The Inverse Association between Margins of Manufacturers and Retailers," *Review of Industrial Organization,* 8, 717-40.

Strenio, A. (1996), "The Aspirin Wars," *Journal of Public Policy & Marketing,* 15 (2), 319-21.

Vakratsas, D. and T. Ambler (1999), "How Advertising Works: What Do We Really Know?" *Journal of Marketing,* 63 (January), 26-43.

10 *Chapter*

The Socioeconomic Consequences of Franchise Distribution

A Policy Retrospective

Patrick J. Kaufmann

Marketing and public policy are inextricably linked. Although this connection is most apparent in the direct impact that marketing activity has on consumers, in areas such as distribution, public policy issues also can arise from the interaction among firms. For example, not only can vertical integration affect competition directly, but its threat also can be a source of opportunistic coercion among channel members. Similarly, asymmetric power in channels can produce arguably problematic phenomena such as slotting allowances and full line forcing. When new forms of distribution appear, therefore, marketing scholars sometimes attempt to anticipate what policy issues these new forms are likely to raise. For example, researchers currently are attempting to understand the likely impact of the Internet on issues such as privacy and encroachment. During the 1970s, marketing scholars were attempting to understand the implications of another burgeoning form of distribution, namely franchising. Now, a quarter of a century later, it is possible to look back and see what has happened to the anticipated policy issues of that new form.

In 1972, Shelby Hunt published a seminal article in the *Journal of Marketing* titled "The Socioeconomic Consequences of the Franchise System of Distribution," the result of a study sponsored by the U.S. Small Business Administration (Hunt 1972). At the time, franchising was a relatively new phenomenon. It has grown to become the dominant method of distribution for many types of goods and services in the United States and is spreading rapidly throughout the rest of the world. Much has changed since Hunt's initial study. The public policy environment is markedly different, and the industry has matured and adjusted. In this chapter, I revisit some of the ideas and predictions made in 1972 relevant to the public policy surrounding franchising and discuss them in light of the intervening 25 years.

Hunt (1972) proposed a number of possible consequences of franchising in the form of five favorable and three unfavorable statements and then reported evidence that either supported or undermined those propositions. Table 10.1 provides a synopsis of Hunt's statements and findings grouped to correspond with the following sections: creation of the franchise relationship, impact of franchising on the franchisee, and impact of franchising on the consumer. Each proposition is discussed in relation to the underlying policy questions and current research.

The Franchising Industry

Franchise-like relationships can be traced back to 18th-century Germany and England, where brewers used them as methods of establishing, growing, and controlling the distribution of their products (Stanworth and Curran 1978). Franchising was introduced into the United States by companies such as McCormick Harvester and Singer Sewing Machine during the mid-19th century (Justis and Judd 1989). Those franchising pioneers soon were followed by automobile, petroleum, and soft drink companies (Luxenberg 1985). The franchisors in this form of franchising, called product franchising, are manufacturers using the franchise relationship as a form of contractual vertical integration.

A new form of franchising, the business format franchise, began in the United States during the early 20th century. In business format franchising, the franchisors are retailers expanding their organizations not by adding more company-owned stores but rather by cloning their retail concepts and licensing them to separate economic entities. Perhaps the earliest example of this form was the Rexall drug store cooperative organized in 1902 (Justis and Judd 1989). But the real prototype of business format franchising was created in 1925 when Howard Johnson began licensing fellow druggists to use his name, his ice cream, and his successful business system in return for an ongoing fee. By 1940, there were 100 orange-roofed Howard Johnson's providing familiar surroundings and consistent quality up and down the East Coast (Luxenberg 1985). By 1960, business format franchising had exploded with the introduction of chains such as Dunkin' Donuts, Holiday Inn, Kentucky Fried Chicken, and McDonald's.

The period of the 1960s and early 1970s was a frenetic time for franchising in general and for business format franchising in particular. Existing chains were expanding rapidly, and new chains were being established at a ferocious pace. There were numerous problems associated with this rapid expansion including examples of outright fraud. There also were vivid examples of strategy shifts that caused some franchisees concern. For example, in 1967 McDonald's embarked on a significant buyback of their franchises, moving from 9% company

TABLE 10.1 Socioeconomic Propositions and Findings

	Hunt's Proposition	Hunt's Findings	Key Changes since 1972	Conclusions
Creation of the franchise relationship	"Franchising greatly increases the opportunities for individuals to become independent business[persons]."	Franchisees saw themselves as independent businesspersons. If not for franchising, 52% of franchisees would not have been self-employed.	More than 50% of the U.S. workforce is employed by small business. Research suggests that franchisees seek established brands and ongoing support, not just independence.	Small business creation still is a major policy goal, and franchising seems to provide at least a significant minority the means to own their own small businesses.
	"Franchising provides opportunities for minority group members to own their own business[es]."	Minority group members held only 1.5% of franchises while comprising 16% of the population.	Current estimates indicate that from 3.0% to 13.6% of franchisees are minorities, but this does not reflect the number of units held by franchisees. By 1995, 26.0% of the population were minorities.	There is little direct research of this question, and estimates are questionable. Minority franchisees sometimes are restricted to minority markets through redlining. The role of women in franchising also has been largely unexamined.
	"Franchisors employ unethical techniques in selling franchises."	Pyramid schemes masquerading as legitimate franchises were a policy concern at the time. The use of celebrities to sell franchises had waned and was decreasing as a problem. Significant evidence was found as to widespread misrepresentation of earnings potential.	In 1978, the FTC commenced the regulation of franchise disclosure. The growth of multilevel marketing has clouded the distinction between franchising and pyramids. The FTC and NASAA are exploring the imposition of mandatory earnings disclosure while setting standards for voluntary disclosure.	Earning claims continue to be the most problematic area of presale disclosure. Because of the FTC's rigid standards, most franchisors do not provide voluntary formal earnings claims. This provides the opportunity for unscrupulous sales personnel to misrepresent the earning potential of franchises.

	Hunt's Proposition	Hunt's Findings	Key Changes since 1972	Conclusions
Impact of franchising on the franchisee	"Franchise agreements are one-sided in favor of protecting the prerogatives of franchisors."	Franchise agreements typically were contracts of adhesion. Nearly 40% of sampled franchisees had not consulted an attorney before signing their agreements.	Recent research confirms that 40% of franchisors allow for no negotiation of agreement terms and reconfirms that only 40% of prospective franchisees seek legal advice before purchase. Courts have begun to restrict franchisor encroachment, and some states have enacted statutory territorial protection.	There is little question that franchise contracts are contracts of adhesion. Even when allowed, negotiation is over peripheral issues. However, the market for franchises is competitive, and franchisees have alternatives. Postcontract changes such as franchisor encroachment on franchisee territories currently are the most serious issue.
	"Franchising is an anti-competitive system of distribution."	Under tying law at the time, the ability of franchisors to strictly control franchisee inputs was limited. Territorial restrictions were considered collusive and illegal per se. Resale price maintenance (both maximum and minimum) was illegal per se. All three practices were prevalent in franchising.	In 1977, the Sylvania case (*Continental TV v. GTE Sylvania*) brought vertical territorial restraints under rule of reason and permitted franchisors to provide exclusive territories. In 1997, the Khan case (*State Oil Company v. Khan*) did the same for maximum resale price maintenance. In 1992, the Kodak case (*Eastman Kodak Company v. Image Technical Services Inc.*) redefined the relevant market for repair parts as that existing after the purchase of copiers.	The Sylvania and Khan cases have direct implications for franchising practice. They permit reasonable franchisor restrictions on franchisee location and maximum pricing decisions. The test of reason, however, is designed to protect consumers from harm as a result of these practices. Tying currently is a serious issue, and the Kodak case has muddied the waters considerably.

209

TABLE 10.1 Continued

	Hunt's Proposition	Hunt's Findings	Key Changes since 1972	Conclusions
	"Franchised businesses have lower failure rates than other businesses."	No conclusive evidence existed.	An often-repeated claim of a 4% franchisee failure rate has been reputed indirectly through research on system failure. New system survival rates of 65% over 4 years, 25% over 10 years, and 30% over 12 years have been reported.	Franchisees in established systems might have better chances for survival, but new systems (and, therefore, franchisees in them) fail at high rates. The commerce department's termination of data collection has prevented systematic research in this area.
Impact of franchising on the consumer	"Franchising decreases economic concentration by providing a viable alternative to completely integrated systems."	There was a move toward ownership redirection obserserved. State and federal legislation made it more expensive to franchise, adding to the impetus to use company stores.	Ownership redirection has become less obvious, although some evidence still exists. Recent analysis indicates that having franchisees might not lead to lower prices, even if less industry concentration exists.	Franchising seems to be a fairly stable phenomenon and does provide an alternative to vertically integrated chains. The beneficial effect on consumers is less obvious given the increasing occurrence of exclusive territories.
	"Franchising assists consumers by providing standardized products to an increasingly mobile public."	Franchising's success proves the population's desire for standardized product/service offerings. Franchisees are not easy to control, and it can be hard to deliver on the promise of uniformity.	Research and analysis have demonstrated that although franchisees work hard, they might not always work in the way that maintains uniformity. There is some indication of a social backlash against uniformity.	Standardization is a function of chain retailing, not of franchising. Its value to consumers might have been greater when it was the exception. As it becomes the norm, idiosyncratic differences might become more attractive.

NOTE: FTC = Federal Trade Commission; NASAA = North American Securities Administrators Association.

210

owned to 33% company owned in just five years (Love 1986). It was a time of turmoil and great wealth creation, much like the excitement that currently surrounds the Internet. A new system of distribution was being created, and marketing scholars such as Hunt (1972) were exploring its socioeconomic implications.

Franchising has continued to flourish. During the late 1990s, more than one-third of all retail dollars flowed through franchise systems each year. Approximately 2,300 franchise systems were listed in the most popular franchise opportunity guide (Bond 1997). The census bureau reported approximately 500,000 franchisees in 1992 (U.S. Bureau of the Census 1992). Research has consistently shown that most franchisees own more than one outlet (Kaufmann and Dant 1996). In fact, in one study, the mean number of fast-food outlets per franchisee was more than four (Baucus, Baucus, and Human 1996). It is clear, therefore, that the actual number of franchised outlets and their impact far exceeds those 500,000 franchisees. Franchising was important to the U.S. economy in 1972 and is much more so today. Some of the policy issues are the same, and some are different; some questions have been answered, and some remain. In the spirit of stock taking, therefore, it is time to revisit Hunt's (1972) propositions.

Creation of the Franchise Relationship

The creation of the franchise relationship raises three important questions relating to the public policy in support of small business creation. Franchising might provide the means for individuals to go into business for themselves where they would not otherwise do so. Moreover, franchising might offer minorities greater opportunity to own their own businesses. On the other hand, there is the lingering concern that some franchisors are involved in fraud and unethical practices in the sale of franchises.

Franchising and Self-Employment

Citing the existence of the Small Business Administration, Hunt (1972) noted that the creation of new, small, independent businesses was a key policy issue in 1972. With actions such as the creation of the Office of Advocacy in 1976, the policy in support of small business start-ups is even greater now. According to the Small Business Administration (1998), small businesses now employ more than 50% of the U.S. workforce, generate more than half of the nation's gross domestic product, and are the principal source of new job creation in the economy. Consequently, Congress has consistently reiterated a strong pro-small business policy, with the House Committee on Small Business declaring its continuing dedication and support for programs on behalf of small business (U.S. House of Representatives 1997) and the Senate clearly recognizing the growing influence that small business has on the U.S. economy (U.S. Senate 1997).

To the extent that franchising helps in the creation of small businesses, therefore, it furthers U.S. public policy. Hunt proposed that franchising is, in fact, responsible for the creation of many new independent businesses. In support of that position, he reported finding that 52% of the franchisees in his study would not have gone into business for themselves if not for franchising.

Since Hunt's original article, there have been several studies dealing with the relationship between franchising and the desire of individuals to become self-employed. The studies, conducted in the United States, the United Kingdom, and Canada, have focused on the characteristics of the individuals who purchase franchises and on the decision process itself. None have asked the direct question that Hunt asked, that is, whether the individuals would have opened their own businesses if not for franchising. Nevertheless, some of the findings indirectly shed light on that issue.

The intuition behind the claim that franchising may foster new small business start-ups is based on the training and support that franchisors give franchisees. Without franchising, the typical path to self-employment would be for an individual to leverage the experience gained in someone's employ to open a new business of his or her own in that sector (Cooper 1981). When no such experience is available, or when the individual does not want to stay in the same line of work, franchising provides the turnkey solution (Perry 1994).

When franchisees (or prospective franchisees) have been asked what factors were important in their decision process, their answers have tended to cluster in two areas: (1) the benefits of self-employment (citing independence and autonomy) and (2) the unique contributions of franchising compared to owning an independent business (Knight 1984; Peterson and Dant 1990; Stanworth and Purdy 1994). Although independence has consistently been found to be a key benefit in these studies, a high level of importance also has been attached to the unique features of franchising. This appears to indicate that, if not for the opportunity to buy a franchise, many of the respondents would not have been able to meet their goals of independence. In another study, Kaufmann and Stanworth (1995) found that 30% of the prospective franchisees surveyed were not also considering independent business start-ups. At least for this significant minority, franchising was viewed as the only possible route to small business creation for them. Unfortunately, the methodologies employed in these studies did not permit complete quantification of franchising's final impact on business creation.

Whereas Hunt focused on the impact that franchising had on franchisees' creation of new businesses, others have argued that franchising is important in providing prospective retailers the wherewithall necessary to create viable new chains (Caves and Murphy 1976; Oxenfeldt and Kelly 1968). Franchisors often are niche retailers with strong growth imperatives. Market preemption, necessary for survival in that context, requires access to significant amounts of capital. Many lenders, however, find new retail concepts unattractive, and the existence of franchisee capital might be the only answer. Although efficient capital market proponents dispute this interpretation (Rubin 1978), some evidence suggests at least a contributing role for capital acquisition in the explanation for franchising (Kaufmann and Dant 1996; Lafontaine 1992b).

More than 25 years after Hunt's initial findings, therefore, we observe public policy in support of the creation of new small business to be even more pronounced. Although there is additional support for the idea that franchising contributes to that creation, quantification of the specific impact has not been forthcoming.

Minorities in Franchising

Ensuring equal opportunities in business for minorities and women continues to be a central goal of U.S. public policy. The current attacks on affirmative action enhance the importance of alternatives to traditional employment in providing paths to prosperity for these segments.

Hunt reported that although minority group members represented about 16% of the total population in 1972, they held only 1.5% of the franchises in his study. This was consistent with other findings at the time. The disappointing representation of minorities in franchising belied the expectation that franchising would provide a unique opportunity to avoid the impediments to success that traditional business settings might present. Hunt offered several explanations for the findings including limited financial resources and managerial skills and the fact that the preferred path to self-employment among African Americans typically was through the professions.[1]

More than 25 years later, finding methods of inclusion for prospective minority business owners is a continuing priority. However, there is no unequivocal answer to the question as to whether franchising has provided significant access to business ownership for minorities. The Federal Trade Commission (FTC) does not track minority franchisees, and the data on minority franchising has been largely anecdotal or piecemeal.[2]

In 1993, Representative LaFalce, then chairman of the House Committee on Small Business, estimated that the percentage of minority franchisees had reached just under 3% (U.S. House of Representatives, 1993); however, this figure is significantly below that reported elsewhere for some fast-food and automobile franchises. Emerson (1998), using statistics compiled from other published sources, noted that not only were the percentages higher than those reported by LaFalce, but they also were increasing. He noted that McDonald's led the major fast-food companies in 1997 with 8.2% of its units owned by minorities, compared to 3.5% for both Burger King and Wendy's. Even this is significantly lower than a more recent figure reported for Burger King. Weingartner (1999) reported that 14% of Burger King's U.S. restaurants were owned by minorities at the time of her study. The domestic automobile manufacturers (Ford, General Motors, and Chrysler) had a combined 4.3% of the dealerships owned by minorities, whereas Asian auto manufacturers had 4.0% and European auto manufacturers had 8.0% minority ownership in the United States.

Although there has been no focused large-sample study of minority franchising, it is possible to glean some insight from the census bureau's characteristics of business owners survey data for 1992 (U.S. Bureau of the Census 1992). Data are provided for a sample of small business owners (proprietorships, partnerships, and subchapter S corporations) broken down by ethnic status and gender. Businesses are characterized as Hispanic, black, or other minority male businesses; female businesses; or nonminority male businesses based on predominant ownership. Included in the survey is the question of whether the business is a franchise. Of the Hispanic businesses, 2.5% reported that they were franchises, compared to 3.5% of the black businesses, 4.5% of other minority businesses, 3.2% of female businesses, and 2.7% of nonminority male businesses. When generalized to the total number of small businesses reported for each category, these percentages would imply that there were 19,293 Hispanic-owned franchises, 21,732 black-owned franchises, 27,289 other minority-owned franchises, 188,444 female-owned franchises (29,507 minority and 158,937 nonminority), and 273,090 nonminority male-owned franchises. In this database, therefore, minority franchisees comprise 13.6% of all franchisees, whereas female franchisees comprise 37.6% and nonminority males comprise 54.5%. (Percentages do not add to 100% because of double counting of minority women.)

These findings should be viewed with considerable caution. First, although taken from census data, they are significantly higher than data reported elsewhere by individual firms. Second, the sample size of approximately 116,000, although large by social science standards, is small by census standards, and there were standard errors associated with the estimates of between 0.2 and 0.5 for each category. Third, only proprietorships, partnerships, and subchapter S corporations were sampled (C corporations were not included). Finally, in this survey, the data specifically refer to firms or economic entities (i.e., the sample is from businesses filing tax forms in 1992) and not establishments. The projected total number of franchised firms in 1992 was approximately equal to the estimated number of franchised establishments reported for 1990 by Trutko, Trutko, and Kostecka (1993). This is hard to understand given the fact that a significant proportion of franchisees have more than one establishment (Kaufmann and Dant 1996).

It also is important to note that ownership percentages must be viewed in light of the overall trends in population percentages. In other words, Hunt was concerned that the proportion of franchise ownership (1.5%) lagged the proportion of minorities in the overall population (then 16.0%). As of 1995, minorities made up 26.0% of the U.S. population, or an increase of 62.5%. If no changes had occurred at all, then we could expect minority franchise ownership to be 2.4%. Emerson (1998) also made the point that when examining the level of minority participation in franchising, the correct comparison is not to the percentage of minorities in the population but rather to the percentage of overall minority business ownership. Using the same census data, the percentage of all small businesses of these types owned by minorities was about 20.0%.

One final point should be made regarding minority franchising. Although a number of franchise systems have initiated affirmative action programs, claims of discrimination in the granting of franchises still are made. One of the more covert discriminatory practices, "redlining," still might exist in some systems (Emerson 1998). Redlining (as used in franchising) is the tacit restriction of minority franchisees to geographic areas with large minority populations. Minority franchisees in a number of systems have sued their franchisors over this practice, claiming that they had been disadvantaged because the likelihood of success was lower in those areas. Emerson suggested that even when companies engage in affirmative efforts to increase the number of minority franchisees, they sometimes match them to markets populated by the same minority, reflecting a form of redlining mind-set.

Unethical Selling of Franchises

In 1972, Hunt identified three problems surrounding the selling of franchises: selling pyramid distribution schemes as legitimate franchise opportunities, using celebrity endorsements, and misrepresenting the potential profitability of the franchise. Each clearly was a violation of public policy. The most significant change in public policy relevant to these issues took place in 1978 when the FTC first promulgated its trade regulation rule, which was titled *Disclosure Requirements and Prohibitions Concerning Franchising and Business Opportunity Ventures* and revised in 1986 (FTC 1986).

Pyramid, or Ponzi, schemes are arrangements in which the victims are sold the rights to distribute some products or services along with the right to sell distributorships to others. Because all or nearly all of the potential revenue comes from the sale of distributorships and not the sale of products, the arrangements resemble economic chain letters. The trend of prohibiting these arrangements through various state statutes, as noted by Hunt in his original article, has continued.

The connection between pyramid schemes and franchising was, and still is, somewhat complicated. Both franchise relationships and the sale of business opportunities are regulated under the FTC's franchise disclosure rule (FTC 1986). So, to the extent that pyramid schemes are classified as business opportunities, they would be subject to the same disclosure regulation as are franchises. Currently, pyramid schemes more often are confused with direct sales organizations (DSOs) and multilevel marketing (MLM) organizations than they are with franchise systems (Biggart 1988). DSOs and MLM organizations historically have not fallen under the definition of business opportunities and so are not regulated under the franchise disclosure rule. However, proposed changes in the FTC's rule have raised the possibility that they soon might come under the definition of business opportunities and face strict disclosure requirements. Although this change is being fought by the MLM and DSO industries because of the added costs of disclosure (FTC 1997), if it does take place, then it might be easier for consumers to distinguish marginal MLM arrangements from unlawful pyramid schemes.

The use of celebrities to endorse franchise systems was in decline even at the time that Hunt wrote his original piece. When the FTC's franchise disclosure rule was promulgated in 1978 and became effective in 1979, it included a section that required extensive disclosure about the relationship between the franchise system and any "public person" used to recommend the purchase of the franchise, used in the name of the franchise, or claimed to be involved in the management. By 1985, this did not seem to be a particularly serious issue. In the survey that formed the basis for the final report on the economic impact of the franchise disclosure rule, the FTC found that only 1.1% of the respondents thought that the role of public figures was among the five most important disclosure items (Opinion Research Corporation 1985).

By far, the most serious policy issue connected with the selling of franchises was, and still is, the provision of legitimate earnings claims to prospective franchisees. When Hunt published his original article, earnings claims were not the subject of federal law. Some states had begun to regulate the disclosures made to prospective franchisees (e.g., California passed the first statute in 1970) including statements made about profitability.[3] In 1975, the Midwest Securities Commissioners Association produced the first Uniform Franchise Offering Circular (UFOC), which set forth guidelines intended to facilitate a uniform disclosure format throughout the country. Section 19 of the UFOC dealt with the disclosure of earnings claims. When the FTC promulgated its own franchise disclosure rule in 1978, it also included a section regulating the disclosure of earnings. Ultimately, compliance with the UFOC was deemed to be equivalent to compliance with the FTC disclosure requirements. In both of these documents, disclosure of earnings was permitted (not required) only when presented in the specified manner and supported by substantial and costly documentation.

The result of these rules and guidelines has been a reticence on the part of franchisors to make earnings claims within their disclosure documents (Mazero and Forseth 1992). For example, in Maryland (a state requiring franchisor registration) in 1987, only 13% of registered franchisors made earnings claims as part of their disclosure documents (Lewis 1988). Consequently, some have argued that earnings claims have become even more the subject of innuendo and puffing by overeager franchise salespersons. Some franchisors have refused requests for earnings disclosure by claiming that they are not permitted to provide prospective franchisees with claims relating to financial performance. Clearly, these results are contrary to the policy goal of providing franchisees with the reliable information they need to make informed investment decisions (Spandorf 1995).

In its most recent amended version of the UFOC, the North American Securities Administrators Association (NASAA, the successor to the Midwest Security Commissioners Association) now requires franchisors who are not making earnings claims to explicitly state (1) that they are not doing so and (2) that they do not allow anyone to make these claims on their behalf (NASAA 1993). The FTC also is considering changes to its franchise disclosure rule that makes it mandatory for such franchisors to disclose that they have chosen not to make any earnings disclosure. More important, recently and for the first time, both the FTC and NASAA have begun to consider whether requiring earnings claims as part of the overall disclosure document is consistent with public policy goals.

The implications of mandatory earnings disclosure are significant (Vincent and Kaufmann 1996). To be useful in comparing various alternative franchise systems, the disclosure presentation must be uniformly structured. However, franchise systems vary widely in what types of performance and earnings information is relevant and available. For example, for many systems gross sales is a good indicator of performance and typically is available, but in hotel chains sales is primarily a function of the size of the property and room rates and might have little to do with the value of converting to the franchisor's brand. Moreover, although aggregation provides existing franchisees with anonymity, average earnings tell little of the distribution of returns, and new systems might not have the number of outlets or geographic coverage that makes better descriptive statistics possible. Nevertheless, there is at least some belief that public policy will only be served by some form of regulated mandatory earnings disclosure.

Impact of Franchising on the Franchisee

Also critical to the public policy interest in franchising are questions surrounding the ongoing impact of this form of distribution on franchisees' ability to operate their businesses free of coercion. These questions typically emerge from the presumed unequal bargaining power of the parties. Franchisees often are characterized as small businesspersons at the mercy of large corporate franchisors. The presumed ability of franchisors to coerce franchisees through contracts of adhesion and to tie unwanted products to the sale of the franchises themselves has increasingly given rise to calls for protection through either regulation or judicial action.

Contracts of Adhesion

In Hunt's (1972) original article, he reported the widespread charge that franchise agreements were contracts of adhesion between powerful franchisors and weak franchisees. These "take it or leave it" contracts contained provisions that gave franchisors extensive unilateral control over franchisees and the ability to terminate franchisees for relatively trivial violations. Exacerbating this problem was the fact that many franchisees (40%) had not sought legal advice before signing the franchise agreements.

It does seem clear that a significant proportion of franchise contracts continue to be contracts of adhesion. Lafontaine (1992b) found that more than 40% of the franchisors surveyed indicated that no negotiations of any terms were allowed in their franchise agreements. The implications of this fact, however, have not always been as clear. In some studies, franchisees have indicated that they still believe they have significant control over their businesses (Hunt 1975) and that they are no less independent than independent business owners (Knight 1984). In fact, under certain conditions, franchisees have even been willing to give up some of the control they have been specifically granted under the agreements (Anand 1987).

Relying on the presumed unequal bargaining position, the Supreme Court refused to uphold the franchisor's right to rely on highly restrictive language in the franchise agreement, finding that the franchisee was forced to accept these terms to obtain access to an otherwise attractive business opportunity (*Perma Life Mufflers Inc. v. International Parts Corporation* 1968). Goldberg (1979) noted that this decision, and the judicial reasoning it represents, is flawed in that it does not distinguish between asymmetric power at the creation of the relationship and asymmetric power within the relationship. He argued that prospective franchisees have free access to alternative franchise systems and enter the agreement freely, accepting all of its provisions, because it is the preferred alternative. Nevertheless, courts have continued to restrict the unbridled power of franchisors in enforcing the letter of the franchise agreement (Trombetta and Page 1978), and some states have enacted fair practice laws that significantly restrict the ability of franchisors to coerce franchisees (Nevin, Hunt, and Ruekert 1980).

One area in which both courts and state legislatures have taken a particular interest in restricting franchisor control has been encroachment. Courts have narrowly interpreted contract provisions allowing franchisors to open new outlets close to existing franchised outlets (*Scheck v. Burger King* 1992), and some states have legislated territorial protection for franchisees (Stassen and Mittelstaedt 1995). Encroachment continues to be among the most contentious areas in franchising and has become one of the subjects of proposed federal legislation (e.g., Small Business Franchise Act of 1998 [H.R. 4841]).

The FTC has taken the position that the best way in which to protect a prospective franchisee is to require disclosure of critical information regarding the franchise agreement far enough in advance that the franchisee can study the provisions and make an informed decision. Under the 1978 franchise disclosure rule, the disclosure of 20 subject areas ranging from litigation history to provisions dealing with termination and cancellation must be made at the first personal meeting or 10 days prior to execution, whichever comes first. Presumably, the timely provision of relevant information and a competitive market for franchises will prevent franchisees from entering into unacceptably onerous contracts. One assumption here is that prospective franchisees will follow the FTC's recommendations and seek professional guidance. As Hunt found in 1972, however, not all franchisees do so. In a recent small unpublished study of 63 prospective franchisees, I found that only 40% had consulted an attorney or an accountant prior to making their decisions, but of those 10 who ultimately had purchased franchises, 7 had consulted an attorney or an accountant.

Anti-Competitive Contracting and Tying

Hunt was concerned about the anti-competitive nature of several franchising practices: territorial restrictions, resale price maintenance, and tying. In each of these areas, there has been significant activity since his original article. In 1972, the law on vertical restraints was contained in the *Schwinn* case (*United States v. Arnold Schwinn & Company* 1967), which treated vertical territorial restrictions as illegal per se, and maximum (in addition to minimum) vertical price restraints were illegal under the *Albrecht* case (*Lester J. Albrecht v. The Herald Company* 1968). The *Carvel* case (*Carvel Corporation* 1965) and the *Chicken Delight* case (*Siegel v. Chicken Delight* 1972) defined the limits of a franchisor's ability to tie various inputs to the sale of the franchise rights. Under the *Carvel* and *Siegel* cases, the franchisor could legally restrict the sources of those inputs necessary to ensure quality control, but nothing more. Hunt, however, asserted that violations of these laws were prevalent in franchising during the early 1970s, and he saw the industry threatened by its dependence on these anti-competitive restraints.

Shortly after Hunt's original article, the *GTE Sylvania* case (*Continental T.V. v. GTE Sylvania* 1977) overturned the *Schwinn* case and ruled that vertical territorial restraints should be examined under a rule of reason test. This effectively permitted franchisors to provide franchisees with exclusive territories (e.g., promising not to put a new store within three miles of the franchised outlet). The decision not to permit a new franchisee to open a store within the territory, however, has to be made unilaterally. Franchisors cannot conspire with existing franchisees to allocate territories by restricting the specific location choices of new franchisees (*American Motor Inns v. Holiday Inns Inc.* 1975). The *GTE Sylvania* case marked a watershed in public policy toward nonprice vertical restraints. In fact, the pro-competitive nature of vertical territorial restraints has become so accepted that legislation introduced in the House during the fall of 1998 not only permits but even requires reasonable territorial protection for franchisees (U.S. House of Representatives 1998).

Since the introduction of "Chicago" school economic reasoning into antitrust law during the late 1970s, legal treatment of all vertical restraints, including resale price maintenance, has come under increased scrutiny (Posner 1976). Because of the economic relationship between franchisor and franchisee, resale price maintenance is more likely to take the form of recommended maximum prices as opposed to minimum prices. This is because the franchisee typically bears all of the fixed costs of the operation. The franchisor who is paid a royalty on the gross sales of the franchise often sees it in his or her own interest to keep prices low and volume high. Consequently, in 1997, when the Supreme Court overruled the decision in the *Albrecht* case and held that maximum resale price maintenance no longer was illegal per se, this had significant implications for franchise practice and represented another major change in public policy since Hunt's original article (*State Oil Company v. Khan* 1997; see also Blair and Lopatka 1998). In other words, many of the restrictions that franchisors place on franchisees that Hunt saw as anti-competitive (as evidenced by their illegality per se) have now been deemed arguably pro-competitive and are tested under a rule of reason.

The law relating to tying also has experienced a significant shift since 1972, primarily because of the decision in the *Kodak* case (*Eastman Kodak Company v. Image Technical Services Inc.* 1992). The *Kodak* case's main impact comes through the court's definition of the relevant market as the market for repair parts that existed after the purchase of the Kodak copier. In franchise systems, this would be the equivalent of the market for supplies that exists after the franchisee is part of the system, one easily monopolized by the franchisor with a tying contract (Blair and Herndon 1995). In a number of recent cases, franchisees have attempted to use the *Kodak* case to argue for the right to obtain inputs from sources other than those approved by the franchisor (Blair and Herndon 1999). Until these cases are decided, however, the applicability of the *Kodak* case to franchising remains a subject of debate.

Even if the *Kodak* case ultimately is not applied to franchising cases, the issue is addressed in the proposed federal legislation referenced earlier (H.R. 4841). Under that bill, franchisees are given the right to obtain inputs from any sources that meet reasonable quality standards promulgated and enforced by franchisors.

It also provides for a right of action against franchisors that prohibits franchisees from doing so. In this area, therefore, policy has shifted to further limit franchisors' right to restrict franchisee action.

Although most of these changes are explicitly rationalized as consistent with a pro-consumer public policy, some clearly align with the interests of franchisees and some with the interests of franchisors. Territorial restrictions reduce intrabrand competition and increase market protection for franchisees. If imposed voluntarily by franchisors, it might be expected that such restrictions would be designed to improve interbrand competition. When mandated in response to the lobbying efforts of franchisees, however, the impact more likely will be market allocation. Disallowing restrictions on sourcing decisions permits franchisees greater economic freedom. If quality control can be maintained, then this pro-franchisee ruling (or legislation) might increase competition in the input market and reduce costs ultimately borne by consumers. On the other hand, permitting maximum resale price maintenance is distinctly a pro-franchisor position. Its impact might be to keep prices lower than could be justified by the fixed-cost position of franchisees. Therefore, although many of the practices that Hunt observed in 1972 still exist, the way in which they are examined with reference to public policy has changed significantly.

Reduced New Business Failure Rate

One of the most important observations made in Hunt's original article dealt with the possibility that franchising lowered the failure rates for small start-up businesses. If proven, then the allocative efficiency implied by this effect clearly would be in the public interest. Hunt, however, found that no credible evidence existed to support it. The one study that dealt with the issue had been conducted by the International Franchise Association and subsequently was withdrawn from distribution when its methodological flaws were exposed (Ozanne and Hunt 1971).

During the intervening years, the number of franchised outlets has grown considerably. One reason for this growth has been the consistent perception that franchising was a relatively low-risk proposition, a perception that understandably was encouraged by the industry. There is theoretical support for the idea that franchise systems may perform better than vertically integrated systems to the extent that they solve basic agency cost problems (Lafontaine 1992a; Rubin 1978). Whether this translates to a reduction in the rate of failure for the systems or for the individual franchisees, however, has become the subject of significant controversy.

During the mid-1980s, the U.S. Department of Commerce published a series of comprehensive reports on the state of franchising (U.S. Department of Commerce 1988). Ostensibly drawing from an analysis of those reports, a spokesperson for the department claimed in the *Wall Street Journal* that fewer than 4% of U.S. franchises were closed during the prior year and added that franchising "is so regulated that failure in the system is almost self-prohibited" (Schlender 1986, p. D14). This figure, and its comparison to the higher overall rates of failure reported for small business start-ups in general, gave rise to the belief that franchising was relatively risk free, and the 4% failure rate became the conventional wisdom in the business press (Dingle 1990; Hartnet 1989). This became especially problematic because the 4% came to be associated with the overall risk of failure, not the yearly rate of attrition. Ultimately, this belief came under increasingly intense scrutiny from policy makers (Cutler 1991) and academic researchers (e.g., Padmanabhan 1988).

One of the factors making the analysis of franchise failure rates so difficult was the termination of the U.S. Department of Commerce's *Franchising in the Economy* annual report in 1988. A similar report using the same name subsequently was published by the franchising industry's leading trade association in conjunction with Horwath International (International Franchise Association Educational Foundation 1990) and later with Arthur Andersen and Company (1992), but the report's lack of industry independence and the inability of the researchers to attain sufficient response rates reduced its impact. The census data on franchising, although extensive, lacks much of the detail that researchers need to analyze the question of franchise failure (U.S. Bureau of the Census 1992). The other data sources for tracking industry trends are commercial indexes compiled primarily for the purposes of advising prospective franchisees of the collection of alternative systems (Bond 1997; Info Press 1998) and special editions of business publications devoted to franchising ("17th Annual Franchise 500" 1996). Lafontaine (1995a), however, found that these data sources are biased toward larger, more established franchise systems and recent entrants, and she argued that government involvement in the gathering and dissemination of data on the franchising industry is warranted so as to facilitate empirical research into, among other things, franchise failure rates. Without good data, therefore, assessing accurate failure rates is impossible and policy makers are operating in the dark.

Another problem in the analysis of franchise failure rates has been the lack of agreement on what constitutes failure (Cross 1994; Walker and Cross 1988). Is "termination for cause" a failure? If the franchisee retires and closes his or her outlet, then is that a failure? These questions are typical of the debate that surrounds interpretation of the data on franchise closings. In fact, even whether an outlet must be closed to constitute a failure is an open question. Franchisors often buy back failing outlets and then sell the franchise rights to other franchisees. Complicating this further is the distinction between franchise system failure and franchisee failure.

Notwithstanding the difficulties with the existing secondary data and the definitional complexity, several recent studies have sought to shed light on the issue of franchise failure rates. Castrogiovanni, Justis, and Julian (1993) found support for the claim that about 4% of franchised outlets fail each year.[4] Other researchers have found the assertion that becoming a franchisee is almost risk free when compared to opening an independent business to be a significant overstatement. Bates (1995) took issue with the industry claim that 96.9% of the franchised units opened within the previous five years still were in operation. Using census data, he found that the survival rate of young franchise firms from 1987 to late 1991 was 65.3% and that this compared badly with the 72.0% for nonfranchised firms. Analyses of franchise systems (i.e., franchisors) produced similar results. Shane (1996) found only 24.6% of new franchise systems surviving after 10 years. Lafontaine and Shaw (1998) found that less than 30% of new franchise systems survived for 12 years or more. This seems to be consistent with findings in the United Kingdom as well (Stanworth 1995).

Clearly, the expectation that purchasing a franchise outlet is a virtually risk-free investment is unrealistic. Although most of the recent empirical research has focused on the survival of the franchisor, it is logical to expect that franchisees fail at an even greater rate than do franchisors (i.e., franchisees of failed systems are joined by failed franchisees of surviving systems). It also is clear that franchisees of established systems fare much better than do those in start-up systems. Whether the differences in franchise fees between established and start-up systems is justified by these risk differences has not been empirically established. Nevertheless, the theorized benefits of owning a franchise remain unproven long after Hunt's original article.

Impact of Franchising on the Consumer

The central focus of public policy in marketing always has been protection of the consumer. It is important, therefore, to explore any suspected impact of franchising not only at the franchisee level but also at the consumer level. Hunt (1972) proposed two such areas of inquiry. Both were thought to be possible benefits of franchising. First, did franchising depress the level of concentration and, by implication, maintain higher levels of competition? In other words, when compared to chains of company-owned outlets, did the independence of franchisees increase competition and, thereby, provide more value to the consumer? Second, did franchising provide a method of ensuring mobile consumers that branded products and services would be of consistent quality?

Lower Levels of Industry Concentration

Hunt was uncertain as to the legitimacy of the claim that franchising would permanently reduce the level of concentration in retail industries. The reason for this was twofold. First, Oxenfeldt and Kelly (1968) had theorized that franchising was a temporary phenomenon in firms. It allowed young firms access to expansion capital in their growth stages. It was predicted that, as internally generated capital became more available to these firms, they would shift to company-owned chains. Second, empirical observation of movement within the fast-food industry suggested that Oxenfeldt and Kelly might have been correct (Love 1986).

Oxenfeldt and Kelly's (1968) thesis of ownership redirection spawned a significant number of studies intent on determining whether such a trend could be found (for a review, see Dant, Paswan, and Kaufmann 1996). Oxenfeldt and Kelly's (1968) idea that franchisors would reacquire successful franchise units, leaving the marginal outlets in the hands of franchisees, also suggested the potential for franchisor opportunism and raised public policy issues relating to the protection of franchisees (Dant, Kaufmann, and Paswan 1992; but see also Williams 1996). As in the case of franchisee failure rates, discerning ownership redirection becomes entangled with definitional complexities. In the nearly 20 studies of ownership redirection, researchers have employed secondary and primary data, aggregate- and firm-level data, cross-sectional and longitudinal data, and a multitude of surrogate operationalizations. Meta-analysis reveals that the single influencing factor as to whether evidence of ownership redirection is found or not is the operationalization of the construct (Dant, Paswan, and Kaufmann 1996). It also should be noted that Hunt's empirical observation of a shift toward company-owned outlets in the fast-food industry coincided with the decision of McDonald's, by far the largest and most visible franchise system, to reacquire many of its franchisees, a decision that subsequently was reversed (Kaufmann and Lafontaine 1994; Love 1986).

The capital acquisition rationale for franchising underlying Oxenfeldt and Kelly's (1968) thesis came under fire from economic theorists, who argued that franchising can be explained as a solution only to the agency problems occasioned by dispersed geographic outlets (Rubin 1978; but see also Lafontaine 1992b). This suggests that no firm-level reversal toward vertical integration should occur and that franchising as a method of distribution should remain a stable phenomenon. Patterns of franchised and company-owned outlets within firms will simply reflect differences in local monitoring costs (Brickley and Dark 1987).

Although the stability of franchising as an organizational form is important, the more significant policy question goes to Hunt's underlying assumption, that is, that having franchisees instead of vertically integrated retail chains would be beneficial to consumers because it implies a lower level of industry concentration and, thus, greater competition. Analysis of channel economics suggests that the opposite might be the case. Lafontaine (1995b) pointed out that royalties as percentages of gross revenues can be thought of as a tax on the franchisee, shifting the demand curve downward. If the franchisee has any local market power, then this sets up a type of double-marginalization problem that leads the franchisee to price higher than the franchisor would if operating a company-owned store. In other words, unless there is a high level of competition at the retail level among franchisees within the same chain, having franchises will lead to higher prices than will having a vertically integrated chain. In her 1995 study, Lafontaine found empirical support for that position. Blair and Esquibel (1996) argued that this is the reason why franchisors should be allowed to set maximum retail prices for their franchisees.

Consistency in the Product/Service Offering

Hunt's final area of inquiry was the question of whether franchising provided mobile consumers with desired standard products. He framed the question, first, as to whether the consumer desired such standardization and, second, as to whether franchising was particularly well suited to providing standardized products and services. He disposed of the first question easily, saying that it was evident from the success of the franchised chains that consumer demand was present. He was not convinced, however, that franchising offered a better way of providing standard offerings than did a company-owned chain.

The ability to deliver a standard product or service at dispersed retail outlets has been at the heart of the subsequent economic analysis of franchising. Agency theory suggests that salaried company employee-managers have incentives to shirk and will underinvest in the effort needed to run their outlets if not closely monitored. On the other hand, franchisees with claims to the profits of their outlets have incentives to work hard (Rubin 1978). To the extent that the franchise concept requires the hard work of the unit manager to ensure a standard product/service offering, franchising should deliver better performance than does a company-owned chain. However, although franchising solves issues of suboptimal effort, it does not solve issues of misdirected effort (Shane 1996). In other words, the same incentives that motivate the franchisee to work hard also motivate the franchisee to work in his or her best interests, not those of the franchisor. If the standardized offering is inconsistent with the demand characteristics of the franchisee's local market, then the franchisee will resist (Kaufmann and Eroglu 1998). Ultimately, however, the likely inability of the franchisor to completely subordinate local tastes to the standard offering might be more consistent with the public interest.

Hunt's assumption that standardized product/service offerings are valued raises sociological issues as well as those policy issues involving the maximization of consumer choice. Hunt's interpretation of the domination of franchising was that the consumer had spoken. Another interpretation, of course, is that it reflects a tyranny of the majority. In fact, as franchising has flourished over the intervening years, it has come under increasingly intense criticism for its role in the homogenization of choice in our culture. Ritzer (1996) referred to the rationalization of every aspect of American life as the "McDonaldization" of society and lamented the lack of creativity implicit in this hyperefficient environment. Luxenberg (1985) complained of how franchise chains have helped to rob small towns of their character. In other words, the standardization that initially was lauded as a way of reducing the anxiety of traveling consumers faced with the questionable quality of unfamiliar eating establishments has become so extensive as to begin to infringe on variety and choice. The resolution of this particular controversy is perhaps more in the realm of philosophy than in that of marketing. It does, however, reflect the depth of impact that franchising continues to have on the social and economic life of the U.S. consumer.

Conclusion

More than 25 years after Hunt published his original article on franchising, significant questions still remain about the specifics of its socioeconomic consequences. Although numerous studies and a substantial body of theoretical work have ensued, some of the more pressing policy issues remain unresolved. Does the lack of earnings disclosures reduce the quality of decision making on the part of prospective franchisees and encourage unethical selling practices? Does franchising reduce the likelihood of failure for new businesses? Much of the difficulty in answering these questions is due to the lack of reliable data. Since the commerce department ceased gathering data during the late 1980s (U.S. Department of Commerce 1988; see also Trutko, Trutko, and Kostecka 1993), there has been no systematic government-sponsored data collection on franchising except for one question on the focused surveys conducted by the census bureau.

Interestingly, there is a relatively easy and inexpensive solution to this problem. The FTC franchise disclosure rule requires that an extensive body of information be provided to prospective franchisees before they sign any franchise contracts. The form of this disclosure (usually following the format prescribed by NASAA) provides a fairly consistent and comparable view of all franchisors. These documents typically run 100 to 200 pages in length, and although some states require filing of the documents by all franchisors operating within the states, there is no federal filing requirement. Proprietary data-gathering companies collect these hard copy documents from states that require filing and sell the analyzed data to interested parties. These data understandably are expensive given the onerous task of collection and data entry, and they are incomplete because of the state-level filing requirements.

The solution is for the FTC to require federal filing of disclosure documents by all franchisors doing business or offering franchises in the United States and for the filing to be done in soft (electronic) form rather than in hard copy form. Those sections amenable to specification within a uniform format should be submitted in machine-readable form; other sections could be submitted in standard word processing format. It is likely that all of these documents are created as word processed documents anyway, so requiring electronic filing would impose no expense or burden on the part of franchisors. In fact, it is quite likely that it would reduce the costs associated with filing. Franchisors complain about the burden of disparate state filing requirements. Prospective franchisees and their advocates, researchers, and policy makers complain of the inability to track or analyze industry trends because of unavailable or prohibitively expensive data. A movement toward standardized electronic filing would seem to be in everyone's best interests.

One of the most remarkable recent changes in the policy environment of franchising has been the shift in the Republican Congress's position on franchise legislation. Under Democratic leadership, the House Committee on Small Business repeatedly introduced legislation designed to regulate the franchise relationship, only to have it defeated by strong Republican opposition. Now, bipartisan support for such legislation suggests that some form of legislation might, in fact, pass in the near future. A key factor in this policy change has been the effective lobbying efforts of franchisee advocacy groups and the increasing difficulty of the franchisor community to speak with one voice. Nevertheless, neither the Republican nor the Democratic position (nor that of the FTC) favors the requirement of disclosing earnings, which are arguably the most important data for a prospective franchisee to have and the area in which there is the greatest possibility of deception if kept informal.

The central question raised by this handbook is what role marketing could play in the discussion of public policy, here relating specifically to franchising. I say *could* because, to date, the direction of public discourse on franchising has been primarily determined by economists and lawyers. This is particularly unfortunate because marketing has a great deal to offer to the subject.

Issues of encroachment (i.e., the harm imposed on franchisees through the placement of new outlets in close proximity to existing franchised outlets), for example, would be much better informed with more explicit reference to research on the interaction of brand preference and store choice behavior rather than on resorting to simplistic legal definitions of permissible distances. Marketers and marketing geographers have provided methodologies for the careful analysis of trade areas and interlocational competition (Ghosh and McLafferty 1987). Marketing can make significant contributions to more relevant and accurate measures of encroachment.

Marketing's expertise in consumer decision processes suggests the potential for significant contributions in several other areas of franchise policy making. The prospective franchisee's decision to purchase a franchise is a complex buying decision. Understanding the role that different types of data play in that decision will help policy makers to determine the wisdom and viability of proposed regulation such as mandatory earnings disclosure. In other words, marketing could provide significant insight into the way in which communication is used and misused in the descriptions of earnings potential. Similarly, research in marketing might help to answer questions about how a prospective franchisee acquires and processes information about the relative risk of becoming a franchisee. Even the structure of the franchisee's decision process as it relates to the overall decision to become self-employed is a topic eminently suited to marketing analysis.

The trade-off between the economic benefits of uniformity and the deterioration of choice is another obvious area for marketing segmentation analysis and explanation. Here again, marketing's expertise in consumer decision making provides the theories and methodologies to examine consumers' reactions to these limitations on choice and the impact of ubiquitous standardization on product/service satisfaction.

Franchising is an important form of distribution and already has received attention from marketing scholars. Most of the attention, however, has been from channels researchers examining, for example, the impact of contractual integration on channel management and control. It is important to recognize that it also provides marketers fertile ground for policy research at both the interorganizational and consumer levels. I believe that policy makers will welcome these contributions.

Because of the format of this chapter, I have not discussed two important policy issues relevant to franchising that were not as central in 1972: the role of franchising in international development and the impact of the Internet on encroachment.

Because of franchising's success in the United States, it has become an important export vehicle (Konnigsberg 1990; Walker 1989). In fact, most of the growth in some of the more established systems now is derived from international expansion. There are clear balance-of-trade benefits from this for the United States. Moreover, franchising provides an efficient method for the transfer of retail know-how to developing countries. Through its impact on local retail distribution and industries supplying inputs to those retailers, it acts as an impetus for internal development (Kaufmann and Leibenstein 1988). Economic development is an accepted policy goal, and international franchising clearly appears to have both domestic and host country benefits.

The Internet has affected most every area of business, and franchising is no exception. The Internet's impact on franchising has been primarily related to the management of the franchise systems. Communication among widely dispersed outlets always has caused franchisors concern, and the ease with which information and training can be disseminated over the Internet (and, in some cases, over intranets) has improved system management significantly. The use of the Internet is likely to have other effects that are more problematic from a policy perspective. The most likely is the distribution of products directly from the franchisor to the end user. Essentially, this is the same problem that occurs when the franchisor distributes products through other channels such as grocery stores (e.g., Carvel Ice Cream) and convenience stores (e.g., Dunkin' Donuts). To the extent that the Internet makes the end user more accessible to franchisors, these forms of electronic encroachment will harm franchisees. Although this is primarily a contract issue and not a policy issue, both the courts and Congress have tended to view franchisees as a group needing protection from unscrupulous franchisors. It seems quite probable that eventually, either the courts or the legislature (or both) will have to deal with this issue.

Notes

1. The topic of women in franchising was not covered in Hunt's (1972) original article, although he discussed this in a subsequent piece (Hunt 1978).

2. Although some relevant articles appear in business magazines such as *Black Enterprise,* there has been little academic attention given to minority franchising (but see Trombetta 1977).

3. As of 1999, 14 states had franchise disclosure and registration requirements.

4. It should be noted that this return to the 4% per year figure is substantially different from a statement that 4% of franchisees fail. Over the five-year horizon usually used to describe small business failures, a 4% annual rate would produce an overall failure rate of close to 20%.

References

American Motor Inns v. Holiday Inns Inc. (1975), 3rd Cir. 521 F.2nd 1230.
Anand, Punam (1987), "Inducing Franchisees to Relinquish Control," *Journal of Marketing Research,* 24 (May), 215-21.
Arthur Andersen and Company (1992), *Franchising in the Economy 1989-1992.* Washington, DC: International Franchise Association.

Bates, Timothy (1995), "Analysis of Survival Rates among Franchise and Independent Small Business Start-Ups," *Journal of Small Business Management,* 33 (2), 26-36.

Baucus, David A., Melissa S. Baucus, and Sherrie E. Human (1996), "Consensus in Franchising Organizations: A Cooperative Arrangement among Entrepreneurs," *Journal of Business Venturing,* 11 (5), 359-78.

Biggart, Nicole W. (1988), *Charismatic Capitalism.* Chicago: University of Chicago Press.

Blair, Roger D. and Amanda K. Esquibel (1996), "The Implications of the Ban on Maximum Resale Price Restraints in Franchising," in *Proceedings of the Society of Franchising.* Minneapolis, MN: Society of Franchising.

———— and Jill B. Herndon (1995), "Franchise Tying Suits after Kodak," *Journal of Public Policy & Marketing,* 14 (1), 149-54.

———— and ———— (1999), "The Misapplication of Kodak in Franchise Tying Suits," *Journal of Business Venturing,* 14 (4), 397-415.

———— and John E. Lopatka (1998), "Albrecht Overruled—At Last," *Antitrust Law Journal,* 66 (3), 537-66.

Bond, Robert (1997), *Bond's Franchise Guide.* Oakland, CA: Source Book Publications.

Brickley, James A. and Frederick H. Dark (1987), "The Choice of Organizational Form," *Journal of Financial Economics,* 18, 401-20.

Carvel Corporation (1965), 68 FTC 128.

Castrogiovanni, Gary, Robert Justis, and Scott Julian (1993), "Franchise Failure Rates: An Assessment of Magnitude and Influencing Factors," *Journal of Small Business Management,* 31 (April), 105-14.

Caves, Richard E. and William F. Murphy (1976), "Franchising: Firms, Markets, and Intangible Assets," *Southern Economic Journal,* 42 (4), 572-86.

Continental T.V. v. GTE Sylvania (1977), 433 U.S. 36.

Cooper, A. C. (1981), "Strategic Management: New Ventures and Small Business," *Long Range Planning,* 14 (5), 39-45.

Cross, James (1994), "Franchise Failures: Definitional and Measurement Issues," in *Proceedings of the Society of Franchising.* Minneapolis, MN: Society of Franchising.

Cutler, Barry J. (1991), *Testimony before the House Committee on Small Business Hearing: Franchising in Hard Times* (Serial No. 102-10, March 20). Washington, DC: Government Printing Office.

Dant, Rajiv P., Patrick J. Kaufmann, and Audhesh K. Paswan (1992), "Ownership Redirection in Franchised Channels," *Journal of Public Policy & Marketing,* 11 (1), 33-44.

Dant, Rajiv P., Audhesh K. Paswan, and Patrick J. Kaufmann (1996), "What We Know about Ownership Redirection in Franchising: A Meta-Analysis," *Journal of Retailing,* 72 (4), 429-44.

Dingle, Derek T. (1990), "Franchising's Fast Track to Freedom," *Money Extra,* 35-44. (*Money* magazine special issue)

Eastman Kodak Company v. Image Technical Services Inc. (1992), 112 S. Ct. 2072.

Emerson, Robert W. (1998), "Franchisee Selection and Retention: Discrimination Claims and Affirmative Action Programs," *Arizona Law Review,* 40, 511-613.

Federal Trade Commission (1986), *Disclosure Requirements and Prohibitions Concerning Franchising and Business Opportunity Ventures,* 16 *CFR* 436 (as revised).

———— (1997), *Hearing in the Matter of the Franchise Rule,* No. R-511003, August 21, Chicago.

Ghosh, Avijit and Sarah McLafferty (1987), *Location Strategies for Retail and Service Firms.* Lexington, MA: Lexington Books.

Goldberg, Victor (1979), "The Law and Economics of Vertical Restrictions: A Relational Perspective," *Texas Law Review,* 58 (1), 91-129.

Hartnet, Michael (1989), "Fired Executives Discover Franchising Is a Route to a Second Chance at Success," *Success,* October, 50-51.

Hunt, Shelby (1972), "The Socioeconomic Consequences of the Franchise System of Distribution," *Journal of Marketing,* 36 (July), 32-38.

——— (1975), "An Examination of Franchisee Independence," *Marquette Business Review,* 19 (1), 9-16.

——— (1978), "Women in Franchising," *MSU Business Topics,* Spring, 25-28.

Info Press (1998), *The 1998 Franchise Annual.* St. Catherines, Ontario: Info Press.

International Franchise Association Educational Foundation (1990), *Franchising in the Economy 1988-1990.* Washington, DC: IFAEF.

Justis, Robert and Richard Judd (1989), *Franchising.* Cincinnati, OH: South-Western.

Kaufmann, Patrick J. and Rajiv P. Dant (1996), "Multi-Unit Franchising: Growth and Management Issues," *Journal of Business Venturing,* 11 (September), 343-58.

——— and Sevgin Eroglu (1998), "Standardization and Adaptation in Business Format Franchising," *Journal of Business Venturing,* 14, 69-85.

——— and Francine Lafontaine (1994), "Costs of Control: The Source of Economic Rents for McDonald's Franchisees," *Journal of Law and Economics,* 37 (2), 417-53.

——— and Harvey Leibenstein (1988), "International Business Format Franchising and Retail Entrepreneurship: A Possible Source of Retail Know-How for Developing Countries," *Journal of Development Planning,* 18, 165-79.

——— and John Stanworth (1995), "The Decision to Become a Franchisee: A Study of Prospective Franchisees," *Journal of Small Business Management,* 33 (4), 22-33.

Knight, Russell M. (1984), "The Independence of the Franchisee Entrepreneur," *Journal of Small Business Management,* 22 (2), 53-61.

Konnigsberg, Alex (1990), *Testimony before the Committee on Small Business Hearing on Franchising in the Economy* (U.S. House of Representatives, Serial No. 101-79, September 27). Washington, DC: Government Printing Office.

Lafontaine, Francine (1992a), "Agency Theory and Franchising: Some Empirical Results," *RAND Journal of Economics,* 23 (2), 263-83.

——— (1992b), "How and Why Do Franchisors Do What They Do?" in *Proceedings of the Society of Franchising.* Minneapolis, MN: Society of Franchising.

——— (1995a), "A Critical Appraisal of Data Sources on Franchising," in *Franchising: Contemporary Issues and Research,* P. Kaufmann and R. Dant, eds. New York: Haworth, 5-26.

——— (1995b), "Within Market Price Dispersion in Franchised Chains," in *Proceedings of the Society of Franchising.* Minneapolis, MN: Society of Franchising.

——— and Katheryn Shaw (1998), "Franchising Growth and Franchisor Entry and Exit in the U.S. Market: Myth and Reality," *Journal of Business Venturing,* 13 (2), 95-112.

Lester J. Albrecht v. The Herald Company (1968), 390 U.S. 145.

Lewis, Warren L. (1988), *Earnings Claim Study: A Study of Franchisors Registered with the Securities Division of the State of Maryland.* Washington, DC: Duncan, Weinberg, Miller, & Pembroke.

Love, John F. (1986), *McDonald's: Behind the Arches.* New York: Bantam Books.

Luxenberg, Stan (1985), *Roadside Empires.* New York: Viking Penguin.

Mazero, Joyce G. and Mark B. Forseth (1992), "Justice before the Mast: State Administrator's Panel," *Annual Forum on Franchising,* October, 28-30.

Nevin John R., Shelby D. Hunt, and Robert W. Ruekert (1980), "The Impact of Fair Practice Laws on a Franchise Channel of Distribution," *MSU Business Topics,* Summer, 27-37.

North American Securities Administrators Association (1993), *Uniform Franchise Offering Circular* (as amended). Washington, DC: NASAA.

Opinion Research Corporation (1985), *Final Report of a Survey to Evaluate the Economic Impact on Franchisors of the FTC Trade Regulation Rule Entitled "Disclosure Requirements and Prohibitions Concerning Franchising and Business Opportunity Ventures."* Princeton, NJ: Opinion Research Corporation.

Oxenfeldt, Alfred R. and Anthony O. Kelly (1968), "Will Successful Franchise Systems Ultimately Become Wholly Owned Chains?" *Journal of Retailing,* 44 (4), 69-87.

Ozanne, Urban B. and Shelby D. Hunt (1971), *The Economic Effects of Franchising.* Washington, DC: Government Printing Office.

Padmanabhan, K. H. (1988), "Are Franchised Businesses Less Risky than the Non-Franchised Businesses?" in *Proceedings of the Society of Franchising.* Minneapolis, MN: Society of Franchising.

Perma Life Mufflers Inc. v. International Parts Corporation (1968), 392 U.S. 134, 139.

Perry, Robert L. (1994), *The 50 Best Low-Investment, High-Profit Franchises,* 2nd ed. Englewood Cliffs, NJ: Prentice Hall.

Peterson, Alden and Rajiv P. Dant (1990), "Perceived Advantages of the Franchise Option from the Franchisee Perspective: Empirical Insights from a Service Franchise," *Journal of Small Business Management,* 28 (July), 46-61.

Posner, Richard A. (1976), *Antitrust Law: An Economic Perspective.* Chicago: University of Chicago Press.

Ritzer, George (1996), *The McDonaldization of Society.* Thousand Oaks, CA: Pine Forge.

Rubin, Paul H. (1978), "The Theory of the Firm and the Structure of the Franchise Contract," *Journal of Law and Economics,* 21 (April), 223-33.

Scheck v. Burger King (1992), 756 F.Supp. 543 (S.D. Fla. 1991); *on rehearing,* 798 F.Supp. 692 (S.D. Fla. 1992).

Schlender, Brenton R. (1986), "Working on the Chain Gang," *The Wall Street Journal,* May 19, D14.

"17th Annual Franchise 500" (1996), *Entrepreneur,* January, 168-316.

Shane, Scott A. (1996), "Hybrid Organizational Arrangements and Their Implications for Firm Growth and Survival: A Study of New Franchisors," *Academy of Management Journal,* 39, 216-34.

Siegel v. Chicken Delight (1972), 448 F.2d 43 (9th Cir. 1971); *cert. den.* 405 U.S. 955 (1972).

Small Business Administration (1998), "SBA Announces Pilot Project to Boost Federal Contracts for 'Very Small Business,'" press release (No. 98-74), September 2.

Spandorf, Rochelle B. (1995), Charting Courses in the Debate over Mandatory Earnings Claims," *Franchise Law Journal,* 15 (1), 34-37.

Stanworth, John (1995), "A European Perspective on the Success of the Franchise Relationship," in *Proceedings of the Society of Franchising.* Minneapolis, MN: Society of Franchising.

———— and James Curran (1978), "Franchising at a Major Crossroads," *Marketing,* April, 22-26.

———— and David Purdy (1994), *The Blenheim/University of Westminster Franchise Survey No. 1.* London: University of Westminster, International Franchise Research Centre.

Stassen, Robert E. and Robert A. Mittelstaedt (1995), "Territory Encroachment in Maturing Franchise Systems," in *Franchising Contemporary Issues and Research,* P. Kaufmann and R. Dant, eds. Binghamton, NY: Haworth, 27-48.

State Oil Company v. Khan (1997), 118 S. Ct. 275.

Trombetta, William L. (1977), "The Black Service Station Franchisee," *Review of Black Political Economy,* 7 (4), 364-72.

————— and Albert L. Page (1978), "Franchisor Control vs. Franchisee Independence," *Atlanta Economic Review,* March-April, 28-34.

Trutko, James, John Trutko, and Andrew Kostecka (1993), "Franchising's Growing Role in the U.S. Economy, 1975-2000," report to the U.S. Small Business Administration (No. SBA-6643-OA-91).

United States v. Arnold Schwinn & Company (1967), 388 U.S. 365.

U.S. Bureau of the Census (1992), *Characteristics of Owners and Their Businesses.* Washington, DC: Government Printing Office.

U.S. Department of Commerce (1988), *Franchising in the Economy.* Washington, DC: Government Printing Office.

U.S. House of Representatives (1993), *Minority Franchising: Is Discrimination a Factor?* (hearing before the House Committee on Small Business, 103rd Congress). Washington, DC: Government Printing Office.

————— (1997), "Report on Small Business Programs Reauthorization and Amendments Act," House Report No. 105-246.

————— (1998), *Small Business Franchise Act of 1998* (H.R. 4841). Washington, DC: Government Printing Office.

U.S. Senate (1997), "Report on Small Business Reauthorization Act," Senate Report No. 105-62.

Vincent, William S. and Partick J. Kaufmann (1996), "Mandatory Earnings Disclosure: Some Comments and Caveats," *Franchising Research: An International Journal,* 1 (3), 21-27.

Walker, Bruce (1989), *A Comparison of International vs. Domestic Expansion by U.S. Franchise Systems.* Washington, DC: International Franchise Association.

————— and James Cross (1988), "Franchise Failures: More Questions than Answers," in *Proceedings of the Society of Franchising.* Minneapolis, MN: Society of Franchising.

Weingartner, Nancy (1999), "Franchisee Accuses Wendy's of Racial Discrimination," *Franchise Times,* January, 22.

Williams, Darrell (1996), "Franchise Contract Terminations: Is There Evidence of Franchisor Abuse?" in *Proceedings of the Society of Franchising.* Minneapolis, MN: Society of Franchising.

11 *Chapter*

Pricing Strategy, Competition, and Consumer Welfare

Joseph P. Guiltinan
Alan G. Sawyer

Perhaps no aspect of public policy thought has been more dominated by neoclassical welfare economics theory than has that of pricing. However, during recent years, scholars from marketing, economic psychology, and game theory have offered new insights on the competitive and consumer welfare consequences of pricing strategies. In addition, consumer researchers have developed extensive insights into how people respond to various ways of presenting price information.

We begin this chapter by examining the welfare effects of pricing practices. Specifically, we examine the consequences for consumer surplus of four selected strategies of interest. Subsequently, we examine broadened notions of consumer welfare, and we review what has been learned about the impact of price presentation practices on consumer behavior. We conclude by offering some suggestions regarding research issues that might be addressed by marketing scholars interested in public policy.

Research Insights from the Traditional Perspective

Consumer Welfare as Consumer Surplus

An individual's consumer surplus for a given product is the difference between the consumer's reservation price (willingness to pay) and the price actually paid.[1] The formulation of *consumer* welfare used in economics is "the expected present value of aggregate consumer surplus" across all customers in a market (Cabral and Riordan 1997, p. 163), and the impact of a given pricing strategy on consumer welfare is judged by traditional welfare economics as positive if lower market prices increase the number of buyers and increase total consumer surplus among existing buyers.

Although strategies that increase output in an industry generally are regarded as enhancing consumer welfare, such strategies might not be optimal for social welfare. In welfare economics, *social* welfare is the sum of consumer surplus plus producers' profits. Thus, when the marginal cost of serving new customers is high and the demand elasticity is relatively low, profits might suffer, so the net welfare effects are less obvious. That is, from an economic efficiency perspective, resources are best allocated when social welfare is maximized as reflected in some "optimal" balance of profits and aggregate consumer surplus (Schmalensee 1981; Varian 1985).

In the following sections, we review what is known or believed about the consumer surplus consequences of four classes of pricing strategies: price discrimination, price bundling, aggressive/predatory pricing, and anti-dumping petitions. Our purpose is to illustrate how traditional (economic-based) policy analysis examines the consequences of various pricing strategies and to clarify the centrality of the consumer surplus metric to that thinking.

Price Discrimination Issues

Firms price discriminate when they charge different prices for the same product to different customers. In the traditional economics perspective, which presumes that consumers are informed about their alternatives, price discrimination occurs because some buyers have higher reservation prices than do others. In "perfect" first-degree price discrimination, a profit-maximizing seller extracts all of each consumer's surplus. This is achievable only if a seller knows each customer's reservation price and can sell its product in a "one-on-one" fashion. The advent of powerful database marketing tools has increased the viability of such policies. Indeed, there also is a significant trend toward "one-to-one" (or "customized") pricing based on the profitability of individual accounts, not just according to individual demand functions (Brooks 1999).

More typically, marketers have used "third-degree" price discrimination in which a market is divided into high- and low-elasticity segments. Couponing and "hi-lo" retail pricing are typical examples of this form of price discrimination; high-elasticity customers are more likely to use coupons, and low-elasticity customers tend not to use coupons (Hoch, Drèze, and Purk 1994; Howell 1991). Other examples of third-degree price discrimination include the yield management systems used by airlines and other service providers (Desiraju and Shugan 1999), senior citizen discounts, discounts for purchasing or using products during "off-peak" periods, and offers of discounted prices for purchases in advance for services such as concert tickets and travel (Shugan and Xie, 2000a) (see Table 11.1).

TABLE 11.1 Alternative Price Discrimination Strategies

Type	Example(s)
Mail/insert distributed coupons	Coupon users may be subsidized by higher shelf prices
Targeted coupons or discounts	Available to targeted geodemographic segments or frequent customers
Periodic discounts	Yield management, "early bird" specials, off-peak use
Noncumulative volume discounts	Buy two, get one free
Cross-selling discounts	Mixed bundling
First-degree discrimination	Negotiated pricing, Internet pricing based on knowledge of past patterns of purchase
Second-market discounting	Dumping, private branding, secondary demographic markets

Third-degree price discrimination is presumed to enhance consumer welfare when aggregate output increases under price discrimination because new markets (segments) are served. This will occur when, as a firm moves from a single price P_i to separate prices P_H and P_L (where $P_H > P_i > P_L$), the increase in sales in the weak market (those who now buy because $P_L < P_i$) is greater than the decrease in sales in the strong market (who now must pay P_H instead of P_i) (Schmalensee 1981). In general, classical economists have accepted the belief that the demand curve in the high-elastic market is more concave than that in the low-elastic market, so that aggregate output will expand (Bork 1978) based on the expectation that demand will expand in the high-elasticity market as new buyers now enter.

But what are the effects of such price discrimination on market maturity when primary demand is stable? Such markets often are characterized by a high level of short-term promotional activity such as coupons, and two studies that have directly examined the issue of coupon practices and consumer surplus argue that couponing can negatively affect consumer welfare in mature markets. According to Howell (1991) and Vilcassim and Wittink (1987), this is so because (1) firms that offer coupons are likely to compensate for these reductions by adjusting shelf prices upward, (2) competitors follow suit in matching coupon offers and raising shelf prices, and (3) there is no expansion of primary demand. Demand elasticities for individual brands are high in such markets, whereas the elasticity of total market demand tends to be low. So, whereas price competition occurs in the high-elasticity segment, its main impact is on brand choice. Under these conditions, the loss of consumer surplus in the low-elasticity segment (from higher shelf prices) is viewed as likely to exceed the gain in consumer surplus in the high-elasticity segment (where no increase in industry volume among coupon buyers results), so that *aggregate* consumer surplus should decline. Although the issue of whether aggregate consumer surplus actually declines would seem to be an empirical question (albeit one not easily researched), the Howell (1991) and Vilcassim and Wittink (1987) arguments are provocative and suggest a need for more systematic analysis of this issue. In any event, it is important to recognize that the view that the effects of third-degree price discrimination are *presumptively* benign rests on a generalized assumption about the relative concavity of low- and high-elasticity markets' demand curves.

Shugan and Xie (2000b) offered further evidence that a particular form of potential price discrimination inevitably leads to positive effects on social welfare. As mentioned earlier, advance selling is the practice of a firm offering lower prices to consumers who, in return for the lower prices, are willing to commit in advance before they are absolutely sure that they will want to buy a service on a particular date. Shugan and Xie's extensive theoretical analysis of the effects of advance selling across a wide variety of conditions proves that, due to the increased sales from early buyers, this practice can "significantly improve sellers' profit without decreasing consumers' surplus" (p. 23). Moreover, "advance selling has no impact on consumer surplus in markets with homogeneous consumers and can increase consumer surplus in markets with heterogeneous consumers" (p. 23). The fact that advance selling, which may take advantage of price discrimination among multiple consumer segments, appears to have no adverse effects on social welfare and often has positive effects on both firms and consumers is an unintuitive result that should be encouraging for both marketing managers and public policy makers. Shugan and Xie's impressive analyses also may serve as a model for other research about the effects of price discrimination.

Bundling

In "pure" bundling, Product *x* is available only if purchased with Product *y*. In that sense, pure bundling is essentially a tying arrangement. In "mixed" bundling, buyers can choose to purchase only *x* or only *y*, or both *x* and *y*, from the same vendor.

Much of the bundling literature has been focused on monopoly bundling scenarios. A general conclusion of this research is that mixed bundling should be preferred to unbundled sales by producers and consumers alike when demands for the two products are negatively correlated (Tellis 1986). With the same assumptions, however, pure bundling reduces consumer surplus (Salinger 1995). But in a typical marketing strategy scenario, bundling is used when the components are complements. In such cases, reservation prices for *x* and *y* ought to be positively correlated in the sense that the utilities for *x* and *y* are somewhat contingent on the purchase of each other (Guiltinan 1987). This can be so, either because *y* has no utility without *x* (so that it is a *necessary* complement), because using both *x* and *y* enhances the functional utility of one or both of the products, or because there are search economies in buying *x* and *y* together.

Applying game theory, some economists view the pure bundling of necessary complements as a product line strategy that enables firms to differentiate their products and, thus, reduce price competition in the primary market (Chen 1997; Whinston 1990). Mixed bundling undermines this differentiation role by allowing more price competition in the market for the second product. Ultimately, however, this results in a reduction in both firms' profits and in aggregate volume of "hybrid" systems, leading to lower social welfare (Matutes and Regibeau

1992). Chen (1997) showed that, in a duopoly setting, pure bundling results not only in increased profits but also in reduced consumer welfare (higher prices in the x market and probably reduced consumption in the y market). If x and y are complementary products used in fixed proportions, however, then a rival for y may allow the market for x to expand if it is differentiated enough to create an expansion in demand. The welfare implications in this case are uncertain (Whinston 1990).

Recent research on bundling has been dominated by such game theoretic formulations. Although insightful, these studies have been limited to duopoly scenarios (for mathematical tractability) and largely to the case of necessary complements. In practice, pure bundles may come with price incentives not attached to mixed bundles (which will enhance the consumer surplus realized on the former), and the reservation price for a bundle is likely to be influenced by the degree of relatedness of the components (Herrmann, Huber, and Coulter 1997). Thus, direct comparisons between the effects of pure and mixed bundles are difficult to generalize based on game theoretic analyses to date.

Another challenge is to compare the effects of bundling versus unbundled sales in the monopolistic competition case. One must look past traditional economic thinking to make such comparisons. That is, consumers' overall evaluations of the utility of the bundle appear to influence reservation prices both for the bundle and its components (Simonin and Ruth 1995). In addition, the utility of the bundle can be analyzed using prospect theory (Yadav and Monroe 1993). If the evaluation is primarily based on the transaction value of the deal, and if consumers pay more because of the framing, is consumer surplus changed? To what extent do our conclusions change depending on the correlation of the products' reservation prices?

Aggressive/Predatory Pricing

Because low-price strategies increase consumer surplus, traditional economic theory would argue that price-based competition ought to be unimpeded by antitrust concerns. This position is most easily supported in the cases of penetration pricing (the practice of reducing new product prices to meet the demands of price-sensitive segments) and experience pricing (the practice of pricing below short-run costs when average costs decline sharply with cumulative experience) (Tellis 1986). In such cases, industry price reductions are likely to hold for the long run.

We use the term *aggressive pricing* to connote low-price strategies specifically directed at harming competitors as opposed to those low-price strategies that are derived from the benefits of experience curve pricing. Aggressive pricing usually is viewed as pro-competitive because it clearly leads to lower consumer prices, at least in the short run. Of concern to public policy makers, however, are the long-term consequences of aggressive pricing, which is so extensive as to be potentially predatory. Successful predation results in the elimination of competitors and higher prices (with reduced consumer surplus) in the long term. As Guiltinan and Gundlach (1996) pointed out, state regulators tend to be excessively concerned with preserving competitors (especially small ones) even when workable competition still is a reality, whereas the prevailing federal perspective is that predation is irrational and, therefore, unlikely. The latter argument generally rests on the presumptions that (1) only "below-cost" pricing could be construed as predatory, (2) these losses could be recouped only through setting supracompetitive prices in the future, and (3) it is unlikely that firms could set supracompetitive prices given that this would encourage new entrants.

Conventional thinking also is challenged as offering too narrow a perspective of what might constitute predatory pricing behavior. Aggressive pricing may be a weapon that is used to influence multiple types of consumer or competitor behaviors and can force competitors to be less competitive in a variety of nonprice ways (e.g., reducing investments in innovation, retreating to core markets). So, although aggregate consumer surplus may be enhanced by the aggressive episode, the resulting market might be less vibrant on nonprice benefits (e.g., innovation, quality, variety, service) and even longer term on price competitiveness if the aggressive episode results in effective monopoly power through the emergence of an acknowledged price "leader" or through collusion (Guiltinan and Gundlach 1996; Gundlach and Guiltinan 1998).

A corollary to this argument is the recognition that pricing strategy must be viewed in the context of a firm's overall competitive strategy. Thus, the Department of Justice (DOJ) filed a predation suit against American Airlines for slashing prices to match low-cost competitors and then adding more flights. The combined strategy was alleged to have driven out competitors, allowing recoupment of short-term losses (Mathews and McCartney 1999). Similarly, some economists noted that giving away software to build an installed base of customers who have high switching costs is likely to be a successful strategy for creating market power sufficient for recoupment (France and Hamm 1998). Thus, understanding the long-term implications of aggressive pricing for competition and consumer welfare is likely to require the continued development of comprehensive models that can link the multiple dimensions of competitive strategy (cf. Chen and Miller 1994; Urbany and Dickson 1994). Indeed, the analyses of predatory pricing might be less relevant than analyses in which predatory behavior is conceptualized as a strategy involving any combination of tactics on which a firm can be aggressively competitive.

Anti-Dumping Petitions

An important strategic weapon in a global economy is the anti-dumping petition. Generally speaking, dumping is said to occur if a competitor's export price is below the ordinary comparable price when the product is destined for home country consumption; thus, dumping is a form of price discrimination. The filing of a charge of illegal dumping against a foreign competitor can be construed as a pricing strategy in that it is designed to influence competitive supply levels and/or prices. Marsh (1998) pointed out that, typically, only some of the domestic competitors in an industry file charges against foreign-sourced competitors, an indication that this often is likely to be a firm-specific strategy with some competitors having more to gain than others from protection from low-priced imports.

Anti-dumping remedies—usually duties or voluntary export restraints negotiated with foreign-sourced firms—would seem to have a negative effect on consumer surplus. Local anti-dumping public policies clearly are designed to protect domestic *firms* from injury (although in the European Union, anti-dumping
policy does contain a "community interest" provision requiring some evaluation
of the impact of potential remedies on upstream and downstream stakeholders
including consumers [Vermulst and Driessen 1997]). If an anti-dumping petition is successfully prosecuted, then the usual result is a duty levied on the foreign competitor to raise the effective price. However, one-third of these petitions
are withdrawn, typically after the domestic industry has negotiated an out-of-
court agreement on price or quantity restrictions and usually with the explicit
cooperation of the government, resulting in higher prices and lower domestic
consumption (Rosendorff 1996).[2] Future research on the welfare consequences
of these policies probably should parallel the suggested path for future research
on aggressive pricing.

Broader Perspectives on Consumer Welfare

Consumer surplus clearly is a useful conceptual metric for evaluating consumer
welfare. However, the acceptance of consumer surplus as the sole criterion for
the evaluation of pricing strategies such as price discrimination, bundling, and
aggressive pricing seems to require acceptance of four assumptions: (1) that
products are homogeneous (so that the *quantity* of aggregate output would be a
good surrogate for the aggregate utility that consumers receive), (2) that consumers have and use perfect information about alternatives, (3) that the aggregate economic welfare outweighs considerations of interpersonal equity in
assessing welfare, and (4) that short-run gains in consumer surplus (from aggressive pricing) can be taken as a guarantor of long-term gains.

In reality, markets are imperfect. Thus, the distribution of imperfectly competitive substitutes and the limited ability and motivation of people to search for
and process incomplete information (as discussed later) limit the robustness of
models that ignore those realities. Long-term and short-term consumer surplus
results may diverge, and changes can occur in the available nonprice benefits
due to changes in market structure. In addition, price knowledge and perceptions (and, thus, perceived quality and reservation prices) may change with different information about alternatives. Thus, it is not surprising that, to more
completely assess the welfare implications of the pricing strategies discussed in
the preceding section, alternative dimensions of consumer welfare might be
sought.

The Risk of Focusing Solely on Consumer Surplus

As noted earlier, consumer surplus is not easily estimated. This is especially
true in a dynamic imperfect market. More important, however, acceptance of
consumer surplus as an overarching goal allows the ends to justify the means.

For example, Gerstner and Hess (1990) presented a model in which "upselling" (i.e., "bait and switch") takes place when a featured brand is out of stock, arguing that consumers actually benefit from bait-and-switch practices when the gain in utility from a higher value product exceeds the sum of the incremental price of the substitute and the cost of waiting for the featured brand to be restocked. Wilkie, Mela, and Gundlach (1998) showed that the consumer benefits in the Gerstner and Hess model really reflect the effects of upselling (the presentation of quality information) instead of the out-of-stock condition. A more fundamental issue, however, is whether consumer welfare can be said to be enhanced—regardless of the impact on consumer surplus—from any deceptive practice (especially one that also might be injurious to competitors).

Distribution of Choices

Marketers generally are interested in aspects of choice that are not readily incorporated in the consumer surplus construct. Some economists also acknowledge the importance of such dimensions. For example, in discussing resale price maintenance, economists note that this practice facilitates the provision of information services (Boyd 1997) and enhanced product quality (Boudreaux and Ekelund 1996). Whinston (1990) is among those economists whose delineation of welfare effects includes *variety*. His view of variety, however, includes only quality variants, which are presumed to be reflected in reservation price differences; absent such differences, no consumer benefit is attached to variety. Ratchford and colleagues (1996) suggested that price and quality variances combined with price-quality correlations are useful measures of market efficiency.

To date, there have been few studies that focused on the impact of price strategy on these dimensions. Yet, the DOJ's suit against Microsoft, which dealt in part with the effects of pure bundling, would seem to indicate a need for developing a multidimensional view of consumer welfare. That is, much of the focus of the case revolves around arguments as to whether Microsoft should be castigated for stifling innovation or praised for enhancing consumer convenience (through standardization).

The Role of "Fairness"

One economist noted that policy analysts "have long considered issues of fairness to be important in evaluating the desirability of different economic outcomes" but that consideration has been given only to the judgments made by economists, not those of the economic actors involved (Rabin 1993, p. 1282). During recent years, empirical and theoretical work has emerged in economics and marketing that considers the concept of fairness from the perspectives of consumers and producers. Studies by Kahneman, Knetsch, and Thaler (1986) suggested that "many actions that are both profitable in the short run and not obviously dishonest are likely to be perceived as unfair exploitations of market power" (p. 737). Following the principle of "dual entitlements," these authors showed that price increases are judged as fair when they reflect the passing on of cost increases but are judged as unfair when they simply reflect the application of monopoly power (see also Urbany, Madden, and Dickson 1989). Campbell (1999) showed that the perceived fairness of a price increase also is influenced by the firm's reputation. Experiments by Franciosi and colleagues (1995) suggested that the fairness of a price increase is only a temporary condition resulting from deviations from expectations, not a component of the buyer's utility function.

Note that all of the forgoing fairness studies focused on price *increases*. However, price *differentials* might be a more relevant fairness issue. Martins and Monroe (1994), drawing from equity theory, argued that the perception that others pay a lower price may influence the perceived economic sacrifice that a consumer is willing to make for a given level of quality, leading to lower reservation prices. The fairness of pricing *procedures* was the central issue in a study by Kimes (1994), who suggested that customers might have no way to assess the fair market (reference) price when firms fail to inform consumers of changes. For example, if customers are not informed of all the ways of obtaining discounted prices (e.g., on airfares or hotel rooms), then they probably will judge the prices they pay as unacceptable (and unfair) if they learn the true available prices after the fact. On the other hand, procedures that allow customers some control over their decisions as to which prices to pay (e.g., taking advantage of the "early bird" dinner special) are less likely to be perceived as unfair.

Research on fairness in other economic and social contexts does, in fact, distinguish between *distributive fairness* (i.e., how rewards and benefits are divided) and *procedural fairness* (as measured by dimensions such as impartiality, explanation of policies, bilateral communication, and refutability). Moreover, procedural fairness appears to have a stronger effect on relationships than does distributive fairness (Kumar, Scheer, and Steenkamp 1995). Because any public policy interest in fairness presumably would be focused on regulating unfair processes rather than unfair outcomes, and because the former type (based on research in other settings) is likely to be of greater concern to consumers, future research on fairness ought to focus on the effects of procedures for determining how price choices and price information are made available. One interesting empirical question is whether greater fairness in information availability results in decreased dispersion in prices paid or in increased aggregate consumer surplus. Another issue is whether the basis for the price discrimination is fair. Senior citizen discounts presume that age is a surrogate for income in many markets, and airlines view required overnight stays on Saturday as a surrogate for distinguishing the more elastic leisure travel market from the less elastic business travel market. Such surrogates might be perceived as less "fair" than off-peak pricing because age-based discounts are not an option for all low-income buyers and because the Saturday restriction is not clearly linked to differences in cost.

Incorporating Insights from Consumer Research

Analyzing consumer surplus is important to the study of welfare, but in the actual marketplace, consumers might have difficulty in finding the lowest

TABLE 11.2 Additional Price Presentation Strategies Affecting Price Knowledge and
Perceptions and Quality Perceptions

Unit pricing

Price-quality signaling

"Sale" pricing

"Low-ball" pricing

Pricing by electronic marketing sources

---

priced product with a particular set of attributes (cf. Kamakura, Ratchford, and
Agrawal 1988). Ratchford and colleagues (1996) showed how inefficiencies can
result from retail price dispersion and price-quality signaling. In addition, consumer researchers are interested in how price presentation strategies (Table
11.2) drive perceptions of quality and value. Thus, a fruitful and important
source of insights from marketing and other consumer research scholars is the
body of work linked to price knowledge and perceptions.

Figure 11.1 is a portrayal of those outcomes and activities that ultimately determine how price strategies can influence the consumer's decision-making process. The variables in ovals are those that have largely been beyond the scope of
traditional welfare economic analyses. Those in rectangles are central elements
of the traditional perspective. (The "distribution of choices" is an element considered in traditional thinking. But, as argued previously, the traditional view
has held a more limited view of the dimensionality of "choice.")

Researchers in marketing have been more interested in how reservation
prices are formed than have economists. Accordingly, consumer research has
contributed more to the understanding of how the price and quality cues used to
communicate a firm's market offering translate into price knowledge and perceptions (which, in turn, affect perceived quality). As per Figure 11.1, price
knowledge and perceptions are influenced by prior prices paid (reference
prices) and by the amount of search. In addition, low levels of knowledge may
motivate search. By understanding the linkages among these variables, more
complete insights can be gained on the effects of pricing strategies on the quality
of consumer decisions and on consumer welfare.

Pricing and Consumers' Perceptions of Price and Value

How Consumers Process Price Information

The goal of many pricing strategies and tactics is to present price information
in a manner that influences consumers' perceptions of the price and the resulting
value of a particular bundle of benefits. Presumably, many firms want consumers to perceive that the value of the firm's products is higher than the value of
competing products. Consumer welfare is decreased to the extent that consum-

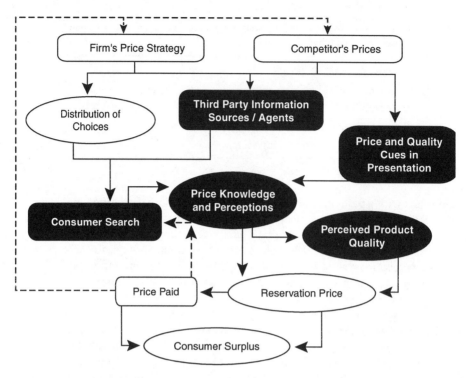

Figure 11.1. Pricing and Consumer Decisions: Influencing Activities and Outcomes

ers misperceive the relative prices of competing goods, and products are purchased that would not have been chosen in the absence of those tactics. Before
reviewing the many areas of pricing that may affect consumer perceptions, we
first review the literature on price knowledge and search by consumers.

It is safe to conclude that consumers are not careful processors of product information including price. It also appears that many consumers are either unable
or disinclined to process price information in a manner that public policy makers
might assume or is ideal. First, consumers do not expend a lot of effort in processing price information or in remembering information that was processed.
Many studies have found that shoppers do not remember prices very well (e.g.,
Gabor and Granger 1961). Dickson and Sawyer (1990) used a method that eliminated short-term memory loss as an explanation for this in their study of four
products: coffee, toothpaste, cold cereal, and margarine. As in past studies (e.g.,
Hoyer 1984), shoppers spent only a few seconds deciding on each purchase.
When asked to recall the price of an item that supermarket shoppers had just
placed into their shopping baskets, only about half (47%) of the shoppers could
remember the price within 5%. When the shoppers were asked whether the item
was priced at a sale price or at the regular price, only about half (53%) accurately
recalled the status of the item they had just selected. Only 13% of those who
bought the item at a sale price could recall the amount of the price reduction, and
58% could not even guess the amount of the reduction. Much of the lack of price
knowledge seems to have resulted from a lack of checking the price. Only 57%

reported checking the price of the item before selecting it, and only 22% reported checking the price of any alternative item. Those shoppers who claimed to have checked the price of the item prior to selecting it were considerably more likely to both know the correct price (71% vs. 17% for those who did not check the price) and correctly perceive whether the item was priced at a special reduced price (60% vs. 26%). Finally, 42% of the shoppers reported that they never compared the prices at different stores, whereas 41% said that they had done so during the past month. These results have been replicated several times. For example, LeBoutiller, LeBoutiller, and Neslin (1994) found similar shopping times and price recall accuracy for coffee. However, price recall accuracy was a much higher 71% for the frequently purchased soda category.

Not only are consumers deficient in terms of the extent of their search and knowledge of prices, but they also have problems in choosing the best value product when all relevant price and product information is right in front of them. Friedman (1966) asked 33 married woman with at least some college education to select the most economical (largest quantity for the price) package for 20 different product categories in a supermarket. He found an average of 14.3 errors for the 20 categories. Friedman attributed the errors to the difficulty of the math in making comparisons and to the difficulty of comparing unlike quantities and packaging. However, Capon and Kuhn (1982) gave supermarket shoppers a simplified task and still found a widespread tendency to not process information to calculate the best buy. Shoppers were asked for the better buy between two alternative packages with different size and price combinations for two different products. Despite being encouraged to get the right answers, being offered paper and pencil, and receiving probes of "Why is that the best buy?" for answers that used simple rules of thumb to determine the answer, the shoppers were prone to use some simple method to choose one of the two packages as the best buy. For the two products, only an average of 32 of 100 shoppers chose to calculate the price per ounce, and an average of 40 of 100 shoppers chose the best buy in a way that made no logical sense.

Many consumers who do process price information do not process the objective price information and remember the price in that manner. Jacoby and Olson (1977) offered a useful descriptive model of how consumers facing price information may or may not attend to the price and may encode and categorize the price as an objective price and/or as some perception or attitude in a more verbal form (e.g., low price, good buy, too high, best buy) while integrating that price perception or attitude with other information about the product or store.

Another cognitive aspect of price information processing that needs to be considered is the notion of a "reference price" (Kalyanarum and Winer 1995). A reference price serves as a standard against which future prices can be compared. Some researchers also consider the "expected price" or "fair price" as a reference price, and there are several other possible definitions (Monroe 1973; Winer 1988). Reference prices presumably are formed through consumers' exposure to prices over time (e.g., past prices paid, prices encountered in advertising, prices encountered at the point of purchase). The notion of a reference price as an expected price can be conceptualized as an adaptation level (Helson 1964). Prices encountered in the future are compared to the reference price and, at the same time, influence the level of the reference price used for future price perceptions. As such, reference prices may mediate the effects of marketing mix variables on consumers' perceptions of current prices, value, and (ultimately) choice.

Although it is not known exactly how reference prices are formed or stored in memory by consumers, it is presumed that some sort of mentally weighted averaging of past prices is used. As we have noted, consumers' indifferent processing of price information often results in incomplete knowledge. Therefore, one would expect that consumers' reference prices often are vague or inconsistent with past and present prices. In empirical research, Puto (1987) directly measured reference prices as "how much you expect to pay," and Urbany and Dickson (1991) used a measure of the "range of prices normally charged" followed up by three examples illustrating that the answer could be a price point or a range. Others, such as Winer (1986), have estimated reference price by a weighted function of recent past prices paid or available at the times of prior purchases in the product category. Winer concluded that consumers act as if they do use reference prices given that models that included reference prices predicted brand choice better than did models that included only current prices. Urbany and Dickson (1991) concluded that internal reference prices significantly affected perceptions of future prices (as low, normal, or high). However, many consumers in their study either did not or could not use their reference prices to judge future prices, and the absolute effects of these internal reference prices was sufficiently small that using external market prices (the objective prices in the product category) was almost as effective. Thus, not much predictive validity is lost when market prices are used as a surrogate for internal reference prices, as Winer (1986) and others (e.g., Kalyanarum and Little 1994) have done. Jacobson and Obermiller's (1990) results were consistent with their assertion that consumers form expectations of future prices and that this expected future reference price, not past prices, is the best predictor of actual future prices. Such a finding is important because consumers perceiving a pattern of prices and price discounts, such as with price promotions, might not have reference prices that vary as dynamically as does the most recent price. Finally, Kalyanarum and Little (1994) found strong support for the notion that, for some products, acceptable reference prices are a range within which consumers are insensitive to small variations, as originally conceptualized by Sherif, Sherif, and Nebergall's (1965) assimilation-contrast theory of attitudes (see also Lichtenstein, Bloch, and Black 1988; Sawyer and Dickson 1984).

A final aspect of consumers' processing of price involves Thaler's (1985) concepts of "acquisition utility" and "transaction utility." Acquisition utility is the overall value of the deal and compares the total package of attributes offered by the product to the selling price. Transaction utility is a function of whether consumers think that they got a "good deal" by comparing the price paid to the regular or expected price. The effect of a perceived price can affect willingness to buy by influencing either or both of these utilities. At a minimum, consumers must perceive adequate acquisition utility to make a purchase. If both utilities are perceived as at least satisfactory, then there is a higher likelihood of immediate purchase. For example, a consumer might perceive that a product offers good enough acquisition utility but decides not to purchase at that time because of in-adequate transaction utility (e.g., the perception that either the price will come down in the near future or the product currently can be purchased elsewhere at a better price). However, if a consumer's knowledge or perception of reference prices is vague with a resulting wide range of indifference, then consumer welfare might be diminished if a reseller increases the transaction utility by, for example, suggesting that the "regular" price is higher than actual and then prompting purchase by "discounting" that regular price with a promoted price "special."

It is important to remember, as we review the effects of price presentation strategies and tactics on the consumer perceptions and welfare, that these perceptions often are not objective, accurate, or the results of much involved processing effort. Moreover, any judgments about the effects on consumers of pricing strategies and tactics must take into account the high variation between the objective prices and the recalled and perceived prices that results from the faulty processing of consumers. Presumably, the errors of information processing and the pricing tactics of firms combine to produce the price inefficiencies observed by Kamakura, Ratchford, and Agrawal (1988) discussed earlier.

We briefly review the evidence of the effects on price perceptions of the following five pricing strategies: unit pricing, price-quality signaling, "sale" pricing, "low-ball" pricing, and pricing by electronic marketing sources.

Unit Pricing

Unit pricing offers the consumer the calculated price per standard unit (e.g., per ounce, per gallon) for each product. Given the findings of Capon and Kuhn (1982) and Friedman (1966), unit pricing would seem to offer high potential to improve consumers' ability to figure out which product is the best buy for them and, hence, increase consumer welfare. A considerable amount of research supports this reasoning. Gatewood and Perloff (1973) and Houston (1972) asked shoppers to find the cheapest per-unit package, and each study found that the number of errors was reduced in stores offering unit price information. Russo and colleagues conducted two studies (Russo 1977; Russo, Krieser, and Miyashita 1975) that monitored sales in stores where the presence and type of unit price information was varied over time. These studies, which did not give any instructions to shoppers, found that the average price paid decreased, more store brands that were low priced were purchased, and more large sizes that were cheaper per unit were purchased. Russo and colleagues found that the most effective type of unit price information was a list of brands and sizes ranked from the lowest to the highest in terms of price per unit. This format resulted in a 3% reduction in the average price paid. Not only was the consumer welfare presumably increased, but these authors estimated that the costs to the store of maintaining the unit cost lists were only about 0.1% of sales.[3]

Russo and colleagues' results were replicated by Zeithaml (1982), who used a laboratory environment closely resembling an actual supermarket to study four shelf-price information format levels in combination with whether the prices were marked on the items themselves or only on the shelves alone. The first three levels of unit price information varied the legibility and size of the unit prices on the shelves, and the fourth level presented both the most legible unit prices and a list of unit prices comparable to the list used in Russo and colleagues' research. Marking the items with the prices resulted in more accurate price recall and lower prices paid, consistent with the results of Allen, Harrell, and Hutt (1976). The level of unit price legibility did not have an effect, probably because many shoppers did not use the unit prices. However, shoppers exposed to the list of the unit prices along with the unit price information on the shelves felt more confident about the accuracy of their price recall, although their recall was not more accurate than that of shoppers who were not exposed to the unit price list. The most notable effect of the unit price list format was that shoppers were more apt to choose lower priced products. Moreover, the savings from the reduced prices were quite large; the savings ranged from 2% to 19% across the 12 products studied, compared to the 3% savings found in Russo and colleagues' field study.

Thus, it is clear that the presence of unit price information has the potential to increase consumer welfare by helping consumers to know the best buy and to pay lower prices. However, the effect of such information will be limited if some consumers choose not to attend or process this information. Dickson and Sawyer (1990) found that only 6% of the shoppers reported checking unit prices to compare brands on that shopping trip and that only 9% had used unit prices to compare different sizes. Similarly, Capon and Kuhn (1982) found that half of the supermarket shoppers they interviewed used a rule of thumb other than comparing the price to the size of the product to indicate a best buy. Thus, requiring that stores make available unit price information will be helpful if shoppers are aware of this unit price information, are educated to consider unit prices as helpful shopping aids, and can find the information in a format (e.g., a list) that is conducive to easy information processing. Future research that investigates how to best educate and motivate consumers to attend to and use unit price information probably is the greatest need in this area. If consumer welfare includes perceived "fairness" and ease of making good choices, then unit pricing might be found to produce positive consumer welfare effects that are more difficult to quantify in economic terms.

Price-Quality Signaling

Consumers sometimes judge the quality of a product by its price (Monroe 1973). For example, McConnell (1968) offered consumers the opportunity to choose among three different brands of beer where a letter was used to indicate the brand. The only thing that differed about the brands (which had, in fact, identical ingredients) was price (low, medium, and high). Consumers tended to choose the higher priced beer and to rate its quality higher, even after keeping the beer and tasting it over a week. This result has been replicated many times in studies where the only piece of information about the brands was the price. This result is not surprising. If one knows nothing else about a product than its price and is asked to differentiate that product from another, then price would be seized as a cue to quality because there is no other information to use. When there are other pieces of information available, the effects of price sometimes become much smaller or have no effect on quality judgments. For example, Jacoby, Olson, and Haddock (1971) used a factorial design to manipulate the level of price, brand name, and composition differences for four beers that were tasted and rated. Price had an effect on perceived quality only when the price information was presented with no other information. When brand image information was present, price had no incremental effect. Surprisingly, however, Rao and Monroe's (1989) meta-analysis of 36 experimental studies found that the overall effect of price was slightly higher when other cues were present. The overall effect of price on perceived quality was found in the meta-analysis to be reasonably large ($\omega^2 = .12$) and almost as large as the effect of the brand name ($\omega^2 = .14$).

Recent research suggests that consumers' use of cues other than price as predictors of quality increases with product familiarity and knowledge. Rao and Monroe's (1988) study about judgments of quality of wool blazers found that more expert participants were less apt to use price (manipulated at four levels from \$49 to \$199) when a cue diagnostic of higher and tight standard quality (Harris Tweed wool) blazers was available. The most knowledgeable consumers did, however, allow a high price to alter their judgments of the quality of the lower quality (virgin wool) blazer that varies more in terms of quality. Thus, although naive consumers are most apt to use price to guess the level of delivered quality, experts also may use price in instances where their market knowledge suggests to them that price is a valid diagnostic cue.

Armed with the general knowledge that higher quality goods cost more and that higher costs usually require a higher price, it is not irrational to guess that higher priced items are higher in quality. This makes sense given the natural positive correlation between price and objective quality (typically estimated from *Consumer Reports* ratings). But the overall correlation, although positive, is quite moderate and ranges from highly positive to no relationship, with some correlations negative. For example, Oxenfeldt (1950) found an average correlation of .25, with a range from .82 to −.81 across 35 product categories. Morris and Bronson (1969) found an average correlation of .29, with a range of .96 to −.66 across 48 product categories. Gerstner (1985) found that 86 higher priced, infrequently purchased product categories had a higher average price-quality correlation (.19) than 59 lower priced, frequently purchased products (.01), with quality and price measured by the Consumer Union in the *Buying Guide*. However, there was a great amount of variance in these price-quality relationships. The proportion of cases in which the price of the best brand was below the *average* price was 36% for the former product category and 68% for the latter. Gerstner's follow-up analysis gave support to the hypotheses that the difference in the results between the two categories was at least partially due to the difference in absolute price levels (perhaps the greater financial commitment of consumers causes them to search more and be more knowledgeable about true quality, and sellers might be more apt to price appropriately in anticipation of this greater knowledge) and to the fact that the lower priced, less frequently purchased items might have more varying unit sizes with smaller, higher price-per-unit sizes reflecting less economic values (in addition to the likely lower incentive for consumers to search and be informed about quality).

Tellis and Wernerfelt's (1987) meta-analysis of extant studies found a positive correlation of .27 for 1,365 product markets. However, these authors also pointed out that this correlation might be inflated because the use of single sources of rated quality and one average price surveyed by *Consumer Reports* eliminates inherent errors that would decrease the size of the correlation. Tellis and Wernerfelt's model offers an understanding that the size of the price-quality correlation will be positive and larger in markets where more consumers search and become more fully and accurately informed. This information helps them to believe and accept price as a valid indicator of quality if markets reach an equilibrium (see also Akerlof 1970).

The preceding empirical results indicate that many markets show a modest but positive correlation between price and quality and also that some markets can be characterized by a zero or even a negative correlation. This suggests at least two interesting questions related to consumers' abilities to process price information. First, how well can consumers judge the correlation between price and quality (if we accept objective ratings as a surrogate for how consumers will rate quality)? Second, to what extent (if any) are these judgments of the price-quality relationship biased by prior overall perceptions about price-quality? The answers to both of these questions seem to depend on the context in which these judgments are made. For example, Lichtenstein and Burton (1989) selected 15 product categories from Gerstner's (1985) study so as to begin with large and small positive and negative price-objective quality correlations and found modest rank-order correlations between these correlations and rated agreement with the statement, "The higher the price of the product, the higher the quality of the product." The size of these correlations was higher for nondurable products than for durables, and although segments emerged in each of four studies that were more likely than other segments to believe in a generalized price-quality relationship, there were no consistent differences between these segments and other segments that did not hold this generalized price-quality belief. Bettman, John, and Scott (1986) exposed consumers to ranked data in different sets of two columns of 10 items that were labeled either as "x" and "y" or as "price" and "quality" and were either shown in perfect rank order for one of the columns (and, hence, easier to analyze) or arranged randomly. In addition, the true correlations between the two columns was varied from strongly positive to strongly negative. These authors found that consumers' ratings of the direction and size of the correlations exhibited clear discrimination between different levels of correlation regardless of the format in which they were presented and, moreover, were quite accurate. In addition, prior beliefs about price-quality had very little effect.

Pechmann and Ratneshwar (1992) examined consumers' ability to detect price-quality relationships when they were allowed to taste orange juice drinks that had been manipulated to alter their objective quality (taste). Also varied were whether the true relationships were positive or null and the ease of diagnosing the relative taste (by allowing either immediate and frequent comparisons or delaying comparisons and intervening these delayed comparisons with eating a cracker). These authors found that, as with Bettman, John, and Scott's (1986) results, consumers were sensitive to the objective ratings, and consumers' prior beliefs about a general positive relationship between price and quality resulted in their ratings of quality being influenced by the price of the drinks only when the tasting procedure made it more difficult to judge the taste. In addition, a second study that allowed consumers to use "external memory aids" (i.e., write down impressions immediately after each tasting) found that the memory aid nearly completely removed any biasing effect of prior beliefs about a general covariation between price and quality. Finally, Ordonez (1998) gave consumers a relatively difficult task of choosing one product from each of more than 100 pairs for which each product was described by its price and overall quality. She found that consumers' choices of products were affected by prior overall beliefs about a positive price-quality relationship, even when the true correlation was zero or strongly negative. Thus, although a consumer's ability to judge objective quality independent of price sometimes is biased by prior beliefs that higher priced products are of a higher quality, this bias tends to exert influence only when the judgment task is a difficult one.

Consumer inefficiencies in selecting the best price-quality alternative (leading to reductions in consumer surplus) could be partially due to their limited ability to process price-quality information (e.g., results discussed earlier by Capon and Kuhn 1982 and Friedman 1966). However, given the preceding results (e.g., those of Bettman, John, and Scott 1986), we conclude that these inefficiencies more likely are due to either consumers' unwillingness to search for and use price information or a lack of reliable nonprice quality cues in the information provided by sellers.

To the extent that the price-quality phenomenon exists when other information is available, this phenomenon appears to emanate from the ways in which consumers process information. There is little blame that can be affixed to firms' pricing tactics other than an occasional attempt to reinforce a positive price-quality belief in advertising and positioning (e.g., "You get what you pay for," "Do you care enough to pay for the best?"). The best way in which to deal with this is to educate the public, as *Consumer Reports* tries to do, with evidence that the highest priced products are not necessarily the best as well as with admonitions to learn more about the quality of products and not depend on price as the only indicator of quality. As with unit pricing, research is needed that attempts to learn how to educate shoppers to learn more about the quality of products and not indiscriminantly use price as a cue.

"Sale" Pricing

There are two instances in which discount prices may affect consumer welfare. The first involves temporary price discounts, typically called price promotions. These typically are promoted at the point of purchase with a label indicating that the price is a deal price or a "shelf talker" (a small sign stating that the price is a special deal). The second situation is when a price discount is advertised, often as a retail store ad in the newspaper but also in other media.

Price promotions typically would increase consumer surplus by offering a product at a reduced price. However, a potential problem would arise if consumers used the mere presence of a promotion as a signal of a "good buy" and as a reason to purchase by itself without regard to whether or how much the price actually was reduced. In fact, there is evidence that such a state of affairs does occur. Guadagni and Little's (1983) statistical analysis of consumer purchase data found that there was a positive statistically significant effect of a product being on promotion, independent of the size of the promotion discount. In other words, even a "zero" discount (e.g., a regular price being labeled "special") can have a positive effect on choice. Grover and Srinivasan (1989) found a similar effect. Dickson and Sawyer's (1990) result that shoppers were less likely to know the amount of a special price reduction than to know that it was a special price also is consistent with the notion that some shoppers might use the fact that an item is being sold at a special promotion price as a signal to buy. Finally, Inman, McAlister, and Hoyer (1990) used an experiment to directly test the effects of a "real" promotion (a sign announcing the sale price accompanied by an approximately 15% price reduction), a "sham" promotion (a sign announcing a "sale" price that was not a discount from the actual past price), and no promotion. The results were that the real promotion had a sizable effect on consumer choice. The sham promotion had a positive effect as well. However, the effect was smaller and occurred only among shoppers who were low in need for cognition; this indicated that the sham promotion influenced only those who were less likely to process relevant information and who were less involved in shopping for the studied items. Inman and McAlister (1993) replicated the lab experiment results with a field experiment that compared sizable real promotions (15% discount) to sham promotions in which the discount was either zero or a token 1%. The results were that the sham promotions were more profitable to the retailer than were the real promotions in six of nine product categories.

Inman, McAlister, and Hoyer's (1990) results suggest that the use of a price promotion as a signal for a good buy can decrease consumer welfare, and the follow-up field study by Inman and McAlister (1993) offers evidence that would be tempting to retailers. Unfortunately, consumers who do not know the regular price or who are less apt to process the size of the alleged price discount will be especially prone to suffer from this retailer practice. Fortunately, the presence of "price vigilantes" (to use John Little's term) or "market mavens" (borrowed by Inman and colleagues from Feick and Price 1987) who do know the price should give pause to retailers who might be tempted to take advantage of unknowing consumers with sham promotions. Also, as Anderson and Simester's (1998) model implies, retailers' incentives to place sale signs on products not at a discount price are not as large as one might initially assume. Such incentives likely are small because misleading sale signs in a store reduce the information value of the correct sale signs; too many misleading sale signs will cause consumers to ignore all of the store's signs and to patronize other stores with more credible sale price sign information. Anderson and Simester's research is particularly valuable because it reminds us that the market can be self-regulating. In addition, the publication of market basket information by consumer groups or local newspapers may offer disincentives for this practice. Even shoppers who are not prone to process detailed price information might pay attention to negative publicity of a retailer doing sham promotions.

The second type of "sale price" that may affect consumer welfare is the situation in which ads promote the new sale price and compare it to the former "regular" sale price. Such ads attempt to offer an "external" reference price that might be used by those consumers who do not have an internal reference price or that might influence the internal reference price for those who are unsure. Thus, the ad might include information such as the sale price, the regular price, the manufacturer's suggested retail price, and one or more of a variety of semantic cues (e.g., percentage off, dollars/cents off, comparison prices). Savings also may be stated in a "tensile" format (e.g., savings up to 40%, save 10% or more [Biswas and Burton 1994]). Here, the prime problem for consumer welfare seems to be the potential for firms to artificially increase the old "regular" price to exaggerate the amount of savings at the advertised reduced price. There are two potentially injurious effects to consumer welfare of this higher advertised reference price. One is that consumers perceiving a more attractive than actual value from the discounted sale price might purchase when they would not have otherwise if an accurate regular price had been presented. The second is that consumers' reference prices might stay artificially high or even increase compared to a possibly lower reference price being formed if the accurate regular price information had been presented (Liefeld and Heslop 1985), thereby biasing future judgments as well.[4] To the extent that competitors are injured by such deceptive "sale" pricing, competition (and, ultimately, consumer welfare) is potentially harmed as well.

There has been a great amount of empirical research in this area (for recent reviews, see Biswas and Blair 1991; Compeau, Grewal, and Grewal 1994; Grewal, Monroe, and Krishnan 1998). Among other things, this research has examined the effects of the level of external reference prices in ads on the believability of those prices, perceptions of the store's regular selling price and the amount of savings, how the sale price compares to the lowest price in the market, and consumers' willingness to buy. Perhaps due to the frequency of these types of ads, consumers are skeptical of the reference price claims and often discount the amount of savings actually available (Blair and Landon 1981; Urbany, Bearden, and Weilbaker 1988). However, despite the fact that implausibly high advertised reference prices are more heavily discounted by consumers than are plausible reference prices, the high reference prices still are more effective in getting consumers to intend to shop at the advertised store. Grewal, Monroe, and Krishnan (1998) found that the level of the advertised regular price increased consumers' internal reference price and their perceptions of the transaction value, that transaction value was influenced by the actual selling price and consumers' internal reference price and mediated the effect of selling price on acquisition value, and that acquisition value was positively related to willingness to buy.

Other research has focused on other variables such as the type of store or product under consideration, the particular semantic description of the two prices, and the knowledge of consumers (Biswas and Blair 1991; Grewal, Krishnan, Baker, and Borin 1998) in attempts to find the boundaries of the effects of advertised reference prices. One particularly interesting result was reported by Gupta and Cooper (1992), who indicated that consumers are skeptical and discount the amount of advertised savings, that there is a threshold below which an advertised discount has no effect on purchase intention, and that this indifference threshold is higher for a store brand than for a name brand as well as for a low-image store than for a high-image store. Overall, the purchase intention effects of the amount of the discount, which was varied from 10% to 70%, resembled an S-curve with no effects, on average, until price was discounted at least 15% and little further impact for price discounts beyond 30%.

It seems clear from this large amount of research that, despite the skepticism with which consumers view "sale" price ads, the fact that the amount of perceived savings is discounted by consumers, and the fact that this discounting is greater for alleged higher savings than for lower savings, such ads announcing high savings do affect consumers' perceptions of the value available and their purchase intentions. It is clear that the Federal Trade Commission and local state regulators need to, as advocated by Compeau and Grewal (1998) and Compeau, Grewal, and Grewal (1994), carefully monitor such practices and take remedial action against retailers that misrepresent the normal sale price. Research that documents the prevalence of such misleading advertising and assesses the effectiveness of regulatory attempts to decrease this practice would be useful.

"Low-Ball" Pricing

The practice of "low-balling" is reputed to be common with auto dealers and is used by others as well. This involves a salesperson asking a customer to make a decision to buy a product at an unusually attractive price. Once the consumer decides to buy at this low price, the salesperson removes that price (e.g., by reporting that the sales manager refuses to sell at such a low price) and then offers the product at a higher price. For this low-ball pricing tactic to be successful, the customer must agree to purchase at the second price, even when that second price is higher than what the customer would have paid if he or she had not first been offered the especially low price.

Unfortunately, the evidence is that low-ball pricing does work, with obvious adverse effects on consumer welfare. Cialdini and colleagues (1978) found that, when a preliminary decision has been made by a consumer to take an action such as purchasing a product, this decision tends not to waiver if the cost of performing the action is increased. Cialdini and colleagues did two more experiments to try to understand the information process by which this effect occurs. They first concluded that the low-ball technique is more effective than the similar "foot-in-the-door" technique in which consumers are allowed to perform the low-cost action before being asked to do the more expensive one. The evidence suggested that the best information processing explanation of the effectiveness of the low-ball technique is consumers' feeling a commitment to the decision and, despite not having a more positive attitude toward the action, being more resistant to changing the decision. Burger and Petty (1981) attempted to better understand the low-ball technique. They concluded, from three experiments, that the commitment underlying the effectiveness of the low ball was not to the behavior being requested but rather to the person offering the product at both the initial lower price and the higher price. Thus, the key to the low-ball technique's effectiveness seems to be that the person is not allowed to actually carry out the initial low-cost decision and that the second, more expensive request is by the same person.

Future research about low-ball pricing ought to first replicate the preceding work (which manipulated the cost of an action by means other than a monetary price) in more realistic marketing situations. Also, given Burger and Petty's (1981) conclusion that a commitment to an individual salesperson making both price offers is key to the effectiveness of the low-ball price, it would be interesting to research whether low-ball pricing works in environments that do not use live persons as sales agents (e.g., Internet marketing). Research that assesses the effects of various tactics to lower the effectiveness of low-ball pricing techniques would be helpful. For example, are buyers who possess cost and typical negotiated price information for products under consideration (e.g., information now available from published buying guides or the Internet) better able to recognize and resist low-ball pricing attempts?

Pricing by Electronic Marketing Sources

Recent years have seen the rapidly expanding development of electronic commerce. The promise of electronic commerce is truly exciting and may revolutionize the way in which products are bought and sold in many instances. Relevant to the goals of this chapter, electronic marketing offers consumers the opportunity to access more information than ever before. A common claim about one of its many benefits is that the Internet can enable the motivated consumer to access nearly complete information about the product offerings in a market much more easily. As such, electronic commerce appears to have the potential of a reality that approximates the assumption of classical microeconomics of complete information for buyers. Alba and colleagues (1997) made several predictions about how information eventually will be provided in electronic commerce. One prediction is that consumers will demand, and eventually be able, to shop for products at one site that will enable searching for designated products and ordering them on various criteria including price. Thus, Alba and colleagues predicted that the demands of consumers will outweigh the reluctance of manufacturers and resellers to join such sites; most manufacturers would rather make price comparisons as difficult as possible.

The increasing presence of various shopping "bots" that aspire to such competitive price transparency, albeit with limited success to date, suggests that electronic commerce might indeed be approaching the ability to easily compare prices with limited effort and with perfect "on-line" memory. Many, adopting the microeconomic view, predict that the dispersion of prices for like items will decrease greatly, perhaps to zero. However, the limited evidence to date suggests that Internet marketing information might not have the large predicted effect on consumer surplus. One way in which to look at this is to assess the dispersion of prices on the Internet given that price dispersion is widely accepted as a measure of efficiency and lack of ignorance in a market (Stigler 1961). Brynjolfsson and

Smith (1999) did an impressive analysis of more than 8,500 individual product observations over 15 months during 1998-99 for two homogeneous consumer product categories: music CDs and books. Preliminary analysis found that prices for books and CDs averaged 9% to 16% less on the Internet compared to traditional channels and that Internet retailers changed prices in smaller increments (likely reflecting the lower menu change costs of electronic markets), which is what would be expected in a more frictionless, efficient market. However, when the price dispersions of Internet retailers were compared to those of traditional retailers, the results were only slightly lower for the former and then only when prices were weighted by market shares. Moreover, Brynjolfsson and Smith found that the dispersion of prices on the Internet was quite substantial (33% for books and 25% for CDs) and that the lowest priced Internet retailers did not obtain the highest sales. Baye and Morgan (1998) discussed the remaining dispersion of prices on Internet sites for commodities such as air travel and home mortgages. Their theoretical analysis suggests a reason why Internet shopping malls still will accommodate sellers with different prices for like items. They cited the role of the "gatekeepers" who own the sites, gather suppliers onto the sites, and earn profits from the sale of products on the sites as well as from advertising on the site and perhaps also from subscriptions from consumers. Baye and Morgan showed how having varying prices might be in the best interests of such gatekeepers. Dispersed prices serve to attract consumers because the more dispersed prices are, the more valuable the information on the sites are to consumers. Dispersed prices also attract advertising from suppliers because they attract more consumers.

Other research suggests that, consistent with another prediction of Alba and colleagues (1997), consumers buying on the Internet will not inevitably be more price sensitive despite the greater wealth of information. Degeratu, Rangaswamy, and Wu (1999) showed that grocery sales on-line may be less price sensitive than sales through traditional channels. Shankar, Rangaswamy, and Pusateri (1999) surveyed consumers who purchased travel from Internet or traditional channels as well as consumers who used both sources. Their results indicated that some aspects of an Internet site can lower price sensitivity. They found lower consumer price sensitivity for Web sites that provide a rich set of both price and nonprice information, are highly interactive, offer a wide range of prices and products, and make it easier to search for nonprice attributes relative to price. Lynch and Ariely's (forthcoming) laboratory experimental results converge with the preceding nonexperimental ones. These experiments sold wine through electronic channels and found that providing nonprice information to consumers lowered price sensitivity and increased consumer loyalty.

We conclude that electronic commerce is not likely to be a panacea for consumer welfare, even though it does offer the potential for many substantial improvements. First, many consumers will not have access to these sources, and these consumers might be the ones most likely to be poor information processors. Second, electronic markets still will be characterized by truncated search by less motivated consumers and by marketing-induced nonprice factors such as how information is presented, consumer trust, and consumer loyalty. Clearly, however, electronic commerce offers marketers and researchers an opportunity to assess whether the ability for consumers (and sellers) to more easily search and retain product and price information results in greater consumer surplus. Research about electronic commerce just now emerging can enable better measurement and understanding of how various marketing tactics and consumer information search patterns and processing affect the efficiency of markets and consumer welfare.

Discussion

In traditional welfare economics, the role of public policy is to see to the efficient allocation of economic resources. Particular cases are informed by the analysis of how the industry structure will affect price and output. To achieve these aims, it makes simplifying assumptions regarding the complexity of both sellers' and buyers' goals and decision-making processes. By contrast, researchers in marketing and consumer research traditionally have been focused on understanding managerial and consumer decision-making processes, recognizing that both sets of actors have complex goals, lack full information, and imperfectly process the information they do receive.

Adopting the latter perspective, the research discussed in this chapter suggests that, in the complex and imperfectly competitive market structures characterizing most markets, reservation prices (and, thus, consumer surplus) are conditioned by (1) reference prices for a given product, (2) the nature and amount of information made available regarding the price and quality of competing offerings, (3) the manner in which information about price and quality is framed, (4) the extent to which consumers use information, and (5) the array of choices provided by the market structure. Whereas traditional economic theory tends to evaluate only the aggregate effect of a given pricing strategy, the welfare of different consumers can vary with differences in the availability of multiple price-quality options and in the quality and quantity of information provided about products and prices. In addition, this chapter has argued that price discrimination strategies that exploit such reservation price differentials ought not to be automatically presumed to be welfare enhancing in the aggregate, especially in those cases where real choice is absent. Finally, consumer surplus seems to be an excessively static indicator of consumer welfare; in new or growth markets, short-term consumer surplus maximization (resulting from aggressive pricing by entrenched market leaders) may well stifle innovation and desirable variety.

Based on the forgoing review, then, there are at least five sets of questions that seem to warrant increased attention from researchers interested in informing public policy debate within the realm of pricing:

1. Do various forms of price discrimination lead to the subsidization of high-elasticity customers by low-elasticity customers without any real gain in output? If so, then what are the consequences for consumers?

2. When price discrimination policies are used, what are the consequences to consumers if information about lower prices is either not conveyed or not accessible to all?

3. How can short-term pricing tactics designed to harm a competitor's ability to compete be assessed in terms of their dynamic (long-term) impact on competition and consumer welfare (e.g., by explicitly considering the consequences when "switching costs" are high)?

4. Under what circumstances is consumer welfare harmed by the provision of price and quality information that is incomplete or framed in a biased or misleading manner?

5. What metrics might be used to supplement the consumer surplus construct when assessing consumer welfare? Is a generalized consumer welfare metric feasible or desirable?

Traditional economists would make the excellent point that the costs of regulation and oversight sometimes can outweigh the social benefits. Moreover, policies aimed at saving inefficient firms in the name of variety and choice can result if the emphasis of public policy focuses on harm to competitors (as currently is the case with policy on dumping) rather than on harm to competition and consumer welfare. In addition, there likely are limited benefits of public policy efforts directed toward the required "force-feeding" of information to consumers who choose not to search.

Yet, in today's digital world, sellers are obtaining increasing amounts of data on individuals' purchase behaviors and are able to target messages and prices to selected customers with greater precision. In this environment, the opportunity to set short-term price discrimination strategies (below cost if necessary) and to be selective in the distribution of information so as to attract or retain customers with different "lifetime values" is substantial. It would seem that researchers within the marketing discipline are equipped to develop an enhanced understanding of how such developments might affect competition and the long-term welfare of consumers.

Notes

1. This definition implicitly assumes that the customer will buy either one unit or not buy at all. Alternatively, the customer sometimes may achieve his or her reservation price by purchasing at quantity discounts.

2. In addition, variety might be affected. In the 1998 anti-dumping petition by U.S. salmon fishing companies against several Chilean firms, a number of U.S. distributors argued (unsuccessfully) that the success of Chilean salmon imports was mainly due to the fact that they were fully deboned filets that were not available from other sources.

3. Monroe and LaPlaca (1972) cited a study by A. T. Kearney for the Consumer Research Institute (1971) that the installation costs for a unit pricing system ranged from 0.01% to 0.04% of sales and that the maintenance costs ranged from 0.007% to 0.1%.

4. A related important issue not discussed here is whether the product ever is sold at the alleged "regular" price or if the item inevitably is priced at the "sale" price (for a review, see Lichtenstein, Burton, and Karson 1991). Many states have laws regulating this practice (Compeau, Grewal, and Grewal 1994).

References

Akerlof, G. (1970), "The Market for Lemons: Quality Uncertainty and the Market Mechanism," *Quarterly Journal of Economics,* 84, 488-500.

Alba, Joseph, John Lynch, Barton Weitz, Chris Janiszewski, Richard Lutz, Alan Sawyer, and Stacy Wood (1997), "Interactive Home Shopping: Consumer, Retailer, and Manufacturer Incentives to Participate in Electronic Marketplaces," *Journal of Marketing,* 61 (July), 54-70.

Allen, John, Gilbert D. Harrell, and Michael D. Hutt (1976), *Price Awareness Study.* Washington, DC: Food Marketing Institute.

Anderson, Eric T. and Duncan I. Simester (1998), "The Role of Sale Signs," *Marketing Science,* 17 (2), 139-55.

Baye, Michael R. and John Morgan (1998), "Information Gatekeepers and the Competitiveness of Homogeneous Product Markets," unpublished working paper, Indiana University.

Bettman, James, Deborah Roedder John, and Carol A. Scott (1986), "Covariation Assessment by Consumers," *Journal of Consumer Research,* 13 (December), 316-26.

Biswas, Abhijit and Edward A. Blair (1991), "Contextual Effects of Reference Prices in Retail Advertisements," *Journal of Marketing,* 55 (July), 1-12.

——— and Scot Burton (1994), "An Experimental Assessment of Effects Associated with Alternative Tensile Price Claims," *Journal of Business Research,* 29, 65-73.

Blair, Edward A. and E. Laird Landon, Jr. (1981), "The Effects of Reference Prices in Retail Advertisements," *Journal of Marketing,* 45 (Spring), 61-69.

Bork, Robert (1978), *The Antitrust Paradox.* New York: Basic Books.

Boudreaux, Donald and Robert Ekelund (1996), "The Resale Price Maintenance Policy Dilemma: Comment," *Southern Economic Journal,* 62 (April), 1079-87.

Boyd, David (1997), "From 'Mom-and-Pop' to Wal-Mart: The Impact of the Consumer Goods Pricing Act of 1975 on the Retail Sector in the United States," *Journal of Economic Issues,* 31 (March), 223-33.

Brooks, Rick (1999), "Alienating Customers Isn't Always a Bad Idea, Many Firms Discover," *The Wall Street Journal,* January 7, A1, A12.

Brynjolfsson, Erik and Michael D. Smith (1999), "Frictionless Commerce? A Comparison of Internet and Conventional Retailers," working paper, Sloan School of Management, Massachusetts Institute of Technology.
Available: http://ecommerce.mit.edu/papers/friction

Burger, Jerry M. and Richard E. Petty (1981), "The Low-Ball Compliance Technique: Task or Person Commitment?" *Journal of Personality and Social Psychology,* 40 (3), 492-500.

Cabral, Luis and Michael Riordan (1997), "The Learning Curve, Predation, Antitrust, and Welfare," *Journal of Industrial Economics,* 45 (June), 155-69.

Campbell, Margaret (1999), "Perceptions of Price Unfairness: Antecedents and Consequences," *Journal of Marketing Research,* 36 (May), 187-99.

Capon, Noel and Deanna Kuhn (1982), "Can Consumers Calculate Best Buys?" *Journal of Consumer Research,* 8 (March), 449-53.

Chen, Ming-Hu and Danny Miller (1994), "Competitive Attack, Retaliation, and Performance," *Strategic Management Journal,* 15 (February), 85-102.

Chen, Yongmin (1997), "Equilibrium Product Bundling," *Journal of Business,* 70 (January), 85-104.

Cialdini, Robert B., John T. Cacioppo, Rodney Bassett, and John A. Miller (1978), "Low-Ball Procedure for Producing Compliance: Commitment Then Cost," *Journal of Personality and Social Psychology,* 36 (5), 463-76.

Compeau, Larry D. and Dhruv Grewal (1998), "Comparative Price Advertising: An Integrative Review," *Journal of Public Policy and Marketing,* 17 (Fall), 257-73.

————, ————, and Diana S. Grewal (1994), "Adjudicating Claims of Deceptive Advertised Reference Prices: The Use of Empirical Evidence," *Journal of Public Policy and Marketing,* 13 (Fall), 312-18.

Consumer Research Institute (1971), "A Study of Consumer Reaction to Unit Pricing and Open Dating in Metropolitan Washington," executive summary, Consumer Research Institute.

Degeratu, Alexandru, Arvind Rangaswamy, and Jeremy Wu (1999), "Consumer Choice Behavior in Online and Regular Stores: The Effects of Brand Name, Price, and Other Search Attributes," paper presented at the Marketing Science Institute Conference on "Marketing Science and the Internet," March, Cambridge, MA.

Desiraju, Ramarao and Steven Shugan (1999), "Strategic Service Pricing and Yield Management," *Journal of Marketing,* 63 (Winter), 44-56.

Dickson, Peter R. and Alan G. Sawyer (1990), "The Price Knowledge and Search of Supermarket Shoppers," *Journal of Marketing,* 54 (July), 42-53.

Feick, Lawrence and Linda L. Price (1987), "The Market Maven: A Diffuser of Marketplace Information," *Journal of Marketing,* 51 (January), 83-97.

France, Mike and Steve Hamm (1998), "Does Predatory Pricing Make Microsoft a Predator?" *Business Week,* November 23, 130-31.

Franciosi, Robert, Praveen Kujal, Roland Michelitsch, Vernon Smith, and Gang Deng (1995), "Fairness: Effect on Temporary and Equilibrium Prices in Posted Markets," *Economic Journal,* 105 (July), 938-50.

Friedman, Monroe Peter (1966), "Consumer Confusion in the Selection of Supermarket Products," *Journal of Applied Psychology,* 50 (6), 529-34.

Gabor, Andre and Clive W. Granger (1961), "On the Price Consciousness of Consumers," *Applied Statistics,* 10 (November), 170-88.

Gatewood, Robert D. and Robert Perloff (1973), "An Experimental Investigation of Three Methods of Providing Weight and Price Information to Consumers," *Journal of Applied Psychology,* 57 (February), 81-85.

Gerstner, Eitan (1985), "Do Higher Prices Signal Higher Quality?" *Journal of Marketing Research,* 22 (May), 209-15.

———— and James D. Hess (1990), "Can Bait and Switch Benefit Consumers?" *Marketing Science,* 9, 114-24.

Grewal, Dhruv, R. Krishnan, Julie Baker, and Norm Borin (1998), "The Effect of Store Name, Brand Name, and Price Discounts on Consumers' Evaluations and Purchase Intentions," *Journal of Retailing,* 74 (3), 331-52.

————, Kent B. Monroe, and R. Krishnan (1998), "The Effects of Price-Comparison Advertising on Buyers' Perceptions of Acquisition Value, Transaction Value, and Behavioral Intentions," *Journal of Marketing,* 62 (April), 46-59.

Grover, Rajiv and V. Srinivasan (1989), "Evaluating the Effects of Retail Promotions on Segmented Markets," Research Paper No. 1059, Graduate School of Business, Stanford University.

Guadagni, Peter M. and John D. C. Little (1983), "A Logit Model of Brand Choice Calibrated on Scanner Data," *Marketing Science,* 2 (Summer), 203-38.

Guiltinan, Joseph (1987), "The Price Bundling of Services: A Normative Framework," *Journal of Marketing,* 51 (April), 74-85.

———— and Gregory Gundlach (1996), "Aggressive and Predatory Pricing: A Framework for Analysis," *Journal of Marketing,* 60 (July), 87-102.

Gundlach, Gregory and Joseph Guiltinan (1998), "A Marketing Perspective on Predatory Pricing," *Antitrust Bulletin* 43 (Fall-Winter), 883-916.

Gupta, Sunil and Lee G. Cooper (1992), "The Discounting of Discounts and Promotion Thresholds," *Journal of Consumer Research,* 19 (December), 401-11.

Helson, Harry (1964), *Adaptation-Level Theory.* New York: Harper & Row.

Herrmann, Andreas, Frank Huber, and Robin Higie Coulter (1997), "Product and Service Bundling Decisions and Their Effects on Purchase Intention," *Pricing Strategy & Practice,* 5, 99-107.

Hoch, Stephen, Xavier Drèze, and Mary Purk (1994), "EDLP, Hi-Lo, and Margin Arithmetic," *Journal of Marketing,* 58 (October), 16-27.

Houston, Michael J. (1972), "The Effects of Unit-Pricing on Choices of Brands and Size in Economic Shopping," *Journal of Marketing,* 36 (July), 51-54.

Howell, Jamie (1991), "Potential Profitability and Decreased Consumer Welfare through Manufacturers' Cents-Off Coupons," *Journal of Consumer Affairs,* 25 (Summer), 164-84.

Hoyer, Wayne D. (1984), "An Examination of Consumer Decision Making for a Common Repeat Purchase Product," *Journal of Consumer Research,* 11 (December), 822-29.

Inman, J. Jeffrey and Leigh McAlister (1993), "A Retailer Promotion Policy Model Considering Promotion Signal Sensitivity," *Marketing Science,* 12 (Fall), 339-56.

————, ————, and Wayne D. Hoyer (1990), "Promotion Signal: Proxy for a Price Cut?" *Journal of Consumer Research,* 17 (June), 74-81.

Jacobson, Robert and Carl Obermiller (1990), "The Formation of Expected Future Price: A Reference Price for Future-Looking Consumers," *Journal of Consumer Research,* 16 (March), 420-32.

Jacoby, Jacob and Jerry C. Olson (1977), "Consumer Response to Price: An Attitudinal, Information Processing Perspective," in *Moving A Head With Attitude Research,* Yoram Wind and Marshall G. Greenberg, eds. Chicago: American Marketing Association, 73-86.

————, ————, and Rafael Haddock (1971), "Price, Brand Name, Product Composition Characteristics as Determinants of Perceived Quality," *Journal of Applied Psychology,* 55 (December), 470-79.

Kahneman, Daniel, Jack Knetsch, and Richard Thaler (1986), "Fairness as a Constraint on Profit Seeking: Entitlements in the Market," *American Economic Review,* 76 (September), 728-41.

Kalyanarum, Gurumurthy and John D. C. Little (1994), "An Empirical Analysis of Latitude of Price Acceptance in Consumer Package Goods," *Journal of Consumer Research,* 21 (December), 408-18.

———— and Russell S. Winer (1995), "Empirical Generalizations from Reference Price Research," *Marketing Science,* 14 (3), G161-69.

Kamakura, Wagner, Brian Ratchford, and Jagdish Agrawal (1988), "Measuring Market Efficiency and Welfare Loss," *Journal of Consumer Research,* 15 (December), 289-302.

Kimes, Sheryl (1994), "Perceived Fairness of Yield Management," *Cornell Hotel and Restaurant Administration Quarterly,* 35 (February), 22-29.

Kumar, Nirmalya, Lisa Scheer, and Jan-Benedict Steenkamp (1995), "The Effects of Supplier Fairness on Vulnerable Resellers," *Journal of Marketing Research,* 32 (February), 54-66.

LeBoutiller, John, Susanna Shore LeBoutiller, and Scott A. Neslin (1994), "A Replication and Extension of the Dickson and Sawyer Price Awareness Study," *Marketing Letters,* 5 (January), 31-42.

Lichtenstein, Donald R., Peter H. Bloch, and William C. Black (1988), "Correlates of Price Acceptability," *Journal of Consumer Research,* 15 (September), 243-52.

────── and Scot Burton (1989), "The Relationship between Perceived and Objective Price-Quality," *Journal of Consumer Research,* 26 (November), 429-43.

──────, ──────, and Eric J. Karson (1991), "The Effect of Semantic Cues on Consumer Perceptions of Reference Price Ads," *Journal of Consumer Research,* 18 (December), 380-91.

Liefeld, John and Louise A. Heslop (1985), "Reference Prices and Deception in Newspaper Advertising," *Journal of Consumer Research,* 11 (March), 868-76.

Lynch, John G. and Dan Ariely (forthcoming), "Interactive Home Shopping: Effects of Search Cost for Price and Quality Information on Consumer Price Sensitivity, Satisfaction with Merchandise, and Retention," *Marketing Science.*

Marsh, Sarah (1998), "Creating Barriers for Foreign Competitors: A Study of the Impact of Anti-Dumping Actions on the Performance of U.S. Firms," *Strategic Management Journal,* 19, 25-37.

Martins, Marielza and Kent Monroe (1994), "Perceived Price Fairness: A New Look at an Old Construct," in *Advances in Consumer Research,* Vol. 21, Chris Allen and Deborah Roedder John, eds. Provo, UT: Association for Consumer Research, 75-78.

Mathews, Anna and Scott McCartney (1999), "American Airlines Faces Changes of Forcing Rivals Out of Hub," *The Wall Street Journal,* May 14, A1, A5.

Matutes, Carmen and Pierre Regibeau (1992), "Compatibility and Bundling of Complementary Goods in a Duopoly," *Journal of Industrial Economics,* 40 (March), 37-54.

McConnell, J. Douglas (1968), "An Experimental Examination of the Price-Quality Relationship," *Journal of Business,* 41 (October), 439-44.

Monroe, Kent B. (1973), "Buyers' Subjective Perceptions of Price," *Journal of Marketing Research,* 10 (February), 70-80.

────── and Peter J. LaPlaca (1972), "What Are the Benefits of Unit Pricing?" *Journal of Marketing,* 36 (July), 16-22.

Morris, Ruby Turner and Claire Sekulski Bronson (1969), "The Chaos in Competition Indicated by Consumer Reports," *Journal of Marketing,* 33 (July), 26-43.

Ordonez, Lisa D. (1998), "The Effect of Correlation between Price and Quality on Consumer Choice," *Organizational Behavior and Human Decision Processes,* 75 (September), 258-73.

Oxenfeldt, Alfred R. (1950), "Consumer Knowledge: Its Measurement and Extent," *Review of Economics and Statistics,* 32, 300-14.

Pechmann, Cornelia and S. Ratneshwar (1992), "Consumer Covariation Judgements: Theory or Data Driven?" *Journal of Consumer Research,* 19 (December), 373-86.

Puto, Christopher P. (1987), "The Framing of Buying Decisions," *Journal of Consumer Research,* 14 (December), 301-15.

Rabin, Matthew (1993), "Incorporating Fairness into Game Theory and Economics," *American Economic Review,* 83 (December), 1281-302.

Rao, Akshay R. and Kent B. Monroe (1988), "The Moderating Effect of Prior Knowledge on Cue Utilization in Product Evaluations," *Journal of Consumer Research,* 15 (September), 253-64.

────── and ────── (1989), "The Effect of Price, Brand Name, and Store Name on Buyers' Perceptions of Product Quality," *Journal of Marketing Research,* 29 (August), 351-57.

Ratchford, Brian, Jagdish Agrawal, Pamela Grimm, and Narasimhan Srinivasan (1996), "Toward Understanding the Measurement of Market Efficiency," *Journal of Public Policy & Marketing,* 15 (Fall), 167-84.

Rosendorff, B. Peter (1996), "Voluntary Export Restraints, Anti-Dumping Procedure, and Domestic Politics," *American Economic Review,* 86 (June), 544-61.

Russo, J. Edward (1977), "The Value of Unit Pricing," *Journal of Marketing Research,* 14 (May), 193-201.

———, Gene Krieser, and Sally Miyashita (1975), "An Effective Display of Unit Price Information," *Journal of Marketing,* 39 (April), 11-19.

Salinger, Michael (1995), "A Graphical Analysis of Bundling," *Journal of Business,* 68 (January), 85-99.

Sawyer, Alan G. and Peter R. Dickson (1984), "Psychological Perspectives on Consumer Response to Sales Promotion," in *Research on Sales Promotion: Collected Papers,* Katherine E. Jocz, ed. Cambridge, MA: Marketing Science Institute, 1-21.

Schmalensee, Richard (1981), "Output and Welfare Implications of Monopolistic Third-Degree Price Discrimination," *American Economic Review,* 71 (March), 242-47.

Shankar, Venkatesh, Arvind Rangaswamy, and Michael Pusateri (1999), "The Online Medium and Customer Price Sensitivity," working paper, Smeal College of Business Administration, Pennsylvania State University.

Sherif, Muzafer, Carolyn Sherif, and R. E. Nebergall (1965), *Attitude and Attitude Change: The Social Judgment-Involvement Approach.* Philadelphia: W. B. Saunders.

Shugan, Steven and Jinhong Xie (2000a), "Advance Pricing of Services and Other Implications of Separating Purchase and Consumption," *Journal of Service Research,* 2 (February), 227-39.

——— and ——— (2000b), "Electronic Tickets, Smart Cards, and Online Prepayments: When to Advance Sell," unpublished working paper, University of Florida, Warrington College of Business Administration.
Available: shugan@dale.cba.ufl. edu

Simonin, Bernard and Julie Ruth (1995), "Bundling as a Strategy for New Product Introduction: Effects on Consumers' Reservation Prices for the Bundle, the New Product, and the Tie-In," *Journal of Business Research,* 33, 219-30.

Stigler, George (1961), "The Economics of Information," *Journal of Political Economy,* 69 (June), 213-25.

Tellis, Gerard (1986), "Beyond the Many Faces of Price: An Integration of Pricing Strategies," *Journal of Marketing,* 50 (October), 146-60.

——— and Birger Wernerfelt (1987), "Competitive Price and Quality under Asymmetric Information," *Marketing Science,* 6 (Summer), 240-53.

Thaler, Richard (1985), "Mental Accounting and Consumer Choice," *Marketing Science,* 4 (Summer), 199-214.

Urbany, Joel E., William O. Bearden, and Dan C. Weilbaker (1988), "The Effect of Plausible and Exaggerated Reference Prices on Consumer Perceptions and Price Search," *Journal of Consumer Research,* 15 (June), 95-110.

——— and Peter Dickson (1991), "Consumer Normal Price Estimation: Market versus Personal Standards," *Journal of Consumer Research,* 18 (June), 45-51.

——— and ——— (1994), "Evidence on the Risk-Taking of Price Setters," *Journal of Economic Psychology,* 15 (1), 127-48.

———, Thomas Madden, and Peter Dickson (1989), "All's not Fair in Pricing: An Initial Look at the Dual Entitlement Principle," *Marketing Letters,* 1 (1), 17-25.

Varian, Hal (1985), "Price Discrimination and Social Welfare," *American Economic Review,* 75 (September), 870-75.

Vermulst, Edwin and Bart Driessen (1997), "New Battle Lines in the Anti-Dumping War," *Journal of World Trade,* 31 (June), 135-57.

Vilcassim, Neufel and Dick Wittink (1987), "Supporting a Higher Shelf Price through Coupon Distributions," *Journal of Consumer Marketing,* 4 (Spring), 29-39.

Whinston, Michael (1990), "Tying, Foreclosure, and Exclusions," *American Economic Review,* 80 (September), 837-59.

Wilkie, William, Carl Mela, and Gregory Gundlach (1998), "Does Bait and Switch Really Benefit Consumers?" *Marketing Science,* 17 (3), 273-82.

Winer, Russell S. (1986), "A Reference Price Model of Brand Choice for Frequently Purchased Products," *Journal of Consumer Research,* 13 (September), 250-56.

——— (1988), "Behavioral Perspectives on Pricing: Buyers' Subjective Perceptions of Price Revisited," in *Issues in Pricing,* Timothy M. Divinney, ed. Lexington, MA: Lexington Books, 35-57.

Yadav, Manjit and Kent Monroe (1993), "How Buyers Perceive Savings in a Bundle Price: An Examination of a Bundle's Transaction Value," *Journal of Marketing Research,* 30 (August), 350-58.

Zeithaml, Valerie A. (1982), "Consumer Response to In-Store Price Information Environments," *Journal of Consumer Research,* 8 (March), 357-69.

Chapter 12

Marketing and Development

Macromarketing Perspectives

Thomas A. Klein
Robert W. Nason

This chapter reviews and evaluates the contributions of marketing to economic and social development. It is based on conceptual, theoretical, and empirical scholarship that, for the most part, has been conducted from a macromarketing point of view. Such a perspective primarily attends to relationships between markets and marketing activities and their economic, social, political, and ecological environments. We update previous reviews, such as those undertaken by Savitt (1988) and Wood and Vitell (1986), and extend the database of Wilkie and Moore's (1999) study to emphasize less developed and transitional economies.

The relationship between marketing and development is necessarily bidirectional. Reactions and feedback more or less continuously affect structures and processes on both sides of the interaction. Marketing is influenced by its environment, as is well known. The character of and outcomes from marketing activities also leave a mark on the economic, social, political, and ecological systems in which they occur. That mark may prompt changes in environmental features such as public policy and investment, income and buying behavior, and resource availability.

The concept of development covers expanded economic opportunities and improved outcomes in domestic and/or export markets, employment, standard of living, and (by implication) social conditions commonly included under the concept of quality of life—access to and quality of health care, education, cultural opportunities, and civic freedom and harmony.

The supposition, of course, is that the functional and structural elements of a marketing system—methods of distribution, channel structure, products and services available, advertising and other forms of marketing information, and pricing methods and policies—have an effect on development. The dynamics of the relationship further imply that an important aspect of this effect is resulting changes in the marketing environment itself.

A proper understanding of development recognizes differences in situations. Challenges differ markedly across varying geographic, social, and economic settings. Commonalities exist, but the task of jump-starting a subsistence economy dominated by self-production differs greatly from situations in which some elements already are in place. The oil-rich Middle East, the former Communist nations in Central and Eastern Europe, the rural hinterlands of industrial countries, and the least developed nations of Latin America and Africa present different problems and opportunities for agents of development, whether public officials, marketers, or nongovernmental organizations (NGOs) (Jain 1993).

Extensive research exists on market development in economies previously dominated by self-production (less developed economies) and command structures (transitional economies). These two settings are the primary focus of this chapter, although other situations are examined when appropriate and possible. An understanding of development also must give some attention to the path of historical change followed in more developed economies.

The Nature of Economic Development: Causes, Processes, and Effects

During the past century and at the dawn of the 21st century, some areas of the world have forged ahead rapidly in per-capita production and material wealth, while many have made only slow progress. Even more troublesome are indications that the gap between the most and least developed nations, at least until very recently, has widened. Absolute levels of economic productivity in less developed countries (LDCs) have grown little, and per-capita measures are aggravated by population increase differentials (United Nations data reported in Baldwin 1966, pp. 3-7, 47-49). Although economic wealth is no guarantor of happiness, those who have little regard improvements in material wealth as clearly desirable. Furthermore, advances in communications and transportation technology have spared few areas of the world of a view of the material comfort of the better off.

From a managerial marketing perspective, LDCs represent a potential opportunity. They constitute a large portion of the global geography and population; they contain a significant share of the world's agricultural, fishery, and mineral resource base; and some are growing more rapidly than advanced mature economies (Jain 1993).

In the economic arena, improved infrastructure and increases in industrial capacity and agricultural productivity are seen as necessary conditions for rapid economic development in LDCs. The application of resources in all these areas has singly or in combination had important effects on development, but these programs rarely have fulfilled the expectations of their architects. Even when technological breakthroughs have been achieved, as in the case of agricultural productivity increases during the 1950s and 1960s, the transfer of benefits to the population has been slower than desired.

Also, there are many noneconomic aspects of development such as its political, cultural, and social effects. However, several studies undertaken during the 1950s and 1960s suggested that the role of the marketing system in the development process had not been examined adequately.

The Theory of Development Stages

Economic development theory commonly begins with understanding Rostow's (1960) stages of growth. Improvements in agricultural technology and the commercial exploitation of natural resources provide marketable commodities that generate income to improve the wage structure, underwrite industrialization, and pay for vital public services. Through successive iterations, personal incomes rise, and the higher incomes can, in turn, be spent on an improved assortment of consumer goods. Profit opportunities attract investment, and a work incentive to the potential labor force is provided by the chance to improve standards of living.

Marketing activities pervade this framework. Production inputs, agricultural surpluses and raw materials, and consumer goods must be channeled to places and times where demand is present and in quantities matching demand. Product development is encouraged. Market research, marketing communications, and business and consumer financing must support this process. A network of distributive and facilitating institutions evolves. This pattern roughly describes economic development in all types of settings, but it is most applicable to a historical understanding of economies that evolve from self-production to domination by industry and/or trade.

It was recognized that in a developing economy, agricultural production and urban consumption of food are interdependent, as are urban industrial producers of nonfoods and rural consumers. Furthermore, links among these sectors make up the marketing system. The general view of theorists and practitioners was that the marketing system, by definition, must follow the development of the industrial and agricultural sectors. Marketing also will automatically distribute this production if and when it becomes available, based on the logic that there must be something to distribute before distribution can take place. Yet, because this logic equates the limited concept of physical distribution with that of marketing, it oversimplifies the development process.

The notion of physical distribution was expanded to include the exchange system for the transfer of property rights and a communication system to disseminate information on product and service characteristics, supply, and demand throughout the channel of distribution. This modification was required because the notion of physical distribution was a limited view of the links between producers and consumers of goods and services, and there was little evidence to support the commonly held proposition that efficient distribution systems will spontaneously develop when there is product to be distributed. Indeed, all evidence pointed to the contrary. Collins and Holton (1964) noted that the dependence of the industrial and agricultural sectors on the development of a distributive sector to bridge the gap between producers and ultimate consumers rarely is recognized. They further argued that it is erroneous to assume that the distributive sector will spontaneously develop in an optimal fashion.

The Role of Marketing in Economic Development

In examining the connection between marketing and economic development, the most fundamental question has been whether marketing actually contributes to development or is merely the result of increases in income and the availability of commercial goods and services. As early as 1957, in a lecture to the Philadelphia chapter of the American Marketing Association, Peter Drucker submitted that "marketing is . . . the most effective engine of economic development" (Drucker 1958, p. 252). Savitt (1988), on the other hand, noted that the view of marketing as an outcome of development generally has prevailed and might, in fact, be the case. Nonetheless, he saw some areas where marketing clearly has supported, if not stimulated, economic growth by facilitating institutional and technological developments. He also recognized that the existence of markets and marketing functions—buying and selling, distribution, information, financing and risk bearing, and establishing quality standards—under conditions of competition might be a critical foundation for effective and efficient development. One may reasonably identify the commercialization of agriculture and fisheries, economic diversification, and activities that expand markets as marketing contributions (Kazgan 1988).

In a more philosophical vein, Kotler (1988) contended that "marketing thinking" is a preferable alternative when the apparent obstacles to development include the rigidities of government planning, ownership, and management; corruption; and a cultural ethos that opposes work, investment, and consumption beyond mere subsistence. Kotler, Jatusripitak, and Maesincee (1997) applied this idea to the whole process of national development including the public policy arena.

Galbraith and Holton (1955), following their work in Puerto Rico, were the first to point out that distribution is an important aspect of economic development that had been neglected. Their field research in 1949 and 1950 attempted to assess the distribution system for both foods and nonfoods in terms of present costs and efficiency as well as improvements that could be made. The idea was introduced that consumers can be better off and the development of a country can be aided if its marketing system operates more efficiently.

This newfound link in development thought was given emphasis by the "Report of the Panel on the World Food Supply" formulated by the President's Science Advisory Committee (1967):

The improvement of food storage, processing, and distribution systems in the developing nations is as important as increasing production. The encouragement of private investment to develop facilities for storing, processing, and distributing goods deserves a high priority. Governments of developing countries must provide a climate hospitable to the kinds of private enterprises that can stimulate change from a subsistence-oriented farming economy to a market-oriented one. (p. 539)

Thus, the first recognized role of marketing in economic development concerned improved systems to distribute existing production efficiently to final consumers. Rural products then could move to urban areas with less loss and spoilage, in greater and more stable volume, and at lower and more stable prices. Both consumers and producers benefited.

There has been a good deal of debate on the role of marketing since the Galbraith and Holton (1955) study. Beyond the notion of simple distribution efficiency, the concept emerged that the marketing system could influence producers to provide increased flows of products at lower costs, of better quality, and in better alignment with market needs. This influence works in two ways. First, it affects the type and amount of goods produced. Second, it supplies production inputs and incentives that facilitate production expansion and improvement. That is, the marketing system influences not only what and how much is produced but also the factors used in production.

Rostow (1964) placed these roles in perspective in a four-point strategy for what he called a "national market":

a build-up of agricultural productivity; a revolution in the marketing of agricultural products in the cities; a shift of industry to the production of simple agricultural equipment and consumers' goods for the mass market; and a revolution in marketing methods for such cheap manufactured goods, especially in rural areas. (p. 136)

These four elements must be carried forward simultaneously. Thus, economic development involves the flow of goods in an interlocking marketing system that allows urban and rural areas to be interdependent and mutually reinforcing in their areas of comparative advantage. Rostow's notion of production for mass consumption parallels closely what Galbraith and Holton (1955, pp. 10-11) termed the "popular consumption criterion," whereby development is organized around the present and prospective consumption requirements of the typical or model consumer. It is notable that development has been greatest when there have been improvements in consumer productivity (McIntyre and Kale 1988), a finding that underscores the need to take a "whole systems approach."

Whatever the intuitive validity of Rostow's (1964) theory, actual situations reveal that advancement is not inevitable. Some nations with the apparent ingredients for economic growth have remained undeveloped for long periods. Why? Sloever (1985) argued that Rostow's theory is both ahistorical and arbitrary. One reason appears to lie in the linkage between production and consumption, that is, the marketing system.

Primary Marketing Problems of Development

From 1965 to the early 1970s, a team of researchers headed by Charles Slater studied and modeled the effect of marketing on the development process. This work was primarily conducted in Latin America (Slater 1968; Slater, Henley et al. 1969, Slater, Riley et al. 1969). The supply of food has a significant effect on the economy in most developing nations; more than half of the urban consumers' income is spent on food, and nearly all members of the rural population produce food. Therefore, Slater and his team placed food distribution at the center of their research.

In later work in Southern Africa, attention also was given to the agricultural input sector (Slater, Walsham, and Shah 1977; Slater et al. 1979). Sorensen (1988) also noted the importance of supply channels in improving agricultural productivity. Although the factor market of the agricultural producer is acknowledged as important, and although there are several possible ways in which marketing can help to increase production and quality, efforts to improve farm technology have been disappointing in many cases. Thus, there must be other reasons for agriculture's nonresponse.

The Marketing System for Foods
from Farm to Consumer

The implication of Rostow's (1964) framework is that if distortions in the system are removed and products can flow more smoothly to ultimate consumers, then producers would respond with increased production. That is, the marketing channel itself is a barrier to production. Faced with price fluctuations, lack of market information, poor transportation facilities, high spoilage rates, high credit costs, small-volume transactions, and inadequate grades and standards, farmers have little confidence that price will cover cost. It does not seem prudent to participate in the market system, as opposed to growing only enough for family use, especially if there is no social safety net, which is the case in most developing nations.

Slater and his team found that the traditional food distribution system in northeastern Brazil had up to eight levels of very small intermediaries for each product. Each intermediary dealt with several baskets of product at a time, for the most part transported by animal. There was no refrigeration; standards or grades were lacking; and there were no protective measures to avoid handling, insect, or rodent damage. These conditions resulted in high spoilage and contributed to extreme fluctuations in farm gate prices. Although spoilage and loss occurred throughout the system, costs tended to be passed on down the channel, resulting in very high prices in urban markets. Of the dry foods that entered the market in Recife, Brazil, in 1966, rice had the lowest spoilage rate—9% of wholesale volume and 10% of retail volume. At the other extreme, perishables often had two to three times these spoilage rates. For bananas, the figures were 30% of wholesale volume and 38% of retail volume. In 1966, different producers of beans in the region received prices that differed by a multiple of more than five. Finally, to add to the difficult channel situation, much of the volume was financed by supplier credit ranging from annualized rates of 113% to 774%, depending on product type (Slater et al. 1969b).

This brief description cannot deal adequately with the causal factors of channel distortions but simply illustrates the magnitude of problems found by Slater's team, both in terms of the stifling effect on market production and in terms of the sheer loss of what was produced. Team members argued that understanding and reducing these distortions and resultant risks and uncertainties constituted one important developmental thrust. It is notable that their perceptions are borne out more recently in China, where market liberalization in the food system produced significant gains for producers, traders, and most consumers but not without problems in many sectors of the economy, prompting the government to intervene again (Rozelle et al. 1997).

Production Response

During the 1960s, many scholars believed that economic modernization was blocked by factors other than a rational consideration of inputs versus the market. It was suggested that those in the traditional economy had a distaste for work and a liking for leisure, the master-servant relationship eliminated any technological creativity, there was a low level of achievement motivation, an independent-experimental frame of mind was lacking, the social structure and rules limited interpersonal bonds to family and kinship groups, and social striving might not be connected to technological progress (see, e.g., Belshaw 1965, pp. 77-110; Brewster 1967, p. 73; Schultz 1966, pp. 43-44).

During this period, some hypothesized that the marketing activity was not a barrier to production but rather was an incentive to increase production in its own right. Slater and his team produced extensive anecdotal and empirical evidence of the vertical coordination and integration effects of the establishment of mass distributors and their positive influence on production efficiency, product development, lower selling prices, market expansion, and the local economy (Latin American Studies Center 1967). At about the same time, Gallagher (1967) illustrated the same effects of the Sears experience in Brazil, Colombia, Mexico, Peru, and Venezuela and, to some degree, in Costa Rica, El Salvador, and Panama.

Income and Demand

Researchers documented that the desire for increased well-being, which results in responses to market factors, also is an important force in resisting modernization by traditional system operators. Wiser and Wiser (1963, pp. 117-18) pointed out that the main barrier to the use of new practices is the perceived risk of failure, which combines the cost of the new practice and the possible loss of production. Brewster (1967) explained,

> So close is life to the bone that their impulse to take a chance on gaining a whole loaf from new and untried techniques is inhibited by anxiety over losing the crumb they feel sure of getting from their old practices. And this progress-blocking anxiety stems from sound economic sense. For innovations carry an immense risk for

the uninitiated, and the risk is magnified by the very poverty they might escape by taking it. Operating at a bare subsistence level, a crop failure or a failure to cover the borrowed money by added harvests would be calamitous. (pp. 66)

The proposal that primitive or peasant societies are not interested in economic maximization is mostly myth. More broadly, most people seek higher income and are willing to work for it. Income is the incentive for both investment and work. Logically, it provides the basis for demand for both producer and consumer goods and services.

It is clear that vigorous markets depend on a high level of demand for goods and services, and a high level of demand presumes a level of income capable of supporting efficient production and distribution. In the absence of a significant infusion of funds to consumers, the market never can expand, which is the economic conundrum of market development.

A chart showing the linkage among food production, distribution, and industrial production is presented as Figure 12.1.

Markets

One approach to resolving this conundrum is to establish market preconditions. Without them, presumably, it will be difficult to achieve the promised benefits of generally higher living standards and economic opportunity. These preconditions include a legal system to establish and protect property rights, contract rights, and choice; adequate information systems; physical infrastructure to facilitate transportation and communications; regard for social aspects such as environmental protection, food safety, and cultural enhancement; and a reliable financial system (Carman and Harris 1986; Harris and Carman 1983, 1984).

Such preconditions are likely to require a public policy foundation, one that probably will differ from that in advanced economies. For example, Nevett (1988) argued that advertising regulation might be necessary in developing countries, whereas self-regulation has proven to be cost-effective in, for example, the United Kingdom and the United States. There also must be incentives that stimulate investment and both organizational and individual productivity and entrepreneurship; progressive tax policies, price controls, and inequities in the distribution of economic gains stifle the individual and corporate efforts necessary for economic growth (Aharoni 1977, pp. 19-26). Macesich (1996) noted that the fall of communism in many parts of the world and the increasing willingness of large corporations to invest in transition economies are critical for development in those settings. Among LDCs, the proposition that the political environment must be hospitable to foreign investment is borne out by the case of Costa Rica (Schuler and Brown 1999). Of course, the prospect that multinational corporations will play a lead role in economic growth is viewed with considerable suspicion in some quarters (Korten 1995).

The early focus on distribution as the key marketing ingredient in economic progress, and the enthusiasm of many of those authors for government interven-

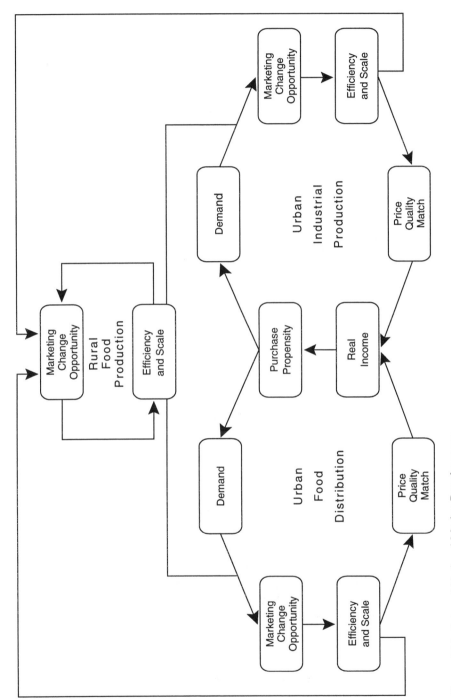

Figure 12.1. Internal National Market Development

tion, suggests that a government-managed distribution system might benefit both producers and consumers of agricultural products more quickly and with greater certainty than do the trials and errors characteristic of market processes. Based on his studies in the Ivory Coast, however, Etgar (1983) argued that such a system is characterized by opportunistic behavior, limited information, and bureaucratic inefficiencies that more than absorb any benefits from improved physical efficiency. Presumably, trade-offs to limit these features would generate little net improvement. A more measured view recognizes a role for both government and private participation in economic development planning (Cundiff 1982).

The Role of Marketing

International scholarship has produced many studies of marketing systems in developing nations. A most encompassing example of this scholarship is that of Glade and colleagues (1970) in Peru. Their extensive study of the Peruvian marketing system for consumer and industrial products (i.e., not limited to the food system) concludes, "Effective marketing, i.e., the set of business policies implied by the marketing concept, can play a valuable part in reducing the manifold market imperfections which tend to depress the efficiency of resource use in the economic system" (p. 214). We next examine evidence that marketing practices influence development.

Technology Transfer

Technological transfer is widely viewed as critical to economic growth. It often is cited in explaining the difference between more and less developed economies. This represents a shift in perspective since the 19th century, when natural resources were commonly viewed as the key difference. Studies in development, ranging from postwar Germany and Japan to more contemporary Taiwan and Korea, indicate that new technology is the primary driver of economic development. Most improvements in economic productivity in the United States are attributable to technology. In agriculture, its effects on production and distribution, primarily financed by the government, are well known (Breimeyer 1963). Bennett (1967) advocated government involvement in new product research, market research, labor force development, and market regulation, although he believed that entrepreneurship should be encouraged. Irrespective of the source of innovation, markets facilitate diffusion and transfer through direct investment, collaboration, and personnel transfers. Barriers to international transfers in the form of taxation, limits to capital repatriation and immigration, religious opposition to technological change, and policy-based disincentives such as employment maintenance regulations, by implication, hinder economic development (Singh 1983).

It is significant that multinational enterprises, rather than governments, have been the most prominent actors in technology transfer (Safarian and Bertin 1987). It is ironic that exported technologies may develop further in different environments (e.g., culture, managerial style, public policies) and may return to influence original host environments and aid yet more development in those settings, as has occurred in the case of the Japanese auto industry (Fuss and Waverman 1987).

Technology transfer under the auspices of multinational enterprises might not be welcomed in all instances. In Chile, for example, a long-standing conflict between the government and International Telephone and Telegraph Company finally was resolved by vesting control of Chile's telecommunications network in an independent "foundation" (Meissner 1988). Similarly, the transfer of technology to industry in Eastern Europe has created considerable frustration (Hayden 1976; Liebrenz 1982).

Product Development

There is little research on product development in the less developed world. For the most part, the role of innovation in such settings is subsumed within the concept of technology transfer. That is, the innovations that have brought significant economic growth to the advanced economies are exported to others, but adaptation strategies are common. Whether these are sufficient is, of course, a matter of some debate (James 1993).

Distribution

Improvements in physical distribution that reduce spoilage and take advantage of scale economies were among the first efforts to improve marketing systems. Research in this area was discussed earlier. Market expansion made possible by participation in export and import markets and by institutional changes, many of which are connected to the physical distribution functions, are examined next.

Import/Export

According to Buzzell (1999), market development and economic growth are inevitably and closely linked to globalization. It is virtually impossible to insulate a local market from global influences in light of the geographic scope of contemporary market organizations and the transportation and communications technology that link both hierarchies and markets.

The economic effects of importing and exporting are both direct and indirect. Mullen (1993), in a study of 155 nations, found that importing primarily improves the ability to meet basic needs, whereas exporting stimulates overall economic activity. Whether the benefits of the latter flow to the whole population depends on the extent of general participation in that activity, a phenomenon that varied across the nations studied. By implication, policies that favor exports at the expense of imports are not in the best interests of the general population un-less there is broad participation in export markets. A less obvious effect of global trade is pressure for common ethical and legal standards, which should lower overall costs in the marketing system (Windsor and Getz 1999).

Trade relationships involving less developed economies are commonly viewed as requiring "colonial" intervention from industrialized nations. However, this sort of relationship may involve nations only slightly more advanced than the least developed partners. For example, Malaysian businesses have jumped into the economic voids created in Guinea when the French left there, presumably to the benefit of both nations' economic circumstances (Montgomery 1999).

Channels/Institutions

Perhaps the most compelling study of marketing channel evolution is by Bucklin (1972). Changes in structure—scope, vertical and horizontal integra-tion, and concentration—and the shifting locus of control from distributors, to manufacturers, to large retailers are cataloged in terms of operating scale, costs and margins, competition, and the ability to respond to buyer requirements. This history also is recounted in the context of 19th-century America by Porter and Livesay (1971).

With respect to economic development, Bucklin (1972, pp. 318-25) argued that the emergence of new distributive institutions and channels brings down consumer costs (of distribution relative to income and overall) and expands the assortment of goods and services available in the marketplace. In a later study, based on work with the United Nations' Food and Agriculture Organization, Bucklin (1976) further outlined improvements in channels that would increase distributive efficiency. Drawing heavily on his work in Java, Layton (1985) sup-ported the proposition that economic growth, distribution system development, and improved living standards in terms of the assortment and cost of goods are interdependent. Specifically, development is aided by larger wholesale and re-tail institutions and shorter channels (Olsen and Granzin 1990). Alternatively, based on their studies in Turkey, Kumcu and Kumcu (1987) found that improve-ments in food retailing could be achieved without major disruptions in the exist-ing structure, and this also was valued by consumers. Ger (1999) argued that the emergence of large-scale distribution, often involving foreign firms, is a com-petitive challenge that can be met by local firms, thereby ratcheting the overall performance of the economy in consumer terms. Even when institutional change is constrained by traditions and lack of investment capital, evolution in distribution brings benefits to segments of the population that are disadvantaged by low income (Ortiz-Buonafina 1992).

Irrespective of the development of formal channels, it should be noted that the informal sector (e.g., gray and black markets, barter, outlawed goods and services), particularly in less developed economies (where markets are severely restricted) and among the poor and unemployed, plays a major role in living standards (Robles and El-Ansary 1988).

More generally, it is possible to map and modify marketing channels based on their performance in delivering benefits to end consumers (Dahringer 1983; Klein 1986).

Nongovernmental Organizations

Another facet of channel development is the emergence of new forms of co-operative or community-based institutions with church sponsorship or affiliation. One alleged advantage is that they are designed to deliver benefits to the community at large, as opposed to individual businesses (Alexander 1997; Mac-Adam 1998). Whether they are more or less effective in this respect, of course, depends on governance structures and processes. Another aspect of NGO activities is their commitment to social goals (Mellor 1998). Their pursuit of economic objectives typically is leavened by concerns for justice for the poorer segments of society; they also may be active in this regard in the political realm.

Marketing Communications

Advertising

The role of advertising in economic and social development has been hotly debated for years. Borden (1942) generally is credited with the first careful analysis of the arguments. He recognized the role of advertising in facilitating the expansion of demand, driving down overall costs due to scale economies. When demand is naturally limited (e.g., for staples), however, competitive advertising increases total costs. Yet, in the context of competitive markets and unfilled demand potential, advertising informs the public regarding product availability and attributes and, thereby, generates value to consumers that typically exceeds any overall cost increases (Nelson 1970).

Advertising, as a potential source of illusory product differentiation, also functions as a barrier to market entry, may distort buyers' evaluations of similar products, and contributes to industrial concentration (Bain 1968). It also contributes to, or at least reinforces, the distortion of consumer values in the sense that social standing and self-image may be manipulated and social meaning is commodified (Dholakia and Levy 1987; Pollay 1986). The indictment of advertising as manipulative, echoing concerns that predate serious academic interest in developing economies (e.g., Galbraith 1958), is viewed as critically flawed by M. Phillips (1997) and Simon (1970). Their defense includes the need to both find and serve exchange partners, provide a motivation to work, and (as with Borden 1942), bring down costs. B. Phillips (1997) addressed the social construction thesis more directly, arguing that information conveyed through advertising is sought because consumers wish to know about socially acceptable consumption in the context of other information they receive from experience and observation. For their part, advertisers will be unsuccessful in advancing modes of consumption that are not aligned with those other social cues.

The context of this scholarship is primarily the United States. What is the significance of these arguments in a less developed economy or one that is undergoing transition? Presumably, the baseline condition in either setting is one of limited supply and demand. Exposure to sponsored information about goods and services that might improve the standard of living, whether foodstuffs or luxury goods, stimulates the supply of market labor (at least in theory) and, thus, income and demand for such goods. In less mature markets, concerns about industry concentration and costs exceeding value might be less relevant. In their place, however, are concerns about cultural homogenization, such as the "McDonaldization" of eating habits to the disadvantage of indigenous businesses and consumption habits (Ritzer 1996). And, as noted previously, advertising, when unregulated, is more likely to produce false or misleading information in LDCs.

Other Forms of Market Information

Apart from advertising, information generally is recognized as contributing to market performance, especially with respect to equitable access to price and quality data. In this respect, market research has played an important role. For example, channel mapping techniques have aided in identifying obstacles in and opportunities for improving the food production and marketing systems of several African nations (Slater, Walsham, and Shah 1977; Slater et al. 1979).

Place Marketing

One of the more obvious applications of marketing in economic development is efforts to promote a community, state, nation, or region as a site for industrial development or tourism. When successful, place marketing directly affects employment and other economic indicators. Of course, place marketing properly includes all the strategic elements of the marketing mix. Targeting and positioning are foundation components of a place marketing strategy. Tax relief packages are an example of pricing in this context. Events and infrastructure development may be viewed as elements of a product offering. We place this concept in the domain of marketing communications to recognize the key role of brochures, sponsored visits, trade shows, advertising, and other communications media as vehicles for informing prospective investors or visitors of the comparative advantages associated with the sponsoring place (Milman and Pizam 1995; Nason, Dholakia, and McLeavey 1987).

Pricing

Whereas economists recognize price as a result of competing forces of supply and demand, marketers recognize price as a strategic element of the marketing mix that can be used to influence demand. In previous comments, we noted the value of bringing down costs through more efficient distribution methods. Lowering costs expands the number of consumers who can buy a given product and, at any given income level, expands access to products. In terms of meeting basic needs, for example, improvements in the nutrition level of the population should result from lower prices. In a totally different realm, the impact of vigorous price competition in the airline industry on total demand generally is recognized.

Other Terms of Sale: Financing

If the concept of pricing is expanded to include other elements of "terms of sale," then it seems appropriate to recognize the economic effects of trade and consumer credit. For example, the demand for autos, home appliances, and other consumer durables undoubtedly has increased as a direct result of improved access to installment credit. The range of these products to be seen in retailer showrooms would be impossible without "floor plans" or factoring. "Dating" programs make it feasible to stabilize the economics of items having seasonal demand or production. These results represent opportunities for investment and employment to producers.

Cultural and Political Barriers to Market Development

An assessment of the relationship between marketing and economic development must take into account more than economic factors (Taylor and Omura 1994, 1995). A comparison of more and less developed economies indicates that cultural and political barriers may be present in the latter. Conversely, some social environments offer fertile ground for moving an economy from agrarian to industrial; for distributing income more equitably such that disposable consumer income is generated; and for stimulating investment and risk taking relative to innovations needed to improve efficiency, increase productivity, and supply expanding markets. When political environments are unstable, the development process, once under way, can be stopped or even reversed. Finally, there is substantial evidence that, absent some external intervention (e.g., foreign investment, government stimulation, even certain artifacts of colonialization), otherwise promising settings might remain undeveloped.

Ray's (1998) thesis is that the economic development process is best understood by identifying barriers to the efficient and equitable functioning of markets. By implication, the improvement of physical and human capital, the reduction of inequality, and enhancement of information flow, together with social institutions that facilitate these developments, are critical to the full realization of a nation's economic potential.

Attitudes toward Profit, Economic Risk, and Security

Schumpeter (1934) generally is credited with recognizing the role of entrepreneurship in development. To the extent that cultures and government policies discourage entrepreneurship, innovations in products and processes will be hindered.

An important barrier to economic growth, common to most less developed settings, is a traditional culture with beliefs and practices that do not recognize the value of work, productivity, risk taking, and material progress. In that case, some major change in the dominant social system, typically brought about through a change in social leadership, is necessary to provide a culture that is hospitable to economic development (Hagen 1962). Similarly, political attitudes that favor economic security, such as in the formerly Communist countries of Eastern and Central Europe, either may prevent market liberalization due to short-term costs in employment and transfer programs or, when liberalization has occurred, may tend to discourage individuals from seeking new sources of employment.

Cundiff and Hilger (1979) proposed that entrepreneurial ingenuity will be the driving force for reform in developing economies. Yet, this "spiritual" resource is not present to the same degree in all societies.

Lack of a Consumption Culture

The motivation to consume is a precondition for both demand that extends beyond meeting basic needs and participation in the labor force. Anderson (1970), in an early study of marketing in Thailand, found that constraints on the propensity to consume (religious asceticism and low income) restricted economic development, whereas market-oriented government policies and investments (notably the construction of all-weather highways) significantly aided it.

Political Instability

Rostow (1971), who believed economic development follows a more or less automatic path, nevertheless recognized the importance of a hospitable and stable political environment. The prospect that public policies, including agreements with governments, will be subject to dramatic change deters investment and other commitments. On the other hand, Costa Rica, which has enjoyed economic growth exceeding that of its neighbors, is distinguished as a stable democracy that has welcomed significant foreign direct investment (Schuler and Brown 1999).

Resistance to External Intervention

Writing during the Great Depression, John Maynard Keynes proposed government intervention to stimulate economic growth in the face of stagnant or declining investment and demand (Keynes 1936). He advocated an incomes policy; government jobs and public works programs, unemployment insurance, and social security are examples of Keynesian theory in action. So-called post-Keynesian theory (Domar 1947; Harrod 1948) added the need for programs that stimulated investment directly such as investment tax credits and interest rate management. These fundamental theoretical propositions have been applied primarily in more developed settings, but they also are relevant in the less developed world (Baldwin 1966, pp. 77-84) and include foreign aid (pp. 105-11).

Limited Natural and Human Resources

Economic development is fostered by a generous natural resource endowment and an educated and trainable labor force (Baldwin 1966, pp. 49-54). Agriculture is the usual economic base of LDCs; marketable agricultural produce depends on soil and climate conditions. In some settings, mineral resources or fisheries are the primary economic base.

In any case, there must be farmers, miners, fishermen, and industrial workers—as well as managers—capable of applying available technology to the task of generating marketable yields. The linkage between poverty and education, which has been explored most thoroughly by Schultz (1963, 1981, 1993), is much more than a statistical relationship observed in advanced economies. Rather, differences in educational investment are a virtually universal factor in explaining variations in economic development. Emphasizing agricultural productivity, Schultz opined that education is the major distinction between more and less productive nations with respect to food and fiber. Places with resource constraints are forced to compete on the basis of low labor costs (McKee and Biswas 1993).

Inadequate Transportation and Communications Infrastructure

The need for transportation and communication networks as a prerequisite for market development and expansion beyond the boundaries of villages and coastal areas has been a fundamental factor in economic history since antiquity. For example, highways, whether built to move armies (as in the Roman Empire or the United States) or to transport agricultural produce from the countryside to urban population centers, have expanded commercial opportunities and attracted new economic ventures. Infrastructure also has been a major outlet for entrepreneurial expression; railroads and other transportation modes, electrical and telephone systems, turnpikes, and (more recently) the Internet typically have involved, if not depended on, substantial private initiative (Kazgan 1988). As noted earlier, Anderson (1970) found that government investment in all-weather highways significantly aided development. Investment in infrastructure also translates into resources in terms of location search criteria (McKee and Biswas 1993).

Failure of Institutions to Protect Individual Property Rights, Facilitate Financial Transactions, and Protect Consumers

The nature of the legal and institutional framework as a precondition of markets was discussed earlier. Underdeveloped nations commonly have a limited framework for establishing, protecting, and exchanging property rights. In such circumstances, uncertainties hinder investments, particularly those calculated to generate long-term returns. The creation of option value measures, based on household endowments and needs in a village in Burkina Faso, provides a basis for establishing property values as a condition of transactions involving both land and agricultural products (Zimmerman and Carter 1999). The inability or unwillingness of financial institutions to make business and consumer loans, which often is related to unstable currencies, is widely recognized as a deterrent to investment and consumption. Savitt (1988, 1994), among others, argued that the absence of consumer protection laws and enforcement is a major weakness in both LDCs and most transitional economies.

Resistance to Foreign Investment

In less developed settings, critical resources are commonly imported from more developed nations, either directly through government-to-government aid or via multinational corporations or indirectly through multilateral organizations. Financing, technology and technical assistance, and management are commonly brought in to take advantage of resource potential. Somewhat more controversial is the importation of institutions, either through colonization or as a required precondition for economic aid.

Layton (1988) argued that, without the involvement of larger companies able to finance and manage (and derive returns from) distribution innovations, those innovations are unlikely to occur. Whether local firms benefit from more efficient methods of distribution depends on whether they actively participate in such changes.

The effect of economic aid also is determined by its delivery. Africa may be cited as an example of failure in these respects given that the distribution of aid is controlled by entrenched forces and is politicized by social concerns such as women's rights, wildlife preservation, and other special interests. Although legitimate and worthy, these groups tend to absorb or deflect investments in agricultural productivity and employment opportunity—and, thereby, the investment and income stimulation needed for growth (Mellor 1998).

Transitional Economies

A broader conceptualization of development is particularly relevant in understanding variations in economies converting from a Communist orientation to a market orientation. When marketing mind-sets and habits, informed consumers who seek a better life, and supportive institutions are in place, we see significant advancement. In other cases, progress has been minimal. Moreover, "advancement" may be accompanied by dislocations (e.g., unemployment, inflation, inequities) that undermine popular support for market reforms. Finally, unregulated entrepreneurship can lead to social disorder, which degrades the quality of life for most citizens and encourages political conservatives who would reinstall the old order (Batra 1999).

Marketing Mind-Sets and Market-Oriented Public Policies

Development assessments in Central and Eastern Europe present mixed results. In large measure, much depends on the extent to which governments embrace the concept of a market economy and, at the same time, establish the institutional and legal framework required for those markets to function efficiently and equitably. The Czech Republic, Hungary, and Poland moved most rapidly to market economies and enjoyed substantial growth during the early 1990s. Because these nations had institutional and legal memories of the pre-Communist period, the disorder that has marked the Russian transition was largely averted. Nevertheless, the shocks of inflation and the end of guaranteed employment have produced a political reaction that has slowed the transition. Experiences vary. On one hand, Poland has persisted in its efforts to improve financial institutions, anti-monopoly laws, and other enabling conditions. On the other hand, the former Russian republics, Bulgaria, and Romania have taken a cautious approach, retaining many of the programs and strictures of the former regime. Accordingly, development has been slower, but the free market hooliganism that has characterized urban Russia also has been largely avoided.

It seems that cultural factors play a major role in transition. Years of dependence on government can create a population unfamiliar with and uncertain about economic risk, unable to see the connection between what is produced and what is consumed, and unwilling to invest effort in improving productivity. In other words, the entrepreneurial mind-set that is considered a precondition of development appears to be quite unevenly distributed among European nations in transition (Savitt 1994, 1996).

The critical agricultural sector has proven especially resistant to market reforms in most settings. In Eastern Europe, the benefits of open markets have been blocked by a reluctance to undertake land reform or allow prices to rise. Farmers revert to subsistence operations because they cannot purchase inputs based on returns from controlled prices. In China, Vietnam, and Ethiopia, by contrast, state procurement programs continued with market-based prices, and production has been encouraged by improved returns (Jones 1996). In Bangladesh, the development of competition in input markets has encouraged productivity without price increases, whereas market liberalization in the agricultural sector has been minimal in India, Pakistan, and Sri Lanka (Ahmed 1996). In most of Africa, liberalization has meant the removal of both production subsidies and price controls, but the emergence of alternative, more efficient, and more competitive channels of distribution has effectively offset the gap that otherwise would have occurred. Price increases have been minimal, and returns to producers have not declined significantly (Jayne et al. 1996).

Tolerance for Dislocations

Throughout history, economic development has been accompanied by a transfer of social status from agricultural to merchant and industrial elites, even as the economic status of those involved in agriculture improved. Even more significant might be changes in the status of different religions insofar as traditional beliefs tend to dominate in rural areas but less so in more urbanized settings (Darian 1985). Social change may have profound political implications and, of course, may be viewed as threatening by the ruling class, which might try to stifle change—and the economic developments that spawned it.

Technological change necessarily affects employment opportunities. These shifts may disadvantage those who already are marginal such that their participation in society is further diminished by their exclusion from the labor force. Grimalda (1999) advocated a "regulated model" of technology adoption that effectively buffers these segments of the population from the adverse consequences of advancement.

Resistance to Competitive Markets and Ethical Deficiencies

Competition is, of course, critical to market performance. Government intervention in markets frequently is directed at insulating local producers from global competition, and this is likely to be a costly and ultimately futile public policy. Porter (1990) argued forcefully for policies that improve competitiveness rather than keep foreign competitors out. Based largely on observations in advanced economies, Porter's thesis has been attacked as inapplicable in less developed situations, where the emphasis often is placed on government-sponsored initiatives such as export incentives. Work by Dominguez and colleagues (Dominguez and Sequeira 1991, 1993; Dominguez, Sequeira, and Rose 1996; Dominguez and Vanmarcke 1987), however, indicated that these initiatives are ineffective; market factors and managerial responses to them are the primary determinants of success. Kaynak's (1986) review of studies of food marketing systems around the world also supports this perspective in relation to domestic markets. Conversely, so-called crony capitalism implies that social factors, often family or political relationships, replace price/quality/service criteria as determinants of transactions. Bribery and extortion also may be an element of exchange equations.

The transition to a market economy often is accomplished by simply switching from one form of oligarchy to another. Yergin and Stanislaw (1998) provided an important historical perspective on the conflict between Socialist and market economies. Socialism triumphed during the 1920s and 1930s because markets failed to deliver a reasonably stable standard of living to the majority of citizens. The return to markets came because the governing elites exercised power in an arbitrary and corrupt manner. Yet, in some settings, markets are effectively governed by a greedy few, regulated by neither individual ethics nor government policies, and hidden from public view by shoddy accounting. This explains the recent economic turmoil in some Asian countries and might signal a return to socialism unless democratic governments exercise greater control over market failure. In short, the public's expectations regarding the economy are ignored by leaders—government officials as well as private businesspeople—at significant peril.

Liberalization Policies

The transition to a market economy may follow full privatization or a more gradual path. In addressing criticisms of full liberalization, Paul, Miller, and Paul (1998) argued for a libertarian state (i.e., no economic intervention) despite the fact that in most advanced economies it is common to find regulation, limited property rights, and government control of some economic sectors such as health care. Alternatively, Goodhue, Rausser, and Simon (1998) favored gradual reform, which allows for less uncertainty than does full liberalization; economic actors (a combination of private and state-owned industries) learn to adjust to market signals, thereby avoiding disorderly markets and their social welfare implications.

A historical perspective on this issue, based primarily on pre- and post-industrial England, was provided by Moore (1998b). Markets were regulated at the local level as early as the 14th century; monopolies, prices, weights and measures, and brokerage rates were commonly subject to legal or administrative control. By the mid-19th century, industrialization brought a reasonable standard of living to a majority of the population. Institutions were in place to resolve disputes related to debt, contracts, trespass, and weights and measures. Socially, moral superiority was accorded those who enjoyed business success. Public goods were associated with economic prosperity (e.g., sewers were built to prevent cholera), and there was vigorous public debate regarding issues such as child labor and fair wages—and the morality of competition (particularly from foreign-made goods). Moore (1998a) noted how various social movements in favor of equality, cooperation, and austerity—often with religious overtones—tended to produce economic productivity and, eventually, broke down in favor of enjoying the rewards of prosperity.

The less developed world and transition economies may be particularly susceptible to the negative byproducts of markets and marketing because they typically lack the sophisticated regulatory structures found in more advanced nations. Questions about environmental preservation and the equitable distribution of income and wealth often receive particular scrutiny. Some argue that personal and corporate standards of morality that exceed the legal minimum are critical to ensure that development brings lasting benefits to the whole society (Singh and Carasco 1996; Tavis 1997). More broadly, Moran and Ghoshal (1999) argued for an integrative approach to understanding both economic development and firm performance. That is, firms are most successful when they create value that can be assessed in terms larger than internal profitability alone, in concert with markets and other institutions.

Marketing and the Quality of Life

What is the relationship between marketing and quality of life? In the case of Thailand, Leelakulthanit, Day, and Ealters (1991) found that overall satisfaction with life depends on family life, material possessions, and self-development. The relationship between marketing and material possessions is intuitively obvious, although Belk (1988) noted the potential for dissatisfaction associated with envy and the gap between desire and fulfillment; this gap occurs when wealth is unevenly distributed and people are exposed to unattainable goods. Economic opportunity provides an important path for self-development and may contribute to improved family life, despite well-known stresses in advanced economies related to work-family conflicts. More broadly, Peterson and Malhotra's (1997) study of measures of culture, freedom, health, and environment in relation to several economic variables indicates a strong and positive connection between economic development and quality of life.

This macroperspective may be extended to considering the balance between private and public goods. More advanced market economies generally provide better health care and educational opportunities and have less crime and more cultural and civic freedom than do those that are less developed. The quality of life in such settings involves more than the assortment of consumer and producer goods and services. Yet, exceptions to this rule can be found. Although the scope of markets is constrained in Western Europe, most citizens enjoy a generous mix of public services and private goods. Furthermore, undernourished education and health care sectors and substantial social disorder are perceived as characteristic of the United States, which is arguably the most economically advanced nation in the world. An aging population in North America and Europe increases the demand for social services and income transfers, yet it might affect tax revenues and global attitudes toward risk. The propagation of a "consumer culture" has obvious implications for resource depletion and the degradation of community values. It also may lead to intolerance for a level of taxation sufficient to bear the cost of an adequate assortment of public goods and services available to all. Nevertheless, Reidenbach and Oliva (1983), who applied principles of entropy to the marketing-society relationship, concluded that the negative externalities of marketing systems ("negentropy") are manageable.

Criticisms of Marketing Effects

A broader theoretical framework to explain economic development implies a more inclusive set of evaluative criteria. Distribution effects usually are viewed as the domain of economics. Market development is commonly accompanied by a widening gap in living standards between rich and poor. Distributive innovations, such as mass market retailing, might be mostly patronized by those who already are better off. Income from expanded trade and improved productivity might not be shared with workers. The exploitation of natural resources, the commercialization of agriculture, and industrialization might be achieved at the expense of deforestation and pollution. The absence of an appropriate combination of business ethics and public regulation can have negative implications for social welfare. In the long run, further economic growth might be undermined and global ecology might be adversely affected.

Distribution Effects: The Gap between Rich and Poor

One troubling thesis is that economic development may lead to higher incomes and living standards, but benefits tend not to be shared equally, at least without significant redistribution efforts by government. To a considerable extent, such inequities arise from unequal access to labor markets (Frank and Cook 1995), and this has income and demand implications. There also is evidence that lower prices available through mass retailers are primarily enjoyed by persons with higher incomes (Leone, Mulhern, and Williams 1998). They are exposed to more information and are better able to postpone certain purchases or take advantage of bargains whenever they are available. In other words, the benefits of large-scale retailing might not actually reach those who need them most.

When Income Gains Are Not Shared

When the benefits of expanded trade and improved productivity are not shared broadly, further trade and productivity gains might be limited. From a moral perspective, there are social justice implications as well. Accordingly, government and corporate strategies directed at economic development need to encompass income distribution effects, both direct and indirect (Goeke 1987; Nason, Dholakia, and McLeavey 1987; Vann and Kumcu 1995).

Cultural and Economic Imperialism

An important social concern connected with global marketing concepts is the plight of dislocated local firms. For example, the embrace of McDonald's and Benetton by consumers in Eastern Europe adversely affects indigenous restaurants and apparel retailers. When there is a significant division between affluent and poor consumers, marketing that targets the former and ignores the latter is predictable (Dholakia, Sharif, and Bhandari 1988).

Another concern is that LDCs suffer social welfare consequences when a portion of food crop production, previously limited to local markets, is sold for export—or replaced with produce targeted to export markets. In theory, this will result in higher local prices (as supplies available to local consumers are reduced) and price fluctuations (as global market conditions are transmitted to previously stable local markets). A contrary finding, based on experience in the Vietnamese rice market, is that greater total demand and expanded employment opportunities will yield a rise in income that exceeds price increases. That is, the proportion of income spent on the exported commodity declines (Minot and Goletti 1998).

Focusing on the consumption effects of development, James (1993) observed resource scarcity effects that raise prices and shift demand from traditional to imported products, a lack of fit between these imported products and the circumstances of consumers (e.g., washing machines too large, infant formula requiring clean water), and an information environment that is confusing and some-times misleading.

The globalization of markets offers other negative prospects. Dholakia and Firat (1988) noted that, under global competition, the economic development of the Third World generally is tied to labor cost differentials. These are transient in nature—partially by design—and place indigenous industry and service organi-zations at a substantial competitive disadvantage relative to "world-class" goods and services. If true, these prospects must limit growth.

An even larger concern is that the focus on economic development, generally defined by Western values, ignores and may conflict with a more authentic an-thropological perspective that takes the values and traditions of less developed cultures into account. By disrupting and subverting those values and traditions, marketing conflicts with development of a more holistic nature (Bennett and Bowen 1988; Hill 1986).

In its extreme form, of course, the use of the size and scope of luxury good markets as a measure of economic progress is misleading (Frank 1999) given that great wealth often coexists with massive poverty. Although one should not overlook the employment opportunities associated with serving the wealthy, the historical economic base of many societies, an authentic anthropology must at-tend to the needs of the poor as a given condition of real development (Klein 1987).

The useful message of these critiques is not that improvements in the stan-dard of living are irrelevant but rather that traditions and beliefs must be taken into account in both planning development initiatives and evaluating economic progress (Dholakia and Sherry 1987; El-Sherbini 1983; Firat, Kumcu, and Karafioglu 1988; Giron and Giron 1993; Joy and Ross 1989; Kaynak 1986; Porter 1993).

Quality of Life Implications

The presumption is that when economic development makes the poorer seg-ments of society comparatively worse off, they are less happy than they were under the previous circumstances (Easterlin 1995). Dissatisfaction with one's share in general economic gains is a critical ingredient in social disorder and possible political instability. Hagerty and Veenhoven (1999) disagreed. Based on a multiyear study of incomes and "life satisfaction," they found significant positive correlations both for individuals and in the aggregate between these measures. In other words, absolute income gains translate into greater life satis-faction, irrespective of whether individual gains are more or less than average. In addition to this self-report approach to assessing the social effect of economic development, economic impact analysis can objectively assess distribution ef-fects through measures of costs and benefits (Klein 1977). The macromarketing perspective, of course, recognizes the value of a multidisciplinary whole sys-tems approach to this task (Meade and Nason 1991).

Environmental Concerns

In all settings, there is concern that economic growth will cause environmental decay through resource depletion and pollution (Barkley and Seckler 1972). Reilly (1999) argued that private enterprise has an obligation to minimize the adverse environmental consequences of its operations, and he provided examples of actions that serve this goal. The debate on this general issue is voluminous. The seminal pessimistic perspective is that of Meadows and colleagues (Meadows, Meadows, and Randers 1992; Meadows et al. 1972). Erekson, Loucks, and Stafford (1999) offered a digestible summary of the relationship between sustainability and the actions of business firms. The late Julian Simon generally was considered the principal champion of the view that human ingenuity, by developing and applying technology in the context of market forces, will produce economic growth and protect or even improve the natural environment (Simon 1998).

The critical perspective in marketing was offered by Fisk (1974) and Kilbourne, McDonagh, and Prothero (1997). Rising consumption levels due to higher incomes necessarily increase resource depletion and pollution. Wants are infinite and mostly socially derived. Consumption in a growing economy is limited only by resource availability. Marketing is primarily about responding to and promoting demand (presumably unconcerned with resource limits). Therefore, once a society exceeds the threshold of delivering a "decent" standard of living—one that is neither opulent nor conspicuous—ecological degradation is predictable.

The environmental consequences of market and economic development—resource depletion and pollution—are third-party effects that seldom are internalized in market transactions. Therefore, it is logical to argue that development degrades natural environments. Apart from the empirical question of whether the environment fares better under socialism, the systemic capability of planned economies to protect the environment probably is greater than that of market economies.

The issue is further complicated by the prospect that any form of economic development may put the environment at risk unless it is controlled to maintain sustainability. The concept of "sustainable development" must be brought into public policy in the economic sphere and recognized in private decisions and conduct (Fisk 1974; Fuller 1999; Lozada 1999; van Dam and Apeldoorn 1996). Fortunately, in many cases, environmental concerns are reflected in economic development projects, and one can argue that, in the absence of economic development, degradation would be inevitable (Hoff 1998).

It also is true that market—and marketing—solutions may be likely to promote sustainability. First, the rationing of scarce resources through market prices tends to limit depletion and to encourage the development and use of more abundant substitutes. Second, markets have emerged—sometimes with government participation—that encourage resource recovery, recycling, and conservation. Within such markets lie opportunities that prompt product and service innovations as well as efficient distribution methods and institutional pathways. These require effective marketing communications.

Conclusions

The Coca-Cola Company is commonly considered *the* icon of global marketers. Its success in LDCs frequently has been cited as a prime example of economic exploitation. To the contrary, Woodward and Teel (1999) revealed that in South Africa, Coke has developed a network of distributors and, in so doing, has provided opportunities for both entrepreneurship and employment. It also may be argued that the emergence of "Coke bars" in LDCs is a motivator for the labor force.

The most encompassing assessment of how marketing affects social and economic development can be obtained through a long-term examination of an advanced economy such as that of the United States. Wilkie and Moore (1999) conducted such an examination. Their searching study began with the simple task of putting breakfast on the table today in comparison to a century ago. The expansion and increased complexity of the aggregate marketing system has been accompanied by efficiency, wider choice, and arguably improved quality in terms of both nutrition and taste. These authors pursued other measures of social influence to note effects such as better safety and health (and, thus, improved longevity), technological developments for home and industry, and general improvement in life satisfaction. They believed that marketing has been either a major or a minor contributor to these measures. They also noted similar patterns emerging in less developed parts of the world. Finally, Wilkie and Moore took a hard look at the major criticisms of marketing, those considered here as well as a few others such as the marketing of dangerous products and consumer privacy. Their assessment is overwhelmingly positive, although challenges continue.

Our general conclusion is that marketing enriches the value of native resources by exploiting commercial opportunities. These are actualized through incentives for productive work, investment, and innovation. Consumer welfare is raised through access to improved products, lower prices, and information (including advertising), particularly under competitive conditions. Thus, the wealth needed to underwrite improvements in public goods is generated.

Economic development is most likely to occur under certain conditions—natural resources; transportation and communications infrastructure; institutions to protect individual property rights, facilitate financial transactions, and provide a measure of consumer protection; a stable and business-friendly political environment; educational resources; and a cultural ethos that values work, entrepreneurship, and material progress. Particularly in LDCs, external intervention might be necessary to provide critical financial, technological, and human resources.

Critics charge that marketing contributes to environmental and cultural degradation and to distortions in consumer values. Markets might not lead to equitable distribution; the benefits of marketing—to both buyers and sellers—might be disproportionately enjoyed by elites relative to the general population.

A comprehensive understanding of this subject takes both positive and negative contributions into account. There is evidence of market failure in all relevant settings; regulatory responses may replace one set of deficiencies with another (i.e., regulatory failure also occurs). Nonetheless, it is difficult to conclude that marketing is not a net positive force in social development and in improving material living standards.

Future Research Needs

The scholarship reviewed in this chapter is voluminous and has touched on virtually every aspect of the relationship between marketing and economic and social development. However, several opportunities for bringing marketing scholarship into the mainstream of development research remain. Those most familiar with the names of principal scholars in marketing subdisciplines such as logistics, consumer behavior, business-to-business marketing, advertising, and product development might notice their absence in this chapter. Indeed, some of these topics have barely been covered, and the coverage provided depends heavily on agricultural economists, economic and social historians, and others whose attention to marketing issues is mostly a byproduct of their primary interests. This implies significant opportunity to develop knowledge and understanding in several areas of primary concern to marketers and to add the multidisciplinary perspective of marketing scholarship to a field of great importance to humanity.

In addition to this broad invitation to marketing scholars to devote their attention to a subject of significant social importance, several lines of research appear particularly rewarding.

Except for the historical works cited, most of this research amounts to short-term studies of particular issues in particular countries. Longitudinal studies (i.e., research that captures movements in related variables over an extended period) would capture the leads and lags that necessarily occur in all complex economic and social settings. Similarly, as each nation presents some idiosyncrasies, comparative studies that control for these differences would give us a firmer grasp of what is salient in economic and social development.

The research reported in this chapter is heavily weighted toward agriculture and food marketing systems. Although these areas are critical, particularly so in poorer countries where inadequate nutrition is common, research devoted to other business and consumer products and services surely would broaden our understanding of development.

Finally, the record is clear that the most advanced economies have developed a measure of independence based on some combination of political, trade, and industrial might, typically traceable to a series of significant product innovations or improvements that amounted to a breakthrough in performance or cost. The reality is that most of the LDCs and transitional economies remain in a state of dependence at this time. We previously noted that research on product development in these nations is virtually nonexistent. If advanced thinking on the process of product—and market—development were brought into these countries, then this dependence might be transformed into the type of interdependence that would provide its own momentum for growth.

References

Aharoni, Yair (1977), *Markets, Planning, and Development.* Cambridge, MA: Ballinger.

Ahmed, Raisuddin (1996), "Agricultural Market Reforms in South Asia," *American Journal of Agricultural Economics,* 78 (August), 815-19.

Alexander, Anne (1997), *The Antigonish Movement: Moses Coady and Adult Education Today.* Toronto: Thompson.

Anderson, Dole A. (1970), *Marketing and Development: The Thailand Experience.* East Lansing: Michigan State University, Graduate School of Business Administration.

Bain, Joe S. (1968), *Industrial Organization,* 2nd ed. New York: John Wiley.

Baldwin, Robert E. (1966), *Economic Development and Growth.* New York: John Wiley.

Barkley, Paul W. and David W. Seckler (1972), *Economic Growth and Environmental Decay: The Solution Becomes the Problem.* New York: Harcourt Brace Jovanovich.

Batra, Rajeev (1999), *Marketing Issues in Transitional Economies.* Norwell, MA: Kluwer.

Belk, Russell (1988), "Third World Consumer Culture," in *Research in Marketing,* Suppl. 4: *Marketing and Development: Toward Broader Dimensions,* Erdogan Kumcu and A. Fuat Firat, eds. Greenwich, CT: JAI, 103-27.

Belshaw, Cyril S. (1965), *Traditional Exchange and Modern Markets.* Englewood Cliffs, NJ: Prentice Hall.

Bennett, John and John Bowen (1988), *Production and Autonomy: Anthropological Studies and Critiques of Development.* New York: University Press of America.

Bennett, P. D. (1967), "Marketing and Public Policy in Latin America," in *Changing Marketing Systems: Consumer, Corporate, and Government Interfaces,* Reed Moyer, ed. Chicago: American Marketing Association, 233-38.

Borden, Neil (1942), *The Economics of Advertising.* Chicago: Irwin.

Breimeyer, Harold F. (1963), "Functioning of Factor Markets and Economic Development," in *Towards Scientific Marketing,* Stephen Greyser, ed. Chicago: American Marketing Association, 409-23.

Brewster, John M. (1967), "Traditional Social Structures as Barriers to Change," in *Agricultural Development and Economic Growth,* Herman M. Southworth and Bruce F. Johnston, eds. Ithaca, NY: Cornell University Press, 66-98.

Bucklin, Louis P. (1972), *Competition and Evolution in the Distributive Trades.* Englewood Cliffs, NJ: Prentice Hall.

——— (1976), "Intermediate Technologies for Improving Food Retailing Efficiency in Developing Asian Countries," in *Macromarketing: Distributive Processes from a Societal Perspective,* Charles Slater, ed. Boulder: University of Colorado Press, 218-37.

Buzzell, Robert D. (1999), "Market Functions and Market Evolution," *Journal of Marketing,* 63, 61-63. (Special issue)

Carman, James M. and Robert G. Harris (1986), "Public Regulation of Marketing Activity, Part III: A Typology of Regulatory Failures and Implications for Marketing and Public Policy," *Journal of Macromarketing,* 6 (Spring), 51-64.

Collins, Norman R. and Richard H. Holton (1964), "Programming Changes in Marketing in Planned Economic Development," in *Agriculture in Economic Development,* Carl Eicher and Lawrence Witt, eds. New York: McGraw-Hill, 359-69.

Cundiff, Edward W. (1982), "A Macromarketing Approach to Economic Development," *Journal of Macromarketing,* 2 (Spring), 14-19.

——— and Mary Hilger (1979), "Marketing and the Product Consumption Thesis in Economic Development," in *Macromarketing: Evolution of Thought,* George Fisk, Robert W. Nason, and Philip D. White, eds. Boulder: University of Colorado Press, 177-86.

Dahringer, Lee D. (1983), "Public Policy Implications of Reverse Channel Mapping for Lesotho," *Journal of Macromarketing,* 3 (Spring), 69-75.

Darian, Jean C. (1985), "Marketing and Economic Development: A Case Study from Classical India," *Journal of Macromarketing,* 5 (Spring), 14-26.

Dholakia, Nikhilesh and A. Fuat Firat (1988), "Development in the Era of Globalizing Markets and Consumption Patterns," in *Research in Marketing,* Suppl. 4: *Marketing and Development: Toward Broader Dimensions,* Erdogan Kumcu and A. Fuat Firat, eds. Greenwich, CT: JAI, 79-101.

——— and John F. Sherry, Jr. (1987), "Marketing and Development: A Resynthesis of Knowledge," in *Research in Marketing,* Vol. 9, Jagdish N. Sheth, ed. Greenwich, CT: JAI, 119-43.

Dholakia, Ruby R. and Sidney Levy (1987), "The Consumer Dream in the United States: Aspirations and Achievements in a Changing Environment," *Journal of Macromarketing,* 17 (Spring), 41-51.

———, Mohammed Sharif, and Labdi Bhandari (1988), "Consumption in the Third World: Challenges for Marketing and Development," in *Research in Marketing,* Suppl. 4: *Marketing and Development: Toward Broader Dimensions,* Erdogan Kumcu and A. Fuat Firat, eds. Greenwich, CT: JAI, 129-47.

Domar, E. (1947), "Expansion and Employment," *American Economic Review,* 37 (March), 34-35.

Dominguez, Luis V. and Carlos Sequeira (1991), "Strategic Options for LDC Exports to Developed Countries," *International Marketing Review,* 8 (5), 27-43.

——— and ——— (1993), "Determinants of LDC Exporters' Performance: A Cross-National Study," *Journal of International Business Studies,* 24 (1), 1-22.

———, ———, and Patricia B. Rose (1996), "Environmental and Managerial Factors in Export-Led Development: An Explorative Test of Porter's Competitive Advantage of Nations," *Journal of Macromarketing,* 13 (Fall), 5-21.

——— and Cristina Vanmarcke (1987), "Market Structure and Marketing Behavior in LDCs: The Case of Venezuela," *Journal of Macromarketing,* 7 (Fall), 4-16.

Drucker, Peter F. (1958), "Marketing and Economic Development," *Journal of Marketing,* 22 (January), 252-59.

Easterlin, Richard A. (1995), "Will Raising the Incomes of All Increase the Happiness of All?" *Journal of Economic Behavior and Organization,* 27 (1), 35-47.

El-Sherbini, Abdel-Aziz (1983), "Behavioral Analysis of the Role of Marketing in Economic Development," *Journal of Macromarketing,* 3 (Spring), 76-79.

Erekson, O. Homer, Orie L. Loucks, and Nigel C. Stafford (1999), "The Context of Sustainability," in *Sustainability Perspectives for Resources and Business,* Orie L. Loucks, O. Homer Erekson, Jan W. Bol, Raymond F. Gorman, Pamela C. Johnson, and Timothy G. Krehbiel, eds. Boca Raton, FL: Lewis, 3-21.

Etgar, Michael (1983), "A Failure in Marketing Technology Transfer: The Case of Rice Distribution in the Ivory Coast," *Journal of Macromarketing,* 3 (Spring), 59-68.

Firat, A. Fuat, Erdogan Kumcu, and Mehmet Karafioglu (1988), "The Interface between Marketing and Development," in *Research in Marketing,* Suppl. 4: *Marketing and*

Development: Toward Broader Dimensions, Erdogan Kumcu and A. Fuat Firat, eds. Greenwich, CT: JAI, 317-41.

Fisk, George (1974), *Marketing and the Ecological Crisis.* New York: Harper & Row.

Frank, Robert H. (1999), *Luxury Fever.* New York: Free Press.

———— and Phillip J. Cook (1995), *The Winner-Take-All Society.* New York: Martin Kessler.

Fuller, Donald A. (1999), *Sustainable Marketing: Managerial-Ecological Issues.* Thousand Oaks, CA: Sage.

Fuss, Melvyn and Leonard Waverman (1987), "The Japanese Productivity Advantage in Automobile Production: Can It Be Transferred to North America?" in *Multinationals, Governments, and International Technology Transfer,* A. E. Safarian and Gilles Y. Bertin, eds. New York: St. Martin's, 191-206.

Galbraith, John Kenneth (1958), *The Affluent Society.* Boston: Houghton Mifflin.

———— and Richard H. Holton, (1955), *Marketing Efficiency in Puerto Rico.* Cambridge, MA: Harvard University Press.

Gallagher, John F. (1967), "Markets as a Basis for Industrial Development," in *The Challenge of Development,* Richard J. Ward, ed. Chicago: Aldine, 318.

Ger, Guliz (1999), "Localizing in the Global Village: Local Firms Competing in Global Markets," *California Management Review,* 41 (Summer), 64-83.

Giron, Jose de la Paz H. and Maria L. H. Giron, (1993), "Structuring Favorable Market Opportunities for the Mixtec Region of Oaxaca, Mexico," *Journal of Macromarketing,* 13 (Fall), 22-31.

Glade, William P., William A. Strang, Jon G. Udell, and James E. Littlefield (1970), *Marketing in a Developing Nation: The Competitive Behavior of Peruvian Industry.* Lexington, MA: Lexington Books.

Goeke, Patricia E. (1987), "State Economic Development Programs: The Orientation Is Macro, but the Strategy Is Micro," *Journal of Macromarketing,* 7 (Spring), 8-21.

Goodhue, Rachel E., Gordon C. Rausser, and Leo K. Simon (1998), "Privatization, Market Liberalization, and Learning in Transition Economies," *American Journal of Agricultural Economics,* 80 (November), 724-37.

Grimalda, Gianluca (1999), "Participation versus Social Exclusion," *Journal of Business Ethics,* 21 (September), 269-79.

Hagen, E. E. (1962), *On the Theory of Social Change.* Homewood, IL: Dorsey.

Hagerty, Michael R. and Ruut Veenhoven (1999), "Wealth and Happiness Revisited: Growing Wealth of Nations Does Go with Greater Happiness," unpublished manuscript, Graduate School of Management, University of California, Davis.

Harris, Robert G. and James M. Carman (1983), "Public Regulation Activity, Part I: Institutional Typologies of Market Failure," *Journal of Macromarketing,* 3 (Spring), 49-58.

———— and ———— (1984), "Public Regulation of Marketing Activity, Part II: Regulatory Responses to Market Failures," *Journal of Macromarketing,* 4 (Spring), 41-52.

Harrod, R. (1948), *Towards a Dynamic Economics.* London: Macmillan.

Hayden, Eric W. (1976), *Technology Transfer to East Europe: U.S. Corporate Experience.* New York: Praeger.

Hill, Polly (1986), *Development Economics on Trial: The Anthropological Case for the Prosecution.* New York: Cambridge University Press.

Hoff, Marie D. (1998), "Sustainable Development: Origins and Essential Elements of a New Approach," in *Sustainable Community Development: Studies in Economic, Environmental, and Cultural Revitalization,* Marie D. Hoff, ed. Boca Raton, FL: Lewis, 5-21.

Jain, Subhash C. (1993), *Market Evolution in Developing Countries: The Unfolding of the Indian Market.* Binghamton, NY: International Business Press.

James, Jeffrey (1993), *Consumption and Development.* London: Macmillan.

Jayne, T. S., Lawrence Rubey, Frank Lupi, David Tschirley, and Michael T. Weber (1996), "Estimating Response to Food Market Reform Using Stated Preference Data: Evidence from Eastern and Southern Africa," *American Journal of Agricultural Economics,* 78 (August), 820-24.

Jones, Stephen (1996), "Creating Markets: Food Policy and Agricultural Reform in the Transition," *American Journal of Agricultural Economics,* 78 (August), 810-14.

Joy, Annama and Christopher Ross (1989), "Marketing and Development in Third World Contexts: An Evaluation and Future Directions," *Journal of Macromarketing,* 9 (Fall), 17-31.

Kaynak, Erdener (1986), *World Food Marketing Systems.* London: Butterworth.

Kazgan, Gulten (1988), "Marketing in Economic Development," in *Research in Marketing,* Suppl. 4: *Marketing and Development: Toward Broader Dimensions,* Erdogan Kumcu and A. Fuat Firat, eds. Greenwich, CT: JAI, 39-61.

Keynes, J. M. (1936), *The General Theory of Employment, Interest, and Money.* New York: Harcourt, Brace.

Kilbourne, William H., Pierre McDonagh, and Andrea Prothero (1997), "Sustainable Consumption and the Quality of Life: A Macromarketing Challenge to the Dominant Social Paradigm," *Journal of Macromarketing,* 17 (Spring), 4-24.

Klein, Saul (1986), "Fostering Development through Backward Integration in Import Channels," *Journal of Macromarketing,* 6 (Spring), 17-27.

Klein, Thomas A. (1977), *Social Costs and Benefits of Business.* Englewood Cliffs, NJ: Prentice Hall.

————— (1987), "Prophets and Profits: A Macromarketing Perspective on 'Economic Justice for All: Catholic Social Teaching and the U.S. Economy,' " *Journal of Macromarketing,* 7 (Fall), 59-77.

Korten, David C. (1995), *When Corporations Rule the World.* San Francisco: Kumarian Press.

Kotler, Philip (1988), "Potential Contributions of Marketing Thinking to Economic Development," in *Research in Marketing,* Suppl. 4: *Marketing and Development: Toward Broader Dimensions,* Erdogan Kumcu and A. Fuat Firat, eds. Greenwich, CT: JAI, 1-10.

—————, Somkid Jatusripitak, and Suvit Maesincee (1997), *The Marketing of Nations: A Strategic Approach to Building National Wealth.* New York: Free Press.

Kumcu, Erdogan and M. Ercan Kumcu (1987), "Determinants of Food Retailing in Developing Economies: The Case of Turkey," *Journal of Macromarketing,* 7 (Fall), 26-40.

Latin American Studies Center (1967), *Food Marketing in the Economic Development of Puerto Rico.* East Lansing: Michigan State University Press.

Layton, Roger (1985), "Marketing Systems in Regional Economic Development," *Journal of Macromarketing,* 5 (Spring), 42-55.

————— (1988), "Industrial Development and Traditional Distribution: Are They Compatible?" in *Research in Marketing,* Suppl. 4: *Marketing and Development: Toward Broader Dimensions,* Erdogan Kumcu and A. Fuat Firat, eds. Greenwich, CT: JAI, 173-98.

Leelakulthanit, Orese, Ralph Day, and Rockney Ealters (1991), "Investigating the Relationship between Marketing and Overall Satisfaction with Life in a Developing Country," *Journal of Macromarketing,* 11 (Spring), 3-23.

Leone, Robert, Francis Mulhern, and Jerome Williams (1998), "Variability of Brand Price Elasticities across Retail Stores: Ethnic, Income, and Brand Determinants," *Journal of Retailing,* 74 (Fall), 427-46.

Liebrenz, Marilyn L. (1982), *Transfer of Technology: U.S. Multinationals and Eastern Europe.* New York: Praeger.

Lozada, Hector R. (1999), "Ecological Sustainability and Marketing Strategy: Review and Implications," in *Marketing Management Association Proceedings,* Dale Varble, Robert Green, and Gene Wunder, eds. Terre Haute: Indiana State University Press, 113-17.

MacAdam, Murray, ed. (1998), *From Corporate Greed to Common Good: Canadian Churches and Community Economic Development.* Ottawa: Novalis.

Macesich, George (1996), *Transformation and Emerging Markets.* Westport, CT: Praeger.

McIntyre, Roger P. and Sudhir Kale (1988), "Buyer-Seller Productivity and Economic Development," *Journal of Macromarketing,* 8 (Fall), 15-28.

McKee, Daryl and Abhijit Biswas (1993), "Community Resources and Economic Development Marketing Strategy: An Empirical Investigation," *Journal of Macromarketing,* 13 (Spring), 33-47.

Meade, William K. and Robert W. Nason (1991), "Toward a Unified Theory of Macromarketing: A Systems Theoretic Approach," *Journal of Macromarketing,* 11 (Fall), 72-81.

Meadows, D. H., D. L. Meadows, and J. Randers (1992), *Beyond the Limits.* Post Mills, VT: Chelsea Green.

———, ———, ———, and W. W. Behrens, III (1972), *The Limits to Growth.* New York: Universe Books.

Meissner, Frank (1988), *Technology Transfer in the Developing World: The Case of the Chile Foundation.* New York: Praeger.

Mellor, John W. (1998), "Closing the Last Chapter on U.S. Foreign Aid: What to Do about Africa," *Choices,* 13 (4), 28-42.

Milman, A. and A. Pizam (1995), "The Role of Awareness and Familiarity with a Destination: The Central Florida Case," *Journal of Travel Research,* 33 (February), 21-27.

Minot, Nicholas and Francesco Goletti (1998), "Export Liberalization and Household Welfare," *American Journal of Agricultural Economics,* 80 (November). 738-49.

Montgomery, Warner M. (1999), "Doing Business in West Africa," *Business and Economic Review,* 45 (July-September), 10-15.

Moore, Barrington, Jr. (1998a), "Austerity and Unintended Riches," in *Moral Aspects of Economic Growth and Other Essays.* Ithaca, NY: Cornell University Press, 54-81.

——— (1998b), "Moral Aspects of Economic Growth: Historical Notes on Business Morality in England," in *Moral Aspects of Economic Growth and Other Essays.* Ithaca, NY: Cornell University Press, 1-53.

Moran, Peter and Sumantra Ghoshal (1999), "Markets, Firms, and the Process of Economic Development," *Academy of Management Review,* 24 (July), 390-412.

Mullen, Michael (1993), "The Effects of Exporting and Importing on Two Dimensions of Economic Development: An Empirical Analysis," *Journal of Macromarketing,* 13 (Spring), 3-19.

Nason, Robert W., Nikhilesh Dholakia, and Dennis W. McLeavey (1987), "A Strategic Perspective on Regional Development," *Journal of Macromarketing,* 7 (Spring), 34-48.

Nelson, Philip (1970), "Information and Consumer Behavior," *Journal of Political Economy,* 78 (March-April), 311-29.

Nevett, Terence (1988), "Advertising Control through Self-Regulation: Some Policy Implications for Developing Countries," in *Research in Marketing,* Suppl. 4: *Marketing and Development: Toward Broader Dimensions,* Erdogan Kumcu and A. Fuat Firat, eds. Greenwich, CT: JAI, 229-51.

Olsen, Janeen E. and Kent L. Granzin (1990), "Economic Development and Channel Structure: A Multinational Study," *Journal of Macromarketing,* 10 (Fall), 61-77.

Ortiz-Buonafina, Marta (1992), "The Evolution of Retail Institutions: A Case Study of the Guatemalan Retail Sector," *Journal of Macromarketing,* 12 (Fall), 16-27.

Paul, Ellen Frankel, Fred D. Miller, Jr., and Jeffrey Paul (1998), *Problems of Market Liberalism.* Cambridge, UK: Cambridge University Press.

Peterson, Mark and Naresh K. Malhotra (1997), "Comparative Marketing Measures of Societal Quality of Life: Substantive Dimensions in 186 Countries," *Journal of Macromarketing,* 17 (Spring), 25-38.

Phillips, Barbara (1997), "In Defense of Advertising: A Social Perspective," *Journal of Business Ethics,* 16 (February), 109-18.

Phillips, Michael J. (1997), *Ethics and Manipulation in Advertising: Answering a Flawed Indictment.* Westport, CT: Quorum.

Pollay, Richard W. (1986), "The Distorted Mirror: Reflections on the Unintended Consequences of Advertising," *Journal of Marketing,* 50 (April), 18-36.

Porter, Gina (1993), "Changing Accessibility and the Reorganization of Rural Marketing in Nigeria," *Journal of Macromarketing,* 13 (Fall), 54-63.

Porter, Glenn and Harold C. Livesay (1971), *Merchants and Manufacturers: Studies in the Changing Structure of Nineteenth Century Marketing.* Baltimore, MD: Johns Hopkins University Press.

Porter, Michael E. (1990), *The Competitive Advantage of Nations.* New York: Free Press.

President's Science Advisory Committee (1967), "Report of the Panel on the World Food Supply," in *The World Food Problem: Report of the Panel on the World Food Supply,* Vol. 2. Washington, DC: Government Printing Office.

Ray, Debraj (1998), *Development Economics.* Princeton, NJ: Princeton University Press.

Reidenbach, R. Eric and Terence Oliva (1983), "Toward a Theory of the Macro Systemic Effects of the Marketing Function," *Journal of Macromarketing,* 3 (Fall), 33-40.

Reilly, William K. (1999), "Private Enterprises and Public Obligations: Achieving Sustainable Development," *California Management Review,* 41 (Summer), 17-26.

Ritzer, George (1996), *The McDonaldization of Society: An Investigation into the Changing Character of Contemporary Life.* Thousand Oaks, CA: Pine Forge.

Robles, Fernando and Adel I. El-Ansary (1988), "Informal Sector and Economic Development: A Marketing Perspective," in *Research in Marketing,* Suppl. 4: *Marketing and Development: Toward Broader Dimensions,* Erdogan Kumcu and A. Fuat Firat, eds. Greenwich, CT: JAI, 199-228.

Rostow, Walter W. (1960), *The Stages of Economic Growth.* Cambridge, MA: Harvard University Press.

——— (1964), *View from the Seventh Floor.* New York: Harper & Row.

——— (1971), *Politics and the Stages of Growth.* London: Cambridge University Press.

Rozelle, Scott, Albert Park, Jikun Huang, and Hehui Jin (1997), "Liberalization and Rural Market Integration in China," *American Journal of Agricultural Economics,* 79 (May), 635-42.

Safarian, A. E. and Gilles Y. Bertin (1987), *Multinationals, Governments, and International Technology Transfer.* New York: St. Martin's.

Savitt, Ronald (1988), "The State of the Art in Marketing and Development," in *Research in Marketing,* Suppl. 4: *Marketing and Development: Toward Broader Dimensions,* Erdogan Kumcu and A. Fuat Firat, eds. Greenwich, CT: JAI, 11-37.

——— (1994), "Understanding Central and Eastern Europe: A Review of Recent Literature," *Journal of Macromarketing,* 14 (Fall), 70-74.

——— (1996), "Russian Market Reform: A Literature Review," *Journal of Macromarketing,* 16 (Spring), 143-47.

Schuler, Douglas A. and David S. Brown (1999), "Democracy, Regional Market Integration, and Foreign Direct Investment: Lessons from Costa Rica," *Business & Society,* 38 (December), 450-73.

Schultz, Theodore W. (1963), *The Economic Value of Education.* New York: Columbia University Press.

——— (1966), *Economic Crises in World Agriculture.* Ann Arbor: University of Michigan Press.

——— (1981), *Investing in People.* Berkeley: University of California Press.

——— (1993), *Origins of Increasing Returns.* Cambridge, MA: Blackwell.

Schumpeter, Joseph (1934), *The Theory of Economic Development.* Cambridge, MA: Harvard University Press.

Simon, Julian (1970), *The Economics of Advertising.* Urbana: University of Illinois Press.

——— (1998), *The Ultimate Resource 2.* Princeton, NJ: Princeton University Press.

Singh, Jang B. and Emily F. Carasco (1996), "Business Ethics, Economic Development, and Protection of the Environment in the New World Order," *Journal of Business Ethics,* 15 (February), 297-307.

Singh, Vidya N. (1983), *Technology Transfer and Economic Development: Models and Practices for the Developing Countries.* Jersey City, NJ: Unz/Scott.

Slater, Charles C. (1968), "Marketing Processes in Developing Latin American Societies," *Journal of Marketing,* 32 (July), 50-53.

———, Donald Henley, John Wish, Vincent Farace, Lloyd Jacobs, David Lindley, Alfred Mercado, and Michael Moran (1969), "Market Processes in La Paz, Bolivia," Research Report No. 3, Latin American Studies Center, Michigan State University.

———, Dorothy G. Jenkins, Laszlo A. Pook, and Lee D. Dahringer (1979), *Easing Transition in Southern Africa: New Techniques for Policy Planning.* Boulder, CO: Westview.

———, Harold Riley, Vincent Farace, Kelly Harrison, Fernando Neves, Alan Bogotan, Mark Doctoroff, Donald Larson, Robert Nason, and Thomas Webb (1969), "The Market Processes of Recife, Brazil and Its Foodshed," Research Report No. 2, Latin American Studies Center, Michigan State University.

———, Geoffrey Walsham, and Mahendra Shah (1977), *KENSIM: A Systems Simulation of the Developing Kenyan Economy, 1970-1978.* Boulder, CO: Westview.

Sloever, William A. (1985), "The Stages of Developing Country Policy toward Foreign Investment," *Columbia Journal of World Business,* 20 (Fall), 3-11.

Sorensen, Olav Jull (1988), "Development of Marketing Channels for Agricultural Supplies," in *Research in Marketing,* Suppl. 4: *Marketing and Development: Toward Broader Dimensions,* Erdogan Kumcu and A. Fuat Firat, eds. Greenwich, CT: JAI, 285-316.

Tavis, Lee A. (1997), *Power and Responsibility: Multinational Managers and Developing Country Concerns.* Notre Dame, IN: University of Notre Dame Press.

Taylor, Charles R. and Glenn S. Omura (1994), "An Evaluation of Alternative Paradigms of Marketing and Economic Development, Part I," *Journal of Macromarketing,* 14 (Fall), 6-20.

——— (1995), "Analyzing Economic Development in the Republic of Korea: An Evaluation of Alternative Paradigms of Marketing and Economic Development, Part II," *Journal of Macromarketing,* 15 (Fall), 66-91.

van Dam, Ynte K. and Paul A. C. Apeldoorn (1996), "Sustainable Marketing," *Journal of Macromarketing,* 16 (Fall), 45-56.

Vann, John W. and Erdogan Kumcu (1995), "Achieving Efficiency and Distributive Justice in Marketing Programs for Economic Development," *Journal of Macromarketing,* 15 (Fall), 5-22.

Wilkie, William L. and Elizabeth S. Moore (1999), "Marketing's Contributions to Society," *Journal of Marketing,* 63, 198-218. (Special issue)

Windsor, Duane and Kathleen A. Getz (1999), "Regional Market Integration and the Development of Global Norms for Enterprise Conduct: The Case of International Bribery," *Business & Society,* 38 (December), 415-49.

Wiser, W. H. and Charlotte V. Wiser, (1963), *Behind Mud Walls, 1930-1960.* Berkeley: University of California Press.

Wood, Van R. and Scott Vitell (1986), "Marketing and Economic Development: Review, Synthesis, and Evaluation," *Journal of Macromarketing,* 6 (Spring), 28-48.

Woodward, Douglas P. and Sandra J. Teel (1999), "Doing Business in South Africa," *Business and Economic Review,* 45 (July-September), 3-9.

Yergin, Daniel and Joseph Stanislaw (1998), *The Commanding Heights: The Battle between Government and the Marketplace that Is Remaking the Modern World.* New York: Simon & Schuster.

Zimmerman, Frederic J. and Michael R. Carter (1999), "A Dynamic Option Value for Institutional Change: Marketable Property Rights in the Sahel," *American Journal of Agricultural Economics,* 81 (May), 467-78.

Corporate Marketing Effects on Consumer Welfare

Short-Term Benefits but Long-Term Costs?

Michael R. Hagerty

A consumer buys a new sport utility vehicle (SUV). Is the net effect on consumer welfare in the United States positive or negative? Public policy makers must consider three types of effects to answer this question fully: (1) short-term effects on the consumer, (2) long-term effects on the consumer, and (3) external effects on *other* consumers affected by the purchase ("externalities"). In this example, the individual consumer gets an initial "bump" in welfare from pride of ownership and satisfaction with the vehicle's performance, adding to consumer welfare. However, in the long term, the individual may become less satisfied with the purchase as maintenance bills mount up beyond expectations and as new models improve performance expectations further. Finally, the purchase may affect other consumers negatively because pollution, commute time, and stress all might increase.

This example demonstrates the three types of effects that this chapter reviews in considering the overall influence of corporate marketing on consumer welfare. The short-term effects are well-known, and market researchers are adept at forecasting them with conjoint analysis, concept tests, or focus groups (Urban and Hauser 1993). The long-term effects are more time-consuming to measure, but marketers now are capturing some of these through satisfaction research at the National Quality Research Center (Fornell et al. 1996). However, marketers almost never measure the third effect because of the difficulty of assessing these "externalities." By contrast, public policy must consider all three of these influences to determine the net effect on consumer welfare. Adding to these difficulties, analysts disagree on *how* to measure consumer welfare itself. Some find that long-term consumer welfare has been rising (Nordhaus and Tobin 1973); Osberg and Sharpe 1999, whereas others find that long-term consumer welfare has been falling (Cobb and Cobb 1994).

The first section of this chapter reviews some long-term costs of marketing hypothesized by critics of marketing. The second section discusses major methods for measuring consumer welfare and introduces the notion of "subjective consumer welfare" (SCW). The third section reviews national surveys of SCW. Finally, the fourth section reviews empirical tests on whether marketing causes negative long-term and externality effects.

Theories of How Marketing Might Reduce Long-Term Consumer Welfare

Are We Doomed to the Hedonic Treadmill with Ever-Rising Consumer Expectations?

Consumer satisfaction is defined as relative to consumers' expectations (Peterson and Wilson 1992). If expectations continue to rise with an expanding economy, then satisfaction with a given purchase would *decline* over time. Brickman and Campbell (1971) and Easterlin (1995) pointed out that, under these assumptions, society might be doomed to the "hedonic treadmill." The treadmill results when each person attempts to increase his or her own happiness (e.g., by consuming more), but as the person adapts to his or her improved consumption, satisfaction returns to its starting value, and the cycle begins all over again. Such an outcome would be disheartening for social planners who wish to increase consumer welfare, and it would support claims of marketing's critics that marketing stimulates short-term demand but fails to improve long-term satisfaction. Do such effects occur? Easterlin (1995) presented preliminary data showing that life satisfaction in eight countries has not increased in 20 years. I examine more extensive data on this hypothesis.

Does Corporate Marketing Impose Negative Externalities on Consumer Welfare?

Other critics of marketing have hypothesized that marketers of private goods (corporate marketing) "steal" welfare from public goods. For example, the SUV example presented earlier suggests that consumer welfare may improve at first and then decline later as the externalities of pollution and congestion reduce welfare. Similarly, the recent criticism of violent computer games suggests that the consumers themselves (often young boys) are well satisfied with the games but that society suffers in the long term because of increased tendencies toward violence. Zinkhan (1994) labeled this "terminal materialism" and argued that marketing can do more to contribute to quality of life (Csikszentmihalyi and Rochberg-Halton 1981).

More generally, Galbraith (1984) argued that people incorrectly spend too much on consumer goods and too little on public goods such as environment, public safety, and family life: "The family which takes its mauve and cerise, air-conditioned, power-steered, and power braked automobile out for a tour passes through cities that are badly paved, made hideous by litter, blighted buildings, billboards, and posts for wires that should long since have been put underground" (p. 192). He blamed marketers and economists for this imbalance in public versus private goods because they overuse persuasive techniques to "stimulate demand by creating new demands." Until recently, the data and methods for testing his assertion were lacking.

These criticisms of marketing are serious because they imply that consumers are myopic. That is, they consume items that increase their short-term welfare but that contribute to long-term *declines* in their welfare. Marketers have, for the most part, ignored these criticisms because they themselves are primarily interested in short-term market share effects. Yet, public policy analysts must seriously consider these theories that the long-term effects of marketing may be negative. If these hypotheses are supported, then government interventions might be necessary to reduce the amount of marketing in the United States. To test these theories, we must have a measure of consumer welfare that takes these long-term and externality effects into account. I review such measures next.

Measures of Consumer Welfare

Consumer welfare is an old concept, but formal measurement has only recently begun. The preamble of the U.S. Constitution mandated more than 200 years ago that one of the purposes of the federal government is "to promote the general welfare." But attempts to formally measure it began during the 1920s with gross national product (GNP) and continue with refinements called measures of economic welfare (MEW). In addition, I introduce a complementary method called subjective consumer welfare that uses the marketing tradition of satisfaction research. Each of these is reviewed in turn.

Gross National Product

GNP measures the amount of goods and services produced in the United States that are exchanged for money. It simply sums the money paid for all goods and services that are consumed or invested in the current year. Its advantage is that it is easy to calculate because all items are measured in the same dollar units. GNP is a very useful measure of economic output that can guide short-term economic policy (Nordhaus and Tobin 1973). But it clearly fails to account for many items that are not exchanged for money such as household work and leisure time. Worse, some items in the GNP seem to *detract* from consumer welfare. For example, growth in burglar alarm sales during the 1980s acted to *increase* GNP, even though it might well have been due to increasing crime rates. Economists have long acknowledged the limitations of GNP in measuring consumer welfare. For example, Abramovitz (1959) wrote, "We must be highly skeptical of the view that long-term changes in the rate of growth of welfare can be gauged even roughly from changes in the rate of growth of output [GNP]" (pp. 21-22).

Figure 13.1 represents how GNP relates to consumer welfare. It shows inputs to consumer welfare on the left-hand side and outputs on the right-hand side. GNP is computed only from the input side and uses only market transactions in which goods or services are exchanged for money. Other inputs that affect consumer welfare are ignored. The measure discussed next attempts to modify GNP to include some of these additional inputs to consumer welfare.

Measures of Economic Welfare

Nordhaus and Tobin (1973) suggested modifications of the GNP accounts to better reflect consumer welfare, which they termed measures of economic welfare. They recommended (1) subtracting capital goods from GNP because they are not consumed in the current period; (2) adding the value of nonmarket effort such as housework; and (3) subtracting purchases for national defense, crime prevention, and pollution abatement. Later refinements of MEW were suggested by Cobb and Cobb (1994) for the United States and by Osberg and Sharpe (1999) for the United States and Canada. Both Nordhaus and Tobin (1973) and Osberg and Sharpe (1999) found that the long-term trend of MEW is increasing rather than decreasing in the United States (although not as fast as is GNP per person).

Although MEW addresses some of the weaknesses of GNP, it still falls short in several areas. First, it assumes that consumer welfare is *linear* in dollars, whereas many psychometric results show that consumers' perception is a non-linear (negatively accelerated) function of dollars. Second, it assumes that all inputs must be given equal weight (after transformation to dollars). By contrast, Slovic (1993) showed that consumers can apply very different weights to the same dollar amount. For example, losing $100 gambling is judged to be a smaller loss in utility than is losing $100 from additional tax because consumers have less choice in the latter. Third, some inputs might be missing from the diagram in Figure 13.1. The next section defines a measure of consumer welfare that avoids these three disadvantages.

Subjective Consumer Welfare

Both GNP and MEW are attempts to define consumer welfare by measuring the *input* side of Figure 13.1. That is, the various inputs such as total consumption (adjusted for environmental and crime damage) are added up. This is typical of the economic approach. A complementary approach is to define consumer welfare by measuring the *output* side. That is, the perceptions and judgments of *consumers* are surveyed to determine their reaction to the inputs of goods, services, and externalities. Using this method, consumers could be asked to judge

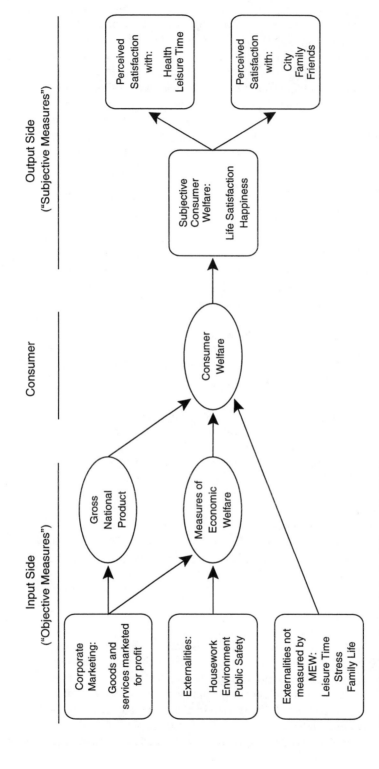

Figure 13.1. Inputs and Outputs of Consumer Welfare

NOTE: MEW = measures of economic welfare.

how satisfied they are with respect to their health, leisure pursuits, families, cities or places of residence, and overall lives. Such a method has a long history of use in marketing to measure micro-satisfaction with individual products and services (Fornell et al. 1996; Peterson and Wilson 1992) but has not been used to measure macro-satisfaction with entire domains of life. To retain parallel nomenclature with the economic measures, I label this measure subjective consumer welfare.

Such a method could avoid all three problems with the previous methods of measuring consumer welfare. It avoids all three problems of nonlinearity in perception, unequal weighting of inputs, and missing inputs because it measures the *perception itself,* not the dollar amounts. This approach is typical in marketing and is evidenced in techniques such as perceptual mapping and Fishbein analysis (see, e.g., Urban and Hauser 1993). I first review national surveys conducted in this style and then review studies on their reliability and validity.

Research Data

A total of 14 countries have been conducting surveys that measure SCW, many for more than 25 years. Of these, 12 are in the European Union, which has used standardized questions since 1973. The remaining 2 are the United States (standardized since 1972) and Japan (standardized since 1958). The question put to European and Japanese consumers (suitably interpreted) was, "On the whole, are you very satisfied, fairly satisfied, not very satisfied, or not at all satisfied with the life you lead?" The question put to consumers in the United States was, "Taken all together, how would you say things are these days—would you say that you are very happy, pretty happy, or not too happy?" Veenhoven (1993) showed that these scales are equal interval, and so averages are meaningful.

In the United States, additional items tap satisfaction with each domain of life. They are asked as a set, using the following introduction: "For each area of life I am going to name, tell me the number that shows how much satisfaction you get from the area." Each area of life is printed on a card, and cards are shuffled to randomize presentation. The domains of life are "your family life," "your health and physical condition," "the city or place you live in," "your friendships," and "your nonworking activities—hobbies and so on." A 7-point response scale was used (7 = *a very great deal,* 6 = *a great deal,* 5 = *quite a bit,* 4 = *a fair amount,* 3 = *some,* 2 = *a little,* 1 = *none*).

The items just described are very broad in nature, asking consumers to give overall judgments of satisfaction across broad categories of their lives. The disadvantage of this breadth is that it averages over many individual corporate decisions. However, the advantage is that we can examine *externalities* across the entire gamut of consumer satisfaction. For example, in the SUV example, traditional marketing research from the National Quality Research Center would assess consumers' satisfaction with their purchases but would miss the broader decline in environment and commute time as more and more are sold. Ultimately, it is desirable to assess *both* specific and broad measures of satisfaction. Many of the other chapters in this handbook collect more specific measures of consumer welfare that will complement the data here.

Research Results

Is SCW Reliable and Valid?

Satisfaction scales have a long history in marketing and have well-documented reliability and validity for measuring individual products (Peterson and Wilson 1992), services (Zeithaml, Parasuraman, and Berry 1990), and even offerings of entire industries (Fornell et al. 1996). For measuring overall consumer satisfaction, Andrews and Withey (1976) and Bradburn (1969) reported satisfactory reliability in national surveys. The two alternative scales that are used most often (life satisfaction and happiness) were found to be highly correlated.

Veenhoven (1993) computed the multimethod validity of welfare measures used in national-level surveys by 55 countries since 1945. He found that alternative measures of self-rated satisfaction correlate with each other as well as with peer-rated measures of life satisfaction. In turn, these satisfaction measures correlate with objective conditions that consumers seek in a country such as high income per capita, education, life expectancy, and women's rights. Andrews and Withey (1976) created perceptual maps of overall life satisfaction, showing how 123 concerns in life can be partitioned into subaccounts or domains. They found that satisfaction with the domains of self-efficacy, family, money, fun/leisure, housing, and health (in that order) contributed most to overall satisfaction (p. 124).

Long-Term Effects: Are We on the Hedonic Treadmill?

Hagerty (1999) analyzed national satisfaction ratings for the eight countries with more than 20 years of satisfaction data as a function of both long-term and short-term effects of consumption per person. He estimated a model containing the following terms:

$$\text{Life Satisfaction}_t = a_0 + bC_t + c\Delta_t,$$

where C_t is the absolute level of consumption per person at Time t and Δ_t is the short-term *change* in consumption per person since some earlier time. If the coefficient b is zero, then that term vanishes and consumers respond only to *short-term* changes Δ in consumption, with no lasting change in life satisfaction. On the other hand, if the coefficient c is zero, then consumers respond only to absolute consumption levels (*long-term* effects) and do not adapt over time. If both coefficients are nonzero, then the relative size of the coefficients reflects the magnitude of each effect.

The model was estimated repeatedly in a grid search for different values of time change Δ. Contingent on each value of Δ, the remaining parameters were fit

TABLE 13.1 Best-Fitting Coefficients for the Pooled Multiple Regression Model
                Predicting Consumer Life Satisfaction

Variable	Coefficient	SE
Δ: number of quarters that short-term effect lasts	10	
c: short-term effect of average quarterly change in consumption per person over past 10 quarters	8.22*	4.0
b: long-term effect of real consumption (dollars per person)	0.0000345**	0.000012
Country dummies		
United Kingdom	0.955**	0.061
Netherlands	1.58**	0.065
France	0.051	0.061
West Germany	0.667**	0.064
Spain	0.384**	0.072
Italy	−0.142*	0.061
Denmark	2.09**	0.068
Japan	0	
R^2 overall	.928	

*$p < .05$; **$p < .01$.

with multiple regression. Table 13.1 shows the coefficients for both the long-term and short-term effects of consumption in the eight countries studied. The best fit was found for $\Delta = 10$ quarters, or $2\frac{1}{2}$ years. That is, short-term changes in satisfaction tend to last about $2\frac{1}{2}$ years, after which they decay as people adapt to their higher consumption. This provides evidence for some adaptation effects. However, a *long-term effect* also is significant in Table 13.1 such that increasing consumption causes a *permanent* increase in consumer life satisfaction. This is contrary to predictions of the hedonic treadmill and consistent with marketers' claim that marketing increases not only short-term welfare but also long-term welfare.[1]

Figure 13.2 gives additional evidence of a positive long-term trend in SCW over time. It plots average SCW (solid circles) from 1973 to 1995 for three countries, with each showing a significant long-term positive trend.

Externality Effects: Does Corporate Marketing of Private Goods "Steal" Welfare from Public Goods?

To estimate any externality effects, we can use the more detailed surveys in the United States to observe whether short-term *increases* in private welfare lead to longer term *declines* in satisfaction with externalities. Figure 13.3 shows

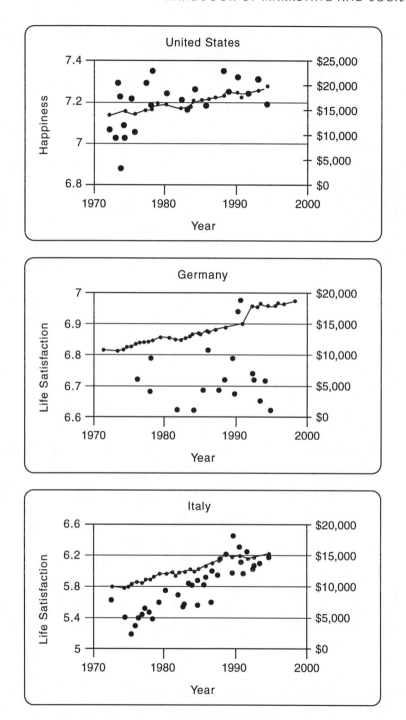

Figure 13.2. Happiness in Three Countries that Showed Significant Correlations with Gross Domestic Product per Capita

NOTE: Happiness or life satisfaction is plotted with solid circles and is scaled on the left-hand side. Gross domestic product per capita in 1987 U.S. dollars is plotted with lines and is scaled on the right-hand side.

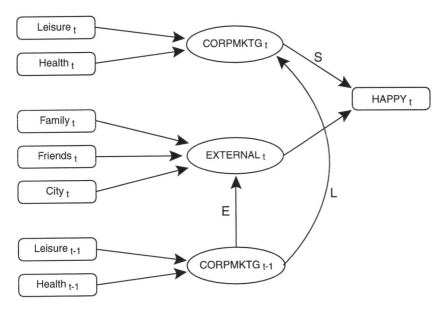

Figure 13.3. Causal Path Model of How Corporate Marketing Affects Overall Consumer Welfare

NOTE: The path labeled *S* is the short-term effect of corporate marketing, *L* is the long-term effect, and *E* is externality.

the path diagram displaying the three types of effects on consumer welfare over time. Manifest variables that can be directly measured are shown as rectangles, and latent variables are shown as ellipses. Beginning on the right-hand side, I attempt to predict national subjective happiness in Year t (HAPPY$_t$). This is affected by the latent variables in the center column, subjective satisfaction with private goods (CORPMKTG$_t$) in Year t and satisfaction with public goods (EXTERNAL$_t$) in Year t. The path labeled S is the short-term effect of marketing private goods on welfare. I expect this to be positive. The path labeled L is the long-term effect of marketing private goods, lagged from Year $t-1$. Finally, the path labeled E is the externality, the effect of marketing private goods in the previous year on current satisfaction with public goods. Critics of marketing predict that this path will be negative.

Proxies for Corporate Marketing Activity

The left-most column in Figure 13.3 contains the indicator variables. Ideally, they would include total corporate marketing activity in Year t. However, I know of no such measures that currently exist. In its place, I use proxy variables that are correlated with marketing activities. These are perceived satisfaction with leisure and health in Year t. There are two reasons why these variables can serve as proxies for corporate marketing activity. First, the leisure and health industries are most correlated with consumer advertising.. To show this, the list of leading national advertisers (Competitive Media Reporting 1997) was used to determine categories most advertised by corporate marketing. Of the 33 indus-

TABLE 13.2 Factor Loadings from U.S. Ratings of Domain Satisfaction

	Loading on Factor 1	Loading on Factor 2
Satisfaction with leisure	.16	.84
Satisfaction with own health	.14	.84
Satisfaction with family	.89	.00
Satisfaction with friends	.59	.59
Satisfaction with city	.81	.22

tries tracked in this list, leisure pursuits were most heavily represented including entertainment and amusements, sporting goods and toys, pets, electronic entertainment equipment, travel and hotels, and cigarettes. The next most heavily represented were health industries including over-the-counter drugs. By contrast, the sectors of family, friends, and city received no mention in the list of leading national advertisers. This is consistent with the partitioning of domains in Figure 13.3.

The second line of evidence for the indicator variables in Figure 13.3 is that factor analysis reveals that leisure and health variables load on the same underlying factor. Table 13.2 shows the loadings from this factor analysis (rotated by varimax). Two factors exceed eigenvalues of 1, indicating the presence of two factors. Consistent with our hypothesis, the three highest loadings on Factor 1 were the low-marketing sectors of family, friends, and city, whereas the two highest loadings on Factor 2 were the high-marketing sectors of leisure and health.

LISREL Estimates

The relationships among the latent variables were tested using LISREL's maximum likelihood estimates. They are given for several models in Table 13.3. The first column estimates the simplest model, constraining long-term (L) and externality (E) effects to zero. It shows significant positive short-term effects, indicating that the short-term effects of marketing increase consumer welfare, as expected. The goodness of fit index (GFI) for this model is .808. (The GFI ranges from 0 to 1, with 1 being perfect prediction.) The next column frees the long-term effect (L) to be nonzero. The parameter estimates show that both L and S are significant and positive, and the GFI increases to .885. The incremental chi-square test shows that this model fits significantly better than the previous one. The final column frees all three effects (S, L, and E) to vary, thereby estimating the complete path diagram in Figure 3.3. Parameter estimates show that all three parameters are significant, and the incremental chi-square test shows that the full model adds significantly to the variance explained. Note that the estimates of short-term and long-term effects are very similar regardless of the model estimates. This indicates that multicollinearity is not affecting the estimates.

In examining the full model estimates in the final column of Table 13.3, the first two rows show that *both* private goods and externalities affect consumer

TABLE 13.3 LISREL Estimates from Figure 13.3

	Short-Term Effects Only	Short-Term and Long-Term Effects Only	Full Model
S: CORPMKTG$_t$ → HAPPY$_t$	.113 (3.46)**	.128 (4.61)**	.122 (8.94)**
EXTERNAL$_t$ → HAPPY$_t$	.580 (10.30)**	.571 (10.10)**	.576 (10.30)**
L: CORPMKTG$_{t-1}$ → CORPMKTG$_t$	—	.822 (6.90)**	.795 (6.60)**
E: CORPMKTG$_{t-1}$ → EXTERNAL$_t$	—	—	.122 (1.93)*
Goodness of fit index	.808	.885	.887
Incremental chi-square ($df = 1$)	—	120.9**	3.5*

NOTE: t statistics are in parentheses.

*$p < .05$; **$p < .01$.

welfare positively and significantly. The magnitude of the effects shows that externalities such as city, family, and friends contribute *more* to welfare than do private goods. This is consistent with consumers' own importance ratings (Andrews and Withey 1976). The estimate of the long-term effect of corporate marketing (*L*) also is positive and significant. This is *contrary* to the hedonic treadmill hypothesis that long-term effects will be zero, but it is consistent with previous findings (Hagerty 1999) that increasing consumption has positive long-term effects on life satisfaction. Finally, the estimate of the externality effect of corporate marketing (*E*) is positive and significant. Again, this is contrary to Galbraith (1984) and other critics of marketing who predict a negative effect. Instead, increasing satisfaction with private goods leads to *increasing* satisfaction with city, family, and friends in the next year. This suggests that consumers are *not* myopic; they make choices of private goods that enhance their enjoyment of public goods and their overall welfare.

Conclusion

I tested two hypotheses that have long been leveled against corporate marketing: (1) that corporate marketing encourages too much consumption of private goods because in the long term consumers *adapt* to ever higher levels of consumption without increasing their satisfaction (the hedonic treadmill) and (2) that corporate marketing "steals" welfare from public goods, creating negative externalities. To test these, I used a new measure of consumer welfare, called subjective consumer welfare, which I argue measures consumer welfare better than do traditional economic measures of GNP or MEW. The subaccounts of SCW were defined as consumers' own perceptual partition of life activities. They include not only items measured by GNP but also important externalities such as environment, stress, leisure time, and family life.

Results from empirical studies so far show that SCW is reliable and valid and that it tracks changes in objective indicators such as real consumption per person. In addition the studies can distinguish among the three important categories of influence on SCW: short-term effects, long-term effects, and externalities.

By examining long-term effects over 20 years in eight countries, I conclude that consumers are *not* on a hedonic treadmill. Instead, improvements in income and consumption have a *positive* and permanent influence, even after factoring out short-term "bumps" in satisfaction. By examining *externality* effects of corporate marketing, I conclude that marketing activities are not negative, as hypothesized by social critics, but rather are significantly positive.

I caution that these are only the first studies of the effects of aggregate corporate marketing on SCW. Future research on long-term effects needs to examine more linkages between objective economic indicators in Figure 13.1, such as environmental quality, to SCW. I also caution that the presence of positive externalities for marketing in these data does *not* imply that current regulation of marketing activities should be dropped. It might be that externalities are positive *because* of the regulations imposed since 1970. My conclusions are simply that the net effect of current regulations and corporate decisions is to *increase,* not decrease, consumer welfare. This should be viewed as a success of the current business/regulatory environment. Future regulation might be able to *further increase* the positive long-term effects and externalities of marketing. Finally, the current research is limited because it tracks consumption effects that are aggregated over many industries. Future research to track specific industries (e.g., over-the-counter drugs) would be helpful to estimate externalities specific to an industry.

Note

1. The bottom rows of Table 13.1 contain estimates for "country dummies" estimated for each country. For example, the dummy for the United Kingdom is 0.955, indicating that the average SCW for the United Kingdom is 0.955 of a scale point higher than that of Japan (the base case). These dummies adjust for conditions that differ across countries such as culture and response bias.

References

Abramovitz, Moses (1959), "The Welfare Interpretation of Secular Trends in National Income and Product," in *The Allocation of Economic Resources,* M. Abramovitz et al., eds. Stanford, CA: Stanford University Press.

Andrews, Frank M. and Stephen B. Withey (1976), *Social Indicators of Well-Being: Americans' Perceptions of Life Quality.* New York: Plenum.

Bradburn, Norman M. (1969), *The Structure of Psychological Well-Being.* Chicago: Aldine.

Brickman, P. and Donald T. Campbell (1971), "Hedonic relativism and planning the good society," in *Adaptation Level Theory: A Symposium,* M. H. Appley, ed. New York: Academic Press, 287-302.

Cobb, Clifford W. and John B. Cobb (1994), *The Green National Product: A Proposed Index of Sustainable Economic Welfare.* New York: University Press of America.

Competitive Media Reporting (1997), *Multi-Media Service: Ad $ Summary.* New York: Competitive Media Reporting.

Csikszentmihalyi, Hihaly and Eugene Rochberg-Halton (1981), *The Meaning of Things: Domestic Symbols and the Self.* Cambridge, UK: Cambridge University Press.

Easterlin, Richard A. (1995), "Will Raising the Incomes of All Increase the Happiness of All?" *Journal of Economic Behavior and Organization,* 27, 35-47.

Fornell, Claes, Michael D. Johnson, Eugene W. Anderson, Jaesung Cha, and Barbara Everitt Bryant (1996), "The American Customer Satisfaction Index: Nature, Purpose, and Findings," *Journal of Marketing,* 60 (October), 7-18.

Galbraith, John K. (1984), *The Affluent Society,* 4th ed. Boston: Houghton Mifflin.

Hagerty, Michael R. (1999), "Unifying Livability and Comparison Theory: Cross-National Time-Series Analysis of Life Satisfaction," *Social Indicators Research,* 47 (July), 343-56.

Nordhaus, W. D. and J. Tobin (1973), "Is Growth Obsolete?" in *The Measurement of Economic and Social Performance,* M. Moss, ed. New York: National Bureau of Economic Research, 509-32.

Osberg, Lars and Andrew Sharpe (1999), *An Index of Economic Well-Being for Canada.* Ottawa: Centre for Study of Living Standards.

Peterson, Robert A. and W. R. Wilson (1992), "Measuring Customer Satisfaction: Fact and Artifact," *Journal of the Academy of Marketing Science,* 20, 61-71.

Slovic, Paul (1993), "Perceived Risk, Trust, and Democracy," *Risk Analysis,* 13 (December), 675-82.

Urban, Glen L. and John R. Hauser (1993), *Design and Marketing of New Products,* 2nd ed. Englewood Cliffs, NJ: Prentice Hall.

Veenhoven, Ruut (1993), *Happiness in Nations.* Rotterdam, Netherlands: Risbo. Data available: http://www.eur.nl/fsw/research/happiness

Zeithaml, Valarie A., A. Parasuraman, and L. L. Berry (1990), *Delivering Quality Service: Balancing Customer Perceptions and Expectations.* New York: Free Press.

Zinkhan George M. (1994), "Advertising, Materialism, and Quality of Life," *Journal of Advertising,* 23 (2), 1-4.

The Effectiveness of Intellectual Property Laws

Alex Simonson

What is a "strong" brand? Ask a manager or a graduate business management student such a question, or read books on branding, and you will inevitably hear some or most of the following: A strong brand is one that has high awareness . . . is liked . . . has high loyalty . . . commands premium pricing . . . has strong "equity" . . . has passed the test of time . . . can effortlessly extend to other categories . . . is desired by other brands to create alliances . . . has high market share . . . has high profitability . . . has a vibrant or distinctive personality.[1]

And, what *makes* a brand strong? That which allows it to grow and thrive makes it strong. That is, sound management; a fertile competitive environment; growing or stable customer interest; budgetary allotments; breadth and consistency of distribution channels; expertise of product designers, graphic designers, marketing managers, and the sales force . . . and not the least, but often the last, *the protection afforded to the brand.*[2]

It is this scope and application of state-sanctioned protection or monopoly that carves out legitimate competition from unfair competition, infringement from permissible encroachment. This chapter introduces the major types of monopoly protection traditionally afforded to marketers and discusses a pressing dilemma facing the future of brands. (It focuses on brands and, therefore, limits attention to the laws affecting brands vs. other intellectual property laws.[3]) The chapter then examines the current legal system's method in handling scientific evidence (empirical data) in determining the course of brand and trade dress protection cases. It concludes with suggested solutions to the issues raised and a discussion of potential future research in this area.

Substance of Intellectual
Property Laws for Marketing

What Is Protected: Traditional Approach

Three articulated types of protection offer monopoly or limited monopoly status to brands (including a broad range of elements such as product configurations and shapes, names and logos, advertising and package copy, trade dress, looks, styles or thematic motifs, and any other identity element). These types of protection for various elements of a brand emanate from three distinct legal concerns. First, is the design *new, original, and ornamental?* Second, is there *original* artistic or creative work embodied in the element or combination of elements? Third, does the element serve to *identify* the product? The first type of protection for new original and ornamental designs, or design patent protection, yields the shortest protection (14 years in the United States). The second level, or copyright protection, yields long protection (75 years from publication in the United States). The strongest and most important protection for brands, or trademark protection, is of endless duration and is afforded to those elements satisfying the third criterion. (The years are provided for the United States and vary by country, but the pattern tends to remain consistent.)

Protection from What: Traditional Approach

It is easy to confuse the realm of protection with the concept of the scope of such protection. Thus, if a design is new, ornamental, and original, for example, then it does not follow that marketers are protected from any design that looks like such a design. Similarly, marketing practitioners often assume that if a mark or logo is registered or otherwise protectable, then anyone who uses such a mark or logo infringes the rights of the brand owner. This, too, does not follow.

There is a common, implicitly false, albeit reasonable, assumption that once a protectable interest is found to exist in a particular element, we can protect that element legally from anyone who copies it. The inaccuracy comes from the separation of (1) defining a protectable interest and (2) defining the scope of protection for any such protectable interest. It is conceivable—and, as we shall see, it is increasingly happening—that a protectable interest is found to exist in a particular element but that no protection is legally afforded to the element in many instances.

Design Patent and Copyright Protection

Design patents and copyrights both afford protection from copying. They mesh well with the intuition that the protection afforded to items of property that are unique is that which stops their proliferation and their reproduction by others—something that would devalue the originality. Design patents further require that the design be a "matter of concern" for the consumer (a very difficult hurdle). For example, if a product configuration has been granted a design patent, then substantially similar designs would be impermissible only to the extent that the consumer indeed cares about the design—that it is important to the consumer.[4]

But trademarks, by far the most useful and sought-after protection for brands, do not provide the type of protection that design patents and copyrights do. Although the protection afforded is perpetual, the scope of the protection is rather limited.

Trademark Protection

Protection from Confusion. Trademark law protects any identifying element (e.g., name, shape, sound) from "confusion." According to the Lanham Act,

> Any person who . . . uses in commerce any word . . ., symbol, or . . . any combination thereof, which is likely to cause confusion . . . as to the affiliation, connection, or association of such person with another person, or as to the origin, sponsorship, or approval of his or her goods, services, or commercial activities by another person, shall be liable in a civil action.

In cases discussing confusion, courts readily accept four types. One is direct confusion or perception confusion, that is, choosing one object, or being lured to one object, thinking that one is seeing another object. For example, Nick & Nora, the makers of the famous sheep and cloud pajamas featured on *Allie McBeal* and in *Victoria's Secret* catalogs, recently complained about being knocked off by a variety of others blatantly copying the cloud pajama designs.[5] A second type is source confusion, that is, thinking that one company makes a product when in fact it does not. An example is thinking that Nicole nail polish emanates from Nicole Miller. A third type is relationship confusion, that is, thinking that the company making a certain product is connected or affiliated with another company. An example is thinking that the Sky Vista brand of television services is related to the Sky View brand. A fourth type is authorization confusion, that is, thinking that the company making the product is authorized or sponsored by another company. An example is thinking that baseball cards emanating from the Baseball Players' Association were approved by Major League Baseball.[6]

Post-Sale Confusion. The law also protects from post-sale confusion, that is, where the packaging at the point of purchase no longer is available to cue consumers into not being confused. Perfume bottle shapes without labels, as was to occur in the recent dispute between Calvin Klein's Eternity and Ralph Lauren's Romance, is a perfect occasion for such post-sale confusion to arise.

Reverse Confusion. The law also protects from reverse confusion (applicable for source and authorization confusion), that is, not that consumers will think that the newcomer emanates from the first brand (or is authorized by the first brand) but rather the reverse—that the newcomer will devote great resources to awareness advertising or other communications such that the first brand will appear as if it comes from the newcomer or is authorized by the newcomer.

Counterfeiting and Palming Off. A Tommy Hilfiger sold on the streets is unlikely to make consumers believe that such a product emanates from Tommy Hilfiger or, indeed, is authorized by him. However, in terms of trademark protection, it causes post-sale confusion. Microsoft counterfeit software, although also involving trademark protection issues, is a substantial copy of copyrighted material and, as such, is prohibited.[7] Receiving a great deal of attention, counterfeiting often is singled out as a source of billions of dollars in damage, notably in the software and entertainment industries (with the ease of copying programs or creating digitized [MP-3] music) but also in pharmaceuticals, where the danger is more than monetary. The problem has resulted in innovative solutions through using seizure and forfeiture legal provisions, through going after landlords of retailers selling counterfeit goods, and through joint corporate and governmental cooperation in investigating and policing organized piracy operations.

Protection from Dilution. Protection discussed and available would not likely protect McDonald's from someone (without intent to confuse and probably without confusion) trying to market a McDonald's line of automotive supplies. The harm complained of by established brands is the "dilution" of their marks, that is, the whittling away of their ability to conjure up the categories in which they do business.[8] Thus, there arose the law of dilution designed to protect famous marks from losing their unique ability to be used in commerce, that is, their ability to conjure up their own product categories. This may very well leave the unscrupulous firm free by placing its own name on a restaurant called "Better than McDonald's." Indeed, confusion law is not geared to address this type of harm, and dilution is not directly designed for it, but the statute for dilution arguably could apply. Although the commentators and law do not discuss it, dilution in this context is akin to copyright in that it stops substantially similar things irrespective of confusion. Because trademarks are perpetual, the law is hesitant to grant such powerful monopolies in both substance and scope, and so dilution is limited to famous marks. It is a move, however, in the direction of viewing a trademark like a copyright. That is, when we protect a mark, we protect its originality from being copied, irrespective of confusion.

Application of Intellectual
Property Laws for Marketing

*The Basis for Effecting Outcomes
in Intellectual Property Cases*

Our system of jurisprudence involves and arose from disputes regarding factual issues. Each side had its rendition of a set of what occurred (the "matters of fact," i.e., the descriptive) and an interpretation of what ought to be the result based on the legal rules or principles (the "matters of law," i.e., the normative). First-year law students and practicing attorneys juxtapose these two pillars as though all aspects of arguing a case can be dichotomized into whether something is a matter of law or a matter of fact. If there is a jury, then the jury decides what is fact and the judge decides what is law. If there is but a judge, which is the case in many intellectual property cases, then the judge acts as both trier of fact and determiner of law. This is what our legal system is designed to handle, for better or for worse.

But when a brand's future is at stake and a brand owner tries to enforce its rights through intellectual property enforcement, scientific evidence often is required. Surveys and expert testimony are commonly proffered in prosecution of trademark cases and in defense of actions. Scientific evidence, however, relies on matters of fact (e.g., what respondents said, what researchers did) and its own normative systems, the principles of consumer behavior and of marketing research. The legal system (with its juxtaposition of fact and law) was not, and indeed is not, designed for handling situations where much of the descriptive (e.g., results of a survey) is itself embedded within a normative context concerning scientific principles of inquiry to discover the facts.

Still, intellectual property rules and adjudications rest on assumptions of consumer behavior and marketing research. Judges, without training and advice in marketing research or consumer behavior, have less than a perfect ability to determine what is likely to occur or proper to do. The danger in effectiveness of the protection of brands is that judges (in bench trials) typically act as though they are determining facts but, indeed, are moving into the territory of opining on the rules of another discipline.

A common example demonstrates the danger. When a rule of law states that we are interested in *actual and potential purchasers,* the researcher might naturally pose the question that is common in marketing research: Has a respondent purchased in the category during the past six months? Courts have deemed such a question "flawed."[9] What exactly are the judges saying here? That this inquiry is not what the law cares about (the finding of law) because what a consumer is doing does not act sufficiently as a proxy for intended prospective purchasers, a finding not of fact but rather of scientific principle or rule. The courts are making an error, however, by not realizing that the latter portion is a finding of consumer behavior or marketing research principles and not a finding of fact. Consider such an open judge. The court would need to state that it assumes that past purchases do not often reflect intention to purchase and that, given such an assumption, a question that inquires into past purchases is irrelevant. Separating out the assumption highlights the types of decisions that the judge really is making; he or she is making decisions about consumer behavior and marketing research.

If this is what is occurring but is not stated, then precedent is not that past purchases are an incorrect way of choosing potential respondents. Instead, precedent is created based on an implicit (untested) assumption given the judge's opinion concerning some aspect of consumer behavior and marketing research—of which he or she may have no knowledge or expertise.

The legal system was not designed for this, and the judge (a subject of the system) is not setting legal precedent but may be obscuring it with various implicit views of consumer research and marketing research masking as matters of fact. It also leaves researchers in the precarious position of doing what they know to be correct about their own field or doing something based on what a judge unlearned in the field assumed about their field because it was implicitly (although not explicitly) part of the legal conclusion the judge had reached.

This chapter seeks to articulate more specifically the challenges in the courts to effectively protect brands and to provide a bridge between the respective disciplines so as to enhance the effectiveness of intellectual property protection of brands.

Background of Scientific Evidence in Protecting Brands

Experts are called in intellectual property cases typically for two purposes: (1) to present opinions about consumer behavior or critiques of other researchers' methods and (2) to present discussions and interpretations of data found through research that they conducted (typically mall intercept or telephone surveys) for the purpose of the litigation.

Surveys are a common empirical method to determine (1) likelihood of confusion, (2) likelihood of dilution, and (3) many other intellectual property aspects (e.g., secondary meaning). Indeed, they are required for plaintiffs in many types of cases.[10] Because surveys are one person's reported responses of others, the substance of what those others are saying normally would be deemed to be hearsay and inadmissible under the federal rules of evidence. The law, however, carves out an exception to this where researchers are allowed to come to substantive conclusions.[11]

Thus, intellectual property cases often revolve around the various experts and their testimony. Each side to a dispute hires its experts and presents direct testimony of such experts at trial. The *Reference Manual on Scientific Evidence,* published by the Federal Judicial Center, sets forth guidelines for judges in interpreting such evidence.[12] Diamond's "Reference Guide on Survey Research" goes a long way toward attempting to educate the legal world on the principles of survey research. Similarly, the *Manual for Complex Litigation*'s discussion on survey evidence provides guidelines to attorneys and courts.[13] But both of these are not sufficient to address the larger issue that I discuss here, that is, the interaction of two worlds—that of lawyers and that of marketing researchers—trained to see the world differently and whose communication is vital to effective protection of intellectual property.

Intellectual Property Law and Marketing Interface

In what follows, I set forth 15 barriers to the effectiveness of protecting brands. The barriers emerge from my personal knowledge, experience, and research in the area but cannot be obtained or supported through empirical research because they deal with findings that experts would tend not to admit (see Barrier 11 for why this is so). They stem from the marketing researcher being injected into the legal system without the legal system truly understanding the rules and principles surrounding marketing research and brands.

Barrier 1: Failure to Protect from the New Style of Copying

Famous marks are difficult to protect given the current legal system.[14] The protection afforded to marketers is cumulative such that one element may be protected by more than one type of law, thus ensuring what appears to be a rich selection of protection options. Indeed, many types of elements are afforded multiple protections. For example, a character such as Mickey Mouse merits copyright protection due to the inherent originality of the embodiment of the mouse as well as trademark protection for the aspects of the mouse (e.g., his ears) that identify one company as the source. The difficulty lies, however, in a growing number of cases (e.g., disputes involving vampire glasses theme, appearance of a coin bank, style of an infomercial, watch design, mobile phone design, wine bottle design, style and theme of a child's toy doll, handbag design, pipette design, cable tie design, sneaker design, Web site design, and barware design) in which savvy marketers copy trademarks and copy trade dress but do so carefully so as to avoid losing on claims of brand confusion or brand dilution.[15] As Simonson and Mostert discussed, this is perhaps the greatest global threat to brands during the coming years.[16]

Barrier 2: Research Objectives Versus Research Methodology

For a researcher to test a particular set of possible outcomes (i.e., brand confusion or no brand confusion), the rules of research implicitly and explicitly require that assumptions be made that define and also constrain the task at hand such as what to test (e.g., the entire point of purchase array or one part of it). Forms for reviewer guidelines typically explicitly separate the judgment of (1) the relevance, importance, or significance of the question and (2) the method by which the question was addressed. A researcher's task in determining consumer perceptions requires (1) creating hypotheses or research questions and (2) designing a method to test those hypotheses or questions. The latter should be the sole province of the researcher. But the former, as with marketing research conducted for brand owners, also is legitimately part of the client's responsibility. The client might desire a particular focus. This goes to the heart of whether the research findings will have relevance for the court's inquiry. When the researcher explicitly states his or her assumptions in the prelude to a report, the proper inquiry for the court is to give deference to the principles of research, that is, to separate the issues as to (1) whether the goals have importance or relevance and (2) how well the research did what it sought to do. Only rarely, however, do courts give such a thorough treatment to the matter. The result is that if the court is not satisfied with the relevance, then the court may conclude that the research was "flawed." Because precedent is so much a part of the case law system, this failure of analysis leads to a situation in which the benefits of relying on precedent might be outweighed by the failure of the court to understand or distinguish the two aspects to a research undertaking. Are we to read out that the method used is "incorrect," or are we to read out particular parts of this case that caused the assumption on which the research was conducted not to be correct.

For example, in a recent trade dress case in the Southern District of New York, *Conopco v. Cosmair,* the plaintiff was claiming that the bottle shape of the defendant was infringing on the plaintiff's bottle shape and that the issue boiled down to whether the bottle would cause confusion (whether direct, source, relationship, or authorization). Based on this hypothesis or question, the researcher may explicitly limit inquiry into whether the bottle without packaging tends to cause confusion if seen, say, on a shelf in a store, in a post-purchase confusion situation, or on someone's bathroom shelf. If the judge believed that confusion with packaging is the appropriate legal standard or that, as a finding of fact, the main method by which this bottle might be seen is with packaging, then he might have rightly declared the findings relevant only where the bottle would be seen without the packaging. Instead, he declared the design flawed by explaining that the packaging was not tested. This leaves future experts and courts at a tremendous disadvantage in not knowing whether the judge was opining that, as a matter of law, full trade dress must be considered in a survey; that, as a matter of fact, the full trade dress must be considered in this case; or that, in a third (and more troubling) possibility, the rules of research are being changed by a judge— where a researcher's ability to rely on testing a question posed by a client no longer is accorded proper deference.

Barrier 3: A "Matter of Consumer Behavior"

In cases dealing with brand confusion, it often is heard concerning the instruction of scientific survey evidence that side-by-side comparisons are not allowed. This collective wisdom, among many other bits of "rules," emerges from legal discussions in which judges do not explicitly separate out the difference between rules of law and rules of research or consumer behavior. One might read, for example, that side-by-side comparisons are not a way in which to test for confusion, but this probably is resting on an assumption of consumer behavior that may or may not be correct in any particular case. Thus, the findings in intellectual property cases must, for justice to prevail and for the laws to be implemented consistency, set out not only the findings of fact and the rules of law that the court is interpreting and applying but also, as important, the assumptions of consumer behavior or marketing research that the court makes. Although courts do this implicitly in each and every decision they make that includes scientific evidence, they are reluctant to do it openly because the opining on the assumptions of consumer behavior and marketing research technique would be seen as wholly out of their expertise on which to comment. Recommendations set forth later would address this shortcoming.

Barrier 4: The Structural Problem in the Adversarial Process

Some have argued that the adversarial system was indeed designed not to mete out truth.[17] One need not take this view, however, to realize that the system is noticeably lacking in discerning truth. Reitter discussed passages from *The Common Law* of Oliver Wendell Holmes that cast light on the adversarial system.[18] (See also Whitton's *The Cartel,* cited later, for similar treatment.) Justice Holmes identified a number of survivals from ancient times as the basis for laws that still are in force. The laws of evidence, although appearing to have reasons for their being that indeed justify their existence, appear strongly to emanate from an ancient set of norms.[19] The heart of the adversarial system of evidence and justice, Reitter aptly analogized, is akin to the medieval system of knights. Reitter opined that the adversarial system of presenting and testing evidence can, indeed, be directly traced to the theory of justice in the culture of knights. That is, each side battles the other in front of the king, with the king acting as judge. The method guarantees that truth shall reign, for God surely will provide strength to the one with virtue. Winning through strength acts as a proxy, therefore, for truth in today's court system.

Yet, the assumption that a force will provide strength to the virtuous to triumph rings distant from the halls of the modern world sensibilities. This is because the correlation between resources and persuasive arguments is not even necessarily positive. The analogy to the knights is, therefore, quite appropriate; the judge is left to decide the merits of the case, often in as intuitive a manner as a king might judge victory. The judge, although experienced in determining truth, might be unaware of individual cues and reactions that are found in research indicating truth. The judge, however well intentioned and although perhaps experienced in hearing about concepts and methods of marketing, science, and marketing research, almost never is given an opportunity to learn and truly understand the concepts to which he or she is exposed on a case-by-case piecemeal basis. The adversarial system, therefore, pits side against side, causing strength and shrewd cunning to be valued attributes, perhaps to the peril of justice.[20]

It is quite common to hear commentators question or complain about the adversarial system and then to reverse course and suggest that, all in all, it still is the best system to mete out justice.[21] It still is the best way in which to get to the truth, they argue, despite the fact that each attorney's job is not to search for truth but rather to question the assertions of the adversary irrespective of the truth. Truth, it goes, shall separate from falsehood and emerge victorious. Although laypersons are quick to criticize the legal system, it is incorrect to infer that their intuitions are not supported by serious shortcomings in the system (so serious in my own mind), that is, that the system is poorly designed for the truth to emerge for a number of reasons.

If truth is what we seek, then the adversarial system might be a poor solution. Yelling and intimidating might not provide a cue to discoverer lying; instead, it might provide a cue to uncover natural nervousness of being "on the stand." Thus, the harsh adversarial tones allowed in court might hinder the proper administration of justice.

Barrier 5: Presence of Judicial "Intuition"

In intellectual property cases, each side presents its results that help the side for which the attorney was hired. Because judges cannot understand much of the science presented to them, they must tend toward their intuitions. Simonson demonstrated that what judges say they consider is not necessarily what they actually do consider.[22] As would be expected, a halo effect can cause a decision to be formed and then evidence selectively chosen to support such a conclusion. This appears readily when evidence contrary to a judge's opinion is not reported in the written opinion. Direct evidence of this is difficult to find given the natural reluctance of judges to admit such processes and of judicial opinions carefully to parse out various portions of trial and deposition transcripts or evidence. Yet, signs of such systemic processes are indeed evident (see the discussion on Judge J. E. Sprizzo pontificating that judges need not necessarily follow the letter of the law if it conflicts with their own views on justice).[23]

Barrier 6: Misconstruing a Pattern of Data

Based on their intuition, judges often distrust the results from studies presented to them. Indeed, what would a statistician think in correctly observing that most of the results of each and every empirical study that appears in court by an expert, hired by one side in the litigation, favors the side that commissioned it? It would, on its face, appear biased.

The implications that derive from this are that researchers must be manipulative and crafty, perhaps even deceptive, in the design, implementation, or analysis. Yet, familiarity with the process reveals a very different conclusion. That is, there are many more studies commissioned for litigation that never see the light of day. Well over half of the studies might reveal negative results for the attorneys commissioning them. The coin is not weighted; the system, at least from the researcher's side, is not rigged. Indeed, it is the researcher's primary interest to maintain credibility. It is the attorneys who will not present or offer results that do not favor their clients' interests. It is the adversarial system that causes the poor results to be hidden away and the good results to be presented. It is the adversarial system that causes the false appearance that experts buck the overwhelming odds that all studies they present turn out to favor the side hiring them. If it were the case that these odds were bucked, then suspicions ought to be raised. But what is offered in court is the choice of the attorneys.

Barrier 7: Poor Standards for Qualifying Experts

Federal rules of evidence provide guidelines as to how to establish whether someone held out as an expert is truly an expert. But in the field of intellectual property and marketing research to support intellectual property cases, some of the experts are duly trained and experienced and are knowledgeable in conducting research or, if being offered for opinions, experts in their fields of study. But unlike in academia, where the academic community can read one's work and create impressions via publications, presentations, and the like, here the judge determines who is an expert based on information provided by the attorney hiring such proposed expert. But the standard of review is poor for two reasons. First, the judge is unaware of the field of study, the journals in the field, and the active researchers in the field. Second, to make matters much worse, the sides to a litigation often do not press this issue in terms of qualification for their own self-interested reasons either because their own expert is questionable or because they desire the opponent's expert to be declared an expert, knowing that the opposing expert is not a challenge to or can actually help their positions (through cross-examination). Yet, although this shortsighted posturing on the part of the attorneys may further their clients' causes, the system is severely damaged because once an expert is "accepted" by one court, this goes a long way toward having that expert accepted in future court appearances, for one judge does not want to go against this prior status having been conferred on the expert.

Some experts brought to conduct marketing research never have been trained in marketing research but act as puppets for the attorneys who funnel for them "appropriate designs," causing them to lie on the stand by saying that the designs are their own—for the experts are to be the persons making such decisions. It is apparent when this occurs (although the judge never would be aware of it) because certain attorneys have themselves invented and used particular distinctive research designs that have inured in the past to their clients' benefit and then used different researchers in succeeding cases who somehow (miraculously) used the identical highly distinctive methods.

Barrier 8: Academic Research Standards Not Adopted

Academic research is designed to test for truth, that is, to learn and to engage ourselves to move forward the field and our own research agendas. Little weight is given to the credibility of the researcher, and great weight is given to scrutinizing the methods for facets such as internal validity, construct validity, external validity, and reliability. Although greater emphasis has been suggested to be placed on credibility and ethics in the place where research has direct implications for deciding commercial practices,[24] the opposite actually is true; an inordinate amount of energy is spent on credibility to show that research, however well conducted, was motivated by a desire to help paying clients. But little attention is paid to many of the safeguards in conducting research that academics have carved out. Mazis explained the differences between legal research and academic research with a number of examples highlighting how legal research, in essence, does not require the type of objectivity that is needed in true academic research but has a greater need for the appearance of objectivity.[25] Such a conclusion highlights the troubling aspects of how science is used in the courts to protect brands. For example, drafts that can help a researcher to grow and learn from prior errors are taboo in the legal world because they can highlight changes in procedures and thoughts as though such a thing is negative. Indeed, they are the heart and blood of conducting research—learning from mistakes. They are, to be sure, taboo because in such an adversarial system they inevitably will be used to cast doubt on credibility; changes were made to effect results, not to better hone the questioning process.

Barrier 9: Flawed Process of Communicating Findings to the Court

When complex issues arise such as deciphering the numerous, and sometimes countervailing, effects of a particular research design, on direct examination the researcher has an opportunity to explain what he or she thought about and designed and to opine about the analysis and results. However, on cross-examination, the process is designed to elicit only yes/no types of answers. The method, however, is not designed to allow, and is not effective in allowing, understanding of principles of marketing research. Consider the following example taken from a recent case. The cross-examiner asks, "Is this statistically significant, *yes* or *no*?" and the researcher answers, "I don't understand your question—statistically significantly different from what?" The cross-examiner states, "Answer my question. Is this statistically significant?" and the researcher comments, "I cannot answer your question because it does not make sense. Would you like me to explain why I cannot answer?" The cross-examiner states, "*No,* answer the question," raising his voice to the researcher." The researcher states, "I cannot answer," whereupon the judge states, "Answer the question— enough already." The researcher answers, "It is statistically significantly different . . ." and is about to continue the sentence ". . . from zero but not from the other stimulus" to explain the truth, but he is abruptly and immediately cut off in midsentence. Once the words "It is statistically significantly different" come out, the cross-examiner abruptly states, "Thank you. That will be all." The court, unless scrutinized by a thoughtful judge and one knowledgeable in understanding why the witness was drawing a distinction, now holds a piece of information that misconstrues the testimony and the truth due to a confluence of factors caused by the adversarial system that is designed to mete out "facts" without, however, the tools to mete out the interpretation of the facts based on principles of research or consumer behavior. A good attorney will try to overcome this particular barrier through a strong "re-direct."

Barrier 10: "Approved" Methods

One could argue that the prior shortcoming might seem rather trivial if it would affect the truth and credibility of only a particular case. But methods sometimes have been "approved" or heralded by courts, even when such methods on their face do not prove what they seek to make the courts believe they prove. Yet, the decisions the courts hand down provide attorneys in future cases the fodder they want to either critique or herald things. Notwithstanding attorneys' unsuspecting role in this greater harm to justice, the harm is inevitable and grows case by case. In each future case, good researchers who need to make decisions based on their ideas of what is sensible must, nevertheless, give great weight to following clearly wrong decisions to avoid the inevitable onslaught showing that they used an already declared "flawed" element or design and the risk that a judge who is less than thoughtful and knowledgeable—and who wants to safely rest on precedent given that he or she wants the decision not to be over-turned at the appellate level—may again praise the wrong method and criticize a correct method.

The recent *Cumberland v. Monsanto* trade dress case illustrates this.[26] One company sued another company over the color of the packaging of a sugar sweetener. The researcher defined the relevant universe as those actual or poten-tial purchasers of sugar substitutes. As most academics would posit without evi-dence to the contrary, past purchasing of disposable goods is one of the best pre-dictors of category use and, thus, future category use. As we might state based on prior research, self-reported data on how likely someone is to purchase might be less correlative with true future purchases than is looking at the past. So, in this context, the researcher defined the relevant universe as those who had used or purchased sugar substitutes during the past six months. The court vehemently attacked this approach because it includes people who might not purchase in the future, and so the correct method is to ask only about future purchase intentions. The court stated,

First, Dr. Rappeport selected a universe for the surveys that was over-inclusive. The survey universe for all three studies was defined as "users or buyers of sugar substitutes within the past six months." To be meaningful, a survey must "rely upon responses by potential consumers of the products in question" (*Universal City Studios Inc. v. Nintendo Co.,* 746 F.2d 112, 118 [2d Cir. 1984]). The relevant confusion in a trademark or dress case is that which affects "the purchasing and selling of the goods or services in question" (*Lang v. Retirement Living Publishing Co.,* 949 F.2d 576, 582-3 [2d Cir. 1991]). Thus, the survey universe must be com-posed of people having a present purchasing interest in the product being sur-veyed. See *Universal City Studios,* 746 F.2d [*572] at 118 (universe improper be-cause it included only former purchasers of Donkey Kong); *American Footwear Corp. v. General Footwear Corp.,* 609 F.2d 655, 661 n. 4 (2d Cir. 1979) (universe improper because although survey participants [**28] were former purchasers of hiking boots, they did not necessarily have any present purchasing interest).

Dr. Rappeport says that past users are good proxies for future purchasers. This may be true for some products. But in the case of sweeteners, the assumption is, to say the least, questionable. Plaintiff's pink packets and the defendant's blue pack-ets are available at most diners and coffee shops and many restaurants. A high per-centage of past users of sugar substitutes may never have purchased sugar substi-tutes and have no intention to do so in the future. The survey did not distinguish between past users who intend to purchase sugar substitutes in the future and those who do not.

It was also improper to use all past "sugar substitute" users without distinguish-ing between saccharin and aspartame users. As noted earlier, there is little overlap between saccharin and aspartame users. Despite EQUAL's instant success upon introduction in 1982, Sweet 'N Low sales remained relatively stable because de-mand for EQUAL came almost entirely from people who had previously never used sweeteners. Thus, past users of saccharin are unlikely to be potential purchasers of aspartame sweeteners and [**29] vice versa.

This logic already has been followed to declare as flawed survey universes that include past purchasers without asking respondents about future purchase intention. Although many who would have purchased in the past would be included in the question about intention to purchase in the future, asking the future intention question might include many who really never have considered the category seriously (an overly broad universe). Why should a court believe that this is any better than asking a past purchase question with the effect of possibly including those who have purchased in the past but might suddenly leave the category (an underinclusive universe)? So, to ensure that those responding are involved in the category, which is the better solution? Reasonable people may indeed differ on the operationalization, but when judges cavalierly cite prior cases claiming that a reasonable choice is "flawed," they infect the process, damage the future, and inhibit researchers from making reasonable choices. Indeed, including only those who have purchased and who also intend to purchase might be an apt solution, but how many researchers will dare to innovate when innovation begets criticism?

Barrier 11: Researchers' Prior Work

Why would innovation beget criticism? Indeed, why could the researcher not learn from the courts' decisions, agree where appropriate and disagree where appropriate, and then design something that seems to be satisfactory? This is a simple solution that not only is not encouraged through the system but is systematically discouraged. Researchers who have testified have faced a barrage of innuendo and even direct attacks when they have diverged from their own prior work. Thus, although the purpose of research is to propel us forward, learn that prior conceptualizations and theories may be updated and disproved, and work toward that end (modifying earlier thoughts), the legal system takes a demonstrably backward view. What one has written or stated in the past, if differing from newer work, is brought to bear to demonstrate lack of consistency, incoherent thoughts, faulty reasoning, or even bad motives. The system forces one to look back to be consistent with prior work even when one learns that prior work could be made better or could have been conceptually revisited. The result is that the researcher who endeavors to be thoughtful and innovative is deterred, for it can only bring criticism of his or her prior work. Admitting that a prior design was not as good can be made to sound, by a trained attorney, as though the current design also might be flawed. But it may take some time in the cross-examination before the researcher comes to understand this. A hypothetical example of a cross-examination demonstrates the difficulty:

> **Cross-Examiner:** You mentioned that you tested for brand dilution not by showing the respondents the plaintiff's brand and then asking what other brands came to mind, but by showing the defendant's brand and asking what other brands came to mind. Is this the correct way to test for brand dilution?

Researcher: It is an appropriate way to test for it.

Cross-Examiner: [Presents document to researcher.] Can you identify this document?

Researcher: Yes, it's a report I wrote for a study conducted last year.

Cross-Examiner: Please turn to Page 2 of that document. Please read for us what it says.

Researcher: I conducted this study to test for brand dilution by showing the respondents the defendant's brand and then asking what came to mind.

Cross-Examiner: Did you choose an incorrect methodology in that study?

Therein lies the dilemma facing the researcher in the continuation of this cross-examination in such a way as not to be forced to disparage his or her own prior work, not to be seen as fickle in what one day he or she perceives as correct and the next day as incorrect, and not to be seen as having changed his or her method due to the goal of helping the client. The cross-examination per se is not the problem; it is the tool by which the law looks backward (incorrectly) to the detriment of methodological advancement or future learning.

Barrier 12: Discrete and Individual versus Stochastic and Collective

Attorneys are trained to examine facts as discrete events, as opposed to stochastic processes. Imagine conducting a large-scale survey concerning brands with various open-ended and closed-ended questions. You give the open-ended questions to coders, who create coding structures and code the open-ended responses that then are tabulated as quantitative data. Assume that you collected data from 300 respondents across eight geographically dispersed markets around the United States (for a test of brand name confusion in a trademark litigation dealing with two services). Say that you found that 70% of respondents were confused (netting "noise" as courts prefer a researcher does). Although not a probability sample, if the sampling was somewhat representative of the underlying population—an issue to determine—then the truth might lie somewhere around 70%. Imagine an attorney taking these 300 questionnaires and treating them as the attorney views evidence—that each questionnaire is a piece of testimony of a respondent and stands, in essence, on its own as testimony that the researcher is granted the right to present. With that mind-set, the attorney meticulously goes through about 20 of the questionnaires to show that you, as researcher, may or may not agree with the coders in how these particular questionnaires and their responses were coded. Hours are spent in deposition or trial going through each "suspect" questionnaire, all to demonstrate either (1) that some questionnaires need to be rejected, (2) that the researcher does not always agree with the coders (in an attempt to cast dispersions on the reliability of the process), and most important (3) that the isolation of these creates a negative halo effect on all the others not discussed. Attorneys think in discrete terms;

either there is a likelihood of confusion, or there is not (respondents will say *yes* to this and *no* to that). They do not think in terms of the way in which consumer processes reveal themselves through marketing research; there are approximately *X%* confused, approximately *X%* of respondents will say *yes,* and each questionnaire standing on its own does *not* have meaning to a market researcher who relies on the large sample processes where a signal emerges from the totality. Although you might not see the signal in any one questionnaire, and indeed the signal may be questioned in any particular one, the signal does emerge in the totality of the questionnaires.

Barrier 13: Ill-Defined Trade Dress and the Inability to Choose Control Groups

A control cell often is used to extract out noise in intellectual property studies. If there ever was an area with more incorrect assumptions about the nature of survey evidence, it is with regard to control stimuli. The reason why the difficulty arises concerns the nature of the disputes.

A control group stimulus in the context of intellectual property cases is designed to exclude the elements of interest (be they for determining secondary meaning or for determining confusion) so that one can determine the effect directly caused by the inclusion of such elements. Unfortunately, in many cases, trade dress is not well defined; it is a look, an entire style.[27] It is hardly a coincidence that trade dress is not defined given that (1) attorneys do not want to define it explicitly because such a definition would be used to carve out and then legitimate copying of the nonspecified elements and (2) often no one knows how the complex interaction effects of the various elements cause the overall trade dress.

Thus, stating that a control stimulus needs to be as close as possible to the test stimulus needs careful review. Judges who imply this again demonstrate the inability of the courts to handle scientific matters. What a control stimulus needs to do is to come as close to the elements in the test cell without including any of the elements that constitute the test at hand. If a package design has not one but rather a series of unique elements, then none of those elements can be present in the test cell. Although this statement sounds similar to the earlier one (i.e., a control stimulus needs to be as close as possible to the test stimulus), it causes dramatic differences. If the control stimulus has any part of the test stimulus that might be in question as comprising its trade dress (or part of the test stimulus that, even if not directly in question, causes unique interaction effects with those elements in question), then the study fails. A control cell cannot be used precisely when the trade dress is ill defined or comprises a "gestalt."

Barrier 14: Being Conservative Can Hurt

Most choices in marketing research are judgment calls in which reasonable people may differ. Thus, imagine choosing a universe to sample and determining that a precise definition is arbitrary to some extent. Should we limit the universe to those purchasing or to those intending to purchase? In a six-month or one-year horizon? As Simonson and Schmitt pointed out, a good rule of thumb is to choose it conservatively, that is, to err on the side against the client's position so that one's integrity cannot be called into question.[28] However, the aggregation of each and every decision being conservative against the client's side might unfairly bias the results against the client. So, where it is too subjective to call, the error often goes toward the other side; where a reasonable position can be gleaned by thinking the problem through, perhaps going with that makes sense. For example, one might note that the target market for a product is females ages 18 to 45 years and, thus, limit the universe to that demographic group despite its not being a conservative choice per se favoring the other side. A deceptive attorney could use this to claim that because one was conservative in the prior choice, one's not being conservative now reflects bias on the part of the client.

Barrier 15: No Position toward Truth: Both Sides Hide Clear Problems

Because both sides to a litigation might have skeletons in their closets in terms of the evidentiary flaws in their cases, it is often the case that one side will keep quiet about something about the other side or its methodology for fear that its side has the same flaw. Although this is a clever strategic tactic, it again reduces the truth from emerging.

Potential Solutions

I have identified numerous structural problems in the effectiveness of the intellectual property laws facing marketers. I looked at the substance of protection and the current system of protecting intellectual property and adjudicating disputes. The critical challenges can be summarized as follows:

- There is a current hole in protection from copying of brand elements—unique experiences—for which the law is finding it tremendously difficult to understand and address.

- There is a preoccupation by attorneys with the veracity of the expert witness, with attempting to show manipulative intent where often none exists (something that arises because attorneys constantly deal with manipulation).

- There is an inherent difficulty for a nonexpert in the position of judge (or jury) to discern what is going on. (What does the question posed to the expert witness really imply, what does the answer to the question mean, and how can I make sense of all of this without training?)

- There is an inability for a judge to ask a third party questions when formulating his or her opinion truly to learn rather than to parse voluminous transcripts without a clue as to what the meaning of most of it is.

- There is a difficulty for the truth to emerge where an expert can discuss rather than respond as a fact witness (yes/no responses), often to deliberately misleading questions where the expert, rather than being able to think clearly about difficult and complex matters, has to be concerned that the attorney might be attempting a trick and not to be caught in a trap—not due to fear that the expert is untruthful but rather due to the knowledge that the attorney's role is to take anything, however innocent or correct, and cast doubt on it. If one looks for doubt, doubt almost always can be found.

Addressing the Copying or Appropriation Issue

Simonson and Greenwald reviewed numerous federal court decisions concerning trademark infringement to find two types of outcomes[29]: (1) those judges employing a strict application of the trademark laws that then allow look-alikes and copies to emerge and (2) those judges interpreting the law as precluding such look-alikes under what amounts to an analysis based on appropriation of a property right—the stealing of one's unique look. According to Simonson and Greenwald, it is arguable that the current laws, indeed, do not support the stopping of look-alikes. They further argued, however, that as a matter of current marketing practices, failing to protect marketers from such acts amounts to failing to have protected them from palming off more than 100 years ago when that was the prevalent mode of unfair competition.

Training for Judges

Judges for intellectual property cases must themselves be knowledgeable in consumer research techniques and principles and should be chosen from a pool of such trained judges. This is a viable technique for them reasonably to be able to opine on research presented to them. Of the myriad problems discussed earlier, a mandatory education program and a judge selection pool program would solve many.

Although we cannot rightly expect a judge to familiarize himself or herself with chemical engineering to determine whether a chemical process was infringed, we ought to be very careful before we cavalierly allow judges without expertise and experience to preside over complex scientific issues, even those including surveys and consumer behavior. The judge in such cases is put in an awkward position (just as a professor of political science might be in reviewing a physics paper); the litigants might not be afforded a procedure where merit wins over shrewd cunning; the experts are not able to be judged as their peers might be judged, and justice simply might not prevail.

Court-Appointed Experts or Advisory Panels

Mazis, in the context of FTC cases, discussed differences in methodologies for legal purposes and for academic research and seemed to indicate that justice might be better served in intellectual property cases by having courts themselves appoint experts or what are termed masters.[30] This approach yields a powerful method to alleviate numerous serious structural problems in the current system.

Declaratory Judgments Concerning Surveys

I am aware of only one attorney who, on a regular basis, makes use of a device that many others do not make use of and that others to whom I have mentioned it did not know it was possible. Perhaps it is not possible in every court, but the concept is compelling. Have a court opine in advance what it will deem to be a proper universe, a proper control, or a proper line of questioning to get at a particular issue.

Team Approach

Teams of two researchers yield better work. They learn from each other's methods, they take comfort in the strength of will they can bring to a client, and each can impose his or her requirements, helping the research to be of higher quality. Such team approaches are rare, and even when conducted as such, only one "expert" is called to testify despite more than one person's involvement in the case. This is to the benefit of the attorney—to avoid inconsistent statements and to have one demeanor on the stand—but it fails to allow the researchers to come forward to a judge or jury with the realistic view that some inconsistencies in memory are normal, that both researchers participated, and that both have insights.

Although the conclusions of the report emerge from both experts and are the result of a series of compromises to get at what might be a more objective statement of truth, attorneys are fearful of one of the experts actually disagreeing with the other in terms of opinions in general or of the possibilities if the wording in the conclusions would differ—where one expert would come out one way and the other expert the other way. The fear is that the other side's attorney will use this to demonstrate that to the judge that even the plaintiff's/defendant's own experts disagree.

What is the damage? None if one—the judge—takes a realistic view that no two experts need to agree on everything for them to be experts and for the side that hired them to feel safe. Indeed, no two professors will agree on everything, and this chapter was intended to generate thought and discussion on a topic so critical to the survival of brands but so overlooked.

Research Streams

Research in the area of trademark protection, both substantive and procedural, is sorely lacking. Four research streams can be identified that relate to protecting brands and may affect the rules concerning how brands compete in the new century.[31]

The first is empirical research on the substantive areas of protecting brands. They include primarily the topics of brand confusion, dilution, secondary meaning, genericism, and appropriation. I. Simonson's work, for example, compared various research methods of testing for brand confusion and for brand genericism, concluding that survey results in this area tend to be the result of a confound between research methodology choice and some true measure of confusion or genericism, as the case may be.[32] In other words, we have no nonbiased or true measure of confusion or genericism as a court might desire. A. Simonson's and Holbrook's empirical study in 1994 on brand dilution and appropriation found that brands with which the courts are most concerned—new brands in product categories close to the product categories of senior users' brands—are precisely those where appropriation would not help and where dilution of original brands would be nonexistent.[33] A recent interesting study by Morrin and Jacoby also moves nicely toward attempting to bridge law and marketing research.[34] Although these researchers have attempted to bridge law and marketing research, the field remains open compared to the body of research on the interface between law and economics, as addressed in works concerning antitrust, tort law, and regulation.

The second, and by far the most common, area of research is that of case reviews of intellectual property cases and implications for public policy.[35] This is the most common because it is the most straightforward and is the type of research most expected from the marketing academic community among those discussing the legal realm. It is characterized by discussion and juxtaposition of cases. It is a useful endeavor because it places changes in rules in the context of the factors causing the changes and, thus, can shed light on hypotheses for further study. However, it also can lend itself to relegating the law to historical review. Although more of this is needed, the next type of research should lead from this type.

Third, conceptual and strategic articles on trademarks are needed. Cohen wrote for marketing academics on trademark law directly.[36] Even Bloch's recent work on the conceptual framework of analyzing design can be used as a stepping-stone to where and how the law should analyze trade dress.[37] But apart from these and a few other articles mainly in the *Journal of Public Policy & Marketing* and *The Trademark Reporter,* conceptual or strategic articles have been written, for the most part, by attorneys for attorneys. Attorneys and legal scholars have written in the legal journals on the conceptual inconsistencies of the law or on the need to change conceptual bases of legal rights based on current changes in marketing. They are, however, driven by marketing theory and practice and would benefit from the creativity and theory of marketing academics. For example, Swann recently *introduced* attorneys[38] to Aaker's 1991 work[39] on branding and used this to explain how the legal concept of genericism is outdated. Although Swann's work is welcome news to bridge the marketing world with the trademark attorney world, it highlights the schism between the two worlds, where attorneys are just now being introduced to theories and strategies of branding developed nearly a decade ago. It will, no doubt, take many more years for these articles in the law journals to enter into courts' decisions. Part of the problem is inherent in the reward structure to marketing academics. Publishing in the legal journals is virtually the only way in which to affect the societal effects of trademark laws. Yet, unfortunately for marketing and society, publishing in this venue (1) is not rewarded as it might be deemed to fall outside the scholar's field and (2) is hardly seen by marketing academics to foster and further the research. The solution is what the Brand Names Education Foundation has sought to do and where I have endeavored to work with the foundation to link legal education with marketing education. Moreover, *The Trademark Reporter* welcomes marketing-related articles concerning intellectual property regulation. Much work is needed at the "top-tier" marketing journals, where the connection between the law and marketing still has not emerged as a major priority or presence.

Finally, research on protecting brands (touching on the effects of the process of the legal system) is needed. This research, both conceptual and empirical, must be designed to offer solutions to the methods used by management to protect intellectual property and by courts and attorneys to adjudicate trademark disputes. This research should offer guidance on the process, where management, trademark lawyers, and judges alike often are working far beyond their formal training and knowledge. Articles in strategic journals addressed to senior-level management can be the most beneficial venue for this type of research, where key management can influence general counsel, who in turn can place pressure on outside counsel to look at things differently—to understand how marketing and law interact.

Notes

1. D. Aaker, *Managing Brand Equity* (New York: Free Press, 1991); K. Keller, *Strategic Brand Management* (Englewood Cliffs, NJ: Prentice Hall, 1998).

2. Bernd Schmitt and Alex Simonson, *Marketing Aesthetics* (New York: Free Press, 1997).

3. The recent discussions of intellectual property often focus on technology and patents; see Lester C. Thurow, "Needed: A New System of Intellectual Property Rights," *Harvard Business Review* (September-October): 95-103 (1997). The discussion of intellectual property as it relates to trademarks, and thus marketing, often is neglected. This chapter focuses on the process of protecting brands.

4. See *Gorham v. White* (81 U.S. 511 [1871]) for the theory of design patents.

5. Interview with Mark Abrams, president of Nick & Nora.

6. *Major League Baseball Properties Inc. v. Pacific Trading Cards Inc.,* 48 U.S.P.Q. 2d (BNA) 1944, 1945 (S.D.N.Y. 1998); *vacated* 150 F.3d 149, 47 U.S.P.Q. 2d (BNA) 1477 (2d Cir. 1998).

7. Utility patents that are violated also are cause for legal action, as where drugs are counterfeited (although this is not the subject of this chapter).

8. P. M. Bible, "Defining and Quantifying Dilution under the Federal Trademark Dilution Act of 1995: Using Survey Evidence to Show Actual Dilution," *University of Colorado Law Review* 70: 295 (1999); A. Simonson, "How and When Do Trademarks Dilute? A Behavioral Framework to Judge 'Likelihood' of Dilution," *The Trademark Reporter,* 83 (2): 149-74 (1993).

9. *Cumberland Packing Corporation v. Monsanto Company,* 32 F.Supp. 2d 561, 1999-1 Trade Cases P 72,447 (E.D.N.Y., January 12, 1999); *Conopco Inc. v. Cosmair Inc.,* 49 F.Supp. 2d 242 (S.D.N.Y., May 7, 1999).

10. J. Thomas McCarthy, *McCarthy on Trademarks and Unfair Competition,* 4th ed. (Clark Boardman Callaghan, 1999).

11. L. S. Pinsky, "The Use of Scientific Peer Review and Colloquia to Assist Judges in the Admissibility of Gatekeeping Mandated by Daubert," *Houston Law Review* 527 (1997).

12. S. S. Diamond, "Reference Guide on Survey Research," in *Reference Manual on Scientific Evidence* (Washington, DC: Federal Judicial Center, 1994), 221-71.

13. Jacob J. Jacoby, Amy H. Handlin, and Alex Simonson, "Survey Evidence in Deceptive Advertising Cases under the Lanham Act: An Historical Review of Comments from the Bench," *The Trademark Reporter* 84 (5): 541-85 (1994). Reprinted in Practising Law Institute Course (B4-7167), "False Advertising and the Law: Coping with Today's Challenges" (September 1996).

14. F. W. Mostert, "Famous Trade Dress: Dilution on Competing Products," *Trademark World* (March 20-26, 1997).

15. These are examples of cases that I worked on and for which details are available on request, subject to any protective orders.

16. A. Simonson and F. Mostert, "Protecting the Exclusivity of Unique Brand Experiences," unpublished manuscript, Georgetown University School of Business (1999).

17. N. M. Crystal, "Limitations on Zealous Representation in an Adversarial System," *Wake Forest Law Review*, 32: 671 (1997).

18. R. Reitter, "Reflections on the Nature of the Ethical in the Judicial System," unpublished working paper (1996).

19. Ibid.

20. E. Whitton, *The Cartel, Lawyers, and Their Nine Magic Tricks* (Herwick, 1998). Available: http://www.ewhitton.com

21. G. Robertson, *The Justice Game* (Chato & Windus, 1998).

22. Simonson, "How and When."

23. *United States v. Lynch,* 952 F.Supp. 167 (S.D.N.Y. 1997).

24. Letter by Jacob Jacoby to the members of the Association for Consumer Research (1995).

25. Michael B. Mazis, "Copy Testing Issues in FTC Advertising Cases," paper presented at Marketing and Public Policy Conference, Summer 1996, Arlington, VA.

26. *Cumberland v. Monsanto,* 32 F.Supp. 2d 561 (E.D.N.Y. 1999).

27. B. Schmitt and A. Simonson, *Marketing Aesthetics* (New York: Free Press, 1997).

28. Ibid.

29. A. Simonson and J. Greenwald, "Brand Appropriation and Confusion: A Conceptual Framework," in progress, Georgetown University (2000).

30. Mazis, "Copy Testing Issues."

31. A fifth type of article/research is not mentioned here—the short strategic article geared to practitioners. Examples of this type abound and offer insights, but they typically fall short of the type of rigor academics seek. See L. Herman, "Research on the Witness Stand," *Quirk's Marketing Research Review*, May, 52-57 (1999). See also T. Hemnes, "How Can You Find a Safe Trademark?" *Harvard Business Review*, March-April, 36-49 (1985); T. Hemnes, "From Experience: Perspectives of a Trademark Attorney on the Branding of Innovative Products," *Journal of Product Innovation Management* 4: 217-24 (1987); A. Simonson, "Surveys on Trademark Confusion: Basic Differences," *The Intellectual Property Strategist* 5 (2): 1, 9-10 (1998). A sixth type also is not discussed—economic modeling of trademark rights that can bear on affecting the laws regulating such rights. See L. Takeyama, "The Intertemporal Consequences of Unauthorized Reproduction of Intellectual Property," *Journal of Law and Economics* 40 (2): 511-22 (1997).

32. I. Simonson, "Trademark Infringement from the Buyer's Perspective: Conceptual Analysis and Measurement Implications," *Journal of Public Policy & Marketing* 13 (2): 181-99 (1994).

33. A. Simonson and M. Holbrook, "Evaluating the Impact of Brand-Name Replications on Product Evaluations," working paper, Georgetown University (1994).

34. M. Morrin and J. Jacoby, "Trademark Dilution: Empirical Measures for an Elusive Concept," *Journal of Public Policy & Marketing* (forthcoming).

35. J. Jacoby and M. Morrin, " 'Not Manufactured or Authorized by . . .': Recent Federal Cases Involving Trademark Disclaimers," *Journal of Public Policy & Marketing* 17 (1): 97-107 (1998); J. D. Mittlestaedt and R. A. Mittlestaedt, "The Protection of Intellectual Property: Issues of Origination and Ownership," *Journal of Public Policy & Marketing* 16 (1): 14-25 (1997).

36. D. Cohen, "Trademark Strategy," *Journal of Marketing* 50 (January): 61-74 (1986); see also L. B. Burgunder, "Trademark Protection of Product Characteristics: A Predictive Model," *Journal of Public Policy & Marketing* 16 (2): 277-88 (1997); see also earlier works such as G. Miaoulis and N. D'Amato, "Consumer Confusion and Trademark Infringement," *Journal of Marketing* 42 (April): 48-55 (1978).

37. P. H. Bloch, "Seeking the Ideal Form: Product Design and Consumer Response," *Journal of Marketing* 59 (July): 16-29 (1995).

38. J. Swann, "Genericism Rationalized," *The Trademark Reporter* 89: 639-56 (1999).

39. Aaker, *Managing Brand Equity.*

Chapter 15

Consumer Response to Warnings and Other Types of Product Hazard Information

Future Public Policy and Research Directions

David W. Stewart
Valerie S. Folkes
Ingrid Martin

How individuals use products can have important implications for consumer welfare and public policy. Risks from product use can be seen in a variety of areas. For example, the environment (e.g., the way in which cars are driven influences air pollution, the way in which toxic substances are used and discarded influences groundwater quality), the health of the individual user and others (e.g., the way in which people smoke cigarettes predisposes them and others to physical ailments), and people's safety (e.g., the ways in which people use tools, sporting equipment, and electrical appliances can lead to injuries) all are areas where this impact is apparent. Marketers and government agencies provide information about how to use products in the form of warnings, disclosures, and instructions, partly because of the many ways in which product use and misuse affects individual consumers and society as a whole. These types of messages inform at-risk consumers of the possible dangers associated with the use or misuse of products. Considering the extreme hazards associated with many products, it might be surprising that a common finding of empirical research is that people often do not comply with such messages.

The objectives of this chapter are to (1) summarize current knowledge about warning messages, (2) discuss the implications of these findings for consumer welfare and public policy makers, and (3) identify directions for future research on warnings and the communication of hazards and potential hazards associated with the use and misuse of products and services. Much like other reviews and meta-analyses in the warnings and disclosure literature, our review takes an information processing approach. If a message is to influence consumers' behavior, then consumers must be motivated to pay attention to the message, comprehend it, be persuaded by it, and remember it. The effects of warning messages that are discussed are influenced by a number of factors: characteristics of the messages themselves, characteristics of consumers, and characteristics of the purchase and usage environments. This chapter examines the influence of each of these sets of factors.

Based on the review of the literature, the chapter offers recommendations for the design of warning messages and directions for future research. Providing such recommendations is somewhat challenging because warning messages can serve multiple goals (e.g., one warning might alert consumers to potential hazards and also protect a manufacturer from liability claims [Schwartz 1998]). In addition, numerous criteria can be used to determine the effectiveness of a warning message (e.g., inform at-risk populations vs. persuade at-risk populations vs. change behavior of at-risk populations).

Function of Warning Messages

This review focuses on warnings that are associated with the individual product, its advertising, or its place of purchase and consumption, as opposed to warnings that reach consumers through other means (e.g., the media, word of mouth). Such warnings are more immediate to the product purchase or usage situation. Their function typically is to interrupt consumers' actions or plans for actions with information about potential negative outcomes arising from those courses of actions. The interrupted actions sometimes are routines established in the service of goals that no longer are salient such as when a long-term smoker, out of habit, picks up a package of cigarettes and encounters a new warning message. In other cases, consumers' actions or plans for actions are explicitly goal driven and purposeful. For example, a consumer might search pesticide packaging to identify how to most effectively eliminate pests, only to be interrupted by the warning against certain types of use. Interrupting a well-developed routine or a goal-driven behavior can be quite difficult. People selectively attend to information that is compatible with their goals. In light of these difficulties, it is not surprising that many warning studies emphasize factors inhibiting or facilitating awareness of the message. For example, many researchers have examined effects of attention-attracting message elements such as color, size of print, and icons or symbols (cf. Stewart and Martin 1994).

The function of many warning messages is not only to interrupt consumers' actions or plans for actions but also to disrupt them. Sometimes, the warning offers information to be included in consumers' evaluations of alternatives. Other warnings change the means for reaching the same goal (e.g., by recommending that gloves be used when handling the product). Some warnings increase the salience of consumers' distal goals rather than more proximal goals (e.g., cigarette warnings attempt to make the long-term health costs of smoking more salient than the immediate benefits of smoking). Others create new goals for product consumption (e.g., when a warning suggests use only after consultation with a physician for users with certain characteristics). The multiple functions of warning messages lend a complexity to the literature that precludes simple conclusions about effects. Furthermore, they highlight the importance of understanding consumers' goals during product use, a point on which we elaborate in the review that follows.

Message Characteristics

Whereas the prototypic warning message might be the brief caution or qualification about usage procedures or prediction of potentially negative outcomes, warning messages are multidimensional in that they can take many forms (Stewart and Martin 1994). Some warnings are short, whereas others are hundreds of words long. Some warnings are informative, whereas others state specific prohibitions. Such messages can provide guidance on what should or should not be done when using the products (e.g., do not inhale), the probabilities of various outcomes from use (e.g., warnings that use of aspirin by children only rarely leads to Reyes syndrome), the circumstances surrounding product use (e.g., use protective goggles when applying the product), and the remedies for misuse (e.g., if it gets in one's eyes, flush with water). Information can be implicit as well as explicit in that a list of product contents can indicate how a product should be used (e.g., the presence of carbon monoxide in cigarettes implicitly warns that its use should be avoided or, at the very least, minimized). Such diversity in the types and functions of messages makes it difficult to derive simple conclusions about the effectiveness of message characteristics. Warning messages also may be composed of many different elements and features. These various features and elements may be combined to create an infinite array of specific messages. Some of these features, such as the meaningfulness and format of warnings, have received considerable attention in empirical research, but there is ample evidence that the interactions of various elements in the messages themselves and characteristics of the users and usage situations play important roles in determining the ultimate effects of warnings. The number and complexity of these interactions represent a formidable challenge for researchers because the main effects of even simple features tend to be complex.

The Meaning of the Message

It is an obvious point that messages have little impact if the recipients cannot understand them. Yet, the intended recipients do not understand many warning messages (Morris et al. 1998). Pyrczak and Roth (1976) examined the readability of various warning messages and statements of caution on 10 aspirin-like products. Such messages and statements required a reading level at or above the 11th or 12th grade. They noted that some of the more difficult words in the language are words that appear frequently in warnings—consult, persists, accidental, immediately, conditions. A failure to comprehend such words does not mean that a warning has failed to convey knowledge of potential hazards, although it does raise a more general question regarding the problem of ensuring that words are meaningful across all potential recipients of a message.

The meaning that a consumer associates with a given hazard also is highly context dependent. Risk is an inherently ambiguous concept that can be communicated in numerous ways and with varying degrees of detail. Research suggests that the way in which risk is described can have a profound effect on the way in which people respond. For example, Smith and colleagues (1990) reported the results of a study encouraging people to think in terms of "thresholds." These thresholds were readings below which a specified radon exposure level would be acceptable and above which it would not. The result of this "framing" significantly affected how people responded to new readings that exceeded the threshold. Another variant on the way in which risk can be presented is in terms of the benefits obtained from preventive efforts (a gain perspective) or the undesirable outcomes to be avoided (a loss perspective). A gain perspective emphasizing the benefits of sunscreen for healthy skin leads to more requests for the product and intentions to use the product frequently than does a loss perspective emphasizing the risks of skin cancer (Detweiler et al. 1999). By contrast, a loss perspective has been demonstrated to be more effective than a gain perspective when the risks are proximal rather than distal (e.g., when the risk of cancer is immediate rather than delayed) (Banks et al. 1995).

These findings are consistent with other empirical evidence (Liu and Smith 1990; Viscusi 1990; Viscusi, Magat, and Huber 1986; Viscusi and O'Connor 1984) and normative suggestions regarding the design of warning messages (Bettman, Payne, and Staelin 1986) that information about risk be presented in a manner consistent with consumer information processing strategies. This does not fully resolve the problem, however, because there are many ways in which to communicate risks, and many risks are inherently probabilistic rather than certain and, therefore, are difficult to quantify with certitude.

Furthermore, individuals vary in how they interpret and use risk information. Rindfleisch and Crockett (1999) identified five different types of risk associated with product use: addiction, financial, health, time, and social. They found that only two of these types of risk were related to smoking behavior. The definition of risk used by experts often is very different from that used by the layman, and even different groups of experts may define risk differently (Fischhoff 1993). This is, in part, an issue of the subjective meaning that individuals assign to risk rather than an issue of right or wrong. Fischhoff (1993) noted that one individual might interpret risk as an increase in the probability of premature death, whereas another might think about risk in terms of the amount of time by which life might be shortened (p. 9). Both interpretations are appropriate but may result in different beliefs about the risk involved and in different actions in response to such interpretations. Fisher (1991), among others, raised similar concerns and suggested the need for further study of the layman's perspective on risk, which often encompasses dimensions other than some determination of the magnitude of a potential hazard. Similarly, Tonn and colleagues (1990) raised concerns "that 'broadly based risk' communications may be ineffective because people differ in their conceptual representation of risk beliefs" (p. 169).

Format of Warning Messages

Studies of alternative designs are among the most common types of research on warnings (for reviews, see Cox et al. 1997; Lehto and Miller 1986). Among the factors that have been studied are the use of signal words, the use of symbols, noticeability, legibility, size and type of font, placement of the warning, readability, and explicitness of conclusions. There is little doubt that the design of a warning is an important determinant of response, but research on design issues has not always produced consistent results or conclusions that are easily reconciled. This literature is quite large and not easily summarized. Thus, the remainder of this section provides a brief review of a representative set of studies rather than a definitive review.

Research on warning design appears to suggest that communication that a potential hazard exists might be more important than the provision of very specific information regarding the nature and severity of the hazard. In a series of experiments, Wogalter and colleagues (1987) found that the deletion of signal words (i.e., hazard, danger) and instructions for product use led to a greater reduction in respondents' perceptions of warning effectiveness than did deletion of other parts of the warning such as the consequences of misuse or continued use of the product. The provision of more detailed information about a potential hazard was not perceived by consumers to make a warning more effective. Likewise, Urzic (1984) found that the use of pictures, large letters, or words implying more or less severe consequences had no effect on either the recall of the warning or perceptions of safety of the product. It is unclear whether such findings generalize to all types of warnings or only to those with which consumers are already familiar.

A number of normative articles on the design of warnings have suggested that the use of symbols may be more effective than words in alerting people to danger (Bettman, Payne, and Staelin 1986; FMC Corporation 1980; Westinghouse Corporation 1981). This might be because symbols are more likely to attract attention, are easier to process, or stimulate greater cognitive elaboration. Kelley, Gaidis, and Reingen (1989) offered empirical evidence that symbols increase recall and the frequency of cognitive elaboration. These researchers attributed their findings to the greater vividness of the symbols used in their study. However, symbols can take many different forms. Thus, general conclusions about the effects of symbols are probably inappropriate. Collins, Lerner, and Pierman (1982) provided a review of research on symbols and concluded that they might be more effective than written communication in cases where the symbols have well-understood meanings. When symbols do not have well-known meanings, they might fail to communicate the potential for hazard and, in some circumstances, might communicate the opposite of what is intended (Lerner and Collins 1980). Research suggests that there is wide variation in the extent to which symbols currently used to represent hazards are understood (Collins and Lerner 1982; Easterby and Hakiel 1981; Easterby and Zwaga 1976; Green and Pew 1978). Comprehension rates appear to range from less than 5% to about 50% (Easterby and Hakiel 1981).

Whether a warning is readily noticed and whether it is legible are important standards by which to evaluate messages. Simply making a warning more noticeable, however, does not mean that it is easier to read or that conclusions can be easily drawn from the message. Indeed, factors that draw attention to a warning might not be optimal for communicating information about a hazard. Pictures and icons might draw attention but might not instruct the user on how to avoid the hazard. Explicit written instructions might be more useful for educating consumers about how to avoid a hazard, but they might not be as effective at attracting attention as are pictures. The characteristics or attributes of a warning that influence noticeability and readability remain a source of controversy in the literature, with considerable contradiction among reports of empirical research. For example, Popper and Murray (1989) found that neither the size of the lettering in a warning nor the background color significantly increased the noticeability and legibility of the message. By contrast, Godfrey, Rothstein, and Laughery (1985) found that by enhancing the lettering and other salient features (e.g., using pictorials and icons, borders, and colors), they were able to increase behavioral compliance. Laughery and colleagues (1993) found that pictorials, icons, and color significantly improved noticeability of a warning but that the use of borders to set off the warning had little impact. These researchers also demonstrated that the number of features employed to draw attention to a warning was not related to improvements in noticeability. That is, adding more features designed to draw attention to a warning did not significantly influence the degree to which people notice a warning. Such contradictory findings suggest that much of the effect of specific characteristics of warnings such as lettering, color, and size are dependent on the context in which they are used and perceived to be salient. They also may suggest that there are diminishing returns to the addition of features to a warning that are designed to increase attention.

Another form of icon is the use of a well-known brand character such as "Joe Camel." There has been limited research on the interaction between these brand characters and warning labels on consumers' information processing strategies. Research in imagery has found that certain types of images may encourage individuals to consume certain types of products (e.g., "Joe Camel makes smoking seem fun and cool") (MacInnis and Price 1987). Research in the medical literature has demonstrated that a large group of young adults evaluated the Joe Camel character as likable, although the link to actual behavior is missing in these studies (DiFranza et al. 1991, Fischer et al. 1989). Likewise, Garretson and Burton (1998) found a positive influence of brand character on attitudes toward the product as well as on the believability of the warning message (p. 44). By contrast, other research has provided conflicting results on the impact of brand characters on compliance with warning messages. For example, Mizerski (1995) found that characters such as Joe Camel did not create a positive attitude toward cigarettes. These conflicting findings indicate that additional research is required to better understand the interaction between brand characters and warning messages and especially the influence of such an interaction on what individuals are motivated to process.

The necessity of considering interactions rather than simple effects also can be seen in studies examining the amount and type of information included in warning messages. For example, Slater and colleagues (1998) examined differences produced by quantitative and qualitative information presented in warning messages on risk perceptions, believability of the warnings, attitudes toward the warning messages, and compliance with the warnings. Their results were contingent on many variables such as the types of information presented in the warnings (e.g., alcohol and cancer risks vs. alcohol and driving) and the types of outcome measures used. This degree of contingency suggests that there is no "simple heuristic for determining whether quantitative information should be used" (p. 59) and clearly illustrates the important role played by interactions among the various elements of features of a warning.

Designing Messages with Consumers in Mind

Little research on warnings has examined consumers' preferences (if any) for the type of information, how the information should be presented, and how they believe the impact of such information should be measured (for exceptions, see Levy, Fein, and Schucker 1991; Lewis and Yetley 1992). However, involving consumers in the design of warnings is not a panacea. Katz and Rose (1976) showed that consumers reported a desire for additional information about light bulbs when, in fact, such information had been available for several years. Apparently, what information consumers say they want and the information they use are not always the same. Likewise Levy, Fein, and Schucker (1991) found that the nutrition labels preferred by consumers were not the most effective for communicating information about nutrition. There has been criticism of previous attempts to use surveys as a means for obtaining what consumers wish to know (Katz and Rose 1976; Viscusi 1990), but surveys that have been used in the past do not begin to exhaust the array of tools that are available for such purposes. Thus, an interesting and potentially useful agenda for research revolves around methodological issues associated with obtaining consumer input into both the design and evaluation of warnings.

Consumer Characteristics and Warning Messages

Outcomes such as whether people pay attention to a warning message, whether they are persuaded by a warning message, and whether their behavior is altered by a warning message are linked directly to recipients' motivation and ability to process the information. Such influences were alluded to in the previous discussion of message meaningfulness and informativeness. It is a certainty that consumers' goals and purposes when using the product, their prior familiarity with the information, their prior beliefs, and their perception of risk influence the degree to which a message is meaningful and informative and, ultimately, their response to the message.

Goals and Purposes of the User

The literature and empirical research on warnings generally have ignored the role of consumer goals in determining how an individual responds to warning information. Consumers' motivation to attend to and use warnings, how they interpret warnings, and the types of warnings they prefer depend on their goals. Goals have been defined as "internal representations of desired states, where states are broadly construed as outcomes, events, or processes" (Austin and Vancouver 1996, p. 338). The hierarchical organizational structure of goals provides the link between cognition and behavior. Higher order goals (e.g., a consumer's desire for safety) guide the lower level or subgoals (e.g., search for warning information on the product label). This, in turn, can be used to move an individual through the processing stages for the warning message. When a salient usage goal (e.g., task safety) guides information search, the warning message becomes the vehicle used to facilitate the consumer's attentional processes, comprehension, persuasion and, compliance (or failure to comply).

People have a variety of types of goals when using products. Ford and Nichols's (1987) well-accepted goal taxonomy provides a sense of this diversity. Some within-person goals include desires for arousal (e.g., excitement), understanding (e.g., making sense of something), and positive self-evaluations. Some person-task goals include desires for self-determination (i.e., a sense of freedom to act or make choices), social responsibility (i.e., conforming to social rules), task mastery (i.e., improving one's situation), and task safety (i.e., being unharmed or free from risk). Although in the Ford and Nichols taxonomy goals are conceptually distinct, they vary in the degree to which they are mutually exclusive and, hence, can be achieved concurrently. For example, the goal of arousal or excitement on an amusement park ride might be incompatible with the goal of feeling safe or free from harm, at least at a given point in time and space.

Most warnings are designed to assist consumers in achieving their task safety goals or attempt to make a task safety goal salient or desirable. At least for food preparation, there is evidence that task safety goals are less important to consumers than are other goals (e.g., task mastery, creativity) (Martin and Folkes

1999). Some of the controversy in the warnings literature can be conceptualized as concerns over whether warnings change people's goals or whether warnings inadvertently serve the wrong types of goals. There has been extensive debate about whether a warning should aim to change a person's goals or whether it should merely identify the means to attain a task safety goal if the person so desires (Stewart and Martin 1994). By making task safety a salient goal, a warning can lead the consumer to relinquish another goal that is perceived as concurrently unattainable. For example, a consumer might replace a desire for superior outcomes from product use with a concern about safety. Research findings that warnings related to drinking while pregnant produce moderate reductions in drinking behavior (Hankin et al. 1993) may be attributable to the displacement of one goal (the immediate benefits associated with drinking) with another (giving birth to a healthy child). Another controversy is whether warnings serve the wrong types of goals. Some consumers might seek risks so that warning information becomes the cue that they use to pursue that risk contrary to the intent of the warning. For example, a warning can serve as a trigger to incite a risk seeker to smoke or to consume alcohol (Ellen, Bone, and Stuart 1998).

Previous research has not always taken into account the fact that warnings will be more effective if they anticipate and reflect people's salient goals. People attend to messages that address their goals and ignore or avoid those that do not (Ford 1992). For example, when the consumer's goal is happiness and maintenance of a good mood, repeated exposure to the same message can lead to irritability and ignoring the warning. Once attended to, messages are interpreted and given meaning in light of the consumer's goals. For example, desires for self-determination might lead a consumer to act contrary to the mandated behaviors in the message (Ellen et al. 1998; Snyder and Blood 1991). Finally, a commitment to adhering to the warning reflects the extent to which the warning is perceived as serving an important goal of the recipient. For example, a belief that a warning is true might not be sufficient to change behavior unless task safety is an important goal.

In sum, consumers might not attend to a particular warning because it lacks relevance to individuals' usage goals. There is evidence that consumers are more likely to attend to other marketing communications when they are personally relevant (Pechmann and Stewart 1990), and a similar phenomenon might exist for warning messages. In a direct examination of this issue, Strawbridge (1985) asked participants why they read only the first part of a warning before skipping to the "uses" portion of the label. The majority of respondents indicated that they were not interested in learning about the dangers of the product and, instead, wished to understand the various product uses. In other words, task mastery was a more salient goal than task safety for this group of respondents.

The importance of goal relevance is underscored in studies comparing more frequent product users to light users or nonusers. Mazis, Morris, and Swasy (1991) found that consumers who were heavy users of alcoholic beverages were most likely to be aware of the warning messages placed on such beverages. Mayer, Smith, and Scammon (1991) found that nonusers of alcohol (a group of devout Mormons in Utah) exhibited by far the least awareness of new warning labels required on all alcoholic beverage containers. This finding probably is attributable, at least in part, to the lack of relevance that alcoholic beverage containers have to the goals of these nonusers. Furthermore, the same sample also exhibited the lowest levels of awareness of alcoholic beverage warnings posted in restaurants. This was despite the fact that Utah had required the posting of restaurant warnings for more than a decade at the time the research was conducted. Such findings are not easily explained by a lack of opportunity for exposure, although it is possible that devout Mormons do not frequent restaurants that serve alcoholic beverages. Such findings more likely reflect the lack of relevance of these warnings for this particular group. Consumers who do not use a product and who do not anticipate using a product will not attend to the warning information.

Prior Familiarity with Warning Information

Relevance seems likely to be related to information seeking about the product and exposure to the product and, hence, to product familiarity and knowledge. Therefore, one might expect greater compliance with warnings by those more familiar with the product and those more knowledgeable about the product. Yet, consumers who already are familiar with the nature and content of a warning might not expend the effort required to attend to a warning once its contents are known. Research suggests that consumers often are aware of the information in warnings even though they might not attend to them on any one occasion. For example, in the case of cigarette warnings, a survey carried out after the 1984 warning labels appeared on cigarette packages in the United States found that 64% of all respondents and 77% of cigarette smokers recalled seeing one or more of the new warning labels (Lieberman Research 1986). Furthermore, the 1989 surgeon general's report indicated that in 1982, 92% of all adults and 85% of all smokers believed that cigarette smoking was the leading cause of lung cancer (Surgeon General 1989, p. 244). Such findings stand in contrast to research finding that only a small percentage of cigarette users pay attention to warning labels on any given occasion (Fischer et al. 1989). Thus, although it might be the case that few individuals attend to a warning on any given occasion, such attention might be unnecessary if the information contained in the warning already is well known. Where the warning information is not well known, consumers might be more likely to attend to the warning. However, the relationship between familiarity and the likelihood of attending to a warning appears to be mediated by other factors.

There are individuals who use products and are in the target population for a warning message but who still fail to attend to a warning. There is a large body of literature that examines compliance rates of patients given instructions for medical regimens. These large-scale studies have found conflicting results concerning the impact of prior familiarity with the instructional information, including warnings, on compliance rates. For example, some studies have found that the patient's familiarity is positively correlated with instructional compliance (Lau et al. 1996), sometimes is negatively correlated (Katz et al. 1998), and sometimes has no relationship with compliance (Sherbourne et al. 1992). Understanding when each of these conditions applies is critical to developing public policy standards for the use and design of various types of warning information.

Recognition of the influence of familiarity, as well as the fact that a given product may be associated with more than one potential hazard, has led policy makers to require multiple warnings that are rotated among packages and advertisements for some products. Such rotation may have the effect of reducing inattention to warnings, at least in the short term. Research on advertising has suggested that variation reduces inattention and increases message processing (Pechmann and Stewart 1988), and a similar effect may occur for warnings. This is an issue that has not received much attention in the warnings literature. An exception is a recent study by Garretson and Burton (1998), who found that familiarity with alcohol warnings is very high. The authors concluded, "In terms of knowledge and attitudes, there is little to be gained from the continuation of these two particular warnings" (p. 44). Instead, they suggested that increasing consumers' knowledge level about the hazards associated with product use would be more effective. In other words, by providing new, little-known information about the hazards of product use to consumers, individuals are continuously learning more about the potential hazards associated with product use.

In a series of studies, Wogalter and colleagues (1991) found that willingness to read product warnings was related to the perceived hazardousness of products. Friedmann (1988) reported similar findings. The perceived hazard associated with a product has, in turn, been shown to decline with increasing familiarity with the product (Godfrey et al. 1983). Thus, a reduction in the perceived risk of a product associated with greater familiarity might result in less attention to a warning. This assertion was tested in a study by Godfrey et al. (1983), who found that, for household products perceived as less hazardous or as having a low probability of a hazard, familiarity tended to reduce the probability that respondents would examine the warning. When products were perceived as more hazardous, familiarity had no effect on the likelihood of examining the warning message. Similarly, Robinson (1977) suggested that individuals with prior product experience might be more likely to ignore warning information because they have not had accidents in the past. A history of avoidance of accidents, for whatever reason, may decrease the perceived risk associated with the product.

Believability and Agreement with Warning Messages

It is almost axiomatic that a message must be believed to have an effect. It does appear that certain types of warnings are more credible than other messages. A number of studies have examined factors that influence the believability of warning messages. For example, Andrews, Netemeyer, and Durvasula (1990) reported finding that information about potential birth defects and driving impairments associated with the consumption of alcoholic beverages was more believable than other warnings associated with these products. They also reported that persons with more favorable attitudes toward consumption and who used of alcoholic beverages more frequently were least likely to believe specific warnings associated with these beverages.

There is a long history of research in social psychology demonstrating that messages with which recipients agree are more likely to be accepted and acted on (Beltramini and Evans 1985; McGuire 1980; Perry 1983). In the medical compliance literature, findings on patients' compliance with instructions and warnings show that they will underuse the prescribed amount of a medication because they believe that they are being overmedicated (Morrow, Von Leirer, and Sheikh 1988). Thus, patients do not believe the messages that they are receiving from their physicians and pharmacists. This effect has been replicated in studies of warnings. Beltramini (1988) found that college students who were more certain of their belief that cigarettes are hazardous were more likely to believe the warning messages on cigarette packages than were those who were less certain. Interestingly, respondents' smoking behavior had no effect on how believable the warning messages were perceived. This latter finding suggests that warning message recipients might believe that a hazard is present without necessarily altering their behavior. There are a number of reasons why this might occur, but one is specifically related to the message evaluation process, that is, how recipients evaluate the relative risks and benefits associated with the use of a product.

Similarly, Andrews, Netemeyer, and Durvasula (1991) found that frequent drinkers tended to perceive warnings on alcoholic beverages as less believable than did infrequent users and nonusers. However, the nature of the warning may influence believability. In the context of warnings for alcoholic beverages, Andrews, Netemeyer, and Durvasula (1993) found that warnings focusing on driving impairment and birth defects tended to be more believable than warnings focusing on hypertension, cancer, addiction, liver disease, and other potential adverse outcomes. These latter results might be explained by both a greater relevance of messages related to driving and pregnancy to consumers' immediate goals and the fact that long-term health consequences such as liver disease and cancer are more distal and probabilistic in nature.

Curiously, the mere presence of a warning seems to increase the likelihood of hazard reduction even when the danger is well-known, perhaps by serving as a reminder. For example, Viscusi, Magat, and Huber (1986) found that different types of information and formats influenced respondents' self-reported propensity for taking precautions. In particular, they found that any of three warnings on two household cleaning products increased respondents' self-reported propensities to engage in precautionary behaviors relative to no warning. Nevertheless, despite well-known information about potential dangers, consumers continue to use products and engage in behaviors that are unsafe, at least at some level. The argument that "if people just knew better, they would change their behavior" is not supported by common experience. Neither is it supported by empirical studies. For example, empirical research on package inserts for pharmaceutical products has found these inserts to be generally effective in providing information to users (Morris, Mazis, and Gordon 1977), but the inserts have not been found to alter behavior (Dwyer 1978; Morris and Kanouse 1982).

Many studies have failed to find strong effects of warning messages on behavior (for a notable but rare exception, see Hankin et al. 1993). Some researchers have argued that such results are attributable to the content of the message rather than an indication of the inherent limitations of warnings. For example, Mayer, Smith, and Scammon (1991) suggested that their failure to find effects of warning labels (for alcohol) on risk perceptions (dangers of drinking while pregnant) and behavior (drinking and driving) might have been because warnings on alcoholic beverages contain well-known information and state the obvious (i.e., risks of drinking and driving). These researchers suggested that warnings would be more effective if they provided specific information that is not widely known. They concluded, "Without such information, one should not be surprised if people ignore labels and rationalize their content" (p. 714). These researchers suggested that when information offered in a warning is not sufficiently compelling (persuasive), perhaps other information not contained in the warning might be more compelling. As Stewart and Martin (1994) observed, this type of argument cannot be refuted. No matter how much information might be provided, there always might be some new or different information that could be offered in a warning in a new and different format. Furthermore, any new information, when repeated often enough, is likely to become well-known and potentially less effective.

There are many reasons why consumers fail to heed warnings even though they are aware of them. As noted in the earlier discussion, consumers might not understand a warning, or they might not find it credible. It also might be the case that consumers understand and accept the content of the warning but choose not to act on it after evaluating the costs and benefits of complying or not complying. A consumer might decide that the risks associated with smoking are not sufficient to give up whatever benefits the consumer believes he or she derives from this activity. Likewise, a consumer might deliberately take a greater dose of an analgesic than is recommended because he or she desires the benefit of a stronger dose. Indeed, the knowledge that an analgesic has been available by prescription in higher doses might lead a consumer to assume that a warning overstates the risk of the product. It also might be the case that the cost or inconvenience of compliance is perceived to be greater than the risk posed by the product. For example, a consumer might find it inconvenient to wear protective glasses when using a power tool for a very brief period, especially if the consumer feels especially skilled and experienced in using the tool. Consumers simply might feel unable to take the recommended steps. Protection motivation theory emphasizes the importance of feelings of self-efficacy in responding to information about a threat. Warnings about the health risks of cigarette smoking are effective only when adolescents and young adults feel that they have the ability to effectively cope with and avert the threatened danger (Sturges and Rogers 1996). Finally, a consumer might decide that the immediate benefits of consumption of a given product are sufficiently desirable that he or she discounts a low probability of harm that might occur only at some point in the distant future. Thus, the consumer might continue to drink heavily because he or she enjoys the immediate relief from tension provided by the alcohol and considers the risk of health impairment to be small. Even if harm were to occur, it might not occur until many years in the future.

Desensitization to Warnings

Another reason why consumers might not attend to warnings could be related to both their ubiquity and the occasional well-publicized retraction of prior warning information (Breznitz 1984). Evidence on this point is quite limited, but it is sufficient to raise questions worthy of future research and to suggest caution in the indiscriminant use of warnings. Magat, Viscusi, and Huber (1988) reported evidence that too frequent exposure to individual warnings or exposure to warnings that are unduly intrusive might diminish or even eliminate their effectiveness. Quite apart from the effects of repeated exposure to any given warning, there is the question of the effects of associating warnings with a vast array of products, services, and environments that differ considerably in the probability of harm and the severity of consequences associated with them.

Although there is no doubt that consumers are well served by better information about the potential risks associated with products, any particular warning exists in a broader context that includes all other warnings, media reports, word-of-mouth communications, and a host of other sources of information about risk. The influence of this context on the effects of warnings has not been well explored in empirical research, nor has it been widely addressed in policy-making forums. The issue is related to current debates in the risk analysis literature over what types of environmental and health risks should be communicated to the public and in what form (Fischhoff 1990; Fisher 1991; Keeney and von Winterfeldt 1991; Weterings and van Eijndhoven 1989). The nexus of this debate is how to ensure an informed public about a wide range of risks without creating a public or segment of the public that either overreacts to small risks or discounts genuine hazards.

Psychological Reactance as a Result of Message Frequency

Although there is evidence that frequent exposure to and familiarity with some warnings tends to reduce subsequent attention, it is unclear whether there are more serious negative effects associated with the ubiquity of warnings. There is empirical evidence that repeated exposures to the same message at high levels of intensity can produce irritation, counterargumentation, and behavior that is inconsistent with the message (Cacioppo and Petty 1979; Calder and Sternthal 1980; Pechmann and Stewart 1988; Petty and Cacioppo 1986). Research in psychology, communications, and marketing also has demonstrated that individuals may react negatively to messages that appear to demand a particular response and/or appear to restrict individual choice (Brehm and Brehm 1981; Clee and Wicklund 1980; McGillis and Brehm 1975; Sensenig and Brehm 1988; Snyder and Wicklund 1976; Wicklund and Brehm 1968; Worchel and Brehm 1970). This phenomenon is referred to as psychological reactance.

Psychological reactance has not been examined carefully within the context of warnings. (For a more in-depth review of this phenomenon in a warning context, see Stewart and Martin 1994.) There is some research (reviewed later) that suggests reactance-like outcomes. That is, behavior that is directly counter to that suggested by the warning may occur in response to exposure to warnings, at least among some consumers. However, the specific processes that produce such outcomes in response to warnings have not been examined. This is a particularly important issue for future research because work in the goal literature suggests that there are ways in which to communicate information without inducing reactance (Austin and Vancouver 1996).

Consumers' Perceptions of Risk

Any discussion of the effectiveness of warnings must consider how consumers make trade-offs between the potentially harmful consequences of a given behavior and the costs and benefits associated with that behavior. Indeed, this is a particularly interesting and important issue because many products that offer important benefits for consumers also have some associated risks. Understanding how consumers make decisions about product use in such circumstances would provide considerable insight into how warning messages influence behavior. Rather little research has examined this important issue. The research that has been conducted indicates that consumers tend to discount consequences that are more distant in time while giving greater weight to more immediate outcomes (Wright and Weitz 1977). Such behavior may be rational in many circumstances in which risks are low and probabilistic, but that is not always the case. Only by understanding how consumers evaluate the full array of positive and negative consequences of product use is it possible to understand why consumers act or fail to act in accordance with warning messages. It might be possible to influence consumer perceptions of risks, hazards, and costs of compliance through the contents or format of a warning, but the final evaluation of the message ultimately will be determined by the specific utilities of the individual consumer.

Message processing might not always produce rational behavior. A risk-averse consumer might choose to avoid a product altogether rather than to exercise the care and prudence suggested by a warning. For example, Rozin, Markwith, and Ross (1990) found that the presence of a warning created the perception of potential hazard even for "safe" products with which consumers were familiar. Such perceptions may arise either because consumers are very risk averse or because they overestimate the hazards associated with a product. Although the frequency of such overestimation effects has not been well established, there is evidence that it occurs. Viscusi (1990) demonstrated that consumers overestimate the actual risk of smoking in response to the warning messages found on tobacco products and advertising. Research on risk perception has shown a general tendency for individuals to overestimate the likelihood of low-probability events, particularly when those events are easily brought to mind as a result of either their salience or their recency (Kahneman, Slovic, and Tversky 1982). One factor that may influence the salience of an event is the presence of a warning.

On the other hand, consumers are likely to underestimate risks associated with many products when warnings are not present. Laughery and Stanush (1989) reported evidence that warning messages that are insufficiently explicit might lead some consumers to underestimate a potential hazard, but their results also are consistent with the proposition that more explicit warnings cause consumers to think that products are more dangerous and that more severe injuries are likely than is actually the case. Because no direct measure of consumers' risk knowledge was obtained in this study, and because there was no comparison of risk perceptions with the actual risk associated with the products, the results of the study are inconclusive. In any case, these researchers found that stronger, more explicit warnings reduced the likelihood of product purchase for only one of the nine products they examined.

There also are situations in which consumers underestimate their personal risk in response to a warning because they view themselves as more careful or more skilled than the average consumer. Such feelings of personal immunity are common and explain a great deal of risk-taking behavior (Slovic, Fischhoff, and Lichtenstein 1980; Svenson, Fischhoff, and MacGregor 1985). Such feelings also provide a partial explanation for the inverse relationship between product familiarity and the perceived hazardousness of a product discussed earlier in the chapter. The dilemma suggested by such findings is that a consumer might not be well informed regardless of whether a warning is present or not. Wildavsky (1991) noted the importance of ensuring that warnings lead to neither underestimates nor overestimates of risk, but this problem has received scant attention from marketing and public policy researchers.

Risk Seekers

Stewart and Martin (1994) observed that a source of excitement for some people, both individually and within certain cliques, could be the transgression of restrictions imposed by law and taboo in a society. For example, Taylor (1976) noted that there are certain segments of society that seek out activities that are high in perceived risk. Warnings might draw attention to risks that some people intentionally choose to take. When asked about their reasons for risk taking, these individuals often indicate that risk taking is a means to other goals such as social acceptance and a thrilling experience. For example, a set of usage instructions for toxic products such as paint thinner may include a set of latex gloves to prevent injury. The instructions and the inclusion of the gloves might trigger a reaction of risk-seeking behavior in which the individual elects not to use the gloves. Warnings may represent a signal of opportunities for risk taking in such circumstances. Little research has examined this issue, but there is some modest support for the proposition that warnings can make products more attractive, at least in certain circumstances.

A study in England found that the presence of warnings on cigarette packages increased the desire to smoke among housewives who smoked but had no effect on nonsmoking housewives (Hyland and Birrell 1979). The authors suggested that the warning creates such extreme dissonance for smokers' belief systems that they reject the validity of the information rather than accept it. Such an explanation is consistent with the concept of reactance discussed earlier. Similarly, Snyder and Blood (1991) found that among young adult consumers of alcoholic beverages, warnings on alcoholic beverages had a "boomerang effect." Young drinkers in the study who were exposed to warnings rated the benefits of drinking more favorably and expressed higher drinking intentions than did comparable respondents who were not exposed to warnings. A similar boomerang effect was found in an earlier study of high school students exposed to anti-drug public service announcements (Feingold and Knapp 1977). Andrews, Netemeyer, and Durvasula (1990) found that the more favorable consumers' attitudes toward drinking, the more likely they were not to believe proximate consequences such as birth defects and driving impairment. The reasons for such findings are unclear. Snyder and Blood (1991) attributed them to teen or subculture rebellion and to the fact that the dangers specified in warnings are temporally remote for young persons. Although such factors undoubtedly are at work, it is unlikely that this is the complete answer to the question of how these effects are produced. Neither is it clear that such effects are unique to products such as cigarettes and alcohol.

Schneider (1977) found that the words "DANGER POISON" increased the attractiveness of a product among children relative to no warning. Even a small written warning was more attractive than no warning. The more information that was provided, the more attractive the package was for children, other things being equal. The use of poison symbols (Mr. Yuk or a skull and crossbones) produced a modest reduction in the attractiveness of the product, but these symbols tended to interact with other product and label characteristics. For example, when the product was scented (either with a pleasant scent or with an antiseptic scent), the presence of a poison symbol increased the attractiveness of the product.

Urzic (1984) also reported results suggesting that people might find products with warnings more attractive, at least in some circumstances. He suggested that one reason for this might be that people infer that products with warnings are more effective or powerful than products without warnings. Some products also may be purchased and used because there is some risk associated with them. For example, sports cars, all-terrain vehicles, various "adventure" vacation packages, and even rides at amusement parks often find their appeal in the risk or perception of risk associated with them. Relevant to this issue are the findings of Boddewyn (1986), who discovered that curiosity about the dangers of smoking were correlated with risk-taking behaviors among adolescents. There also have been suggestions that violence ratings on records and television shows might attract individuals who use such ratings as a signal for a particular type of entertainment. Warning labels for violent television programs increase interest in those programs more than do information labels (Bushman 1996). The effect is strongest for high-reactance individuals and for labels citing authoritative sources. Likewise, labels on alcoholic beverages that report high levels of alcohol content might make certain beverages more attractive to some consumers by virtue of the higher alcohol content. A warning label about the dangers of high-fat food elicited more interest in tasting a full-fat food than a reduced-fat food compared to a label merely providing information about the food's fat content (Bushman 1998).

These empirical findings regarding risk-seeking and curiosity effects, modest as they are, would suggest caution about indiscriminant and uninformed use of warning messages. Warnings that produce psychological reactance, that serve as signals for risk-taking opportunities, or that make a product more attractive may produce behavior that is exactly the opposite of that intended by the placement of the warning, at least among certain groups of individuals. Such effects clearly are unintended, but their consequences may, under some circumstances, make the use of warning messages less desirable than no message at all. Certainly, an understanding of how such undesirable effects might be diminished or eliminated would be useful for guiding public policy. Such findings also provide further evidence that the responses of consumers to warnings are not uniform. Individual differences appear to have an important influence on responses to warnings. Rather little research has sought to systematically examine what individual differences determine the differential responses of consumers to warnings and how these individual differences interact with message characteristics to produce cognitive, affective, and behavioral outcomes. This is an area where examination of the influence of goals within the context of the specific goals of the message recipient may be especially useful.

Suggestibility and Risk Perception

Although evidence suggests that warnings can increase risk taking among some individuals, there also have been suggestions that warnings may increase risk aversion in some situations and among certain recipients. A number of researchers have suggested that the listing of various side effects or adverse consequences of product use may cause people to "experience" such effects, particularly in the context of medicinal products (Loftus and Fries 1979). The logic behind this suggestion is that certain individuals may be highly suggestible and, therefore, experience effects in response to a warning that they would not otherwise experience but for the warning. These effects may lead these individuals to believe that the product is more dangerous or potent than it really is. Such effects also may cause individuals to avoid or discontinue use of the product.

Empirical studies of this issue, which are few in number and not of especially recent origin, generally have failed to find support for such suggestibility effects. Myers and Calvert (1973, 1976, 1978) and Weibert (1977) examined this issue and found no evidence that someone informed that a medication had greater numbers of side effects believed the medication to be more risky than did someone not so informed. On the other hand, there is evidence that knowledge of side effects makes consumers more likely to attribute any side effects that do occur to the product, even when the specific side effects are not explicitly identified (Dwyer 1978; Morris and Kanouse 1982). Such effects could be detrimental to a consumer's welfare if they caused the consumer to forgo use of the product. However, this does not appear to be the case. Morris and Kanouse (1982) reported that informing individuals of potential side effects did not increase the probability of discontinuance. Dwyer (1978) also found that informing individuals about side effects of medications did not increase their anxiety about the drug treatment. Morris and Kanouse (1982) suggested that information about side effects might even have the positive effect of increasing consumers' involvement in monitoring their health.

The research on this issue has largely focused on changes in perception and behavior in monadic tests, that is, tests involving the presentation of a single product. In many purchase situations, consumers confront choices among competing products where warnings might not provide comparable information (because the risks differ) but where consumers might need to make comparisons of the relative risk associated with the available alternatives. Such comparisons are especially daunting because they require that consumers generate some assessment of risk that is comparable across alternatives when both the information available and the nature of the risk may differ across products. For example, when comparing insecticides or over-the-counter analgesics, consumers may confront products that differ in the types of risk, degrees of risk associated with particular types of risk, and differences in the amount and specificity of information provided on the warning labels. In such situations, consumers might well conclude that a product with a warning containing less information about hazards is safer than one with a warning containing far more information when, in fact, the reality might be the opposite. This problem has especially important implications for social welfare and public policy because it suggests that warnings for any one product in a category should not be designed without consideration of the warnings present on competitive products.

Characteristics of the Purchase and Usage Environment

Research on the processing of warnings makes it clear how difficult it is to separate the efficacy of a given warning message from the prior experience of the message recipient. In addition, the effects of warnings cannot be easily divorced from other types of communication about safe practices, instructions on the use of the product, and the meaning of specific symbols and words that may indicate the presence of a hazard or a means for avoiding potential harm. Such findings also are consistent with more general research on consumer behavior suggesting that the interaction of the individual differences, characteristics of occasions, and specific environmental stimuli provides a more robust explanation for consumer behavior than does an examination of individual effects (Punj and Stewart 1983).

Context Effects

Several studies have demonstrated higher levels of comprehension of warning messages or symbols when they are placed within the specific usage context rather than presented to respondents without a context (Cahill 1976; Galer 1980; Simpson and Williams 1980). Likewise, several empirical studies have shown that strong cultural differences exist with respect to the meaning of nonverbal symbols (Cairney and Sless 1982; Easterby and Zwaga 1976; Sinaiko 1975; Winter 1963). Cahill (1975, 1976) suggested that warning messages, particularly those communicated by symbols, may be most helpful to individuals with intermediate levels of knowledge and experience. The assumption underlying this proposition is that the novice does not understand the symbol, whereas the highly experienced individual is unlikely to need or want a reminder.

The earlier discussion of factors related to attention to warnings suggested that contextual factors such as prior familiarity with a product, prior familiarity with warning information, and the perceived hazardness of the product influence the ways in which consumers interact with warnings. These factors, among others, also appear to influence the ways in which warning information is processed. For example, Smith (1990) found that respondents who consumed beer generally were less concerned about the safety of alcohol. Warnings on alcoholic beverages had less effect on their beliefs about the safety of alcohol than on a group of respondents for whom alcohol was less relevant (see also Andrews, Netemeyer, and Durvasula 1990). Lehto and Miller (1986) noted that research on risk perceptions suggests that higher levels of risk are more acceptable when the risk is perceived as voluntary, controllable, and familiar. These authors speculated that warnings may serve to make risk more acceptable by making it more voluntary, controllable, and familiar (see also Fisher 1991).

The Role of Distraction

The phenomenon of selectively choosing to attend to certain information while ignoring other information has been described as selective exposure (Zillmann and Bryant 1985). As seen previously, two factors that may trigger this behavior are the lack of personal relevance (e.g., the information does not fit with the individual's salient goal) and familiarity with the stimulus. Some policy makers and researchers have attributed results showing that consumers often ignore warnings to the structure and content of the packages or advertisements that have been posited as drawing attention away from the warning (Surgeon General 1989). Similarly, Johnston and Dark (1990) suggested that an object might fail to attain awareness because another object is selected instead.

Some empirical research on warnings suggests that selective exposure consists mainly of low attention to the warning message and not heightened attention to other elements of the message (e.g., product label, packaging) (Chaffee and Miyo 1985). Other research suggests that distraction may occur under certain conditions; that is, the content and characteristics of an advertisement or a package are most likely to distract the consumer from the information contained in a warning when the consumer is unfamiliar with a product and there are constraints placed on the time available for examining the product.[1] For example, Morris, Mazis, and Brinberg (1989) reported a study of warnings for fictional drugs demonstrating that higher awareness and knowledge of product risks were accompanied by lower awareness of product benefits. Likewise, higher awareness of product benefits tended to be associated with lower awareness of product risks. Such research suggests that consumers may make trade-offs about what information to attend to when confronted with large amounts of information in a short time. These trade-offs might be driven by the types of usage goals that guide consumers' information processing. Consumers who are not previously acquainted with a product are more likely to focus on information about what a product is and what benefits it provides. Only after determining whether the product is relevant to their own individual goals will consumers become interested in warning information.

Research by Strawbridge (1985) and Friedmann (1988) supports the view that consumers' product familiarity and goals guide attention to specific product information and the order in which they attend to information. These researchers found that when consumers are less familiar with a product, they are more likely to focus on information about product attributes and uses than on warning information. This does not mean, however, that consumers do not attend to warning information on subsequent exposure occasions. It does suggest that more than one opportunity for exposure might be required before a warning is attended to and processed by consumers. There also is evidence that a warning can distract consumers from other information on a product or in an advertisement. Clark and Brock (1993) reported results of a study demonstrating that moving a warning to a central location within an advertisement where it was more likely to gain the attention of consumers distracted participants from processing the advertisement's positive information about the product. This distraction resulted in a less positive attitude toward the advertised product than was the case when the warning was in a less prominent location, at least on initial exposure.

Although trade-offs when processing information might be necessary in some circumstances, it is likely that distraction will decline as exposure opportunities increase for three reasons. First, there are additional opportunities to attend to the warning. Second, selective attention is not confined to warnings. As consumers learn the content of a product package or an advertisement, they are less likely to attend to those elements with which they are already familiar and more likely to attend to those elements that remain novel. Third, if and when consumers decide that a product is something they should use, their goals will shift to product use and the acquisition of information relevant to product use. The potential for distraction effects on first exposure to a product or an advertisement does suggest that research on the efficacy of warnings needs to account for the effects of repeated exposures and the prior familiarity of consumers with a product or an advertisement. Research on distraction, familiarity, and desensitization effects would appear to suggest that the greatest attention to warning messages will occur at intermediate stages of product familiarity and use, after consumers have determined what the product is and how it is used and before becoming so familiar with the product and information about it that warnings are largely ignored and/or discounted.

Availability of Enabling Factors

There also is evidence that warnings that provide instructions for reducing or eliminating the potential hazard or that provide the means for reducing the hazard are more likely to induce compliance (Leventhal, Singer, and Jones 1965; Wogalter et al. 1987). For example, if a warning calls for the use of gloves, then the cost of compliance can be reduced by providing disposable gloves with the product. Bettman, Payne, and Staelin (1986) recommended organizing warnings in a manner that clearly associates the means for avoiding dangers with the dangers. Instructions about how to avoid a hazard may be most effective in situations in which consumers are unlikely to know how to cope with the potential hazard. When the coping response is well-known, the warning itself may be sufficient to induce compliance (Lehto and Miller 1986). This is consistent with self-efficacy beliefs regarding the personal resources (e.g., time, effort) that individuals believe they have to accomplish a goal such as avoiding a hazard (Bandura 1986). Protection motivation theory predicts that the efficacy of the warning (and its recommended actions) can be the most important predictor of behavioral compliance. Thus, when an individual sees a direct link between a particular behavior (e.g., drinking while pregnant) and the desired outcome (e.g., giving birth to a healthy child), then the health warning will be adopted (Block and Keller 1995).

Lowering the costs of compliance also should increase the probability of behavior consistent with the warning message. Lowering the costs of compliance, however, is likely to require more than a change in a warning message. Rather, lowering the costs of compliance may require providing protective equipment, telephone hotlines, and/or comprehensive safety training programs. Research suggests that the greater and more probable the perceived danger, the more likely consumers will take precautions (Friedmann 1988). Although this would appear to suggest that warning messages should be written in the strongest language possible, there might be a danger that an exaggerated threat will be less credible or will discourage use of the product in some cases. Finally, there is evidence that consumers differ with respect to their perceptions about the effectiveness of their own precautionary behaviors. Laux and Brelsford (1989) reported results suggesting that compliance with a warning might be increased if consumers' beliefs about their ability to prevent accidents were increased. Such findings suggest that warnings or instructions that reinforce beliefs about consumers' ability to control accidents may be useful.

The presence of a warning, even one that consumers attend to and comprehend, is no assurance that consumers will behave in a manner consistent with the contents of the warning. Research to date, however limited, demonstrates that some consumers persist in potentially harmful activities even when they are well aware of potentially harmful consequences. This has led to some pessimistic conclusions about the efficacy of warnings (McCarthy et al. 1984). On the other hand, there is evidence that warnings can affect behavior, at least in some circumstances and among certain individuals (Hankin et al. 1993; Hankin, Sloan, and Sokol 1998). The critical question begging further research is not whether warnings can affect behavior but rather under what circumstances and among what types of consumers various types of warnings influence message processing, behavioral intention, and actual behavior. Future research should consider consumers' motivation, opportunity, and ability to process warning information (Moorman and Matulich 1993).

Implications for the Design of Warning Messages

A central feature of the debate surrounding warnings is the question of what constitutes an effective warning. Some contend that warnings are effective insofar as they inform consumers (Laughery et al. 1993; Lehto and Miller 1986). This perspective holds that manufacturers cannot be held responsible for the actions of consumers who have been reasonably informed of the potential hazards associated with a product and its use. For example, tobacco manufacturers in product liability cases have used this argument as a defense (see, e.g., *Cippolone v. Liggett Group Inc. et al.* 1988). At the other extreme in the effectiveness debate are those who suggest that warnings are effective only if they alter behavior (Beltramini 1988; Hadden 1991; Hilton 1993; Peters 1984). For example, Hilton (1993) argued that the principal criterion for judging the effectiveness of warning labels on alcoholic beverages should be a measurable change in the risk behavior described in the warning. The latter view tends to discount the role of the individual in determining whether to take precautions against a potential hazard.

The criteria used to evaluate the effectiveness of warnings have direct implications for their design. Messages designed to inform may take a very different form from those designed to persuade individuals to behave in a particular fashion. For example, an explicit statement of the consequences associated with a particular action (or inaction) and of the probability that a particular action (or inaction) will reduce the potential for harm might be more important in a message designed to persuade than in one designed only to inform (Bettman, Payne, and Staelin 1986). Thus, any effort to understand the effects and effectiveness of warnings must consider multiple and potentially inconsistent effects. Lehto and Miller (1986) noted that warning messages often are "arbitrarily assumed to be either effective or ineffective without adequate research upon which to base such assumptions" (p. 51). Categorizing warnings as either effective or ineffective is naive at best. The question is not one of effectiveness in the abstract but rather one of effectiveness in accomplishing specific objectives. For example, objectives might be defined in terms of attitude change or actual behavioral compliance, responses that can differ for the same message. Bushman (1998) offered empirical evidence that a warning label about the consequences of a high-fat diet was less effective than a label merely providing information about a food's fat content in discouraging people from wanting to taste the food, but the same label related to consequences was equally effective in discouraging consumers from eating high-fat foods.

Further complicating the problem of defining an effective warning is the aggregation problem. Warnings generally are designed to reach large groups of people, and each individual recipient may respond to a warning in a different way. Some individuals may consider warning information irrelevant or too technical to be of use. Some individuals may already know about the potential hazard or may have information about how to avoid the hazard. Some message recipients may be predisposed to believe warning messages, whereas others may be inclined to reject the information. The net utility of such communication is the sum of its effects on all recipients. Individual-level effects might not necessarily be the same and might even be contradictory. This is consistent with the findings of a meta-analysis conducted by Cox and colleagues (1997). In this examination of the literature, the authors stated that the behavioral effectiveness of warnings among different target segments is an important area for future research.

Given the wide variance in types, purposes, and measures of the effects of warning messages and the number of products for which some adverse event can be imaged, it is not surprising that the use of warnings has sparked considerable debate (Calfee 1992; Freedman 1989). This debate has been all the more heated as a result of studies suggesting that warnings might have unintended negative effects such as discouraging use of a product that offers important benefits when used appropriately and signaling the opportunity for risk taking (Stewart and Martin 1994). A warning, at least in some form, may create the impression that a product is more dangerous than it really is or may be more dangerous than an alternative that does not contain a warning (Rozin, Markwith, and Ross 1990; Viscusi 1990, 1991). In an important meta-analysis, Cox and colleagues (1997) provided support for this view. As noted earlier, there also is some evidence that warnings might make products more attractive to some individuals (Hyland and Birrell 1979; Snyder and Blood 1991).

A possible solution to the unintended negative consequences of warnings and other usage information is to use a goal hierarchy framework in the design of messages. The hierarchical structure of goals can provide a framework to construct marketing communications that are consistent with the underlying motivational structure of consumers (cf. Austin and Vancouver 1996). Placing usage information into an "in order to" structure facilitates comprehension and use of the information to comply with the intended meaning.

Finally, information directed at very specific target populations might not be relevant to consumers who are not in such populations. Thus, an understanding of the effects of warnings must include an explicit consideration of the relevance of the information. This suggests that research on warnings employing convenience samples that are not representative of the intended audience(s) for a warning might not provide results that are generalizable to a larger population. It also suggests that results obtained within one segment of a larger population might not be representative of results that would be obtained within another segment of the population, even if a warning were relevant to both segments. Table 15.1 summarizes the multiple considerations involved in designing an effective warning.

TABLE 15.1 Steps in Designing Warning Messages

1. Identify the objective(s) for providing information:
   - Influence consumers
   - Protect manufacturers from product liability
   - Satisfy special interest groups
   - Conform to regulations and laws
   - Conform to societal norms

2. Characterize the information recipient:
   - Ascertain the recipient's ability to respond to information in the message (e.g., vocabulary, cognitive skills, product knowledge)
   - Determine the recipient's motivation to respond to information (e.g., reactance, predisposition toward message, feelings of personal immunity, message involvement, salient usage goals, risk perceptions)

3. Specify the desired type of influence on the message recipient (often includes finding out what recipient wants from information):
   - Awareness
   - Knowledge
   - Comprehension
   - Persuasion
   - Behavior
   - Product satisfaction

4. Describe the context within which information will be received:
   - Distracters in the message environment
   - Salience of message relative to other aspects of the product

5. Identify message factors that achieve the desired goal within the usage context (includes the impact of various elements when used in combination with the message):
   - Relevance of the information to the individual
   - Meaningfulness of negative information to the individual
   - Use of words versus symbols or icons
   - Repetition of the information
   - Alternating messages

6. Recognize negative and unintended consequences of message (often includes identifying what recipient does not want as well as what recipient truly wants):
   - Creating beliefs about side effects from noncompliance
   - Changing beliefs about product efficacy
   - Instigating risk-seeking behavior
   - Provoking curiosity about proscribed product or procedure
   - Desensitizing message recipient to warnings
   - Creating false alarms

7. Select the best option to achieve the desired goal(s)

8. Test effects of the message on relevant target populations (e.g., use strategic research and copy testing techniques)

9. Make the necessary revisions

Implications for Public Policy

From a public policy perspective, extant research on warning messages and their effects makes clear that the issues are far more complex than the simple question of whether to warn or not to warn. The effects and effectiveness of warnings tend to be multidimensional, context dependent, and population specific. It is probably overly optimistic to expect that warning messages will produce changes in behavior beyond those that are attributable to informing the consumer of potential hazards and, perhaps, how these hazards might be avoided. Ensuring that consumers are adequately informed is a challenging task, and the complexity of this task requires the same types of copy testing research that are common in the design of advertising messages. Furthermore, it is clear that different messages might be required for different populations and for different settings, although it also is clear that individuation of messages is not economically feasible. Policy makers should have a clear understanding of what motivates consumers to use products and how consumers use products. This information would help to guide the policy-making strategies that are undertaken to inform various target populations concerning the risks of product use.

The law of unintended consequences certainly applies to the design and use of warning messages. Because warning messages can have unintended yet predictable consequences, it is important to test for these consequences and seek ways in which to reduce or eliminate them. One way to better understand and predict the potential for negative consequences from warning information is to understand the underlying motivational structure of target populations. For example, a target population that is motivated by the usage goals of risk seeking and excitement might need to have risk information presented in a different form and format (e.g., education program on the risks associated with noncompliance).

Such unintended consequences include both increasing the attractiveness of a product in some populations and creating an unrealistic fear of product use that reduces the likelihood that consumers will buy and use the product for the benefits that are actually provided. Aside from issues associated with the design of specific warnings for individual products, there is a need for policy makers to consider the impact of the proliferation of warnings. If everything is hazardous or requires precautions in use, then products with greater hazards might not be distinguished from those that require lesser precautions and carry lower risks of harm. A critical issue for public policy is helping consumers to differentiate greater risks from lesser risks associated with the use of products. Another public policy challenge is that of ensuring that the risks of all real and imagined hazards for all consumers are not borne solely by the product provider. Consumers who ignore warnings or who do not make reasonable efforts to become informed about product hazards and the means for reducing them must bear responsibility for their own decisions, however catastrophic the outcomes of product use. Indeed, the empirical evidence appears to suggest that some government-mandated warnings produce unintended and adverse outcomes for some consumers.

Implications for Future Research

Many substantive issues that require further research have been identified throughout this chapter. However, it may be helpful to underscore some of the more general points. That some consumers fail to act on warning messages does not mean that warnings in general or any specific warnings are ineffective. Virtually all empirical studies to date suggest that an individual who reads a warning message or remembers its contents is more likely to comply with it (Hilton 1993; Laughery et al. 1993). The presence of a warning alone, however, has not been demonstrated to be sufficient to ensure that all persons will act on the information contained in the warning by changing either their attitudes or their behaviors. Nevertheless, evidence that compliance increases with attention to and processing of warnings suggests that the factors contributing to a higher probability that consumers will attend to and process warning labels represent important areas for future inquiry.

Processing of information remains one of the most infrequently studied facets of consumers' responses to warnings. This is unfortunate given that there is a considerable body of theory and research in marketing and cognitive psychology on which such work might build. Indeed, a great deal of research has examined the general issue of risk perception, but this research has not been widely applied in the design of warnings for consumer products, nor has much research on warnings to consumers built on these more general research efforts been widely applied. In addition, there is an extensive literature on the processing of goal-related information that could be used as a basis to better understand what consumers do with warning information. Research on goals and processing of warnings might well help to explain why individuals differ in their responses to warnings and to provide better insight into the reasons for the conflicting findings regarding the influence of warnings on behavior. Table 15.2 provides a description of the various issues related to the design and use of warnings, the effects of warnings, and extant theory that may inform research questions related to warnings.

Investigators have examined the influence of a variety of message, consumer, and context characteristics but have not always clarified at what stage that influence occurs or how factors interact to moderate effects of other factors. Table 15.3 indicates the ways in which some factors may facilitate or hinder the extent to which consumers pay attention to, comprehend, are persuaded by, and act on usage information. Some of these factors seem to have the same effect directionally regardless of the information processing stage; for example, distracting influences in the environment are likely to hinder attention, comprehension, persuasion, and adherence to the behaviors. Other factors seem to be particularly influential at certain stages; for example, the use of color seems to be more important in influencing attention than at later points in the communication process.

The numerous conflicting findings in the literature on the influence of warnings appear to be the result of a failure to explicitly recognize that the same

TABLE 15.2 Warning Messages and Theory

Type of Warning	Example	Literature(s)
Usage messages		
Conceptual information	Alcohol causes birth defects	Attribution theory
		Motivated reasoning
Product category information	Poison symbol	Categorization theory
		Product knowledge/expertise
Context	Use in well-ventilated area	Decision making
Procedures to follow	Use gloves when applying	Attitudes and behavior
		Cognitive reassurance theory
		Categorization theory
		Goals and goal-directed behavior
		Product knowledge/expertise
		Motivated reasoning
Procedures to avoid	Do not inhale	Psychological reactance theory
		Protection motivation theory
		Categorization theory
		Benefit-cost analysis
		Goals and goal-directed behavior
Outcomes from usage messages		
Probabilities	Use of aspirin rarely leads to Reyes syndrome	Perceived risk
		Risk communication
		Counterargumentation
		Message framing effects
Remedies for misuse	Flush with water	Gain-loss
		Motivated reasoning
		Goal-derived categorization
		Product knowledge/expertise

factor can facilitate the processing, evaluation, and actions associated with a message at one stage but can hinder these processes and outcomes at other stages. For example, consumers appear to pay less attention to usage information that is familiar to them, but when they do pay attention, they comprehend the information better. Furthermore, factors interact; a sufficiently motivated consumer's comprehension of a message might not be hindered by message complexity. Such interactions have been given less attention but may explain why the literature appears to be filled with seemingly contradictory results. In sum, there are many research opportunities in identifying those factors that influence consumers and how these many factors interact with one another.

TABLE 15.3 Stages in the Hierarchy of Effects Model at Which Some Factors Influence the Processing of Usage Information

Types of Influencer	Attention	Comprehension	Persuasion	Behavior
Consumer related	+ Goal congruency + Relevance − Familiarity with message − Familiarity with low-risk product	+ Goal congruency + Familiarity	+ Goal congruency + Preexisting consistent attitudes − False alarm experiences − Voluntary controllable risks − Product familiarity − Warning familiarity	+ Goal congruency + Simple message − Perceived benefits from noncompliance − Feelings of personal immunity − Risk-seeking behavior
Message related	+ Pictures, symbols, and icons + Simple message + Variation in the messages − Complexity of message − Pictures and icons (e.g., Joe Camel)	+ Explicit, precise written message + Simple message + Novel information + Well-understood symbols and signal words − Pictures and icons − Use of probabilistic information − Risk information	+ Warning messages sponsored by the marketer of the product + Actions specified − Unduly intrusive messages − Overly simplistic	+ Behavioral instructions for avoiding hazards + Immediate benefits stated − Distal negative consequences − Inconvenience
Situation related	+ Novelty of situation[a] − Distractions − Retraction of prior warning information	+ Message received in the usage context − Time	+ Consistent experiences − Novel information[a]	+ Convenient implements − Obstacles to compliance

Note

1. Such constraints may be imposed by the characteristics of the study in which a consumer participates (e.g., a forced-exposure task with time limits) or by the consumer as a result of other demands on his or her time.

References

Andrews, J. Craig, Richard G. Netemeyer, and Srinivas Durvasula (1990), "Believability and Attitudes toward Alcohol Warning Label Information: The Role of Persuasive Communications Theory," *Journal of Public Policy and Marketing,* 9 (1), 1-15.

———, ———, and ——— (1991), "Effects of Consumption Frequency on Believability and Attitudes toward Alcohol Warning Labels," *Journal of Consumer Affairs,* 25 (2), 323-38.

———, ———, and ——— (1993), "The Role of Cognitive Responses as Mediators of Alcohol Warning Label Effects," *Journal of Public Policy & Marketing,* 12 (1), 57-68.

Austin, James T. and Jeffrey B. Vancouver (1996), "Goal Constructs in Psychology: Structure, Process, and Content," *Psychological Bulletin,* 120 (3), 338-75.

Bandura, A. (1986), *Social Foundations of Thought and Action.* Englewood Cliffs, NJ: Prentice Hall.

Banks, S. M., Peter Salovey, S. Greener, Alexander J. Rothman, A. Moyer, J. Beauvais, and E. Epel (1995), "The Effects of Message Framing on Mammography Utilization," *Health Psychology,* 14, 178-84.

Beltramini, Richard F. (1988), "Perceived Believability of Warning Label Information Presented in Cigarette Advertising," *Journal of Advertising,* 17 (2), 26-32.

——— and K. R. Evans (1985), "Perceived Believability of Research Results Information in Advertising, *Journal of Advertising,* 14, 18-24, 31.

Bettman, James R., John W. Payne, and Richard Staelin (1986), "Cognitive Considerations in Designing Effective Labels for Presenting Risk Information," *Journal of Public Policy & Marketing,* 5, 1-28.

Block, Lauren G. and Punam Anand Keller (1995), "When to Accentuate the Negative: The Effects of Perceived Efficacy and Message Framing on Intentions to Perform a Health-Related Behavior," *Journal of Marketing Research,* 32 (May), 192-203.

Boddewyn, J. J. (1986), *Why Do Juveniles Start Smoking? An International Study of the Role of Advertising and Other Contributory Factors in Australia, Hong Kong, Norway, Spain, and the United Kingdom.* New York: International Advertising Association, Children's Research Unit.

Brehm, S. S. and J. W. Brehm (1981), *Psychological Reactance: A Theory of Freedom and Control.* New York: Academic Press.

Breznitz, S. (1984), *Cry Wolf: The Psychology of False Alarms.* Hillsdale, NJ: Lawrence Erlbaum.

Bushman, Brad J. (1996), "Forbidden Fruit versus Tainted Fruit: Effects of Warning Labels on Attraction to Television Violence," *Journal of Experimental Psychology: Applied,* 2 (3), 207-26.

——— (1998), "Effects of Warning and Information Labels on Consumption of Full-Fat, Reduced-Fat, and No-Fat Products," *Journal of Applied Psychology,* 83 (1), 97-101.

Cacioppo, John T. and Richard E. Petty (1979), "Effects of Message Repetition and Position on Cognitive Response, Recall, and Persuasion," *Journal of Personality and Social Psychology,* 37 (January), 97-109.

Cahill, M. C. (1975), "Interpretability of Graphic Symbols as a Function of Context and Experience Factors," *Journal of Applied Psychology,* 60 (3), 376-80.

———— (1976), "Design Features of Graphic Symbols Varying in Interpretability," *Perceptual and Motor Skills,* 42 (2), 647-53.

Cairney, P. T. and D. Sless (1982), "Communication Effectiveness of Symbolic Safety Signs with Different User Groups," *Applied Ergonomics,* 13 (June), 91-97.

Calder, Bobby J. and Brian Sternthal (1980), "Television Commercial Wearout: An Information Processing View," *Journal of Marketing Research,* 17 (May), 173-86.

Calfee, John E. (1992), "FDA's Ugly Package: Proposed Label Rules Call for Vast Changes, *Advertising Age,* March 16, 25.

Chaffee, Stephen H. and Y. Miyo (1985), "Selective Exposure and the Reinforcement Hypothesis: An Intergenerational Panel Study of the 1980 Presidential Campaign," *Communication Research,* 10 (1), 3-36.

Cippolone v. Liggett Group Inc. et al. (D.N.J. June 7, 1988), C.A. 83-8846.

Clark, Eddie M. and Timothy C. Brock (1993), "Warning Label Location, Advertising, and Cognitive Responding," in *Attention, Attitude, and Affect in Response to Advertising,* E. M. Clark, T. C. Brock, and D. W. Stewart, eds. Hillsdale, NJ: Lawrence Erlbaum.

Clee, Mona A. and Robert A. Wicklund (1980), "Consumer Behavior and Psychological Reactance," *Journal of Consumer Research,* 6 (March), 389-405.

Collins, B. L. and N. D. Lerner (1982), "Assessment of Fire-Safety Symbols," *Human Factors,* 24 (1), 75-84.

————, ————, and B. C. Pierman (1982), *Symbols for Industrial Safety* (NBSIR 82-2485). Washington, DC: National Bureau of Standards.

Cox, Eli P., III, Michael S. Wogalter, Sara L. Stokes, and Elizabeth J. Tipton-Murf (1997), "Do Product Warnings Increase Safe Behavior? A Meta-Analysis," *Journal of Public Policy & Marketing,* 16 (2), 195-204.

Detweiler, Jerusha B., Brian T. Bedell, Peter Salovey, Emily Pronin, and Alexander J. Rothman (1999), "Message Framing and Sunscreen Use: Gain-Framed Messages Motivate Beach Goers," *Health Psychology,* 18 (2), 189-96.

DiFranza, Joseph D., John W. Richards, Paul M. Freeman, Nancy Wolf-Gillespie, Christopher Fletcher, Robert D. Jaffe, and David Murray (1991), "RJR Nabisco's Cartoon Camel Promotes Camel Cigarettes to Children," *Journal of the American Medical Association,* 266 (22), 3149-53.

Dwyer, F. Robert (1978), "Consumer Processing and Use of Supplemental Drug Label Information," in *Advances in Consumer Research,* Vol. 10, Keith Hunt, ed. Provo, UT: Association for Consumer Research, 220-26.

Easterby, R. S. and S. R. Hakiel (1981), "Field Testing of Consumer Safety Signs: The Comprehension of Pictorially Presented Messages," *Applied Ergonomics,* 12 (3), 143-52.

———— and H. J. G. Zwaga (1976), "Evaluation of Public Information Symbols ISO Tests: 1975 Series," Report No. 60, University of Aston, College House.

Ellen, Pam Schroder, Paula Fitzgerald Bone, and Elnora W. Stuart (1998), "How Well Do Young People Follow the Label? An Investigation of Four Classes of Over-the-Counter Drugs," *Journal of Public Policy & Marketing,* 17 (1), 70-85.

Feingold, P. C. and M. L. Knapp (1977), "Anti-Drug Abuse Commercials," *Journal of Communication,* 27, 20-28.

Fischer, Paul M., James W. Richards, Edward J. Berman, and Daniel M. Krugman (1989), "Recall and Eye Tracking Study of Adolescents Viewing Tobacco Advertisements," *Journal of the American Medical Association,* 261, 84-89.

Fischhoff, Baruch (1990), "Understanding Long-Term Environmental Risks," *Journal of Risk and Uncertainty,* 3, 315-30.

——— (1993), "Controversies over Risk: Psychological Perspective on Competence," *Psychological Science Agenda,* 6 (2), 8-9.

Fisher, Ann (1991), "Risk Communication Challenges," *Risk Analysis,* 11 (2), 173-79.

FMC Corporation (1980), *Product Safety Signs and Label System,* 3rd ed. Santa Monica, CA: FMC Corporation.

Ford, M. E. (1992), *Motivating Humans: Goals, Emotions, and Personal Agency Beliefs.* Hillsdale, NJ: Lawrence Erlbaum.

——— and C. W. Nichols (1987), "A Taxonomy of humans goals and Some Possible Applications," in *Humans as Self-Constructing Systems: Putting the Framework to Work,* M. E. Ford and D. H. Ford, eds. Hillsdale, NJ: Lawrence Erlbaum, 289-311.

Freedman, A. M. (1989), "Rebelling against Alcohol, Tobacco Ads," *The Wall Street Journal,* November 14, B1.

Friedmann, K. (1988), "The Effect of Adding Symbols to Written Warning Labels on User Behavior and Recall," *Human Factors,* 30 (4), 507-15.

Galer, M. (1980), "An Ergonomics Approach to the Problem of High Vehicles Striking Low Bridges," *Applied Ergonomics,* 11 (March), 43-46.

Garretson, Judith A. and Scot Burton (1998), "Alcoholic Beverage Sales Promotion: An Initial Investigation of the Role of Warning Messages and Brand Characteristics among Consumers over and under the Legal Drinking Age," *Journal of Public Policy & Marketing,* 17 (1), 35-47.

Godfrey, Sandra S., Laurel Allender, Kenneth R. Laughery, and Victoria L. Smith (1983), "Warning Messages: Will the Consumer Bother to Look?" in *Proceedings of the Human Factors Society—27th Annual Meeting.* Santa Monica, CA: Human Factors Society, 950-54.

———, Pamela R. Rothstein, and Kenneth R. Laughery (1985), "Warnings: Do They Make a Difference?" in *Proceedings of the Human Factors Society 29th Annual Meeting.* Santa Monica, CA: Human Factors Society, 669-73.

Green, P. and R. W. Pew (1978), "Evaluating Pictographic Symbols: An Automotive Application," *Human Factors,* 20 (1), 103-14.

Hadden, Susan G. (1991), "Regulating Product Risks through Consumer Information," *Journal of Social Issues,* 47 (1), 93-105.

Hankin, Janet R., Ira J. Firestone, James J. Sloan, Joel W. Ager, Allen Goodman, Robert Sokol, and Susan S. Martier (1993), "The Impact of the Alcohol Warning Label on Women during Pregnancy," *Journal of Public Policy & Marketing,* 12 (1), 10-18.

———, James J. Sloan, and Robert J. Sokol (1998), "The Modest Impact of the Alcohol Beverage Warning Label on Drinking during Pregnancy among a Sample of African-American Women," *Journal of Public Policy & Marketing,* 17 (1), 61-69.

Hilton, Michael E. (1993), "An Overview of Recent Findings on Alcoholic Beverage Warning Labels," *Journal of Public Policy & Marketing,* 12 (Spring), 1-9.

Hyland, Michael and James Birrell (1979), "Government Health Warnings and the 'Boomerang' Effect," *Psychological Reports,* 44, 643-47.

Johnston, W. A. and V. J. Dark (1990), "Selective Attention," *Annual Review of Psychology,* 36, 43-75.

Kahneman, Daniel, Paul Slovic, and Amos Tversky (1982), *Judgment under Uncertainty: Heuristics and Biases.* New York: Cambridge University Press.

Katz, Benjamin J. and Jane A. Rose (1976), "Information Utilization and the Awareness Criterion in Labeling Regulation," in *Proceedings of the American Marketing Association Educators' Conference,* Kenneth Bernhardt, ed. Chicago: American Marketing Association, 202-4.

Katz, Roger C., Jay Ashmore, Elvia Barboa, Karen Trueblood, Veronica McLaughlin, and Lisa Mathews (1998), "Knowledge of Disease and Dietary Compliance in Patients with Endstage Renal Disease," *Psychological Reports,* 82 (February), 331-36.

Keeney, Ralph L. and Detlof von Winterfeldt (1991), "A Prescriptive Risk Framework for Individual Health and Safety Decisions," *Risk Analysis,* 11 (3), 523-33.

Kelley, Craig A., William C. Gaidis, and Peter H. Reingen (1989), "The Use of Vivid Stimuli to Enhance Comprehension of the Content of Product Warning Messages," *Journal of Consumer Affairs,* 23 (2), 243-66.

Lau, Hong S., Karin S. Beuning, Ennie Postma-Lim, Liesbeth Klein Beernik, Anthorios Deboer, and Arjan J. Porsius (1996), "Noncompliance in Elderly People: Evaluation of Risk Factors," *Pharmacy World and Science,* 18 (April), 63-68.

Laughery, Kenneth L. and Julie A. Stanush (1989), "Effects of Warning Explicitness on Product Perceptions," in *Proceedings of the Human Factors Society: 31st Annual Meeting.* Santa Monica, CA: Human Factors Society, 111-16.

———, Stephen L. Young, Kent P. Vaubel, and John W. Brelsford, Jr. (1993), "The Noticeability of Warnings on Alcoholic Beverage Containers," *Journal of Public Policy & Marketing,* 12 (Spring), 38-56.

Laux, L. F. and J. W. Brelsford (1989), "Locus of Control, Risk Perception, and Precautionary Behavior," in *Interface 89: The Sixth Symposium on Human Factors and Industrial Design in Consumer Products.* Santa Monica, CA: Human Factors Society, 121-24.

Lehto, Mark R. and James M. Miller (1986), *Warnings: Fundamentals, Design, and Evaluation Methodologies.* Ann Arbor, MI: Fuller Technical Publications.

Lerner, N. D. and B. L. Collins (1980), *The Assessment of Safety Symbol Understandability by Different Testing Methods* (No. PB81-185647). Washington, DC: National Bureau of Standards.

Leventhal, H., R. Singer, and S. Jones (1965), "The Effects of Fear and Specificity of Recommendations upon Attitudes and Behavior," *Journal of Personality and Social Psychology,* 2 (July), 20-29.

Levy, Alan S., Sara B. Fein, and Raymond E. Schucker (1991), "Nutrition Labeling Formats: Performance and Preference," *Food Technology,* July, 116-21.

Lewis, Christine J. and Elizabeth A. Yetley (1992), "Focus Group Sessions on Formats on Nutrition Labels," *Journal of the American Dietetic Association,* 92 (January), 62-66.

Lieberman Research (1986), *A Study of Public Attitudes toward Cigarette Advertising and Promotions Programs Conducted for American Cancer Society, American Heart Association, and American Lung Association.* Los Angeles: Lieberman Research.

Liu, J. T. and V. K. Smith (1990), "Risk Communication and Attitude Change: Taiwan's National Debate over Nuclear Power," *Journal of Risk and Uncertainty,* 3, 331-49.

Loftus, Elizabeth F. and J. F. Fries (1979), "Informed Consent may Be Hazardous to Health," *Science,* 204, 11.

MacInnis, Deborah J. and Linda L. Price (1987), "The Role of Imagery in Information Processing: Review and Extensions," *Journal of Consumer Research,* 13 (4), 473-91.

Magat, W., W. K. Viscusi, and J. Huber (1988), "Consumer Processing of Hazard Warning Information," *Journal of Risk and Uncertainty,* 1 (2), 201-32.

Martin, Ingrid M. and Valerie S. Folkes (1999), "Product Instructions as a Means to Fulfill Usage Goals," working paper, Economics Institute, University of Colorado.

Mayer, Robert N., Ken R. Smith, and Debra L. Scammon (1991), "Evaluating the Impact of Alcohol Warning Labels," in *Advances in Consumer Research,* Vol. 18, Rebecca H.

Holman and Michael R. Soloman, eds. Provo, UT: Association for Consumer Research, 706-14.

Mazis, Michael B., Louis A. Morris, and John L. Swasy (1991), "An Evaluation of the Alcohol Warning Label: Initial Survey Results," *Journal of Public Policy & Marketing,* 10 (1), 229-41.

McCarthy, R. L., J. P. Finnegan, S. Krumm-Scott, and G. E. McCarthy (1984), "Product Information Presentation, User Behavior, and Safety," in *Proceedings of the Human Factors Society 28th Annual Meeting.* Santa Monica, CA: Human Factors Society, 81-85.

McGillis, D. B. and J. W. Brehm (1975), "Compliance as a Function of Inducements that Threaten Freedom and of Modeling Behavior that Implies Restoration of Freedom," working paper, Department of Psychology, Williams College.

McGuire, William J. (1980), "The Communication-Persuasion Model and Health-Risk Labeling," in *Product Labeling and Health Risks,* Banbury Report No. 6, L. A. Morris, M. B Mazis, and I. Barofsky, eds. Cold Spring Harbor, NY: Cold Spring Harbor Laboratory, 99-122.

Mizerski, Richard (1995), "The Relationship between Cartoon Trade Character Recognition and Attitude toward Product Category in Young Children," *Journal of Marketing,* 59 (3), 58-71.

Moorman, Christine and Erika Matulich (1993), "A Model of Consumers' Preventive Health Behaviors: The Role of Health Motivation and Health Ability," *Journal of Consumer Research,* 20 (2), 208-28.

Morris, Louis A. and D. E. Kanouse (1982), "Informing Patients about Drug Side Effects," *Journal of Behavioral Medicine,* 5, 363-73.

———, Karen Lechter, Michael Weintraub, and Debra Bowen (1998), "Comprehension Testing for OTC Drug Labels Goals, Methods, Target Population, and Testing Environment," *Journal of Public Policy & Marketing,* 17 (1), 86-96.

———, Michael B. Mazis, and David Brinberg (1989), "Risk Disclosures in Televised Prescription Drug Advertising to Consumers," *Journal of Public Policy & Marketing,* 8 (1), 64-80.

———, ———, and E. Gordon (1977), "A Survey of the Effects of Oral Contraceptive Patient Information," *Journal of the American Medical Association,* 238, 2504-8.

Morrow, Daniel, Von Leirer, and Javaid Sheikh (1988), "Adherence and Medication Instructions: Review and Recommendations," *Journal of American Geriatrics Society,* 36, 1147-60.

Myers, E. D. and E. J. Calvert (1973), "The Effect of Forewarning on the Occurrence of Side Effects and the Discontinuance of Medication in Patients on Amitriptyline," *British Journal of Psychiatry,* 122, 461-64.

——— and ——— (1976), "The Effect of Forewarning on the Occurrence of Side Effects and Discontinuance of Medication in Patients on Dothiepin," *Journal of International Medical Research,* 4, 237-40.

——— and ——— (1978), "Knowledge of Side Effects and the Perseverance with Medication," *British Journal of Psychiatry,* 132, 526-27.

Pechmann, Cornelia and David W. Stewart (1988), "Advertising Repetition: A Critical Review of Wearin and Wearout," *Current Issues and Research in Advertising,* 11, 285-330.

——— and ——— (1990), "The Role of Comparative Advertising: Documenting Its Effects on Attention, Recall, and Purchase Intentions," *Journal of Consumer Research,* 17, 180-91.

Perry, R. W. (1983), "Population Evacuation in Volcanic Eruptions, Floods, and Nuclear Power Plant Accidents: Some Elementary Comparisons," *Journal of Community Psychology,* 11 (January), 36-47.

Peters, G. A. (1984), "A Challenge to the Safety Profession," *Professional Safety,* 29, 46-50.

Petty, Richard and John Cacioppo (1986), *Communication and Persuasion: Central and Peripheral Routes to Attitude Change.* New York: Springer-Verlag.

Popper, Edward T. and Keith B. Murray (1989), "Format Effects on In-Ad Disclosure," in *Advances in Consumer Research,* Vol. 16, Thomas Srull, ed. Provo, UT: Association for Consumer Research, 221-30.

Punj, Girish and David W. Stewart (1983), "An Interaction Framework of Consumer Decision Processes," *Journal of Consumer Research,* 10 (September), 181-96.

Pyrczak, F. and D. H. Roth (1976), "The Readability of Directions on Non-Prescription Drugs," *Journal of the American Pharmaceutical Association,* 16 (May), 242-43, 267.

Rindfleisch, Aric and David X. Crockett (1999), "Cigarette Smoking and Perceived Risk: A Multidimensional Investigation," *Journal of Public Policy & Marketing,* 18 (2), 159-71.

Robinson, G. H. (1977), "Human Performance in Accident Causation: Toward Theories on Warning Systems and Hazard Appreciation," in *Proceedings of the Third International System Safety Conference,* 55-69. (Washington, DC)

Rozin, P., M. Markwith, and B. Ross (1990), "The Sympathetic Magical Law of Similarity, Nominal Realism, and Neglect of Negatives in Response to Negative Labels," *Psychological Science,* 1 (6), 383-84.

Schneider, Kenneth C. (1977), "Prevention of Accidental Poisoning through Package and Label Design," *Journal of Consumer Research,* 4 (September), 67-74.

Schwartz, Victor E. (1998), "Continuing Duty to Warn: An Opportunity for Liability Prevention or Exposure," *Journal of Public Policy & Marketing,* 17 (1), 124-26.

Sensenig, J. and J. W. Brehm (1968), "Attitude Change from an Implied Threat to Attitudinal Freedom," *Journal of Personality and Social Psychology,* 8, 324-30.

Sherbourne, C., R. Hays, L. Ordway, M. DiMatteo, and R. Kravitz (1992), "Antecedents of Adherence to Medical Recommendations: Results from the Medical Outcome Study," *Journal of Behavioral Medicine,* 15, 447-67.

Simpson, C. A. and D. H. Williams (1980), "Response Time Effects of Alerting Tone and Semantic Context for Synthesized Voice Cockpit Warnings," *Human Factors,* 22 (3), 319-30.

Sinaiko, H. W. (1975), "Verbal Factors in Human Engineering: Some Cultural and Psychological Data," in *Verbal Factors in Human Engineering.* Washington, DC: Smithsonian Institution, 159-77.

Slater, Michael D., David Karan, Donna Rouner, Kevin Murphy, and Federick Beauvais (1998), "Developing and Assessing Alcohol Warning Content: Responses to Quantitative Information and Behavioral Recommendations in Warnings with Television Beer Advertisements," *Journal of Public Policy & Marketing,* 17 (1), 48-60.

Slovic, Paul, Baruch Fischhoff, and Sarah Lichtenstein (1980), "Facts and Fears: Understanding Perceived Risk," in *Societal Risk Assessment: How Safe Is Safe Enough?* R. C. Schwing and W. A. Albers, Jr., eds. New York: Plenum, 181-214.

Smith, Sandra J. (1990), "The Impact of Product Usage Warnings in Alcoholic Beverage Advertising," *Journal of Public Policy & Marketing,* 9 (1), 16-29.

Smith, V. Kerry, William H. Desvousges, F. Reed Johnson, and Ann Fisher (1990), "Can Public Information Programs Affect Risk Perception?" *Journal of Policy Analysis and Management,* 9, 41-59.

Snyder, H. L. and R. A. Wicklund (1976), "Prior Exercise of Freedom and Reactance," *Journal of Experimental Social Psychology,* 12, 120-30.

Snyder, Leslie B. and Deborah J. Blood (1991), "Alcohol Advertising and the Surgeon General's Alcohol Warnings may Have Adverse Effects on Young Adults," paper presented at the annual meeting of the International Communication Association, May, Chicago.

Stewart, David W. and Ingrid Martin (1994), "Intended and Unintended Consequences of Warning Labels," *Journal of Public Policy & Marketing,* 13 (Spring), 1-19.

Strawbridge, J. (1985), "The Influence of Position, Highlighting, and Imbedding on Warning Effectiveness," unpublished master's thesis, California State University, Northridge.

Sturges, James W. and Ronald W. Rogers (1996), "Preventive Health Psychology from a Developmental Perspective: An Extension of Protection Motivation Theory," *Health Psychology,* 15 (3), 158-66.

Surgeon General (1989), *Reducing the Health Consequences of Smoking.* Rockville, MD: U.S. Department of Health and Human Services.

Svenson, Ola, Baruch Fischhoff, and Daniel MacGregor (1985), "Perceived Driving Safety and Seatbelt Usage," *Accident Analysis and Prevention,* 17, 119-33.

Taylor, D. H. (1976), "Accidents, Risks, and Models of Explanation," *Human Factors,* 18, 371-80.

Tonn, Bruce E., Cheryl B. Travis, Richard T. Goeltz, and Raymond H. Phillip (1990), "Knowledge-Based Representations of Risk Beliefs," *Risk Analysis,* 10 (1), 169-84.

Urzic, H. (1984), "The Impact of Safety Warnings on Perception and Memory," *Human Factors,* 28, 677-82.

Viscusi, Kip (1990), "Do Smokers Underestimate Risk?" *Journal of Political Economy,* 98 (6), 1253-69.

——— (1991), "Hazard Warnings," in *Reforming Product Liability,* Kip Viscusi, ed. Cambridge, MA: Harvard University Press, 132-56.

Viscusi, Kip, W. A. Magat, and J. Huber (1986), "Informational Regulation of Consumer Health Risks: An Empirical Evaluation of Hazard Warnings," *RAND Journal of Economics,* 17 (3), 351-61.

Viscusi, Kip and C. J. O'Connor (1984), "Adaptive Responses to Chemical Labeling: Are Workers Bayesian Decision Makers?" *American Economic Review,* 74, 942-56.

Weibert, R. (1977), "Potential Distribution Problems: Joint Symposium on Drug Information for Patients—Patient Package Inserts," *Drug Information Journal,* 11, 455-95. (Supplement)

Westinghouse Corporation (1981), *Westinghouse Product Safety Label Handbook.* Trafford, PA: Westinghouse Printing Division.

Weterings, Rob A. P. M. and Josee C. M. van Eijndhoven (1989), "Informing the Public about Uncertain Risks, *Risk Analysis,* 9 (4), 473-82.

Wicklund, R. A. and J. W. Brehm (1968), "Attitude Change as a Function of Felt Competence and Threat to Attitudinal Freedom," *Journal of Experimental Social Psychology,* 4, 64-75.

Wildavsky, Aaron (1991), *Searching for Safety* (Studies in Social Philosophy and Policy, No. 10). New Brunswick, NJ: Transaction Publishers.

Winter, W. (1963), "The Perception of Safety Posters by Bantu Industrial Workers," *Psychologia Africana,* 10, 263-70.

Wogalter, Michael S., John W. Brelsford, David R. Desaulniers, and Kenneth R. Laughery (1991), "Consumer Product Warnings: The Role of Hazard Perception," *Journal of Safety Research,* 22 (Summer), 71-82.

————, S. S. Godfrey, G. A. Fontenelle, David R. Desaulniers, P. R. Rothstein, and Kenneth R. Laughery (1987), "Effectiveness of Warnings," *Human Factors,* 29 (5), 599-612.

Worchel, S. and J. W. Brehm (1970), "Effect of Threats to Attitudinal Freedom as a Function of Agreement with the Communicator," *Journal of Personality and Social Psychology,* 14, 18-22.

Wright, Peter P. and Barton Weitz (1977), "Time Horizon Effects on Product Evaluation Strategies," *Journal of Marketing Research,* 14 (November), 429-43.

Zillmann, D. and J. Bryant (1985), *Selective Exposure to Communication.* Hillsdale, NJ: Lawrence Erlbaum.

Chapter

Do Food Labels Work?

*Gauging the Effectiveness of
Food Labels Pre- and Post-NLEA*

Brenda M. Derby
Alan S. Levy

Food labeling today is the result of landmark legislation passed by Congress in 1990. Lengthy and complex implementing regulations govern the content and format of food labels. Much is expected from the food label. The food label is viewed as a uniquely valuable tool to help consumers acquire and use product-specific health and nutrition information on food packages, with the goal of improving the American diet and reducing the toll of chronic diet-related diseases. It also is seen as a versatile tool for food manufacturers to promote their products and as an incentive to encourage food manufacturers to develop more healthful food products.

The history of food labeling regulation sometimes has been contentious, particularly for issues such as the use of health claims on labels (Cooper, Frank, and O'Flaherty 1990; Hutt 1986). After the intense activity associated with developing the implementing regulations, the Food and Drug Administration (FDA) and interested industry and consumer organizations have continued to grapple with unresolved issues (see, e.g., the Keystone Center [1996] report on the *Keystone National Policy Dialogue on Food, Nutrition, and Health*) and to address advances in scientific knowledge that require modifying specific regulations (e.g., proposal to add trans fatty acids to the "Nutrition Facts" label [FDA 1999]).

It has been six years since the food labeling regulations went into effect. Has the food label fulfilled its promise? Has the label helped consumers to make more informed food choices? Are there more healthful food alternatives in the marketplace today? This chapter examines data that shed light on how effective the new food labels have been and identifies remaining issues and concerns for the future.

To provide a context for understanding how the food label has changed, we briefly review food labeling prior to 1990 and identify the major consumer-related objectives included in the legislation. We examine a variety of types of research including experimental studies, national surveys, qualitative studies (e.g., focus groups), food consumption trends, and marketplace studies.

Regulatory Background

In 1990, the U.S. Congress passed the Nutrition Labeling and Education Act (NLEA). This culminated a process within and outside the FDA to dramatically change the food label. It has been called "the most significant food labeling legislation in the United States in at least fifty years" (Scarbrough 1995, p. 30).

The FDA adopted voluntary nutrition labeling regulations in 1973, focusing on concerns of the time such as deficiencies in essential vitamins and minerals. Labels were mandatory on foods that were fortified or that made claims about the nutritional properties of the foods. Developments in nutrition science during the 1970s and 1980s that linked diet to chronic diseases, such as heart disease and cancer, brought macronutrients to center stage (National Research Council 1989; U.S. Department of Health and Human Services 1988). The mass media, public education campaigns, and food manufacturers effectively presented information about diet-disease relationships to the general public and alerted consumers to health-related components of foods such as sodium, fat, and cholesterol (Levy, Fein, and Stephenson 1993; Schucker et al. 1991). Consumer awareness and concern about these food components grew significantly during the 1980s (Food Marketing Institute [FMI] 1991; Guthrie, Derby, and Levy 1999).

Labeling Pre-NLEA

A report on nutrition labeling prepared by the Committee on the Nutrition Components of Food Labeling (Porter and Earl 1990) identified major deficiencies in the pre-NLEA requirements for food labeling such as incomplete nutrition labeling of packaged foods (estimated at 40% of FDA-regulated packaged foods), deficiencies in the information about nutrient content required on labeled products (e.g., nutrients of public health significance such as cholesterol, saturated fat, and fiber were not required, whereas vitamins and minerals that were not deficient in American diets had to be listed), misleading label disclosures of nutrient contents (nutrient content claims), and a lack of established standard definitions. The report also identified a need for labeling and labeling changes to be accompanied by consumer education.

There also was continuing controversy concerning the use of health claims on food labels. The Federal Food, Drug, and Cosmetic Act of 1938 and the Drug Amendments of 1962 provided the statutory framework for health claims on foods. The FDA's position was that any product with a claim that the food or any component of the food could treat or prevent disease was legally considered a drug. Because health claims for foods could not satisfy the drug standards for proof, health claims were not allowed to appear on food packaging. Controversy arose during the mid-1980s when the Kellogg Company bypassed the FDA and began using a National Cancer Institute-sanctioned health claim related to fiber and cancer for its All-Bran cereal. This initiated a period of change that, combined with court decisions, led the FDA to adopt a hands-off approach to health claims (Cooper, Frank, and O'Flaherty 1990; Shank 1992). As a result, nutrient and health claims proliferated during the late 1980s, and the credibility of claims were called into question (Roper Organization 1993).

The NLEA

The FDA published final regulations on January 6, 1993, after an extensive comment and rule-making process. The regulations are necessarily complex and detailed, but some fundamental changes of significance to consumers include the following:

- Mandatory nutrition labeling for nearly all packaged foods
- Per-serving information on nutrients of public health concern such as saturated fat, cholesterol, and dietary fiber
- Nutrient reference values (Percent Daily Values) to help consumers put the nutrient information into the context of total daily diet
- Uniform definitions for nutrient contents (nutrient content claims) such as "light," "low," "reduced," and "lean"
- A limited and strictly defined set of allowable health claims that describe the relationship between a food or food component and a disease such as sodium and hypertension, fat and cancer, and calcium and osteoporosis

The final regulations took into account FDA and other consumer research on alternative nutrition label formats to ensure that the new label met the NLEA goal of conveying information in a way that consumers could readily comprehend and use for making healthful dietary choices. The label format incorporated features found to help consumers use the label for a variety of possible purposes (e.g., to compare two products, to judge overall healthfulness, to put a serving into the context of a total daily diet, to comprehend whether a nutrient was relatively high or low in a key nutrient) (Levy, Fein, and Schucker 1996).

The NLEA acknowledged that the massive changes proposed for food labels needed a complementary education effort to have the desired effects on Americans' diets including a mandate to educate consumers about (1) the availability of nutrition information in the label or labeling of food and (2) the importance of that information in maintaining healthy dietary practices.

Given the enormity of the task of creating new food labels for virtually all packaged food products, a lengthy time period was needed for the industry to comply. In addition, the implementation date for the new regulations was changed to permit packages labeled prior to that date to be sold rather than requiring all packages on the shelf by the implementation date to show new labels. As a result, new food labels appeared over a prolonged time period. This eased the burden on the industry but also lengthened the transition period for consumers.

The FDA identified three major objectives for the NLEA regulations: (1) to clear up consumer confusion about label information and claims on food labels to restore consumer confidence, (2) to help consumers make healthful food choices, and (3) to encourage manufacturers to produce healthier food products.

Measuring Food Label Effects

Roles Food Labels Play

Food labels are at the nexus between sellers and buyers of food products. In addition to their role in food marketing and product selection, they are expected to assist consumers in dietary management and to contribute to nutrition education (Levy and Derby 1996; Scarbrough 1995). Their roles in these complex domains are essentially informational rather than motivational. Food labels operate in the context of other factors that influence consumer food purchases, consumption decisions, and the marketing of food products. Food labels provide a great deal of information about the product that is not easily available anywhere else and provide more information than typically would be used at any one time. Consumers use food labels selectively, focusing on certain label information based on their own particular interests and needs (Levy and Derby 1996).

The practical impacts of the NLEA depend very much on whether and how manufacturers and consumers choose to use food labels for a variety of possible purposes. The multiple potential impacts of the food labeling regulations cannot easily be separated from ongoing trends in consumer attitudes toward diet and heath and associated developments in food marketing. The post-NLEA food label is both the result of and a contributing cause of these developments.

Possible Impact Measures

Given the diverse possible uses for the food label, there are several ways in which to measure the impacts of the NLEA regulations. Impacts can be categorized in terms of the behavior of manufacturers, of consumers, or of markets. Possible measures differ in terms of precision, sensitivity, feasibility, and practical significance.

Consumer Behavior

There are a variety of short- and long-term measures for consumer response to the changed food labels. In the short term, measures include awareness of the new food labels and trends in consumer perceptions and practices related to food labels (e.g., reported frequency of use, reported purposes for using food labels, confidence in label information). Data on consumer perceptions and practices are available from consumer surveys conducted by industry, public health, consumer, and government organizations. In the long term, measures such as changes in overall diet quality and reduced morbidity and mortality from diet-related diseases represent possible label effects. Data on nutrition and health status of the general public are available from several federal government-sponsored dietary intake and health status surveys that are part of the National Nutrition Monitoring and Related Research Program (Bialostosky 1998). Such long-term effects are the result of many factors occurring over long time periods and, therefore, are not easily connected to labels per se.

Manufacturer and Market Behavior

Measures of manufacturer behavior include compliance with NLEA labeling requirements (e.g., prevalence of nutrition labeling), prevalence of voluntary information (e.g., nutrient content claims, health claims), and the number and type of new product introductions. Data on compliance and claims are available from the FDA's Food Label and Package Survey (FLAPS) surveillance system (see Bialostosky 1998, pp. 150-51). Marketing databases track new product introductions. Information about product reformulations generally is not available. Ad hoc procedures to estimate nutrient changes in brands over time have been developed for specific research projects (Moorman 1998).

Measures of market behavior include market share trends for nutrition-promoted product segments within a given product category (e.g., sales of low-fat, reduced-fat, or fat-free products for a given product category). Data on food market trends are available from a number of proprietary market research databases used by the food industry. The FDA purchases proprietary market data to support various regulatory analyses. A preliminary study of selected food product categories pre- and post-NLEA provides insights into market responses to the food labeling regulations (Levy and Derby 1996).

Assessing the Impacts of the NLEA

Consumer Impacts

When the NLEA went into effect in 1994, American consumers were provided with an unprecedented amount of nutrition information about the packaged foods they eat. To help evaluate the impact of the new regulations, the FDA conducted two national telephone surveys: the 1994 Food Label Use and Nutrition Education Survey (FLUNES) and the 1995 FLUNES (one replicate of the

1995 Health and Diet Survey). In 1994, most of the interviews were conducted in the spring (March-April), prior to the NLEA implementation date, whereas a smaller number were conducted during August and September, when a growing number of products had new labels. Some products had new labels well before the implementation date, but there is evidence that these represented a small part of the market. For example, in a supermarket study, Moorman (1998) found that only 1% of the products checked during the five months preceding implementation of the NLEA had new nutrition labels. The 1995 FLUNES interviews were conducted in the fall of 1995 (November-December), about 18 months after the implementation of NLEA. The FLUNES interviews provide data on the ways in which consumers used food labels (purposes, parts of the label) as well as the credibility of label information. Relevant data on consumer responses to the new food label also are available from a variety of other national surveys including national samples of grocery shoppers (FMI Supermarket Trends Surveys, FMI/ Prevention Shopping for Health Surveys) and samples of adults (American Dietetic Association Trends Surveys).

Awareness of the New Food Label

As noted previously, the new food label appeared on market shelves over an extended period. Because some new labels had appeared prior to the May 1994 implementation date, the FDA included a question about awareness of new labels in the 1994 survey. In March and April, 30% of consumers said that they had seen new labels. By September, about half (49%) said that they had seen new labels (Derby and Levy 1994). A CNN/Prevention poll reported that 44% of consumers had seen the new labels by early August (" 'Premature' Survey" 1994). The FMI/Prevention (1994) Shopping for Health survey, conducted in February, reported that more than one in three shoppers had seen the new Nutrition Facts label. Surprisingly, when this question was repeated a year later, there was only a modest increase in the percentage of shoppers who said that they had seen the Nutrition Facts label (43%, up 5%).

Consumers who noticed the new food label gave it positive ratings. In the FLUNES, 72% of those who noticed the new label rated it somewhat better (33%) or much better (39%) than the old label (Derby and Levy 1994). In a follow-up open-ended question, consumers who rated the new label as somewhat or much better gave as reasons that it was easier to read, easier to understand, and provided more specific information that they wanted (e.g., information on fat). In the FMI/Prevention (1994) survey, two-thirds of the shoppers who said that they noticed the new label rated it as more clear and understandable than the old label. Those who said that they noticed the new label in 1995 also rated the new label positively; fully 57% said that the labels were very clear and understandable, and another 32% rated them as somewhat clear and understandable (FMI/Prevention 1995). Similarly, national surveys by the American Dietetic Association (ADA) showed a significant increase from 1993 to 1995 in the percentage of consumers who gave high ratings to "ease of understanding" and "usefulness of information"(ADA 1993, 1995).

The FMI Trends surveys also found positive reactions to new labels. In 1995, among the 78% of grocery shoppers who said that they had seen recent changes in the food label, 79% rated the new label as more understandable (FMI 1995). In 1996 and 1997, grocery shoppers were asked how useful they found the nutrition label wording and format. Close to half said that they were very useful, and nearly all (90%) found the label to be somewhat useful or very useful (FMI 1996, 1997). Consistent with other studies, fat was identified as useful by the largest proportion of shoppers (61% in 1997, up 5% from 1996), followed by ingredients (37% in 1997), calories, and salt (each 30% in 1997).

Overall Label Use

The FDA Health and Diet Surveys showed that pre-NLEA, a majority of consumers reported using the food label the first time they purchased a food product (Bender and Derby 1992). There was virtually no change in the proportion of consumers who reported this behavior during the 1990s. The FDA surveys found that about three-quarters of consumers looked at the food label the first time they purchased a food product. Among grocery shoppers an even higher percentage reported reading the nutrition label when buying a food product the first time (FMI 1990, 1995, 1997). This type of question provides little insight into the impact of improved food labels because reported label use already was high. To better understand the effects of the new food label, more specific questions are needed.

Trends in Label Use

One of the key objectives of the new labeling regulations was to make it easier for consumers to use the quantitative nutrition information on the food label. To meet this objective, the regulations prescribed a new format for the Nutrition Facts panel. There were significant changes in reported label use practices and beliefs of the general public during the 18 months between the two FDA food labeling surveys, suggesting that this objective is being achieved (Levy and Derby 1996).

Consumers were asked how often they used the label for eight different purposes (Table 16.1). Four purposes increased significantly between 1994 and 1995. The predominant use, by a large margin, was to see how high or low a food is in specific nutrients such as calories or fat. By 1995, 70% of consumers said that they used the label often for this purpose. Other frequent purposes were to "get a general idea of the nutritional content of the food" and to "compare different food items with each other." Use of the label to control portions increased to nearly one in three in 1995.

Consumers were asked how often they used different parts of the food label when the information was available. The macronutrient amounts from the nutrition panel was the information used most often, and it also was the part of the label that showed the greatest increase in use following implementation of the labeling regulations (Table 16.2). Absolute nutrient content claims (descriptors such as "low") were used about as often as macronutrient amounts in 1994 but showed little change with new labels. Information about vitamins and minerals

TABLE 16.1 Percentages of Consumers Who Used Different Parts of the Food Label "Often": 1994-95

Label Purpose	Spring 1994	Fall 1995
See how high/low in nutrients	62	70
Judge overall nutrition quality	48	55
Compare foods	43	48
Avoid ingredient	45	44
Decide which brand to buy	44	44
Control portions	27	32
Check claims	30	33
Plan meals	26	29

SOURCES: 1994 Food Label Use and Nutrition Education Survey (FLUNES; N = 1,653); 1995 Health and Diet Survey (FLUNES replicate; N = 1,001).

TABLE 16.2 Percentages of Consumers Who Used the Food Label for Different Purposes "Often": 1994-95

Part of Food Label	Spring 1994	Fall 1995
Nutrient amounts	43	56
High/low descriptors	41	44
Ingredient list	39	36
Serving size	30	28
Light/healthy/reduced claims	28	29
Vitamin/mineral amounts	22	27
Health claims	20	25

SOURCES: 1994 Food Label Use and Nutrition Education Survey (FLUNES; N = 1,653); 1995 Health and Diet Survey (FLUNES replicate; N = 1,001).

and health claims increased significantly, although they were the parts of the food label used often by the fewest number of consumers.

These findings on purposes and parts of the label used suggest that consumers rely on the label primarily for product-specific information to use in making product choices, not as a source of information about dietary science or dietary guidance.

A statewide survey conducted in Washington State pre- and post-NLEA found similarly positive results. Kristal and colleagues (1998) reported that more consumers usually read food labels during 1995-96 than during 1992-93, although they also noted that the percentage saying that they never use labels was unchanged at about 25% (comparable to the 25% in FDA surveys who said that they rarely or never read labels the first time). Their data also showed that a strong majority had noticed the new label format during 1995-96, and those consumers rated food labels more positively. For example, post-NLEA, more consumers said that they usually found the information they were looking for on the label.

Among regular label users, there were large post-NLEA increases in the percentage who looked for fat information (84%, up 15%), calories (69%, up 11%), and serving size (45%, up 10%). There were more modest increases for cholesterol and fiber information. Barriers to label use also decreased. For example, fewer consumers said that nutrition labels are too hard to understand or take too much time. However, improvements were not consistent across age and education groups. There was little or no change among those age 60 years or over, and both older consumers and less educated consumers were more likely to find nutrition labels too difficult to understand. The FDA studies of possible new label formats also found that older and less educated consumers had more difficulty in using food labels (Levy and Fein 1998).

Changing a Decision Based on Label Information

A more revealing label use question focuses on the impact of looking at the food label on consumers' product choices. In the 1990 Health and Diet Survey, consumers were asked, "In the last two weeks, can you remember an instance when your decision to buy or use a food product was changed because you read the nutrition label?" Nearly one-third (30%) of consumers said that they had changed their minds as a result of looking at the nutrition label. In the 1994 FLUNES, 47% of consumers said that they changed their minds, comparable to the percentage that said so in 1995 (48%). This large increase between 1990 and 1994 cannot easily be attributed to implementation of the NLEA. Although there were new labels available to consumers in the spring of 1994, it is not known whether many of the consumers in 1994 who reported changing their minds were answering based on a new food label. There had been considerable publicity in the mass media about food labels and the coming changes prior to implementation, and so early exposure to new labels, by providing novel information on those products, might have made a strong impression on those consumers. In the 1994 FMI/Prevention survey, those shoppers who had noticed the new label were more likely to say that they had changed their minds based on the food label than were those who had not yet noticed the new label.

Several surveys elaborated on the question of whether consumers changed their minds as a result of looking at the food label by specifying the type of change, for example, starting to buy a product not previously purchased based on information on the label or stopping the purchase of a product used before because of information on the label.

The 1995 FMI/Prevention survey asked about starting and stopping during the past month, whereas the 1996 and 1997 surveys referred to the past six months. Despite the change in the time reference, there was little or no change between 1995 and 1996. In 1996, one-third of shoppers said that they stopped buying a product that they had regularly purchased and used because they read the nutrition label, and one in four started to buy or use a product not used before based on the nutrition label. Shoppers overwhelmingly cited fat as the specific information that influenced their decisions (as to whether to start or stop buying a product), with sodium a far second. In 1997, somewhat fewer shoppers stopped buying a product based on the nutrition label (28%, down 6% from 1996), but slightly more said that they started buying a new product (25%, up 3% from 1996). Far fewer cited fat in 1997 (down about 20% from the 1995 level).

A majority of American adults surveyed in 1997 (American Dietetic Association 1997) reported changing their buying habits as a result of looking at nutrition labels—buying some foods less often (69%) or more often (65%), eliminating an item altogether (59%), or switching brands (56%).

Moorman (1996) conducted a longitudinal field experiment to look at effects of the NLEA on nutrition information processing. Her research focused on the acquisition and comprehension of nutrition information from food packages in a sample of shoppers randomly selected in supermarkets pre- and post-NLEA (October 1993 and 1994). The shoppers spent more time searching for nutrition information post-NLEA and had greater comprehension of the information. Moorman concluded that consumers acquired and comprehended more nutrition information following the introduction of new labels and that the goal of the NLEA—that most consumers should be able to use the new labels—was partially successful; consumers who varied in measures of motivation and some types of nutrition knowledge had greater comprehension with the new labels, but consumers who were more motivated and less skeptical acquired more information post-NLEA.

Percent Daily Value

Research on alternative nutrition label formats showed that "Percent Daily Value (%DV) information helped consumers to make certain types of judgments about the nutritional characteristics of labeled foods (FDA 1993, pp. 2125-28; Levy, Fein, and Schucker 1996). Pre-NLEA nutrition labels showed the amounts of nutrients such as fat, cholesterol, and sodium in gram or milligram amounts. Despite high levels of concern with these nutrients over the years (FMI 1991, 1999), few consumers are able to correctly interpret this quantitative information or to recall what the appropriate amounts of these nutrients are in the diet (Derby and Fein 1995).

Some have criticized the %DV information as too difficult for consumers to understand and use (FDA 1993, pp. 2125-28). The 1991 FDA label format study (Levy, Fein, and Schucker 1996) found that even a very brief introduction to the percent daily value concept resulted in more accurate use of this information. Even without an explanation, consumers were better able to judge how high or low a food was in specific nutrients than when this information was not present or when only the daily values themselves were provided.

In a comparison of the %DV with an average-brand reference, Barone and colleagues (1996) reported more accurate evaluation of a product's healthfulness using the average-brand reference. However, the label task did not involve putting the food into the context of a total daily diet, an explicit objective under the NLEA and one that the alternative reference would not be able to assist given that it only put a product into the context of a defined food category. This also would limit its usefulness for comparisons across product categories.

Other critiques of the %DV emphasize the inability of most consumers to correctly define the term. In the 1996 FMI/Prevention survey, shoppers who read the nutrition label were asked what a %DV for fat of 5% meant from a choice of four alternatives (FMI/Prevention 1996). A plurality (43%) answered correctly, but fewer had answered with the previous year's question correctly. The question was repeated in 1997, with the addition of a question about the percentage daily value for fiber (FMI/Prevention 1997). There was no change in the percentage responding correctly for fat, but more shoppers answered the fiber question correctly (57%).

Some consumer confusion might be due less to a fundamental misunderstanding of the concept than to the complexity of dietary advice related to the nutrient of top concern to most consumers—fat. The evidence from the label format studies suggests that consumers can use the %DV information appropriately, even if they do not fully understand it.

Label Claims

Label claims include two types of information: nutrient content descriptors (e.g., "fat-free") and statements of health benefits ("health claims"). Health claims explicitly link a food or food component with a disease or health condition. While content and health claims have important regulatory distinctions, discussions of claims sometimes confuse the two. Recent qualitative and quantitative research on claims showed that nutrient content claims often were viewed by consumers as health information or as a reminder of a known diet-disease relationship (Levy 1996; Levy, Derby, and Roe 1997). For example, in an open-ended question about the health benefits of a particular food product, participants in an experimental study responded in terms of nutrients (e.g., "It is low in fat") rather than in terms of a diet-disease relationship, even though a health claim was present on the package (Levy, Derby, and Roe 1997).

A key objective of the new labeling regulations was to restore the credibility of nutrition and health claims being made for food products by requiring that such claims adhere to established standards and be limited to products that meet FDA requirements (Scarbrough 1995). The FDA established nutritional criteria for nutrient content claims to ensure that consumers could rely on content claims in making healthful food choices. Under the NLEA, nutrient content claims must comply with strict guidelines designed to minimize the risk of consumer confusion. For example, cholesterol claims are permitted only if the food does not contain more than a specified amount of saturated fat. Foods that are naturally low in a nutrient cannot use a nutrient content claim unless it is phrased in terms of the product category.

A recent study of cholesterol-free claims shed some light on this debate (Burke, Milberg, and Moe 1997). This study focused on "features-absent" inferences to see if (1) consumers would interpret the presence of a nutrient-free content claim (e.g., cholesterol-free) on one product in a product category to mean that only products with the claim shared the attribute, which is in fact typical of all brands of the product and (2) presence of the claim affected food choices among brands. A narrow "cholesterol-free" claim resulted in "feature-absent" inferences and choices in favor of the brand with the claim for subjects who believed it was atypical in the product category. A broader claim ("All peanut oils are cholesterol free") was less deceptive and helped less knowledgeable consumers. However, food marketers are often reluctant to use broad claims that benefit the entire category. The authors concluded that the results support the FDA's position that nutrient-free claims alone may mislead consumers.

To ensure that health claims were truthful and not misleading, the NLEA required that the FDA review proposed health claims against a rigorous "significant scientific agreement" standard. Of 10 potential health claims included in the NLEA, 7 were approved. Critics viewed this standard as too stringent, limiting claims to already well-established relationships while information based on emerging science could not be made available to consumers on the label (Keystone Center 1996). Since the publication of the 1993 regulations, several other health claims have been approved (Kurtzweil 1998).

Pre-NLEA, the level of consumer confidence in the accuracy or believability of label information was found to be moderate at best (Derby and Fein 1995). Confidence varied by part of the label. For example, about 1 in 3 thought that the ingredient list and nutrient label were accurate, whereas for comparative claims (e.g., "light"), fewer than 1 in 5 believed that they were accurate. Only 1 in 10 regarded health claims as accurate. The 1990 FMI Trends Survey also found that few shoppers considered health claims to be very believable (8%), yet many (73%) said that such statements influenced their purchase decisions. One factor that may underlie lack of confidence in label claims is the belief that this type of label information is like advertising. The Roper Organization (1993) reported that, although significantly fewer consumers could recall seeing health claims in advertising on food packages in 1992 than in 1989, their degree of skepticism did not change. A plurality said that they believed that only some claims were accurate, and few believed that many of them or just about all of them were accurate. Half of the sample participants were asked about claims in advertising, and half were asked about claims on food labels. Ratings of accuracy were virtually identical, suggesting that consumers did not distinguish between advertisements and labels.

Another factor that may underlie consumer skepticism is the widely held belief that label claims are not regulated. Pre-NLEA, the Roper Organization (1993) found that nearly half of consumers felt that there was not enough monitoring of health claims by the government. Post-NLEA, many consumers remained unaware that the government regulates the nutrient content and health claims on food labels (Derby and Guthrie 1999; Levy 1996). For example, focus group participants expressed surprise that claims are regulated but thought that it was important for consumers to know this (Levy 1996). They remained skeptical about the use of health information on food packages. Similarly, most respondents in the U.S. Department of Agriculture's (USDA) Diet and Health Knowledge Survey did not believe that the government defines and enforces specific label terms such as "light" and "low cholesterol" (Derby and Guthrie

1999). These findings suggest that strict government regulation of label claims was an aspect of the new food label that was poorly communicated to American consumers.

Survey data suggest some progress post-NLEA. Although there still was widespread skepticism about the veracity of label claims among the general public, during the 18 months between the 1994 and 1995 FLUNES, there was significant improvement in public confidence in such claims (Levy and Derby 1996). More consumers said that they used the health claim information on the label when it was available (25%, up 5%), and more considered nutrient and health claims to be accurate; fully 34% rated absolute content claims as accurate (up 5%), and 31% rated health claims as accurate (up 6%), although there was no improvement for comparative content claims such as "light" and "reduced." Fewer consumers agreed with the statement, "Claims on food labels are more like advertising than anything else" (39% strongly agreed, down 8%).

The 1999 FMI Trends survey asked shoppers whether they had sought out and purchased products with specific types of label claims. From 1996 to 1999, products labeled "low fat" were the most frequently purchased type of product (more than 80% from 1996 to 1998, dropping to 77% in 1999). Although cholesterol has declined as a nutritional concern in the Trends surveys, a majority of shoppers said that they purchased products labeled "low cholesterol" (60% in 1999, down 10% from 1996). More than half of the shoppers (53% in 1999, down 8% from 1996) purchased products labeled "low salt."

In the health claim regulations, the FDA (1993) provided model health claims. The industry argued that these claims were too lengthy and complex. Diverse perspectives on the effectiveness and practicality of the FDA's health claim regulations led to a two-year dialogue among interested parties (Keystone Center 1996).

In focus groups, participants were highly skeptical of health claims on foods and preferred simpler statements than those included in FDA model health claims (Levy 1996). Even for a relationship that was unknown to most participants (folic acid and neural tube defects), a shortened health claim was preferred. The participants believed that nutrition information is important but also that it is widely available. Food labels were not viewed as a good place to learn new information about nutrition science. They regarded health claims, like nutrient content claims, as reminders. Their skepticism about health claims also reflected mistrust of food manufacturers' motives in putting health claims on food packages.

There have been attempts to measure the impact of health claims on consumer knowledge and concern about diet-disease relationships. Consumer awareness of diet-disease links for heart disease, hypertension, and cancer have been tracked in FDA Health and Diet Surveys since 1982 (Guthrie, Derby, and Levy 1999). Consumer awareness increased significantly over the 1980s.

Mathios and Ippolito (1999) documented dietary improvements that they suggested could be attributed, in part, to health claims on food products, citing as examples the impact of fiber-cancer claims on ready-to-eat cereal and improvements in fat and cholesterol consumption associated with the pre-NLEA period when the FDA no longer prohibited the use of health claims. These authors also reported positive effects on the marketplace during this health claims period (e.g., more healthful innovations within the cereal market to respond to consumer interest in high-fiber cereals). This period also was associated with several major public health education campaigns (e.g., the National Heart, Lung, and Blood Institute's Cholesterol Awareness Campaign) and growing media coverage of health news. To what extent consumers' growing awareness can be attributed to advertising or health claims on food packages versus other sources of information is difficult to assess.

Recently, Teisl, Levy, and Derby (1999) examined this question by looking at trends in awareness as measured by the FDA Health and Diet Surveys (where awareness indicates "top of mind" awareness in response to an open-ended question) in conjunction with data on the same diet-disease relationships provided by the news media (newspaper articles) and health-related information in magazine advertising for foods and beverages. The study used regression techniques to predict awareness as a function of education, other socioeconomic characteristics, and the quantity of health-related information provided in news media and food advertising.

Diet-disease awareness increased with education level, indicating an education gap in awareness. Higher awareness levels were associated with time periods of increased newspaper article activity. Increased use of nutrient content claims in advertising tended to follow significant increases in consumer awareness suggesting that advertising responded to change in consumer awareness rather than the converse.

The analysis of food and beverage advertising revealed that very few health claims were being used in ads; most health-related information consisted of nutrient content information. This suggests that health claims were not the vehicle for increased consumer awareness during the post-1984 period. Although this analysis suggests that health claims were not responsible for making more consumers aware of emerging diet-disease relationships, they could play an important role in consumers' food choices.

There have been a variety of experimental studies on how consumers are affected by nutrient content and/or health claims on food packages. FDA research on new label formats has provided some insight into how consumers use front panel label claims, particularly nutrient content claims (Levy, Fein, and Schucker 1996). Participants evaluated a product more favorably when just the front panel claims were presented. Once they looked at the nutrition label, their judgments were moderated (i.e., the food was given lower healthfulness ratings) and their ratings came closer to the judgments of nutrition experts (Levy and Fein 1998). Consumers were quite competent at evaluating the truthfulness of nutrient content claims, but they also showed a bias toward believing claims. They were more likely to err in saying a false claim was true than in saying a true claim was false (Levy and Fein 1998).

Keller and colleagues (1997) examined the effects of nutrition claims that were either consistent or inconsistent with information in the Nutrition Facts panel. The study partially replicated an earlier study (Ford et al. 1996) that had concluded that consumers will not draw incorrect conclusions about overall nutrition and product evaluations from claims when specific nutrient information is readily available in the Nutrition Facts label. Keller and colleagues (1997) looked at motivation to determine whether claims might have a greater effect for less motivated consumers who are hypothesized to be less willing to spend time processing label information. The participants were primary grocery shoppers in one state. Inconsistent claims resulted in lower evaluations of the manufacturer's credibility but did not lead to more favorable nutrition or product evaluations, supporting the earlier finding (Ford et al. 1996) that consumers rely on Nutrition Facts to a greater extent than they do nutrient claims on the front. Keller and colleagues (1997) concluded that if the findings extend to more realistic purchase settings, then a less restrictive approach to front panel claims is preferable. They also suggested that consumers would benefit from awareness that there are specific government restrictions on the use of claims. However, the study also found motivation differences, such that less motivated consumers were less likely to correctly evaluate the nutritional qualities of the food product, particularly when the Nutrition Facts information was inconsistent with the claim.

Similarly, in a study of an implied health claim ("It does your heart good") (Mitra et al. 1999), the health claim alone affected product ratings, but in the presence of the Nutrition Facts panel, both educationally disadvantaged and advantaged consumers made appropriate nutritional ratings. The authors concluded that when consumers relied on health claims only, they tended to make overly broad healthfulness judgments.

The FDA Health Claims Study (Levy, Derby, and Roe 1997) helps to illuminate the issues raised in the experimental studies cited previously. Using a mall-intercept procedure, the FDA tested variations in health claim language and placement to help resolve issues raised by industry and consumer groups concerning the FDA's health claims regulations, such as wording flexibility and claim length. The primary focus of the study was the communication effectiveness of alternative health claim statements. The study used realistic mock-ups of three types of food that qualified for the claims being tested; there was no inconsistency between the claims and the Nutrition Facts panel, as there was in the studies cited previously. Label-looking behavior was assessed by recording which part of the package (the front or the Nutrition Facts label on the side or back) the participants referred to in answering a series of questions. Participants had access to the package throughout the question series, so they were free to look at one part of the label, to look at both parts, or not look at the label at all while answering a given question. When a health claim or a nutrient content claim was present, respondents tended to truncate their information search to the front of the package, resulting in more positive product ratings and greater weight to the information in the claim (Roe, Levy, and Derby 1999). Regular label users were less likely to truncate their information search. Less educated consumers were more likely to rely on the front panel only. The findings suggested that consumers cannot be assumed to take advantage of all the information that is available when making judgments about food products. In this experimental study, time constraints were minimal and participants were likely to be more conscientious than could be expected in the time-pressed and information-rich environments in which food choices often are made such as supermarket aisles.

Dietary Changes

One goal of the new food label was to help American consumers make more healthful dietary choices, with the long-term goal of improving their diets and health (Scarbrough 1995). Many factors influence consumer food choices. The food label represents a valuable point-of-purchase source of product-specific nutrition information. It provides a tool for motivated consumers to make food choices consistent with their dietary goals. But information alone will not change behavior. Motivation and concern also are critical. And even motivated consumers might find dietary improvement elusive.

A study based on USDA dietary intake data pre-NLEA found awareness of diet-disease relationships to be associated with reduced intake of fat and cholesterol (Variyam 1999). Pre-NLEA, aware consumers needed nutrition knowledge about the foods that contain important nutrients so as to act on their awareness to make healthful food choices. In an analysis of food label users, Levy and Derby (1995) found significant correlations among awareness of dietary risk factors, concern about these risk factors, and label use. With the greater availability and clarity of nutrition information on labels post-NLEA, it seems likely that the relationship between awareness and dietary choice would play a greater role than before in helping motivated consumers to achieve healthful diets. Data to support this view are very limited to date.

One recent study, conducted post-NLEA, examined label use among a representative sample of adults in one western state as it related to an estimate of fat consumption (Neuhouser, Kristal, and Patterson 1999). The strongest predictor of label use was understanding the importance of eating a low-fat diet. A regression analysis showed a strong association between label reading and fat consumption as measured by a Dietary Health Questionnaire. It appears that consumers who wanted to reduce their fat intake were using nutrition labels to help them make food choices.

Some commentators have suggested that food labels have failed at the objective of improving Americans' health, as demonstrated by increasing obesity (Gugliotta 2000). Obesity, like other serious chronic health problems and diseases, has multiple causes. The label provides relevant information to help concerned consumers control their food intake and to choose healthful foods. But other dietary factors can moderate the effects of labels on overall diet. For example, a growing proportion of the foods that Americans consume come from unlabeled sources.

A recent study of "away-from-home foods" provides useful insights into this phenomenon (Lin, Guthrie, and Frazao 1999). The trend in fat consumption over the past two decades has shown some encouraging patterns such as a decreasing percentage of calories from fat (e.g., from 41.1% during 1977-78 to 33.6% in 1995) and an increase in the proportion of people who meet the dietary recommendation of consuming 30% or less of total calories from fat (from 13% during

1977-78 to 37% in 1995). On the other hand, average daily intake of total fat in grams, which fell between 1977-78 (86.3) and 1989 (72.0), has increased steadily since 1990, reaching 76.2 in 1995.

When consumption is categorized in terms of foods eaten at home and away-from-home foods, it is apparent that one problem is that away-from-home foods have declined very little in their fat content compared to home foods. As American lifestyles move toward more away-from-home foods, the beneficial effects of the label in choosing foods may well be overwhelmed by such changes. Lin, Guthrie, and Frazao (1999) documented a significant increase in dining out over the past 20 years, from 16% to 27% of meals and snacks. This away-from-home food provided one-third of calories in 1995 compared to 18% during 1977-78.

The pattern for saturated fat diverges from that of total fat. Average daily intake has declined, modestly, from 1987-88 to 1995, in concert with a decline in the percentage of calories from saturated fat. There has been a similar increase in the proportion of people who meet the guideline for saturated fat, as was noted previously for total fat. Saturated fat is less pervasive in the food supply than is total fat, so concerned consumers might be able to reduce this food component in their diets more easily than they can total fat. The different patterns also might reflect changes within the food industry such as the switch from meat-based frying fats (e.g., lard, beef tallow) to hydrogenated vegetable oils and the widespread use of hydrogenated fats in processed foods (e.g., cookies, crackers). The apparent dietary improvements for saturated fat may be offset by these uses of hydrogenated fats.

There has been growing concern in the public health community regarding trans fatty acids in the diet. In response, the FDA published a proposal to require adding trans fatty acid content to the saturated fat amount on the Nutrition Facts label along with quantitative information on trans fatty acids in an accompanying footnote (FDA 1999). This information, although limited to labeled products, would help consumers to identify foods with higher levels of fats that are linked with heart disease. To ensure that the label continues to communicate clearly to consumers, major modifications in the content of the Nutrition Facts label are considered only when there is a compelling public health rationale for the change.

USDA food consumption trend data have revealed numerous changes during recent years in the average American diet (e.g., switching from whole milk to low-fat and skim milk) that have helped move consumers toward the public health goal of 30% of total calories from fat (Tippett and Cleveland 1999). But accompanying these healthful food choices is a trend toward higher calorie consumption. Consumption of food from certain categories such as grains and grain mixtures has increased during recent years, as has consumption of particular nutrients such as added sugars and added sodium (Tippett and Cleveland 1999, Guthrie and Morton 2000).

Dietary patterns and consumer awareness and concerns suggest that low-fat messages were well communicated to consumers, but the food consumption trends suggest that the advice proved difficult to apply effectively. Food manufacturers succeeded in developing more palatable reduced-fat and fat-free food options, but consumers failed to reduce their calorie intake while improving their percentage of calories from fat. In part, this might reflect the mistaken belief that cutting fat naturally would cut calories as well (Gugliotta 2000; Schwartz and Borra 1997). Effective use of calorie information on the label is more difficult than for specific nutrients such as fat because it requires quantitative regulation to work.

When consumers make food choices based on label information, they often are deciding based on the nutrition profile or a comparison across products. Dietary regulation comes into play when foods are consumed. The label helps consumers to identify lower fat options or products that are a good source of a nutrient, but the dietary impact of choosing particular foods also depends on how much of the food consumers eat and whether they balance this food in the context of their total diets. Throughout the 1990s, nutrition messages to the public focused on fat consumption to the point where some nutrition experts warn that consumers have become obsessed with fat yet remain confused about how to translate their concerns into healthful dietary choices (Schwartz and Borra 1997).

Sigman-Grant (1997) explored how two theoretical models, diffusion of innovation and stages of change, can provide useful frameworks for understanding adoption of healthful dietary changes. For example, she used the diffusion of innovations perspective to analyze sales of fluid milk, showing how in 1987 there was a crossover of whole milk sales to low-fat milk sales. She noted that it took 25 years for adoption of skim milk to begin to move from a "fad" to a slowly diffusing innovation. She also examined assumptions and expectations related to fat-modified foods, in particular the impact on individual- and population-level dietary status and health outcomes such as obesity. Research on intake of fat-modified foods has shown that most consumers use only one or two such products daily. Depending on whether consumers substitute the modified food for its regular counterpart, use some combination of both, or otherwise "compensate" for the reduced fat, there may or may not be a decline in total fat or calories. Sigman-Grant drew a parallel to the disappointing impact of artificially sweetened beverages on obesity; as substitutes, these beverages were found to be related to weight loss in research studies, but at the population level, this was not the case. Her article underscores the difficulty of changing the total diet. The benefits of one healthful behavior can be modest at best and might be reversed by other choices.

Putler and Frazao (1991) observed a similar phenomenon when they examined food intakes among women. Well-educated women made health-related dietary changes such as reduced consumption of certain foods (e.g., red meat, eggs). Surprisingly, the authors found that these women had total fat consumption identical to that of women who had not made these changes. The nutritionally aware women had increased their consumption of salads and high-fat dairy products; in other words, they substituted one type of fat with another rather than decreasing overall consumption as they probably had intended to do. As Mathios (1996) found in his regional study, pre-NLEA, many salad dressings in the supermarket were not labeled. Post-NLEA, consumers have greatly increased access to relevant nutrient information to assist them in regulating their diets. But the inherent difficulty of keeping track of dietary intake in addition to the other factors that are highly important to consumers when making food choices, notably taste, creates major challenges to nutrition educators.

According to a recent survey sponsored by the Calorie Control Council (1999), consumer interest in reduced-fat products remains high. For example, most Americans said that they consume reduced-fat foods or beverages on a regular basis (85%, up 12% since 1993). Most do so for overall health benefits (77%) or to maintain weight (57%). A majority (62%) said that they always check the nutrition label for fat content, and more than half said that they check for calories (55%). According to the survey, the most popular reduced-fat products were skim and low-fat milk (62%); salad dressings, sauces, and mayonnaise (56%); and cheese and other dairy products (e.g., yogurt, sour cream) (50%).

The FMI/Prevention (1999) Shopping for Health survey reported that about two-thirds of grocery shoppers make purchase decisions based on a desire to reduce the risk of a health condition or an illness or to manage or treat a condition or an illness on their own. Reducing fat intake was a motivating factor to 81% of these consumers. Similarly, 82% of the sample reported being concerned about the fat in their diets. A comparable proportion of shoppers in this survey said that they purchase foods with reduced fat (78%) and reduced salt (57%), as in the 1999 Trends survey.

There is some evidence that consumer enthusiasm for low-fat and fat-free foods, although still high, is starting to wane ("Good Nutrition" 1997; Ralston 1999). In the FMI Trends surveys, grocery shoppers continued to identify fat content as their top nutritional concern, but the percentage of consumers who mentioned fat in 1999 was significantly lower than that in the previous year and was down 15% from the decade peak of 65% in 1995. In 1996, 81% of shoppers said that they had sought out low-fat products; this level remained consistent for two years but dropped to 77% in 1999. The drop in the proportion of shoppers who sought out low-cholesterol products was greater, from 70% in 1996 to 60% in 1999. Low-salt products, already lower, dropped as well, from 61% in 1996 to 53% in 1999. Nevertheless, in 1999, a majority (59%) said that they had changed their purchases because of information on the product nutrition label. This still is a respectable level.

Marketplace Impacts

Prevalence of Claims

One goal of the NLEA was to provide nutrition labeling on virtually all packaged foods. The FDA conducts a biennial tracking study of food labels, called the Food Label and Package Survey (FLAPS), to identify market response to regulations via changes in product package labels. FLAPS data have been used to estimate the prevalence of nutrition labeling on product packages (O'Brien 1996) as well as the extent of quantitative labeling of various nutrients such as fatty acids and the prevalence of various nutrient content and health claims on food products.

O'Brien (1996) reported that the percentage of sales accounted for by products with nutrition labeling rose from 41.9% in 1978 to 65.9% in 1991. In 1993, prior to the implementation of the NLEA, it reached 75.5%, and in 1995 it was nearly universal at 96.1%. Nutrition labels prior to the implementation date in 1994 were unlikely to be Nutrition Facts labels, but it is noteworthy that significantly more products carried nutritional labeling in 1993 than in 1991. This would help account for the finding noted earlier that a significant increase in use of the label for decision making occurred prior to implementation of the new label regulations.

In a preliminary analysis of 1997 FLAPS data to estimate the sale-based percentages of brands with nutrient content and health claims (M. M. Bender, personal communication, December 1999), about 40% of the sampled packages included some type of claim on the label. About 4% showed a health-related claim (this included not only FDA-approved diet-disease claims but also implied claims such as use of the American Heart Association heart check and accompanying statement or other health-related statements). Two types of nutrient content claims increased between 1991 and 1997: Fat claims increased to about 23.0% in 1997 (up 5%), and fiber claims increased from less than 1.0% in 1991 to about 2.5% in 1997. Other nutrient content claims either decreased (cholesterol, sugar, sodium, and saturated fat) or stayed about the same (calories).

The health claims regulations limit both the types of allowable claims and the products that qualify for health claims. The use of health claims is entirely voluntary, and there is some evidence that food manufacturers use health claims on few of their qualified products. In a recent review of the regulatory history of health claims and health claims research, Geiger (1998) cited an informal survey of the top 100 cereal brands showing that only 7% displayed a health claim, although virtually all (97%) qualified for at least one approved health claim.

Marketplace Innovations

Another key objective of the NLEA was to provide more incentives to food manufacturers to introduce healthier versions of traditional foods into the marketplace. The development of low-fat, reduced-fat, and fat-free versions of traditional types of food is a clear indicator of food manufacturers' interest in meeting the demand for lower fat foods created by the public's increased awareness of fat as a primary dietary risk factor for disease. Since the passage of the NLEA in 1990, there have been impressive changes in the availability and market share of food products promoted on the basis of health and nutrition. In an analysis of market response in a select number of product categories suitable for the introduction of fat-modified versions of traditional products—cookies, cheese, crackers, peanut butter, and tortilla/corn chips—Levy and Derby (1996) found impressive simultaneous increases in new product introductions and market share for the fat-modified products. Fat-modified cookies increased from a negligible market share of nearly zero in the second quarter of 1991 (35 fat-modified cookie products out of approximately 2,000 total) to 15% by the second quarter of 1995, when nearly 300 fat-modified products were available. Fat-modified cheeses more than doubled their share of cheese sales, from 4% to 10% of the market, while tripling the number of fat-modified cheese items available to consumers. Similar patterns were found for crackers, peanut butter, and corn chips, with the number of fat-modified products increasing in concert with sharp increases in market share. For these three product categories, most of the new product introductions and sales gains occurred after the 1994 effective date for the new food labeling regulations. Two additional product categories, frozen dinners and salad dressing, were examined to see the pattern for products that were likely to have included fat-modified products, and therefore nutrition labeling, pre-NLEA. These products were, not surprisingly, less likely to show changes in market share or new product introductions post-NLEA.

Weimar (1999) described a symbiotic relationship between the industry and consumers, noting that the food industry responded to consumer health concerns by providing products with less fat and other nutrients. Thousands of new food products have been promoted with fat and other nutrient content claims to appeal to health-conscious consumers. Weimar presented trend data on the use of nutrient content claims in new food products introduced each year from 1991 to 1997 (for complete data, see Table 1 in Weimar 1999). With the exception of fat claims, nutrient content claims peaked during the early 1990s (e.g., calorie and cholesterol claims peaked in 1991; salt, sugar, and fiber claims peaked in 1992). By 1997, fewer new products made nutrient content claims except those related to fat. Fat claims peaked in 1996. This pattern could mean that consumers are less interested in nutrient-modified foods. Alternatively, the decline might reflect less interest in new modified foods because so many have been introduced over the past decade and have established themselves in the marketplace.

In a study of selected product categories, Mojduszka and Caswell (forthcoming) tested the signaling of nutritional quality pre-NLEA by examining the correspondence between nutritional quality and the presence or absence of a nutrition label. The authors suggested that if more healthful foods showed a nutrition label while less healthful foods did not, then consumers could rely on the presence or absence of a nutrition label as an indicator of nutritional value, making mandatory labeling less necessary. Data on products in 33 categories sold in a New England supermarket during 1992 and 1993 showed that quality signaling was not a reliable indicator prior to implementation of the new food labeling regulations. The authors reported that there was no clear and consistent pattern in the types of products that had labels versus those that did not.

Although the presence of a label was an unreliable cue, it is not known to what extent consumers might have assumed that the absence of a label was a sign of a less healthful product. There is some suggestive evidence from Mathios (1996) that, in one product category (salad dressing), some consumers might have used the presence of a food label as a cue in product selection pre-NLEA. Mathios studied sales of labeled and unlabeled salad dressing in 20 supermarkets that varied in terms of the income and education levels of their customers. Mathios found that 44% of salad dressings did not have nutrition labeling prior to mandatory food labeling (data were collected during 1992 and 1993). Regression analyses showed a significant correlation between the socioeconomic status characteristics of grocery store shoppers and the proportion of salad dressing sales accounted for by unlabeled high-fat products. Stores with more elderly, lower income, and less educated shoppers reported higher sales of unlabeled high-fat salad dressings. Stores with more female shoppers reported fewer sales of unlabeled high-fat salad dressings. This study could not isolate the impact of labeling, and there are alternative hypotheses that could account for the results, but it raises the possibility that health-conscious consumers used the presence of a label as a cue about the characteristics of both labeled and unlabeled options in a product category.

Market response also is complex. Moorman (1998) examined base brands (brands not positioned with respect to nutrition) and brand extensions (brands positioned as healthier than the base by reducing negative nutrients, such as sodium or fat, or increasing positive nutrients, such as vitamin C or calcium) pre- and post-NLEA. She found that different strategies were employed simultaneously as food companies adjusted to the changes required by mandatory food labeling. There were more healthy brands introduced post-NLEA (18.5%, up from 14.4% before). For base brands, there were improvements in terms of the addition of positive nutrients but no significant deletion of negative nutrients. On the other hand, brand extensions did not significantly increase the number of positive nutrients, but there was a significant increase in the number of extensions that deleted negative nutrients. When brand "healthiness" was low, there was a significant relationship between year and price promotion, suggesting that these brands were promoted more after the NLEA was implemented, whereas healthy brands were unchanged over time. Moorman's pattern of findings revealed a strategic response to the NLEA by food manufacturers by changing base and brand extensions in opposite ways so as to allow products to occupy distinct niches in the marketplace.

Conclusion

Research on label use before and after implementation of the NLEA showed increasing awareness of the new label over time and significant levels of reported label use to make product choices. The food label caused some consumers to stop buying products or to try new products. The food label provided the types of information that consumers are most concerned about (e.g., dietary fats) and presented the information more clearly than before.

Experimental studies demonstrated that most consumers have no difficulty in understanding the nutritional characteristics of food products, and when they pay attention to both claims and Nutrition Facts information, they draw appropriate conclusions about the product's healthfulness. In their day-to-day lives, consumers face an information-rich environment, time constraints, and strong habits and beliefs about foods that affect what information they notice and attend to when making product choices. It is hard to estimate the extent to which consumers rely on front panel claims in choosing foods rather than confirming the information by examining the nutrition label. Although consumers tended to express skepticism in research settings, they also have reported greater probability of buying products with health claims.

The FDA Health Claims Study findings offer support for maintaining health claim regulations that limit claims to relationships meeting standards of scientific certainty and limit use of claims to products not exceeding disqualifying levels for other health-relevant nutrients. Even without time constraints and in a situation where participants are likely to be more vigilant and conscientious, the presence of front panel claims reduced the likelihood that participants would check the Nutrition Facts label. So long as claims are limited to products that meet defined standards, a lack of vigilance on the part of consumers will not be likely to result in misjudging the nutritional characteristics of foods or in making choices that do not support consumers' intentions.

Consumer research on label use and consumer perceptions of label information revealed that the food label is not an ideal vehicle for disseminating generic nutrition education messages. Consumers use the label for product-specific purposes. Health-related information is likely to be seen as a reminder or signal; consumers generally are reluctant to accept food labels as a source of new information about diet-disease relationships. Health and nutrition information is widely available to consumers and has become a standby of broadcast and print news reporting. This information creates a context, and also might provide motivation, for consumers' use of food labels. For example, public awareness of major dietary risk factors, successfully communicated to the public through a wide variety of campaigns and media, enabled consumers to use food labels to help make food choices consistent with their dietary concerns.

Data from the FLUNES indicated that newer findings of nutrition science are being successfully disseminated to the general public. For example, there were sharp increases in the percentage of adults who had heard of health problems related to not eating enough folic acid (41% in 1995, up 16% from 1994) and antioxidant vitamins (45% in 1995, up 12% from 1994). The food label was not likely to be the source of this information given that health claims for these nutrients had not been approved by the FDA; the FDA subsequently approved a folic acid and neural tube defects health claim in conjunction with a folate fortification policy that went into effect in 1998. The fact that the public seems eager to know about the newest findings of nutrition science is an indication of the important role that the food label can play as a source of accurate, reliable, and relevant information about the nutrition characteristics of foods.

One aspect of the NLEA that has not been systematically studied is the effect of the "education mandate" that was incorporated into the legislation. In the NLEA, Congress explicitly acknowledged that for the labeling regulations to achieve their objectives, consumers would need to be educated about the availability of nutrition information in the label or labeling of food and the importance of that information in maintaining healthful dietary practices.

The FDA and the USDA worked together to develop education initiatives in collaboration with partners such as public health organizations, consumer interest groups, trade associations, and individual industries (Kulakow 1995; Swann 1995). The FDA provided a variety of resources to the media when the new food labels were launched in 1994. The Nutrition Facts label was the major focus of most educational efforts. Practical guidance for consumers on how to use the new label was incorporated into general dietary guidance (e.g., the 2000 Dietary Guidelines for Americans) and specific educational programs (e.g., USDA nutrition education programs). Diet programs such as Weight Watchers emphasize use of the Nutrition Facts label as a tool to help program participants make food choices.

The extent to which food label education materials and programs have reached the American public and helped consumers to make effective use of the label is not known. With respect to nutrient content and health claims, research showed little consumer awareness that claims are regulated, and a majority of consumers remain skeptical of health claims on food labels. This suggests that, to date, consumer education has not adequately addressed the credibility issue.

The NLEA food label now is a well-known and ubiquitous part of the food marketplace. The level of interest in tracking label use has declined during recent years. The latest ADA Nutrition Survey did not ask specific questions about label use (ADA 1999), and there were few label-related questions in the FMI Trends and FMI/Prevention Surveys during the late 1990s. Current concerns have centered on diet and health topics such as dietary guidance, dietary supplements, and foods marketed for their special properties (e.g., organic foods, "functional foods").

References

American Dietetic Association (1993), *Survey of American Dietary Habits 1993: Executive Summary.* Chicago: ADA.

——— (1995), *Nutrition Trends Survey 1995: Executive Summary.* Chicago: ADA.

——— (1997), *Nutrition Trends Survey 1997: Executive Summary.* Chicago: ADA.

——— (1999), *Nutrition Trends Survey 1999: Executive Summary.* Chicago: ADA.

Barone, M. J., R. L. Rose, K. C. Manning, and P. W. Miniard (1996), "Another Look at the Impact of Reference Information on Consumer Impressions of Nutrition Information," *Journal of Public Policy & Marketing,* 15 (1), 55-62.

Bender, M. M. and B. M. Derby (1992), "Prevalence of Reading Nutrition and Ingredient Information on Food Labels among Adult Americans: 1982-1988," *Journal of Nutrition Education,* 24, 292-97.

Bialostosky, K., ed. (1998), *Nutrition Monitoring in the United States: The Directory of Federal and State Nutrition Monitoring and Related Research Activities.* Hyattsville, MD: National Center for Health Statistics.

Burke, S. J., S. J. Milberg, and W. W. Moe (1997), "Displaying Common but Previously Neglected Health Claims on Product Labels: Understanding Competitive Advantages, Deception, and Education," *Journal of Public Policy & Marketing,* 16 (2), 242-55.

Calorie Control Council (1999), *Trends and Statistics* [on-line]. Available: http://www.caloriecontrol.org/survey4.html

Cooper, R. M., R. L. Frank, and M. J. O'Flaherty (1990), "History of Health Claims Regulation," *Food Drug Cosmetic Law Journal,* 45, 655-91.

Derby, B. M. and S. B. Fein (1995), "Meeting the NLEA Education Challenge: A Consumer Research Perspective," in *The Nutrition Labeling Handbook,* R. Shapiro, ed. New York: Marcel Dekker, 315-52.

——— and J. F. Guthrie (1999), "Trends in Food Label Use and Associated Knowledge, Attitudes, and Personal Characteristics, 1994-1996," paper presented at the annual meeting of the Society for Nutrition Education, July, Baltimore, MD.

———— and A. S. Levy (1994), "Consumer Use of Food Labels: Where Are We? Where Are We Going?" paper presented at the annual meeting of the American Dietetic Association, October, Orlando, FL.

Food and Drug Administration (1993), "Food Labeling; Label Format; Percent DV Format," *Federal Register,* 58 (3), 2125-28.

———— (1999), "Food Labeling; Trans Fatty Acids in Nutrition Labeling, Nutrient Content Claims, and Health Claims; Proposed Rule," *Federal Register,* 64 (221), 62745-825.

Food Marketing Institute (1990), *Trends in the United States: Consumer Attitudes and the Supermarket 1990.* Washington, DC: FMI.

———— (1991), *Trends in the United States: Consumer Attitudes and the Supermarket 1991.* Washington, DC: FMI.

———— (1995), *Trends in the United States: Consumer Attitudes and the Supermarket 1995.* Washington, DC: FMI.

———— (1996), *Trends in the United States: Consumer Attitudes and the Supermarket 1996.* Washington, DC: FMI.

———— (1997), *Trends in the United States: Consumer Attitudes and the Supermarket 1997.* Washington, DC: FMI.

———— (1999), *Trends in the United States: Consumer Attitudes and the Supermarket 1999.* Washington, DC: FMI.

Food Marketing Institute/Prevention (1994), *Shopping for Health 1994: Eating in America—Perception and Reality.* Washington, DC: FMI/Prevention.

———— (1995), *Shopping for Health 1995: New Food Labels, Same Eating Habits?* Washington, DC: FMI/Prevention.

———— (1996), *Shopping for Health 1996: Americans Look for Answers about the Foods They Eat.* Washington, DC: FMI/Prevention.

———— (1997), *Shopping for Health 1997: Balancing Convenience, Nutrition, and Taste.* Washington, DC: FMI/Prevention.

———— (1999), *Shopping for Health 1999: The Growing Self-Care Movement.* Washington, DC: FMI/Prevention.

Ford, G. T., M. Hastak, A. Mitra, and D. J. Ringold (1996), "Can Consumers Interpret Nutrition Information in the Presence of a Health Claim? A Laboratory Investigation," *Journal of Public Policy & Marketing,* 15 (1), 16-27.

Geiger, C. J. (1998), "Health Claims: History, Current Regulatory Status, and Consumer Research," *Journal of the American Dietetic Association,* 98 (11), 1312-22.

"Good Nutrition: The Bloom Is Off the Bud" (1997), *Wirthlin Report.* McLean, VA: Wirthlin Organization.

Gugliotta, G. (2000), "Food Labels: By Some Measures, a Well-Read Success," *The Washington Post,* January 3, A3.

Guthrie, J. F., B. M. Derby, and A. S. Levy (1999), "What People Know and Don't Know about Nutrition," in *America's Eating Habits: Changes and Consequences,* Agriculture Information Bulletin No. 750, E. Frazao, ed. Washington, DC: U.S. Department of Agriculture, 243-80.

———— and J. F. Morton (2000), "Food Sources of Added Sweeteners in the Diets of Americans," *Journal of the American Dietetic Association,* 100(1), 43-48, 51.

Hutt, P. B. (1986), "Government Regulation of Health Claims in Food Labeling and Advertising," *Food Drug Cosmetic Law Journal,* 41, 3-73.

Keller, S. B., M. Landry, J. Olson, A. M. Velliquestte, S. Burton, and J. C. Andrews (1997), "The Effects of Nutrition Package Claims, Nutrition Facts Panels, and Motivation to Process Nutrition Information on Consumer Product Evaluations," *Journal of Public Policy & Marketing,* 16 (2), 256-69.

Keystone Center (1996), *The Final Report of the Keystone National Policy Dialogue on Food, Nutrition, and Health.* Keystone, CO: Keystone Center.

Kristal, A. R., L. Levy, R. E. Patterson, S. S. Li, and E. White (1998), "Trends in Food Label Use Associated with New Nutrition Labeling Regulations. *American Journal of Public Health,* 88 (8), 1212-15.

Kulakow, N. (1995), "NLEA: Linking Education to Regulation," in *The Nutrition Labeling Handbook,* R. Shapiro, ed. New York: Marcel Dekker, 299-314.

Kurtzweil, P. (1998), "Staking a Claim to Good Health: FDA and Science Stand behind Health Claims on Foods," *FDA Consumer,* 32 (6), 16-21.

Levy, A. S. (1996), "Summary Report on Health Claims Focus Groups," in *The Final Report of the Keystone National Policy Dialogue on Food, Nutrition, and Health.* Keystone, CO: Keystone Center, 141-50.

———— and B. M. Derby (1995), *Food Label Use and Nutrition Education Survey: Selected Results Prepared for the Dietary Guidelines Advisory Committee.* Washington, DC: U.S. Food and Drug Administration.

———— and ———— (1996), "The Impact of the NLEA on Consumers: Recent Findings from FDA's Food Labeling and Nutrition Tracking System," paper prepared for the Office of the FDA commissioner, Food and Drug Administration.

————, ————, and B. E. Roe (1997), *Consumer Impacts of Health Claims: An Experimental Study* [on-line]. Available: http://vm.cfsan.fda.gov/label.html

———— and S. B. Fein (1998), "Consumers' Ability to Perform Tasks Using Nutrition Labels." *Journal of Nutrition Education,* 30 (4), 210-17.

————, ————, and R. E. Schucker (1996), "Performance Characteristics of Seven Nutrition Label Formats," *Journal of Public Policy & Marketing,* 15 (1), 1-15.

————, ————, and M. Stephenson (1993), "Nutrition Knowledge Levels about Dietary Fats and Cholesterol: 1983-1988," *Journal of Nutrition Education,* 25, 60-66.

Lin, B-H., J. F. Guthrie, and E. Frazao (1999), *Away-from-Home Foods Increasingly Important to Quality of American Diet* (Agricultural Information Bulletin No. 749). Washington, DC: U.S. Department of Agriculture.

Mathios, A. D. (1996), "Socioeconomic Factors, Nutrition, and Food Choices: An Analysis of the Salad Dressing Market," *Journal of Public Policy & Marketing,* 15 (1), 45-54.

Mathios, A. D. and P. Ippolito (1999), "Health Claims in Food Advertising and Labeling: Disseminating Nutrition Information to Consumers. In *America's Eating Habits: Changes and Consequences,* Agriculture Information Bulletin No. 750, E. Frazao, ed. Washington, DC: U.S. Department of Agriculture, 189-212.

Mitra, A., M. Hastak, G. T. Ford, and D. J. Ringold (1999), "Can the Educationally Disadvantaged Interpret the FDA-Mandated Nutrition Facts Panel in the Presence of an Implied Health Claim?" *Journal of Public Policy & Marketing,* 18 (1), 106-17.

Mojduszka, E. M. and J. A. Caswell (2000), "A Test of Nutritional Quality Signaling in Food Markets Prior to Implementation of Mandatory Labeling," *American Journal of Agricultural Economics,* 82, 289-309.

Moorman, C. (1996), "A Quasi-Experiment to Assess the Consumer and Informational Determinants of Nutrition Information Processing Activities: The Case of the Nutrition Labeling and Education Act," *Journal of Public Policy & Marketing,* 15 (1), 28-44.

———— (1998), "Market-Level Effects of Information: Competitive Responses and Consumer Dynamics," *Journal of Marketing Research,* 35 (1), 82-98.

National Research Council (1989), *Diet and Health: Implications for Reducing Chronic Disease.* Washington, DC: National Academy Press.

Neuhouser, M. L., A. R. Kristal, and R. E. Patterson (1999), "Use of Nutrition Labels Is Associated with Lower Fat Intake," *Journal of the American Dietetic Association,* 99 (1), 45-53.

O'Brien, T. (1996), *Status of Nutrition Labeling of Processed Foods: 1995* (Food Label and Package Survey). Washington, DC: Food and Drug Administration.

Porter, D. V. and R. O. Earl, eds. (1990), *Nutrition Labeling: Issues and Directions for the 1990s.* Washington, DC: National Academy Press.

" 'Premature' Survey on Food Label's Effects Finds One" (1994), *Food Labeling News,* August 11, 27.

Putler, D. S. and E. Frazao (1991), "Assessing the Effects of Diet/Health Awareness on the Consumption and Composition of Fat Intake," in *Economics of Food Safety,* J. A. Caswell, ed. New York: Elsevier, 247-70.

Ralston, K. (1999), "How Government Policies and Regulations Can Affect Dietary Choices," in *America's Eating Habits: Changes and Consequences,* Agriculture Information Bulletin No. 750, E. Frazao, ed. Washington, DC: U.S. Department of Agriculture, 331-69.

Roe, B. E., A. S. Levy, and B. M. Derby (1999), "The Impact of Health Claims on Consumer Search and Product Evaluation Outcomes: Results from FDA Experimental Data," *Journal of Public Policy & Marketing,* 18 (1), 89-105.

Roper Organization (1993), *Roper Reports: Food and Health* (93-1). New York: Roper Organization.

Scarbrough, F. E. (1995), "Perspectives on Nutrition Labeling and Education Act," in *The Nutrition Labeling Handbook,* R. Shapiro, ed. New York: Marcel Dekker, 29-52.

Schucker, B., J. T. Wittes, N. C. Santanello, W. J. Weber, D. McGoldrick, K. Donato, A. S. Levy, and B. M. Rifkind (1991), "Change in Cholesterol Awareness and Action: Results from National Physician and Public Surveys," *Archives of Internal Medicine,* 151, 666-73.

Schwartz, N. E. and S. T. Borra (1997), "What Do Consumers Really Think about Dietary Fat?" *Journal of the American Dietetic Association,* 97 (7), S73-75. (Supplement)

Shank, F. R. (1992), "The Nutrition Labeling and Education Act of 1990," *Food and Drug Law Journal,* 47, 247-52.

Sigman-Grant, M. (1997), "Can You Have Your Low-Fat Cake and Eat It too? The Role of Fat-Modified Products," *Journal of the American Dietetic Association,* 97 (7), S76-81. (Supplement)

Swann, L. (1995), "Consumer Communications: Informing, Educating, and Persuading the Public to Use the New Food Label," in *The Nutrition Labeling Handbook,* R. Shapiro, ed. New York: Marcel Dekker, 355-71.

Teisl, M. F., A. S. Levy, and B. M. Derby (1999), "The Effects of Education and Information Source on Consumer Awareness of Diet-Disease Relationships," *Journal of Public Policy & Marketing,* 18 (2), 197-207.

Tippett, K. and L. E. Cleveland (1999), "How Current Diets Stack Up: Comparison with the Dietary Guidelines," in *America's Eating Habits: Changes and Consequences,* Agriculture Information Bulletin No. 750, E. Frazao, ed. Washington, DC: U.S. Department of Agriculture, 51-95.

U.S. Department of Health and Human Services (1988), *The Surgeon General's Report on Nutrition and Health.* Washington, DC: U.S. Government Printing Office.

Variyam, J. N. (1999), "Role of Demographics, Knowledge, and Attitudes," in *America's Eating Habits: Changes and Consequences,* Agriculture Information Bulletin No. 750, E. Frazao, ed. Washington, DC: U.S. Department of Agriculture, 281-94.

Weimar, H. (1999), "Accelerating the Trend toward Healthy Eating: Private and Public Efforts," in *America's Eating Habits: Changes and Consequences,* Agriculture Information Bulletin No. 750, E. Frazao, ed. Washington, DC: U.S. Department of Agriculture, 385-401.

The Effectiveness of Environmental Marketing Claims

The Roles of Consumers, Competitors, and Policy Makers

Robert N. Mayer
Linda A. Lewis
Debra L. Scammon

Consumers, businesses, and governments all contribute to environmental degradation and, therefore, have a responsibility to protect the natural environment. During the 1970s, primary attention was focused on the role that businesses and governments could play in environmental improvement, but during the latter half of the 1980s, there was a distinct growth of interest in how individual consumers (both before and after the act of purchase) could help to mitigate their environmental impact.

The interest of consumers in environmental stewardship set in motion a complex and interrelated set of responses from businesses and public policy makers. First, sellers of consumer products responded to the perceived demand for environmentally preferable brands by making claims about the environmentally relevant attributes of their brands. While some firms touted features that had existed prior to the kindling of consumer interest in environmental matters (e.g., biodegradable detergent, CFC-free aerosols), other firms redesigned products and/or packages to improve their environmentally relevant attributes (e.g., mercury-free batteries, items packaged in cardboard made from post-consumer recycled paper).

To encourage consumers to notice and try their brands, firms made environmental claims in advertising and on labels. Some of these claims were trivial or misleading. As a result, public interest groups and competitors lodged complaints with governmental authorities and self-regulatory bodies (e.g., Council of Better Business Bureaus). In response, these authorities took a variety of actions to promote honest and meaningful claims. In some nations, public policies were undertaken, not just to rein in potentially deceptive claims, but also to encourage the use of third-party environmental seals of approval. The availability of seals of approval expanded the means by which environmental marketing claims could be made, indirectly influencing corporate competition via environmental attributes, consumer decision making regarding brands, and (ultimately) the natural environment itself.

The actions of firms to gain competitive advantage through environmental marketing as well as the efforts of government and self-regulatory bodies to control environmental marketing occurred in a context of key assumptions. First, it was largely assumed that environmental claims and seals of approval influenced the behavior of consumers. Second, feedback in the form of consumer behavior was presumed to influence the further actions of firms and regulators.

The chain of events just described raises a number of important questions about environmental marketing:

1. What evidence was available to businesses as to the strength of consumer demand for environmental marketing efforts?

2. What types of environmental marketing claims were available to businesses to promote the environmental attributes of their brands?

3. What patterns of growth across time and product classes characterized environmental marketing claims?

4. How and how well have first-party environmental claims been regulated in various countries?

5. How and how well have third-party seals of approval been promoted in various countries?

6. How effective are first-party claims and third-party seals in changing consumer behavior and affecting competition?

7. What are the current trends in the use of first-party environmental claims and third-party seals of approval?

This chapter is organized around answers to these questions.

The Demand for Environmental Marketing Claims

The marketing story of the growth of environmental marketing usually begins around 1989 with opinion poll results showing renewed public concern about the state of the natural environment and the willingness of consumers to do something to improve it. The sociological story, however, needs to go back further to explain why public concern about the environment had noticeably increased by 1989, when marketers "discovered" it. The reasons, which are beyond the scope of this chapter, no doubt would include a string of environmental disasters including houses built on top of toxic wastes at Love Canal, New York, in 1978; the release of radioactive gas from Pennsylvania's Three Mile Island nuclear power plant in 1979; the explosion at a Union Carbide chemical plant in Bhopal, India, in 1984; the meltdown of the Chernobyl nuclear reactor in the former Soviet Union in 1986; and the running aground of the Exxon *Valdez* oil tanker in 1989. The oil spilled by the *Valdez* in March 1989, plus oil from three additional spills in June of that year, did more than pollute the oceans; it may have ignited long-simmering public anxieties about humankind's treatment of the natural environment.

Whatever the exact catalyst, by 1989, marketers could see that consumers wanted to do their part in addressing environmental problems. The results of numerous surveys of consumers supported this perception. Not only did people declare high levels of environmental concern, but they also indicated that this concern was changing their behavior in the marketplace. The majority of the 1,000 respondents in a 1989 study conducted by the Michael Peters Group in the United States said that they had declined to buy a product during the past year because of concern that it or its packaging might be harmful to the environment (cited in Elkington, Hailes, and Makower 1990, p. 6). In another national study conducted in the United States in 1989, more than 90% of respondents reported that they would "make a special effort to buy products from companies trying to protect the environment" and would "give up some convenience, such as the disposability of items, in return for environmentally safer products or packaging" (Hume and Strnad 1989). Other studies indicated that the majority of consumers consider environmental attributes when buying (Wells and Stoeckle 1990) and actually select or reject brands based on their environmental impact ("Cambridge Reports" 1992; Gerstman and Meyers 1991; Wells and Stoeckle 1990).

Perhaps most tantalizing to marketers were survey findings that consumers were willing to pay higher prices for environmentally preferable brands ("Cambridge Reports" 1992; Farhar 1994; Gutfeld 1991; Levin 1990; S. C. Johnson & Son 1990, 1992; Wells and Stoeckle 1990). This is despite the finding that green brands were not necessarily more expensive (Cude 1993; Purcell and Keil 1990). The exact price increases that consumers said they were willing to bear varied across studies and products, and skepticism would have been warranted about the degree to which actual behavior would match articulated willingness. Nevertheless, all the survey evidence seemed to point in the same direction:

Consumers wanted the opportunity to express their environmental concerns through their purchases.

Types of Environmental Marketing Claims

The apparent interest of consumers in environmental improvement dovetailed nicely with the perception of some firms that they could gain a competitive advantage by emphasizing the superior environmental attributes of their brands. The strategic question for these firms was how to communicate with consumers.

Broadly speaking, firms have two options for communicating brand-specific environmental information: first-party claims and third-party seals of approval. A first-party claim is one whose content is completely controlled by the firm. It typically extols, in the company's own words and images, one or more brand attributes. For example, a firm might claim that the packaging of its current brand of detergent has been engineered to use 50% less cardboard and plastic than its previous version. Some environmental claims, instead of referring to brand attributes, refer to the behavior of the brand's parent. A firm might claim that 1% of the proceeds from a detergent's sales are donated to environmental organizations or that paper consumption at the firm's corporate headquarters has been reduced by 35% during the previous year. Whereas these latter claims are environmental claims, this chapter focuses on claims about the environmental attributes of a product or its packaging.

Like first-party claims, third-party claims are voluntary, but their content is partly controlled by an impartial body that is independent of the seller. There are two important types of third-party claims. The first and most common type is a seal of approval indicating that an objective organization deems the brand to be relatively good (or less bad) within its product class in terms of its environmental impact. The oldest such seal is Germany's Blue Angel, but more than 20 such seals now exist around the world (U.S. Environmental Protection Agency [EPA] 1998; Yang 1998). Typically, these seals of approval consider multiple dimensions of a brand's environmental performance and are potentially applicable across a wide range of product classes. There are, however, a number of single-attribute certification programs that tend to be applicable to a narrower range of products (e.g., a dolphin-safe seal of approval for tuna products). A particularly notable example of a single-attribute seal of approval is the Energy Star program run by the EPA. Initiated for office equipment and recently expanded to other electric products, the use of the Energy Star logo now is so common for computers, monitors, and printers that it has become a de facto energy conservation standard (Cavanagh 1998).

A second and less common type of third-party claim provides a way of displaying a brand's attributes along multiple dimensions but without indicating that the brand under consideration is superior to other brands. These "environmental report cards" show a brand's environmental performance in the same way as nutritional labels reveal a food's nutritional performance. One food item might be loaded with calories, saturated fat, and sodium, whereas another might be low on these dimensions; either way, the "Nutrition Facts" panel would be used. Similarly, companies could use a standard format to disclose the environmental performance of their brands. Scientific Certification Systems has been the major advocate of the environmental report card, but the issuance of this type of third-party claim has been very limited to date.

The International Standards Organization (ISO) has been working on principles to guide the use of both first- and third-party claims (Hedblom 1998). As of the beginning of 2000, the ISO was nearing completion of its guidelines for making first-party claims containing statements about the environmental impact of a brand's attributes (as opposed to claims about corporate environmental practices that are not reflected directly in the company's products or packaging). The ISO also is working on standards for third-party, multi-attribute environmental seals of approval. First-party claims and third-party seals account for the majority of environmental marketing communications sent by firms to consumers. Accordingly, these two types of claims are the focus of the discussion that follows.

Patterns of Growth in Environmental Marketing Claims

During the late 1980s, when firms became interested in making environmental marketing claims, first-party claims were virtually the only option (except in Germany, which had the Blue Angel program since 1978) for communicating brand-specific environmental information. There is no definitive source of information about the content of these pioneering first-party claims or about the types of products to which they referred. One of the best sources of data, however, is the ProductScan service run by Marketing Intelligence Service (MIS). Beginning in 1986, MIS collected information on the percentage of *new* brand introductions for nondurable goods that made "green promises" on their package labels. These claims include terms such as "biodegradable," "recyclable," "recycled," "no fluorocarbons," and "no phosphates" as well as claims such as being organic and pesticide free, which can be viewed by consumers to be environmental claims, health claims, or both (Janet Mansfield, Marketing Intelligence Service Ltd., personal communication, February 9, 1999).

Table 17.1 shows the rates of brand introductions accompanied by green claims between 1986 and 1998 in product categories such as foods, health and beauty aids, and pet-related products. The data show that environmental marketing claims for new brands increased dramatically between 1988 and 1990, peaked during the early 1990s, and declined only modestly through the remainder of the 1990s. Claims were most common in the household category (e.g., detergents, cleaners, trash bags, paper towels) and least prevalent in the foods and beverages categories despite the counting of claims such as "organic" and "pesticide free" (Mansfield, personal communication, February 9, 1999).

Whereas the MIS data are based on claims appearing on packages, several studies examined environmental claims appearing in advertisements. The purpose of these studies was not to quantify the frequency of first-party environ-

TABLE 17.1 Green Product Introductions, 1986-1998: Percentages of Total
Introductions Making Green Claims

Year	Total	Foods	Beverages	Cosmetics	House-hold	Other	Pet-Related Products
1986	1.1	1.4	2.3	0.4	2.7	0.5	0.9
1987	2.0	2.1	2.3	0.4	7.4	1.7	3.9
1988	2.8	3.4	5.4	0.6	9.4	2.2	3.2
1989	4.5	4.9	10.1	1.6	15.7	4.2	1.4
1990	11.4	9.2	11.4	13.0	25.9	6.5	11.6
1991	13.4	9.3	13.4	14.7	32.9	19.5	22.9
1992	11.5	8.7	8.9	12.0	30.5	6.3	18.2
1993	13.1	10.4	15.1	13.6	29.6	8.6	15.3
1994	10.5	5.7	7.7	14.2	37.2	14.4	17.2
1995	9.7	8.2	7.5	10.8	25.9	8.2	8.9
1996	12.1	6.8	8.3	9.3	30.4	8.1	9.9
1997	12.5	8.0	8.5	9.5	29.5	8.8	10.7
1998	8.7	7.1	12.0	7.7	25.4	6.8	6.8

SOURCE: 1999 ProductScan by Marketing Intelligence Service Ltd.

mental claims in advertising but rather to investigate the various types of information presented in these ads and to evaluate these claims for their potential to mislead consumers (Banerjee, Gulas, and Iyer 1995; Carlson, Grove, and Kangun 1993; Kangun, Carlson, and Grove 1991; Polonsky et al. 1997). Nevertheless, these studies revealed that environmental claims were common by the late 1980s and early 1990s.

A way of tracking the types of environmental claims that were made in both labels and advertisements is by following enforcement actions taken by the U.S. Federal Trade Commission (FTC), Council of Better Business Bureau (CBBB), and other regulatory bodies. Scammon and Mayer (1995) found that, within the United States, these cases peaked in 1991 among state and local regulatory authorities, in 1992 in the CBBB's National Advertising Division, and in 1993 at the FTC. In terms of the product classes involved, they found that plastic products (e.g., "degradable" trash bags) and aerosol sprays (e.g., "ozone-friendly" cleaners) were most common among those whose claims were challenged by regulators. Despite being biased toward the most questionable claims, the enforcement data suggest the same conclusions as do the new brand introduction figures: The presence of environmental marketing claims intensified markedly during the late 1980s and early 1990s, and claims were most prevalent among nonfood, nondurable items.

In the United States at least, the use of third-party seals of approval has lagged far behind that of first-party claims. In 1990, the first companies were given permission to use the logo of the Green Cross Certification Company (now Scientific Certification Systems) to show that their claims regarding levels of recycled content had been verified. For example, it certified that Willamette Industries' paper grocery bags contained 40% recycled content. (The Green Cross was not a true seal of approval inasmuch as it did not indicate conformity to a minimum standard but merely verified a manufacturer's first-party claim.) Green Seal, a true multi-attribute seal of approval program, was established in 1990 but was slow to issue standards. Its first standard was issued in 1992 and covered toilet and facial tissues. Despite the issuance of standards for more than 20 product classes by 1995, marketers in the United States were slow to embrace the seal in their ads and on their labels. Seals outside of the United States have been more successful (discussed later in this chapter).

Regulation of First-Party Environmental Claims

What ground rules were developed by regulatory and self-regulatory authorities to deal with perceived deficiencies in the quality of first-party environmental claims? How did the intensity and focus of these initiatives vary by country?

In the United States, regulation of environmental marketing claims did not stop with case-by-case action by regulatory authorities and self-regulatory bodies. By the early 1990s, there was considerable pressure for a more encompassing approach. Some states (e.g., New York, California, Rhode Island) passed their own rules, but both state and local regulators as well as business groups pressed the FTC for national guidance. The state and local regulators had been happy to play the role of gadflies, but they lacked the resources to regulate environmental marketing claims over the long run (Scammon and Mayer 1995). Businesses were distressed by the prospect of having to meet different, and potentially inconsistent, state mandates when marketing brands on a national scale.

Although the FTC could have issued formal rules regarding environmental marketing claims, it opted for a quicker and more flexible approach by issuing comprehensive national guidelines in 1992 (*Code of Federal Regulations* 1993). The guidelines explained how the FTC would enforce its general mandate forbidding deceptive claims by offering a set of principles as well as specific examples of claims that would fall either within or outside of acceptable boundaries. The principles included the injunctions that (1) claims should not exaggerate environmental benefits; (2) qualifications in claims should be clear, prominent, and understandable; (3) whether a claim refers to a product, its packaging, or both should be clear; and (4) the basis for any comparative claims should be clear.

The specific examples in the guidelines were designed to provide manufacturers with a "safe harbor" for making environmental claims by illustrating deceptive and nondeceptive claims. For example, the claim that plastic trash bags are degradable, with no qualification or other disclosure and based on soil burial tests showing that the product will decompose in the presence of water and oxygen, would be deceptive if the trash bags are customarily disposed of in incineration facilities or at sanitary landfills that are managed in a way that inhibits degradation by minimizing moisture and oxygen. By contrast, a commercial agricultural plastic mulch film advertised as "photodegradable," if qualified with the phrase "will break down into small pieces if left uncovered in sunlight" and supported by competent and reliable scientific evidence that the product will break down in a reasonably short period of time after being exposed to sunlight and into sufficiently small pieces to become part of the soil, would not be deceptive.

The FTC guidelines have been widely adopted. Not only have several U.S. states replaced their regulations with the FTC's guidelines, but several other countries (e.g., Australia) and international bodies (e.g., ISO [Standard 14021]) have used the FTC guidelines to shape their own regulatory efforts.

As important as the FTC's 1992 guidelines have been, they were not the first such guidelines. Nor are guidelines the only method of regulation of environmental claims that have been tried. In 1991, Consumer and Corporate Affairs Canada (CCAC), a branch of the Canadian national government, issued "Guiding Principles for Environmental Labelling and Advertising." The guidelines were developed by a working group consisting of government and industry representatives, the latter including groups such as the Association of Canadian Advertisers, the Grocery Products Manufacturers of Canada, and the Packaging Association of Canada. Similar to the FTC in the United States, the CCAC administers general statutes against deceptive advertising and labeling (e.g., Consumer Packaging and Labelling Act, Competition Act). Hence, the guiding principles issued by the CCAC serve to define how it will enforce the existing law in relation to environmental marketing claims. In several respects, the Canadian guidelines are stronger than those of the FTC. For example, the Canadian guidelines express the presumption that claims about recycled content will refer to "post-use" or "post-consumer" material (e.g., newspapers, aluminum cans), whereas the FTC guidelines allow firms to call "pre-consumer" material "recycled." Pre-consumer waste includes material generated during the manufacturing process (e.g., scraps, by-products) that never leaves the factory grounds.

Besides issuing guidelines that interpret broad government statutes, other approaches were tried to combat misleading advertisements and labels. In 1986, the Swiss federal government passed an "Ordinance Relating to Environmentally Hazardous Substances." In addition to prohibiting misleading statements, the law explicitly banned words such as "degradable," "ecologically harmless," "environmentally favourable," and "harmless to waters" (J. Salzman, personal communication, December 31, 1991).

Other nations relied heavily on self-regulatory efforts. In the Netherlands, for example, the nongovernmental Advertising Steering Group collaborated with the governmental Ministries of Environment and Economic Affairs to produce the "Dutch Environmental Advertising Code" in 1991. The International Chamber of Commerce also drew up a "Code of Advertising Practice" in 1991 (Consumers International 1998).

To its credit, the FTC reviewed the effectiveness of its 1992 guidelines. It held hearings in 1995 and issued revisions to the guidelines in 1996 and again in 1998 (*Code of Federal Regulations* 1997, 1999). In its July 31, 1995 request for public comments, the FTC sought information on what changes had occurred regarding consumer perceptions, environmental technology, and regulation at the state and local levels that might call for changes in the guidelines. In terms of evaluating the impact of the guidelines to that point, the FTC defined several yardsticks including: (1) benefits and costs to consumers, including reduced consumer skepticism and confusion about environmental claims; (2) benefits and costs to firms, including manufacturer uncertainty about which claims might lead to FTC law enforcement actions; and (3) impacts on the development of environmentally beneficial innovations in technology and products. The "gold standard" for evaluating the guidelines, however, was their effect on "the prevalence and accuracy of various environmental claims."

The FTC's 1995 request for comments elicited the views of a broad array of interested groups, each with its own particular suggestions for improving the guidelines. For example, Helene Curtis, a manufacturer of aerosol-propelled personal care products, urged the FTC to view the term "no CFCs" as truthful and not misleading, even though CFCs have long been banned in consumer products. Ford Motor Company wanted to make sure that it could make unqualified recyclability claims, even though there may be no curbside or drop-off recycling programs for automobile parts. Important differences of opinion existed among participants concerning the meaning of recycled content, the ways of properly qualifying recyclability claims, and the value of "eco-labels," but there was a consensus that the guidelines were working well and should remain in place.

If the guidelines were indeed working well, then there was very little systematic evidence submitted to support this view. The results of several surveys on consumer interpretations of particular claims were debated (e.g., impacts on the ozone layer, recyclability, and recycled content), but most comments offered only weak evidence of the impact of the guidelines on claims themselves. For example, the head of Green Seal, grantor of the United States' only third-party multi-attribute seal of approval, made the comment, "The guides have undeniably had a positive impact on the flow of accurate, truthful information about environmental claims . . ., [but] we have no factual data to support this assertion" (Dean 1995). Instead, Green Seal offered the observation, "In our many contacts with manufacturers . . ., we constantly hear the concern that any claims they make be consistent with the FTC guides." In a similar vein, 3M's director of corporate product responsibility submitted the following comment:

I am unable to quantify my perceptions that I believe that the guides have had a beneficial effect on the improved flow of truthful information and a reduction in the flow of deceptive information to consumers. . . . During the 3M environmental marketing claim review process, roughly 25% of claims initially submitted are unsuitable primarily because they have the potential for being misleading. In most instances, the initial claim has been successfully modified to be compatible with the FTC guides. In the remaining instances, the claim has been eliminated. (Theissen 1995)

Only one set of comments reported the results of a study designed to assess the impact of the guidelines by examining any changes in the quantity and quality of claims. The Utah Tracking Study (Cude and Mayer 1995; Mayer et al.

1995) collected data at six-month intervals, starting immediately after issuance of the FTC guidelines in 1992 and continuing through the fall of 1995. Using supermarkets in five geographically dispersed markets in the United States, the researchers coded the content and prominence of claims made for all brands in 16 product categories. The study found no evidence for the contention that the FTC guidelines would have a "chilling" effect on claims and would reduce their frequency. It found a reduction in the frequency of several categories of problematic claims (e.g., unqualified general claims, degradability claims, ozone-friendly claims) and an increase in the specificity of several categories of claims (especially recycled content and source reduction claims). The study also found that the vast majority of recyclability claims remained unqualified or vaguely qualified. The Utah Tracking Study, although providing some policy-relevant data, stopped far short of constituting a rigorous evaluation study in which competing explanations for any observed changes are controlled. Thus, the study did little to change the overall conclusion that the FTC's evaluation of its guidelines was based more on accounts of personal experience and internal corporate decision making than on systematic empirical data. And as limited as the FTC's evaluation was, there have been no other such efforts in other nations, at the state or local level within the United States, or within self-regulatory bodies.

Promotion of Third-Party Environmental Seals of Approval

In the development of a national regulatory regime for first-party environmental claims, the United States was one of the world's leaders. In the case of third-party environmental seals of approval, however, the United States has been a laggard. The first such label, the Blue Angel, was established in West Germany in 1978. The second such label was announced in Canada in 1988 and was called the Environmental Choice Program. The following year, Japan launched its Eco-Mark label. A report issued by the EPA in 1993, *Status Report on the Use of Environmental Labels Worldwide* (Abt Associates 1993b), listed 12 national programs plus a European Community-wide seal. (In addition, the report cited several programs that either focused on a single attribute, such as dolphin safety, or were run by individual businesses or industry-wide groups.) By 1998, the number of seals had climbed to at least 25 (Yang 1998). Of these national and regional programs, all except the United States' Green Seal and Sweden's Environmental Choice program (which is largely funded by retailers) have been assisted with public funds for operations and publicity. Although fees charged to manufacturers for using the seals are a source of revenue, government funding has been essential as well. In a review of environmental labeling programs, Salzman (1991) concluded, "At present, no national programmes are self-financing or are expected to become so in the immediate future" (p. 24). Hence, it is no coincidence that the Green Seal program, run entirely with private funds, has gained relatively little visibility compared to its international counterparts.

Although the effectiveness of third-party seals of approval per se has been summarized in three reports (Abt Associates 1994; U.S. EPA 1998; Organization for Economic Cooperation and Development [OECD] 1997), no evaluation of policies designed to promote the success of these certification programs has been conducted. Such public policies include giving preferential treatment to eco-labeled brands in government procurement decisions, recognizing stores with a special commitment to green buying, building partnerships with environmental and consumer organizations, and providing financial support. The procurement policies of several departments within the Canadian federal government and of individual Canadian provinces encourage the purchase of brands that meet the standards of the Environmental Choice labeling program (Gesser 1998). In Sweden, a program implemented by regional environmental officials awards environmental diplomas to stores that offer their customers a broad range of green products. To receive a diploma, a store must meet standards regarding the proportion of items within each product group that are labeled with either eco-labels or organically grown labels (OECD 1997). In Germany, coverage by the local media and campaigns by consumer organizations played an important role in educating members of the public about the Blue Angel (OECD 1997). Thus, public policies can strengthen eco-seal programs, but knowledge of what works, and under what conditions, is only beginning to accumulate.

Effectiveness of First-Party Claims and Third-Party Seals

Given the proliferation of first-party environmental marketing claims and third-party seals of approval over the past decade, as well as the effort expended by regulatory and self-regulatory bodies to optimize the roles of these types of environmental marketing efforts, one would think that there would be substantial empirical evidence concerning the impact of these claims and seals. Such evaluations, first, would have to specify what these intended effects are and on whom. Then, they would have to determine whether any apparent effects can reasonably be attributed to the claims or seals.

First-party claims and third-party seals typically are aimed at consumers, so the examination of their effects should begin with and concentrate on individual consumers (even though industrial buyers also may be the targets of environmental claims). Claims and seals may influence the behavior of competitive producers and retailers as well, but any such effects presume effects on consumers. For example, a company may react to an environmental claim made by a competitor by improving the environmental attributes of its brand (Wong, Turner, and Stoneman 1996), but only if the company perceives that consumers are responding positively to its competitor's claim. Similarly, a retailer may choose to stock more of a brand bearing an environmental claim or to improve its shelf position (Strong 1995), but this action presumes the retailer's belief that consumers will respond positively to the seal. Because upstream changes in environmental strategies likely are predicated on knowledge of or assumptions about consumer responsiveness to those strategies, examination of the effectiveness of first-party claims and third-party certifications should focus primarily on their impact on consumers.

As with any communication directed at consumers, the effectiveness of environmental claims and seals can be defined in terms of an increasingly stringent set of criteria. The easiest criteria to satisfy typically are awareness, recall, and/ or accurate interpretation of the communication. More difficult to establish is the interpretation of a communication and its effect on attitudes and intentions. Still more difficult to demonstrate is the communication's effect on individual behavior, in this case, the selection of particular brands. At a level beyond individual consumers, effectiveness of claims and seals may be judged in terms of their impact on the behavior of competitors and, ultimately, the quality of the natural environment.

The simplest measure of a claim's impact is whether people report having been exposed to it. No publicly available study reports exposure to particular claims for individual brands, but a national telephone survey conducted for J. Walter Thompson Company in 1990 found that 34% of respondents remembered an ad that discussed a brand's environmental safety (Levin 1990). A three-country study conducted two years later (S. C. Johnson & Son 1992) found much higher reported exposure to labels or advertisements that proclaim the environmental benefits of a specific brand. Fully 72% and 80% of U.S. and Canadian respondents, respectively, reported having seen environmental claims on labels. The corresponding percentages for advertising claims were 66% in the United States and 82% in Canada. In Mexico, 42% of consumers in a national sample said that they had seen environmental claims on labels, and 44% said that they had seen them in advertisements.

A U.S.-only study commissioned by S. C. Johnson & Son in 1990 contains information on whether consumers search for environmental information on product labels, information that presumably is offered in the form of first-party claims. In the 1990 study, 26% of U.S. consumers claimed to "read the labels on products to see if the contents are environmentally safe" on a regular basis, and another 36% claimed to do so from time to time.

There are several studies (Cude 1991; Ellen 1994; J. W. Thompson 1991; Mayer, Scammon, and Zick 1992; Morris, Hastak, and Mazis 1995; "Public Confused" 1990-91) that have examined consumer understanding of the terms used in environmental marketing claims (e.g., "recyclable," "degradable"). This research reveals that consumers are highly aware of environmental marketing claims but often misunderstand their contents. Even if consumers understand these claims perfectly, the claims might not be effective in altering consumer behavior or improving the natural environment. For example, claims could be highly ineffective as a sales tool precisely because they are correctly understood by consumers and, therefore, are perceived as not terribly important. (Conversely, claims could be highly effective at increasing sales if consumers misunderstand and exaggerate their meanings.)

Closely related to consumer understanding of environmental claims is the perceived credibility of claims. Studies of the credibility of environmental marketing claims have reported fairly high levels of skepticism regarding these claims (Chase and Smith 1992; Environmental Research Associates, cited in Abt Associates 1993a; Gerstman and Meyers 1991; Mayer, Zick, and Scammon 1992; Roper Starch Worldwide, cited in Stisser 1994; S. C. Johnson & Son 1990), a factor that should tend to undercut their effectiveness.

Even if an environmental claim is accurately understood and perceived as credible, it might not be effective if consumers make unintended negative interpretations of the claim. In particular, environmental claims might connote to consumers that a brand is higher in price and/or lower in quality than its less environmentally oriented competitors. Questions about consumers' willingness to pay more or their willingness to give up convenience, efficiency, or performance for environmentally friendly brands *presume* that some type of sacrifice is necessary when buying these brands. Very few questions actually test whether consumers hold this presumption. Wells and Stoeckle (1990) found that only 31% of consumers believed that environmentally oriented brands "cost more." In another study (S. C. Johnson & Son 1990), people were asked about the reasons why they do not do more for the environment. More than half (52%) cited the expense of environmentally friendly brands, and 48% mentioned that these brands "don't work as well." To the extent that environmental claims contribute to consumer perceptions that brands are higher in price and/or lower in quality, these claims have had an impact, but not in the way that sellers intended.

Assuming that the intended effects of environmental claims are stronger than their unintended effects, the most meaningful measure of the effectiveness of environmental marketing claims would be their impact on behavior. One 1992 study contained a question asking people whether environmental claims have influenced their purchase behaviors (Chase and Smith 1992). Fully 75% of respondents believed that environmental marketing claims sometimes or very often influenced their purchasing decisions. There also are survey questions about whether a person has bought a "green product" (Roper Starch 1994 Survey, cited in Raymond Communications 1994; S. C. Johnson & Son 1992; Scott and Willits 1994), but it is not clear whether such purchases can be attributed to first-party claims. For example, a person might buy a particular brand because it appears to have less packaging, independent of any claim about the packaging.

The biggest obstacle to determining whether environmental claims "work" is isolating a brand's environmental claims from its nonenvironmental claims and, by extension, isolating its environmental attributes from its nonenvironmental attributes. For all but the most environmentally concerned consumers, environmental attributes are only a subset of desirable brand features. Indeed, environmental attributes may be less important than features such as price and quality (Speer 1997). Thus, it should not be surprising that an environmental claim has little impact on sales if the brand is relatively weak in terms of the overall value that it offers consumers.

From a research point of view, then, one needs to control for brand competitiveness when examining the effectiveness of environmental claims. Ackerstein and Lemon (1999) tried to do this in an experimental setting with four product classes: laundry detergent, disposable diapers, single-serving juice boxes, and toilet paper. For each product class, they compared two well-known brands (e.g., Huggies and Pampers) and found that both environmental claims on a label and environmental brand extensions had a positive impact on sales, even assuming that environmental brands would be 5% more expensive. Unfortunately, the study was based on only 66 respondents and was not based on actual purchases, but it points the way toward more rigorous evaluation of the impact of environmental marketing claims.

Overall, then, there is limited evidence in surveys conducted with the general public as to whether environmental marketing claims have affected consumer knowledge about, attitudes toward, or actual purchase of particular brands. What other evidence of effectiveness can be mustered? There is some anecdotal evidence that a brand's sales or market share took off after making a specific environmental marketing claim, but such evidence is scarce and difficult to interpret. In 1993, for example, 3M redesigned Scotch-Brite Never Rust soap pads so that they contained recycled polyester film waste (rather than metal as with competitive brands) and biodegradable soap (3M 1998). The brand captured more than a 20% share during its first year, but how much of that percentage was a result of any claims made by 3M in its advertising or on its package labels? How much was the result of 3M's strong brand image and/or other features of the product or package? (Ironically, cases brought by regulatory and self-regulatory authorities presume that claims lead to increased sales and market share advantages; otherwise, the challenged claims, although possibly misleading, would not have the requisite detrimental effect on consumers or competitors to warrant legal action.)

Evidence of the effectiveness of third-party environmental seals of approval is a bit more extensive and convincing than that of first-party claims. There are even two EPA-funded studies—one titled *Determinants of Effectiveness for Environmental Certification and Labeling Programs* (Abt Associates 1994) and the other titled *Environmental Labeling Issues, Policies, and Practices Worldwide* (U.S. EPA 1998)—and an OECD (1997) report titled *Eco-Labelling: Actual Effects of Selected Programmes.* But these documents contain fairly little in the way of nonanecdotal evidence of the impacts of these programs.

Several studies attest to the visibility of the seal programs. A 1988 survey reported that 80% of Germans were familiar with the Blue Angel (Abt Associates 1994). High levels of awareness also have been reported for seal programs in Canada, the Nordic countries, and Japan (Abt Associates 1994; OECD 1997; Yang 1998). Additional studies have suggested that consumers understand the purpose of the seals and attach substantial credibility to them (Abt Associates 1994; Hemmelskamp and Brockmann 1997; OECD 1997; Ramm 1996; Rhodes and Brown 1997).

Do consumers actually use the seals of approval? West Germans, who have had two decades to become familiar with the Blue Angel seal, say that they do. In a 1996 survey, 51% of West German respondents said that they paid attention to brands bearing the Blue Angel label when shopping (Hemmelskamp and Brockmann 1997), and 50% of West Germans reported that they used the Blue Angel to identify environmentally superior brands (OECD 1997).

Whereas evidence that consumers rely on and use environmental seals is confined to Germany, data on the impact of seals on sales or market share are broader in geographic scope but are largely anecdotal. The data fall into two general categories. First are stories about sales increases of a particular company's brand that are attributable to an environmental seal of approval. For example, Hoover Manufacturing Company was one of the first companies to use the European Union environmental seal of approval, and with its use, the company "has seen its sales in Germany soar" (OECD 1997, p. 40). In a similar case, the market share of Scribona photocopiers rose by 20% in Scandinavia after a promotional campaign stressing its qualification for the Nordic Swan seal (OECD 1997).

The second type of sales data refers to the share of sales within a product category that are accounted for by brands bearing eco-labels. An increase in the market share attained by eco-labeled brands could result from a fixed number of firms increasing their sales and/or an increased number of companies meeting the criteria for and using the seal. In Sweden, large detergent producers initially were not interested in eco-labels, but after smaller producers started winning market share from the large ones, the large producers modified their brands to earn the seal. "Consequently, when the [detergent] criteria were published in 1990, the market share for eco-labelled products was negligible, and in 1993 it was close to 50 percent" (OECD 1997, p. 43). Note that some companies might adopt seals of approval defensively, that is, to protect market share. Thus, seals could spur product improvement without changing market shares.

Given the length of time that the Blue Angel program has been in effect in Germany, it is surprising that the data on its impacts are not more systematic. The market share for eco-labeled sanitary paper brands increased from 32% to 64% between 1986 and 1993. The market share for eco-labeled office paper went from 13% to 24% during the same time period. In the market for varnishes and similar coatings in Germany, the overall trend was away from any product containing solvents, but the market share for low- and no-solvent products awarded the Blue Angel increased faster than did that for low- and no-solvent products without the seal (Hemmelskamp and Brockmann 1997).

The sheer increase in the number of brands seeking label certification and the cumulative weight of anecdotes concerning sales increases are impressive, but they stop far short of a convincingly positive evaluation of the impact of the labels. Any increases in the market share of eco-labeled brands might be attributable to their environmental superiority but not the label per se. This superiority could be communicated to consumers via word-of-mouth recommendations or first-party claims. Also, any increases in sales or market share might be the result of superiority in nonenvironmental attributes. Ideally, one would like to set up a research design that could rule out some of these potentially confounding factors. For example, one could compare market share trends for two items that are equivalent in their environmental impacts and first-party claims but only one of which has applied for environmental certification. Or, one could compare sales across time for two brands, both of which have been awarded a seal of approval but which differ in their performances along nonenvironmental dimensions. Sadly, this type of evaluation data is completely lacking.

Recently, environmental seals of approval have received attention in the arena of international trade, with the concern that they could constitute unfair barriers to trade (Mayer 1998). The basic argument is that the criteria and processes used to award seals will favor domestic manufacturers, especially those in more developed nations. On one hand, business groups, which oppose eco-labels for a variety of reasons, argue that the labels are extremely powerful in altering consumer behavior but lack strong empirical support for their position. On the other hand, environmental groups, because they support the use of eco-labels to steer consumer purchases in environmentally beneficial directions, are afraid to acknowledge that there is virtually no evidence that environmental seals have a substantial impact on markets. Ironically, a dispassionate look at the data might end the debate, but neither side wishes to know the truth.

New Directions in the Use of First-Party Claims and Third-Party Seals

At the end of the 1990s, environmental marketing claims for brands have become familiar to most consumers, but a new type of claim for a particular *service* is becoming more predominant and raising public policy issues. That service is electricity, and the claims have been tripped off by state-level policies to deregulate electricity markets. The purpose of electricity deregulation is to spur competition and give consumers more choices. One of these choices would be to purchase electricity that has been generated by environmentally superior energy sources, especially renewable sources. To convince consumers to select "green power," companies have begun to make environmental marketing claims.

Even more so than the environmental marketing claims made for tangible products and their packages, claims for energy are difficult for consumers to verify. Most important, the electric power that consumers actually use cannot be traced back to an exact source. Energy is created at multiple sources and added to a power grid, where it is mixed together with energy from other sources before being delivered to consumers. Moreover, a company's power sources change over time, even within the course of a single day.

Given the unverifiable nature of environmental claims for electricity, it is important that there be a strong regulatory and/or self-regulatory presence to encourage honesty in environmental claims regarding electricity. One source of surveillance has been the National Association of Attorneys General (NAAG). Just as the NAAG focused attention on problematic environmental claims for products in 1990 with the publication of *The Green Report* (NAAG 1990), in July 1998, the NAAG released for public comment a first draft of "Green Guidelines for Electricity." The guidelines, which were adopted in December 1999, are intended for use by industry and law enforcement agencies to clarify how environmental marketing claims can be made in a nondeceptive manner. Of particular concern is the use of terms such as "renewable," "green," and "clean."

In October 1998, Public Citizen, a consumer organization founded by Ralph Nader, also increased scrutiny of environmental marketing claims for energy by issuing a report titled *Green Buyers Beware: A Critical Review of "Green Electricity" Products* (Public Citizen 1998). The report claimed that the marketing of green electricity in California is "largely a hoax" in which consumers pay extra for supposedly cleaner power but without any real benefit for the environment. Sellers of renewable energy in California responded by claiming that "Public Citizen is completely out of touch" ("Ralph Nader Group" 1998), and many environmental groups took exception to the report as well (Green Power Network 1998).

The prodding by the NAAG and Public Citizen has brought forth responses from national regulatory and self-regulatory authorities. The FTC, for its part, believes that environmental claims for energy can be handled within the framework of its environmental marketing guides. For example, terms such as "green" and "clean" should be treated as general environmental benefit claims, meaning that they require qualification (FTC 1998). The National Advertising Division of the CBBB also took action. It sided with the Natural Resources Defense Council in its challenge of claims by the Nuclear Energy Institute that nuclear power was "environmentally clean." Citing the FTC guidelines, the National Advertising Division ruled that general environmental claims such as "environmentally clean" and "produces electricity without polluting the environment" should be qualified or avoided ("Cleaning Up Environmental Claims" 1999).

The area of energy choice also exemplifies recent trends with respect to third-party seals of approval, namely, the proliferation of certification programs run by private entities and focusing on a narrow set of products. A "Green-e" certification program for clean electricity is run by the Center for Resource Solutions. The logo means that (1) at least 50% of the electricity supply for the product comes from renewable electricity sources, (2) any nonrenewable part of the product has lower air emissions than does a traditional mix of electricity (i.e., if the consumers had not switched energy suppliers), and (3) the company offering the product agrees to abide by the Green-e program's code of conduct, which requires that providers disclose the sources of their electricity ("What Is Greene?" 1999).

Privately run seals of approval are not entirely new. In Sweden, the Society for the Conservation of Nature has offered a multi-attribute seal of approval since 1990. Earthtrust, a nonprofit wildlife conservation organization, began offering the Flipper Seal of Approval in 1992 to indicate that firms have obtained their tuna from fishermen who use certain dolphin-safe practices. In addition, retailers such as Wal-Mart, Fred Meyers, Whole Earth Access, and Home Depot have used shelf tags in their stores to indicate environmentally superior brands.

What distinguishes the current time period is the rapid proliferation of new seals of approval, usually focusing on a single environmentally relevant attribute. For example, the Chlorine Free Products Association provides a logo certifying that a firm uses chlorine-free methods in the production of its paper products. The Smithsonian Migratory Bird Center certifies coffee cultivation that has occurred in songbird-friendly shaded forests. The Rainforest Alliance certifies forests that are being managed in a sustainable yield fashion, and the Forest Stewardship Council certifies the certifiers of forest management. Growers and food companies may qualify for a Salmon-Safe certification from the Pacific Rivers Council by preserving and restoring salmon habitat along the rivers and streams of the Pacific Northwest. For consumers concerned about the impact of pesticides and other toxic substances on the environment (and on themselves), there are labels such as Core Values for apples grown in the northeastern United States, Stemilt Responsible Choice for Washington orchardists, and BuyGreen Virginia for Virginia farm produce. There also are several "fair trade" labels (e.g., Transfair, Fair TradeMark Canada) attesting that products have been grown in a manner that is respectful both of the natural environment and of workers.

Will this new generation of environmental seals of approval be effective in influencing consumer and corporate behavior? To the extent that their predecessors have been successful, the new generation is likely to be less so. A large number of separate certifications, each covering a fairly narrow domain and run by a variety of relatively unknown and resource-strapped organizations, is unlikely to lead to the level of public awareness and credibility needed for a successful labeling program. Marketers, for their part, have little incentive to apply and pay for a seal of approval that carries little recognition and weight among consumers.

Conclusion

What does the story of environmental marketing tell us about the interactions among public policy decisions, corporate marketing decisions, competition within markets, and consumer welfare? Moreover, what role did research play in these interactions?

A string of environmental disasters during the late 1970s and 1980s led marketers to believe that consumers were interested in using their purchasing power to slow the pace of environmental degradation. Survey research, primarily conducted by prominent consulting firms, indicated strong consumer interest in buying environmentally superior brands and supported corporate decisions to make environmental marketing claims. The prevalence of environmental marketing claims increased sharply during the 1989-90 period as firms felt pressure to match or exceed the claims of their competitors. Although many claims reflected genuine environmental benefits, other claims were vague, exaggerated, or misleading. The poor quality of some environmental claims led to action by regulatory and self-regulatory authorities, acting on behalf of honest competition, consumer welfare, and/or environmental welfare. Outside of the United States, governments took the additional step of promoting programs that awarded environmental seals of approval. Both the regulation of first-party claims and the support of third-party labeling programs were undergirded by survey research indicating that consumers were confused about the meaning of individual environmental claims and were skeptical about the entire genre of first-party claims.

First-party claims and third-party certification remained popular among marketers during the entire 1990s. Even during the latter half of the decade, survey researchers continued to report that consumers were willing to pay extra for green brands (Dunn 1997; Gesser 1998; Hemmelskamp and Brockmann 1997; Scher 1997), and marketers continued searching for ways in which to bridge the gap between that willingness and actual sales of green brands. Research on the impact of first-party claims and third-party seals on the behavior of consumers and competitors remained largely anecdotal. By the same token, research on public policies designed to control first-party claims and promote third-party seals rarely was undertaken. Thus, 10 years after the explosion of environmental marketing claims, we have accumulated little systematic knowledge about whether, and under what conditions, corporate and public policy decisions can increase consumer welfare through environmental marketing efforts. Instead, we have a landscape in which corporate decision makers would be justified in thinking that environmental claims and seals do work—or do not—and in which public policy makers would be justified in devoting more resources—or less—to claims regulation and the promotion of seals of approval.

There are several top priorities for researchers interested in whether and how communicating brand-specific environmental information to consumers makes any difference. First, researchers must go beyond simple willingness-to-pay measures when assessing the potential impact of environmental claims and seals of approval. It is just too easy for a person to respond affirmatively to a hypothetical question of whether he or she would be willing to pay a 5% premium for an environmentally superior brand. Second, researchers must examine the impact of environmental claims and seals in real markets while controlling, as thoroughly as possible, for other factors that might explain any shifts in brand share. Finally, researchers should build an understanding of how environmental claims and seals affect not only consumers but also the behavior of competitors and markets. For example, an environmental improvement made by one firm might quickly cascade into a series of improvements by all competitors, in which case brand shares might be unchanged but the natural environment would be enhanced.

Fortunately, social issues operate in cycles, and there likely will be a time in the not-so-distant future when consumers will show even stronger interest in buying green brands and when firms again will see a potential advantage in promoting them. When the next peak of the cycle occurs, one can hope that social research will play a larger and more useful role in informing decision making and, thereby, in enhancing consumer welfare.

References

Abt Associates (1993a), *Evaluation of Environmental Marketing Terms in the United States.* Washington, DC: U.S. Environmental Protection Agency.

———(1993b), *Status Report on the Use of Environmental Labels Worldwide.* Washington, DC: U.S. Environmental Protection Agency.

——— (1994), *Determinants of Effectiveness for Environmental Certification and Labeling Programs.* Washington, DC: U.S. Environmental Protection Agency.

Ackerstein, Daniel S. and Katherine A. Lemon (1999), "Greening the Brand: Environmental Marketing Strategies and the American Consumers," in *Greener Marketing,* Martin Charter and Michael Jay Polonsky, eds. Sheffield, UK: Greenleaf, 233-54.

Banerjee, Subhabrata, Charles S. Gulas, and Easwar Iyer (1995), "Shades of Green: A Multidimensional Analysis of Environmental Advertising," *Journal of Advertising,* 24 (Summer), 21-31.

"Cambridge Reports Benchmarks Green Consumerism" (1992), *Green Market Alert,* October, 7-8.

Carlson, Les, Stephen J. Grove, and Norman Kangun (1993), "A Content Analysis of Environmental Advertising Claims: A Matrix Method Approach," *Journal of Advertising,* 22 (3), 27-39.

Cavanagh, Kimberly C. (1998), "It's a Lorax Kind of Market! But Is It a Sneetches Kind of Solution? A Critical Review of Current Laissez-Faire Environmental Marketing Regulation," *Villanova Environmental Law Journal,* 9, 133-224.

Chase, Dennis and Therese Kauchak Smith (1992), "Consumers Keen on Green but Marketers Don't Deliver," *Advertising Age,* June 29, S2, S4.

"Cleaning Up Environmental Claims" (1999), *NACAA News,* February, 2.

Code of Federal Regulations (1993), Title 16, Part 260, 118-27.

———— (1997), Title 16, Part 260, 222-31.

———— (1999), Title 16, Part 260, 213-23.

Consumers International (1998), *Green Guidance: How Consumer Organizations Can Give Better Advice on Putting Sustainable Consumption into Practice—An International Study.* London: Consumers International.

Cude, Brenda J. (1991), Comments prepared for the U.S. Environmental Protection Agency hearings on the use of the terms "recycled," "recyclable," and "recycling emblem" in environmental marketing claims, November 13, Washington, DC.

———— (1993), "Does It Cost More to Buy 'Green'?" in *Proceedings of the 39th Annual Conference of the American Council on Consumer Interests,* Theresa Mauldin, ed. Columbia, MO: University of Missouri Press, 108-13.

———— and Robert N. Mayer (1995), "Comments on the Federal Trade Commission's Guides for the Use of Environmental Marketing Claims," September 27. Available: http://www.ftc.gov/bcp/grnrule/comments.htm

Dean, Norman (1995), "Comments by Green Seal Inc. on the Federal Trade Commission's Guides for the Use of Environmental Marketing Claims," September 18. Available: http://www.ftc.gov/bcp/grnrule/comments.htm

Dunn, Seth (1997), "Power of Choice," *Worldwatch,* September-October, 30-36.

Elkington, John, Julia Hailes, and Joel Makower (1990), *The Green Consumer.* New York: Penguin.

Ellen, Pam Scholder (1994), "Do We Know What We Need to Know? Objective and Subjective Knowledge Effects on Pro-Ecological Behaviors," *Journal of Business Research,* 30 (May), 43- 52.

Farhar, B. C. (1994), "Trends in U.S. Public Perceptions and Preferences on Energy and Environmental Policy," *Annual Review of Energy and the Environment* 19, 211-39.

Federal Trade Commission (1998), "FTC Files Comment with State Attorneys General about Green Guidelines for Electricity," press release, August 12.

Gerstman and Meyers (1991), *Consumer Solid Waste: Awareness, Attitude, and Behavior Study III.* New York: Gerstman and Meyers.

Gesser, Avi (1998), "Canada's Environmental Choice Program: A Model for a 'Trade-Friendly' Eco-Labeling Scheme," *Harvard International Law Journal,* 39 (Spring), 501-44.

Green Power Network (1998), "Environmentalists Respond to Public Citizen Green Power Report," press release, October 29 [on-line]. Available: http://www. eren.doe.gov/greenpower/blast4_1198_pr.html

Gutfeld, Rose (1991), "Shades of Green: Eight of 10 Americans Are Environmentalists, at Least so They Say," *The Wall Street Journal,* August 2, A1, A8.

Hedblom, Mats-Olov (1998), "Environment, for Better or Worse (Part 3)," *Ericsson Review,* No. 1, 1-15.

Hemmelskamp, Jens and Karl Ludwig Brockmann (1997), "Environmental Labels: The German 'Blue Angel,' " *Futures,* 29 (1), 67-76.

Hume, Scott and Patricia Strnad (1989), "Consumers Go 'Green,' " *Advertising Age,* September 25, 3, 92.

J. W. Thompson (1991), "The Meaning of Green," *JWT Greenwatch,* No. 3 (Spring/ Summer), 1.

Kangun, Norman, Les Carlson, and Stephen J. Grove (1991), "Environmental Advertising Claims: A Preliminary Investigation," *Journal of Public Policy & Marketing,* 10 (Fall), 47-58.

Levin, Gary (1990), "Consumers Turning Green: JWT Survey," *Advertising Age,* November 12, 74.

Mayer, Robert N. (1998), "Protectionism, Intellectual Property, and Consumer Protection: Was the Uruguay Round Good for Consumers?" *Journal of Consumer Policy,* 21 (June), 195-215.

———, Brenda J. Cude, Jason Gray-Lee, and Debra L. Scammon (1995), "Trends in Environmental Marketing Claims since the FTC Guides: Two-Year Auditing Results," in *Consumer Interest Annual: Proceedings of the Annual Conference of the American Council on Consumer Interests,* Karen Folk Fox, ed. Columbia, MO: American Council on Consumer Interests, 161-66.

———, Debra L. Scammon, and Cathleen D. Zick (1992), "Turning the Competition Green: The Regulation of Environmental Claims," in *Proceedings of the 1992 Marketing and Public Policy Conference,* Paul N. Bloom and Richard G. Starr, eds. Washington, DC: Public Policy and Marketing Association, 152-65.

———, Cathleen D. Zick, and Debra L. Scammon (1992), "Poisoning the Well: Do Environmental Claims Strain Consumer Credulity?" in *Advances in Consumer Research,* Leigh McAlister and Michael L. Rothschild, eds. Provo, UT: Association for Consumer Research, 698-703.

Morris, Louis A., Manoj Hastak, and Michael B. Mazis (1995), "Consumer Comprehension of Environmental Advertising and Labeling Claims," *Journal of Consumer Affairs,* 29 (Winter), 328-50.

National Association of Attorneys General (1990), *The Green Report: Findings and Preliminary Recommendations for Responsible Environmental Advertising.* Washington, DC: NAAG.

Organization for Economic Cooperation and Development (1997), *Eco-Labelling: Actual Effects of Selected Programmes.* Paris: OECD.

Polonsky, Michael Jay, Les Carlson, Stephen Grove, and Norman Kangun (1997), "International Environmental Marketing Claims: Real Changes or Simple Posturing?" *International Marketing Review,* 14 (4), 218-32.

Public Citizen (1998), *Green Buyers Beware: A Critical Review of "Green Electricity" Products.* Washington, DC: Public Citizen.

"Public Confused over 'Green' Marketing Terms" (1990-91), *COPPE Quarterly,* Winter, 1, 3.

Purcell, Bill and Fritz Keil (1990), "Will Consumers Pay More for Green Products?" *Progressive Grocer,* June, 64-66.

"Ralph Nader Group Says California's 'Green Electricity' is a Hoax on Consumers" (1998), *Salt Lake Tribune,* October 23, F9.

Ramm, Jorun Skoglund (1996), *Consumers' Environment-Motivated Attitudes and Actions.* Lysaker, Norway: Statens Institutt for Forbruksforrskning.

Raymond Communications (1994), *State Recycling Law Update.* Riverdale, MD: Raymond Communications.

Rhodes, Stanley P. and Linda G. Brown (1997), "Consumers Look for the Ecolabel," *Forum for Applied Research and Public Policy,* 12 (Spring), 109-15.

S. C. Johnson & Son (1990), *The Environment: Public Attitudes and Individual Behavior.* New York: Roper Organization.

——— (1992), *Environmental Behavior, North America: Canada, Mexico, United States.* New York: Roper Organization.

Salzman, James (1991), *Environmental Labelling in OECD Countries.* Paris: Organization for Economic Cooperation and Development.

Scammon, Debra L. and Robert N. Mayer (1995), "Agency Review of Environmental
Market Claims: Case-by-Case Decomposition of the Issues," *Journal of Advertising,*
24 (Summer), 33-44.

Scher, Abby (1997), "Green Labels: Can They Build a New Marketplace?" *Dollars &
Sense,* May-June, 22-28.

Scott, David and Fern W. Willits (1994), "Environmental Attitudes and Behavior: A
Pennsylvania Survey," *Environment and Behavior,* 26 (March), 239-60.

Speer, Tibbett L. (1997), "Growing the Green Market," *American Demographics,* 19
(August), 45-49.

Stisser, Peter (1994), "A Deeper Shade of Green," *American Demographics,* March, 24-29.

Strong, Carolyn (1995), "Are Grocery Retail Buyers Making Greener Purchasing Decisions?" *Greener Management International,* 11 (July), 103-12.

Theissen, Donald R. (1995), "Comments on the Federal Trade Commission's Guides for
the Use of Environmental Marketing Claims," September 27.
Available: http://www.ftc.gov/bcp/grnrule/comments.htm

3M (1998), *Developing Environmentally Improved Products* [on-line].
Available: http://www.mmm.com/profile/envt/product.html

U.S. Environmental Protection Agency (1998), *Environmental Labeling Issues, Policies,
and Practices Worldwide.* Washington, DC: EPA.

Wells, Richard and Andrew Stoeckle (1990), "Consumer Purchasing Behavior and the
Environment: Results of an Event-Based Study," report on a study conducted by Abt
Associates.

"What Is Green-e?" (1999), [On-line.]
Available: http://www.igc.org/crs2/what/index.html

Wong, Veronica, William Turner, and Paul Stoneman (1996), "Marketing Strategies and
Market Prospects for Environmentally-Friendly Consumer Products," *British Journal of Management,* 7, 263-81.

Yang, Wanhua (1998), "Ecolabelling: Its Role in Promoting Sustainable Production and
Consumption," paper prepared for the International Symposium on Policy Instruments for Sustainable Consumption and Production, November, Oslo, Norway.

Chapter 18

Insights from Consumer Research on the Effects of Deceptive Advertising Regulations

John E. Calfee

This is an appraisal of the impact of consumer research on assessing the effectiveness of deceptive advertising regulation in the United States. Before looking at research findings, however, we must consider what variety of advertising regulation is being assessed and how to assess it. The Federal Trade Commission (FTC) regulates most, but by no means all, advertising. The Food and Drug Administration (FDA) regulates prescription drug advertising and wields a strong influence over FTC regulation of advertising for foods and over-the-counter drugs. This often has caused the FTC to move against advertising that arguably was nondeceptive but violated FDA standards (Calfee and Pappalardo 1991). The Securities and Exchange Commission (SEC) exercises stringent regulation over advertising of stocks and bonds (McChesney 1988; Wolfson 1990). However, the FDA and SEC pay rather little attention to consumer deception. Because they regulate not just advertising but also the products being advertised, these agencies have been free to write highly specific advertising rules, the enforcement of which consists mainly of a factual determination of whether the rules were violated with little or no regard to whether advertising is deceptive (on the FDA, see Calfee 1996; on the SEC, see McChesney 1988; Wolfson 1990).

AUTHOR'S NOTE: The author acknowledges the research assistance of Randolph Stempski of the American Enterprise Institute.

Also important is a complex set of self-regulation organizations. The largest is the National Advertising Division of the Council of Better Business Bureaus, which also operates the Children's Advertising Review Unit (with funding from major toy manufacturers). In addition, the television networks operate their own in-house review systems. These self-regulation groups wield influence of varying scope and strength while relying on the FTC to take action when firms resist complying with their rulings.[1]

There also are legislative restrictions or bans on various types of advertising such as for cigarettes and alcoholic beverages. Those bans sometimes are justified on the grounds that the advertising subject to the bans is inherently deceptive. In practice, however, ad bans are a substitute for assessing deceptiveness in advertising. This review does not address ad bans, partly because the extensive literature on bans seldom, if ever, attempts to assess their impact on deception as opposed to consumption, prices, and other variables.

Finally, the FTC itself has taken at least two disparate approaches to advertising regulation. One is the case-by-case enforcement of the FTC Act's general prohibition on deceptive business practices (FTC 1983). The other is the promulgation and enforcement of trade regulation rules. The latter require disclosures and prohibit specific practices including advertising claims that the FTC has deemed inherently deceptive. The balance between these two approaches has fluctuated widely. Rule making gained great prominence during the mid-1970s and rapidly receded thereafter (see Andrews's chapter in this volume [Chapter 1]). However, the rule-making approach always has played a subsidiary role. Even in industries subject to trade regulations, most advertising is governed by the general prohibition on deceptive advertising. This review, therefore, focuses on what marketing knowledge can tell us about the effects of the FTC's core activity of case-by-case enforcement of the prohibition on deceptive advertising.

Assessing Case-by-Case Advertising Regulation by the FTC

The FTC Act's prohibition on "deceptive acts or practices" contains no definition of "deceptive." This gave rise to decades of confusion and debate over what the law actually proscribes. In 1983, the FTC promulgated a policy statement on deception that defined deception as a "representation, omission, or practice that is likely to mislead the consumer acting reasonably in the circumstances, to the consumer's detriment." Controversial when it was issued, the 1983 policy statement was rapidly implemented through formal FTC decisions on cases and has remained the commission's benchmark for determining what advertising claims are deceptive.[2]

At the heart of deceptive advertising regulation is the "advertising substantiation doctrine." Established during the early 1970s and encapsulated in a policy statement on advertising substantiation in 1984, this doctrine states that claims lacking a "reasonable basis" are deceptive. It has formed the core of deceptive advertising regulation for nearly three decades and probably will continue to do so.[3]

We must recognize the difficulties in assessing the effectiveness of deceptive advertising regulation in general and of the substantiation doctrine in particular. The most direct approach would be simply to assess the extent to which deceptive claims have been eliminated from advertising. Such an approach raises several problems. One is determining which claims are deceptive and how prevalent such claims are. The FTC and others define deception in ways that depend on the context in which claims appear and the reactions of reasonable consumers. Contextual issues include consumer knowledge as well as problematic matters such as distinguishing between consumer deception and miscomprehension, the extent to which reasonable consumers rely on claims, and the probable truthfulness of claims.[4] A second problem is determining the causal relationship between regulation and changes in the prevalence of deceptive claims. Regulation does not operate alone. Market forces, including self-regulation, also limit deception. Equally important is the FTC's policy (described later) of giving substantial weight to the trade-off between the costs of suppressing useful claims and the benefits of suppressing deceptive claims. This ensures that even with the most efficient advertising regulation, deceptive claims still will exist to some unknown extent. In fact, the FTC largely ignores advertising in substantial sections of the media except when consumer complaints arise. A notable example is the scientific literature, which contains a great deal of advertising making highly specific claims.[5]

Most of the difficulties in assessing the effects of advertising regulation arise from the fact that its primary goals involve the second-order effects of both advertising and sound regulation. The substantiation doctrine is based on the proposition that advertising is a tool for competition, whereas deceptive advertising is an impediment to competition. The implication is that sound regulation promotes competition and its benefits. Most of the benefits from advertising, however, are "downstream"—more consumer information, better information, lower prices, better products—rather than simply better or cleaner advertising. Hence, in advertising regulation, the relevant variables are not just the truthfulness of advertising claims but also matters such as the plentitude of accurate information, the delivery of such information to relevant consumer segments, the vigor of competition, and (most notably) not suppressing useful claims.[6] Thus, in 1996 the chairman of the FTC noted, "Unnecessary restraints on truthful advertising can be as harmful to consumers as deceptive or unfair advertising" (Pitofsky 1996, p. 56, quoted in Abernathy and Franke 1998). The 1984 Advertising Substantiation Statement is, accordingly, quite explicit about the necessity of balancing of the costs and benefits of permitting claims that might turn out not to be true versus prohibiting claims that might not be deceptive. One must keep this cost-benefit balance in mind when judging the value of advertising regulation so as to avoid the error of concluding that a complete ban on advertising is valuable because it eliminates deceptive advertising.

Even if we can determine the second-order effects of advertising, we have to relate them to changes in regulation. That requires identifying and perhaps measuring changes in the law or the enforcement of law. The problems in measuring changes in the law and related policies are well-known and not easily solved (Priest 1987). Moreover, substantial changes in deceptive advertising regulation have been rare. The exceptions are the development of specific remedies such as corrective advertising and the occurrence of few specific regulatory episodes that have offered opportunities for indirect assessment of regulation. Even then, the research problems are imposing (Kinnear 1997).

A thorough evaluation of advertising regulation would involve economic reasoning and analysis combined with consumer research and other tools for creating marketing knowledge. The power and necessity of this combination of disciplines is evident in much of the work by FTC staff, who typically start out as pure economists and end up with one foot in consumer research as they participate in consumer research conferences and work with consumer researchers as coauthors and sometimes as temporary colleagues (when consumer research academics consult with or join FTC staff as visitors).[7]

The Scarcity of Assessments of Deceptive Advertising Regulation

The difficulties in assessing the effects of advertising regulation are reflected in the scarcity of research results. This is not to say that consumer research on topics related to advertising regulation is scarce. The advertising regulation literature is large, numbering hundreds or thousands of articles and scores of books. But it is devoted almost entirely to topics such as determining when advertising is deceptive, the impact of specific advertising campaigns or themes, advertising for controversial products (e.g., alcohol, food, tobacco, drugs), the impact of advertising restrictions, and the effects of specific regulatory remedies such as mandated disclosures—to the near exclusion of the *effects* of regulation aimed specifically at deception. The exception is work on corrective advertising (discussed later in some detail).

The sparseness of research on the effectiveness of deceptive advertising regulation is apparent from reviews of the literature. Examples include Preston's comprehensive surveys during the 1980s (Preston 1983, 1987). These were written well after the burst of advertising regulation during the FTC's activist period of the 1970s. Yet, they cited virtually nothing on the effects of regulation beyond a few legal or semipopular works that essentially debated the merits of the deregulatory trend of the Reagan years. A few years later, the Gardner and Leonard (1989) survey, titled "Research in Deceptive and Corrective Advertising: Progress to Date and Impact on Public Policy," contained nothing on the effects of case-by-case regulation except for work on the effects of specific remedies such as corrective advertising orders.

One can reach much the same conclusion from reviewing the tables of contents of leading marketing journals including the *Journal of Consumer Research, Journal of Marketing, Journal of Advertising,* and *Journal of Advertising Research.* All reveal very little in the way of overt attempts to assess the effects of deceptive advertising regulation. For example, the 16 articles in a 1999 special issue of the *Journal of Marketing* on "fundamental issues and directions for marketing" contained nothing on regulation and its effects. The same is true of the articles listed in the "deceptive advertising" and "public policy" sections of the most recent index of the *Journal of Consumer Research* (although there are articles on related topics such as determining when advertising is deceptive).

What is more remarkable is that work assessing the effectiveness of deceptive advertising regulation is almost absent from the pages of the *Journal of Public Policy & Marketing* and other leading journals that devote substantial space to policy issues including the *Journal of Current Issues and Research in Advertising, International Journal of Advertising,* and *Journal of Consumer Policy.* This is not to say that none of the research in these and other journals has anything to say about what advertising regulation has done. A few research themes are of value and are discussed in the next section. But the scarcity of explicit assessments is striking.

The views set forth in recent retrospective looks at consumer research and public policy include the following. Bloom's (1997) review of the impact of consumer research and related disciplines described the impact of that research on public policy but not its role in assessing FTC regulation generally (as opposed to examining specific tools, notably corrective advertising). In fact, assessing the effects of deceptive advertising regulation is hardly on the research agenda at all. In Mazis's (1997) review of the status of marketing and public policy research, the short section on researching deception is on the effects of advertising, not the effects of regulation (pp. 141-42). Wilkie's (1997) largely historical review of research on public policy and marketing did not mention this topic at all.

Research that Casts Light on the Effectiveness of Deceptive Advertising Regulation

Several strands of research have shed useful light on the workings of FTC regulation of deceptive advertising, despite the difficulties in devising strong tests of regulatory effects. I begin with a central topic, information in advertising, and then move on to credibility in advertising, the value of advertising to consumers, the influence of specific regulatory events, and corrective advertising (the most thoroughly studied single topic in advertising regulation effects).

Information in Advertising

The most extensive consumer research literature related to deceptive advertising regulation is on the information content of advertising. Much of that research was undertaken with the goal of assessing advertising itself rather than regulation, but when matched with regulatory events, these findings can, within severe limits, be used to assess the effects of regulation. The idea is to take advantage of the fact that a central purpose of the advertising substantiation program is to increase the credibility of advertising claims, which would in turn encourage sellers to make specific claims and, therefore, increase the total amount of information in advertising. This section deals with information in advertising, and the next section deals with credibility. Regarding information, the strongest hypothesis is that information should increase after the substantiation program was established. Moreover, one can address the question of what level of enforcement is necessary to maintain incentives to provide information because a substantial weakening of the substantiation program should reduce credibility and, therefore, reduce information in advertising.

Most scholars investigating regulatory change at the FTC have focused on two landmarks.[8] One occurred during the 1970s when the consumer protection functions of the FTC were greatly strengthened through infusions of new staff and larger budgets, new legislation that broadened the FTC's tools to include rule-making authority and expanded use of civil penalties, much more activity in the form of investigations and demands for industry materials, a flurry of proposed trade regulation rules, and (most important for our purposes) the establishment of the advertising substantiation doctrine during 1971-72.[9] These same years also saw the creation of the major self-regulation groups described earlier. The second landmark is the deregulatory years of the Reagan administration, which began late in 1981 when James C. Miller assumed the chairmanship and continued through most of the decade, during which time overt enforcement of the advertising substantiation doctrine declined, even as the FTC issued its 1983 and 1984 policy statements on deception and substantiation.

We are fortunate to have at hand a recent and thorough meta-analysis incorporating new research on the quantity of information in advertising through time, broken down into periods corresponding to major changes in FTC regulation. The Abernathy and Franke (1998) study forms the basis for most observations in this section. Its central premise was that the substantiation doctrine and its regulatory apparatus were designed to increase the incentives to make specific advertising claims (because regulation enhanced the credibility of claims), suggesting that the informational richness of advertising should have peaked during the activist decades of the 1970s.

Unfortunately, very little of this stream of research permits comparisons starting before the substantiation doctrine was established. Abernathy and Franke (1998) cited only two studies. Chou, Franke, and Wilcox (1987), focusing on the impact of the FTC's advocacy of comparative advertising, found no change in the informational content of magazine advertisements for the years 1970, 1975, and 1985. Kassarjian and Kassarjian (1988), a follow-up study to Healey and Kassarjian (1983), reached strongly mixed results across a few product categories and concluded that there was little, if any, evidence that the substantiation program improved information or that information suffered during the more relaxed regulation of the mid-1980s.

The bulk of the Abernathy and Franke (1998) meta-analysis (which included the authors' own original research) dealt with studies that measured the quantity of information in advertising during the 1970s and 1980s. Most studies used the methods developed by Resnick and Stern (1977), which involved counting how many of 14 different types of information (e.g., prices, safety claims, performance claims) were represented in an ad. Working with approximately 36 studies, the authors constructed a multitude of measures of the quantity of information including the mean number of informational cues, percentage of ads containing *n* or more cues (with *n* ranging from 1 to 3), and the percentage of ads containing certain types of information (e.g., taste, nutrition). They found that the mean number of cues increased from 1.73 during the 1970s to 2.18 during the 1980s, with roughly similar improvements in nearly all other measures. The results survived or were strengthened when robustness was tested by removing several studies that could have wielded exceptional influence. The results also were robust (although less decisively) after introducing a time trend to take into account unmeasured secular developments in consumer behavior, the technology of advertising, and so on. Perhaps the most interesting of the various robustness investigations was the authors' meta-analysis of the much smaller group of studies that examined advertising outside the United States, where the shifts in FTC policy presumably had little impact. This revealed a decline in information content during the 1980s.

These intriguing results would appear to rule out the possibility that incentives to provide information through advertising were substantially weakened during the 1980s. It should be borne in mind, however, that the 1980s were not a sharp break from the late 1970s in terms of what types of claims would trigger FTC scrutiny. The 1983 and 1984 policy statements were presented as encapsulations of recent cases rather than as rejections of them, and the 1984 statement on advertising substantiation was unanimously passed by the FTC with virtually no controversy. Abernathy and Franke (1998) also noted that, during the 1980s, the FTC continued to work at reducing private, state, and local restrictions on advertising and that the commission unleashed numerous health claims for foods when it prevailed over the FDA on the standards for such claims (discussed later). All else being equal, then, the FTC apparently was facilitating additional information in advertising during the 1980s.

The Abernathy and Franke (1998) results are limited in other ways in their ability to address the effects of deceptive advertising regulation. As the authors noted, the studies they examined did not assess the quality of information. This raises the question of whether the slight increase in the quantity of claims during the 1980s simply reflected a proliferation of less truthful claims, a possibility whose likelihood was reduced, although not eliminated, by the parallel meta-analysis of foreign advertising. But the most important limitation, in my opinion, is the simple fact that the gyrations in the type and level of advertising regulation were rather limited. We cannot learn much from this study about what would happen to information in advertising if there were either a drastic relaxation or a substantial tightening of regulation. A later section on prominent episodes in regulation discusses this point.

Credibility of Advertising

In theory at least, enhancing the credibility of truthful information is the central goal of modern advertising regulation (Abernathy and Franke 1998; FTC 1984; Sauer and Leffler 1990). However, assessing the impact of regulation on the credibility of advertising poses especially difficult questions. One must take into account consumer perceptions rather than simply looking at advertising content, as is done in most information studies. One can do this directly (by attempting to measure credibility) or indirectly (by using measures correlated with credibility).

A leading example of the indirect approach is Sauer and Leffler (1990). They found that after the substantiation doctrine was implemented, advertising for four infrequently purchased durables (autos, furniture, household equipment, and office equipment) increased relative to that for four inexpensive frequently purchased goods (cosmetics and toiletries, foods, soft drinks, and sweets). This was interpreted as reflecting increased credibility in advertising because sellers of the first type of goods tend to employ claims that cannot be ascertained directly by consumers. The authors placed a similar interpretation on other findings: increased sales for over-the-counter drugs introduced during 1973-75 relative to those introduced during 1967-69 and gains in the value of television broadcasting stocks in the aftermath of three of four events associated with the introduction of the substantiation doctrine.

Calfee and Ringold (1994) examined national consumer surveys on a variety of attitudes toward advertising since the 1930s including consumer skepticism. They found little change in the perceived credibility of advertising as FTC regulation evolved from the slightly regulated 1960s through the activist 1970s and then through the relative inactivity of the 1980s. What changes there were tended to be in the direction of less skepticism and suspicion of advertising during the 1980s. It should be borne in mind, however, that the tendency to distrust advertising appears to be quite universal in the face of radically different regulatory environments. In a 1991 Canadian survey, for example, 76% of respondents agreed that "advertising is often misleading" (Crane 1991). A 1995 Roper Starch survey of 38,000 consumers in 40 countries found that 73% of consumers "believe advertisers regularly mislead or exaggerate a product's benefits" (Parker-Pope 1995).

Unfortunately, these two studies, with their contrasting results, are another illustration of the difficulties in obtaining persuasive results on the effects of regulation. The results of the two studies probably could be reconciled or confuted by appealing to a number of factors including trends in the technology and content of advertising; in consumer understanding of advertising; and even the extent to which advertising standards become ensconced in the thinking, practices, and institutions of the advertising business itself. On the whole, the Calfee and Ringold (1994) result seems less susceptible to such influences, but the authors noted that the survey data they examined did not reach to the level of advertising for specific brands or specific claims.

The Value of Advertising to Consumers

One also could focus on how regulation affects the perceived benefits of advertising, which FTC regulation is designed to buttress, rather than examining the narrower attributes of information or credibility in advertising. Measurement is an obvious problem because advertising manifests its value in subtle ways. The much-extolled benefits from competition, in the form of lower prices and better products, are only part of what needs to be taken into account. Advertising also tends to provide "generic" information in addition to brand-specific information, and this provides positive externalities (i.e., spillover benefits) that attenuate the tendency for competitive markets to under-produce valuable information (Calfee 1997, chap. 2). Thus, the literature on the measured benefits of advertising is itself fairly rare, and research connecting those benefits to regulation is even more so.

The only relevant study I have come across takes the simplest approach, which is to measure consumer valuations of advertising during periods of changing regulation. Public opinion polls have touched on the perceived benefits of advertising in various ways since the 1930s. The Calfee and Ringold (1994) survey of poll results found little change through the decades (in some cases in responses to essentially identical questions) as a persistent and relatively stable majority of consumers found advertising useful. This is, of course, consistent with a conclusion that fluctuations in the type and intensity of FTC regulation, including the imposition of the substantiation doctrine, had little influence on the value of advertising. But again, regulation is only one of many factors that affect the value of advertising, and as I noted earlier, these results tell us little about how consumers would respond to more radical changes in the regulatory environment. On the other hand, the fact that such persistent majorities found advertising useful even through the lightly regulated decades of the 1930s and 1940s is suggestive.

The Influence of Specific Regulatory Events

There is a large consumer research literature devoted to narrowly drawn regulatory episodes (as opposed to broad shifts in regulatory philosophy such as the adoption of the advertising substantiation doctrine). Much of this literature, however, examines the antecedents and consequences of advertising restrictions targeted at specific products, usually cigarettes or alcoholic beverages. I noted earlier that such research is largely peripheral to assessing deceptive advertising regulation. However, the ad ban results do tell us a little. The dominant research finding on both cigarette and alcoholic beverage advertising restrictions is an absence of substantial reductions in consumption associated with restrictions or bans (Calfee 1997, chap. 5). This finding tends to contradict the notion that such advertising is systematically deceptive. It also is consistent with the observation that advertising for these products, in fact, seldom is attacked as deceptive by the FTC or European regulatory bodies (Calfee 1997, chaps. 5-6).

One regulatory episode very worthy of note, however, is the remarkable and much-studied evolution of health claims for foods.[10] A number of studies examined events surrounding the advent of health claims for foods in 1984, when the FDA was forced to defer to FTC regulation and abandon its de facto ban on health claims. Here, the main regulatory variable is not FTC standards but rather the shift in regulatory dominance away from the FDA, which simply prohibited health claims regardless of deception, to the FTC and its substantiation doctrine. Hence, we can learn something of the benefits of the FTC's policy of permitting or encouraging claims that possess reasonable substantiation. The dominant research finding has been that health claims for foods during the mid- to late 1980s improved consumer information, consumer choices, and products.[11] This suggests that regulation based explicitly on limiting deception is superior to regulation consisting of blanket prohibitions of wide classes of claims.

The Effects of Information Remedies: Corrective Advertising

Information-based remedies for deceptive advertising have come to form an independent topic in the literature on advertising regulation. Two remedies stand out. One consists of mandated disclosures, especially warnings. These usually are created through legislation rather than FTC rules or cases (see Stewart, Folkes, and Martin's chapter in this volume [Chapter 15]). The other remedy, which is entirely a creation from FTC case law, is corrective advertising. This tool was born during the early 1970s when the newly activist FTC staff worked closely with consumer researchers and funded research on the impact of its own actions. Corrective advertising disappeared from the FTC tool kit during the 1980s, not to return until a 1998 action against Novartis's decades-long campaign for Doan's Pills, a case that remained in litigation at the time of this writing (Ingersoll 1999; Rose and Freeman 1998).

The FTC's corrective advertising episode left an extremely important legacy, however, in the form of what appears to be the largest single body of empirical research devoted specifically to the effects of deceptive advertising regulation. This legacy includes several excellent reviews on which this section relies (Armstrong, Gurol, and Russ 1983; Gardner and Leonard 1989; Wilkie, McNeill, and Mazis 1984), with special attention to Wilkie, McNeill, and Mazis's (1984) thorough description of the genesis and mechanics of FTC corrective advertising litigation and related activities.

Corrective advertising was designed to fix mistaken consumer impressions without affecting truthful information. To assess whether its tools worked as intended, the FTC commissioned consumer surveys and other research on some of its corrective advertising orders, especially in connection with the largest and best-known cases concerning a claim (found to be false) that Listerine mouthwash cured or prevented the common cold and claims for the STP motor oil additive. Most research focused on the two topics of greatest interest to the FTC: the "precision" of corrective advertising as a tool for correcting the original mistaken consumer impressions (the "target belief") without affecting other claims from the same advertiser and the possible negative effects of corrective advertising on the offending firm's overall image or credibility.

Research results began to appear in the academic literature as early as 1973 (Hunt 1973) and remained a fixture through the 1970s and early 1980s. On both topics—correction of the target belief and effects on company image—results were very mixed. Some studies found the desired effect on the target belief with little effect on other beliefs (see, e.g., the controlled field study by Mizerski, Allison, and Calvert 1980). Others detected evidence of a negative effect on nontarget beliefs (Kuehl and Dyer 1976; Mazis and Adkinson 1976). Some research even found extensive consumer misunderstanding or miscomprehension of corrective advertising messages (Jacoby, Nelson, and Hoyer 1982).

Regarding company image, several field studies found no effect on company image (Bernhardt, Kinnear, and Mazis 1986; Mizerski, Allison, and Calvert 1980). Other work, including the field research by Armstrong, Franke, and Russ (1982) and more than one experimental study (e.g., Dyer and Kuehl 1974) found significant but not necessarily large effects on firm credibility and image.

Although the bulk of corrective advertising research examined consumer attitudes or beliefs, very few studies addressed purchase intentions or behavior. Again, results were mixed. Bernhardt and colleagues (1981), for example, found effects on purchase intentions but not on behavior, whereas Mizerski, Allison, and Calvert (1980), looking only at intentions, found no effects.

Arguably more important than what research revealed about a few corrective advertising orders, however, is what it revealed about the more general problems of measuring the effects of information remedies in advertising regulation. The fact that the FTC commissioned research to predict *and* evaluate the effects of corrective advertising permitted researchers to address long-standing research problems such as the validity of predictions based on laboratory exercises with student participants. They generally found that the experiments greatly overestimated actual effects in the marketplace. For example, the review by Armstrong, Gurol, and Russ (1983) noted that, of the seven studies of Listerine corrective advertising, the five using experimental settings gave fairly strong corrective results for target beliefs (sometimes with undesired side effects), whereas the two studies of actual campaigns found disappointingly small results for target beliefs.

Researchers also had occasion to measure the persistence of information imparted through advertising campaigns including corrective advertising. They generally found that the effects of corrective advertising dissipated fairly rapidly, that is, within a few weeks (Gardner and Leonard 1989, p. 293).

As useful as these findings are, the fact remains that corrective advertising is a very limited tool that never will play more than a subsidiary role in deceptive advertising regulation. It is notable that the major corrective advertising cases of the 1970s tended to involve very long-running and much-criticized campaigns (e.g., Listerine, STP oil additives), and the same is true of the 1999 resurrection of corrective advertising for a case attacking decades of advertising for Doan's Pills. Whether corrective advertising will resume a prominent spot in the FTC arsenal and prompt a new wave of consumer research on the effects of deceptive advertising regulation remains to be seen.

Conclusion

Consumer research and other contributions to marketing knowledge have provided important insights into the effects of FTC regulation of deceptive advertising. These findings include the relative stability of the quantity and quality of information in advertising through the 1970s and 1980s and beyond, the benefits of encouraging additional truthful claims in advertising, substantial indirect evidence that contemporary advertising does not contain large quantities of deceptive claims, and illuminating details from the corrective advertising remedies of the 1970s.

But a larger finding is negative: the relative paucity of research beyond a few narrow areas on the effects of deceptive advertising regulation. This can be attributed primarily to two causes. One is the inherent difficulty of assessing the effects of advertising regulation. This difficulty arises from the fact that FTC regulation is designed to facilitate the second-order benefits of advertising such as better information, lower prices, and improved products. The second cause is the lack of large changes in regulation itself. Despite the controversy surrounding the most activist elements of FTC policy during the late 1970s and the deregulatory years of the early 1980s, the core principles of advertising regulation have remained quite stable since the advertising substantiation doctrine was established during the early 1970s. This lack of variation has offered but few opportunities to assess the impact of changes. Public policy research in marketing was, of course, still in its infancy when advertising regulation really did change during the early 1970s. On the other hand, economic analysis of regulation was well established during the 1960s. Yet, the economics literature also offers very few attempts to assess the effects of advertising regulation. This is testimony to the challenges in this type of research, which requires a combination of economic reasoning, the tools of consumer research and allied disciplines, and specially created data sets.

This suggests at least two areas for further research. One is the delineation of additional indirect measures of the effectiveness of deceptive advertising regulation. Measures such as information and credibility are useful but often are ambiguous in their implications for regulatory effects. More is needed.

Second, researchers can seek to identify and exploit more "natural experiments" in regulation. Promising arenas include the dramatic changes in advertising regulation for dietary supplements (where the legal and policy literature already is plentiful but empirical work remains scarce), the arrival of Internet advertising that is necessarily more loosely regulated than traditional media, the massive escalation of direct-to-consumer prescription drug advertising after the FDA relaxed its rules for broadcast advertising in 1997, and the shifting nature of securities advertising and its regulation by the SEC and FTC. In considering research in these areas, scholars should take note of the value of rich case studies such as those performed on a few corrective advertising campaigns during the 1970s.

Notes

1. Chapter 6 of my book, *Fear of Persuasion,* describes self-regulation in the context of advertising, competition, and government regulation (Calfee 1997). A brief review of self-regulation is included in Petty (1997, p. 7). Boddewyn (1992) provides an older and more complete worldwide review.

2. The deception statement is listed in the references as FTC (1983). The genesis and contents of this statement are analyzed in Ford and Calfee (1986). A useful summary of later developments is included in Beales and Muris (1993).

3. See FTC (1984).

4. In addition to the FTC policy statements already cited, see Beales, Craswell, and Salop (1981); Craswell (1985); and Ford and Calfee (1986). On the distinction between deception and miscomprehension, see Jacoby and Hoyer (1982) and the contrasting views of Preston and Richards (1986). The entire debate is summarized in Gardner and Leonard (1989).

5. Thus, the FDA scrutinizes prescription drug advertising in medical journals, whereas the FTC pays no attention to voluminous scientific and medical device advertising in *Science* and other scholarly journals.

6. In 1996, the FTC chairman noted "an understanding that unnecessary restraints on truthful advertising can be as harmful to consumers as deceptive or unfair advertising" (Pitofsky 1996, p. 56, quoted in Abernathy and Franke 1998).

7. Two useful sources on the institutional history of consumer research and economic analysis at the FTC are Murphy and Wilkie (1990) and the special historical section of the Spring 1997 issue of the *Journal of Public Policy & Marketing* (cf. Bloom 1997).

8. Among many sources on the recent history of FTC advertising regulation, Abernathy and Franke (1998) provided a convenient and reasonably complete summary.

9. On the origins of the substantiation doctrine, see Pitofsky (1977) and the very useful FTC staff memo by Guerard and Niemasik (1978).

10. This section relies on Ippolito and Mathios (1991) and Calfee and Pappalardo (1991).

11. See Ippolito and Mathios (1991).

References

Abernathy, Avery and George Franke (1998), "FTC Regulatory Activity and the Information Content of Advertising," *Journal of Public Policy & Marketing,* 17 (2), 239-56.

Armstrong, G., G. Franke, and F. Russ (1982), "The Effects of Corrective Advertising on Company Image," *Journal of Advertising,* 11 (4), 39-47.

————, Metin N. Gurol, and Frederick A. Russ (1983), "Corrective Advertising: A Review and Evaluation," *Current Issues and Research in Advertising: 1983,* 6, 93-114.

Beales, Howard, Richard Craswell, and Stephen Salop (1981), "The Efficient Regulation of Consumer Information," *Journal of Law and Economics,* 24 (December), 491-539.

———— and Timothy J. Muris (1993), *State and Federal Regulation of National Advertising.* Washington, DC: AEI Press.

Bernhardt, K. L., T. C. Kinnear, and M. Mazis (1986), "A Field Study of Corrective Advertising Effectiveness," *Journal of Public Policy & Marketing,* 5, 146-62.

————, ————, ———— and Bonnie Reese (1981), "Impact of Publicity on Corrective Advertising Effects," in *Advances in Consumer Research,* Vol. 8, Kent Monroe, ed. Ann Arbor, MI: Association for Consumer Research, 414-15.

Bloom, Paul N. (1997), "Field of Marketing and Public Policy: Introduction and Overview," *Journal of Public Policy & Marketing,* 16 (Spring), 126-28.

Boddewyn, Jean (1992), *Global Perspective on Advertising Self-Regulation.* Westport, CT: Quorum Books.

Calfee, John E. (1996), "The Leverage Principle in FDA Regulation of Information," in *Competitive Strategies in the Pharmaceutical Industry,* Robert Helms, ed. Washington, DC: American Enterprise Institute, 306-21.

———— (1997), *Fear of Persuasion: A New Perspective on Advertising and Regulation.* London: Agora. (North American distribution by the American Enterprise Institute)

———— and Janis K. Pappalardo (1991), "Public Policy Issues in Health Claims for Foods," *Journal of Public Policy & Marketing,* 10 (Spring), 33-54.

———— and Debra Jones Ringold (1994), "The Seventy Percent Majority: Enduring Consumer Beliefs about Advertising," *Journal of Public Policy & Marketing,* 13 (Fall), 228-38.

Chou, Linly, George Franke, and Gary Wilcox (1987), "The Information Content of Comparative Magazine Advertisements: A Longitudinal Analysis," *Journalism Quarterly,* 64 (Spring), 119-24, 250.

Crane, F. G. (1991), "Consumers' Attitudes towards Advertising: A Canadian Perspective," *International Journal of Advertising,* 10 (2), 111-16.

Craswell, Richard (1985), "Interpreting Deceptive Advertising," *Boston University Law Review,* 65, 657-732.

Dyer, Robert and Phillip Kuehl (1974), "The 'Corrective Advertising' Remedy of the FTC: An Empirical Evaluation," *Journal of Marketing,* 38 (January), 48-54.

Federal Trade Commission (1983), "Statement on Deception," *Antitrust and Trade Regulation Report,* October 27, 689. (Reprinted as an appendix to *FTC v. Cliffdale Associates Inc. et al.* [1984], 103 FTC 110, 174-84)

———— (1984), "Advertising Substantiation Policy Statement," *Antitrust and Trade Regulation Report,* August 2, 234-35. (Reprinted as an appendix to *Thompson Medical Company* [1984], 104 FTC 648, 839-942)

Ford, Gary T. and John E. Calfee (1986), "Recent Developments in FTC Policy on Deception," *Journal of Marketing,* 50 (July), 82-103.

Gardner, David M. and Nancy Leonard (1989), "Research in Deceptive and Corrective Advertising: Progress to Date and Impact on Public Policy," *Current Issues and Research in Advertising,* 12 (2), 275-309.

Guerard, Collot and Julie Niemasik (1978), "Evolution and Evaluation of the Ad Substantiation Program since 1971," Federal Trade Commission staff memorandum, December 1.

Healey, J. and H. Kassarjian (1983), "Advertising Substantiation and Advertiser Response: A Content Analysis of Magazine Advertisements," *Journal of Marketing,* 47 (January), 107-17.

Hunt, H. Keith (1973), "Effects of Corrective Advertising," *Journal of Advertising Research,* 13 (October), 15-22.

Ingersoll, Bruce (1999), "FTC Orders Novartis to Run Ads to Correct 'Misbeliefs' about Pill," *The Wall Street Journal,* May 28.

Ippolito, Pauline and Alan Mathios (1991), "Health Claims in Food Marketing: Evidence on Knowledge and Behavior in the Cereal Market," *Journal of Public Policy & Marketing,* 10 (Spring), 15-32.

Jacoby, J. and W. Hoyer (1982), "Viewer Miscomprehension of Televised Communication: Selected Findings," *Journal of Marketing,* 46 (October), 12-26.

————, M. Nelson, and W. Hoyer (1982), "Corrective Advertising and Affirmative Disclosure Statements: Their Potential for Confusing and Misleading the Consumer," *Journal of Marketing* 46 (January), 61-72.

Kassarjian, Harold and Waltraud Kassarjian (1988), "The Impact of Regulation on Advertising: A Content Analysis," *Journal of Consumer Policy,* 11, 269-85.

Kinnear, Thomas (1997), "An Historic Perspective on the Quantity and Quality of Marketing and Public Policy Research," *Journal of Public Policy & Marketing,* 16 (Spring), 144-46.

Kuehl, Phillip and Robert Dyer (1976), "Applications of the 'Normative Belief' Technique for Measuring the Effectiveness of Deceptive and Corrective Advertisements," in *Advances in Consumer Research,* Vol. 4, William R. Perrault, ed. Valdosta, GA: Association for Consumer Research, 204-12.

Mazis, Michael B. (1997), "Marketing and Public Policy: Prospects for the Future," *Journal of Public Policy & Marketing,* 16 (Spring), 139-43.

———— and Janice Adkinson (1976), "An Experimental Evaluation of a Proposed Corrective Advertising Remedy," *Journal of Marketing Research* 13 (April), 178-83.

McChesney, Fred S. (1988), "A Positive Regulatory Theory of the First Amendment," *Connecticut Law Review,* 20, 355-82.

Mizerski, R., N. Allison, and S. Calvert (1980), "A Controlled Field Study of Corrective Advertising Using Multiple Exposures and a Commercial Medium," *Journal of Marketing Research,* 17, 341-48.

Murphy, Patrick and William Wilkie, eds. (1990), *Marketing and Advertising Regulation: The Federal Trade Commission in the 1990s.* Notre Dame, IN: University of Notre Dame Press.

Parker-Pope, Tara (1995), "Consumers Say They Aren't Buying Advertisers' Hard Sell, Survey Finds," *The Wall Street Journal,* July 14, B5.

Petty, Ross (1997), "Advertising Law in the United States and European Union," *Journal of Public Policy & Marketing,* 16 (Spring), 2-13.

Pitofsky, Robert (1977), "Beyond Nader: Consumer Protection and the Regulation of Advertising," *Harvard Law Review,* 90, 661-701.

———— (1996), "Advertising Regulation's 'State of the Union,'" *Editor & Publisher,* April 6, 56.

Preston, I. (1983), "A Review of the Literature on Advertising Regulation," *Current Issues and Research in Advertising: 1983,* 6, 1-37.

———— (1987), "A Review of the Literature on Advertising Regulation," *Current Issues and Research in Advertising: 1987,* 10, 297-325.

———— and Jef I. Richards (1986), "Consumer Miscomprehension as a Challenge to FTC Prosecutions of Deceptive Advertising," *John Marshall Law Review,* 19, 605-35.

Priest, George L. (1987), "Measuring Legal Change," *Journal of Law, Economics, and Organization,* 3 (2), 193-225.

Resnick, A. and B. Stern (1977), "An Analysis of Information Content in Television Advertising," *Journal of Marketing,* 41 (January), 50-53.

Rose, Lew and D. Reed Freeman, Jr. (1998), "ALJ Finds Liability, Refuses to Order Corrective Advertising in Doan's Case," *National Law Journal,* May 18.

Sauer, R. and K. Leffler (1990), "Did the Federal Trade Commission's Advertising Substantiation Program Promote More Credible Advertising?" *American Economic Review,* 80 (1), 191-203.

Wilkie, William (1997), "Developing Research on Public Policy and Marketing," *Journal of Public Policy & Marketing,* 16 (Spring), 144-46.

————, Dennis L. McNeill, and Michael B. Mazis (1984), "Marketing's 'Scarlet Letter': The Theory and Practice of Corrective Advertising," *Journal of Marketing,* 48 (April), 11-31.

Wolfson, Nicholas (1990), *Corporate First Amendment Rights and the SEC.* Westport, CT: Quorum Books.

The Effectiveness of Product Safety Regulation and Litigation

Fred W. Morgan

This review covers the effectiveness of product safety regulation and litigation, two important avenues for enhancing overall safety within both living and working environments.[1] Safety regulation, a public approach in that the state initiates laws and enforcement mechanisms, usually focuses on ubiquitous issues, such as fresh food and automobile performance, that affect all of us. Safety regulations sometimes are intended to help groups of people, such as children and the elderly, who might be unable to make informed choices in free markets. Safety-related litigation, generally a private dispute between two or more parties, helps to resolve a specific problem, such as what or who caused someone's injuries,[2] and generally is aimed at redressing the injuries. Litigation often is the precursor to safety regulation because laws frequently are enacted in response to a series of lawsuits centering on repeated problems with a product, product category, or consumption situation.

Safety regulation and litigation both have their own origins, processes, and goals.[3] Laws encouraging safer products emanate from the give and take of partisan politics, the influence of interest groups, assessments of the competitiveness of products manufactured in the United States, and the visibility and graphic nature of product-related dangers. Litigation occurs somewhat more spontaneously than regulation but also can achieve momentum as society gains an awareness of the widespread nature of safety issues. Although the judiciary is more removed from the factors that influence legislative action, pointed social criticism can result in judicial attention and eventual response.

In this chapter, I first discuss the macro process by which safety goals are established and scrutinized. I then look at safety regulation and litigation, specifically at their similarities and differences in terms of goals and processes. Finally, I review the costs and effectiveness of these two avenues to product safety and highlight policy issues that should be examined in greater detail.

Establishing Safety Goals

As a starting point, the societal goal of product safety generally is regarded as "good" and worthy of pursuing. The question of "how much safety" is not easily answered because increased safety generally comes at the price of forgoing certain products and important features of others. Indeed, greater levels of safety require trade-offs in terms of lifestyle and convenience. Common household products such as knives and drain cleaners lack functional utility if manufactured so that they absolutely cannot harm people. Increases in safety sometimes come at costs that consumers will not assume unless mandated by law (e.g., automobile air bags [Garber 1998]), making unilateral safety improvements by individual companies a poor investment.

Several social forces interact to influence the consensus regarding the appropriate level of safety, both for society in general and with respect to specific industries and products. The most visible and persistent of these factors are as follows (in no particular order):

1. current technology, projected technological developments, and the rate of movement toward these innovations;

2. political processes (e.g., legislative and administrative law making, election of politicians, interplay among governmental branches);

    a. competitiveness of U.S. firms relative to firms from other countries and within specific markets and industries;

    b. interest groups representing (at least purportedly) affected or soon-to-be-affected parties (e.g., industry trade associations, consumer groups, professional lobbyists);

3. judicial processes and decisions and the resultant common law; and

4. dissemination of information (i.e., the degree to which involved and affected parties and the general public are accurately informed).

The complexity of the interaction among these factors borders on unfathomable, particularly in a discussion of a topic as amorphous as the "overall level of product safety in the United States." An example illustrates the confluence of these forces on safety within an industry as well as the existence of rival explanations for safety levels.

From the late 1970s through the mid-1980s, American manufacturers of single-engine piston aircraft experienced greatly reduced demand for their products. During this time period, industry members were sued several hundred times because of aircraft crashes leading to fatalities. Beech Aircraft, after analyzing litigation arising from more than 200 crashes during the 1980s, concluded that its cost per lawsuit was $530,000, with dismissed cases costing as much as $200,000. Beech further claimed that federal investigators found no evidence of faulty design or manufacture in any of these cases (Brickman 1994; Bulkeley 1993). Industry spokespersons publicized the view that the unfettered product liability climate was causing the demise of the industry. The industry produced more than 17,000 planes in 1978,[4] about 2,600 in 1983, and fewer than 1,000 in 1993 (Meyer 1993). Safety advocates adopted the position that small aircraft were inherently unsafe and were being driven from the market because they could not be made safe at prices that the market would bear (Ausness 1996; Tarry and Truitt 1995).

During this time period, proponents of tort reform, using the litigation history of the aircraft and other industries, argued that the American business sector was experiencing a product liability crisis of unprecedented magnitude (Huber 1988; Mitts 1983; Neely 1988; Viscusi 1991). Trade associations and attorneys representing corporate defendants promulgated the reform position ("The Devils" 1979). The purported increase in product liability lawsuits and the geometric growth of punitive damages awards were cited as examples of how runaway juries were holding businesses hostage because of the unforeseeable behavior of foolish and careless consumers (Schwartz and Behrens 1993; Twerski 1994). Critics noted that fear of product liability exposure squelched innovation (Barrett 1995; Thomas and Theall 1995). Many firms stated that product liability insurance was prohibitively expensive, forcing them to operate with minimum or no coverage (Riggs 1986; Whitmore 1987).

Conversely, plaintiffs' attorneys, consumer groups, and legal scholars argued that the product liability crisis was a public relations effort on the part of American industry (Schwartz 1988; Work 1982). They also contended that reliable data indicated normal inflation in jury awards (Merritt and Barry 1999) and that punitive damages rarely were awarded and almost always were reduced on appeal (Baker 1998; Daniels and Martin 1998; Galanter 1998; Perczek 1993). Some analysts concluded that the insurance industry took advantage of the product liability hype to increase rates without concomitant increases in payouts (Berger 1988; Meyer 1997; Miller 1997).

Within this regulatory and litigation milieu, debate about the small aircraft industry resulted in the passage of the General Aviation Revitalization Act of 1994 (GARA), the first major legislation Congress enacted to reform the product liability environment (GARA 1994). GARA ended 8 years of lobbying by general aviation producers to provide "some predictability to an industry which has stopped building small airplanes because of liability costs" (Glickman 1994). Probably the most important aspect of GARA is a statute of repose barring lawsuits against manufacturers of general aviation aircraft when the aircraft are more than 18 years old. GARA enjoyed broad-based support including the backing of pilot groups and general aviation passengers, typically the plaintiffs in general aviation litigation (Sanger 1995).

So, what is the safety level within the general aviation industry after all these developments, trends, claims, and counterclaims? National Transportation

Safety Board (NTSB) data reveal 1.35 deaths per 100,000 flight hours for general aviation aircraft in 1998, compared to 1.50 in 1996 and 1.75 in 1986 (Fallows 1999). Preliminary data for 1999 show an improvement over 1998. In 1998, 1,907 general aviation accidents were reported, compared to 3,233 in 1982, the first year in which such data were recorded (Schneider 1999). Industry output also has begun to rebound. Ending a 10-year hiatus, Cessna commenced production of single-engine aircraft immediately after the enactment of GARA and sold about 2,000 planes in 1998 ("Cessna Meets Demand" 1999). Piper emerged from a 4-year bankruptcy in 1995 and now is financially healthy ("Honors and Awards" 1999).

Are safety improvements due to the impact of product liability claims and the vigilance of the NTSB and the Federal Aviation Administration (FAA)? Are safety improvements due to technological advances in the areas of air traffic control, global positioning systems, ergonomic cockpit design, visual pathway imagery, heads-up instrumentation, voice-command controls, and lighter-stronger alloys. The answers are *yes* and *yes*.

Will improvements in safety levels continue to be made? The answer is *probably*. The FAA has voiced a goal of reducing general aviation deaths by 20% by the year 2007, even with increasing general aviation traffic ("FAA Ready to Act" 1999). Analysts seem to think that this is an attainable goal, albeit a lofty one ("FAA Considers" 1999; Fiorino 1999; "Industry, FAA" 1999).

Even with technological developments, regulatory oversight, and the threat of litigation, the key to improved general aviation safety is increased skill of pilots, the consumers of general aviation goods and services. The NTSB estimates that 87% of the 621 general aviation fatalities in 1998 were due to pilot error. Developing "better consumers" is critical for enhanced safety in most product markets ("GAO Says" 1999). Improper consumer behavior can be anticipated in terms of product design and warnings, but such behavior cannot be eliminated.

Safety goals reflect the measurable performance of safety-based processes beginning with product design; continuing through manufacture, distribution, and sale (including consumption or use); and following up with accident or misuse analysis (leading to product redesign, recall, or market withdrawal). Safety processes are repetitive in the context of the overarching goal of continuous improvement. Both regulatory and judicial procedures play critical signaling roles in the process of achieving greater levels of product safety.

An Overview of Regulation and Litigation

The regulatory and judicial systems are complementary in their role as mechanisms for achieving social goals such as product safety (Smith 1993). Regulatory activities, in some ways a fourth branch of the government, are ubiquitous, dwarfing the decisions of the other three branches in terms of volume (Croley 1998, p. 3). Agencies are created and authorized by Congress to focus on specific topics not fully addressed by legislative action (Kerwin 1979) such as overcoming types of free market failures (e.g., concentrated power, imperfect information) (Breyer 1982, 1993). Agencies are not directly accountable to the citizenry; however, regulators do act on behalf of elected legislators (Croley 1998; Shapiro and Levy 1995). Prominent agencies with general responsibilities for product safety include the Food and Drug Administration (FDA), the Consumer Product Safety Commission (CPSC), the Federal Trade Commission (FTC), the Environmental Protection Agency (EPA), and the National Highway Traffic Safety Administration.

Regulatory agencies operate within the framework of administrative law, which pertains to doctrines and rules that govern relationships between private parties and regulators (Croley 1998, p. 6). Smith (1985) defined administrative law as a "comprehensive system of specific legal rules and judicial precedents governing the way government makes decisions affecting the private rights of individuals" (p. 433).

The federal judiciary also has a role in the functioning of regulatory agencies. A court may be called on to settle a disagreement about a regulatory agency decision or with respect to how a regulatory agency has interpreted its congressional directive (Dorf and Sabel 1998; Seidenfeld 1992; Sunstein 1989; Werhan 1996). The interdependence of administrative and judicial concerns for safety is illustrated by a comment by Abner Mikva, then circuit judge for the U.S. Court of Appeals for the District of Columbia circuit:

> The proper division of labors between courts and administrative agencies is a subject that is never far from most federal judges' minds. This relationship determines, in no small measure, how the agencies carry out their statutory mandates. Judicial review of agency action also affects how Congress governs and how judges go about their business. Indeed, in our modern administrative state, Congress delegates much of the day-to-day lawmaking to the agencies. In some regulatory areas requiring heavy technical expertise and daily or frequent oversight, neither Congress nor the courts can ride close enough herd on the agency's lawmaking. In these fields, judicial review for fidelity to the agency's statute is the primary means for a democracy to ensure that the agencies are carrying out the will of the politically accountable branches of government. (Mikva 1986, p. 3)

A discussion of the extent of judicial review of agency comportment is beyond the scope of this chapter. However, the aggressiveness of judicial oversight is a topic that engenders strong reactions in both directions (Cogan 1987; Krent 1997; Levine and Forrence 1990).

Judicial influence on product safety is most widely felt through private litigation. Consumers initiate lawsuits when they have been injured either by products or by how others have used products. The term "product liability" refers to this dynamic legal area. Plaintiff recovery can be based on several legal theories including breach of warranty, negligence, strict liability, misrepresentation, and fraud. These approaches to recovery, although differing in terms of the legal elements required to prove the plaintiff's claim, require that the product be defective. The term "defect" includes improper design, errors in manufacture, and/or inadequate warning. Because strict liability is the most common approach to recovery, the tort law system, circumscribing strict liability, provides the dominant framework for achieving product safety.

Thus, we have both public (regulatory action initiated by the state) and private (judicial action initiated by individuals) paths for reducing product-related risks. These two approaches can be compared with respect to goals, processes, and results.

Goals Setting and Product Safety

Regulatory Goals

The defined goals of regulatory agencies typically are set forth in statutes that legitimize the agencies. For example, the general purpose of the CPSC is to reduce injuries caused by consumer products (Mayton 1986), and the federal code establishing the CPSC describes its purpose as follows:

1. to protect the public against unreasonable risks of injury associated with consumer products;

2. to assist consumers in evaluating the comparative safety of consumer products;

3. to develop uniform safety standards for consumer products and to minimize conflicting state and local regulations; and

4. to promote research and investigation into the causes and prevention of product-related deaths, illnesses, and injuries. (CPSC 1999b)

This language, while providing guidance, allows the CPSC broad latitude in carrying out its duties. The agency must define "unreasonable risk" in the context of market segments, technology, and comparable products. Delineating these terms amounts to a balancing of costs and benefits (Megara 1998, p. 964), quite a subjective undertaking. Of course, this analysis requires identifying relevant costs and benefits and then assessing the balance between them, again subjective determinations.

If Congress does not go beyond general language to prescribe specific measures to be used as goals to assess performance, then agencies do. For example, the FDA requires that newly emerging therapies be evaluated in three-stage clinical trials, with Phase 3 trials guided by the general goals of safety and efficacy (Anastasio 1998-99). Phase 3 involves controlled randomized comparative trials (Graham and Rhomberg 1996) and establishes "whether the median disease-free survival time in the experimental group is superior to [that in] the control group" (Lahr 1997, p. 621).

Goals of regulatory agencies eventually are narrowed to numerical objectives that can be measured over time. If appropriate, as with the FDA example, goals are compared to existing benchmarks. Or, a goal may be developed to be reached within a specific number of years such as the reduction in number of annual fatalities associated with a product class. For example, the CPSC's 1999 goals were as follows:

1. reduce the product-related head injury rate to children by 10%;

2. prevent any increase in the death rate to children under 5 years [of age] from unintentional poisoning by drugs or hazardous household substances;

3. reduce the fire-related death rate by 10%;

4. reduce the carbon monoxide poisoning death rate by 20%; and

5. reduce the electrocution death rate by 20%. (CPSC 1999a)

Judicial Goals

This discussion focuses on the goals of tort law, which includes the law of product liability. Scholars have discussed and proposed various goals for tort law for decades, not so much in terms of disagreeing about the goals but focused more on goal hierarchies. From a descriptive perspective, the tort system should lead to predictable and uniform results ("Class Certification" 1983, p. 1154; Green and Matasar 1990, p. 656; Rabin 1997, pp. 5-6). Similar facts should lead to similar outcomes (Pace 1997, p. 1623) unless crucial factual differences account for varying adjudication. Without predictable outcomes, companies will be unable to look to the law for direction regarding the line between acceptable and unacceptable behavior.

At a more operational level, the purposes of tort law are (1) to compensate injured parties, (2) to deter wrongful conduct, (3) to encourage socially responsible behavior, and (4) to spread the costs of accidents (Gripman 1997, p. 176; Judges 1993, p. 141; Lee et al. 1999, p. 874; Madden 1999, p. 542). The compensation component returns the victim to his or her original condition, as nearly as possible within the parameters of the law. The deterrence component bespeaks a warning that similar behavior will be met with similar punishment. The encouragement component suggests that proper (opposite of the punished) behavior is the "right" conduct to mimic in future activities. The cost-spreading component assigns liability costs to future consumers of injury-causing products in the form of higher prices.

From a philosophical viewpoint, the original goal of tort law is grounded in corrective justice, that is, reversing the effects of tortious behavior (Madden 1999, pp. 555-56). Corrective justice theories are noninstrumental in that they emphasize the achievement of justice and the elimination of wrong and fault (Benson 1992; Coleman 1992; O'Connell 1997). Theories of corrective justice vary in their emphases on formal structures for achieving justice and on functional systems for separating right from wrong (Coleman 1995; Henderson and Twerski 1998; Keating 1996).

A second philosophical view of the tort system looks at economic efficiency. This approach considers the social costs of tort rules, that is, effects on all plaintiffs and defendants, product availability, and prices (Coase 1960). Some analysts view the situation from a societal level (Green 1997; Posner 1984), whereas others emphasize the distributive effects across different sectors of society (Coase 1960).

These various goal hierarchies resonate in the background during each product liability trial. The court seeks to render a verdict that is just and fair to the litigants in the context of the facts under review and with consideration of earlier decisions involving combinations of the same facts. The various goals are not always mutually consistent (i.e., they do not always lead to the same outcome), so the court must determine which goal should dominate. A more realistic view of the impact of tort goals on product liability litigation is that tort goals have little effect on the outcome of a single dispute. Allegations, arguments, evidence, facts, jurisdiction, and opinions combine to determine the outcome.

Processes and Product Safety

Regulatory Processes

The processes of regulatory agencies justify and delimit agencies' capacities to promulgate regulations, prosecute violators, and adjudicate enforcement actions (Wainstein 1988, p. 762). Individual citizens cannot readily organize themselves to produce public goods (e.g., build highways, control airways, provide consumers with information about products), at least not consistently and effectively (Croley 1998, pp. 22-23). Incapable of effective collection action, citizens delegate authority to provide these public goods to legislators who, in turn, delegate authority to administrative agencies to handle recurring regulatory decisions. Regulatory agencies are vested with power to resolve relatively homogeneous issues. The functioning of these agencies involves the interplay of (1) legislators, (2) regulators, (3) public interest groups and their leaders, (4) special interest groups and their leaders, and (5) regulated parties and their leaders (Rodriguez 1994; Rossi 1997; Seidenfeld 1992; Zywicki 1999).[5]

Regulatory agencies trying to advance the level of product safety can be influenced or compromised in several ways. For example, legislators can reduce the level of financial support for agencies, making it very difficult or impossible for them to accomplish their objectives. Agencies must compete with each other on an annual basis for a percentage of the designated appropriations (Posner 1974). Regulators might have to choose between administrative goals and personal goals, for example, when career advancement goals conflict with administrative duties (Langevoort 1987). Interest groups pressure, cajole, and threaten regulators to bring about the adoption of positions favoring the groups (Vreeland 1990). The independence of relationships between regulated sectors and regulators can be questioned when administrative agency personnel come from regulated industries that are the source of the most qualified experts in an area (Graham 1997; Romano 1996).

Within the pressures of this operating environment, agencies with product safety responsibilities must determine which products and markets need scrutiny and the establishment of standards. Regulated industries generally seek minimal safety standards that can be met without undue difficulty (Schwartz 1988, p. 1146). In addition, regulatory budgets affect the extent to which agencies can monitor technological developments so as to enforce up-to-date standards. Because regulated industries are paramount sources of information about their technologies, regulators are again battling for full disclosure of information (Lyndon 1995, 1997).

Beyond this, technology often frames regulators' understanding of its capabilities. So, when regulators make decisions about risks of alternative technologies, they are doing so by using frameworks that are, at least in part, defined by the alternatives being considered (Lyndon 1997). Technology framing is especially important when regulatory agencies adopt a technology-forcing approach to promulgating safety standards (Rest and Ashford 1988; Viscusi 1996). Technology-forcing agencies require that industries adopt a specific technology or perhaps develop new technology, often in the absence of cost-benefit analysis, that is, achieving safety standards via prescribed technology rather than least cost technology.

Some agencies have the authority to require approval of products prior to their being marketed. For example, the FDA regulates drug products and medical devices through an approval process that involves reviewing testing protocols and marketplace information such as labels. The FDA's multi-tier[6] scheme results in new products being subject to lengthy pre-market approval, whereas proposed products deemed bioequivalent to existing products face a lesser standard. The CPSC, by way of contrast, relies mainly on voluntary standards, recalls of marketed products that have harmed consumers, and standards for product performance and labels and warnings (McGarity 1992).

Judicial Processes

From the standpoint of product safety, the judicial system first used a contract paradigm in which the plaintiff consumer had to be in a contractual relationship with the seller of the harm-causing product. Vestiges of this paradigm still exist today in the form of warranties of merchantability and fitness. As consumers and marketers became separated from each other with the advent of mass production and intermediate sellers, negligence emerged as the primary approach to recovery for injured consumers. During the 1960s, strict liability was popularized, leading to its adoption as the primary criterion for recovery today.[7]

The principal source of product safety standards applied and evaluated by courts is the common law, that is, prior court decisions within the jurisdiction in which the dispute is being litigated. Courts also apply federal and state statutes, when appropriate, in product liability trials, and courts sometimes are called on to validate administrative law decisions.

In their pursuit of product safety, courts differ most in comparison to regulatory agencies in that juries often make the initial evaluation of the harm-causing product.[8] This contrasts sharply with the expertise found within regulatory bodies. Although courts provide for the use of expert testimony and technical evidence, jurors represent a cross section of the population and might have little appreciation for the technical aspects of products that are being examined.[9] Appellate review of trial court decisions helps to ensure uniformity, fairness, and a general matching of the outcome with the facts being disputed.

Tort system procedures have been criticized generally because of state-to-state variations in common law and specifically because of the following:

- *The lack of guidelines for determining damages (compensatory awards) and punishments* (punitive awards). In response, several states have placed limits on compensatory awards and have restricted punitive awards to some multiple of compensatory awards (Galanter 1998; Kang 1999; Mogin 1998; Schwartz 1993).

- *The uncertain time that elapses between the consumer's use of a product and the consumer's injury.* In response, several states have passed statutes of repose, making it difficult for a consumer to litigate if the injury occurs after a prescribed time period (Baughman 1996; Werber 1995).

- *The relationship between regulatory compliance and tort liability.* Regulatory standards are treated as minimum safety standards, perhaps insufficient to exculpate defendants. Companies would like to see compliance treated as an affirmative (i.e., complete) defense (Warren 1997).

In addition to state responses, federal product liability reform has been discussed intermittently for the past two decades, as was noted earlier in the discussion of general aviation (Schwartz, Behrens, and Mathews 1999; Viscusi 1991). The politics of crafting an acceptable federal statute is formidable, and federalism stands as another roadblock for those seeking such reform (Chemerinsky 1995; Moulton 1999; Razook 1995). In the absence of statutory tort reform, the *Restatement (Third) of Torts* (American Law Institute 1997) influences product safety by providing a synthesis of relevant common law and by suggesting recommended treatment of issues for which common law consensus is lacking (Henderson and Twerski 1998; Massey 1997-98).

Results: Costs and Effectiveness of Regulation and Litigation

Assessments of the effectiveness of regulations and litigation in enhancing product safety can be carried out at several levels. At the societal level, U.S. consumers seem to be living in an environment characterized by greater levels of product safety than ever before. But because this is a perceptual judgment, how is aggregate product safety measured and what time interval is appropriate? Are products safer than they were a decade ago? The answer is *probably.* Are they safer now than in 1950? The answer is *most certainly,* but in what proportion or at what level? Aggregate safety is achieved at some overall cost, also difficult to measure at the societal level. Effectiveness assessments call our attention back to the goals of regulation and litigation, thereby illustrating the continuous and circular nature of the pursuit of product safety.

Regulatory Costs and Effectiveness

Estimates of the annual cost of federal regulations range from $400 billion to more than $1.5 trillion ("Government in Retreat" 1998; Hopkins 1992; Laffer and Bord 1992; Viscusi, Vernon, and Harrington 1995). Hahn and Hird (1991) found that total costs and benefits of regulations were roughly equal, although they cautioned about uncertainty in their work. The cost of federal regulations per household is approximately $6,000 per year by one estimate (Hopkins 1992).

One fully supportable conclusion is that individual regulations vary enormously in terms of their effectiveness. Discussions of regulation effectiveness usually center on cost-benefit comparisons, that is, the cost per life saved or cost per injury prevented.[10] Other studies estimate the reduction in injuries or deaths resulting from a specific regulation. In spite of inherent uncertainty, studies of regulatory effectiveness have been widely discussed and reprinted. For example, an economist with the Office of Management and Budget prepared estimates of the cost per life saved of a number of federal regulations (Table 19.1) (Lutter and Morrall 1994; Morrall 1986). Heinzerling (1998) commented that these "numbers are ubiquitous in the literature on risk regulation" (p. 1982) and went on to cite dozens of reports and numerous scholarly treatises using all or part of these results to support arguments about regulatory reform and risk trade-offs.[11]

Assuming that Table 19.1 data are valid, reliable, and based on consensual assumptions, this type of information permits comparisons of regulatory effectiveness. These data can be used to determine where to invest regulatory budgets and effort. However, numerical data, although appearing objective, reflect both the explicit normative assumptions and choices and implicit normative values of researchers. Examples of these assumptions, choices, and values in assessing overall regulatory effectiveness include the following:

1. *equivalency of lives:* whether every person in society is of "equal value" or whether some segments (e.g., the wealthy or politically influential) merit greater protection (Keeney 1990);

2. *balancing of catastrophic and individual risks:* whether large-scale losses of life (e.g., airline crashes) deserve greater preventive efforts than do individual losses of life (Zeckhauser and Viscusi 1996);

3. *implicated costs and benefits:* what indirect costs or savings to include in the analysis (lifesaving regulations [e.g., seat belts] do just that, whereas health-enhancing regulations [e.g., air purification] save lives but also improve quality of life, a complex benefit to quantify) (Keeney 1996);

4. *risk latency:* understanding and estimating the impact of long-term exposure to incalculable or minuscule risks relative to known and instantaneous risks (Revesz 1999); and

5. *voluntary and involuntary exposure to risk:* whether these are equivalent and whether consumers can assess risk levels (Cross 1997, 1999; Graham 1997).

As compared to cost-benefit analyses, evaluating the effectiveness of regulations in lowering the number of injuries is somewhat easier. Most studies use pre- and post-regulation measures of injury levels, adjusting for other causal factors. Nearly every study of regulations has reported lower injury levels fol-

TABLE 19.1 Lives Saved and Costs of Various Regulations

Benefit-Cost Test Regulation	Year	Agency	Cost per Life Saved (millions of 1984 dollars)	Cost per Life Saved (millions of 1992 dollars)
Unvented space heaters	1980	CPSC	0.1	0.1
Cabin fire protection	1985	FAA	0.2	0.3
Passive restraints/belts	1984	NHTSA	0.3	0.4
Underground construction	1989	OSHA	0.3	0.4
Alcohol and drug control	1985	FDA	0.5	0.7
Servicing wheel rims	1984	OSHA	0.5	0.7
Seat cushion flammability	1984	FAA	0.6	0.8
Floor emergency lighting	1984	FAA	0.7	0.9
Crane suspension personal platform	1988	OSHA	1.2	1.2
Concrete and masonry construction	1988	OSHA	1.4	1.9
Hazard communication	1983	OSHA	1.8	2.4
Asbestos	1986	OSHA	89.3	2.8
Benzene/fugitive emissions	1984	EPA	2.8	3.8
Grain dust	1987	OSHA	5.3	8.8
Radionuclides/uranium mines	1984	EPA	6.9	9.3
Benzene	1987	OSHA	17.1	23.1
Ethylene oxide	1984	OSHA	25.6	34.6
Uranium mill tailings inactive	1983	EPA	27.6	37.3
Acrylonitrile	1978	OSHA	—	50.8
Uranium mill tailings active	1983	EPA	53.0	71.6
Asbestos	1989	EPA	104.2	72.9
Coke ovens	1976	OSHA	—	83.4
Arsenic	1978	OSHA	—	125.0
DES (cattlefeed)	1979	FDA	—	178.0
Arsenic/glass manufacturing	1986	EPA	142.0	192.0
Benzene/storage	1984	EPA	202.0	273.0
Radionuclides/Department of Energy facilities	1984	EPA	210.0	284.0
Radionuclides/elementary phosphorus	1984	EPA	270.0	365.0
Benzene/ethylbenzenol styrene	1984	EPA	483.0	416.0
Benzene/maleic anhydride	1984	EPA	820.0	1,107.0
Formaldehyde	1987	OSHA	72,000.0	119,000.0

SOURCE: Adapted from Lutter and Morrall (1994) and Morrall (1986).

NOTE: CPSC = Customer Product Safety Commission; FAA = Federal Aviation Administration; NHTSA = National Highway Traffic Safety Administration; OSHA = Occupational Safety and Health Administration; FDA = Food and Drug Administration; EPA = Environmental Protection Agency.

lowing regulatory enactment. For some regulations (e.g., mandated auto seat belts or air bags), effectiveness measurement is straightforward—reduction in the number of fatalities and injuries (Cochran 1989). For others (e.g., mandated warnings and information disclosures), effectiveness is subtle and multidimensional including appraisals of injury level, behavior, and attitude (Latin 1994; Stewart and Martin 1994).

Additional factors also influence the effectiveness of regulations. Sunstein (1990, p. 413) argued that stringent regulatory standards may cause administrative agencies to police less vigilantly for fear of the onerous burden that the standards place on companies. Sunstein (p. 417) also proposed that severe restrictions on new market entrants, accompanied by exempt status for current marketers, actually increase risks because potential entrants disappear and earlier outdated technologies remain in place. Similarly, regulations endorsing the best available technology might discourage technological innovation because of the indeterminate costs associated with new technologies (Latin 1985). Finally, required information may result in less informed consumers because of the burden of processing the volume of information in required disclosures (Grether, Schwartz, and Wilde 1986; Hahn 1997; Latin 1994; Sunstein 1990).

Determining the effectiveness of regulations is difficult because of the contemporaneous influence of so many factors that are not independent of each other and that often have a lagged impact on product safety. With supportive assumptions and selective data analyses, studies of regulatory effectiveness can be crafted to support arguments for increased regulation, regulatory reform, or deregulation. Add interpretive license to the mix, and one can choose from a number of proffered positions regarding the efficacy of regulations with regard to product safety.

Judicial Costs and Effectiveness

Many commentators have expressed opinions about the impact of judicial decisions on productivity, competitiveness of U.S. companies, and new product development. These reports often are based on skewed interpretations of information, depending on the vested interests of the writers. Scholarly and statistical analyses generally conclude that defendants file few lawsuits and lose most of them, whereas representatives of product manufacturers and insurers portray plaintiff consumers and their attorneys as careless, vindictive, and opportunistic (Daniels and Martin 1990; Koenig and Rustad 1993; Peterson, Sharma, and Shanley 1987).

Lacking data on cost per life saved, analysts have a more difficult time evaluating the effectiveness of the judicial system in preventing deaths and injuries. The direct effect of judicial activities on product safety is difficult to determine; hence, only circumstantial indicators exist. Most evaluations are found in studies of trends in tort litigation (e.g., operating costs, number of lawsuits, size of jury awards). For example, former Vice President Quayle popularized $300 billion as the amount spent on litigation annually in the United States.[12] At about the same time, the research group Tillinghast estimated these costs to be $132 billion in 1991 (Thornburgh 1996, p. 1). A RAND Institute study concluded that these costs ranged from \$30 billion to \$35 billion in 1985 (Kakalik and Pace 1986). In light of several commentators' opinions and other cost studies, the lower numbers seem more reasonable.

The number of product liability claims also has been overstated by proponents of tort reform. In a study of the 75 largest U.S. counties during the 12 months beginning July 1, 1991, product liability filings comprised 4.4% of tort filings (Bureau of Justice Statistics 1995).[13] These counties generated a total of 647 product liability verdicts. During this period, the number of federal product liability verdicts totaled 218. Plaintiffs prevailed in about 40% of these trials (Eisenberg et al. 1996, p. 437). Product liability awards are considerably larger than other tort awards, with the average federal award exceeding the average state award (pp. 438-50). The few studies that examined the relationship between plaintiffs' injuries and awards or settlements found strong correlations (Merritt and Barry 1999; Vidmar 1998). Defendants' settlement offers did not correlate with the severity of plaintiffs' injuries (Merritt and Barry 1999, p. 344). In general, judicial trends (number of filings and awards) seemed to favor plaintiffs from the late 1970s until about 1985. Since then, researchers show evidence of a "truly national pro-defendant shift in trial and pretrial awards" (Eisenberg and Henderson 1992, p. 796). This shift reflects, to some extent, the tort reform statutes enacted by nearly every state.[14]

These elemental conclusions emanate from the preceding trends and outcomes:

1. The few cases that proceed to jury awards are the ones that frame the product safety environment.

2. Most product liability claims (approximately 95% according to several researchers) settle before judges or juries render verdicts (Koenig 1998).[15] Specifics of many of these settlements are not disclosed, thereby not directly affecting the product safety environment.

3. Verdicts reported by national media (i.e., the newsworthy outcomes) are atypical of the "average" product liability case. Thus, most of us know only about extreme characteristics of the product safety environment.[16]

Although the debate continues, most experts argue that the tort system saves lives and lowers the likelihood of injury.[17] Product liability awards signal the marketplace with regard to several decisions that manufacturers/marketers must make:

1. the minimum levels of quality that products must achieve including quality level on an attribute-by-attribute basis;

2. the types of information that consumers should have available to make sound purchase and use decisions;

3. the relationships between product designs and product warnings (i.e., to what extent warnings can be used to offset design deficiencies); and

4. the extent to which product designs and warnings must anticipate consumer misuse of products.

State-to-state differences in thresholds for these decisions may, at first glance, augur for national product liability standards. But products sold in interstate commerce that could end up in any of several states must comply with the most stringent standards of the various states in which the product is sold. In effect, national marketers face a relatively uniform product liability environment—that of the states with the most pro-consumer product liability tradition.[18]

A major source of uncertainty about the effectiveness of judicial approaches to product safety is plaintiff self-selection. Most viable product liability claims are not filed, according to several observers of the judicial system (Merritt and Barry 1999; Viscusi 1989).[19] As a result, the only products involved in enough lawsuits to fully define the parameters of product liability as applied to them are products that have injured hundreds or thousands of consumers before product causation becomes manifest. Most marketers must assess their own product liability obligations (1) through their own minimal experience with litigation or (2) by making inferences from the litigation history of other products.

Conclusions and a Research Agenda

The consensus is that both regulatory and judicial incentives have improved product safety in the United States in comparison to an unconstrained market system. The essential questions being discussed are whether these systems provide incentives to increase product safety on a cost-effective basis and whether each system needs to be reformed. From the standpoint of process mechanisms, Ausness (1997, p. 453) contended that direct regulation looks to be more efficient in terms of lowering product-related accident costs. Regulatory agencies possess the expertise to understand product technologies, and they enforce specific and broad-reaching regulations that blanket entire industries, thereby raising safety levels. By comparison, tort statutes vary from state to state in both content and enforcement diligence, and judges and juries are not product technology experts. However, state tort reform, particularly caps on damages, creates the potential for much greater uniformity in tort outcomes.

The politics and funding of administrative agencies diminish their effectiveness in fully implementing their goals. Without adequate budgets, agencies must choose where to focus their resources, sometimes choosing between safety battles that need to be fought and battles that the agencies can realistically win. Consumer interest groups can influence these choices, but industry pressures also can be strong. By contrast, the tort system is much more of a free market mechanism than is the regulatory system. A single injured consumer can initiate a product liability lawsuit that forces an industry to rethink and perhaps change its product safety stance. Although large corporate defendants have advantages in terms of wealth and technical product knowledge, experienced plaintiffs' attorneys can marshal the resources necessary to litigate aggressively.

Regulatory agencies can fine companies that disobey guidelines or fail to follow pre-market procedures. For very large organizations, these fines can be insignificant relative to corporate revenues and profits. Court-awarded damages, however, can be substantial and can more closely match the punishment with the offense. The combination of compensatory damages to provide a monetary equivalent to the plaintiff's loss and punitive damages to punish the offending organization can be a noticeable financial burden. Compared to regulatory fines, the tort system provides greater financial incentives/threats for companies to develop safer products.[20]

Thus, we have complementary systems for improving product safety for which a number of important issues are in need of additional discussion and research. Marketing experts could contribute to and benefit from an examination of the following research questions:

1. How could we determine the proportional impact of regulations and judicial decisions on the level of product safety? Regulators take action on behalf of all potential consumers, whereas individuals litigate on their own behalf and indirectly help all other consumers and users of the products in question. Which is more instrumental with respect to product safety levels? Research could try to assess the following:

    a. comparative time lags of signals (passage of regulations or judicial decisions) on behavior changes within affected industries or product categories; and

    b. regulatory and tort system costs by industry or product category or market segment.

2. How could regulatory and judicial approaches to product safety be better coordinated? The independence of the judiciary prevents any formal cooperation, so agencies and legislators must anticipate and accommodate judicial review and response. How is this best accomplished in the context of the public (regulatory enhancement of safety) versus private (judicial deterrence of unsafe products and compensation of victims) orientations of the two systems?

3. What measures of success or goal accomplishment are most appropriate? Many experts can contribute to progress here including economists, public policy officials, and legal scholars. Marketers also have a role to play (see any issue of the *Journal of Public Policy & Marketing;* see also Wilkie and Moore 1999).

4. Which market segments are insufficiently covered by product safety regulations? Regulations focus on industries or products, not markets. A review of the regulatory environment from a marketing perspective would yield useful insights for future regulatory action.

5. How can regulatory agencies better publicize (and perhaps better understand) the interdependence of their goals? Agencies with multiple goals need to understand the tensions among goals and make the public aware of goal trade-offs. For example, the FDA's fundamental public health orientation conflicts with its other goal of promoting technological innovation.

Market, regulatory, and product liability incentives all play a part in encouraging the development of safe products. If we can better understand the role of each type of incentive and how it contributes to the overall level of product safety, then we can make appropriate funding allocations to regulatory and judicial systems. Safety as a product/service attribute affords a base level of safety across all products, markets, and consumers. Regulations shore up safety deficiencies as defined by the politics of the legislative and executive branches of government and as scrutinized by various interest groups. Judicial action fills in the gaps in the product safety environment that are overpowered by other market forces or political agendas.

Notes

1. Although state regulatory agencies and courts also influence product safety, this discussion focuses primarily on the effectiveness of federal safety imperatives. This emphasis on federal issues does not imply that actions to improve product safety by states are unimportant; rather, state efforts, including statutes and regulatory agencies, often are modeled after their federal counterparts.

2. Litigation can arise in response to regulations when a party disputes the outcome of a regulation as applied to a given set of circumstances.

3. This review is an abbreviated discussion of these issues. Thousands of economics, law, and political science scholars have studied aspects of this topic in detail. I summarize the central arguments and positions. For illustrative and detailed discussions, see Croley (1998), who describes theories of regulation and the administrative process; Heinzerling (1998), who looks at risk regulation and an alternative to estimate costs of regulation; Kelman (1988), who describes how externalities can be corrected by regulation and when some situations should be unregulated; Lebow (1997), who looks at the relationship between federalism and state efforts to reform product liability law; Merrill (1997b), who presents different views of comparative institutional choice; Merritt and Barry (1999), who study in detail the effects of tort reform in Ohio; Meyer (1997), who reviews the goals of tort law; Rose-Ackerman (1988), who examines the roles of law and economics in the modern welfare state; Schwartz (1988), who highlights the relationship between regulatory and tort systems; Schwartz and Shapiro (1997), who discuss proposed changes to the tort system and the importance of regulatory standards; and Sunstein (1990), who presents examples of self-defeating regulatory strategies.

4. Other sources estimate 1978 production at about 14,000 units (GAMA 1993, p. 6; see also Boswell and Coats 1994-95).

5. Croley (1998) provided an overview of regulatory processes by describing and examining competing theories of administrative regulation: public choice, neopluralist, public interest, and civil republican. He argued that these four theories have their roots in the pluralist theory of politics popularized during the 1950s. For additional reading, see Brietzke (1999), Colombatto and Macey (1996), Kelman (1988), Merrill (1997a), and Wiener (1999).

6. See Walsh and Pyrich (1996) for a history of the FDA and a review of its procedures.

7. Contractual relationships favored sellers over consumers because sellers developed the contracts (Owen 1998). In 1916, privity of contract was repudiated in the New York case of *MacPherson v. Buick Motor Company* (1916), ushering in negligence as the primary cause of action in litigation over product-related injuries. However, warranty actions continue to be tenable under the Uniform Commercial Code. Strict liability in tort was introduced in California in 1963 in the case of *Greenman v. Yuba Power Products Inc.* (1963), relying in part on *Henningsen v. Bloomfield Motors Inc.* (1960).

8. Juries serve these functions in the United States: (1) an effective means to resolve disputed facts fairly; (2) a means to protect against abuses of power by legislatures, judges, prosecutors, businesses, and other powerful political elites; (3) a vehicle for bringing community values into dispute processing; (4) a check against the bureaucratization and professionalization of the legal system; and (5) a means for legitimizing the outcome of dispute processing and facilitating citizens' knowledge about the legal process (American Bar Association/Brookings Institution 1992, pp. 8-11; Smith 1994, p. 80).

9. The U.S. Supreme Court made efforts during the 1990s to make expert testimony more reliable (*Daubert v. Merrell Dow Pharmaceuticals* 1993; Kapsa and Meyer 1999; Wood 1999).

10. This approach dates back to President Reagan's Executive Order 12291 (1981).

11. Morrall (1986) used agencies' estimates of compliance costs and discounted future compliance costs and number of lives saved by 10%. Morrall began with agencies' estimates of risks and effectiveness and adjusted them based on other information sources.

12. Such cost estimates for the U.S. civil justice system illustrate how opinions become facts via the process of "saying it makes it so." Marc Galanter, law professor at the University of Wisconsin, said the following of the $300 billion figure: "Three hundred billion? Where does that come from? The vice-president has it from the Council on Competitiveness (which he chairs), whose 'Agenda for Civil Justice Reform,' released August 13, 1991, borrows it from an article in *Forbes,* which in turn took it from liability guru Peter Huber, who, it is fair to say, made it up" (Gallanter 1992, p. 84).

13. This number excludes 199 asbestos verdicts in federal courts. Merritt and Barry (1999, p. 383) suggested that this study might overstate the percentage of product liability lawsuits because smaller counties likely encounter fewer product liability lawsuits on a per capita basis.

14. As of this writing, at least 46 states have passed tort reform legislation (Stewart 1998-99).

15. Cases settle for a variety of reasons including arbitration, dismissal, and agreement following motions (Eisenberg and Henderson 1992; Galanter and Cahill 1994).

16. According to Merritt and Barry (1999, p. 317), most versions of the McDonald's spilled coffee verdict omit the details that (1) the woman was parked, not driving, when the coffee spilled; (2) she was hospitalized with third-degree burns for eight days; (3) McDonald's was aware of more than 700 complaints about coffee-related scaldings; (5) McDonald's served its coffee hotter than did its competitors; (6) the woman offered to settle for $20,000; (6) the trial judge lowered the punitive award to $480,000; and (7) the parties finally settled for an undisclosed amount.

17. Kimmelman (1990) stated that 6,000 lives are saved and injuries are reduced by millions because of the product liability system. Legal scholars have provided countless arguments supporting the deterrent effect of strict product liability (Craswell 1999).

18. Several states vie for this honor. Developing a list of pro-consumer states is well beyond the scope of this chapter and depends on the products/markets in which the firm is competing. Historically, California, Louisiana, and New Jersey have been at the forefront of product liability developments. With the advent of tort reform, state-to-state variations have diminished.

19. Reasons for not filing claims include being unaware of legal rights, lack of access to competent legal counsel, not knowing how to assert one's legal rights, and being distracted from taking legal recourse due to the seriousness of the injury.

20. The tobacco settlement provides a recent example of the potential magnitude of tort awards and settlements (Hanson and Logue 1998). One of the potential drawbacks of tort reform is the limitation that many states have placed on punitive damages. By capping punitive damages, either as a multiple of compensatory damages or in absolute dollars, tort reformers have made punitive damages more predictable. This allows companies to incorporate punitive damages into their cost-benefit decision calculus. Predictable legal penalties now can be factored into the cost of potential safety improvements (Daniels and Martin 1998; Garber 1998).

References

American Bar Association/Brookings Institution (1992), *Charting a Future for the Civil Jury System.* Washington, DC: ABA/Brookings Institution.

American Law Institute (1997), *Restatement (Third) of Torts: Products Liability.* Philadelphia: American Law Institute.

Anastasio, Julia (1998-99), "Legislative Developments in the Regulation of Insurance Coverage: Will These New Regulations Benefit Women with Breast Cancer?" *American University Journal of Gender, Social Policy & Law,* 7, 55-85.

Ausness, Richard C. (1996), "The Case for a 'Strong' Regulatory Compliance Defense," *Maryland Law Review,* 55, 1210-66.

——— (1997), "Product Category Liability: A Critical Analysis," *Northern Kentucky University Law Review,* 24 (Summer), 423-55.

Baker, Tom (1998), "The Incidence, Scope, and Purpose of Punitive Damages: Reconsidering Insurance for Punitive Damages," *Wisconsin Law Review,* 101-30.

Barrett, Dirk (1995), "Introduction: Product Liability Aspects of Innovation," *Canada-United States Law Journal,* 21, 305-6.

Baughman, Jan Allen (1996), "The Statute of Repose: Ohio Legislators Attempt to Lock the Courthouse Doors to Product-Injured Persons," *Capital University Law Review,* 25, 671-703.

Benson, Peter (1992), "The Basis of Corrective Justice and Its Relation to Distributive Justice," *Iowa Law Review,* 77 (January), 515-624.

Berger, Robert G. (1988), "The Impact of Tort Law Development on Insurance: The Availability/Affordability Crisis and Its Potential Solutions," *American University Law Review,* 37 (Winter), 285-321.

Boswell, John H. and George Andrew Coats (1994-95), "Saving the General Aviation Industry: Putting Tort Reform to the Test," *Journal of Air Law and Commerce,* 60 (December-January), 533-73.

Breyer, Stephen (1982), *Regulation and Its Reform.* Cambridge, MA: Harvard University Press.

——— (1993), *Breaking the Vicious Circle: Toward Effective Risk Regulation.* Cambridge, MA: Harvard University Press.

Brickman, Lester (1994), "On the Relevance of the Admissibility of Scientific Evidence: Tort System Outcomes Are Principally Determined by Lawyers' Rates of Return," *Cardozo Law Review,* 15 (April), 1755-97.

Brietzke, Paul H. (1999), "Democratization and ... Administrative Law," *Oklahoma Law Review,* 52 (Spring), 1-47.

Bulkeley, William M. (1993), "Small-Plane Makers May Get a Big Lift from Congress," *The Wall Street Journal,* October 19, B1.

Bureau of Justice Statistics (1995), *Special Report: Civil Jury Cases and Verdicts in Large Counties—Civil Justice Survey of State Courts, 1992.* Washington, DC: Government Printing Office.

"Cessna Meets Demand for Planes with Mazak Palletech Cells" (1999), *Metalworking Production & Purchasing,* March, 4.

Chemerinsky, Edwin (1995), "The Values of Federalism," *Florida Law Review,* 47 (September), 499-540.

"Class Certification in Mass Accident Cases under Rule 23(b)(1)" (1983), *Harvard Law Review,* 98 (March), 1143-60.

Coase, Ronald H. (1960), "The Problem of Social Cost," *Journal of Law & Economics,* 3 (October), 1-44.

Cochran, Robert F., Jr. (1989), "New Seat Belt Defense Issues: The Impact of Air Bags and Mandatory Seat Belt Use Statutes on the Seat Belt Defense, and the Basis of Damage Reduction under the Seat Belt Defense," *Minnesota Law Review,* 73 (June), 1369-450.

Cogan, Efrat Massry (1987), "Executive Nonacquiescence: Problems of Statutory Interpretation and Separation of Powers," *Southern California Law Review,* 60 (May), 1143-77.

Coleman, Jules L. (1992), *Risks and Wrongs.* Cambridge, UK: Cambridge University Press.

——— (1995), "The Practice of Corrective Justice," *Arizona Law Review,* 37 (Spring), 15-30.

Colombatto, Enrico and Jonathan R. Macey (1996), "A Public Choice Model of International Economic Cooperation and the Decline of the Nation-State," *Cardozo Law Review,* 18 (December), 925-56.

Consumer Product Safety Commission (1999a), *1999 Annual Performance Plan: Consumer Product Safety Commission* [on-line].
Available: http://www.cpsc. gov/about/gpra/annpln99.pdf

——— (1999b), Public Law 92-573, §2, *Statutes,* 86, §1207, *United States Code Service,* 15, §2051.

Craswell, Richard (1999), "Deterrence and Damages: The Multiplier Principle and Its Alternatives," *Michigan Law Review,* 97 (June), 2185-238.

Croley, Steven P. (1998), "Theories of Regulation: Incorporating the Administrative Process," *Columbia Law Review,* 98 (January), 1-168.

Cross, Frank B. (1997), "Making Risk Policy in the Face of Expert/Public Conflicts: The Subtle Vices behind Environmental Values," *Duke Environmental Law & Policy Forum,* 8 (Fall), 151-70.

——— (1999), "Common Law Conceits: A Comment on Mainers & Yandle," *George Mason Law Review,* 7 (Summer), 965-81.

Daniels, Stephen and Joanne Martin (1990), "Myth and Reality in Punitive Damages," *Minnesota Law Review,* 75 (October), 1-64.

——— and ——— (1998), "Punitive Damages, Change, and the Politics of Ideas: Defining Public Policy Problems," *Wisconsin Law Review,* 71-100.

Daubert v. Merrell Dow Pharmaceuticals (1993), *reversed and remanded,* 509 U.S. 579, 113 S.Ct. 2786, 125 L.Ed.2d 469; 951 F.2d 1128 (9th Cir. 1991); 727 F.Supp. 570 (S.D. Cal. 1989).

"The Devils in the Product Liability Laws" (1979), *Business Week,* February 12, 72.

Dorf, Michael C. and Charles F. Sabel (1998), "A Constitution of Democratic Experimentalism," *Columbia Law Review,* 98 (March), 267-371.

Eisenberg, Theodore, John Goerdt, Brian Ostrom, and David Rottman (1996), "Litigation Outcomes in State and Federal Courts: A Statistical Portrait," *Seattle University Law Review,* 19 (Spring), 433-53.

———— and James A. Henderson, Jr. (1992), "Inside the Quiet Revolution in Products Liability," *UCLA Law Review,* 39 (April), 731-809.

Executive Order 12291 (1981), *Federal Register,* February 17, 13193.

"FAA Considers Draft Safety Goal of 20 Percent Drop in GA Accidents," (1999), *The Weekly of Business Aviation,* September 27, 142.

"FAA Ready to Act on Reducing Runway Incursions" (1999), *Aviation Daily,* November 10, 8.

Fallows, James (1999), "Turn Left at Cloud 109," *The New York Times,* November 21, 84. (Sunday late edition, Section 6)

Fiorino, Frances (1999), "General Aviation Trainer's Safety Benefits No Illusion," *Aviation Week & Space Technology,* November 29, 66.

Galanter, Marc (1992), "Pick a Number, Any Number," *American Lawyer,* April, 82-88.

———— (1998), "Shadow Play: The Fabled Menace of Punitive Damages," *Wisconsin Law Review,* 1-14.

———— and Mia Cahill (1994), "'Most Cases Settle: Judicial Promotion and Regulation of Settlements," *Stanford Law Review,* 46 (July), 1339-91.

"GAO Says More Data Needed to Link Computer-Based Training to Safety" (1999), *Aviation Daily,* July 22, 4.

Garber, Steven (1998), "Product Liability, Punitive Damages, Business Decisions, and Economic Outcomes," *Wisconsin Law Review,* 237-91.

General Aviation Manufacturers Association (1993), *General Aviation Statistical Databook.* Washington, DC: GAMA.

General Aviation Revitalization Act (1994), Public Law 103-298, *Statutes,* 108, 1522.

Glickman, Dan (1994), "Statement of Representative Dan Glickman," *Congressional Record,* June 27, H5001.

"Government in Retreat?" (1998), *Industry Week,* September 21, 84.

Graham, John D. (1997), "Legislative Approaches to Achieving More Protection against Risk at Less Cost," *University of Chicago Legal Forum,* 13-58.

———— and Lorenz Rhomberg (1996), "Uncertainty and Risk Assessment: How Risks Are Identified and Assessed," *Annals of the American Academy of Political and Social Science,* 545 (May), 15-23.

Green, Michael D. (1997), "Negligence = Economic Efficiency: Doubts," *Texas Law Review,* 75 (June), 1605-43.

———— and Richard A. Matasar (1990), "The Supreme Court and the Products Liability Crisis: Lessons from *Boyle's* Government Contractor Defense," *Southern California Law Review,* 63 (March), 637-726.

Greenman v. Yuba Power Products Inc. (1963), 59 Cal.2d 57, 377 P.2d 897, 27 Cal.Rptr. 697, 13 A.L.R.3d 1049.

Grether, David M., Alan Schwartz, and Louis L. Wilde (1986), "The Irrelevance of Information Overload: An Analysis of Search and Disclosure," *Southern California Law Review,* 59 (January), 277-303.

Gripman, David L. (1997), "The Doors Are Locked but the Thieves and Vandals Are Still Getting In: A Proposal in Tort to Alleviate Corporate America's Cyber-Crime Problem," *John Marshall Journal of Computer & Information Law,* 16 (Fall), 167-95.

Hahn, Robert W. (1997), "Achieving Real Regulatory Reform," *University of Chicago Legal Forum,* 143-58.

———— and John A. Hird (1991), "The Costs and Benefits of Regulation: Review and Synthesis," *Yale Journal on Regulation,* 8, 233-78.

Hanson, Jon D. and Kyle D. Logue (1998), "The Costs of Cigarettes: The Economic Case for Ex Post Incentive-Based Regulation," *Yale Law Journal,* 107 (March), 1163-361.

Heinzerling, Lisa (1998), "Regulatory Costs of Mythic Proportions," *Yale Law Journal,* 107 (May), 1981-2070.

Henderson, James A., Jr. and Aaron D. Twerski (1998), "Achieving Consensus on Defective Product Design," *Cornell Law Review,* 83 (May), 867-919.

Henningsen v. Bloomfield Motors Inc. (1960), 32 N.J. 358, 161 A.2d 69, 75 A.L.R.2d 1.

"Honors and Awards" (1999), *Aerospace America,* November, B20.

Hopkins, Thomas D. (1992), "The Costs of Federal Regulation," *Journal of Regulation and Social Costs,* 2 (August), 1-45.

Huber, Peter W. (1988), *The Legal Revolution and Its Consequences.* New York: Basic Books.

"Industry, FAA Look at CFIT, Weather to Reduce GA Accidents by 20 Percent" (1999), *The Weekly of Business Aviation,* November 1, 198.

Judges, Donald P. (1993), "Of Rocks and Hard Places: The Value of Risk Choice," *Emory Law Journal,* 42 (Winter), 1-142.

Kakalik, James S. and Nicholas M. Pace (1986), *Cost and Compensation Paid in Tort Litigation,* Santa Monica, CA: RAND Corporation, Institute for Civil Justice.

Kang, Michael S. (1999), "Don't Tell Juries about Statutory Damage Caps: The Merits of Nondisclosure," *University of Chicago Law Review,* 66 (Spring), 469-92.

Kapsa, Marilee M. and Carl B. Meyer (1999), "Scientific Experts: Making Their Testimony More Reliable," *California Western Law Review,* 35 (Spring), 313-32.

Keating, Gregory C. (1996), "Reasonableness and Rationality in Negligence Theory," *Stanford Law Review,* 48 (January), 311-84.

Keeney, Ralph L. (1990), "Mortality Risks Induced by Economic Expenditures," *Risk Analysis,* 10 (1), 147-59.

———— (1996), "The Process of Risk Management: The Role of Values in Risk Management," *Annals of the American Academy of Political and Social Science,* 545 (May), 126-34.

Kelman, Mark (1988), "On Democracy-Bashing: A Skeptical Look at the Theoretical and 'Empirical' Practice of the Public Choice Movement," *Virginia Law Review,* 74 (March), 199-273.

Kerwin, Cornelius M. (1979), "Judicial Implementation of Public Policy: The Courts and Legislation for the Judiciary," *Harvard Journal on Legislation,* 16, 415-44.

Kimmelman, Gene (1990), "Current System Said to Work," *Daily Report for Executives,* April 6, A6.

Koenig, Thomas (1998), "The Shadow Effect of Punitive Damages on Settlements," *Wisconsin Law Review,* 169-209.

———— and Michael Rustad (1993), "The Quiet Revolution Revisited: An Empirical Study of the Impact of State Tort Reform of Punitive Damages in Products Liability," *Justice System Journal,* 21, 27-55.

Krent, Harold J. (1997), "Reviewing Agency Action for Inconsistency with Prior Rules and Regulations," *Chicago-Kent Law Review,* 72, 1187-251.

Laffer, William G., III and Nancy A. Bord (1992), "George Bush's Hidden Tax: The Explosion in Regulation," *Heritage Foundation Reports: Backgrounder,* July 10. (Washington, DC: Heritage Foundation)

Lahr, J. Gregory (1997), "What Is the Method to Their 'Madness?' Experimental Treatment Exclusions in Health Insurance Policies," *Journal of Contemporary Health Law & Policy,* 13 (Spring), 613-36.

Langevoort, Donald C. (1987), "Statutory Obsolescence and the Judicial Process: The Revisionist Role of the Courts in Federal Banking Regulation," *Michigan Law Review,* 85 (February), 672-733.

Latin, Howard (1985), "Ideal versus Real Regulatory Efficiency: Implementation of Uniform Standards and 'Fine-Tuning' Regulatory Reforms," *Stanford Law Review,* 37 (May), 1267-332.

———— (1994), " 'Good' Warnings, Bad Products, and Cognitive Limitations," *UCLA Law Review,* 41 (June), 1193-310.

Lebow, Cynthia C. (1997), "Federalism and Federal Product Liability Reform: A Warning not Heeded," *Tennessee Law Review,* 64 (Spring), 665-90.

Lee, Michael, Sean Pak, Tae Kim, David Lee, Aaron Schapiro, and Tamer Francis (1999), "Electronic Commerce, Hackers, and the Search for Legitimacy: A Regulatory Proposal," *Berkeley Technology Law Journal,* 14 (Spring), 839-85.

Levine, Michael E. and Jennifer L. Forrence (1990), "Regulatory Capture, Public Interest, and the Public Agenda: Toward a Synthesis," *Journal of Law, Economics, & Organizations,* 6, 167-95.

Lutter, Randall and John F. Morrall, III (1994), "Health-Health Analysis: A New Way to Evaluate Health and Safety Regulation," *Journal of Risk & Uncertainty,* 8 (1), 43-66.

Lyndon, Mary L. (1995), "Tort Law and Technology," *Yale Journal on Regulation,* 12 (Winter), 137-76.

———— (1997), "Tort Law, Preemption, and Risk Management," *Widener Law Symposium Journal,* 2 (Fall), 69-86.

MacPherson v. Buick Motor Company (1916), 217 N.Y. 382, 111 N.E. 1050.

Madden, M. Stuart (1999), "Component Parts and Raw Materials Sellers: From the Titanic to the New Restatement," *Northern Kentucky University Law Review,* 26 (Spring), 535-71.

Massey, Gary, Jr. (1997-98), "Interpreting the Restatement of Torts Section 402B after the Changes to Section 402A," *Cumberland Law Review,* 28, 177-214.

Mayton, William T. (1986), "The Possibilities of Collective Choice: Arrow's Theorem, Article I, and the Delegation of Legislative Power to Administrative Agencies," *Duke Law Journal,* December, 948-69.

McGarity, Thomas O. (1992), "Some Thoughts on 'Deossifying' the Rulemaking Process," *Duke Law Journal,* 41 (June), 1385-462.

Megara, John M. (1998), "The Rose Industry Exception for Early Entry into Pesticide Treated Greenhouses: Romance in Regulation," *Boston College Environmental Affairs Law Review,* 25 (Summer), 941-88.

Merrill, Thomas W. (1997a), "Capture Theory and the Courts: 1967-1983," *Chicago-Kent Law Review,* 72, 1039-116.

———— (1997b), "Review of *Imperfect Alternatives: Choosing Institutions in Law, Economics, and Public Policy,* by Neil K. Komesar, Chicago: University of Chicago Press, 1994, 287 pp.," *Law and Social Inquiry,* 22 (Fall), 959-98.

Merritt, Deborah Jones and Kathryn Ann Barry (1999), "Is the Tort System in Crisis? New Empirical Evidence," *Ohio State Law Journal,* 60, 315-98.

Meyer, Linda Ross (1997), "Review of *Just the Facts? Exploring the Domain of Accident Law: Taking the Facts Seriously,* by Don Dewees, David Duff, and Michael Trebilcock, NY: Oxford University Press, 1996, 452 pp.," *Yale Law Journal,* 106 (January), 1269-312.

Meyer, Russell W., Jr. (1993), Testimony of chief executive officer, Cessna Aircraft Company, before the House Public Works and Transportation Subcommittee on Aviation on H.R. 3087, October 27.

Mikva, Abner J. (1986), "How Should the Courts Treat Administrative Agencies?" *American University Law Review,* 36 (Fall), 1-9.

Miller, Gregory T. (1997), "Behind the Battle Lines: A Comparative Analysis of the Necessity to Enact Comprehensive Federal Products Liability Reforms," *Buffalo Law Review,* 45 (Winter), 241-75.

Mitts, Diane E. (1983), "The Products Liability Crisis: A Federal Statutory Solution," *University of Illinois Law Review,* 757-86.

Mogin, Paul (1998), "Why Judges, not Juries, Should Set Punitive Damages," *University of Chicago Law Review,* 65 (Winter), 179-222.

Morrall, John F., III (1986), "A Review of the Record," *Regulation,* November-December, 25-34.

Moulton, H. Geoffrey, Jr. (1999), "The Quixotic Search for a Judicially Enforceable Federalism," *Minnesota Law Review,* 4 (April), 849-925.

Neely, Richard (1988), *The Product Liability Mess: How Business Can Be Rescued from State Court Politics.* New York: Free Press.

O'Connell, Matthew S. (1997), "Correcting Corrective Justice: Unscrambling the Mixed Conception of Tort," *Georgetown Law Journal,* 85 (May), 1717-37.

Owen, David (1998), "Products Liability Law Restated," *South Carolina Law Review,* 49 (Winter), 273-91.

Pace, Kimberly A. (1997), "Recalibrating the Scales of Justice through National Punitive Damage Reform," *American University Law Review,* 43 (June), 1573-638.

Perczek, Jacqueline (1993), "On Efficiency, Punishment, Deterrence, and Fairness: A Survey of Punitive Damages Law and a Proposed Jury Instruction," *Suffolk University Law Review,* 27 (Fall), 825-78.

Peterson, Mark A., Syam Sharma, and Michael G. Shanley (1987), *Punitive Damages: Empirical Findings.* Washington, DC: RAND Corporation, Institute for Civil Justice.

Posner, Richard A. (1974), "Theories of Economic Regulation," *Bell Journal of Economics & Management Science,* 5 (Autumn), 335-58.

———— (1984), "Wealth Maximization and Judicial Decision-Making," *International Review of Law & Economics,* 4, 131-45.

Rabin, Robert L. (1997), "Federalism and the Tort System," *Rutgers Law Review,* 50 (Fall), 1-30.

Razook, Nim (1995), "Legal and Extralegal Barriers to Federal Product Liability Reform," *American Business Law Journal,* 32, 541-80.

Rest, Kathleen M. and Nicholas A. Ashford (1988), "Regulation and Technological Options: The Case of Occupational Exposure to Formaldehyde," *Harvard Journal of Law & Technology,* 1 (Spring), 63-96.

Revesz, Richard L. (1999), "Environmental Regulation, Cost-Benefit Analysis, and the Discounting of Human Lives," *Columbia Law Review,* 99 (May), 941-1016.

Riggs, Rod (1986), "Casualty Insurance Firms Continue to Suffer from Expansive Payouts," *San Diego Union-Tribune,* January 27, 16. (Perspective section)

Rodriguez, Daniel B. (1994), "The Positive Political Dimensions of Regulatory Reform," *Washington University Law Quarterly,* 72 (Spring), 1-73.

Romano, Roberta (1996), "A Thumbnail Sketch of Derivative Securities and Their Regulation," *Maryland Law Review,* 55, 1-82.

Rose-Ackerman, Susan (1988), "Progressive Law and Economics—And the New Administrative Law," *Yale Law Journal,* 98 (December), 341-68.

Rossi, Jim (1997), "Participation Run Amok: The Costs of Mass Participation for Deliberative Agency Decision Making," *Northwestern University Law Review,* 92 (Fall), 173-249.

Sanger, Ladd (1995), "Will the General Aviation Revitalization Act of 1994 Allow the Industry to Fly High Once Again?" *Oklahoma City University Law Review,* 20 (Summer-Fall), 435-67.

Schneider, Martin (1999), "Plane Lands on Fairfax Road," *The Washington Times,* July 27, C4.

Schwartz, Alan (1988), "Proposals for Products Liability Reform: A Theoretical Synthesis," *Yale Law Journal,* 97 (February), 353-419.

Schwartz, Teresa Moran (1988), "The Role of Federal Safety Regulations in Products Liability Actions," *Vanderbilt Law Review,* 41 (November), 1121-69.

——— (1993), "Punitive Damages and Regulated Products," *American University Law Review,* 42 (Summer), 1335-63.

——— and Maurice C. Shapiro (1997), "Regulatory Standards and Products Liability: Striking the Right Balance between the Two," *University of Michigan Journal of Legal Reform,* 30 (Winter-Spring), 431-60.

Schwartz, Victor E. and Mark A. Behrens (1993), "Punitive Damages Reform: State Legislatures Can and Should Meet the Challenge Issued by the Supreme Court of the United States in *Haslip,*" *American University Law Review,* 42 (Summer), 1365-85.

———, ———, and Leavy Mathews, III (1999), "Federalism and Federal Liability Reform: The United States Constitution Supports Reform," *Harvard Journal on Legislation,* 36 (Summer), 269-322.

Seidenfeld, Mark (1992), "A Civil Republican Justification for the Bureaucratic State," *Harvard Law Review,* 105 (May), 1512-76.

Shapiro, Sidney A. and Richard E. Levy (1995), "Judicial Incentives and Indeterminacy in Substantive Review of Administrative Decisions," *Duke Law Journal,* 44 (April), 1051-80.

Smith, Christopher E. (1994), "Imagery, Politics, and Jury Reform," *Akron Law Review,* 28 (Summer), 77-95.

Smith, Laura A. (1993), "Justiciability and Judicial Discretion: Standing at the Forefront of Judicial Abdication," *George Washington Law Review,* 61 (June), 1548-615.

Smith, Loren A. (1985), "Judicialization: The Twilight of Administrative Law," *Duke Law Journal,* 427-66.

Stewart, Chad E. (1998-99), "Damage Caps in Alabama's Civil Justice System: An Uncivil War within the State," *Cumberland Law Review,* 29, 201-37.

Stewart, David W. and Ingrid M. Martin (1994), "Intended and Unintended Consequences of Warning Messages: A Review and Synthesis of Empirical Research," *Journal of Public Policy & Marketing,* 13 (Spring), 1-21.

Sunstein, Cass R. (1989), "On the Costs and Benefits of Aggressive Judicial Review of Agency Action," *Duke Law Journal,* June, 522-37.

——— (1990), "Paradoxes of the Regulatory State," *University of Chicago Law Review,* 57 (Spring), 407-41.

Tarry, Scott E. and Lawrence J. Truitt (1995), "Rhetoric and Reality: Tort Reform and the Uncertain Future of General Aviation," *Journal of Air Law and Commerce,* 61 (September-October), 163-201.

Thomas, Bruce A. and Lawrence G. Theall (1995), "Product Liability and Innovation: A Canadian Perspective," *Canada-United States Law Journal,* 21, 313-22.

Thornburgh, Dick (1996), "High Noon for Civil Justice Reform," *The Metropolitan Corporate Counsel,* February, 1-5.

Twerski, Aaron D. (1994), "Punitive Damages Awards in Product Liability Litigation: Strong Medicine or Poison Pill?" *Villanova Law Review,* 39, 353-62.

Vidmar, Neil (1998), "The Performance of the American Civil Jury: An Empirical Perspective," *Arizona Law Review,* 40 (Fall), 849-99.

Viscusi, W. Kip (1989), "Toward a Diminished Role for Tort Liability: Social Insurance, Government Regulation, and Contemporary Risks to Health and Safety," *Yale Journal on Regulation,* 6 (Winter), 65-107.

———— (1991), "The Dimensions of the Product Liability Crisis," *Journal of Legal Studies,* 20, 147-81.

———— (1996), "The APA at Fifty: Regulating the Regulators," *University of Chicago Law Review,* 63 (Fall), 1423-60.

————, John M. Vernon, and Joseph E. Harrington, Jr. (1995), *Economics of Regulation and Antitrust,* 2nd ed. Cambridge: MIT Press.

Vreeland, Cindy (1990), "Public Interest Groups, Public Law Litigation, and Federal Rule 24(a)," *University of Chicago Law Review,* 57 (Winter), 279-309.

Wainstein, Kenneth L. (1988), "Judicially Initiated Prosecution: A Means of Preventing Continuing Victimization in the Event of Prosecutorial Inaction," *California Law Review,* 76 (May), 727-67.

Walsh, Charles J. and Alissa Pyrich (1996), "Rationalizing the Regulation of Prescription Drugs and Medical Devices: Perspectives on Private Certification and Tort Reform," *Rutgers Law Review,* 48 (Spring), 883-962.

Warren, Ashley W. (1997), "Compliance with Governmental Regulatory Standards: Is It Enough to Immunize a Defendant from Tort Liability?" *Baylor Law Review,* 49 (Summer), 763-816.

Werber, Stephen J. (1995), "The Constitutional Dimension of a National Products Liability Statute of Repose," *Villanova Law Review,* 40, 985-1052.

Werhan, Keith (1996), "Delegalizing Administrative Law," *University of Illinois Law Review,* 423-66.

Whitmore, Julie (1987), "Gallagher Pins Hopes on New Markets," *Crain's Chicago Business,* May 18, 40.

Wiener, Jonathan Baert (1999), "On the Political Economy of Global Environmental Regulation," *Georgetown Law Journal,* 87 (February), 749-93.

Wilkie, William L. and Elizabeth A. Moore (1999), "Marketing's Contribution to Society," *Journal of Marketing,* 63, 198-218. (Special issue)

Wood, James M. (1999), "The Judicial Coordination of Drug and Device Litigation: A Review and Critique," *Food and Drug Law Journal,* 54, 325-61.

Work, Clemens P. (1982), "Product Safety: A New Hot Potato for Congress," *U.S. News & World Report,* June 14, 62.

Zeckhauser, Richard J. and W. Kip Viscusi (1996), "Risk Management Studies: The Risk Management Dilemma," *Annals of the American Academy of Political and Social Science,* 545 (May), 144-55.

Zywicki, Todd J. (1999), "Environmental Externalities and Political Externalities: The Political Economy of Environmental Regulation and Reform," *Tulane Law Review,* 73 (February), 845-921.

The Effectiveness of Self-Regulated Privacy Protection

A Review and Framework
for Future Research

George R. Milne

In the marketing and public policy field, information privacy is an issue of growing importance. Although the marketing discipline has begun to investigate this area, it is a topic that would benefit from more research that would advance the discipline significantly (Mazis 1997). The use of consumer information is fundamental to the marketing function. Marketers' desire to gather consumer information so that they can provide consumers with offers tailored to their individual needs. At the same time, information technology and the explosion of organizational databases allow easy acquisition, storing, and transferring of consumer data in a manner that might violate consumer privacy rights (Bloom, Milne, and Adler 1994). The increased use of technology in marketing efforts has made privacy protection more salient to consumers, organizations, and public policy makers. In marketing, consumer privacy has been conceptualized along the dimensions of consumer knowledge and control (Culnan 1995; Nowak and Phelps 1995). From this perspective, self-regulated privacy protection is tantamount to whether organizations have provided consumers with the knowledge and opportunity to control the type of information that the organizations collect, use, and transfer to third parties.

Introduction

Self-Regulation

Self-regulation has been, and should continue to be, the primary mechanism to ensure consumers' privacy protection from business activities in the United States.[1] The "Code of Fair Information Practices," proposed in 1973 by the Secretary's Advisory Committee on Automated Personal Data Systems for the U.S. Department of Health, Education, and Welfare, has been the foundation of much of the self-regulation efforts of the 1970s and 1980s (Jones 1991) as well as throughout the 1990s. The principles of this code are as follows:

1. Personal data record-keeping practices should not be kept secret.

2. An individual should have the ability to find out what information about him or her is on record and how it is disclosed.

3. An individual should have the ability to correct or amend a record of identifiable information about him or her.

4. An individual should have the ability to limit the disclosure of information about him or her that was obtained for one purpose from being disclosed for other unrelated purposes.

5. An organization creating, maintaining, using, or disseminating records of identifiable personal data must guarantee the reliability of the data for their intended use and must take precautions to prevent the misuse of the data.

Industry groups, such as the Direct Marketing Association (DMA), have attempted to communicate these principles to their members. They have done this by offering codes similar to the fair information practices (DMA 1994) and by creating mechanisms (e.g., Mail Preference Service, Telephone Preference Service, E-mail Preference Service [in development]) that help individuals to protect their individual privacy. Other organizations, such as the Better Business Bureau, also have developed codes.

Purpose

Against the backdrop of limited federal legislative efforts and strong industry pushes for self-regulation, the marketing and public policy and the direct marketing academic subgroups have been researching privacy issues. The impetus for this emerging stream of research is threefold. First, it is widely recognized that consumer concern continues to be high. Research polls, most notably the Harris-Equifax polls, have suggested that consumers have lost control over how information about them is circulated and used by companies. The level of concern has increased over the years—71% in 1990, 71% in 1991, 76% in 1992, 80% in 1993, 80% in 1995, 83% in 1998 (Harris, Louis & Associates 1990, 1991, 1992, 1993, 1995, 1998). Second, the rapid growth of information technology, and of the Internet in particular, is creating new privacy issues that need

TABLE 20.1 Examples of Privacy Violations by Marketers

A national drug store chain and a national supermarket chain provided patients' medical information to an outside database marketing firm so as to send prescription reminders and promotional literature for new drugs. Even though the drug companies never received access to these consumer files, widespread consumer complaints suggested privacy concerns about the use of consumers' personal medical information. (O'Harrow 1998a)

A Web community of more than two million members secretly sold personal information about its members. At the time of sign-up, members provided the Web community with their names and addresses and answered optional questions about their incomes, occupations, and so forth. The sign-up form also asked whether applicants wanted to receive offers from other companies. The Federal Trade Commission charged the Web community with misleading consumers because personal information was sold to third parties not specifically mentioned in the agreement. Also, optional information was sold to third parties without consumer approval. (O'Harrow 1998b)

A company that produces a popular software program for listening to music on computers was found to have the ability to have the software transmit information about users' listening practices to company headquarters. The software provided details about to which type of music customers listen, the number of songs they copy, and serial numbers that could identify the consumers. ("Privacy Suit Filed" 1999)

to be addressed. Marketers' policies on "spam," "cookies," and disclosure of information collection on the Web are issues that consumers do not fully understand and are not self-regulated very well. Third, the gap between business practices and consumer concern is not closing over time. Organizations continue to not adhere to fair information practices and continue to make poor decisions regarding consumer privacy (Table 20.1). Consumers continue to be poorly educated about privacy protection actions that they can take.

The purpose of this chapter is to review the emerging privacy literature, propose a framework to identify privacy research issues, and suggest future research directions that will address the effectiveness of self-regulated privacy protection. In the next section, I review the conceptual and empirical literature that emerged during the 1990s in the marketing and public policy and direct marketing areas. Next, building on the literature review, I present a framework that places existing research and future research opportunities in a broad industry context. In the final section, I discuss possible directions for future research.

Literature Review

This literature review is primarily comprised of conceptual and empirical articles published during the 1990s[2] in the *Journal of Public Policy & Marketing, Journal of Marketing, Journal of Direct Marketing,* and *Journal of Interactive Marketing.*[3] A few other articles not published in these journals are included because they often were cited in this literature or because they present important findings for marketing researchers. (The Appendix provides a cross-citation analysis of the 27 articles in this review.) Although the review is not intended to be exhaustive, it does focus on the range of issues that have been addressed in the marketing literature.

Conceptual Literature

The stream of conceptual articles, which reflects the changing business and technological environment, identified research questions examined by subsequent empirical studies. Table 20.2 depicts a brief overview of 10 nonempirical privacy articles listed in chronological order.

Early articles by Baker, Dickinson, and Hollander (1986) and McCrohan (1989) examined the issue of computer matching and the possibility that government agencies misused survey data. McCrohan warned that misuse of survey data could lower consumers' willingness to participate. Whereas concerns over government abuse are curtailed in part through the Computer Matching and Privacy Protection Act of 1988, concern about falling survey response due to privacy concerns and abuses remains (Bearden, Madden, and Uscategui 1998). Interestingly, in commercial settings, addressing what happens to information when it is transferred to third parties remains an unanswered question and an important one to resolve.

The privacy debate shifted from government to business behavior when Jones (1991) reviewed industry practices and the role that marketers played in the collection, dissemination, and use of information. Her recommendations focused on developing better safeguards for the collection and handling of mailing lists. She also advocated data dissemination that would restrict disclosure of information to third parties and would require gaining voluntary informed consent from consumers. Empirical research verifies that the disclosure of personal information to third parties without consumer consent continues to be a major concern of consumers (Milne and Boza 1999).

Goodwin (1991) conducted the first review of the dimensions of privacy. Her often-cited article (see Appendix) provides a very thorough review of previous privacy literature from the behavioral sciences. Goodwin defined consumer privacy realms in terms of consumers' control over their personal information and the environment in which the transactions take place. The environment dimension has been criticized (Foxman and Kilcoyne 1993) because such situational factors are individual specific and the desire to be left alone is not absolute. Still, the concept of control introduced by Goodwin has been used in subsequent definitions of privacy realms, and subsequently, consumer knowledge has been incorporated as a second dimension (Culnan 1995; Foxman and Kilcoyne 1993; Nowak and Phelps 1995). Privacy states often are conceptualized in terms of consumer knowledge (high/low) and control (high/low) dimensions. Empirical research built on these conceptualizations would be useful to confirm or expand on the privacy dimensions. Qualitative research that gathers consumer and business subjective views on privacy might yield new dimensions not discussed in the literature.

TABLE 20.2 Overview of Nonempirical Privacy Literature in Marketing

Citation	Overview
Richards (1997)	Provides review of how Internet raises legal risks for managers; invasion of privacy is highlighted; legal issues and cases pertaining to intrusiveness, access to personal information, collection methods (cookies), use of information, and protection of children are reviewed
Thomas and Maurer (1997)	Explores two legal developments that could affect the database industry and the privacy of individuals; one issue is the regulation of credit databases (via Federal Credit Reporting Act), and the second is the consumer protection in noncredit databases
Davis (1997)	Suggests that consumers have property rights to the personal information that database marketers buy and sell for direct marketing purposes
Nowak and Phelps (1995)	Develops framework addressing privacy concerns that arise when direct marketers use consumer information; privacy is an issue when consumers are not given an opportunity to control the collection, use, and transfer of their information to third parties
Bloom, Milne, and Adler (1994)	Discusses legal and societal issues caused by new information technologies such as computer matching and automatic order entry systems; consumer privacy is highlighted as one of four types of problems faced by managers using information technologies; focus is on how managers and researchers can reduce chance of problems
Foxman and Kilcoyne (1993)	Discusses concepts of consumer privacy and examines ethical issues relating to privacy and marketing practices; describes marketing practices that affect consumer privacy and evaluates policies to protect consumer privacy; provides comprehensive set of privacy recommendations for marketers
Cespedes and Smith (1993)	Database marketers should pay more attention to consumers' fears about privacy and use of their personal information; the conflicts between database marketers and consumers are discussed; suggests using sunshine principles that allow consumers access and control of their personal information
Goodwin (1991)	Provides a comprehensive overview of privacy literature in the public policy and behavioral literature; privacy is defined as "the consumer's ability to control (a) presence of other people in the environment during a market transaction or consumption behavior and (b) dissemination of information related to or provided during such transactions or behaviors to those who were not present"; privacy taxonomy is based on control over environment and/or information disclosure (or neither)
Jones (1991)	Reviews industry practices and marketers' role in collection, dissemination, and use of consumer information; reviews existing privacy protections and suggests future regulatory options facing marketers
McCrohan (1989)	Examines cost to society if consumers fail to provide information to market researchers, who provide information to government agencies, which then use computer matching programs; the rise in consumer privacy concerns is justified given potential benefits of information to society; more rigorous procedures to ensure consumer privacy are needed
Baker, Dickinson, and Hollander (1986)	Reviews the issues of sale of marketing research data to the Internal Revenue Service and possible "big brother" abuse through use of computer matching programs; recommends that government make distinctions between survey data and registration, administrative, and facilitative data

Whereas much of the nonempirical privacy literature has been positioned from an advocacy position, several articles have provided managers with advice on how to avoid problems when using information technologies with consumers' personal information (Bloom, Milne, and Adler 1994; Cespedes and Smith 1993). Reviews of legal statutes and cases have been used to illustrate situations in which companies have gotten in trouble by not adhering to fair information practices (Bloom, Milne, and Adler 1994; Thomas and Maurer 1997). Researchers have suggested principles for companies to follow. Cespedes and Smith (1993) suggested a set of "sunshine principles." Foxman and Kilcoyne (1993, p. 117) outlined a comprehensive set of consumer privacy recommendations and implementation suggestions for marketers. Davis (1997) recommended approaches for making direct marketer-consumer contacts more mutually beneficial.

The Internet, which was only starting to be seriously used by businesses in 1995, has created new privacy issues for public policy researchers to address (Richards 1997). For example, the widespread use of unsolicited e-mail (i.e., spam) is of rising concern. This intrusion may have a bigger impact on consumers than does junk mail. On another front, Internet technology has enabled organizations to collect information about consumers without their knowledge. Cookies (i.e., hidden files) can be placed on consumers' computers and used to track Web site visits. Log files are used to track consumers' mouse clicks and activity and movement through the Internet. Moreover, the ease with which information can be disseminated makes the organization's use of consumers' personal information a very sensitive topic for consumers. The nature of the Internet brings with it the possibility of alternative forms of self-regulation. These include technological solutions (e.g., privacy software that helps consumers to control the type of information they provide to Web sites) and the use of consumer agent "infomediaries" (Hagel and Singer 1999).

Empirical Literature

The empirical literature has explored many of the issues identified by the nonempirical literature as well as other topics. The 16 articles summarized in Table 20.3 (in reverse chronological order) cover issues of measuring consumer attitudes and knowledge (domestically and internationally), media coverage, cost/benefit analysis, business perspectives, measurement issues, and a trust/relationship marketing perspective.

Some of the early empirical privacy research focused on measuring consumer attitudes and levels of concern toward privacy as well as levels of consumer knowledge (Culnan 1995; Nowak and Phelps 1992). Attitudes or concerns about privacy were found to be lower for consumers who had more knowledge (Nowak and Phelps 1992) and who knew how to control their personal information (Culnan 1993). The fact that only 48% of the public was aware of name removal procedures (Culnan 1995) suggests the need for more research that evaluates approaches for increasing awareness. Other important findings established by research were that situational factors (Wang and Petrison 1993) and demographic

TABLE 20.3 *Overview of Empirical Privacy Literature in Marketing*

Study	Primary Focus	Sample	Empirical Results	Summary Comments
Milne and Boza (1999)	Supports the claim that improving trust and reducing concern are two distinct approaches for managing consumer information	1,508 survey responses by direct mail users belonging to Metromail list	Trust and concern negatively correlated and vary across 17 industries; trust was more positively associated with direct marketing use than was concern reduction	Customers do not mind organizations using data to serve them better (68%); the primary concern is the sharing of data; 71% were against organizations transferring data to third parties
Culnan and Armstrong (1999)	Examines whether organizations can address privacy issues by following procedural fairness and building interpersonal trust	Raw data from 1994 Harris-Equifax consumer privacy surveys (1,000 U.S. adults)	When people are not explicitly told that fair procedures will be used, people with greater privacy concerns will be less willing to have their personal information used for profiling	Procedural fairness will make customers more likely to engage in relationships with organizations, allowing organizations to benefit from the relationships
Milne and Boza (1998)	Contrasts business's privacy perspective with that of consumers; measures levels of privacy practices implemented by businesses; notes differences in practices	365 key informants from Direct Marketing Association companies with consumer databases	38% notified customers about the gathering of personal information, 33% indicated the use of the information, and 26% asked permission for the information	Organizations that made greater use of customer information were more likely to have privacy practices in place; still, privacy practices are not widespread
Campbell (1997)	Exploratory investigation of consumer and direct marketers' attitudes in one Canadian city toward information privacy issues; examines consumer concerns about collection and use as well as differences across individuals; do managers and consumers share same views about information privacy?	105 mall intercept surveys in Toronto area; 12 structured personal interviews of senior managers using firms using database marketing	Using Smith, Milberg, and Burke's (1996) Information Privacy Concerns scale, found that consumers were concerned about collection, error potential, and unauthorized access/secondary use concerns; most managers considered industry self-regulation preferable to government regulation	Consumers' and managers' views differ; consumers focus on potential abuses; managers focus on potential benefits to consumers of better-targeted direct marketing campaigns; managers want to exploit consumer information while avoiding regulation

Study	Purpose	Sample/Method	Findings	Conclusions
Milne (1997)	Measures consumers' willingness to provide marketers with personal information and permission to rent this information given varied permission formats, types of information requested, and levels of disclosure	2,694 consumers (age 18 years or over) who filled out promotion/information cards and were asked to sign up to be on a mailing list at a retail store	68% signed up; more likely to join list when not asked for phone number and asked directly; 40% allowed personal information to be transferred to third parties; transfer was more likely when euphemisms were used and specific third parties were identified	Consumers are not willing to transfer their names to third parties; consumers prefer a more direct communication approach when being asked for permission; first behavior-based study of privacy
Smith, Milberg, and Burke (1996)	Develops and validates a measurement instrument of control that can be used in future privacy research	Structured interviews, focus group, and expert judges; survey of 704 employees and 147 graduate students	Developed 15-item scale with four dimensions: Collection, Errors, Unauthorized Secondary Use, and Improper Access; confirmatory factor analysis results suggest valid scale	Scale identified important dimensions to be studied and to assist managers with taking corrective actions regarding privacy policies and actions
Milne, Beckman, and Taubman (1996)	Develops and tests a conceptual model of international consumers' attitudes toward direct marketing and privacy	Convenience sample of 169 Argentinean respondents	Only 11% of respondents were very concerned about privacy; 28% found target marketing acceptable	Argentinean consumers were not familiar with database tactics where data sharing and customer privacy issues are central
Culnan (1995)	Characterizes consumers who are aware/not aware of name removal procedures; assesses whether consumer information problem is related to implied social contract	Raw data from 1991 Harris-Equifax consumer privacy survey (1,000 U.S. adults)	52% of the public, including 45% of those who shop by mail, are not aware of name removal procedures	Consumer information problems exist for direct marketers based on low consumer awareness of existing name removal information
Taylor, Vassar, and Vaught (1995)	Examines marketing professionals' attitudes toward buying and selling names and addresses, the role of government protection, and the use of automatic number identification	Survey of 190 marketing professionals from American Marketing Association, National Association of Purchasing Managers, and Direct Marketing Association	38% found buying and selling names acceptable, 56% thought that businesses should get written permission from consumers to sell or rent information, and 55% believed that government should regulate the types of information collected	Business results differed from consumer attitudes in previous studies; still, business sample indicates that more privacy controls are needed; notes possibility of a pro-privacy sample

TABLE 20.3 Continued

Study	Primary Focus	Sample	Empirical Results	Summary Comments
Petrison and Wang (1995)	Examines how consumer privacy issues have been perceived over time and across cultures; involves the analysis of media coverage of privacy in England and United States from 1960 to 1993	Compares the New York Times and London Times across various privacy infringements	Americans take a relativist approach to privacy, concerned about potential infringements and the possible harm; Britons are more philosophical and are concerned about protecting privacy for its own sake	Privacy is a construct that can have varying meanings to different cultures and over time; still, in the cases of the United States and England, it remains an important topic
Milne and Gordon (1994)	Forms segments based on individual utilities derived from a conjoint study that measured consumers' attitudes toward privacy and direct marketing	Sample from Milne and Gordon (1993)	Three segments found: Demanding Middle (51%), Potential Lobbyists (31%), and New Right (18%); segments differ by attributes they want from direct marketer relationships	Segmenting consumers by attitudes toward direct marketing, and not contacting these individuals, can reduce "bad will"
Phelps, Gonzenbach, and Johnson (1994)	How much coverage has the press given to consumer privacy issues relating to direct marketing? How important have consumer privacy issues been to the public over time? Does media attention influence public concern?	Analysis of five leading newspapers' coverage of privacy issues related to direct marketing	Big increase in articles: 10 in 1984, 105 in 1991, and 69 in 1992; the New York Times published a disproportionately high percentage; consumer concern between 77% and 79% over the time period, with no correlation with number of articles	Public concern about privacy was high even before increased media coverage during the mid-1980s; concern and media coverage are not related
Milne and Gordon (1993)	Presents a theoretical framework for examining the privacy-efficiency trade-off consumers make; uses conjoint analysis to examine the trade-off	75 adults from continuing education, M.B.A. students, and university staff; 100 mall intercepts across the United States	Consumers perform a cost/benefit analysis of the attributes associated with a particular direct mail environment; derived utilities suggest that consumers prefer privacy policy in which they are compensated for their information	The conceptual model of direct mail as an implied social contract provides a basis for evaluating attitudes toward direct mail and temporal changes in attitudes

Wang and Petrison (1993)	Determines how consumers feel about particular types of information-handling activities and whether different types of consumers have different attitudes about privacy-related issues	Based on two survey questions added to omnibus telephone survey of 1,000 Chicago residents	Consumers rated the company's own use of information more positively than its selling information to other companies; consumers believed that hospitals using height and weight from driver's licenses was more appropriate than a large clothing store doing the same	Consumers' concern about privacy issues varies by situation and need for the products being sold; some consumers more negative about privacy threats than others
Culnan (1993)	Profiles consumers based on their attitudes toward secondary information use; determines variables that discriminate between consumers who are information sensitive and those who are not	Written questionnaires of 126 undergraduate students	People who are less sensitive about secondary use of personal information have more positive attitudes toward shopping by mail, better coping mechanisms for unwanted mail, and a lower concern for privacy	Control is an important variable in differentiating individuals with positive attitudes toward secondary information from those with negative attitudes
Nowak and Phelps (1992)	Attempts to increase direct marketers' understanding of privacy issues by examining how well informed consumers are about information gathering and information use practices	Regional telephone survey of 266 adults (age 18 years or over)	59% had heard of the Direct Marketing Association's mail preference service; 35% had heard of the telephone preference service; 78% believed that it was wrong for marketers to buy or sell names/addresses without consumers' knowledge; 91% believed that companies should get written permission before they sell or rent personal information	Consumers are against renting of personal information without permission; consumer ignorance may be a significant contributor to privacy concern; a strong commitment to consumer education might be necessary to avoid government regulation and legislation

background variables (Culnan 1993; Nowak and Phelps 1992; Wang and Petrison 1993) affect privacy attitudes. Comparative international research found consumers in Argentina to be less concerned about privacy than consumers in the United States (Milne, Beckman, and Taubman 1996). Like U.S. consumers, Argentinean privacy attitudes were found to differ by demographic background. In summary, many of the background factors affecting consumer attitudes have been identified and confirmed by research. However, further research is needed to understand how situational factors affect consumer privacy attitudes. For example, differences in concern about privacy have been found based on the sensitivity of data collected (Rohm and Milne 1999), and the channel of distribution used to collect information (Milne and Rohm 1999).

Phelps, Gonzenbach, and Johnson (1994) examined whether media coverage of privacy topics was related to levels of consumer concern. For the period from 1984 to 1992, they found no relationship, partly due to the fairly flat (yet high) level of public concern during this time period. Interestingly, with the emergence of the Internet, public concern about controlling personal information has increased (Harris, Louis & Associates 1998). A cross-national comparison of media was examined to understand how Americans and English differ in their privacy attitudes (Petrison and Wang 1995). Taken together, these research studies show how newspaper media can be used as a rich data source. Clearly, the role of media is a factor in shaping policy (e.g., the film *Wag the Dog*), and additional research might be needed to study its influence (as well as new Internet media's influence) in shaping legislative efforts.

Because of its database orientation, much of the privacy research has been conducted in the context of direct marketing. In a direct marketing relationship, consumers give information to marketers for some implied benefit such as better targeted offers in the future. Milne and Gordon (1993) conceptualized situations in which consumers provide organizations with information about themselves in return for offers that might be of interest to them as a social contract. Based on a conjoint study, Milne and Gordon's results suggested that compensation may be an important attribute of a social contract. In a follow-up study, Milne and Gordon (1994) found consumer segments based on the attributes that consumers desire in a contract. Subsequently, compensating consumers for information has been advocated by consultants addressing Internet privacy issues (Godin 1999; Hagel and Singer 1999) and might deserve more research.

Information exchange, and proper handling of consumer information, not only requires consumers to be aware and to use controls such as "opt-out" but also requires managers and organizations to follow fair information practices. Given the importance of business activities in regard to consumer privacy, it is surprising that not more research has examined marketers' and businesses' perspectives and behaviors toward privacy. Exploratory research has shown that business perspectives differ from consumer perspectives (Campbell 1997; Taylor, Vassar, and Vaught 1995). Findings have indicated that businesses focus on how the collection of personal information can help to improve targeting efforts and consumers' focus on potential abuses of information. Other research has reported that many businesses are not in compliance with industry self-regulation policies (Milne and Boza 1998). As self-regulation continues, additional research will be needed to measure business compliance of fair information policies. An area in marketing that has not been addressed is the procedures and policies that marketing organizations employ to ensure privacy and to protect the confidentiality of databases. Literature in the management area (Smith 1994), as well as on the marketing auditing function (Kotler, Gregor, and Rogers 1989), may be useful to marketing scholars interested in this direction.

Relationship marketing recently was suggested as an approach for managing consumer markets (Sheth and Parvatiyar 1995). Consultants and scholars in the direct marketing area have suggested relationship marketing as an alternative approach for managing consumer privacy issues (Campbell 1997; Peppers and Rogers 1993; Milne and Boza 1999; Shaver 1996). The relationship marketing concept suggests that consumers are more likely to provide information to marketers to enable them to serve consumers better when marketers are forthcoming about their information practices. Milne and Boza (1999) empirically demonstrated that building trust is a key positive factor that can reduce consumer privacy concerns and improve relationships between consumers and organizations. In another study, Culnan and Armstrong (1999) empirically found that consumers were more likely to engage in relationships when procedural fairness was implemented. Relationship marketing appears to be a perspective that aligns consumers' and marketers' interests and, as such, might serve as a platform for self-regulation efforts.

Another important dimension from which to review the empirical privacy literature is the rigor of the methods and measures employed. There has been a move from simple descriptive studies to research that employs multivariate research tools. An area that needs further research is the development of measures. Smith, Milberg, and Burke (1996) created and validated a much-needed measure of consumer concern. Campbell (1997) used this measure in her research. The rigor of privacy research can be improved if more existing, validated, multiple-item scales are created and reused. In addition, most of the research has relied on consumer and business perceptions. Measuring self-reported behavior (Milne and Boza 1998) and measuring actual behavior (Milne 1997) are other measurement approaches that add value to understanding public policy decisions (Kinnear 1997).

The empirical research on privacy has included both purely empirical studies and more theoretically driven research. Theory bases that have been introduced and used to test empirical relationships include exchange theory (Milne and Gordon 1993), information theory (Milne and Boza 1998), social contracts (Culnan 1995; Milne and Gordon 1993), trade-off analysis (Milne and Gordon 1993), procedural justice (Culnan and Armstrong 1999), and relationship marketing (Campbell 1997; Milne and Boza 1998, 1999). Most of these theoretical approaches have been used to understand consumer risks and trade-offs of participating in information exchanges.

The literature review shows that the emerging area of privacy research has not been viewed from a holistic overarching framework. To date, much research has examined privacy from the consumer's perspective, identifying background and situational factors that predict consumer concern. Other research has viewed privacy from the marketer's perspective, identifying risks to managers of misusing information technologies. Finally, some research has focused on the marketer-consumer information interaction. This research has looked at social contracts, the role of trust, and trade-offs involved in information exchanges. Putting together findings from across specific studies within a larger framework is useful for evaluating our current understanding and identifying directions for future empirical research. In the next section, I develop a privacy issues framework based on relationship marketing and information exchange theories used in the marketing literature.

Privacy Research Issues Framework

The framework in Figure 20.1 describes the process of information exchange and the influences affecting marketers and consumers. The framework is comprised of three major components. The first and central component is the "marketer-consumer information interaction." This is the process connecting a marketer's information strategy to consumers' decisions of whether to provide the marketer with the requested information. Grounded research that led to some of the ideas in this first component is from a study by Milne, Rohm, and Boza (1999). The second component is "marketer influences," and the third is "consumer influences." As shown in the figure, both marketer influences and consumer influences affect the marketer-consumer information interaction.

Marketer-Consumer Information Interaction

The marketer-consumer information interaction is based on relationship marketing and trust (Morgan and Hunt 1994; Smith and Barclay 1997). This framework also draws on social contract theory (MacNeil 1980), exchange theory (Bagozzi 1975; Houston and Gassenheimer 1987), trade-off analysis (Milne and Gordon 1993), and market signaling theory (Spence 1973). Overall, the framework shows how trust, along with existing privacy controls, can assist consumers in deciding whether to provide organizations with their personal information. The framework indicates that marketing strategy, which contains privacy policies, affects a consumer's perceived risk through trust and market communication. The consumer then decides whether to engage in the information exchange. I now discuss the process that leads to trust and consumers providing personal information to marketers.

To begin, a consumer's risk/benefit perception is a key condition leading to whether the consumer will provide a marketer with personal information. In a situation where a consumer is asked to provide personal information, the consumer is forced to make a cost/benefit trade-off (Milne and Gordon 1993). The level of risk is based on the type and sensitivity of information that is requested by the marketer, how the marketer uses the information, and whether the marketer will transfer information to third parties. Risk is balanced by the potential benefit of being rewarded directly or receiving benefits of better targeting and service from the organization. Of course, there is a high level of uncertainty

Consumer Influences

Marketer - Consumer Information Interaction

Marketer Influences

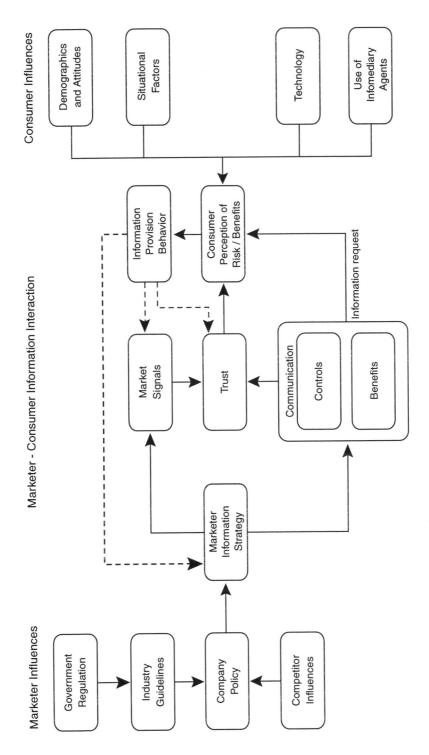

Figure 20.1. Privacy Research Framework

about how organizations will use the information, and this makes consumers vulnerable. Organizations, for example, could misuse the information by transferring it to third parties without the consent of consumers. This level of uncertainty is a prerequisite for trust (Moorman, Deshpande, and Zaltman 1993).

The level of communication between the marketer and the consumer also affects the consumer's risk perception by helping to align mutual perceptions between exchange partners (Morgan and Hunt 1994). Consistent with relationship marketing findings, communication also is shown to indirectly affect perceptions through increasing levels of trust.

Trust directly affects consumers' perceptions of risks/benefits. When trust is established, consumers will perceive less risk and greater benefits in providing organizations with personal information than in situations where trust does not exist. In the privacy context, frequent, meaningful, and timely communication about both privacy policies and practices (controls) and discussion of benefits should increase trust.

The marketer's information strategy has two facets that affect trust. The first is through creating market signals. Market signals can be reputations that organizations develop through their past business dealings. Reputation can exist in the marketplace due to word of mouth and established brand equity. Or, organizations could use a third-party seal, such as the Better Business Bureau or Truste, to signal best information practices. This market presence leads to credibility, which in turn leads to trust. The second strategic facet is to increase trust by communicating information controls. This can encompass opt-out notices, the type of information collected, how it is used, and whether it will be transferred to third parties.

The framework also shows the dynamic impact that results when a consumer exchanges information with an organization. Consumer feedback loops in Figure 20.1 are shown by dashed lines. The first feedback loop shows that when a consumer evaluates and complies with an organization's request for information, this action directly affects the level of trust because the consumer makes a commitment. The second feedback loop directly affects market signals through possible word of mouth. The third feedback loop flows back to the organization and its respective marketing strategy. Once the organization receives the consumer's personal information, it is possible for the organization to customize future communications to that specific customer.

Marketer Influences

The framework shows that company policy will have a direct impact on the marketer information strategy. Within an organization, it is possible that numerous databases will exist across the divisions and departments that contain consumer information. Formal company policies, security measures and internal audits, corporate norms, and accepted practices all will influence the manner in which data are handled.

Company policy is, in turn, influenced by industry guidelines. For example, the DMA issued a set of guidelines that member companies will need to abide by if they wish to be affiliated with the association (Magill 1998). On the other hand, industry policy is affected by government regulation. Government can force self-regulation by threats to impose legislation or mandate behavior through passed legislation. The Federal Trade Commission (FTC) recently has influenced industry guidelines and behavior by periodically examining Web sites for privacy policy notices (Culnan 1999; FTC 1998).

Company policy also can be influenced by competitor influences. In the spring of 1999, IBM announced that it would not do business with organizations that did not follow fair information practices. Competitor practices also can include foreign competition. Businesses in the European Union, with its stricter privacy practices, might put pressure on U.S. companies to alter their policies so as to conduct transactions.

Consumer Influences

In Figure 20.1, I show consumer perceptions of risk and benefits to be affected by demographic and attitudinal background, situational factors, technology, and use of infomediary agents. The first two factors have been incorporated in previous research, and the last two are new elements that might have an influence.

Demographic background, such as age and education, can affect an individual's risk tolerance. A consumer's attitudes toward direct marketing and technology, and whether he or she has experience with the company, all can affect perceptions. Situational factors that can influence perceptions include the type and sensitivity of data requested and the channel through which the information request is made (e.g., regular mail, telephone, e-mail).

The consumer also can use technology and infomediary agents to reduce his or her level of perceived risk. Software is available to help the consumer review the privacy policies of the Web site that he or she is visiting. If a Web site does not meet predetermined standards, then the software will alert the consumer; otherwise, the consumer has assurances that the site meets his or her specified level of control. Infomediary agents allow the consumer to be anonymous while the agent conducts the business transaction with an organization. The agent can provide business with some personal information that is not linked to the individual's name, phone number, or address. Organizations that want to contact the consumer do so through the infomediary.

Directions for Future Research

Marketer-Consumer Interaction Research

To date, the majority of research has focused on consumer perceptions of the risks of providing personal information given existing marketer controls. A central issue is the effectiveness of marketers in communicating their information policies to consumers. This is an important topic that could use more research.

Industry effort has focused on posting disclosure statements and information policies. Do consumers notice or fully comprehend policies and statements that are posted? Do some formats for data permission work better than others? Are there alternative methods of educating consumers that will improve consumer knowledge and welfare? For example, incorporating theories used in other public policy research on how consumers react to product warnings (Stewart and Martin 1994) and disclosures (Andrews 1998) might further our understanding of the effectiveness of privacy disclosure statements. A better understanding of disclosure statements can help marketers to capture the goodwill of consumers to make informed choices. This will have the social advantage of reducing unwanted communications.

Because the decision to provide information involves a trade-off, more research is needed that considers the risks and benefits simultaneously. A range of benefits should be explored including the compensation of consumers for information. Economic models measuring choices under different risk assumptions might provide useful insights. From a relationship marketing perspective, it would be interesting to learn whether consumers believe that they are gaining value beyond the immediate compensation they might receive. Are consumers willing to provide additional information as their relationships with marketers deepen? Promotions often are used as an offered benefit to gather personal information. Research could include investigating the ethics of these promotions and consumer awareness that such "games" are compiling personal information for marketing purposes. Do the promotions use proper notification?

Behavioral research is needed to measure the extent that consumers willingly provide information and understand the conditions that lead to this compliance. With Web site log files, it is possible to analyze "clickstream" data. These individual-level data might be used in natural occurring experiments. The impact of different disclosure statements, whether these statements were read (or at least the screen was opened), and the role of trust seals (e.g., Truste) or brand equity could be evaluated.

What makes individuals trust organizations with their information? Milne and Boza (1999) found that, in general, past experience and reputation were the leading reasons. More detailed research should investigate the empirical strength of the relationship between consumer trust and the type of controls in place—or consumer trust and market signals. Research conducted in the vein of brand equity research (Keller 1993) could be used to investigate how controls and signals affect trust levels.

Marketers now are starting to use a diversity of marketing information strategies to gather consumer information. One area that needs additional research is the relative viability of an opt-out policy of direct marketers versus opt-in policies used by Web businesses. For example, organizations such as CVS and Giant, which have relied on opt-out polices, have found themselves in difficult situations when they transferred lists to third parties without getting explicit opt-in permission (O'Harrow 1998a). Other controls, as specified in the fair information practices, need research to determine whether consumers are aware of their rights and whether businesses are in compliance. These include whether organizations provide individuals access to their data records and afford them the opportunity to correct mistakes.

Marketer Influences

Research is needed to investigate the policies that companies and marketers follow in guaranteeing the reliability of the data they store about consumers and what precautions they undertake to prevent the misuse of data. How long should information be stored? Can or should it be combined with other information without the permission of consumers? For example, most surveys do not warn consumers about the possibility of future combination with other data. Research should be undertaken to understand the data sensitivity orientation of businesses. Exemplars for this research might be found in research on marketing orientation (Jaworski and Kohli 1993) and corporate social responsibility (Drumwright and Murphy 1999). Within an organization, there are multiple data situations that could be investigated using data sensitivity measures. For example, many companies have multiple databases. Does the organization need to gain consumer permission for intraorganizational merging of databases for cross-selling efforts?

How do public policy makers evaluate the effectiveness of self-regulation across an industry? For companies using the Internet, there have been two large-scale sweeps of Web sites to look for compliance with fair information practices. Preliminary reports suggest that a higher percentage of firms were in compliance during the second study than during the first study. But the second study warned about making direct comparisons between the two studies (Culnan 1999). What, then, is the role of replication research in evaluating self-regulation? Do new methodologies need to be developed to track changes over time?

To what extent does a data provider's policies affect a company's information policy? If a marketer uses data from a data provider for prospecting (i.e., finding new customers), and the data were acquired using methods not condoned by company policy, then how does this affect the marketer's credibility? In many respects, data providers are the "guilty" parties in database marketing. Although ignored by researchers, these organizations are collecting the majority of consumer data for reselling. Although the impact on an individual organization might not be apparent, the use of databases from unethical data suppliers hurts the industry as a whole. This may result in general distrust, lower survey response rates, and lower likelihood of consumers entering into data partnerships with organizations. Because the data provider industry is such a large contributor to the privacy problem, research needs to document and assess its policies. Such research may aid in legislative efforts to curtail unethical practices.

International privacy laws and data exchange standards likely will continue to plague the United States. As Richards (1997) noted, the Internet's global reach brings with it new and challenging policy issues including privacy. Certainly, marketers using the Internet to sell products to global consumers will need to be aware of the laws and statutes that affect them. Research on privacy will need to extend to global contexts in terms of legal reviews, business practices, and consumer attitudes.

Consumer Influences

Demographics and attitudes have been mentioned frequently as antecedents to measuring consumer concern or risk assessment. The research findings should be integrated to learn more about specific demographic subsets (Moorman and Price 1989). Are these natural clusters of individuals who have different privacy attitudes? Some groups, such as children and older adults, might be naive and might not have the assessment skills to make effective choices.

Future research also should investigate how situational factors affect consumer risk perceptions. Two important situational factors include sensitivity of data type and channel for data collection. Company information policies could be amended based on knowledge of what type of information is necessary and prudent to collect. Disclosure forms could be amended to allow consumers to allow some (but not all) information to be used. Consumer sensitivity also may vary by the type of data collection channel. Consumers may be less likely to provide information to a telemarketer than to respond to regular mail or e-mail requests. A better basic understanding of the differences among intrusion, annoyance, and privacy might provide insights as to why consumers react differently to information requests across information channels.

Finally, the role of technology and infomediaries may transform the business models used to collect personal information. In the future, consumers might approach businesses with requests for information and products and use technology to protect their privacy—or at least get full economic value for surrendering their privacy. Hagel and Singer (1999) suggested that technologies such as anonymizer software, cookie suppressors, e-mail filters, anonymous payment mechanisms, and reverse cookies (i.e., those allowing consumers to track stores) already are turning the tide in favor of consumers. If these technologies are employed, will there be a segment of the population that is left behind? What will be the societal costs, if any, and the risks to consumer privacy?

Appendix

Citation Analysis of Privacy Literature in Marketing

Article Cited	| Source Article 1	2	3	4	5	6	7	8	9	10	11	12	13	14	15	16	17	18	19	20	21	22	23	24	25	26	Number of Cities
1. Baker, Dickinson, and Hollander (1986)		•							•				•		•	•	•		•					•			6
2. McCrohan (1989)		†							•						•	•	•			•				•	•	•	9
3. Jones (1991)				•			•		•							•	•		•	•					•	•	9
4. Goodwin (1991)				•	•		•	•							•	•	•		•	•	•				•		10
5. Nowak and Phelps (1992)					•			•				•		•	•	•	•		•	•		•					8
6. Culnan (1993)									†										•	•		•	•	•	•		8
7. Cespedes and Smith (1993)															•	•	•		•	•		•	•		•		7
8. Foxman and Kilcoyne (1993)									•					•	•	•	•			•		•	•	•		•	10
9. Milne and Gordon (1993)														•	•	•	•		•	•				•	•	•	9
10. Bloom, Milne, and Adler (1994)							†				•		•	•	•	•	•						•				8
11. Wang and Petrison (1993)							†								•	•		•				•	•				6
12. Phelps, Gonzenbach, and Johnson (1994)															•		•						•				3
13. Milne and Gordon (1994)																•						•	•	•	•		5
14. Nowak and Phelps (1995)																•						•		•			3
15. Petrison and Wang (1995)																											0
16. Taylor, Vassar, and Vaught (1995)															†									•	•	•	3
17. Culnan (1995)																				•				•	•	•	4
18. Milne, Beckman, and Taubman (1996)																							•				1
19. Smith, Milberg, and Burke (1996)																							†				1
20. Milne (1997)																				•							1
21. Thomas and Maurer (1997)																					•						1
22. Richards (1997)																											0
23. Campbell (1997)																			•								1
24. Davis (1997)																											0
25. Milne and Boza (1998)																											1
26. Culnan and Armstrong (1999)																											0
27. Milne and Boza (1999)																									†		1

NOTE: † = working paper cited; • = published article cited.

481

Notes

1. Federal legislation aimed to protect privacy has focused on protecting citizens from government privacy violations with little broad-based legislation aimed at regulating business activity (Bloom, Milne, and Adler 1994). Examples of such federal legislation that restricts governmental actions include the Privacy Act of 1974, the Right to Financial Privacy Act of 1978, the Privacy Protection Act of 1980, the Family Education and Privacy Right Act of 1984, the Computer Security Act of 1987, and the Computer Matching and Privacy Protection Act of 1988. The federal legislation that has been passed to protect consumers from business actions has been industry specific. Such legislation includes the Fair Credit Reporting Act of 1970, the Electronic Transfer Funds Act of 1980, the Cable Communications Act of 1984, the Electronic Communications Privacy Act of 1988, the Video Privacy Protection Act of 1988, and the Driver's Privacy Protection Act of 1994. Recent legislation has been passed establishing rules for collecting information from children (Children's Online Privacy Protection Act of 1998). With the emergence of the Internet, there has been an influx of legislation proposed to help protect the privacy of individuals on-line (Melillo 1999).

2. Note that articles published in the Spring 2000 issue of the *Journal of Public Policy & Marketing,* a special issue on privacy issues, are not included in this chapter.

3. The *Journal of Direct Marketing* was changed to the *Journal of Interactive Marketing* in 1998.

References

Andrews, Craig (1998), "Warnings and Disclosures: Special Editor's Note," *Journal of Public Policy & Marketing,* 19 (Spring), 1-2.

Bagozzi, Richard P. (1975), "Marketing as Exchange," *Journal of Marketing,* 39 (October), 32-39.

Baker, R. C., Roger Dickinson, and Stanley Hollander (1986), "Big Brother 1994: Marketing Data and the IRS," *Journal of Public Policy & Marketing,* 5, 527-42.

Bearden, William O., Charles S. Madden, and Kelly Uscategui (1998), "The Pool is Drying Up," *Marketing Research,* Spring, 27-33.

Bloom, Paul, George R. Milne, and Robert Adler (1994), "Avoiding Misuse of New Information Technologies: Legal and Societal Considerations," *Journal of Marketing,* 58 (January), 98-110.

Campbell, Alexandra (1997), "Relationship Marketing in Consumer Markets: A Comparison of Managerial and Consumer Attitudes about Informational Privacy," *Journal of Direct Marketing,* 11 (Summer), 44-58.

Cespedes, Frank V. and H. Jeff Smith (1993), "Database Marketing: New Rules for Policy and Practice," *Sloan Management Review,* Summer, 7-22.

Culnan, Mary (1993), "How Did They Get My Name? An Exploratory Investigation of Consumer Attitudes toward Secondary Information Use," *MIS Quarterly,* 17 (September), 341-64.

———— (1995), "Consumer Awareness of Name Removal Procedures: Implications for Direct Marketing," *Journal of Direct Marketing,* 9 (Spring), 10-19.

———— (1999), *Georgetown Internet Privacy Policy Study* [on-line]. Available: http://www.msb.edu/faculty/culnanm/gippshome.html

———— and Pamela K. Armstrong (1999), "Information Privacy Concerns, Procedural Fairness, and Impersonal Trust: An Empirical Investigation," *Organizational Science,* 10 (1), 104-15.

Davis, Judy (1997), "Property Rights to Consumer Information: A Proposed Policy Framework for Direct Marketing," *Journal of Direct Marketing,* 11 (Summer), 32-43.

Direct Marketing Association (1994), *Fair Information Practices Manual.* New York: DMA.

Drumwright, Meme and Pat Murphy (1999), "Corporate Social Awareness and Marketing Initiatives," paper presented at the Public Policy and Marketing Conference, June, South Bend, IN.

Federal Trade Commission (1998), *Privacy Online: A Report to Congress.* Washington, DC: FTC.

Foxman, Ellen R. and P. Kilcoyne (1993), "Information Technology, Marketing Practice, and Consumer Privacy," *Journal of Public Policy & Marketing,* 12 (Spring), 106-19.

Godin, Seth (1999), "The Power of Permission," *The DMA Insider,* Fall, 20-23.

Goodwin, Cathy (1991), "Privacy: Recognition of a Consumer Right," *Journal of Public Policy & Marketing,* 10 (Spring), 149-66.

Hagel, John, III, and Marc Singer (1999), *Net Worth.* Boston: Harvard Business School Press.

Harris, Louis & Associates (1990), *The Equifax Report on Consumers in the Information Age.* Atlanta, GA: Equifax Inc.

———— (1991), *Harris-Equifax Consumer Privacy Survey 1991.* Atlanta, GA: Equifax Inc.

———— (1992), *Harris-Equifax Consumer Privacy Survey 1992.* Atlanta, GA: Equifax Inc.

———— (1993), *Health Information Privacy Survey 1993.* Atlanta, GA: Equifax Inc.

———— (1995), *Equifax-Harris Mid-Decade Consumer Privacy Survey.* Atlanta, GA: Equifax Inc.

———— (1998), *E-commerce and Privacy: What Net Users Want.* Hackensack, NJ: Privacy & American Business.

Houston, Franklin and Jule B. Gassenheimer (1987), "Marketing and Exchange," *Journal of Marketing,* 51 (October), 3-18.

Jaworski, Bernard J. and Ajay K. Kohli (1993), "Market Orientation: Antecedents and Consequences," *Journal of Marketing,* 57 (July), 53-70.

Jones, Mary Gardiner (1991), "Privacy: A Significant Marketing Issue for the 1990s," *Journal of Public Policy & Marketing,* 10 (Spring), 133-48.

Keller, Kevin Lane (1993), "Conceptualizing, Measuring, and Managing Customer-Based Brand Equity," *Journal of Marketing,* 57 (January), 1-22.

Kinnear, Thomas (1997), "An Historic Perspective on the Quantity and Quality of Marketing and Public Policy Research," *Journal of Public Policy & Marketing,* 16 (Spring), 44-46.

Kotler, Philip, William Gregor, and William Rogers (1989), "The Marketing Audit Comes of Age," *Sloan Management Review,* Winter, 49-62.

MacNeil, Ian R. (1980), *The New Social Contract.* New Haven, CT: Yale University Press.

Magill, Ken (1998), "DMA Mails Privacy Draft to Members: Debate Begins," *DM News,* June 8, 1, 50.

Mazis, Michael (1997), "Marketing and Public Policy: Prospects for the Future," *Journal of Public Policy & Marketing,* 16 (Spring), 139-43.

McCrohan, Kevin (1989), "Information Technology, Marketing Practice, and Consumer Privacy," *Journal of Public Policy & Marketing,* 8, 265-78.

Melillo, Wendy (1999) "UncleSam.reg," *Interactive Report,* May 3, 12-14.

Milne, George R. (1997), "Consumer Participation in Mailing Lists: A Field Experiment," *Journal of Public Policy & Marketing,* 16 (Fall), 298-309.

———, James Beckman, and Marc L. Taubman (1996), "Consumer Attitudes toward Privacy and Direct Marketing in Argentina," *Journal of Direct Marketing,* 10 (1), 22-29.

——— and Maria-Eugenia Boza (1998), "A Business Perspective on Database Marketing and Consumer Privacy Practices," Working Paper No. 98-110, Marketing Science Institute.

——— and ——— (1999), "Trust and Concern in Consumers' Perceptions of Marketing Information Management Practices," *Journal of Interactive Marketing,* 13 (Winter), 5-24.

——— and Mary Ellen Gordon (1993), "Direct Mail Privacy-Efficiency Tradeoffs within an Implied Social Contract Framework," *Journal of Public Policy & Marketing,* 12 (Fall), 206-15.

——— and ——— (1994), "A Segmentation Study of Consumers' Attitudes toward Direct Mail," *Journal of Direct Marketing,* 8 (Spring), 45-52.

——— and Andrew Rohm (1999), "Consumers' Perspectives on the Control of Personal Information across Mail, Telephone, and Internet Direct Channels," unpublished working paper, University of Massachusetts.

———, ———, and Maria-Eugenia Boza (1999), "Trust Has to Be Earned: An Exploration into the Antecedents of Trust in Database Marketing," in *Frontiers in Direct Marketing Research,* Joseph Phelps, ed. New York: John Wiley, 31-41.

Moorman, Christine, Rohit Deshpande, and Gerald Zaltman (1993), "Factors Affecting Trust in Marketing Research Relationships," *Journal of Marketing,* 57 (January), 81-101.

——— and Linda L. Price (1989), "Consumer Policy Remedies and Consumer Segment Interactions," *Journal of Public Policy & Marketing,* 8, 181-203.

Morgan, Robert M. and Shelby D. Hunt (1994), "The Commitment-Trust Theory of Relationship Marketing," *Journal of Marketing,* 58 (July), 20-38.

Nowak, Glenn J. and Joseph Phelps (1992), "Understanding Privacy Concerns: An Assessment of Consumers' Information-Related Knowledge and Beliefs," *Journal of Direct Marketing,* 6 (Autumn), 28-39.

——— and ——— (1995), "Direct Marketing and the Use of Individual-Level Consumer Information: Determining How and When 'Privacy' Matters," *Journal of Direct Marketing,* 9 (Summer), 46-60.

O'Harrow, Robert, Jr. (1998a), "CVS also Cuts Ties to Marketing Service; Like Giant, Firm Cites Privacy on Prescriptions," *The Washington Post,* February 19.

——— (1998b), "FTC Curbs Web Site's Data Use; Agency Limits Sales of Personal Details," *The Washington Post,* August 14.

Peppers, Don and Martha Rogers (1993), *The One-to-One Future.* New York: Doubleday/Currency.

Petrison, Lisa and Paul Wang (1995), "Exploring the Dimensions of Consumer Privacy: An Analysis of Coverage in British and American Media," *Journal of Direct Marketing,* 9 (Autumn), 19-37.

Phelps, Joseph, William Gonzenbach, and Edward Johnson (1994), "Press Coverage and Public Perceptions of Direct Marketing and Consumer Privacy," *Journal of Direct Marketing,* 8 (Spring), 9-22.

"Privacy Suit Filed vs. Real Networks" (1999), *USA Today* [on-line]. Available: http://www.usatoday.com/life/cyber/tech/ctg638.htm

Richards, Jef I. (1997), "Legal Potholes on the Information Superhighway," *Journal of Public Policy & Marketing,* 16 (Fall), 319-26.

Rohm, Andrew and George R. Milne (1999), "Consumers' Privacy Concerns about Direct Marketers' Use of Personal Medical Information," in *Advances in Health Care Research,* Joe Hair, Jr., ed. Madison, WI: Omnipress, 27-37.

Shaver, Dick (1996), *The Next Step in Database Marketing.* New York: John Wiley.

Sheth, Jagdish and Atul Parvatiyar (1995), "Relationship Marketing in Consumer Markets: Antecedents and Consequences," *Journal of the Academy of Marketing Science,* 23 (4), 255-71.

Smith, Jeff (1994), *Managing Privacy: Information Technology and Corporate America.* Chapel Hill: University of North Carolina University Press.

————, Sandra Milberg, and Sandra Burke (1996), "Information Privacy: Measuring Individuals' Concerns about Corporate Practices," *MIS Quarterly,* 20 (2), 167-96.

Smith, J. Brock and Donald W. Barclay (1997), "The Effects of Organizational Differences and Trust on the Effectiveness of Selling Partner Relationships," *Journal of Marketing,* 61 (January), 3-21.

Spence, Michael (1973), "Job Market Signalling," *Quarterly Journal of Economics,* 87 (August), 355-77.

Stewart, David and Ingrid M. Martin (1994), "Intended and Unintended Consequences of Warning Messages: A Review and Synthesis of Empirical Research," *Journal of Public Policy & Marketing,* 13 (Spring), 1-19.

Taylor, Raymond E., John Vassar, and Bobby C. Vaught (1995), "The Beliefs of Marketing Professionals Regarding Consumer Privacy," *Journal of Direct Marketing* 9 (Autumn), 38-46.

Thomas, Robert E. and Virginia G. Maurer (1997), "Database Marketing Practice: Protecting Consumer Privacy," *Journal of Public Policy & Marketing,* 16 (Spring), 147-55.

Wang, Paul and Lisa A. Petrison (1993), "Direct Marketing Activities and Personal Privacy: A Consumer Survey," *Journal of Direct Marketing,* 7 (Winter), 7-19.

Social Marketing and Development

Ruby Roy Dholakia
Nikhilesh Dholakia

The second half of the 20th century witnessed the determined application of managerial techniques to social problems. Flush with the success of modern management methods during World War II and subsequently in a booming post-war American economy, management theorists and practitioners came to believe that key principles of management could be extended to large-scale social problems in America as well as globally (Drucker 1958). In the field of marketing, a forceful argument was presented to the effect that the "marketing concept"—the successful postwar operating philosophy that emphasized the formulation of marketing programs based on perceived consumer needs (Borch 1957; McKitterick 1957; Togeson 1956)—could be extended well beyond for-profit business organizations (Kotler and Levy 1969; Levy and Kotler 1969). This "broadening of the marketing concept" paved the way for the application of marketing methods in a variety of nonbusiness sectors such as politics, popular culture, and religion.

A major offshoot of the "broadening" argument was the emergence of the concept of "social marketing" (Kotler and Zaltman 1971). Social marketing translated the conceptual thrusts of the broadening argument into programmatic marketing elements—goals, techniques, methods, strategies, plans—relevant to social sectors such as health care, family planning, traffic safety, substance abuse prevention, literacy, and sanitation.

In this chapter, we review the evolution of social marketing and its application to problems of economic and social development. Although such problems traditionally are associated with the so-called developing nations, we take a broader view (Dholakia and Dholakia 1984; Kumcu and Firat 1989). All societies and nations are "developing" from their existing states to, hopefully, better meliorative states (Dholakia and Firat 1989). We reflect on the challenges that arise when social marketing methods are applied with the intent of promoting major categories of national, regional, or global social change. We explore some of the limitations and contradictions of social marketing in such settings and provide suggestions for further research to enhance the effectiveness of social marketing—indeed, marketing in general—in the context of globalization, economic dislocations and transitions, and major cultural shifts.

A brief review of social marketing is provided in the next section. Using three major examples, the second section discusses the complex relationship of social marketing and development. The third section reflects on some of the dilemmas and challenges that arise during the course of social marketing interventions, particularly in the context of developing countries. In the concluding section, we reflect on the major theoretical and practical challenges for social marketing in the foreseeable future, and we provide some recommendations for addressing these challenges.

Social Marketing

According to Kotler and Zaltman (1971),

> Social marketing is the design, implementation, and control of programs calculated to influence the acceptability of social ideas and involving considerations of product planning, pricing, communication, distribution, and market research. . . . It is the explicit use of marketing skills to help translate present social action efforts into more effectively designed and communicated programs that elicit desired audience response. (p. 5)

Among the application areas for social marketing, health care-oriented issues (Zaltman and Vertinsky 1971)—including family planning (El-Ansary and Kramer 1973; Farley and Leavitt 1971; Roberto 1975)—and environment-oriented issues (Zikmund and Stanton 1971) received early attention and have continued to generate ongoing interest (see, e.g., Greenlee 1997; Rangan, Karim, and Sandberg 1996). With its roots in social advertising and social communication, social marketing has evolved to include at least four additional elements—market research, product development, use of incentives, and facilitation—not included in the communication approach (Fox and Kotler 1980) as well as an emphasis on voluntary behavior of target audiences, not just behaviors desired by social marketers (Andreasen 1995; Kotler and Roberto 1989; Rothschild 1999).

Developing nations and the disadvantaged groups within affluent nations emerged as obvious targets for social marketing programs. Social problems such as overpopulation, illiteracy, malnutrition, substance abuse, and poor sanitation loomed large for these groups. Social marketing was seen as a powerful addition to the arsenal of social interventions available to government agencies and nongovernmental organizations that had to deal with such problems (Murthy 1991). In fact, in developing nations, marketing often was viewed as capable of delivering an effective one-two punch: Conventional marketing (of the commercial variety) would ignite the engine of economic development (Cundiff 1982), whereas social marketing would assuage existing and emerging social problems (Duhaime, McTavish, and Ross 1985). As a result, social marketing received ready and quick acceptance in the field of marketing (Fox and Kotler, 1980).

Social Marketing and Development

Figure 21.1 shows a simplified four-sector view of how social marketing addresses some of the economic development problems. Starting from a macro social objective such as health care for the population, social marketing programs are built on specific actionable goals. Thus, emphasis on disease prevention leads to immunizing of children. With specific measurable goals such as DPT (diphtheria, polio, tetanus), MMR (measles, mumps, rubela), and polio immunizations of young children in view, targeted social marketing programs are designed to achieve such goals. All the techniques of integrated marketing are brought to bear on the problem, along with the best of management and medical practices.

Such targeted, well-designed, and well-implemented social marketing programs deliver results but may cause systemic impacts that are not always easy to foresee. We discuss three cases to illustrate the systemic complexities.

Family Planning

As social marketing approaches emerged, family planning became one of the most popular focus areas for social marketing; it was seen as more effective in meeting population control targets than were the existing bureaucratic approaches (El-Ansary and Kramer 1973; Roberto 1975). At first, the emphasis was to generate knowledge about contraception. In India, for example, government-run family planning agencies started using the country's top advertising agencies to develop the communication campaigns. Abandoning the earlier insipid messages, family planning campaigns became colorful with memorable slogans. A simple and easily recognizable logo, an inverted red triangle, was developed for the nation's family planning program. In addition to the broadcast media, outdoor media such as posters, billboards, and wall paintings were employed in a massive way. With increasing awareness of social marketing, advertising pertaining to family planning underwent tremendous changes.

Second, channels of distribution were targeted to reach the millions of people. Lacking a good infrastructure of clinics and hospitals, especially in the rural areas of India, it was decided that commercial retail channels would be used for the subsidized distribution of condoms. In Sri Lanka, similar efforts were made by the government to achieve widespread use of condoms as a means of birth control (Fox and Kotler 1980). In Bangladesh, contraceptives were prominently

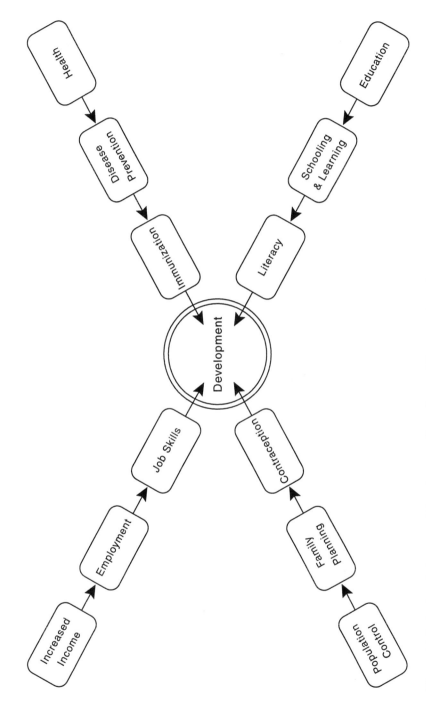

Figure 21.1. Social Marketing and Development: From Sectoral Targets to Specific Behaviors

merchandised and sold in public markets rather than distributed free in medical clinics (Brown, Waszak, and Childers 1989). According to several sources, these efforts led to significant increases in the availability of condoms as well as changes in knowledge, attitudes, and birth control practices of consumers (Bogue and Tsui 1979; Brown, Waszak, and Childers 1989; Population Information Program 1980; Rangan, Karim, and Sandberg 1996).

Meeting family planning targets, however, required more than condom distribution. Many innovative approaches were tried. One of these approaches, the "mass camp" approach to family planning in India, showed both the success potential of and the problems with social marketing methods (R. Dholakia 1984). Vasectomy was chosen as the preferred technique for controlling pregnancies. Traveling mass camps for vasectomies were set up in rural areas. Teams of doctors performed vasectomies in makeshift operating rooms set up under tents. Incentives were offered to village leaders to motivate the men in the villages to undergo vasectomies. Individual incentives—cash, bags of food grain, transistor radios—were offered to the men who lined up to get vasectomies.

As a social marketing approach, the mass camp met all the requirements of effective integrated marketing. It conducted market research, employed multiple media, relied on integrated marketing communications, used opinion leaders in an effective way, created an efficient and speedy service delivery system, and provided point-of-sale incentives that resulted in desired behaviors.

These mass vasectomy camps did achieve the family planning agency's immediate goals, but with major side effects. To take advantage of the incentives, all types of men underwent the operation including unmarried males and older males not married to childbearing women. The camps were set up during the low season in the agricultural cycle. This presumably was to facilitate participation by the men who were extremely busy during the high agricultural season. But it also meant that incomes, savings, and food stocks were low in the villages, and people saw the mass camp as a way of getting extra money or food. Many of the men did not understand the nature of the vasectomy operation and went through the procedure just to take advantage of the incentives. Some of the men later wanted to reverse the procedure, but no clinics were available for this; the camps and the doctors moved on to other locations when they were finished with a village.

Recycling

Social marketing programs are not restricted to economically developing countries. In economically advanced countries such as the United States, health care issues have been less concerned with infectious diseases and birth control than with lifestyles associated with excessive drinking, unhealthy diet, lack of exercise, or the use of tobacco (Walsh et al. 1993). Social marketing programs have been designed to address a whole host of issues including alcohol and other drug problems on college campuses (Zimmerman 1997) and traffic safety among broader communities (Hastings and Elliott 1993).

One consequence of economic development and rising incomes is an increase in solid waste that results from an affluent throw-away culture. According to one estimate, the annual production of municipal solid waste in the United States alone grew from 88 million tons in 1960 to 217 million tons in 1997 (Gavzer 1999). This does not include other waste materials such as old automobiles and scrap metals.

With this phenomenal increase in waste, developing reverse channels and encouraging recycling behaviors have become application targets for social marketing. In the poorer nations, economic incentives still are in place to encourage recycling behaviors. In India, for example, there is a flourishing trade in which recycled paper and clothes can be exchanged for shiny new stainless steel utensils or for cold hard cash. In Ghana, everything from newspapers and bottles to scrap auto parts can be recycled profitably. Newspapers are converted into packages for use by vendors such as roasted peanut sellers. Discarded auto parts are converted into anchors, toys, and cooking grills. In the United States, such specialized waste recycling channels existed in the past, but these became unprofitable and disappeared with growing affluence (Zikmund and Stanton 1971).

The typical approach to managing recycling in Europe has been to circumvent the market and to rely on legislative measures. High container deposit fees (to motivate container recycling), mandatory separation of solid waste by type of waste at the consumer level, and design-for-recycling of products at the manufacturer level (e.g., cars) so that they are recyclable after being junked have been used by various European nations. Although laws and legislation are one method of changing individual and group behaviors, the recent emphasis on exchange and voluntary behaviors has led some scholars to eliminate these approaches as social marketing approaches (Andreasen 1995; Rothschild 1999).

In the fragmented political and more market-oriented U.S. environment, the challenge of recycling has been addressed by more conventional social marketing approaches. The first focus of social marketing programs has been to overcome the information gaps regarding recycling. The problem existed at all levels of the supply chain—manufacturers, intermediaries, and consumers (Johnson 1991). Research by Rathje (1989) showed that it was paper—newspapers and telephone books—that contributed in a big way to landfills, not diapers and fast-food packaging as popular media liked to portray.

The second emphasis has been to stimulate recycling behaviors. The "green" marketing in the United States and Canada shows that consumers are ready and willing to change their behaviors to achieve societal objectives such as saving the environment for future generations. Despite good intentions, however, most people recycle less than their expressed goals. Such gaps between knowledge and behaviors are common in social marketing programs (Hornik 1989). Various researchers have attempted to identify the necessary conditions for overcoming such barriers (see, e.g., Rangan, Karim, and Sandberg 1996; Rothschild 1999). As a result of these various measures, there have been significant increases in recycling behaviors. Globally, the percentage of fiber supply for paper derived from recycled sources increased from 23% in 1970 to 36% in 1998 (Worldwatch Institute 1999). In the United States, according to the Environmental Protection Agency, the rate of recycling has reached nearly 94% for auto batteries but is only 22% for auto tires (cited in Gavzer 1999).

In terms of factors motivating recycling behavior, affluent nations seem to be no different from poor nations in that money talks. In the United States, with regard to recycling behavior, Rathje (1989) concluded, "The only reliable predictor is the price paid for the commodity at the buyback centers. When prices rose for, say, newsprint, the number of newspapers found in local garbage suddenly declined" (p. 9).

No matter how successful and effective social marketing programs are in promoting responsible recycling behaviors, they remain vulnerable to the systemic critique that marketing is a primary cause of wasteful consumption practices in the first place. According to Ewen (1988),

> From a marketing point of view, disposability is the golden goose. It conflates the act of using with that of using up and promotes markets that are continually hungry for more. . . . The ever mounting glut of waste materials is a characteristic byproduct of [the] modern "consumer society." It might even be argued that capitalism's continual need to find or generate markets means that disposability and waste have become the spine of the system. . . . It must be acknowledged that, for most people living within a consumer society, waste is seen as an inherent part of the processes by which they obtain replenishment and pleasure.

Micro-credit

Although such programs do not self-identify as social marketing, micro-credit programs have emerged as widely used social interventions that use business (including marketing) techniques to alleviate poverty by making very small (micro-) loans to the poorest people in the world, usually women. The source and inspiration of such programs is Bangladesh's Grameen Bank, the pioneering micro-credit institution founded by economist Muhammad Yunus, who started the venture in 1976 by making small personal loans to skilled but destitute Bangladeshi women. Grameen was formally launched in 1983 and by 1998 had grown into a $2.5 billion socially oriented financial institution. A host of enterprises dealing with telecommunications, textiles, and electricity were created under the Grameen (the word means "rural" in Bangla language) umbrella during the 1990s.

The lore of Grameen Bank has been richly celebrated (Bornstein 1996; Jackelen and Rhyne 1991; MacKeen 1998; Todd 1996; Wahid 1993, 1994). Grameen uses a well-crafted mix of target marketing, service positioning, product development, relationship marketing, and word-of-mouth communication to run a $2.5 billion micro-credit operation in Bangladesh. To obtain a loan, cells of five unrelated women members are formed among the poor in a village. At first, two members of a cell (selected by the cell itself) are given micro-loans in the range of $30 to $150. The interest rate is 18%, except for housing loans, which are given at a subsidized rate of 8%. When a successful repayment record is established with the initial two members, other members of the cell become eligible for loans. After a loan is paid back, members become eligible for subsequent slightly larger loans.

The loan repayment is the collective responsibility of the group. Grameen field-workers hold weekly meetings with groups of six cells. Repayments are made weekly in a public forum. Peer pressure ensures that members do not default; if a single member defaults, then other members in the cell cannot receive credit. Several other methods are used to facilitate loan repayment and to augment the loan-paying capacity of members. Members have to open savings accounts and are encouraged by the field-workers and cell chairpersons to save tiny amounts in a disciplined weekly pattern. As soon as sufficient savings accumulate, members have to buy one dividend-paying share in the bank, costing about $3. Bank members are expected to memorize and adhere to Grameen Bank's 16 development-oriented principles (e.g., grow vegetables, exercise, no dowries, keep family size small).

Grameen Bank provides products and services such as seed, saplings, oral rehydration kits, and emergency disaster loans (Bangladesh is subject to severe flooding). All these are provided at a price, often subsidized but not free of charge. Grameen's experience is that women are conscientious borrowers, use the funds for essential family needs such as nutrition and education, and are far more likely to stick to a repayment schedule than are men.

Grameen Bank embarked on an ambitious product development and diversification strategy during the 1990s. Subsidiaries dealing with textiles, electricity, and telecommunications were created. Grameen Telecom, for example, established a joint venture with Norway's Telenor (now merged with Telia) and Japanese and U.S. partners to offer cellular phones to some of its members. The women who acquire Grameen cellular phones rent out air time to other villagers and use the revenue to repay the loans for the phones and to make small profits. They use the wireless phones to keep abreast of agricultural prices so as not to be cheated by middlemen. Grameen plans to branch out into fax, voice messaging, and Internet services.

Although Grameen Bank has received laudatory comments from the world over and its system is being replicated in more than 50 countries (including Chicago's South Shore Bank), there have been critics. Some of the studies have shown that the benefits to Grameen's borrowers have not been substantial or sustainable (Goetz and Gupta 1996; Neff 1996). Grameen's commendable preference for women also has come under criticism. The system sometimes has strained gender relations and at other times has been manipulated by men who use the women in their families as a front to get loans but are the true beneficiaries of the credit (Goetz and Gupta 1996; Neff 1996). Other critics have commented on the single-minded emphasis of Grameen on credit and repayment, neglecting other women's issues such as health, child care, legal aid, job training, and unionizing (De Sarkar and Ahmad 1997; Labelle 1998). The cultlike adherence to Grameen's "principles" has been criticized as an instance of a top-down enforcement of a development ethos that might not be in tune with local realities. Finally, the ideology of micro-credit-based capitalism has come under attack. It is seen as a part of the global process, supported by Western governments and the World Bank, of rollback of the welfare system and throwing the poor at the mercy of the market (Neff 1996; Solomon 1997-98).

Dilemmas and Challenges

Disconnected Worldviews and Systemic Complexity

The view in Figure 21.1 assumes that social marketing programs are specific interventions targeted at distinct socioeconomic development sectors and goals. In reality, development activities are enmeshed in a thick cultural-historical context in ways such that interventions cannot be surgically precise. Figure 21.2 shows a view of social marketing interventions with the contextual backdrop of politics, technology (at work and at home), gender relations, and infrastructure (transport, communications, and education). Needless to say, this is a highly simplified view of the multidimensional contextual backdrop of development activities. Not only is there a thick contextual backdrop, but this backdrop is being shaped and transformed by the interactions of local and global factors (Appadurai 1996). In such settings, it is a challenge to achieve congruence between what the managers of social marketing programs offer and what the target recipients ("beneficiaries") want.

The disconnect between the program managers' goals and worldviews and the goals and worldviews of other actors in the systems in which social marketing programs intervene is a major problem. In the case of India's family planning program, the program managers who instituted the mass vasectomy camps wanted rapid adoption of vasectomy as a means of population control. The poor villagers, however, simply wanted cash or food during the lean agricultural season. Many underwent the vasectomy operation just to get the money, with little understanding of the procedure or its consequences.

In the case of recycling programs in the United States, the program managers wanted reductions in garbage and increases in waste delivered to buy-back centers. Scrap dealers wanted to make money by maximizing the spread between their "buy" and "sell" prices. Despite good intentions, consumers wanted to minimize the effort involved in recycling waste, with the exceptions of those periods when waste fetched attractive prices.

Grameen has provided a social business model that is extremely well liked by international aid agencies and Western governments, but this model often has not harmonized with local realities. International agencies and Grameen-style social entrepreneurs want poverty alleviation and social upliftment through self-help methods, which they believe can be jump-started through micro-credit. The rural poor often just want to meet their pressing consumption and personal social needs. Recipients of micro-credit often use the money for traditional consumption-oriented purposes. They often pay lip service to the principles of development so as to maintain the impression that they are "good credit risks." Because of Grameen's strict weekly repayment schedule, servicing the loans often becomes a problem and, just to remain in Grameen's good books, borrowings may occur from usurious local moneylenders.

The issues discussed in the preceding paragraphs arise because of the holistic and connected nature of social marketing and development activities. It rarely is possible to limit the impact of a program to a strictly circumscribed and specific

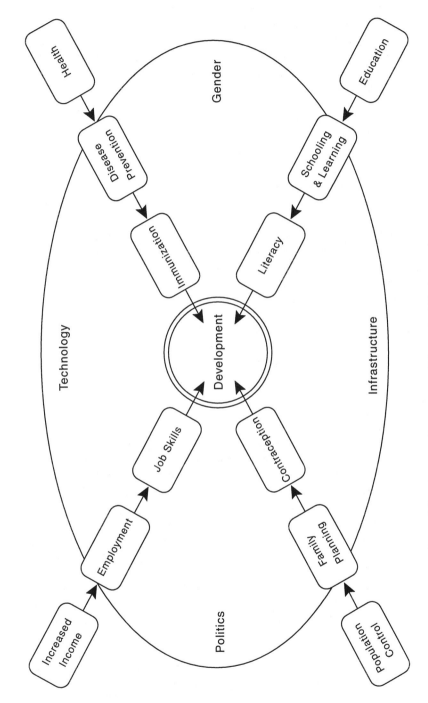

Figure 21.2. Social Marketing and Development: Importance of Contextual Background

social dimension. Intervention in one area usually has spillover—not always predictable—impacts on other areas (Figure 21.3). In enacting mandatory beverage container deposit legislation, the short-term effect was to reduce alcohol sales (Sjolander and Chen 1989) without significantly reducing total litter (Ferretti and Lesser 1985). It creates significant problems for planning, implementing, and evaluating social marketing programs (Andreasen 1995; Bloom and Novelli 1981).

Gender Issues: Some Targeting Dilemmas

One of the generic approaches in marketing is the segmentation of the market and targeting specific groups and individuals for marketing programs. For a variety of social or pragmatic reasons, gender has become a primary criterion for targeting in social marketing programs. In India's family planning programs, earlier efforts targeted rural women with birth control solutions such as an intrauterine device (or the so-called "loop") and the pill. This approach did not always work; in the tradition-bound rural society, women were unapproachable and, even if approached by a female social worker, were not willing to talk about conception and birth control issues. In such instances, the target was changed to men. Male sterilization, frequently performed at the mass vasectomy camp, obviated such problems. The medical procedure was simple enough to be performed in makeshift tent clinics. Incentives and effective use of village opinion leaders overcame the resistance from men and brought them into the clinics by the thousands. In Bangladesh, the initial focus on men for family planning efforts was changed to include women when surveys revealed that women were more receptive to family planning messages (Rangan, Karim, and Sandberg 1996).

In the case of Grameen Bank, women were specifically targeted for a variety of reasons. They were perceived as good credit risks, more cooperative in nature (for the cells to work), and likely to use the funds for income-generating or family-oriented needs (e.g., nutrition, education, health care).

The use of gender as a segmentation and targeting variable has ramifications beyond immediate effectiveness of the social marketing programs. When a program is successful, as in the case of the Grameen Bank in Bangladesh, it strains gender relations in the local society. In the case of the mass vasectomy camps in India, the targeting of males raises cries of exploitation and discrimination.

Ignoring gender as a segmentation/targeting variable also has its problems and critics. In examining the impact of global trade expansion and liberalization on gender issues, Fontana, Joekes, and Masika (1998) urged more research as well as specific policies to promote women's role in economic activities of developing countries. They argued,

> Women's economic activity . . . has wider human resource development as well as gender benefits. . . . Women tend to have more family—and "socially"—oriented expenditure patterns than men, i.e., they invest in social networks and reciprocal support relationships. Therefore, as women's share of total wage payments rises with trade expansion, child nutritional status and other human resource develop-

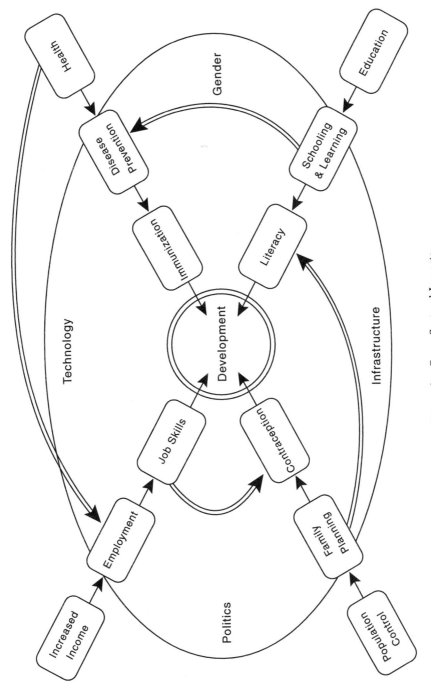

Figure 21.3. Social Marketing and Development: Illustrative Cross-Sectoral Impacts

ment indicators may be expected to rise. . . . [This] strengthens the incentive for investment in the human capital of girls, with all the wider benefits that the education of girls brings. (p. 49)

Incentives: Effectiveness and Externalities

In most social marketing programs, incentives play a crucial role in motivating or sustaining desired behaviors. In fact, it is the use of incentives that differentiates a social marketing program from a social advertising or social communication program (Fox and Kotler 1980). Experience with social marketing programs indicates that incentives usually are effective in inducing desired types of short-term behavioral responses from target groups.

In India's family planning mass camps, incentives helped meet the vasectomy goals of the program administrators. Grameen Bank succeeded in creating millions of micro-loan takers. In the case of recycling, refunds on returned bottles and cans stimulated container returns directly among end users as well as among scavengers (Grabowski 1980). Thus, incentives have the effect of spurring very specific forms of behavior that social marketers seek from their target groups.

A critical issue in social marketing is designing the appropriate incentives. In terms of value of the incentives, the higher the value, the greater the chances of motivating the targeted behavior. In Sweden, for example, only after doubling the refund rate did the recycling programs achieve desired levels of beverage container returns (Svenska Dagbladet 1988). In general, the process of economic development keeps raising the bar in terms of incentives; more affluent countries need higher incentives than do less affluent countries. There is a sort of acclimatization effect, ultimately leading to a state where very high incentives—at levels that cannot be sustained by social marketing programs—have to be legislated.

In this process, however, unintended external consequences could arise. Under certain conditions, incentives could act as bait that attracts and then traps the recipient into an alien, poorly understood system. Under such circumstances, incentive-driven social marketing efforts may degenerate into quasi-bribery or even quasi-coercion. Such circumstances may easily arise in poor developing nations, where a sack of rice or a cash incentive during the lean agricultural season may have an almost compelling effect of driving men in a village into a mass vasectomy camp. In the case of Grameen Bank of Bangladesh, women and their families might have been pushed into new types of credit dependencies. In affluent countries, incentives might not have such a compelling effect. This creates a further dilemma. Either the incentives have to be continually raised to motivate the desired behavior, or the planners have to abandon social marketing approaches and turn to mandatory regulation of behavior.

Market-Led Development

Although social marketing has gained wide acceptance in marketing academia as well as in marketing practice, the tool kit of social marketing was not without problems. Because social marketing entailed the annexation of the social services domain into the expansionary fold of conventional marketing methods, there were frequent mismatches between business-derived techniques and the objectives and organizational cultures of social service agencies (Bloom and Novelli 1981; Zimmerman 1997). After reviewing several of the mismatches between commercial and social marketing domains, Bloom and Novelli (1981) came to the following conclusion:

> The relationship between social marketing and the more conventional commercial marketing may be somewhat like the relationship between [American] football and rugby. The two marketing games have much in common and require similar training, but each has its own set of rules, constraints, and required skills. The good player of one game may not necessarily be a good player of the other. (p. 87)

In arguing for a market-led social marketing program, Rangan, Karim, and Sandberg (1996) pointed to some of the challenges and complexities created by multiple constituencies typically involved in such programs. Whereas multiple constituencies, conflicting goals, and constraints stemming from political, social, and cultural factors make social marketing processes complex in economically advanced countries, this is even more so in the case of economically developing nations and in economies undergoing major transformations. To examine these challenges, the relationship between social marketing and development needs to be located in the wider conceptual frame representing the relationship between marketing and development.

The relationship between marketing and development has evolved from ideological discussions to an examination of connections between political-economic changes and consumption patterns. During the 1970s and 1980s, the arguments regarding the relationship between marketing and development often were seen as emanating from antagonistic or at least deeply divided camps (N. Dholakia 1984). On one hand were the arguments recognizing and promoting the causative role of marketing as an engine of capitalist market development (Cundiff 1982; Wood and Vitell 1986). On the other hand were arguments drawing from the critical theories of development and cautioning against both the intranational and international inequities that market-led development created (Dholakia and Dholakia 1984; Dholakia and Sherry 1987). Other approaches urged a historical analysis of the relationship between marketing and development during both capitalist (Dixon 1981) and pre-capitalist eras (Darian 1985).

By the 1980s, it had become evident that materialism and rising consumption aspirations were both a driving force for and a vivid result of the political-economic changes occurring across the globe. The relationship between marketing and economic development has become more tumultuous and controversial as the margins and peripheries of the global political economy expand rapidly and get connected mightily to the technology and finance-driven centers of the global political economy (Appadurai 1996). Attention has shifted from the threatening aspects (e.g., exploding populations, hungry hordes) to the commendatory aspects (e.g., new mass markets, billions of buyers) of these countries. This has brought an additional dimension to the study of the relationship between marketing and development. Material possessions (Belk 1984, 1985), consumption aspirations and frustrations (Belk 1997), consumption values (Ahuvia and Friedman 1998, Leelakulthanit, Day, and Walters 1991), and consumption patterns (Firat and Dholakia 1982, 1998) became subjects of study in the context of both advanced and developing societies.

One conclusion from the growing body of work on marketing and development is that limiting the focus of social marketing programs to economic and managerial aspects is not very useful. Looking at social marketing and information campaigns only in terms of criteria specified by the marketing organization ignores the fundamental societal processes of social control and social change (Salmon 1989). This was readily evident in the three cases discussed earlier. Development is a multifaceted process. During the course of development, marketing affects not just economic institutions but also political, social, and cultural patterns (Dholakia and Firat 1989). Whenever economic development occurs, there are social impacts that need attention. In fact, it can be argued that neglecting the social side of development will derail the economic engine of growth (Escobar 1995). For social marketing campaigns, the implication is that analysis of the social marketer's goals and strategies must be situated in a wider context of socioeconomic development. Impacts of such campaigns should be examined in both instrumental and broader developmental terms.

Concluding Comments

At the beginning of the 21st century, there is an unprecedented openness to marketing ideas across the globe including the ideas of social marketing. From just a curious extension of marketing concepts from the business sector to the social sector, social marketing has graduated to an accepted and widely practiced social change strategy. Social marketing programs have created changes in a wide variety of areas including family planning, recycling, and use of credit for economic activities.

Despite this salutary environment, social marketing (and indeed marketing in general) continues to run into roadblocks. Crises keep punctuating the processes of economic development and social change. In such circumstances, social marketing solutions often seem like the application of a Band-Aid™ to a trauma victim. Social marketing, however, does have the *potential* to address some of the root causes that lead to economic and social crises. To be a more credible source of policy and practice, social marketing has to reinvent itself. This is a multipronged challenge.

First, the complexity of the linkages among economic development, social change, and marketing processes needs to be remapped, updating earlier works such as those of Dholakia and Dholakia (1984), Dholakia and Sherry (1987), and Joy and Ross (1989). In this endeavor, the rapidly growing literature dealing with cultural analysis of marketing and consumption processes is particularly valuable (see, e.g., Howes 1996). This endeavor also requires engagement with emerging literature pertaining to the social aspects of economic development (see, e.g., Escobar 1995).

Second, social marketing needs to be reconceptualized in the transformed setting of globalization, pervasive marketization, and cultural changes that are eroding received ideas of modernization and modernity (Firat and Dholakia 1998). The implied flow of influence in social marketing programs—from the developed, modern, knowledgeable core to the underdeveloped, traditional, uninformed periphery—might not exhibit the suggested linearity and might instead follow complex global circuits in the emerging postmodern world (Appadurai 1996).

Finally, social marketing needs to be integrated with the broader range of social change theories, techniques, and practices. Because of its managerial bias, social marketing often sits on a high horse, dismissive of other social change approaches. In reality, social marketing needs a greater understanding of sociocultural processes.[1] Techniques and methods that bring long-term, often multigenerational, goals into the planning process need to be injected into social marketing. Such methods require reference to fields such as evolutionary economics (Daly 1997) and environmental policy (Peet and Watts 1996). In general, studies in social marketing have to open the disciplinary floodgates and let the currents from various social science and humanistic inquiries flow in. Through a healthy exchange of ideas, social marketing can gain in relevance and stature in terms of addressing issues of social change and economic development.

Note

1. Conventional marketing faces this same challenge in a massive way. During the 1990s, the study of marketing processes and consumption has mushroomed in the humanities and social sciences. This burgeoning body of knowledge makes scant reference to the literature in marketing (Firat and Dholakia 1998).

References

Ahuvia, Aaron C. and Douglas C. Friedman (1998), "Income, Consumption, and Subjective Well-Being: Toward a Composite Macromarketing Model," *Journal of Macromarketing,* 18 (Fall), 153-68.

Andreasen, Alan R. (1995), *Marketing Social Change.* San Francisco: Jossey-Bass.

Appadurai, Arjun (1996), *Modernity at Large: Cultural Dimensions of Globalization.* Minneapolis: University of Minnesota Press.

Belk, Russell W. (1984), "Three Scales to Measure Constructs Related to Materialism: Reliability, Validity, and Relationships to Measure of Happiness," in *Advances in Consumer Research,* Vol. 11, T. C. Kinnear, ed. Provo, UT: Association for Consumer Research, 154-60.

——— (1985), "Materialism: Trait Aspects of Living in the Material World," *Journal of Consumer Research,* 3 (December), 265-79.

——— (1997), "Everyday Life for Eastern European Consumers," in *Marketing Challenges in Transition Economies: Proceedings of Sixth International Conference on Marketing and Development,* Dana-Nicoleta Lascu, Iacob Catoiu, Nikhilesh Dholakia, and Sanford Grossbart, eds. Muncie, IN: International Society for Marketing and Development, 1-8.

Bloom, Paul N. and William D. Novelli (1981), "Problems and Challenges in Social Marketing," *Journal of Marketing,* 45 (Spring), 79-88.

Bogue, Donald J. and Amy Ong Tsui (1979), "Zero World Population Growth?" *The Public Interest,* 55 (Spring), 99-113.

Borch. Fred J. (1957), "The Marketing Philosophy as a Way of Business Life," in *The Marketing Concept: Its Meaning to Management,* Marketing series, No. 99, Elizabeth Martin and Albert Newgarden, eds. New York: American Management Association, 3-16.

Bornstein, David (1996), *The Price of a Dream: The Story of the Grameen Bank.* New York: Simon & Schuster.

Brown, Jane D., Cynthia S. Waszak, and Kim Walsh Childers (1989), "Family Planning, Abortion, and AIDS: Sexuality and Communication Campaigns," in *Information Campaigns: Balancing Social Values and Social Change,* Charles T. Salmon, ed. Newbury Park, CA: Sage, 85-112.

Cundiff, Edward W. (1982), "A Macromarketing Approach to Economic Development," *Journal of Macromarketing,* 2 (Spring), 14-19.

Daly, Herman (1997), *Beyond Growth: The Economics of Sustainable Development.* Boston: Beacon.

Darian, Jean C. (1985), "Marketing and Economic Development: A Case Study from Classical India," *Journal of Macromarketing,* 5 (Spring), 14-26.

De Sarkar, Dipankar and Tahmina Ahmad (1997), "Microfinance 'not the Panacea' for Women," *Panos,* January 20. Available: http://www.panos.org.uk

Dholakia, Nikhilesh (1984), "Marketing in the LDCs: Its Nature and Prospects," in *Marketing in Developing Countries,* G. S. Kindra, ed. London: Croom Helm, 10-28.

———— and Ruby Roy Dholakia (1984), "Missing Links: Marketing and the Newer Theories of Development," in *Marketing in Developing Countries,* G. S. Kindra, ed. London: Croom Helm, 57-75.

———— and A. Fuat Firat (1989), "Development in the Era of Globalizing Markets and Consumption Patterns," in *Marketing and Development: Toward Broader Dimensions,* E. Kumcu and A. F. Firat, eds. Greenwich, CT: JAI, 79-101.

———— and John F. Sherry, Jr. (1987), "Marketing and Development: A Re-Synthesis of Knowledge," in *Research in Marketing,* Vol. 9, J. N. Sheth, ed. Greenwich, CT: JAI, 119-43.

Dholakia, Ruby Roy (1984), "A Macromarketing Perspective on Social Marketing: The Case of Family Planning in India," *Journal of Macromarketing,* 4 (Spring), 53-60.

Dixon, Donald F. (1981), "The Role of Marketing in Early Theories of Economic Development," *Journal of Macromarketing,* 1 (Fall), 19-35.

Drucker, Peter F. (1958), "Marketing and Economic Development," *Journal of Marketing,* 23 (January), 252-59.

Duhaime, Carole P., Ronald McTavish, and Christopher A. Ross (1985), "Social Marketing: An Approach to Third-World Development," *Journal of Macromarketing,* 5 (Spring), 3-13.

El-Ansary, Adel I. and Oscar E. Kramer (1973), "Social Marketing: The Family Planning Experience," *Journal of Marketing,* 37 (July), 1-7.

Escobar, Arturo (1995), *Encountering Development: The Making and Unmaking of the Third World.* Princeton, NJ: Princeton University Press.

Ewen, Stuart (1988), *All Consuming Images: The Politics of Style in Contemporary Culture.* New York: Basic Books.

Farley, John U. and Harold Leavitt (1971), "Marketing and Population Problems," *Journal of Marketing,* 35 (July), 28-33.

Ferretti, William M. and William Lesser (1985), *The New York Returnable Beverage Container Law: The First Year* (report of the Nelson A. Rockefeller Institute of Government to the Temporary State Commission on Returnable Beverage Containers). Albany: State University of New York Press.

Firat, A. Fuat and Nikhilesh Dholakia (1982), "Consumption Choices at the Macro Level," *Journal of Macromarketing,* 2 (Fall), 6-15.

—— and —— (1998), *Consuming People: From Political Economy to Theaters of Consumption.* London: Routledge.

Fontana, Marzia, Susan Joekes, and Rachel Masika (1998), "Global Trade Expansion and Liberalisation: Gender Issues and Impacts," Report No. 42, University of Sussex, Institute of Development Studies.

Fox, Karen F. and Philip Kotler (1980), "The Marketing of Social Causes: The First 10 Years," *Journal of Marketing,* 44 (Fall), 24-33.

Gavzer, Bernard (1999), "Take Out the Trash and Put It . . . Where?" *Parade Magazine,* June 13, 4-6.

Goetz, Anne Marie and Rina Sen Gupta (1996), "Who Takes the Credit? Gender, Power, and Control over Loan Use in Rural Credit Programs in Bangladesh," *World Development,* 24 (1), 45-63.

Grabowski, Barbara (1980), *The Michigan Bottle Bill: One Year after.* Lansing: Michigan United Conservation Clubs.

Greenlee, Timothy (1997), "Alternative Communication Strategies to Influence Risky Behavior: Addressing AIDS Pandemic," doctoral dissertation, University of Rhode Island.

Hastings, G. B. and B. Elliott (1993), "Social Marketing Practice in Traffic Safety," in *Marketing of Traffic Safety.* Paris: Organization for Economic Cooperation and Development, 35-53.

Hornik, Robert (1989), "The Knowledge-Behavior Gap in Public Information Campaigns: A Development Communication View," in *Information Campaigns: Balancing Social Values and Social Change,* Charles T. Salmon, ed. Newbury Park, CA: Sage, 113-38.

Howes, David, ed. (1996), *Cross-Cultural Consumption: Global Markets, Local Realities.* London: Routledge.

Jackelen, Henry R. and E. Rhyne (1991), "Towards a More Market Oriented Approach to Credit and Savings for the Poor," *Small Enterprise Development,* 2 (December).

Johnson, Arthur (1991), "Eco-Hype: Consumer Beware—'Green' Products Might not Be What They Seem," *The Financial Post Magazine,* May, 17-22.

Joy, Annamma and Christopher A. Ross (1989), "Marketing and Development in Third World Contexts: An Evaluation and Future Directions," *Journal of Macromarketing,* 9 (Fall), 17-31.

Kotler, Philip and Sidney J. Levy (1969), "Broadening the Concept of Marketing," *Journal of Marketing,* 33 (January), 10-15.

—— and Eduardo L. Roberto (1989), *Social Marketing Strategies for Changing Public Behavior.* New York: Free Press.

—— and Gerald Zaltman (1971), "Social Marketing: An Approach to Planned Social Change," *Journal of Marketing,* 35 (July), 3-12.

Kumcu, Erdogan and A. Fuat Firat, eds. (1989), *Marketing and Development: Toward Broader Dimensions.* Greenwich, CT: JAI.

Labelle, Huguette (1998), *CBC Radio World Report* [on-air interview], August 3.

Leelakulthanit, Orose, Ralph Day, and Rockney Walters (1991), "Investigating the Relationship between Marketing and Overall Satisfaction with Life in a Developing Country," *Journal of Macromarketing,* 11 (Spring), 3-23.

Levy, Sidney J. and Philip Kotler (1969), "Beyond Marketing: The Furthering Concept," *California Management Review,* 12 (Winter), 67-73.

MacKeen, Dawn (1998), "A Few Good Men Banking on Poor Women," *Salon,* February 12. Available: http://www.salon.com/mwt/fgm/1998/02/12fgm.html

McKitterick, J. B. (1957), "What Is the Marketing Management Concept?" in *The Frontiers of Marketing Thought and Science,* Frank M. Bass, ed. Chicago: American Marketing Association.

Murthy, Kinnera (1991), "Development and Social Change: Need for a Social Marketing Approach," in *Third International Conference on Marketing and Development,* Ruby R. Dholakia and Kiran C. Bothra, eds. Muncie, IN: International Society for Marketing and Development, 82-87.

Neff, Gina (1996), "Microcredit, Microresults," *Left Business Observer,* October. Available: http://www.panix.com/~dhenwood/micro.html

Peet, Richard and Michael Watts, eds. (1996), *Liberation Ecology: Environment, Development, Social Movements.* London: Routledge.

Population Information Program (1980), "Social Marketing: Does It Work?" in *Population Reports,* Family Planning Programs, Series J, No. 21. Baltimore, MD: Johns Hopkins University Press.

Rangan, V. Kasturi, Sohel Karim, and Sheryl K. Sandberg (1996), "Do Better at Doing Good," *Harvard Business Review,* 74 (May-June), 42-54.

Rathje, William L. (1989), "Rubbish!" *Atlantic Monthly,* December, 1-10.

Roberto, Eduardo (1975), *Strategic Decision-Making in a Social Program: The Case of Family Planning Diffusion.* Lexington, MA: Lexington Books.

Rothschild, Michael (1999), "Carrots, Sticks, and Promises: A Conceptual Framework for the Management of Public Health and Social Issue Behaviors," *Journal of Marketing,* 63 (October), 24-37.

Salmon, Charles T. (1989), "Preface," in *Information Campaigns: Balancing Social Values and Social Change,* Charles T. Salmon, ed. Newbury Park, CA: Sage, 7-13.

Sjolander, Richard and Henry C. K. Chen (1989), "The Macromarketing Effects of Beverage Container Legislation," *Journal of Macromarketing,* 9 (Spring), 24-34.

Solomon, Lawrence (1997-98), "Planners from Hell: The Little Bank that Couldn't," *The Next City,* Winter [on-line]. Available: http://www.nextcity.com/main/town/10planners.htm

Svenska Dagbladet (1988), *Hojre Pant Satte Fart pa Returerna* (Higher Deposit Increased Returns). Stockholm, Sweden: Svenska Dagbladet.

Todd, Helen (1996), *Women at the Center: Grameen Bank Borrowers after One Decade.* Boulder CO: Westview.

Togeson, A. A. (1956), "The Switch from a Sales to a Marketing Concept," in *Broadening Horizons in Marketing,* Marketing series, No. 96, M. J. Dooher and Elizabeth Marting, eds. New York: American Management Association, 26-37.

Wahid, Abu N. M. (1993), *The Grameen Bank: Poverty Relief in Bangladesh.* Boulder CO: Westview.

———— (1994), "The Grameen Bank and Poverty Alleviation in Bangladesh: Theory, Evidence, and Limitations," *American Journal of Economics and Sociology,* 53 (January), 1-15.

Walsh, Diana Chapman, Rima E. Rudd, Barbara A. Moeykens, and Thomas W. Moloney (1993), "Social Marketing for Public Health," *Health Affairs,* Summer, 104-19.

Wood, Van R. and Scott J. Vitell (1986), "Marketing and Economic Development: Review, Synthesis, and Evaluation," *Journal of Macromarketing,* 6 (Spring), 28-48.

Worldwatch Institute (1999), *Providence Journal,* July 4, D3. (Chart)

Zaltman, Gerald and Ilan Vertinsky (1971), "Health Service Marketing: A Suggested Model," *Journal of Marketing,* 35 (July), 19-27.

Zikmund, William G. and William J. Stanton (1971), "Recycling Solid Wastes: A Channel-of-Distribution Problem," *Journal of Marketing,* 35 (July), 34-39.

Zimmerman, Robert (1997), *Social Marketing Strategies for Campus Prevention of Alcohol and Other Drug Problems.* Newton, MA: Education Development Center.

Theories and Models in Social Marketing

R. Craig Lefebvre

Theories and models for social marketing abound, with little formal consensus on which types of models for what types of social problems in what types of situations are most appropriate. In defining what social marketing is, many authors include the notion of exchange theory to link it to its marketing roots (Kotler and Roberto 1989; Lefebvre and Flora 1988; Novelli 1990). Other writers on the subject omit any mention of exchange theory either in their definitions of social marketing or in their discussions of its key elements (Andreasen 1995; Manoff 1985). Elliott (1991), in a review of the exchange concept's place in social marketing, concluded that it "is either absent or obtuse" (p. 157). Adding to this confusion are other authors who refer to a "social marketing theory" (Gries, Black, and Coster 1995; Tomes 1994).

Although authors such as Lefebvre and Rochlin (1997) and Novelli (1990) recognized the value of the exchange concept in describing social marketing, both held open the idea that many other theoretical models may be applied in the actual development of social marketing programs. "Marketing is theory based. It is predicated on theories of consumer behavior, which in turn draw upon the social and behavioral sciences" (Novelli 1990, p. 343). In fact, this is what happens in the practice of social marketing. However, Walsh and colleagues (1993) noted that "professional social marketers tend to be broadly eclectic and intuitive tinkerers in their use of available theory" (p. 115). So, although a review of theoretical models used in social marketing seems relevant to advance the field, it also is speculative. Many social marketers do not report on their work in professional journals or at conferences, and of those who do, only a few focus on the theoretical models that affected their judgments on selection of target audiences, questions posed during formative research studies, strategies selected, how program elements were selected and developed, what outcomes were intended, and how they were measured.

The theories selected for review reflect my own experience and interaction with a broad array of social marketers and social marketing programs. The theories also reflect a public health bias in that most social marketing programs in this field are designed by people with advanced degrees in social and behavioral science advancing public health goals, not by people with training in other fields (e.g., business management, economics) or focusing on other issues (e.g., environment, education, justice). As a benchmark, a review of the most commonly used theories and models in 497 health education/health promotion articles over a two-year period found that the health belief model, social cognitive theory, theory of reasoned action, community organization, stages of change, and social marketing were the most frequently cited ones (in that order) among the 67% of cases in which theories or models were mentioned at all (Glanz, Lewis, and Rimer 1997, p. 29).

Health Belief Model

As already noted, the health belief model (HBM) is one of the most widely used theories among public health practitioners, and many of its major tenets have found their way into social marketing projects. The HBM originally was designed to explain why people did not participate in programs to prevent or detect diseases. The core components of the HBM are as follows:

- *Perceived susceptibility:* the subjective perception of risk of developing a particular health condition

- *Perceived severity:* feelings about the seriousness of the consequences of developing a specific health problem

- *Perceived benefits:* beliefs about the effectiveness of various actions that might reduce susceptibility and severity (the latter two taken together are labeled "threat")

- *Perceived barriers:* potential negative aspects of taking specific actions

- *Cues to action:* bodily or environmental events that trigger action

More recently, the HBM has been appended to include the notion of self-efficacy as another predictor of health behaviors, especially more complex ones in which lifestyle changes must be maintained over time (Strecher and Rosenstock 1997). A wide variety of demographic, social, psychological, and structural variables also may affect individuals' perceptions and, indirectly, their health-related behaviors. Some of the more important ones include educational attainment, age, gender, socioeconomic status, and prior knowledge.

The HBM has been one of the more empirically studied theoretical models. A mid-1980s review of this research (Janz and Becker 1984), conducted across numerous health and screening behaviors (e.g., receiving flu shots, practicing breast self-examinations, using seat belts, attending screening programs), found not only substantial support for the model but also that the perceived barriers component was the strongest predictor across studies and behaviors. Among studies that looked at sick role behaviors (e.g., compliance with medication regimens, self-help behaviors among people with diabetes), perceived benefits proved to be the strongest predictor of engaging in health behaviors. As social marketers make choices about the theoretical models they use in their programs, this finding of different predictors of various types of behaviors needs to be heeded so that a particular theory or model is not wrongly applied.

For social marketing research and practice, the HBM becomes a salient theoretical model when addressing issues for at-risk populations who might not perceive themselves as such. Issues of fear- or anxiety-arousing messages often take place within the context of increasing perceived threat. The HBM components of barriers and benefits seem to be common issues addressed by many social marketing programs, especially in price and placement decisions. Finally, the cues to action component, although the least researched among the components, is another piece of the HBM that many social marketing programs attempt to address either explicitly or implicitly.

Theory of Reasoned Action

The theory of reasoned action (TRA) organizes itself around the constructs of behavioral and normative beliefs, attitudes, intentions, and behavior. An extension of the TRA, the theory of planned behavior (TPB), adds the construct of self-efficacy or one's perceived control over performance of the behavior. In the TRA, the most important predictor of subsequent behavior is one's intention to act. This behavioral intention is influenced by one's attitude toward engaging in the behavior and the subjective norm that one has about the behavior. Attitude, in turn, is determined by one's beliefs about both the outcomes and attributes associated with the behavior. Subjective norms are based on one's normative beliefs that reflect how significant referent people apprise the behavior, either positively or negatively. Referents may range from one's family to one's physician, peers, or models. The TPB adds the construct of perceived behavioral control that is determined by one's "control beliefs" (the presence or absence of resources and impediments to engage in the behavior) and "perceived power" (the weighting of each resource and barrier).

In their review of the TRA and TPB, Montano, Kasprzyk, and Taplin (1997) reported that they "cannot stress enough the importance of conducting in-depth, open-ended elicitation interviews to identify the behavioral outcomes, referents, and facilitators and constraints that are relevant to the particular behavior and population" (p. 109). These elicitation interviews are conducted during the early planning stages of the project and usually include 15 to 20 participants equally divided between those who currently are engaging or planning to engage in the behavior and those who are not. The authors noted that the TRA and TPB provide a framework for these interviews on which programs should focus to ascertain what beliefs should be the focus of intervention efforts.

Social marketers often employ the TRA and TPB, although they usually are implicit and incomplete. Subjective norms and referents, for example, often are the focus of social marketing programs (e.g., teen tobacco use prevention), even though the theoretical model might not be familiar to the planners. Although one sees great attention given to this half of the TRA "equation," one rarely sees the same level of concern given to how to change the attitudes toward the behavior itself. An exception was the 5 A Day for Better Health program (Sutton, Balch, and Lefebvre 1995) in which formative research discovered that members of the target audience perceived people who ate five servings of fruits and vegetables a day as less capable, less dependable, less gentle, and less friendly than themselves. This insight helped the program planners to design and develop materials that could counter these negative attitudes as they fashioned the image of the program.

Social Cognitive Theory

Social cognitive theory (SCT) explains behavior in terms of triadic reciprocality ("reciprocal determinism") in which behavior, cognitive and other interpersonal factors, and environmental events all operate as interacting determinants of each other. In contrast to the previous theoretical models, SCT explicitly recognizes that behavior is not determined by just intrinsic factors or that individuals are products of their environments but rather that individuals have an influence on what they do, their personal characteristics, how they respond to their environments, and what their environments are. Changes in any of these three factors are hypothesized to render changes in the others.

One of the key concepts in SCT is an environmental variable, observational learning. In contrast to earlier behavioral theories, SCT views the environment as one that not only reinforces or punishes behaviors but also provides a milieu where one can watch the actions of others and learn the consequences of those behaviors. Processes governing observational learning are as follows:

- *Attentional:* gaining and maintaining attention

- *Retention:* being remembered

- *Production:* reproducing the observed behavior

- *Motivational:* being stimulated to produce the behavior

Other core components of SCT include the following:

- *Self-efficacy:* a judgment of one's capability to accomplish a certain level of performance

- *Outcome expectation:* a judgment of the likely consequences that such behavior will produce

- *Outcome expectancies:* the value placed on the consequences of the behavior

- *Emotional coping responses:* strategies used to deal with emotional stimuli including psychological defenses (e.g., denial, repression), cognitive techniques (e.g., problem restructuring), and stress management

- *Enactive learning:* learning from the consequences of one's actions (vs. observational learning)

- *Rule learning:* generating and regulating behavioral patterns, most often achieved through vicarious processes and capabilities (vs. direct experience)

- *Self-regulatory capability:* much behavior motivated and regulated by internal standards and self-evaluative reactions to people's own actions

SCT is viewed as one of the more comprehensive efforts to explain human behavior (Baranowski, Perry, and Parcel 1997). Its focus on reciprocal determinism and self-efficacy (the latter, as we have seen, has been adopted by other theoretical models as well) gives social marketers a strong theoretical base from which to launch environmental interventions that complement individually focused ones such as with the Team Nutrition program for fourth graders (Lefebvre, Olander, and Levine 1999). A major finding of this research project was that it was the number of different channels through which children were exposed to Team Nutrition messages, rather than any particular component, that was most predictive of self-reported behavior change. SCT also reminds program planners to assess audience members' perceptions of their ability to perform the desired behavior, the anticipated consequences of that action, and the value that they place on those consequences. The theory also underlies many attempts to model new behaviors for the target audience and that attention, retention, production, and motivational processes all must be addressed for effective learning and performing of new behaviors.

The Transtheoretical Model of Health Behavior Change

The transtheoretical model of health behavior change, popularly known as "stages of change," has become one of the more often used models in social marketing programs. Although this model was being applied by social marketing programs during the early 1990s to increase physical activity levels of community residents (Marcus et al. 1992), its incorporation by Andreasen (1995) as the theoretical model for *Marketing Social Change* no doubt has influenced its adoption by many social marketing practitioners.

The model emerged from an analysis of leading theories of psychotherapy and behavior change in which 10 distinct processes of change were identified. These processes suggest certain types of interventions that will be most appropriate for moving people through six specific stages of change. Some of the processes identified by Prochaska and Velicer (1997) include the following:

- *Consciousness raising:* increases awareness of the causes and consequences of, as well as the cures for, a problem behavior (feedback, education, confrontation, and media campaigns are possible intervention modalities)

- *Self-reevaluation:* uses assessments of one's self-image with and without a particular unhealthy behavior (value clarification, healthy role models, and imagery techniques can help people to move evaluatively)

- *Social liberation:* increases the social opportunities or alternatives, especially for people already relatively deprived or oppressed (advocacy, empowerment techniques, and policy changes are procedures that can be used to meet these goals)

- *Helping relationships:* combines caring, trust, openness, acceptance, and support for health behavior change (strategies such as relationship building, counselor calls, and buddy systems can be sources for such support)

The most popular and utilized aspect of the model are the stages themselves. They consist of the following:

- *Precontemplation:* people not intending to take action in the foreseeable future, usually measured as the next six months

- *Contemplation:* people indicating that they are planning to take action (change behavior) within the next six months

- *Preparation:* people indicating that they will take action during the next month and have a plan of action

- *Action:* people having made specific behavioral changes during the past six months

- *Maintenance:* people working at preventing relapse and using many of the processes described earlier to help them maintain their changes (lasts anywhere from six months to three years)

- *Termination:* described as "the stage in which individuals have zero temptation and 100% self-efficacy" (people sure that they will not return to their old behaviors or habits) (Prochaska and Velicer 1997, p. 39)

Other concepts in the model include decisional balance (weighing the pros and cons of changing), self-efficacy, and temptation (the role of negative affect or emotional distress, positive social situations, and craving). What the model attempts to drive home to social marketers is that relatively few members of a target audience are ready for action-oriented programs and that more time and energy must be directed to moving people out of the earlier stages in which they are "stuck" through attention to other processes (e.g., consciousness raising, social liberation). Prochaska and Velicer's (1997) research indicates that people use specific processes in specific phases and that, generally speaking, experiential processes (consciousness raising, environmental reevaluation, self-reevaluation, and dramatic relief) are most appropriate for people in the pre-contemplation and contemplation stages. People in the action and maintenance phases are more likely to use behavioral processes such as contingency management, helping relationships, counterconditioning, and stimulus control.

Matching interventions to the stages individuals are in then becomes a critical factor in the effectiveness of the program to lead to behavior change.

Prochaska and Velicer (1997) also reported on a series of 12 studies looking at how pros and cons change as people progress through the stages for a variety of health behaviors. In all cases, the cons clearly outnumbered the pros for changing with people in the precontemplation phase. By the time people were in the contemplation phase, the number of pros had increased and surpassed the number of cons (which had not changed). Moving from contemplation to action required the number of cons to begin decreasing while the number of pros remained steady or even increased slightly. The mathematical relationships between pros and cons led the authors to conclude that pros must increase twice as much as cons decrease to move an individual from precontemplation to action. The implication for social marketers is that perhaps twice as much effort should be spent on raising the benefits for change as on reducing perceived costs and barriers.

Diffusion of Innovations

What should be one of the more important models for people who are attempting to influence the behavior of large groups of people is diffusion of innovations. Kotler and Roberto (1989) reviewed diffusion of innovations research and its application to social marketing programs. One of the first points they made was that there are different types of adopters in every target audience that, based on hundreds of studies, usually are represented in certain proportions and have unique motivations for adopting new behaviors. These five adopter segments and their motives are as follows:

- *Innovator (2.5%):* need novelty and need to be different

- *Early adopter (13.5%):* recognize the value of adoption from contact with innovators

- *Early majority (34.0%):* need to imitate or match up with others with a certain amount of deliberateness

- *Late majority (34.0%):* need to jump on the bandwagon when seeing that the early majority has legitimated the change

- *Laggard (16.0%):* need to respect traditions

In other work, Rogers (1983) went into great detail as to how these five segments differ with respect to demographics, communication patterns, and other variables.

A second group of diffusion of innovation concepts centers around the determinants of the speed and extent of diffusion (Oldenburg, Hardcastle, and Kok 1997). Some of these attributes include the following:

- *Relative advantage:* whether the new behavior is better, easier, and simpler than what people currently do

- *Compatibility:* whether the behavior fits into people's lifestyles, cultural/ethnic beliefs and practices, and self-images

- *Trialability:* whether the behavior be tried before making a final commitment

- *Communicability:* whether the behavior can be understood clearly and easily

- *Risk:* whether the behavior can be adopted with minimal risk and uncertainty

Rothman and colleagues (1983) provided the best integrated discussion of how diffusion research influenced the development of a social marketing campaign directed at community mental health workers. Some of their theoretical concerns, which led to empirical investigations, centered on the notion of "reference group appeals." In their case, the question was how to position the offering. Should the benefit be a bureaucratic or agency one (e.g., more efficient operations), a professional one (e.g., improving knowledge and skills), or a community/client one (e.g., in people's best interest)? Their review of diffusion research, especially in organizational settings, led the authors to quickly conclude that the community/client appeal was likely to be the least effective of the three. Consequently, they focused their project on the other two appeals.

Rothman and colleagues (1983) also looked at the varying effects of high-intensity "personal selling" approaches to diffusion/marketing, as contrasted with a low-intensity "mass communication" approach. In their analysis of cost versus utilization (adoption) patterns, the authors concluded, "For half the cost, the low-intensity approach resulted in twice the amount of high utilization" (p. 222).

Diffusion of innovations research and concepts offer a tremendous amount of insight for social marketers to use in designing their programs, yet we see very little active discussion of it in social marketing circles (e.g., Andreasen [1995] does not index the term). Diffusion of innovations has many "big" ideas that, when meeting constrained budgets and short time horizons, might receive short shrift. Basic to the notion of adopter segments, for example, is the implication that one starts with one or two segments (innovators and early adopters), and only when adoption is successful with them does one move to the "bigger numbers." Phased approaches over time often are impossible to plan and implement when priorities change and when budgets contract and expand with little warning. Yet, other concepts related to how to make adoption happen more quickly and efficiently can be applied in most contexts with minimal impact on resources. As was mentioned at the beginning of this section, the diffusion model is one of the few population-focused models available to social marketers. Although the point can be made that behavior change ultimately happens on an individual level, diffusion research suggests that there are processes available to manage widespread behavior change and not leave it to chance (cf. Redmond's [1996] discussion of diffusion of the adoption of nonsmoking).

Other Theories and Models

As was noted at the beginning at this chapter, there are few guides as to what theories and models many social marketers use in planning and implementing social change programs because not enough is written about that aspect of their work. However, several segmentation studies have suggested other possible theories and models, applications of social marketing in nontraditional settings offer other models, and ongoing social marketing projects focused on specific health behaviors have developed their own models based on their research findings and experiences.

Morris, Tabak, and Olins (1992) reported on a segmentation analysis of prescription drug information-seeking motives among the elderly. The authors used the HBM, information-seeking research (usually subsumed under the transactional model of stress and coping [Lerman and Glanz 1997]), information processing models, consumer involvement models, and a typology for consumer motivation. Slater and Flora (1991) reviewed data from the Stanford Five-City Project and identified seven healthy lifestyle segments. Their theoretical approach to segmentation included SCT, the HBM, and the TRA. In an extension of this work to Hispanic audiences, Williams and Flora (1995) also noted the use of several concepts drawn from the fields of anthropology, advertising research, and communications literature.

Murray and Douglas (1988) examined the role that social marketing could play in the alcohol policy arena. Their analysis of the many ways in which social marketing could be used in helping to shape social policies about alcohol (and other issues as well) brings to light the political science and public opinion research and theories that also could be employed in designing certain social marketing projects.

A number of large-scale social marketing programs were conducted in community settings where community organization theories played a role in program development and implementation. Some examples include the Stanford Five-City Project (Farquhar, Maccoby, and Solomon 1984) and the Pawtucket Heart Health Program (Lefebvre et al. 1987). McKee (1992) discussed several different programs that have combined social marketing with social mobilization strategies; Lefebvre (1990) outlined how social marketing can be used to facilitate institutionalization, or long-term sustainability, of community-based programs; and Bryant and colleagues (1999) combined community organization theories and social marketing principles into a "community-based prevention marketing" model. Because many social marketing programs are developed by state and local agencies, we can expect that even more work along these lines will help to increase our understanding of how to effectively engage and leverage "the community" to achieve social change objectives.

Piotrow and colleagues (1997) summarized their 25 years of work in reproductive health and family planning overseas. They developed a theoretical framework, based on their experience, termed "steps to behavior change" (SBC). As they described it, the SBC "is an adaptation of diffusion of innovations theory and the input/output persuasion model, enriched by social marketing experience and flexible enough to use other theories within each of the steps, or stages, as appropriate" (p. 21). The five major stages are knowledge, approval, intention, practice, and advocacy, each with three "steps" subsumed under it (e.g., can name family planning methods and/or sources of supply, approves of family planning, intends to consult a provider, chooses a method and begins family planning use, advocates practice to others). Other theoretical models that the authors mentioned included SCT; the TRA; social influence, social comparison, and convergence theories; theories of emotional response; and the cultivation theory of mass media.

Conclusion

Trying to depict what theories and models social marketers use in designing and implementing programs is a daunting task. Social marketers who have advanced degrees, and who thus have studied "theories," might be using this knowledge in an a priori fashion to influence decisions as to what problem to tackle, how to segment audiences, what program objectives should be, which target audiences to choose and how to characterize them, what questions to ask in formative research activities, how to develop program strategies and tactics, which ones to choose, how to go about developing and testing them, how to organize and manage the implementation/distribution process, which message may best resonate with the target audience, what benefits and barriers are most in need of attention, and how to best promote their messages and products/services (to list just a few key decision points). My suspicion is that in 20% of the cases, this is a conscious process. As was noted at the beginning of the chapter, when Walsh and colleagues (1993) conducted more than 30 interviews with leading social marketers, one of their conclusions was that eclecticism and intuition seemed to be the primary determinants of theories used in social marketing.

Another disquieting finding is that there is little understanding of when social marketers are using "theory," "models," or the results of specific research studies. There also is the question of whether they know for certain what is a theory versus a model. Although there are indications of models ascending to theory status (e.g., people referring to diffusion theory or stages of change theory), what appears to be happening is that social marketers are more "model based" (with stages of change being the most popular at this particular point in time) and that there is some theory (model) creep (i.e., one model or theory is applied regardless of whether the situation or previous research supports its application).

When behavior change theories are employed, they are used in a context of changing individuals' behavior. Although this objective is a bottom-line focus for many social marketers, the promise of social marketing over other approaches to social change is its overall focus on influencing population groups to achieve social change objectives. Yet, aside from the diffusion of innovations model, one can see no evidence of "population-based" theories and models being reflected in social marketing literature or discourse.

Behavior change is a complex process, and there are dozens of theories and models to choose from to meet social marketing objectives. Too much attention seems to be given to individual theories of change in the published literature. Social marketing is not an alternative to individual behavior change strategies; rather, it is a process to increase the prevalence of specific behaviors among target audiences (Lefebvre et al. 1995). Social marketers need to expand their knowledge and use of divergent theoretical frameworks as the situations dictate. Winett (1995) demonstrated one approach to integrating social marketing constructs with behavioral theories. In examining the "four Ps," he argued that various theories might be most appropriate for thinking through each component:

Variable	Theory
Product	Diffusion theory
	Stages of change
Price	Behavior analysis
	Social cognitive theory
Promotion	Theory of reasoned action
	Health belief model
	Protection motivation theory
	Social cognitive theory
	Behavior analysis
Place	Public health
	Ecological

In his discussion of this integrative approach, Winett (1995) also noted that most of the behavioral theories seem to focus predominantly on the promotion elements of the marketing mix. His suggestion—and one echoed here—is that perhaps more attention needs to given to theoretical models that might add insight to other elements of the marketing process and marketing mix.

Social change is an enormous undertaking, and to paraphrase a graduate adviser, "The one with the biggest toolbox wins." Using multiple theories and models that fit or explain the behavior and situation with which one is challenged, including not only the ones discussed here but also motivational theories to inform message development, social network theories to inform message dissemination, organizational development and business-to-business marketing models to inform coalition and partnership development and management, political theories and agenda-setting research to inform policy initiatives, and cross-cultural theories to inform international social marketing efforts, is what social marketers must aspire to do so as to meet both the personal and social goals of "doing good."

References

Andreasen, Alan R. (1995), *Marketing Social Change.* San Francisco: Jossey-Bass.
Baranowski, Tom, Cheryl L. Perry, and Guy S. Parcel (1997), "Social Cognitive Theory," in *Health Behavior and Health Education,* 2nd ed., Karen Glanz, F. M. Lewis, and B. K. Rimer, eds. San Francisco: Jossey-Bass, 153-78.
Bryant, Carol A., Melinda S. Forthofer, Kelli McCormack Brown, and Robert J. McDermott (1999), "Community-Based Prevention Marketing," *Social Marketing Quarterly,* 5 (3), 54-59.

Elliott, Barry J. (1991), "A Re-Examination of the Social Marketing Concept," unpublished master's thesis, University of New South Wales.

Farquhar, John W., Nathan Maccoby, and Douglas S. Solomon (1984), "Community Applications of Behavioral Medicine," in *Handbook of Behavioral Medicine,* W. Doyle Gentry, ed. New York: Guilford, 437-78.

Glanz, Karen, Frances Marcus Lewis, and Barbara K. Rimer, eds. (1997), *Health Behavior and Health Education,* 2nd ed. San Francisco: Jossey-Bass.

Gries, Julie A., David R. Black, and Daniel C. Coster (1995), "Recruitment to a University Alcohol Program: Evaluation of Social Marketing Theory and Stepped Approach Model," *Preventive Medicine,* 24, 348-56.

Janz, Nancy K. and Marshall H. Becker (1984), "The Health Belief Model: A Decade Later," *Health Education Quarterly,* 11, 1-47.

Kotler, Philip and Eduardo L. Roberto (1989), *Social Marketing.* New York: Free Press.

Lefebvre, R. Craig (1990), "Strategies to Maintain and Institutionalize Successful Programs: A Marketing Framework," in *Health Promotion at the Community Level,* Neil Bracht, ed. Newbury Park, CA: Sage.

———— and June A. Flora (1988), "Social Marketing and Public Health Intervention," *Health Education Quarterly,* 15, 299-315.

————, Thomas M. Lasater, Richard A. Carleton, and Gussie Peterson (1987), "Theory and Delivery of Health Programming in the Community: The Pawtucket Heart Health Program," *Preventive Medicine,* 16, 80-95.

————, Deborah Lurie, Laura Saunders Goodman, Linda Weinberg, and Kathleen Loughrey (1995), "Social Marketing and Nutrition Education: Inappropriate or Misunderstood?" *Journal of Nutrition Education,* 27 (3), 146-50.

————, Carol Olander, and Elyse Levine (1999), "The Impact of Multiple Channel Delivery of Nutrition Messages on Student Knowledge, Motivation, and Behavior: Results from the Team Nutrition Pilot Study," *Social Marketing Quarterly,* 5 (3), 90-98.

———— and Lisa Rochlin (1997), "Social Marketing," in *Health Behavior and Health Education,* 2nd ed., Karen Glanz, F. M. Lewis, and B. K. Rimer, eds. San Francisco: Jossey-Bass, 384-402.

Lerman, Caryn and Karen Glanz (1997), "Stress, Coping, and Health Behavior," in *Health Behavior and Health Education,* 2nd ed., Karen Glanz, F. M. Lewis, and B. K. Rimer, eds. San Francisco: Jossey-Bass, 113-38.

Manoff, Richard K. (1985), *Social Marketing.* New York: Praeger.

Marcus, Bess H., Stephen W. Banspach, R. Craig Lefebvre, Joseph S. Rossi, Richard A. Carleton, and David B. Abrams (1992), "Using the Stages of Change Model to Increase the Adoption of Physical Activity among Community Participants," *American Journal of Health Promotion,* 6 (6), 424-29.

McKee, Neill (1992), *Social Mobilization and Social Marketing in Developing Communities.* Panang, Malaysia: Southbound.

Montano, Daniel E., Danuta Kasprzyk, and Stephen H. Taplin (1997), "The Theory of Reasoned Action and the Theory of Planned Behavior," in *Health Behavior and Health Education,* 2nd ed., Karen Glanz, F. M. Lewis, and B. K. Rimer, eds. San Francisco: Jossey-Bass, 85-112.

Morris, Louis A., Ellen Tabak, and Nancy J. Olins (1992), "A Segmentation Analysis of Prescription Drug Information-Seeking Motives among the Elderly," *Journal of Public Policy & Marketing,* 11 (2), 115-25.

Murray, Glen G. and Ronald R. Douglas (1988), "Social Marketing in the Alcohol Policy Arena," *British Journal of Addiction,* 83, 505-11.

Novelli, William D. (1990), "Applying Social Marketing to Health Promotion and Disease Prevention," in *Health Behavior and Health Education,* 2nd ed., Karen Glanz, F. M. Lewis, and B. K. Rimer, eds. San Francisco: Jossey-Bass, 342-69.

Oldenburg, Brian, Deborah M. Hardcastle, and Gerjo Kok (1997), "Diffusion of Innovations," in *Health Behavior and Health Education,* 2nd ed., Karen Glanz, F. M. Lewis, and B. K. Rimer, eds. San Francisco: Jossey-Bass, 270-86.

Piotrow, Phyllis Tilson, D. Lawrence Kincaid, Jose G. Rimon, II, and Ward Rinehart (1997), *Health Communication.* Westport, CT: Praeger.

Prochaska, James O. and Wayne F. Velicer (1997), "The Transtheoretical Model Of Health Behavior Change," *American Journal of Health Promotion,* 12 (1), 38-48.

Redmond, William H. (1996), "Product Disadoption: Quitting Smoking as a Diffusion Process," *Journal of Public Policy & Marketing,* 15 (1), 87-97.

Rogers, Everett M. (1983), *Diffusion of Innovations.* New York: Free Press.

Rothman, Jack, Joseph G. Teresa, Terrence L. Kay, and Gershom Clark Morningstar (1983), *Marketing Human Service Innovations.* Beverly Hills, CA: Sage.

Slater, Michael D. and June A. Flora (1991), "Health Lifestyles: Audience Segmentation Analysis for Public Health Interventions," *Health Education Quarterly,* 18 (2), 221-33.

Strecher, Victor J. and Irwin M. Rosenstock (1997), "The Health Belief Model," in *Health Behavior and Health Education,* 2nd ed., Karen Glanz, F. M. Lewis, and B. K. Rimer, eds. San Francisco: Jossey-Bass, 41-59.

Sutton, Sharyn M., George I. Balch, and R. Craig Lefebvre (1995), "Strategic Questions for Consumer-Based Health Communication," *Public Health Reports,* 9, 725-33.

Tomes, Keith (1994), "Marketing and the Mass Media: Theory and Myth," *Health Education Research,* 9 (2), 165-69.

Walsh, Diana Chapman, Rima E. Rudd, Barbara A. Moeykens, and Thomas W. Maloney (1993), "Social Marketing for Public Health," *Health Affairs,* Summer, 104-19.

Williams, Janice E. and June A. Flora (1995), "Health Behavior Segmentation and Campaign Planning to Reduce Cardiovascular Disease Risk among Hispanics," *Health Education Quarterly,* 22 (1), 36-48.

Winett, Richard A. (1995), "A Framework for Health Promotion and Disease Prevention Programs," *American Psychologist,* 50, 341-50.

Index

About the Authors

Editors:

Paul N. Bloom is Professor of Marketing in the Kenan-Flagler Business School at the University of North Carolina at Chapel Hill. He holds a Ph.D. in marketing from the Kellogg School at Northwestern University and an M.B.A. from the Wharton School at the University of Pennsylvania. His undergraduate degree is from Lehigh University. He is a frequent contributor to marketing journals on topics related to consumer protection, antitrust, and social marketing. One of his articles won the award for the outstanding article published in the *Journal of Public Policy & Marketing* for 1987 to 1991. He also has authored or co-authored several books including *Knowledge Development in Marketing: The MSI Experience* (1987). He has served on a variety of editorial review boards and in leadership roles within the American Marketing Association (AMA) and the Association for Consumer Research. He was a member of the AMA's Task Force on the Development of Marketing Thought and, most recently, served as chair of the AMA's Marketing and Society special interest group. He formerly held posts as a visiting scholar at the Marketing Science Institute and with the faculty of the University of Maryland at College Park.

Gregory T. Gundlach is Associate Professor of Marketing in the College of Business Administration at the University of Notre Dame. His primary research interests focus on the legal aspects of marketing, particularly interorganizational trade relations, competition, and governance. His articles have appeared in the *Journal of Marketing, Journal of Marketing Research, Marketing Science, Journal of Business Research, Journal of Public Policy & Marketing, Antitrust Bulletin, Journal of Business Venturing, Journal of Retailing,* and *Journal of the Academy of Marketing Science* as well as in numerous American Marketing Association (AMA) publications. He currently is editor of the Legal Developments section of the *Journal of Public Policy & Marketing* and is a member of the editorial boards of the *Journal of Marketing, Journal of Public Policy & Marketing, Journal of Retailing,* and *Journal of the Academy of Marketing Science.* He also has served as chair of the AMA's Marketing and Society special interest group.

Contributors:

Andrew V. Abela is Lecturer in Marketing in the McIntire School of Commerce at the University of Virginia. Prior to this position, he was an engagement manager with McKinsey & Company, where he led marketing strategy and implementation projects in the United States, Canada, Central and South America, the United Kingdom, and Russia. He was a co-leader of McKinsey's Digital Marketing practice and a regular faculty member at the firm's global training programs. Before this, he was the brand manager of Procter & Gamble's Clearasil brand in Canada. He has an M.B.A. from the Institute for Management Development in Switzerland, where he received the American Express Award for Outstanding Achievement. He studied theology and philosophy at the John Paul II Institute in Washington, D.C., and currently is pursuing a doctorate in marketing and business ethics at the Darden Business School at the University of Virginia.

Alan R. Andreasen is Professor of Marketing in the McDonough School of Business at Georgetown University. He is a specialist in consumer behavior and the application of marketing to nonprofit organizations, social marketing, and the marketing problems of disadvantaged consumers. He is the author or editor of 12 books and numerous monographs. His most recent books are *Strategic Marketing in Nonprofit Organizations* (co-authored with Philip Kotler, 5th ed., 1996), *Marketing Social Change* (1995), and *Cheap but Good Marketing Research* (1988). He also has published more than 100 articles and presented conference papers on a variety of topics and serves on the boards of reviewers of the *Journal of Consumer Research, Journal of Consumer Policy, Social Marketing Quarterly,* and *Journal of Public Policy & Marketing.* He is past president of the Association for Consumer Research.

J. Craig Andrews is Professor and the Charles H. Kellstadt Chair in Marketing at Marquette University. He received his Ph.D. in marketing from the University of South Carolina. He is the current editor of the *Journal of Public Policy & Marketing.* He served as a consumer research specialist with the Federal Trade Commission in its Division of Advertising Practices. In addition, he is a former chair of the American Marketing Association's Marketing and Society special interest group. His research on nutrition labeling and claims, warnings and disclosures, cross-cultural advertising, and advertising involvement has appeared in the *Journal of Marketing, Journal of Consumer Research, Journal of Public Policy & Marketing, Journal of Advertising,* and *Journal of Consumer Affairs,* among others.

John E. Calfee is Resident Scholar at the American Enterprise Institute (AEI), where he has been since 1995. He holds a Ph.D. in economics from the University of California, Berkeley. From 1980 to 1986, he served in the Bureau of Economics at the Federal Trade Commission (FTC), where he worked on consumer protection policy including the regulation of advertising. After leaving the FTC, he taught marketing and consumer behavior in the business schools at the University of Maryland at College Park and Boston University and spent a year as a visiting senior fellow at the Brookings Institution. His scholarly work on advertising has been published in numerous journals, and his op-ed pieces have appeared in several major newspapers and other publications. At AEI, he conducts research on advertising, tort liability, and regulation. His books include *Fear of Persuasion*, which analyzes a wide variety of issues in advertising (particularly its impact on markets and consumers), and *Prices, Markets, and the Pharmaceutical Revolution.*.

Brenda M. Derby is Statistician in Consumer Studies, Division of Market Studies, U.S. Food and Drug Administration. She holds a Ph.D. and an M.A. in applied social psychology from Claremont Graduate University and an undergraduate degree from the University of British Columbia. Her research has focused on consumer responses to dietary supplements, labeling, and food safety information.

Nikhilesh Dholakia is Professor of Marketing at the University of Rhode Island. Among his books are *Consumption and Marketing: Macro Dimensions* (1996) and *Consuming People: From Political Economy to Theaters of Consumption* (1998). He is an area editor of *CMC: Consumption, Markets, & Culture,* an interdisciplinary journal. He serves on the advisory board for the International Society of Marketing and Development. He holds a B.Tech. in chemical engineering from the Indian Institute of Technology, an M.B.A. from the Indian Institute of Management, and a Ph.D. in marketing from Northwestern University.

Ruby Roy Dholakia is Professor of Marketing at the University of Rhode Island (URI). She was the first president of the International Society of Marketing and Development. Her work on social marketing, macromarketing, and marketing in developing countries has appeared in the *Journal of Macromarketing* and *Journal of Business Research* as well as in edited volumes. She also is founder and director of the Research Institute for Telecommunications and Information Marketing at URI and has written extensively on topics related to marketing of telecom and information technologies. She holds a B.S. and an M.B.A. from the University of California, Berkeley, and a Ph.D. in marketing from Northwestern University.

Minette E. Drumwright has a joint appointment in the College of Communication (Department of Advertising) and the College of Liberal Arts at the University of Texas at Austin. Previously, she has been on the faculties of the University of Texas Business School and the Harvard Business School. Her current research is in the area of business and society, particularly in marketing and advertising. Her articles and cases have been published in a variety of books and journals. She is on the editorial review boards of the *Journal of Marketing* and *Social Marketing Quarterly.* She has won two schoolwide teaching awards at the University of Texas for her M.B.A. courses. She teaches in various corporate executive education programs in North America and abroad. She has a Ph.D. in business administration from the University of North Carolina at Chapel Hill. Prior to graduate school, she worked for seven years in advertising and public relations.

Julie Edell is Associate Professor in the Fuqua School of Business at Duke University. She received her Ph.D. from Carnegie Mellon University in 1982. Her primary research areas are advertising and consumer choice. Her current advertising research includes how the structure of an advertisement affects a consumer's cognitive and affective responses and the impact of these responses on a brand's equity. Her consumer choice work examines the role that emotional reactions play in the decision-making process. She serves on the editorial review boards of the *Journal of Consumer Research, Journal of Consumer Psychology, Journal of Business Research,* and *Quarterly Journal of Business and Economics.* She teaches courses in marketing research, customer relationship management, and marketing communications. In 1987, she received the Kraft Award for Excellence in Management Education. She serves on the board of directors of the Colon Cancer Alliance and on the National Cancer Institute's Clinical Trials Advisory Panel.

Paul W. Farris is Landmark Communications Professor of Business at the Darden Graduate School of Business Administration at the University of Virginia. Prior to his current appointment, he earned degrees from the University of Missouri, University of Washington, and Harvard University. He also taught at the Harvard Business School and has worked as a product manager for UNILEVER in Germany and in account management for the LINTAS advertising agency. His teaching and research have focused on understanding marketing costs and developing ways in which to improve marketing productivity. He has published in the *Harvard Business Review, Journal of Marketing, Marketing Science, Management Science, Sloan Management Review, Journal of Retailing, Journal of Advertising Research, International Journal of Marketing Research, Journal of Brand Management,* and several other professional and academic journals.

Valerie S. Folkes is Professor of Marketing and Chairperson of the Department of Marketing in the Marshall School of Business at the University of Southern California. She earned her Ph.D. from the University of California, Los Angeles, and her undergraduate degree from the University of Texas at Austin. Her research interests focus on consumer decision making, particularly customer satisfaction with products and services. She has been selected as a fellow of the Consumer Psychology division of the American Psychological Association and has served as treasurer of the Association for Consumer Research (for which she currently is president-elect). She is an editorial review board member of the *Journal of Consumer Research* as well as president of the policy board of the journal. She also serves on the editorial review board of the *Journal of Consumer Psychology.*

Joseph P. Guiltinan is Professor of Marketing at the University of Notre Dame, where he has served as department chair and as associate dean for M.B.A. programs. Prior to joining the faculty at Notre Dame, he was a member of the faculties at the University of Kentucky and University of Massachusetts. A graduate of the University of Notre Dame with a B.B.A. in marketing, he holds both the M.B.A. and D.B.A. degrees from Indiana University. His current research interests are in pricing, product line management, and new product strategy. His work has appeared in the *Journal of Marketing, Journal of Consumer Research, Journal of Retailing, Journal of Product Innovation Management, the Antitrust Bulletin,* and *Social Forces.* He also has authored two texts on marketing.

Michael R. Hagerty is Associate Professor in the Graduate School of Management at the University of California, Davis. His research has been in choice and attitude models of consumer behavior, emphasizing how consumers become happy and fulfilled. He currently is investigating the link between consumers' satisfaction and their voting support in national elections for the governing party. He has published articles in the *Journal of Marketing Research, Marketing Science, Journal of Consumer Research, Journal of International Forecasting,* and *Social Indicators Research.*

Patrick J. Kaufmann joined Boston University's faculty in 1998. He received a B.A. in economics from Georgetown University in 1968, a J.D. from Boston College Law School in 1974, an M.B.A. from the Wharton School at the University of Pennsylvania in 1980, and a Ph.D. in marketing from Northwestern University in 1985. From 1985 to 1991, he was an assistant professor at the Harvard Business School, and from 1991 to 1998, he was an associate professor and professor of marketing at Georgia State University. His research is in the areas of franchising, channels of distribution, and public policy. He has published articles in a wide variety of scholarly journals including the *Journal of Marketing, Journal of Law and Economics, Journal of Public Policy & Marketing,* and *Journal of Retailing.* He serves on the editorial boards of the *Journal of Retailing, Journal of Public Policy & Marketing,* and *Journal of Marketing Channels.*

Thomas A. Klein is Professor of Marketing at the University of Toledo and previously was director of business research and dean of the university's College of Business Administration. He is a longtime member of the editorial policy board of the *Journal of Macromarketing.* His research and teaching specialties are market organization and ethical issues in business.

R. Craig Lefebvre is Chief Technical Officer and Vice President of Health Communications at Prospect Associates. The social marketing projects and public health programs he has been involved with include the development and implementation of the Office of Cancer Communications' 5 A Day for Better Health program and the development of the global behavior change communication strategy for HIV prevention for the AIDSCAP project. He was project director for health communications support to the Centers for Disease Control and Prevention and for the U.S. Department of Agriculture's Team Nutrition program. Prior to joining Prospect Associates, he was the intervention director of the Pawtucket Heart Health Program and associate professor of community health at Brown University. He is a fellow in the American Heart Association Council of Epidemiology and Preventive Cardiology, holds faculty positions at both the Johns Hopkins University and the University of South Florida Schools of Public Health, and serves as co-editor of *Social Marketing Quarterly.*

Alan S. Levy is Team Leader in Consumer Studies, Division of Market Studies, U.S. Food and Drug Administration. He holds a Ph.D. in social psychology from Columbia University and an undergraduate degree from Michigan State University. His research has focused on consumer responses to dietary supplements, labeling, and food safety information.

Linda A. Lewis is a doctoral student in the Department of Marketing at the University of Utah. She earned her B.A. at Gonzaga University in 1978 and her M.B.A. at Eastern Washington University in 1995. She worked in the private sector for firms such as IBM, Hewlett-Packard, and Sun Microsystems, and she has done volunteer work for local environmental organizations.

Ingrid Martin is Assistant Professor of Marketing, Division of Economics and Business, Economics Institute, University of Colorado. She received her Ph.D. in marketing from the Marshall School of Business at the University of Southern California in 1994. Her research interests focus on the impact that goals have on how consumers make decisions and use both market and nonmarket products (i.e., public lands) and the public policy implications of these processes. In addition, she is investigating the impact that goals have on how managers learn competitive market information.

Robert N. Mayer is Professor of Family and Consumer Studies at the University of Utah. He received his Ph.D. in sociology from the University of California, Berkeley, in 1978. His research examines the U.S. and global consumer movements and also evaluates consumer protection policies. His current research projects cover electronic commerce and life insurance aspects of genetic testing. He is author of *The Consumer Movement: Guardians of the Marketplace* (G. K. Hall/Twayne, 1989) and editor of *Enhancing Consumer Choice* (ACCI, 1991). He is associate editor (with Stephen Brobeck and Robert Herrmann) of the *Encyclopedia of the Consumer Movement* (1997). His research also has appeared in numerous scholarly journals. He currently is a board member of the American Council on Consumer Interests and the National Consumers League. Previously, he served as the consumer representative on the Direct Selling Education Foundation's board of directors.

George R. Milne is Associate Professor at the University of Massachusetts–Amherst. He teaches marketing management, Internet marketing, marketing research, applied multivariate statistics, and research methods. His areas of research specialization are interactive marketing and Internet/database privacy. He has been working in the area of marketing information privacy since 1992 and has published numerous articles appearing in the *Journal of Marketing, Journal of Public Policy & Marketing, Journal of Direct Marketing,* and *Journal of Interactive Marketing.* He was the special issue editor of the Spring 2000 edition of the *Journal of Public Policy & Marketing,* focusing on privacy and ethics issues of interactive/database marketing.

Christine Moorman is Professor of Marketing in the Fuqua School of Business at Duke University. Her research focuses on understanding the nature and effects of market information utilization activities by consumers, managers, and organizations. She is particularly interested in how information utilization activities affect the design and implementation of marketing strategies and new product development as well as the effective functioning of markets. She has published research in the *Journal of Marketing Research, Journal of Consumer Research, Journal of Marketing,* and *Journal of Public Policy & Marketing.* She is a member of the editorial review boards for all of these journals as well as *Marketing Letters* and the *Journal of Strategic Marketing.* She previously taught at the University of Wisconsin–Madison for 10 years and won numerous teaching awards there. Her teaching interests are in marketing strategy, new product development, and consumer behavior.

Fred W. Morgan is Ashland Professor of Marketing at the University of Kentucky. Before that, he served on the marketing faculties at the University of Oklahoma and University of Missouri–Columbia. He has been a visiting faculty member at the University of Michigan, University of California, Berkeley, and University of San Francisco. His research interests center on the impact of the legal environment on marketing and business strategy and the effect of distribution practices on product liability exposure. His research has been published in the *Journal of Marketing, Journal of Consumer Research, Journal of Public Policy & Marketing, Journal of the Academy of Marketing Science, Journal of Business, Journal of Retailing, Journal of Advertising, American Behavioral Scientist,* and *American Business Law Journal,* among other scholarly journals.

Patrick E. Murphy is Professor and Chair of the Department of Marketing, College of Business Administration, University of Notre Dame. He was a Fulbright scholar in the Department of Management and Marketing at University College Cork in Ireland during 1993-94. Previously, he was on the faculty at Marquette University. He is a former editor of the *Journal of Public Policy & Marketing* and serves on the editorial boards of four journals. He holds a Ph.D from the University of Houston, an M.B.A. from Bradley University, and a B.B.A. from Notre Dame. He has written a number of scholarly articles on business and marketing ethics. He is a member of the advisory board for *Annual Editions: Business Ethics.* In 1999, he was co-chair of the Marketing and Public Policy Conference and was organizer of the Symposium on Teaching Ethics in Marketing held at Notre Dame University.

Robert W. Nason is Professor of Marketing and Chair of the Department of Marketing and Supply Chain Management in the Broad Graduate School of

Business Administration at Michigan State University. He is a past editor of the *Journal of Macromarketing*. His research and teaching specialty is economic development.

Alan G. Sawyer is J. C. Penney Professor of Marketing at the University of Florida. He received a B.A. from the University of Maine, an M.B.A. from Northeastern University, and a Ph.D. from Stanford University. He also has taught at the Ohio State University, University of Massachusetts, and State University of New York at Buffalo and has been a visiting professor of marketing at several European business schools. He has more than 50 publications in academic journals and proceedings. His research has focused on research methods, market segmentation, advertising, pricing and consumer promotions, and consumer search behavior in the marketplace. He is a member of the editorial review boards of the *Journal of Consumer Research, Journal of Marketing Research,* and *Marketing Letters.* In addition, he is an active consultant to many corporations and law firms. Each summer, he returns to his other life as a visiting researcher in South Harpswell, Maine.

Debra L. Scammon is Emma Eccles Jones Professor of Marketing, and Associate Dean for Academic Programs in the David Eccles School of Business at the University of Utah. She earned her M.S. in marketing from the University of California, Los Angeles, and her Ph.D. in marketing from the University of California, Los Angeles. Her areas of emphasis in teaching and research include consumer behavior, public policy and marketing, and health care marketing. Her recent research has focused on nutrition and health claims in both advertising and labeling. She has published in numerous journals including those dealing with consumer affairs, consumer protection, and antitrust issues. She is past editor of the *Journal of Public Policy & Marketing* and is active in the American Marketing Association's Marketing and Society special interest group and in the Association for Consumer Research.

Mary Jane Sheffet received her Ph.D. and M.B.A. degrees from the University of California, Los Angeles. She was an assistant professor of marketing at Indiana University from 1979 to 1986, when she became an associate professor at Michigan State University. In 1997, she moved to the University of Northern Iowa as a full professor and head of the Department of Marketing. Her research is focused on legal issues in marketing and has appeared in numerous journals and proceedings. She has served on the editorial board of the *Journal of Marketing* and the editorial review board of the *Journal of Macromarketing,* and she currently is on the editorial board of the *Journal of Public Policy & Marketing.* In 1993, she was program and arrangements chair for the Marketing and Public Policy Conference, which met at Michigan State University. She has consulted for law firms, corporations, and nonprofit organizations.

Alex Simonson is Visiting Associate Professor of Marketing, Seton Hall University, Stillman School of Business (and a member of the full-time faculty of marketing at Georgetown University School of Business, on leave). He is an Associate Member of the International Trademark Association and a member of the Editorial Board of *The Journal of Public Policy and Marketing* and of *The Trademark Reporter.* He is also a marketing consultant and researcher. He holds a Ph.D. in marketing, *with distinction,* from Columbia Business School, a J.D. from New York University School of Law, and an A.B., *magna cum laude,* from Columbia College, Columbia University. Dr. Simonson specializes in brands "in distress" and advertising communications. He has designed and conducted survey research in the context of trademark and advertising litigation for about ten years and has been accepted as an expert in marketing research by various federal courts. Dr. Simonson has worked for IBDC, a strategic marketing consulting firm in New York, and has been a consultant to a variety of organizations including the United States Federal Trade Commission on survey design. He has published in academic marketing, strategic and intellectual property journals such as the *Journal of Public Policy & Marketing, Long Range Planning,* and *The Trademark Reporter,* respectively. He is co-author of the best-selling book on brands and marketing communications entitled *Marketing Aesthetics: The Strategic Management of Brands, Identity and Image* 1997) (German trans., Japanese trans., Spanish trans., Chinese trans.; other translations forthcoming).

N. Craig Smith is Associate Professor of Marketing at London Business School. He joined Georgetown in 1991, prior to which he was on the faculties of the McDonough School of Business, Georgetown University, Graduate School of Business Administration, Harvard University, and the Cranfield School of Management, Cranfield Institute of Technology. His current research projects examine ethical decision making in an increasingly global business environment, bribery, ethical issues in consumer research, vulnerable consumers, consumer boycotts, and corporate citizenship. He is the author of *Morality and the Market: Consumer Pressure for Corporate Accountability* (1990) and the co-author (with John A. Quelch) of *Ethics in Marketing* (1993/1996). He consults with various organizations on problems of good marketing practice including marketing ethics.

Richard Staelin is Edward and Rose Donnell Professor of Business Administration at Duke University. Prior to joining Duke's faculty, he served as professor and associate dean in the Graduate School of Industrial Administration at Carnegie Mellon University. His professional activities include performing consulting work for both the public and private sectors, serving as executive director of the Marketing Science Institute, and publishing a book and more than 50 journal articles. He also has supervised more than 30 doctoral students, many of whom currently are teaching in top-ranked business schools. He was associate dean for faculty in the Fuqua School of Business for eight years and was the editor of *Marketing Science* from 1995 to 1997. He was the initial managing director of Fuqua's Global Executive M.B.A. program and currently is area coordinator for the marketing group. His current research interests include information search, channel management, strategy formulation, and managerial decision making.

David W. Stewart is Robert E. Brooker Professor of Marketing and Deputy Dean of Faculty in the Marshall School of Business at the University of Southern California. He previously served as chairman of the Department of Marketing in the Marshall School. Prior to moving to Southern California in 1986, he was senior associate dean and associate professor of marketing in the Owen Graduate School of Management at Vanderbilt University. He currently is editor of the *Journal of Marketing*. He has served as vice president of finance and on the board of directors of the American Marketing Association (AMA). He also has served on the board of the AMA Foundation. He has authored or co-authored more than 150 publications and six books. His research has examined a wide range of issues including marketing strategy, the analysis of markets, consumer information search and decision making, effectiveness of marketing communications, and methodological approaches to the analysis of marketing data. His research and commentary are frequently featured in the business and popular press.

William L. Wilkie is Aloysius and Eleanor Nathe Professor of Marketing at the University of Notre Dame. His primary research interests focus on issues of marketing, consumer behavior, and public policy. He has served as president of the Association for Consumer Research, an international professional group with members in 30 nations. He also has served as a member of the editorial boards of several journals. He is the author of numerous books, monographs, and articles on marketing and consumer behavior. His research has received a number of awards and recognitions. He received his undergraduate degree from the University of Notre Dame and received his M.B.A. and Ph.D. degrees from Stanford University, where he also was a fellow in the year-long Stanford-Sloan Executive Development Program. Prior to joining Notre Dame's faculty, he served as an in-house consultant to the Federal Trade Commission; as a research professor at the Marketing Science Institute; and as a faculty member at Purdue University, Harvard University, and the University of Florida.